The Confessions *of* Our Faith

The Westminster Confession of Faith

The Larger Catechism

The Shorter Catechism

The Fortress Edition

Historical Introduction
Dr. David B. Calhoun

Editor
Rev. Brian W. Kinney

Tanglewood Publishing
www.tanglewoodpublishing.org

Tanglewood Publishing
800-241-4016
www.tanglewoodpublishing.org

Grateful acknowledgment is made to the following:

The Dean and Chapter of Westminster for permission to use a picture of the Jerusalem Chamber and quotations; Crossway/Goodnews Publishers for quotations from the English Standard Version of the Bible; and Christy Rodriguez for pictures of Westminster used in this publication.

ISBN-13: 978-0-9793718-8-2
ISBN-10: 0-9793718-8-0

Printed in the United States of America

Book design, layout, and production by
Martha Nichols/aMuse Productions®

TABLE OF CONTENTS

PREFACE

BY THE EDITOR,
THE REV. BRIAN KINNEY

"If you confess with your mouth that Jesus is Lord and believe in your heart that God raised him from the dead, you will be saved" (Romans 10:9). Thus the Apostle Paul tells us the importance of our confession of what Scripture testifies are the truths about Jesus Christ.

Yet how shall we know which truths are most important for us to confess? Surely we could confess all of the Bible, if we were capable even of remembering all the truths contained in the 66 books of God's revelation. Most of us, however, do much better with a summary of the central truths of the faith, a summary that we can hold in our hands and retain in its essence in our minds, perhaps even to memorize its doctrinal core. Such a summary is found in the great documents of the Reformation known as the Westminster Confession of Faith and the Larger and Shorter Catechisms.

What we present to you in this Fortress Edition are those three confessional writings, the doctrinal heart of the Reformed faith. These confessions are both for believers, who have them as a guide for life and faith, and for unbelievers, who need them in order to understand the teachings of Jesus Christ and to distinguish between the mandates of God and the opinions of man — and perhaps turn to God and be saved by confessing that Jesus is their Lord.

The Fortress Edition begins with the assumption that God's truths are eternal and universal. God is not a man that He should change His mind.

However, the language of man does change over the centuries to the point at which some English words of the 1640s no longer are understood in the English speaking world, expressions such as "Therefore it pleased the Lord, at sundry times, and in divers manners. ..." Thus have we undertaken to follow standard English usage for clarity, while at the same time leaving the statement of doctrines unchanged. Specifically, we have avoided any changes to vital theological terms that bear heavily on our doctrinal standards, words such as predestination, election, justification, sanctification, propitiation, and the like, along with words such as recreations that have been at the center of doctrinal controversies. The councils and courts of our church are the forums for defining these terms, not the computer screen of an editor.

In our attempt to make the Westminster Confession and the Catechisms clearer to the twenty-first century reader, we hope that believers from various backgrounds will use them for an understanding of the central teachings of the Christian faith. Many Christians have so little understanding of systematic theology that they are almost helpless in the defense of what they believe. Yet the Confession and Catechisms are so thoroughly and solely based on Scripture that they provide a wonderful framework for the understanding and articulation of the message of the Bible. The writers of these documents have provided us with many "proof texts" from Scripture to support this framework. Therefore we have included the citations for the proof texts handed down to us from the Westminster Divines.

Editor's Note: Other than substituting standard English usage where necessary, our primary documents (the Burgess manuscript and the Caruthers edition of the Confessions) are the same as those approved by the First General Assembly of the Presbyterian Church in America in 1973. We are grateful to the PCA for their approval and official use of the Westminster Standards and to Crossway Bibles for permission to use quotations from the English Standard Version of the Bible.

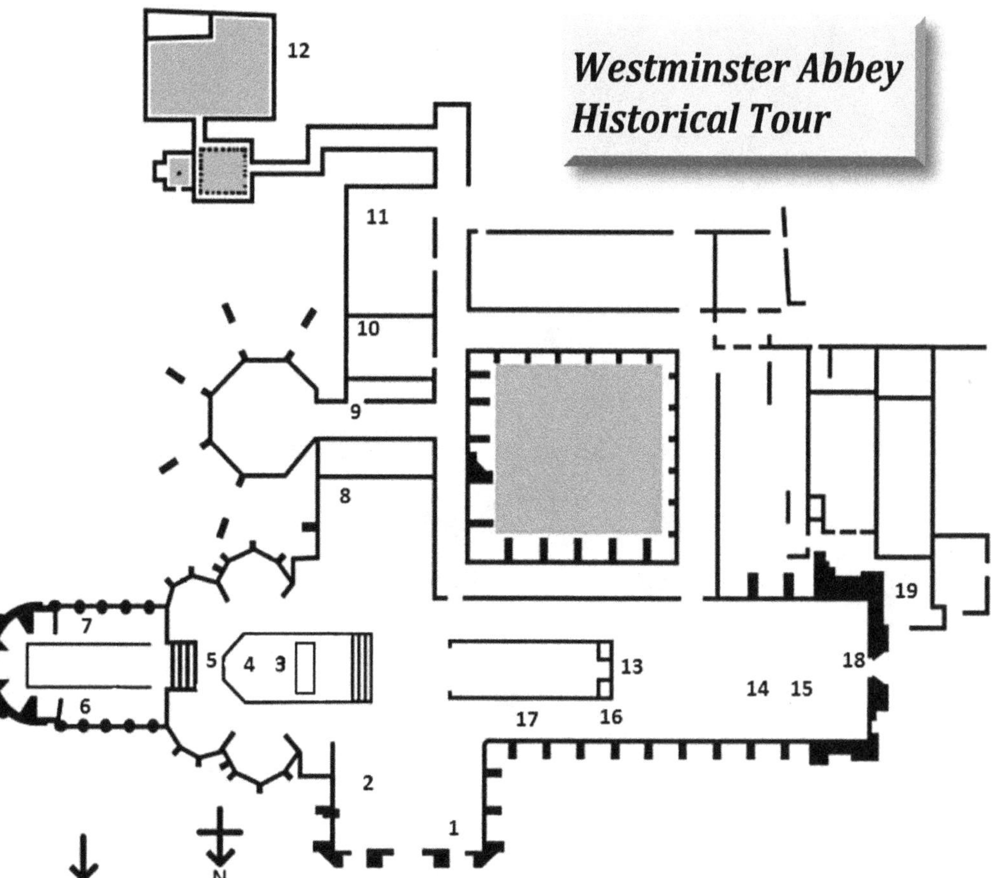

1 Tour entrance
2 Statesman's Corner: Graves of William Gladstone, William Pitt, William Wilberforce
3 Chapel of Edward the Confessor (1042-1066), builder of Westminster; outside the chapel are several medieval tombs, including Aveline (daughter-in-law of Henry III), her husband Edmund, and Anne of Cleves (fourth wife of Henry VIII)
4 Tomb of Henry V
5 Coronation Chair, used for every coronation since 1297
6 Tomb of Elizabeth I; underneath the tomb of Elizabeth I is the tomb of Mary I, her half-sister
7 Tomb of Mary, Queen of Scots
8 Poet's Corner: Graves include Robert Browning, Geoffrey Chaucer, Charles Dickens, John Dryden, George Frederick Handel, Thomas Harvey, Samuel Johnson, Rudyard Kipling, Laurence Olivier, Edmund Spenser, Alfred Tennyson
9 Oldest surviving door in England
10 Pyx Chamber, dates from between 1065 and 1090. Contains a rare pre-Reformation stone altar. Held the nation's silver and gold coinage
11 Abbey Museum. Contains artifacts removed from the Abbey for preservation
12 College Garden. Oldest garden in England
13 Graves and commemorations for Isaac Newton, Michael Faraday, and other scientists
14 Grave of missionary David Livingstone. His body lies here; his heart is buried in Africa
15 Grave of the Unknown Warrior
16 Musician's Aisle, grave of Henry Purcell
17 Statue of William Wilberforce
18 Tour exit
19 Jerusalem Chamber (now part of the Dean's private residence). Site of the translation of the King James Bible and writing of the Westminster Confession of Faith and Catechisms

Great West Door and Jerusalem Chamber Window

Jerusalem Chamber

The view of the West Front of Westminster Abbey is one of the best known in the world. The gothic lower part was completed in the fifteenth century; the towers, designed by Nicholas Hawksmoor in a more classical stye, were added at the beginning of the eighteenth century. (Anthony Harvey, Sub-Dean of Westminster)

The Rose Window and the North Transept of Westminster where William Wilberforce is buried next to his friend William Pitt the Younger.

Above: Jerusalem Chamber

Right: Great West Door Towers

Above: Rose Window

Left: Great West Door Towers

Statue of composer George Frederick Handel holding the musical score to "I Know that My Redeemer Liveth." ©Westminster Abbey

BROUGHT BY FAITHFUL HANDS
OVER LAND AND SEA
HERE RESTS
DAVID LIVINGSTONE,
MISSIONARY,
TRAVELLER,
PHILANTHROPIST,
BORN MARCH 19.1813,
AT BLANTYRE, LANARKSHIRE,
DIED MAY 1. 1873,
AT CHITAMBO'S VILLAGE, ULALA.

FOR 30 YEARS HIS LIFE WAS SPENT
IN AN UNWEARIED EFFORT
TO EVANGELIZE THE NATIVE RACES,
TO EXPLORE THE UNDISCOVERED SECRETS,
TO ABOLISH THE DESOLATING SLAVE TRADE,
OF CENTRAL AFRICA,
WHERE WITH HIS LAST WORDS HE WROTE,
"ALL I CAN ADD IN MY SOLITUDE, IS,
MAY HEAVEN'S RICH BLESSING COME DOWN
ON EVERY ONE, AMERICAN, ENGLISH, OR TURK,
WHO WILL HELP TO HEAL
THIS OPEN SORE OF THE WORLD."

"OTHER SHEEP I HAVE, WHICH ARE NOT OF THIS FOLD:
THEM ALSO I MUST BRING, AND THEY SHALL HEAR MY VOICE."

"TANTUS AMOR VERI, NIHIL EST QUOD NOSCERE MALIM,
QUAM FLUVII CAUSAS PER SÆCULA TANTA LATENTES."

Grave of missionary David Livingstone. His body lies here; his heart is buried in Africa. ©Westminster Abbey

Part of the inscription on the statue of William Wilberforce reads "HIS NAME WILL EVER BE SPECIALLY IDENTIFIED WITH THOSE EXERTIONS WHICH, BY THE BLESSING OF GOD, REMOVED FROM ENGLAND THE GUILT OF THE AFRICAN SLAVE TRADE, AND PREPARED THE WAY FOR THE ABOLITION OF SLAVERY IN EVERY COLONY OF THE EMPIRE."
©Westminster Abbey

Twin towers above the the entrance to the Nave of Westminster, which has served as the coronation church of kings and queens for over a thousand years.

THE WESTMINSTER ASSEMBLY (1643-1648)

BY DR. DAVID B. CALHOUN
Professor of Church History and Chair of the Church History and World Mission Department
Covenant Theological Seminary, St. Louis, Missouri

Sixteenth-century Puritans were disappointed with the middle-of-the-road reform of the Church of England favored by Elizabeth I. Their successors had great hopes that the Scottish King James VI (who in 1603 became James I of England) would bring the Church of England into greater conformity with the Presbyterian Church in Scotland. Soon it became obvious that King James had no intention of doing this. In fact, he was determined to make Scotland's church more like the English church. Puritan disillusionment with James quickly became despair with Charles I, the son and successor of James, and with the fiercely anti-Puritan Archbishop William Laud.

Tensions heightened and fighting broke out in both Scotland and England. In 1638, the National Covenant rallied Presbyterian determination after the king's attempt to introduce a revised English *Book of Common Prayer* for Scottish worship. The Bishops' Wars of 1639 and 1640 failed to put down the uprising. In 1642, war erupted in England between the king and the Puritan Parliament (the so-called "Long Parliament" that began on November 3, 1640, and continued until dissolved by Oliver Cromwell on April 20, 1653). The

Parliament insisted on a larger role in government against the royal absolutism of Charles, and greater reform in the church against Laud's high-church policies and Arminian doctrine. This Civil War was "not a selfish and ferocious conflict like the Wars of the Roses, but a war fought mainly for political and religious ideals."[1] It "made England at last the stronghold of constitutional liberty in Europe, and laid the foundation for a Protestant republic in America."[2] After some early uncertainty, the war resulted in victory for the Parliament, and the executions of Archbishop Laud in 1645 and King Charles I in 1649. Meanwhile, the hierarchy and liturgy of the Church of England were abolished. "The old building was destroyed," comments Philip Schaff, "before a new building was agreed upon."[3]

On May 13, 1643, the Parliament organized an assembly of ministers (or "divines") to create standards for a Church of England that would be reformed in worship, government, and doctrine. A few weeks later, on July 1, the opening session of the Westminster Assembly was held, with both houses of Parliament in attendance. The prolocutor (presiding officer), William Twisse, preached from John 14:18—"I will not leave you comfortless: I will come to you." The Assembly sent fraternal greetings to the Reformed churches in the Netherlands, France, Switzerland, and elsewhere, and settled down to its first task—a modest revision of the Thirty-Nine Articles to clarify or strengthen, where necessary, the Reformed theology of these defining statements of Anglican doctrine.

The Assembly comprised 151 members, including 30 laymen, chosen by Parliament to represent the counties, the universities, the House of Lords, and the House of Commons. Three of the divines were ministers of the Reformed Church of France, serving congregations in Canterbury and London. Three New England ministers were invited to take part, but declined to make the long journey. Twenty-eight of the divines did not attend (mainly because of the king's prohibition), and twenty-one, called "superadded divines," were appointed later to replace members who did not attend or who died during the proceedings. Some outstanding Puritan pastors and theologians, such as Richard Baxter and John Owen, were not included in the Assembly list. A few months later, eight commissioners were chosen by the Church of Scotland "to propone [put forward], consult, treat and conclude"

1 F. E. Halliday, *A Concise History of England*, 116.
2 Philip Schaff, *The Creeds of Christendom* 1: 702-703.
3 Schaff 1:734.

with the Westminster divines. The Scots arrived in London "fresh from the battle 'with lordly bishops, popish ceremonies, and royal mandates.'"[1]

The Westminster divines, mostly teachers and pastors of churches, were described by the Parliament as "learned, godly, and judicious." And they were. "Puritanism had been doing its work of making great men in England for a century."[2] Richard Baxter held that "the Christian world, since the days of the Apostles, had never a synod of more excellent divines" than Westminster and the Synod of Dort.[3] Church historian Philip Schaff wrote that "not a few" of the Westminster divines "combined rare learning, eloquence, and piety in beautiful harmony."[4] John Leith described the Westminster divines as "very competent men, as competent as composed any synod in Church history."[5] William Barker's Puritan Profiles summarizes the lives and accomplishments of many of the Westminster divines (and some other influential Puritans who lived during the time of the Westminster Assembly).

The Assembly's members were all Calvinists in theology and could all be called Puritans in the broad sense. The main difference among them was in their views of church government and discipline. This resulted in a number of groups or parties—moderate Episcopalians (most of whom declined to attend out of loyalty to the king), Presbyterians (much the largest group), and Congregationalists (who gained influence through the growing support of Oliver Cromwell and the army). There was a small but learned group of Erastians who held that church discipline was to be carried out only with approval of the state.

The Assembly met at first in Westminster Abbey's imposing Henry VII Chapel, its ornate medieval architecture and decoration forming a striking contrast to Puritan simplicity of worship and dress. As the weather turned cooler, the divines were glad to move to the more comfortable Jerusalem Chamber. Every member took a vow (which was read every Monday morning) to "maintain nothing in point of doctrine but what I believe to be most agreeable to the Word of God; nor in point of discipline, but what may make most for God's glory and the peace and good of his Church." The Assembly met every day except Saturday and Sunday, from nine o'clock until one or

---

1 Schaff 1:745.

2 "The Origin and Formation of the Westminster Confession of Faith," prepared for the 1906 General Assembly of the Presbyterian Church in the United States of America. Reprinted in *The Westminster Confession of Faith* (Atlanta: Committee for Christian Education & Publications, 1990), xv.

3 William Barker, *Puritan Profiles*, 288. Schaff 1:729.

4 Schaff 1:740.

5 John Leith, *Assembly at Westminster: Reformed Theology in the Making*, 49.

two. Forty members constituted a quorum. In the afternoons, the divines worked in committees. One of the rules guiding the deliberations required that "what any man undertakes to prove as necessary, he shall make good out of Scripture." The minutes and other reports of the Assembly's work reveal a strong commitment to this rule.

Much of the time of the Westminster divines was taken up with preaching and hearing sermons. More than 240 sermons were delivered to the Parliament during the 1640s, most of them by members of the Westminster Assembly. Because of their efforts to apply Scripture to their times, these preachers have been called "England's Deuteronomists." Many hours were spent in corporate prayer and discussion concerning the lessons of God's providence in the successes and failures of the Parliamentary army and the progress or lack thereof of the Assembly itself. Scottish commissioner Robert Baillie described the "fast" observed on May 17, 1644, as "the sweetest day" he had spent in England, although the prayers, psalms, and sermons of that day lasted eight hours without interruption. "We cannot read such accounts," Schaff comments, "without amazement at the devotional fervor and endurance of the Puritan divines."[1]

There were 1,163 numbered sessions of the Westminster Assembly, the last coming on February 22, 1649 (although the doctrinal standards were completed by 1648). For several more years the Assembly continued as a ministerial examining committee. It was never formally dissolved.

The Westminster Assembly's first project of revising the Thirty-Nine Articles was abandoned, and work on new documents begun, after the Presbyterians of Scotland joined with the English Puritans in August 1643 in the *Solemn League and Covenant* for "the preservation of the reformed religion in the Church of Scotland ... the reformation of religion in the kingdoms of England and Ireland, in doctrine, worship, discipline, and government, according to the Word of God, and the example of the best reformed churches."

Over the course of five and a half years, during a time of political and religious chaos, the Westminster Assembly created five great documents of theological orthodoxy and ecclesiastical stability for the church in England, Ireland, and Scotland.

The Directory for Public Worship set forth a middle ground between a fixed liturgy and a completely open form of worship in which everyone would be "left to his own will." The *Directory* contains what has been called "the finest brief description of expository preaching to be found in the English

1 Schaff 1:752.

language."[1] The divines also approved Francis Rous's revised version of the Psalter for congregational worship.

The Form of Church Government set forth a Presbyterian polity tempered by the debate between the Presbyterians and the competent and outspoken small group of Independents (their leaders were called "the five dissenting brethren" by the Presbyterians). It was tempered as well by the disagreement between the stricter Presbyterians who insisted on the "divine right" of Presbyterianism, and others who held that Presbyterian polity was "lawful and agreeable to the Word of God," but subject to change according to the needs of the church.

The Westminster Confession of Faith, the Assembly's most important work, is a model of mainstream Calvinism, setting forth what B. B. Warfield called "the generic doctrine of the Reformed churches."[2] Drawing on the richness of the creeds and confessions of church history, especially the Thirty-Nine Articles, the Lambeth Articles, and the Irish Articles of Archbishop James Ussher (one of the greatest "doctrinal Puritans" of the time, who though not in attendance at Westminster was present "in spirit"), the Westminster divines with "remarkable comprehensiveness, balance and precision"[3] summed up in thirty-three chapters "what man is to believe concerning God, and what duty God requires of man."[4] The *Confession* is noted for its strong opening chapter on the authority of the Scripture, its uncompromising allegiance to God's sovereignty in providence and predestination, its covenant theology, its Protestant and evangelical soteriology, its unique chapter on adoption, and its emphasis on the Christian life—both personal and communal. Chapters 10 through 33, comprising two-thirds of the Confession, deal with the Christian life (supplemented by the substantial commentary on the Ten Commandments in the *Larger Catechism*.) It is abundantly clear that the creators of the Westminster standards "were not simply concerned with sound doctrine but also with the embodiment of doctrine in life."[5]

The *Confession* was presented to Parliament for approval in December 1646. Fifteen hundred "proof texts" were added (by order of Parliament), and the complete document was published, with the title *The Humble Advice*

1 S. B. Ferguson, *Dictionary of Scottish Church History and Theology*, 864.
2 B. B. Warfield, *The Westminster Assembly and Its Work*, 96.
3 David F. Wright, *New Dictionary of Theology*, 156.
4 *Westminster Shorter Catechism*, question 3.
5 John Leith, *Assembly at Westminster*, 97.

of the Assembly of Divines, Now by Authority of Parliament sitting at Westminster, concerning a Confession of Faith. After further discussion, Parliament published another "authorized" edition of the *Confession*, with the new title of "Articles of Religion approved and passed by both Houses of Parliament." It differed from the Assembly's *Confession* by the omission of parts of chapters 20 and 24 and all of chapters 30 and 31, touching on issues of church–state relations and responsibilities.

The Westminster Assembly produced two catechisms—"one more exact and comprehensive, another more easy and short for new beginners." *The Larger Catechism* was completed in October 1647, and *The Shorter Catechism* a month later. *The Shorter Catechism*, originally intended for children and beginners, made the greater impact and remains a beloved expression of Reformed doctrine. For millions of children (and adults) it laid what John G. Paton (nineteenth-century missionary to the New Hebrides from Scotland's Reformed Presbyterian Church) called "the solid rock-foundations" of their Christian lives.[1] The famous *New England Primer*, for more than a hundred years the beginning textbook for America's children, contained *The Shorter Catechism*. An 1843 printing of the *Primer* states:

> *Our Puritan fathers brought the Shorter Catechism with them across the ocean and laid it on the same shelf with the family Bible. They taught it diligently to their children. ... If in this catechism the true and fundamental doctrines of the Gospel are expressed in fewer and better words and definitions than in any other summary, why ought we not now to train up a child in the way he should go?*[2]

The Westminster Confession served, in a limited way, the church in England until the Restoration in 1660 (although Presbyterianism functioned effectively, it seems, only in London and Lancashire). The General Assembly of the Church of Scotland received the *Confession* as its theological standard (alongside the Scots Confession of 1560) on August 27, 1647. The General Assembly declared it "to be most agreeable to the Word of God, and in nothing contrary to the received doctrine, worship, discipline, and government of this Kirk," and thankfully acknowledged the great mercy of the Lord "in that so excellent a Confession of Faith is prepared, and thus far agreed upon in both kingdoms." *The Westminster Confession*, with modifications in church polity, was adopted in 1648 by the Congregational churches of Massachusetts, as

---

1 James Paton, ed., *John G. Paton—Missionary to the New Hebrides: An Autobiography (1889, 1965)*, 16.

2 *The New-England Primer* (1777, 1991), 4.

their *Cambridge Platform.* It was adopted as the *Savoy Declaration* by the English Congregational churches in 1658. *The Westminster Confession*, altered in baptism as well as polity, was accepted by the London Baptists in 1677 and, as *The Philadelphia Confession*, by Baptists in America in 1742. In 1729 the newly organized Presbyterian Church in the American colonies adopted *The Westminster Confession* ("good forms of sound words," they called it), with the provision that ministers could take exceptions to the *Confession*, provided the presbytery agreed that those exceptions did not compromise the theological integrity of the *Confession. The Westminster Confession* was amended in chapters 20, 23, and 31 (dealing with issues of church and state) by the American Presbyterian Church and approved in 1789 at its first General Assembly.

The Westminster Confession has been translated into many languages (most recently into Lithuanian) and has shaped Reformed churches and thought throughout the world. Its "solidity and majesty"[1] have inspired many people, and its biblical faithfulness has helped them to know "how we may glorify and enjoy" God.

In 1843, Princeton Seminary's Archibald Alexander wrote concerning *The Westminster Confession and Catechisms:*

> *We venerate these standards, partly because they embody the wisdom of an august Synod; because they come down to us associated with the memory and faith of saints and martyrs and embalmed with their blood; but we love them most of all because they contain the truth of God—that truth which forms the foundation of our hopes. As our fathers prized them, and we prize them, so may our children and our children's children love and preserve them.*[2]

In his opening address to Princeton Seminary students on September 20, 1903, B. B. Warfield recommended some books that the students should read in order to nurture their spiritual life. He ended, somewhat surprisingly, with the statement that the *Creeds of Christendom* are "more directly, richly, and evangelically devotional" than any other writings, apart from the Bible. He recommended especially *The Westminster Confession of Faith* and *The Heidelberg Catechism.* Warfield said: "He who wishes to grow strong in his religious life, let him, I say, next to the Bible, feed himself on the great creeds of the church." They are not "metaphysical speculation," said Warfield, but "compressed and weighted utterances of the Christian heart."[3]

---

1 David F. Wright, *New Dictionary of Theology*, 156.
2 *Biblical Repertory and Princeton Review* (1843), 586.
3 *Shorter Works of Benjamin B. Warfield* 2:492-94.

John Murray paid high tribute to *The Westminster Confession of Faith* when he wrote that "in respect to fidelity to Scripture, precision of thought and formulation, fullness of statement, balanced proportion of emphasis, studied economy of words, and effective exposure of error, no creedal confession attains to the same level of excellence characterizing that of Westminster." Murray revealed his Protestant and Presbyterian convictions when he added that this praise did not mean that the confession was "a perfect document" and "not susceptible to improvement or correction ... an estimate and veneration that belong only to the Word of God."[1]

Prayer

Our Father, we thank you that you have given us your own
counsel in the inspired Scripture concerning those things which
we need to know for your glory and our salvation—and that by your
singular care and providence you have kept that Scripture pure in all ages.

We thank you for the inward illumination of the Holy Spirit that enables us to
come to the saving knowledge of those things that are revealed in your Word.

We thank you that for the better government and further
edification of the church you raised up assemblies
such as the one that met at Westminster Abbey.

Help us, our Father, to profit from its diligent example and learn
from its careful documents, while always remembering that the
Supreme Judge by which all controversies of religion are to be determined,
all theologies are to be examined, and in whose sentence we are to rest,
is no other than the Holy Spirit speaking in the Scripture.

In Jesus's name we pray, in obedience to His commands,
and with confidence in His promises.
Amen.

1 *Collected Writings of John Murray* 4:241-63.

BRIEF BIBLIOGRAPHY

Barker, William S. *Puritan Profiles: 54 Influential Puritans at the Time When the Westminster Confession of Faith Was Written* (1996).

Carson, John L., and Hall, David W., eds. *To Glorify and Enjoy God: A Commemoration of the 350th Anniversary of the Westminster Assembly* (1994).

Leith, John H. *Assembly at Westminster: Reformed Theology in the Making* (1973).

Warfield, Benjamin Breckinridge. *The Westminster Assembly and Its Work* (1931).

The Westminster Confession of Faith

The Jerusalem Chamber was ... the meeting place of the Westminster Assembly, the committee of divines appointed by Parliament in 1643 to reform the Church of England. Among the documents to emerge from the Assembly was the Westminster Confession, which was to be the definitive doctrinal statement of English Presbyterianism.

—The Dean and Chapter of Westminster

CHAPTER 1

OF THE HOLY SCRIPTURE.

1. Although the light of nature, and the works of creation and providence do so far make known the goodness, wisdom, and power of God, as to leave men without excuse,[1] they are not sufficient to give that knowledge of God, and of his will, that is necessary for salvation.[2] Therefore it pleased the Lord, at various times, and in a variety of ways, to reveal Himself, and to declare His will to His Church;[3] and afterward, for the better preserving and propagating of the truth, and for the more sure establishment and comfort of the Church against the corruption of the flesh, and the malice of Satan

---

1 **Rom. 1:19-20,32.** For what can be known about God is plain to them, because God has shown it to them. For his invisible attributes, namely, his eternal power and divine nature, have been clearly perceived, ever since the creation of the world, in the things that have been made. So they are without excuse...Though they know God's decree that those who practice such things deserve to die, they not only do them but give approval to those who practice them. **Rom. 2:1,14-15.** Therefore you have no excuse, O man, every one of you who judges. For in passing judgment on another you condemn yourself, because you, the judge, practice the very same things...For when Gentiles, who do not have the law, by nature do what the law requires, they are a law to themselves, even though they do not have the law. They show that the work of the law is written on their hearts, while their conscience also bears witness, and their conflicting thoughts accuse or even excuse them. **Ps. 19:1-3.** The heavens declare the glory of God, and the sky above proclaims his handiwork. Day to day pours out speech, and night to night reveals knowledge. There is no speech, nor are there words, whose voice is not heard.

2 **1 Cor. 1:21.** For since, in the wisdom of God, the world did not know God through wisdom, it pleased God through the folly of what we preach to save those who believe. **1 Cor. 2:13-14.** And we impart this in words not taught by human wisdom but taught by the Spirit, interpreting spiritual truths to those who are spiritual. The natural person does not accept the things of the Spirit of God, for they are folly to him, and he is not able to understand them because they are spiritually discerned.

3 **Heb. 1:1.** Long ago, at many times and in many ways, God spoke to our fathers by the prophets

and of the world,[1] to commit His same will to writing: which makes the Holy Scripture to be most necessary;[2] those former ways of God's revealing His will to His people being now ceased.[3]

2. Under the name of Holy Scripture, or the Word of God written, are now contained all the books of the Old and New Testaments, which are these,

---

1 **Prov. 22:19-21**. That your trust may be in the LORD, I have made them known to you today, even to you. Have I not written for you thirty sayings of counsel and knowledge, to make you know what is right and true, that you may give a true answer to those who sent you? **Isa. 8:19-20**. And when they say to you, "Inquire of the mediums and the necromancers who chirp and mutter," should not a people inquire of their God? Should they inquire of the dead on behalf of the living? To the teaching and to the testimony! If they will not speak according to this word, it is because they have no dawn. **Matt. 4:4,7,10**. But he answered, "It is written, 'Man shall not live by bread alone, but by every word that comes from the mouth of God.'"...Jesus said to him, "Again it is written, 'You shall not put the Lord your God to the test.'"...Then Jesus said to him, "Be gone, Satan! For it is written, 'You shall worship the Lord your God and him only shall you serve.'" **Luke 1:3-4**. It seemed good to me also, having followed all things closely for some time past, to write an orderly account for you, most excellent Theophilus, that you may have certainty concerning the things you have been taught. **Rom. 15:4**. For whatever was written in former days was written for our instruction, that through endurance and through the encouragement of the Scriptures we might have hope.

2 **2 Tim. 3:15**. ...and how from childhood you have been acquainted with the sacred writings, which are able to make you wise for salvation through faith in Christ Jesus. **2 Pet. 1:19**. And we have something more sure, the prophetic word, to which you will do well to pay attention as to a lamp shining in a dark place, until the day dawns and the morning star rises in your hearts

3 **Heb. 1:1-2**. Long ago, at many times and in many ways, God spoke to our fathers by the prophets, but in these last days he has spoken to us by his Son, whom he appointed the heir of all things, through whom also he created the world.

OF THE OLD TESTAMENT		OF THE NEW TESTAMENT	
Genesis	Ecclesiastes	Matthew	Titus
Exodus	The Song of Solomon	Mark	Philemon
Leviticus	Isaiah	Luke	Hebrews
Numbers	Jeremiah	John	James
Deuteronomy	Lamentations	Acts	1 Peter
Joshua	Ezekiel	Romans	2 Peter
Judges	Daniel	1 Corinthians	1 John
Ruth	Hosea	2 Corinthians	2 John
1 Samuel	Joel	Galatians	3 John
2 Samuel	Amos	Ephesians	Jude
1 Kings	Obadiah	Philippians	Revelation
2 Kings	Jonah	Colossians	
1 Chronicles	Micah	1 Thessalonians	
2 Chronicles	Nahum	2 Thessalonians	
Ezra	Habakkuk	1 Timothy	
Nehemiah	Zephaniah	2 Timothy	
Esther	Haggai		
Job	Zechariah		
Psalms	Malachi		
Proverbs			

all which are given by inspiration of God to be the rule of faith and life.[1]

1 **Lk. 16:29-31**. But Abraham said, 'They have Moses and the Prophets; let them hear them.' And he said, 'No, father Abraham, but if someone goes to them from the dead, they will repent.' He said to him, 'If they do not hear Moses and the Prophets, neither will they be convinced if someone should rise from the dead.'" **2 Tim.3:16**. All Scripture is breathed out by God and profitable for teaching, for reproof, for correction, and for training in righteousness, **Eph. 2:20**. built on the foundation of the apostles and prophets, Christ Jesus himself being the cornerstone. **Rev. 22:18-19**. I warn everyone who hears the words of the prophecy of this book: if anyone adds to them, God will add to him the plagues described in this book, and if anyone takes away from the words of the book of this prophecy, God will take away his share in the tree of life and in the holy city, which are described in this book.

3. The books commonly called Apocrypha, not being of divine inspiration, are no part of the canon of the Scripture, and therefore are of no authority in the Church of God, nor to be any otherwise approved, or made use of, than other human writings.[1]

4. The authority of the Holy Scripture, for which it ought to be believed, and obeyed, depends not on the testimony of any man, or Church; but wholly on God (who is truth itself) the author thereof: and therefore it is to be received, because it is the Word of God.[2]

5. We may be moved and induced by the testimony of the Church to a high and reverend esteem of the Holy Scripture.[3] And the heavenliness of the matter, the efficacy of the doctrine, the majesty of the style, the unity of all the parts, the purpose of the whole (which is, to give all glory to God), the full revelation it makes of the only way of man's salvation, the many other incomparable excellencies, and the entire perfection thereof, are abundant evidence that Holy Scripture is the Word of God: yet our full persuasion and assurance of its infallible truth and

---

1 **Lk. 24:27,44**. For who is the greater, one who reclines at table or one who serves? Is it not the one who reclines at table? But I am among you as the one who serves... And being in an agony he prayed more earnestly; and his sweat became like great drops of blood falling down to the ground. **Rom. 3:2**. Much in every way. To begin with, the Jews were entrusted with the oracles of God. **2 Pet. 1:21**. For no prophecy was ever produced by the will of man, but men spoke from God as they were carried along by the Holy Spirit.

2 1 **Thess. 2:13**. And we also thank God constantly for this, that when you received the word of God, which you heard from us, you accepted it not as the word of men but as what it really is, the word of God, which is at work in you believers. **2 Tim. 3:16**. All Scripture is breathed out by God and profitable for teaching, for reproof, for correction, and for training in righteousness. **2 Pet.1:19,21**. And we have something more sure, the prophetic word, to which you will do well to pay attention as to a lamp shining in a dark place, until the day dawns and the morning star rises in your hearts. **1 Jn. 5:9**. If we receive the testimony of men, the testimony of God is greater, for this is the testimony of God that he has borne concerning his Son.

3 **1 Tim. 3:15**. if I delay, you may know how one ought to behave in the household of God, which is the church of the living God, a pillar and buttress of the truth.

divine authority is from the inward work of the Holy Spirit bearing witness by and with the Word in our hearts.[1]

6. The whole counsel of God concerning all things necessary for His own glory, man's salvation, faith and life, is either expressly set down in Scripture, or by good and necessary logic may be shown from Scripture: to which nothing at any time is to be added, whether by new revelations of the Spirit or traditions of men.[2] Nevertheless, we acknowledge the inward illumination of the Spirit of God to be necessary for the saving understanding of such things as are revealed in the Word:[3] and that there are some circumstances concerning the worship of God, and government of the Church, that arise from time to time and which are to be decided according to natural principles governed by a

---

1 **Isa. 59:21.** "And as for me, this is my covenant with them," says the LORD: "My Spirit that is upon you, and my words that I have put in your mouth, shall not depart out of your mouth, or out of the mouth of your offspring, or out of the mouth of your children's offspring," says the LORD, "from this time forth and forevermore." **Jn. 16:13-14.** When the Spirit of truth comes, he will guide you into all the truth, for he will not speak on his own authority, but whatever he hears he will speak, and he will declare to you the things that are to come. He will glorify me, for he will take what is mine and declare it to you. **1 Cor. 2:10-12.** these things God has revealed to us through the Spirit. For the Spirit searches everything, even the depths of God. For who knows a person's thoughts except the spirit of that person, which is in him? So also no one comprehends the thoughts of God except the Spirit of God. Now we have received not the spirit of the world, but the Spirit who is from God, that we might understand the things freely given us by God. **1 Jn. 2:20.** But you have an anointing from the Holy One, and all of you know the truth.

2 **Gal. 1:8-9.** But even if we or an angel from heaven should preach to you a gospel contrary to the one we preached to you, let him be accursed. As we have said before, so now I say again: If anyone is preaching to you a gospel contrary to the one you received, let him be accursed. **2 Thess. 2:2.** not to be quickly shaken in mind or alarmed, either by a spirit or a spoken word, or a letter seeming to be from us, to the effect that the day of the Lord has come. **2 Tim. 3:15-17.** and how from childhood you have been acquainted with the sacred writings, which are able to make you wise for salvation through faith in Christ Jesus. All Scripture is breathed out by God and profitable for teaching, for reproof, for correction, and for training in righteousness, that the man of God may be competent, equipped for every good work

3 **Jn. 6:45.** It is written in the Prophets, 'And they will all be taught by God.' Everyone who has heard and learned from the Father comes to me. **1 Cor. 2:9-12.** But, as it is written, "What no eye has seen, nor ear heard, nor the heart of man imagined, what God has prepared for those who love him"—these things God has revealed to us through the Spirit. For the Spirit searches everything, even the depths of God. For who knows a person's thoughts except the spirit of that person, which is in him? So also no one comprehends the thoughts of God except the Spirit of God. Now we have received not the spirit of the world, but the Spirit who is from God, that we might understand the things freely given us by God

Christian heart, according to the general rules of the Word, which are always to be observed.[1]

7. All things in Scripture are not equally obvious, nor equally clear to everyone:[2] yet those things that are necessary to be known, believed, and observed for salvation, are so clearly stated and explained in some place of Scripture or other, that not only the learned, but the unlearned, by paying reasonable attention, may attain a sufficient understanding of them.[3]

8. The Old Testament in Hebrew (which was the native language of the people of God of old), and the New Testament in Greek (which, at the time of the writing of it, was most generally known to the nations), being immediately inspired by God, and, by His special care and providence, kept pure in all ages, are therefore authentic;[4] so as, in all controversies of religion, the Church is to appeal ultimately to them.[5] But, because these original languages are not known to all the people of God, who have the right to read and the desire to know the Scriptures, and are commanded, in the fear of God, to read and search them,[6]

---

1 **1 Cor. 11:13-14**. Judge for yourselves: is it proper for a wife to pray to God with her head uncovered? Does not nature itself teach you that if a man wears long hair it is a disgrace for him. **1 Cor. 14:26,40**. What then, brothers? When you come together, each one has a hymn, a lesson, a revelation, a tongue, or an interpretation. Let all things be done for building up. ... But all things should be done decently and in order.

2 **2 Pet. 3:16**. as he does in all his letters when he speaks in them of these matters. There are some things in them that are hard to understand, which the ignorant and unstable twist to their own destruction, as they do the other Scriptures.

3 **Ps. 119:105,130**. Your word is a lamp to my feet and a light to my path... The unfolding of your words gives light; it imparts understanding to the simple.

4 **Mt. 5:18**. For truly, I say to you, until heaven and earth pass away, not an iota, not a dot, will pass from the Law until all is accomplished.

5 **Isa. 8:20**. To the teaching and to the testimony! If they will not speak according to this word, it is because they have no dawn. **Jn. 5:39,46**. You search the Scriptures because you think that in them you have eternal life; and it is they that bear witness about me. **Acts 15:15**. And with this the words of the prophets agree, just as it is written.

6 **Jn. 5:39**. You search the Scriptures because you think that in them you have eternal life; and it is they that bear witness about me,

therefore they are to be translated into the common language of every nation where they are brought,[1] that, the Word of God dwelling plentifully in all, they may worship Him in an acceptable manner;[2] and, through patience and comfort of the Scriptures, may have hope.[3]

9. The infallible rule of interpretation of Scripture is the Scripture itself: and therefore, when there is a question about the true and full sense of any Scripture (which is not multiple, but one), it must be searched and known by other places that speak more clearly.[4]

10. The supreme judge by which all controversies of religion are to be determined, and all decrees of councils, opinions of ancient writers, doctrines of men, and private illuminations are to be examined, and on whose decisions we are to rely, can be no other but the Holy Spirit speaking in the Scripture.[5]

---

1 **1 Cor. 14:6,9,11-12,24,27-28**. Now, brothers, if I come to you speaking in tongues, how will I benefit you unless I bring you some revelation or knowledge or prophecy or teaching?... So with yourselves, if with your tongue you utter speech that is not intelligible, how will anyone know what is said? For you will be speaking into the air...but if I do not know the meaning of the language, I will be a foreigner to the speaker and the speaker a foreigner to me. So with yourselves, since you are eager for manifestations of the Spirit, strive to excel in building up the church...But if all prophesy, and an unbeliever or outsider enters, he is convicted by all, he is called to account by all...If any speak in a tongue, let there be only two or at most three, and each in turn, and let someone interpret. But if there is no one to interpret, let each of them keep silent in church and speak to himself and to God.

2 **Col. 3:16**. Let the word of Christ dwell in you richly, teaching and admonishing one another in all wisdom, singing psalms and hymns and spiritual songs, with thankfulness in your hearts to God.

3 **Rom. 15:4**. For whatever was written in former days was written for our instruction, that through endurance and through the encouragement of the Scriptures we might have hope.

4 **Acts 15:15-16**. And with this the words of the prophets agree, just as it is written, "After this I will return, and I will rebuild the tent of David that has fallen; I will rebuild its ruins, and I will restore it." **2 Pet. 1:20-21**. knowing this first of all, that no prophecy of Scripture comes from someone's own interpretation. For no prophecy was ever produced by the will of man, but men spoke from God as they were carried along by the Holy Spirit.

5 **Mt. 22:29,31**. But Jesus answered them, "You are wrong, because you know neither the Scriptures nor the power of God... And as for the resurrection of the dead, have you not read what was said to you by God? **Acts 28:25**. And disagreeing among themselves, they departed after Paul had made one statement: "The Holy Spirit was right in saying to your fathers through Isaiah the prophet: **Eph. 2:20**. built on the foundation of the apostles and prophets, Christ Jesus himself being the cornerstone

CHAPTER 2

OF GOD, AND OF THE HOLY TRINITY.

1. There is but one only,[1] living, and true God,[2] who is infinite in being and perfection,[3] a most pure spirit,[4] invisible,[5] without body, parts,[6]

---

1 **Deut. 6:4**. Hear, O Israel: The LORD our God, the LORD is one. **1 Cor. 8:4-6**. Therefore, as to the eating of food offered to idols, we know that "an idol has no real existence," and that "there is no God but one." For although there may be so-called gods in heaven or on earth—as indeed there are many "gods" and many "lords"—yet for us there is one God, the Father, from whom are all things and for whom we exist, and one Lord, Jesus Christ, through whom are all things and through whom we exist.

2 **Jer. 10:10**. But the LORD is the true God; he is the living God and the everlasting King. At his wrath the earth quakes, and the nations cannot endure his indignation. **1 Thess. 1:9**. For they themselves report concerning us the kind of reception we had among you, and how you turned to God from idols to serve the living and true God,

3 **Job 11:7-9**. Can you find out the deep things of God? Can you find out the limit of the Almighty? It is higher than heaven—what can you do? Deeper than Sheol—what can you know? Its measure is longer than the earth and broader than the sea. **Job 26:14**. Behold, these are but the outskirts of his ways, and how small a whisper do we hear of him! But the thunder of his power who can understand?

4 **Jn. 4:24**. God is spirit, and those who worship him must worship in spirit and truth.

5 **1 Tim. 1:17**. To the King of ages, immortal, invisible, the only God, be honor and glory forever and ever. Amen.

6 **Deut. 4:15-16**. Therefore watch yourselves very carefully. Since you saw no form on the day that the LORD spoke to you at Horeb out of the midst of the fire, beware lest you act corruptly by making a carved image for yourselves, in the form of any figure, the likeness of male or female. **Lk. 24:39**. See my hands and my feet, that it is I myself. Touch me, and see. For a spirit does not have flesh and bones as you see that I have. **Jn. 4:24**. God is spirit, and those who worship him must worship in spirit and truth.

or human frailty;[1] unchangeable,[2] immense,[3] eternal,[4] incomprehensible,[5] almighty,[6] most wise,[7] most holy,[8] most free,[9] most absolute;[10] working all things according to the counsel of His own unchangeable and most righteous will,[11] for His own glory;[12] most

---

1 **Acts 14:11,15**. And when the crowds saw what Paul had done, they lifted up their voices, saying in Lycaonian, "The gods have come down to us in the likeness of men!" "Men, why are you doing these things? We also are men, of like nature with you, and we bring you good news, that you should turn from these vain things to a living God, who made the heaven and the earth and the sea and all that is in them.

2 **Mal. 3:6**. For I the LORD do not change; therefore you, O children of Jacob, are not consumed. **Jas. 1:17**. Every good gift and every perfect gift is from above, coming down from the Father of lights with whom there is no variation or shadow due to change.

3 **I Kings 8:27**. But will God indeed dwell on the earth? Behold, heaven and the highest heaven cannot contain you; how much less this house that I have built! **Jer. 23:23-24**. Am I a God at hand, declares the LORD, and not a God far away? Can a man hide himself in secret places so that I cannot see him? declares the LORD. Do I not fill heaven and earth? declares the LORD.

4 **Ps. 40:2**. He drew me up from the pit of destruction, out of the miry bog, and set my feet upon a rock, making my steps secure. **1 Tim. 1:17**. To the King of ages, immortal, invisible, the only God, be honor and glory forever and ever. Amen.

5 **Ps. 145:3**. Great is the LORD, and greatly to be praised, and his greatness is unsearchable.

6 **Gen. 17:1**. When Abram was ninety-nine years old the LORD appeared to Abram and said to him, "I am God Almighty; walk before me, and be blameless. **Rev. 4:8**. And the four living creatures, each of them with six wings, are full of eyes all around and within, and day and night they never cease to say, "Holy, holy, holy, is the Lord God Almighty, who was and is and is to come!"

7 **Rom. 16:27**. to the only wise God be glory forevermore through Jesus Christ! Amen.

8 **Isa. 6:3**. And one called to another and said: "Holy, holy, holy is the LORD of hosts; the whole earth is full of his glory!" **Rev. 4:8**. And the four living creatures, each of them with six wings, are full of eyes all around and within, and day and night they never cease to say, "Holy, holy, holy, is the Lord God Almighty, who was and is and is to come!"

9 **Ps. 115:3**. Our God is in the heavens; he does all that he pleases.

10 **Ex. 3:14**. God said to Moses, "I AM WHO I AM." And he said, "Say this to the people of Israel, 'I AM has sent me to you.'"

11 **Eph. 1:11**. In him we have obtained an inheritance, having been predestined according to the purpose of him who works all things according to the counsel of his will

12 **Prov. 16:4**. The LORD has made everything for its purpose, even the wicked for the day of trouble. **Rom. 11:36**. For from him and through him and to him are all things. To him be glory forever. Amen.

loving,[1] gracious, merciful, patient, abundant in goodness and truth, forgiving iniquity, transgression, and sin;[2] the one who rewards those who diligently seek Him;[3] and along with this, most just, and terrifying in His judgments,[4] hating all sin,[5] and who will by no means acquit the guilty.[6]

2. God has all life,[7] glory,[8] goodness,[9] blessedness,[10] in and of Himself; and is alone in and of Himself all-sufficient, not standing in need of

1 **1 Jn. 4:8-16**. Anyone who does not love does not know God, because God is love. In this the love of God was made manifest among us, that God sent his only Son into the world, so that we might live through him. In this is love, not that we have loved God but that he loved us and sent his Son to be the propitiation for our sins. Beloved, if God so loved us, we also ought to love one another. No one has ever seen God; if we love one another, God abides in us and his love is perfected in us. By this we know that we abide in him and he in us, because he has given us of his Spirit. And we have seen and testify that the Father has sent his Son to be the Savior of the world. Whoever confesses that Jesus is the Son of God, God abides in him, and he in God. So we have come to know and to believe the love that God has for us. God is love, and whoever abides in love abides in God, and God abides in him.

2 **Ex. 34:6-7**. The LORD passed before him and proclaimed, "The LORD, the LORD, a God merciful and gracious, slow to anger, and abounding in steadfast love and faithfulness, keeping steadfast love for thousands, forgiving iniquity and transgression and sin, but who will by no means clear the guilty, visiting the iniquity of the fathers on the children and the children's children, to the third and the fourth generation."

3 **Heb. 11:6**. And without faith it is impossible to please him, for whoever would draw near to God must believe that he exists and that he rewards those who seek him.

4 **Nah. 9:32-33**. Now, therefore, our God, the great, the mighty, and the awesome God, who keeps covenant and steadfast love, let not all the hardship seem little to you that has come upon us, upon our kings, our princes, our priests, our prophets, our fathers, and all your people, since the time of the kings of Assyria until this day. Yet you have been righteous in all that has come upon us, for you have dealt faithfully and we have acted wickedly.

5 **Ps. 5:5-6**. The boastful shall not stand before your eyes; you hate all evildoers. You destroy those who speak lies; the LORD abhors the bloodthirsty and deceitful man.

6 **Ex. 34:7**. keeping steadfast love for thousands, forgiving iniquity and transgression and sin, but who will by no means clear the guilty, visiting the iniquity of the fathers on the children and the children's children, to the third and the fourth generation." **Nah. 1:2-3**. The LORD is a jealous and avenging God; the LORD is avenging and wrathful; the LORD takes vengeance on his adversaries and keeps wrath for his enemies. The LORD is slow to anger and great in power, and the LORD will by no means clear the guilty. His way is in whirlwind and storm, and the clouds are the dust of his feet.

7 **Jn. 5:26**. For as the Father has life in himself, so he has granted the Son also to have life in himself.

8 **Acts 7:2**. And Stephen said "Brothers and fathers, hear me. The God of glory appeared to our father Abraham when he was in Mesopotamia, before he lived in Haran.

9 **Ps. 119:68**. You are good and do good; teach me your statutes.

10 **Rom. 9:5**. To them belong the patriarchs, and from their race, according to the flesh, is the Christ who is God over all, blessed forever. Amen. **1 Tim. 6:15**. which he will display at the proper time—he who is the blessed and only Sovereign, the King of kings and Lord of lords.

any creatures which He has made,[1] nor deriving any glory from them,[2] but only displaying His own glory in, by, to, and upon them. He is the only fountain of all being, of whom, through whom, and to whom are all things[3] and has most sovereign dominion over them, to do by them, for them, or upon them whatever pleases Him.[4] In His sight all things are open and known,[5] His knowledge is infinite, infallible, and independent of the creature,[6] so as nothing is to Him contingent, or uncertain.[7] He is most holy in all His counsels, in all His works, and in all His commands.[8] To Him is due from angels

1 **Acts 17:24-25**. The God who made the world and everything in it, being Lord of heaven and earth, does not live in temples made by man, nor is he served by human hands, as though he needed anything, since he himself gives to all mankind life and breath and everything.

2 **Job 22:2-3**. "Can a man be profitable to God? Surely he who is wise is profitable to himself. Is it any pleasure to the Almighty if you are in the right, or is it gain to him if you make your ways blameless?

3 **Rom. 11:36**. For from him and through him and to him are all things. To him be glory forever. Amen.

4 **Dan. 4:25,35**. that you shall be driven from among men, and your dwelling shall be with the beasts of the field. You shall be made to eat grass like an ox, and you shall be wet with the dew of heaven, and seven periods of time shall pass over you, till you know that the Most High rules the kingdom of men and gives it to whom he will; all the inhabitants of the earth are accounted as nothing, and he does according to his will among the host of heaven and among the inhabitants of the earth; and none can stay his hand or say to him, "What have you done?" **1 Tim. 6:15**. which he will display at the proper time—he who is the blessed and only Sovereign, the King of kings and Lord of lords. **Rev. 4:11**. "Worthy are you, our Lord and God, to receive glory and honor and power, for you created all things, and by your will they existed and were created."

5 **Heb. 4:13**. And no creature is hidden from his sight, but all are naked and exposed to the eyes of him to whom we must give account.

6 **Ps. 147:5**. Great is our Lord, and abundant in power; his understanding is beyond measure. **Rom. 11:33-34**. Oh, the depth of the riches and wisdom and knowledge of God! How unsearchable are his judgments and how inscrutable his ways!" For who has known the mind of the Lord, or who has been his counselor?"

7 **Ezek. 11:5**. And the Spirit of the LORD fell upon me, and he said to me, "Say, Thus says the LORD: So you think, O house of Israel. For I know the things that come into your mind. **Acts 15:18**. known from of old.

8 **Ps. 145:17**. The LORD is righteous in all his ways and kind in all his works. **Rom. 7:12**. So the law is holy, and the commandment is holy and righteous and good.

and men, and every other creature, whatever worship, service, or obedience He is pleased to require of them.[1]

3. In the unity of the Godhead there are three persons, of one substance, power, and eternity: God the Father, God the Son, and God the Holy Spirit:[2] the Father is not created by another, nor is He begotten or proceeding; the Son is eternally begotten of the Father;[3] the Holy Ghost is eternally proceeding from the Father and the Son.[4]

---

1 **Rev. 5:12-14**. saying with a loud voice, "Worthy is the Lamb who was slain, to receive power and wealth and wisdom and might and honor and glory and blessing!" And I heard every creature in heaven and on earth and under the earth and in the sea, and all that is in them, saying, "To him who sits on the throne and to the Lamb be blessing and honor and glory and might forever and ever!" And the four living creatures said, "Amen!" and the elders fell down and worshiped.

2 **Mt. 3:16-17**. And when Jesus was baptized, immediately he went up from the water, and behold, the heavens were opened to him, and he saw the Spirit of God descending like a dove and coming to rest on him; and behold, a voice from heaven said, "This is my beloved Son, with whom I am well pleased." **Mt. 28:19**. Go therefore and make disciples of all nations, baptizing them in the name of the Father and of the Son and of the Holy Spirit. **2 Cor. 13:14**. The grace of the Lord Jesus Christ and the love of God and the fellowship of the Holy Spirit be with you all. **1 Jn. 5:7**. For there are three that testify

3 **Jn. 1:14,18**. And the Word became flesh and dwelt among us, and we have seen his glory, glory as of the only Son from the Father, full of grace and truth. No one has ever seen God; the only God, who is at the Father's side, he has made him known.

4 **Jn. 15:26**. But when the Helper comes, whom I will send to you from the Father, the Spirit of truth, who proceeds from the Father, he will bear witness about me. **Gal. 4:6.** And because you are sons, God has sent the Spirit of his Son into our hearts, crying, "Abba! Father!"

CHAPTER 3

OF GOD'S ETERNAL DECREE.

1. God from all eternity did, by the most wise and holy counsel of His own will, freely and unchangeably ordain whatever comes to pass.[1] Yet neither is God the author of sin;[2] nor are creatures forced to act contrary to their wills; nor is the liberty or contingency of second causes taken away, but rather established.[3]

---

1 **Rom. 9:15,18**. For he says to Moses, "I will have mercy on whom I have mercy, and I will have compassion on whom I have compassion."; So then he has mercy on whomever he wills, and he hardens whomever he wills. **Rom. 11:33**. Oh, the depth of the riches and wisdom and knowledge of God! How unsearchable are his judgments and how inscrutable his ways! **Eph. 1:11**. In him we have obtained an inheritance, having been predestined according to the purpose of him who works all things according to the counsel of his will. **Heb. 6:17**. So when God desired to show more convincingly to the heirs of the promise the unchangeable character of his purpose, he guaranteed it with an oath.

2 **Jas. 1:13,17**. Let no one say when he is tempted, "I am being tempted by God," for God cannot be tempted with evil, and he himself tempts no one; Every good gift and every perfect gift is from above, coming down from the Father of lights with whom there is no variation or shadow due to change. **I Jn. 1:5**. This is the message we have heard from him and proclaim to you, that God is light, and in him is no darkness at all.

3 **Prov. 16:33**. The lot is cast into the lap, but its every decision is from the LORD. **Mt. 17:12**. "But I tell you that Elijah has already come, and they did not recognize him, but did to him whatever they pleased. So also the Son of Man will certainly suffer at their hands." **Jn. 19:11**. Jesus answered him, "You would have no authority over me at all unless it had been given you from above. Therefore he who delivered me over to you has the greater sin." **Acts 2:23**. This Jesus, delivered up according to the definite plan and foreknowledge of God, you crucified and killed by the hands of lawless men. **Acts 4:27-28**. For truly in this city there were gathered together against your holy servant Jesus, whom you anointed, both Herod and Pontius Pilate, along with the Gentiles and the peoples of Israel, to do whatever your hand and your plan had predestined to take place.

2. Although God knows whatever may or can come to pass under all hypothetical conditions,[1] He has not decreed anything because He foresaw it as future, or as that which would come to pass under such conditions.[2]

3. By the decree of God, for the display of His glory, some men and angels[3] are predestined to everlasting life; and others foreordained to everlasting death.[4]

4. These angels and men, thus predestined and foreordained, are individually and unchangeably designed, and their number so certain and definite, that it cannot be either increased or decreased.[5]

5. Those of mankind who are predestined to life, God, before the foundation of the world was laid, according to His eternal and unchangeable purpose and the secret counsel and good pleasure of His will,

---

1 **1 Sam. 23:11-12.** Will the men of Keilah surrender me into his hand? Will Saul come down, as your servant has heard? O LORD, the God of Israel, please tell your servant." And the LORD said, "He will come down." Then David said, "Will the men of Keilah surrender me and my men into the hand of Saul?" And the LORD said, "They will surrender you." **Mt. 11:21,23.** "Woe to you, Chorazin! Woe to you, Bethsaida! For if the mighty works done in you had been done in Tyre and Sidon, they would have repented long ago in sackcloth and ashes; And you, Capernaum, will you be exalted to heaven? You will be brought down to Hades. For if the mighty works done in you had been done in Sodom, it would have remained until this day. **Acts 15:18.** 'known from of old.'

2 **Rom. 9:11,13,16,18.** though they were not yet born and had done nothing either good or bad—in order that God's purpose of election might continue, not because of works but because of him who calls; As it is written, "Jacob I loved, but Esau I hated." So then it depends not on human will or exertion, but on God, who has mercy; So then he has mercy on whomever he wills, and he hardens whomever he wills.

3 **Mt. 25:41.** "Then he will say to those on his left, 'Depart from me, you cursed, into the eternal fire prepared for the devil and his angels." **1 Tim. 5:21.** In the presence of God and of Christ Jesus and of the elect angels I charge you to keep these rules without prejudging, doing nothing from partiality.

4 **Prov. 16:4.** The LORD has made everything for its purpose, even the wicked for the day of trouble. **Rom. 9:22-23.** What if God, desiring to show his wrath and to make known his power, has endured with much patience vessels of wrath prepared for destruction, in order to make known the riches of his glory for vessels of mercy, which he has prepared beforehand for glory. **Eph. 1:5-6.** He predestined us for adoption as sons through Jesus Christ, according to the purpose of his will, to the praise of his glorious grace, with which he has blessed us in the Beloved.

5 **Jn. 13:18.** I am not speaking of all of you; I know whom I have chosen. But the Scripture will be fulfilled; He who ate my bread has lifted his heel against me.' **2 Tim. 2:19.** But God's firm foundation stands, bearing this seal: "The Lord knows those who are his," and, "Let everyone who names the name of the Lord depart from iniquity."

chose in Christ for everlasting glory,[1] out of His mere free grace and love, without foreseeing faith, or good works, or perseverance in either faith or works, or any other quality of the creature, as conditions or causes moving Him to do so;[2] and all to the praise of His glorious grace.[3]

6. As God has appointed the elect to glory, so has He, by the eternal and most free purpose of His will, foreordained all the means to accomplish this.[4] They who are elected, being fallen in Adam, are redeemed by Christ;[5] are effectually called to faith in Christ by His

---

1 **Rom. 8:30**. And those whom he predestined he also called, and those whom he called he also justified, and those whom he justified he also glorified. **Eph. 1:4,9,11**. even as he chose us in him before the foundation of the world, that we should be holy and blameless before him; making known to us the mystery of his will, according to his purpose, which he set forth in Christ; In him we have obtained an inheritance, having been predestined according to the purpose of him who works all things according to the counsel of his will. **1 Thess. 5:9**. For God has not destined us for wrath, but to obtain salvation through our Lord Jesus Christ. **2 Tim. 1:9**. who saved us and called us to a holy calling, not because of our works but because of his own purpose and grace, which he gave us in Christ Jesus before the ages began.

2 **Rom. 9:11,13,16**. though they were not yet born and had done nothing either good or bad—in order that God's purpose of election might continue, not because of works but because of him who calls; As it is written, "Jacob I loved, but Esau I hated." So then it depends not on human will or exertion, but on God, who has mercy. **Eph. 1:4, 9**. even as he chose us in him before the foundation of the world, that we should be holy and blameless before him; making known to us the mystery of his will, according to his purpose, which he set forth in Christ.

3 **Eph. 1:6,12**. to the praise of his glorious grace, with which he has blessed us in the Beloved; So that we who were the first to hope in Christ might be to the praise of his glory.

4 **Eph. 1:4-5**. Even as he chose us in him before the foundation of the world, that we should be holy and blameless before him. In love he predestined us for adoption as sons through Jesus Christ, according to the purpose of his will. **Eph. 2:10**. For we are his workmanship, created in Christ Jesus for good works, which God prepared beforehand, that we should walk in them. **2 Thess. 2:13**. But we ought always to give thanks to God for you, brothers beloved by the Lord, because God chose you as the firstfruits to be saved, through sanctification by the Spirit and belief in the truth. **1 Pet. 1:2**. According to the foreknowledge of God the Father, in the sanctification of the Spirit, for obedience to Jesus Christ and for sprinkling with his blood: May grace and peace be multiplied to you.

5 **1 Thess. 5:9-10**. For God has not destined us for wrath, but to obtain salvation through our Lord Jesus Christ, who died for us so that whether we are awake or asleep we might live with him. **Titus 2:14**. who gave himself for us to redeem us from all lawlessness and to purify for himself a people for his own possession who are zealous for good works.

Spirit working in due time; and are justified, adopted, sanctified,[1] and kept by His power, through faith, for salvation.[2] None are redeemed by Christ, effectually called, justified, adopted, sanctified, and saved, but the elect only.[3]

7. The rest of mankind God was willing, according to the unsearchable counsel of His own will, by which He extends or witholds mercy as He pleases, for the glory of His sovereign power over His creatures, to pass by and to ordain to dishonor and wrath for their sin, to the praise of His glorious justice.[4]

---

1 **Rom. 8:30**. And those whom he predestined he also called, and those whom he called he also justified, and those whom he justified he also glorified. **Eph. 1:5**. He predestined us for adoption as sons through Jesus Christ, according to the purpose of his will. **2 Thess. 2:13**. But we ought always to give thanks to God for you, brothers beloved by the Lord, because God chose you as the firstfruits to be saved, through sanctification by the Spirit and belief in the truth.

2 **1 Pet. 1:5**. who by God's power are being guarded through faith for a salvation ready to be revealed in the last time.

3 **Jn. 6:64-65**. But there are some of you who do not believe." (For Jesus knew from the beginning who those were who did not believe, and who it was who would betray him.) And he said, "This is why I told you that no one can come to me unless it is granted him by the Father." **Jn. 8:47**. "Whoever is of God hears the words of God. The reason why you do not hear them is that you are not of God." **Jn. 10:26**. but you do not believe because you are not part of my flock. **Jn. 17:9**. I am praying for them. I am not praying for the world but for those whom you have given me, for they are yours. **Rom. 8:28**. And we know that for those who love God all things work together for good, for those who are called according to his purpose. **1 Jn. 2:19**. They went out from us, but they were not of us; for if they had been of us, they would have continued with us. But they went out, that it might become plain that they all are not of us.

4 **Mt. 11:25-26**. At that time Jesus declared, "I thank you, Father, Lord of heaven and earth, that you have hidden these things from the wise and understanding and revealed them to little children; yes, Father, for such was your gracious will. **Rom. 9:17-18**. For the Scripture says to Pharaoh, "For this very purpose I have raised you up, that I might show my power in you, and that my name might be proclaimed in all the earth." So then he has mercy on whomever he wills, and he hardens whomever he wills. **Rom. 9:21-22**. Has the potter no right over the clay, to make out of the same lump one vessel for honorable use and another for dishonorable use? What if God, desiring to show his wrath and to make known his power, has endured with much patience vessels of wrath prepared for destruction. **2 Tim. 2:19-20**. But God's firm foundation stands, bearing this seal: "The Lord knows those who are his," and, "Let everyone who names the name of the Lord depart from iniquity." Now in a great house there are not only vessels of gold and silver but also of wood and clay, some for honorable use, some for dishonorable. **1 Pet. 2:8**. and "A stone of stumbling, and a rock of offense." They stumble because they disobey the word, as they were destined to do. **Jude 4**. For certain people have crept in unnoticed who long ago were designated for this condemnation, ungodly people, who pervert the grace of our God into sensuality and deny our only Master and Lord, Jesus Christ.

8. The doctrine of this high mystery of predestination is to be handled with special prudence and care,[1] so that men, seeking to know the will of God revealed in His Word, and yielding obedience to it, may, from the certainty of their effectual calling, be assured of their eternal election.[2] So shall this doctrine bring praise, reverence, and admiration of God;[3] and humility, diligence, and abundant consolation to all who sincerely obey the Gospel.[4]

1 **Deut. 29:29.** "The secret things belong to the LORD our God, but the things that are revealed belong to us and to our children forever, that we may do all the words of this law." **Rom. 9:20**. But who are you, O man, to answer back to God? Will what is molded say to its molder, "Why have you made me like this?" **Rom. 11:33**. Oh, the depth of the riches and wisdom and knowledge of God! How unsearchable are his judgments and how inscrutable his ways!

2 **2 Pet. 1:10**. Therefore, brothers, be all the more diligent to make your calling and election sure, for if you practice these qualities you will never fall.

3 **Rom. 11:33**. Oh, the depth of the riches and wisdom and knowledge of God! How unsearchable are his judgments and how inscrutable his ways! Eph. 1:6. to the praise of his glorious grace, with which he has blessed us in the Beloved.

4 **Lk. 10:20**. Nevertheless, do not rejoice in this, that the spirits are subject to you, but rejoice that your names are written in heaven." **Rom. 8:33**. Who shall bring any charge against God's elect? It is God who justifies. **Rom. 11: 5-6,20**. So too at the present time there is a remnant, chosen by grace. But if it is by grace, it is no longer on the basis of works; otherwise grace would no longer be grace; That is true. They were broken off because of their unbelief, but you stand fast through faith. So do not become proud, but fear. **2 Pet. 1:10**. Therefore, brothers, be all the more diligent to make your calling and election sure, for if you practice these qualities you will never fall.

CHAPTER 4

OF CREATION.

1. It pleased God the Father, Son, and Holy Ghost,[1] for the display of the glory of His eternal power, wisdom, and goodness,[2] in the beginning, to create, or make out of nothing, the world, and all things in it whether visible or invisible, in the space of six days; and all very good.[3]

---

1 **Gen. 1:2**. The earth was without form and void, and darkness was over the face of the deep. And the Spirit of God was hovering over the face of the waters. **Job 26:13**. By his wind the heavens were made fair; his hand pierced the fleeing serpent. **Job 33:4**. The Spirit of God has made me, and the breath of the Almighty gives me life. **Jn. 1:2-3**. He was in the beginning with God. All things were made through him, and without him was not any thing made that was made. **Heb. 1:2**. But in these last days he has spoken to us by his Son, whom he appointed the heir of all things, through whom also he created the world.

2 **Ps. 33:5-6**. He loves righteousness and justice; the earth is full of the steadfast love of the LORD. **Ps. 104:24**. O LORD, how manifold are your works! In wisdom have you made them all; the earth is full of your creatures. **Jer. 10:12**. It is he who made the earth by his power, who established the world by his wisdom, and by his understanding stretched out the heavens. **Rom. 1:20**. For his invisible attributes, namely, his eternal power and divine nature, have been clearly perceived, ever since the creation of the world, in the things that have been made. So they are without excuse.

3 **Gen. 1**. All of Gen. 1. **Acts 17:24**. The God who made the world and everything in it, being Lord of heaven and earth, does not live in temples made by man. **Col. 1:16**. For by him all things were created, in heaven and on earth, visible and invisible, whether thrones or dominions or rulers or authorities—all things were created through him and for him. **Heb. 11:3**. By faith we understand that the universe was created by the word of God, so that what is seen was not made out of things that are visible. **Ps. 33:6**. By the word of the LORD the heavens were made, and by the breath of his mouth all their host. **Ex. 20:11**. For in six days the LORD made heaven and earth, the sea, and all that is in them, and rested on the seventh day. Therefore the LORD blessed the Sabbath day and made it holy.

2. After God had made all other creatures, He created man, male and female,[1] with reasoning minds and immortal souls,[2] having knowledge, righteousness, and true holiness, after His own image,[3] having the law of God written in their hearts,[4] and power to fulfill it:[5] and yet with the possibility of transgressing, being left to the liberty of their own will, which was subject to change.[6] Besides this law written in their hearts, they received a command, not to eat of the Tree of the Knowledge of Good and Evil,[7] which while they kept, they were happy in their communion with God and had authority over the creatures.[8]

---

1 **Gen. 1:27.** So God created man in his own image, in the image of God he created him; male and female he created them.

2 **Gen. 2:7.** then the LORD God formed the man of dust from the ground and breathed into his nostrils the breath of life, and the man became a living creature. **Eccl. 12:7.** and the dust returns to the earth as it was, and the spirit returns to God who gave it. **Mt. 10:28.** And do not fear those who kill the body but cannot kill the soul. Rather fear him who can destroy both soul and body in hell. **Lk. 23:43.** And he said to him, "Truly, I say to you, today you will be with me in Paradise."

3 **Gen. 1:26.** Then God said, "Let us make man in our image, after our likeness. And let them have dominion over the fish of the sea and over the birds of the heavens and over the livestock and over all the earth and over every creeping thing that creeps on the earth." **Eph. 4:24.** and to put on the new self, created after the likeness of God in true righteousness and holiness. **Col. 3:10.** and have put on the new self, which is being renewed in knowledge after the image of its creator.

4 **Rom. 2:14-15.** For when Gentiles, who do not have the law, by nature do what the law requires, they are a law to themselves, even though they do not have the law. They show that the work of the law is written on their hearts, while their conscience also bears witness, and their conflicting thoughts accuse or even excuse them

5 **Eccl. 7:29.** See, this alone I found, that God made man upright, but they have sought out many schemes.

6 **Gen. 3:6.** So when the woman saw that the tree was good for food, and that it was a delight to the eyes, and that the tree was to be desired to make one wise, she took of its fruit and ate, and she also gave some to her husband who was with her, and he ate. **Eccl. 7:29.** See, this alone I found, that God made man upright, but they have sought out many schemes.

7 **Gen. 2:17.** but of the tree of the knowledge of good and evil you shall not eat, for in the day that you eat of it you shall surely die. **Gen. 3:8-11,23.** And they heard the sound of the LORD God walking in the garden in the cool of the day, and the man and his wife hid themselves from the presence of the LORD God among the trees of the garden. But the LORD God called to the man and said to him, "Where are you?" And he said, "I heard the sound of you in the garden, and I was afraid, because I was naked, and I hid myself." He said, "Who told you that you were naked? Have you eaten of the tree of which I commanded you not to eat?"... therefore the LORD God sent him out from the garden of Eden to work the ground from which he was taken

8 **Gen. 1:26,28.** Then God said, "Let us make man in our image, after our likeness. And let them have dominion over the fish of the sea and over the birds of the heavens and over the livestock and over all the earth and over every creeping thing that creeps on the earth."... And God blessed them. And God said to them, "Be fruitful and multiply and fill the earth and subdue it and have dominion over the fish of the sea and over the birds of the heavens and over every living thing that moves on the earth."

CHAPTER 5

OF PROVIDENCE.

1. God the great Creator of all things does uphold,[1] direct, make willing, and govern all creatures, actions, and things,[2] from the greatest even to the least,[3] by His most wise and holy providence,[4] according to His infallible foreknowledge,[5] and the free and unchangeable

---

1 **Heb. 1:3**. He is the radiance of the glory of God and the exact imprint of his nature, and he upholds the universe by the word of his power. After making purification for sins, he sat down at the right hand of the Majesty on high,

2 **Job 38-41**—all of Job 38-41. **Ps. 135:6**. Whatever the LORD pleases, he does, in heaven and on earth, in the seas and all deeps. **Dan. 4:34-35**. At the end of the days I, Nebuchadnezzar, lifted my eyes to heaven, and my reason returned to me, and I blessed the Most High, and praised and honored him who lives forever, for his dominion is an everlasting dominion, and his kingdom endures from generation to generation; all the inhabitants of the earth are accounted as nothing, and he does according to his will among the host of heaven and among the inhabitants of the earth; and none can stay his hand or say to him, "What have you done?" **Acts 17: 25-26,28**. nor is he served by human hands, as though he needed anything, since he himself gives to all mankind life and breath and everything. And he made from one man every nation of mankind to live on all the face of the earth, having determined allotted periods and the boundaries of their dwelling place, ... In him we live and move and have our being; as even some of your own poets have said, "For we are indeed his offspring."

3 **Mt. 10:29-31**. Are not two sparrows sold for a penny? And not one of them will fall to the ground apart from your Father. But even the hairs of your head are all numbered. Fear not, therefore; you are of more value than many sparrows.

4 **Ps. 104:24**. O LORD, how manifold are your works! In wisdom have you made them all; the earth is full of your creatures. **Ps. 145:17**. The LORD is righteous in all his ways and kind in all his works. **Prov. 15:3**. The eyes of the LORD are in every place, keeping watch on the evil and the good.

5 **Ps. 94:8-11**. Understand, O dullest of the people! Fools, when will you be wise? He who planted the ear, does he not hear? He who formed the eye, does he not see? He who disciplines the nations, does he not rebuke? He who teaches man knowledge—the LORD—knows the thoughts of man, that they are but a breath. **Acts 15:18**. known from of old.

counsel of His own will,[1] to the praise of the glory of His wisdom, power, justice, goodness, and mercy.[2]

2. Although, in relation to the foreknowledge and decree of God, the first Cause, all things happen as God intended, without change and without fail;[3] yet, by the same providence, He orders them to come about through second causes, either necessarily, freely, or contingently.[4]

1 **EPH. 1:11.** In him we have obtained an inheritance, having been predestined according to the purpose of him who works all things according to the counsel of his will.

2 **GEN. 45:7.** And God sent me before you to preserve for you a remnant on earth, and to keep alive for you many survivors. **PS. 145:7.** They shall pour forth the fame of your abundant goodness and shall sing aloud of your righteousness. **ISA. 63:14.** Like livestock that go down into the valley, the Spirit of the LORD gave them rest. So you led your people, to make for yourself a glorious name. **ROM. 9:17.** For the Scripture says to Pharaoh, "For this very purpose I have raised you up, that I might show my power in you, and that my name might be proclaimed in all the earth." **EPH. 3:10.** so that through the church the manifold wisdom of God might now be made known to the rulers and authorities in the heavenly places.

3 **ACTS 2:23.** this Jesus, delivered up according to the definite plan and foreknowledge of God, you crucified and killed by the hands of lawless men.

4 **GEN. 8:22.** While the earth remains, seedtime and harvest, cold and heat, summer and winter, day and night, shall not cease." **EX. 21:13.** But if he did not lie in wait for him, but God let him fall into his hand, then I will appoint for you a place to which he may flee. **DEUT. 19:5.** as when someone goes into the forest with his neighbor to cut wood, and his hand swings the axe to cut down a tree, and the head slips from the handle and strikes his neighbor so that he dies—he may flee to one of these cities and live. **1 KINGS 22:28,34.** And Micaiah said, "If you return in peace, the LORD has not spoken by me." And he said, "Hear, all you peoples!" **ISA. 10:6-7.** Against a godless nation I send him, and against the people of my wrath I command him, to take spoil and seize plunder, and to tread them down like the mire of the streets. But he does not so intend, and his heart does not so think; but it is in his heart to destroy, and to cut off nations not a few. **JER. 31:35.** Thus says the LORD, who gives the sun for light by day and the fixed order of the moon and the stars for light by night, who stirs up the sea so that its waves roar—the LORD of hosts is his name:

3. God, in His ordinary providence, makes use of means,[1] yet is free to work without,[2] above,[3] and against them,[4] at His pleasure.
4. The almighty power, unsearchable wisdom, and infinite goodness of God make themselves known in His providence, such that it extends itself even to the first fall, and all other sins of angels and

---

1 **Isa. 55:10-11.** "For as the rain and the snow come down from heaven and do not return there but water the earth, making it bring forth and sprout, giving seed to the sower and bread to the eater, so shall my word be that goes out from my mouth; it shall not return to me empty, but it shall accomplish that which I purpose, and shall succeed in the thing for which I sent it. **Acts 27:31,44.** Paul said to the centurion and the soldiers, "Unless these men stay in the ship, you cannot be saved."... and the rest on planks or on pieces of the ship. And so it was that all were brought safely to land.

2 **Job 34:10.** Therefore, hear me, you men of understanding: far be it from God that he should do wickedness, and from the Almighty that he should do wrong. **Hos. 1:7.** But I will have mercy on the house of Judah, and I will save them by the LORD their God. I will not save them by bow or by sword or by war or by horses or by horsemen." **Mt. 4:4.** But he answered, "It is written, "'Man shall not live by bread alone, but by every word that comes from the mouth of God.'"

3 **Rom. 4:19-21.** He did not weaken in faith when he considered his own body, which was as good as dead (since he was about a hundred years old), or when he considered the barrenness of Sarah's womb. No distrust made him waver concerning the promise of God, but he grew strong in his faith as he gave glory to God, fully convinced that God was able to do what he had promised.

4 **2 Kings 6:6.** Then the man of God said, "Where did it fall?" When he showed him the place, he cut off a stick and threw it in there and made the iron float. **Dan. 3:27.** And the satraps, the prefects, the governors, and the king's counselors gathered together and saw that the fire had not had any power over the bodies of those men. The hair of their heads was not singed, their cloaks were not harmed, and no smell of fire had come upon them.

men;[1] and that not merely by God's permission,[2] but such as has joined with it a most wise and powerful setting of limits,[3] and otherwise establishing of order, and governing of them, in many ways, to His own holy ends;[4] yet so, as this sinfulness proceeds only from the creature, and not from God, who, being most holy and righteous, neither is nor can be the author or approver of sin.[5]

---

1 **2 SAM. 16:10**. But the king said, "What have I to do with you, you sons of Zeruiah? If he is cursing because the LORD has said to him, 'Curse David,' who then shall say, 'Why have you done so?'" **2 SAM. 24:1**. Again the anger of the LORD was kindled against Israel, and he incited David against them, saying, "Go, number Israel and Judah." **1 KINGS 22:22-23**. And the LORD said to him, 'By what means?' And he said, 'I will go out, and will be a lying spirit in the mouth of all his prophets.' And he said, 'You are to entice him, and you shall succeed; go out and do so.' Now therefore behold, the LORD has put a lying spirit in the mouth of all these your prophets; the LORD has declared disaster for you." **1 CHR. 10:4,13-14**. Then Saul said to his armor-bearer, "Draw your sword and thrust me through with it, lest these uncircumcised come and mistreat me." But his armor-bearer would not, for he feared greatly. Therefore Saul took his own sword and fell upon it....So Saul died for his breach of faith. He broke faith with the LORD in that he did not keep the command of the LORD, and also consulted a medium, seeking guidance. He did not seek guidance from the LORD. Therefore the LORD put him to death and turned the kingdom over to David the son of Jesse. **1 CHR. 21:1**. Then Satan stood against Israel and incited David to number Israel. **ACTS 2:23**. this Jesus, delivered up according to the definite plan and foreknowledge of God, you crucified and killed by the hands of lawless men. **ROM. 11:32-34**. For God has consigned all to disobedience, that he may have mercy on all. Oh, the depth of the riches and wisdom and knowledge of God! How unsearchable are his judgments and how inscrutable his ways! "For who has known the mind of the Lord, or who has been his counselor?"

2 **ACTS 14:16**. In past generations he allowed all the nations to walk in their own ways.

3 **2 KINGS 19:28**. Because you have raged against me and your complacency has come into my ears, I will put my hook in your nose and my bit in your mouth, and I will turn you back on the way by which you came. **PS. 76:10**. Surely the wrath of man shall praise you; the remnant of wrath you will put on like a belt.

4 **GEN. 50:20**. As for you, you meant evil against me, but God meant it for good, to bring it about that many people should be kept alive, as they are today. **ISA. 10:6-7**. Against a godless nation I send him, and against the people of my wrath I command him, to take spoil and seize plunder, and to tread them down like the mire of the streets. But he does not so intend, and his heart does not so think; but it is in his heart to destroy, When the Lord has finished all his work on Mount Zion and on Jerusalem, he will punish the speech of the arrogant heart of the king of Assyria and the boastful look in his eyes. and to cut off nations not a few;

5 **PS. 50:21**. These things you have done, and I have been silent; you thought that I was one like yourself. But now I rebuke you and lay the charge before you. **JAS. 1: 13-14,17**. Let no one say when he is tempted, "I am being tempted by God," for God cannot be tempted with evil, and he himself tempts no one. But each person is tempted when he is lured and enticed by his own desire.... Every good gift and every perfect gift is from above, coming down from the Father of lights with whom there is no variation or shadow due to change. **1 JN. 2:16**. For all that is in the world—the desires of the flesh and the desires of the eyes and pride in possessions—is not from the Father but is from the world.

5. The most wise, righteous, and gracious God does often leave, for a time, His own children to many temptations, and the corruption of their own hearts, to chastise them for their former sins, or to show them the hidden strength of corruption and deceitfulness of their hearts, that they may be humbled;[1] and, to raise them to a more close and constant dependence for their support on Him, and to make them more watchful against all future occasions of sin, and for various other just and holy ends.[2]

---

1 **2 Sam. 24:1**. Again the anger of the LORD was kindled against Israel, and he incited David against them, saying, "Go, number Israel and Judah." **2 Chr. 32:25-26,31**. But Hezekiah did not make return according to the benefit done to him, for his heart was proud. Therefore wrath came upon him and Judah and Jerusalem. But Hezekiah humbled himself for the pride of his heart, both he and the inhabitants of Jerusalem, so that the wrath of the LORD did not come upon them in the days of Hezekiah....And so in the matter of the envoys of the princes of Babylon, who had been sent to him to inquire about the sign that had been done in the land, God left him to himself, in order to test him and to know all that was in his heart.

2 **Ps. 73**. all of Ps. 73. **Ps. 77:1,10,12**. I cry aloud to God, and he will hear me.... Then I said, "I will appeal to this, to the years of the right hand of the Most High."... will ponder all your work, and meditate on your mighty deeds. **Mk. 14:66-72**. And as Peter was below in the courtyard, one of the servant girls of the high priest came, and seeing Peter warming himself, she looked at him and said, "You also were with the Nazarene, Jesus." But he denied it, saying, "I neither know nor understand what you mean." And he went out into the gateway and the rooster crowed. And the servant girl saw him and began again to say to the bystanders, "This man is one of them." But again he denied it. And after a little while the bystanders again said to Peter, "Certainly you are one of them, for you are a Galilean." But he began to invoke a curse on himself and to swear, "I do not know this man of whom you speak." And immediately the rooster crowed a second time. And Peter remembered how Jesus had said to him, "Before the rooster crows twice, you will deny me three times." And he broke down and wept. **Jn. 21:15-17.** When they had finished breakfast, Jesus said to Simon Peter, "Simon, son of John, do you love me more than these?" He said to him, "Yes, Lord; you know that I love you." He said to him, "Feed my lambs." He said to him a second time, "Simon, son of John, do you love me?" He said to him, "Yes, Lord; you know that I love you." He said to him, "Tend my sheep." He said to him the third time, "Simon, son of John, do you love me?" Peter was grieved because he said to him the third time, "Do you love me?" and he said to him, "Lord, you know everything; you know that I love you." Jesus said to him, "Feed my sheep." **2 Cor. 12:7-9**. So to keep me from becoming conceited because of the surpassing greatness of the revelations, a thorn was given me in the flesh, a messenger of Satan to harass me, to keep me from becoming conceited. Three times I pleaded with the Lord about this, that it should leave me. But he said to me, "My grace is sufficient for you, for my power is made perfect in weakness." Therefore I will boast all the more gladly of my weaknesses, so that the power of Christ may rest upon me.

6. As for those wicked and ungodly men whom God, as a righteous Judge, for former sins, does blind and harden,[1] from them He not only withholds His grace through which they might have been enlightened in their understandings, and convicted in their hearts;[2] but sometimes also withdraws the gifts that they had,[3] and exposes them to such objects as their corruption make occasions for sin;[4] and, with this, gives them over to their own lusts, the temptations

1 **Rom. 1:24,26,28**. Therefore God gave them up in the lusts of their hearts to impurity, to the dishonoring of their bodies among themselves,... For this reason God gave them up to dishonorable passions. For their women exchanged natural relations for those that are contrary to nature;... And since they did not see fit to acknowledge God, God gave them up to a debased mind to do what ought not to be done. **Rom. 11:7-8**. What then? Israel failed to obtain what it was seeking. The elect obtained it, but the rest were hardened, as it is written, "God gave them a spirit of stupor, eyes that would not see and ears that would not hear, down to this very day."

2 **Deut. 29:4**. But to this day the LORD has not given you a heart to understand or eyes to see or ears to hear.

3 **Mt 13:12**. For to the one who has, more will be given, and he will have an abundance, but from the one who has not, even what he has will be taken away. **Mt. 25:29**. For to everyone who has will more be given, and he will have an abundance. But from the one who has not, even what he has will be taken away.

4 **Deut. 2:30**. But Sihon the king of Heshbon would not let us pass by him, for the LORD your God hardened his spirit and made his heart obstinate, that he might give him into your hand, as he is this day. **2 Kings 8:12-13**. And Hazael said, "Why does my lord weep?" He answered, "Because I know the evil that you will do to the people of Israel. You will set on fire their fortresses, and you will kill their young men with the sword and dash in pieces their little ones and rip open their pregnant women." And Hazael said, "What is your servant, who is but a dog, that he should do this great thing?" Elisha answered, "The LORD has shown me that you are to be king over Syria."

of the world, and the power of Satan,[1] so that they harden themselves, even under those means that God uses for the softening of others.[2]

7. As the providence of God does, in general, reach to all creatures; so, after a most special manner, it takes care of His Church, and works all things to the good of it.[3]

---

1 **Ps. 81:11-12**. But my people did not listen to my voice; Israel would not submit to me. So I gave them over to their stubborn hearts, to follow their own counsels.
2 Thess. 2:10-12. and with all wicked deception for those who are perishing, because they refused to love the truth and so be saved. Therefore God sends them a strong delusion, so that they may believe what is false, in order that all may be condemned who did not believe the truth but had pleasure in unrighteousness.

2 **Ex. 7:3**. But I will harden Pharaoh's heart, and though I multiply my signs and wonders in the land of Egypt. **Ex. 8:15,32**. But when Pharaoh saw that there was a respite, he hardened his heart and would not listen to them, as the LORD had said...But Pharaoh hardened his heart this time also, and did not let the people go. **Isa. 6:9-10**. And he said, "Go, and say to this people: "'Keep on hearing, but do not understand; keep on seeing, but do not perceive.' Make the heart of this people dull, and their ears heavy, and blind their eyes; lest they see with their eyes, and hear with their ears, and understand with their hearts, and turn and be healed." **Isa. 8:14**. And he will become a sanctuary and a stone of offense and a rock of stumbling to both houses of Israel, a trap and a snare to the inhabitants of Jerusalem. **Acts 28:26-27**. 'Go to this people, and say, You will indeed hear but never understand, and you will indeed see but never perceive. For this people's heart has grown dull, and with their ears they can barely hear, and their eyes they have closed; lest they should see with their eyes and hear with their ears and understand with their heart and turn, and I would heal them.' **2 Cor. 2:15-16**. For we are the aroma of Christ to God among those who are being saved and among those who are perishing, to one a fragrance from death to death, to the other a fragrance from life to life. Who is sufficient for these things? **1 Pet. 2:7-8.** So the honor is for you who believe, but for those who do not believe, "The stone that the builders rejected has become the cornerstone," and "A stone of stumbling, and a rock of offense." They stumble because they disobey the word, as they were destined to do.

3 **Isa. 43:3-5,14**. For I am the LORD your God, the Holy One of Israel, your Savior. I give Egypt as your ransom, Cush and Seba in exchange for you. Because you are precious in my eyes, and honored, and I love you, give men in return for you, peoples in exchange for your life. Fear not, for I am with you; I will bring your offspring from the east, and from the west I will gather you....Thus says the LORD, your Redeemer, the Holy One of Israel: "For your sake I send to Babylon and bring them all down as fugitives, even the Chaldeans, in the ships in which they rejoice. **Am. 9:8-9**. Behold, the eyes of the Lord GOD are upon the sinful kingdom, and I will destroy it from the surface of the ground, except that I will not utterly destroy the house of Jacob," declares the LORD. "For behold, I will command, and shake the house of Israel among all the nations as one shakes with a sieve, but no pebble shall fall to the earth. **Rom. 8:28**. And we know that for those who love God all things work together for good, for those who are called according to his purpose. **1 Tim. 4:10**. For to this end we toil and strive, because we have our hope set on the living God, who is the Savior of all people, especially of those who believe.

CHAPTER 6

OF THE FALL OF MAN, OF SIN, AND OF THE PUNISHMENT THEREOF.

1. Our first parents, being seduced by the cunning and temptation of Satan, sinned, in eating the forbidden fruit.[1] This sin, God was willing, according to His wise and holy counsel, to permit, having intended it for His own glory.[2]
2. By this sin they fell from their original righteousness and communion, with God,[3] and so became dead in sin,[4] and wholly defiled in all the parts and faculties of soul and body.[5]

---

1 **Gen. 3:13**. Then the LORD God said to the woman, "What is this that you have done?" The woman said, "The serpent deceived me, and I ate." **2 Cor. 11:3**. But I am afraid that as the serpent deceived Eve by his cunning, your thoughts will be led astray from a sincere and pure devotion to Christ.

2 **Rom 11:32**. For God has consigned all to disobedience, that he may have mercy on all.

3 **Gen. 3:6-8**. So when the woman saw that the tree was good for food, and that it was a delight to the eyes, and that the tree was to be desired to make one wise, she took of its fruit and ate, and she also gave some to her husband who was with her, and he ate. Then the eyes of both were opened, and they knew that they were naked. And they sewed fig leaves together and made themselves loincloths. And they heard the sound of the LORD God walking in the garden in the cool of the day, and the man and his wife hid themselves from the presence of the LORD God among the trees of the garden. **Eccl. 7:29**. See, this alone I found, that God made man upright, but they have sought out many schemes. **Rom. 3:23**. For all have sinned and fall short of the glory of God

4 **Gen. 2:17**. But of the tree of the knowledge of good and evil you shall not eat, for in the day that you eat of it you shall surely die." **Eph. 2:1**. And you were dead in the trespasses and sins.

5 **Gen. 6:5**. The LORD saw that the wickedness of man was great in the earth, and that every intention of the thoughts of his heart was only evil continually. **Jer. 17:9**. The heart is deceitful above all things, and desperately sick; who can understand it? **Rom. 3:10-18**. "None is righteous, no, not one; no one understands; no one seeks for God. All have turned aside; together they have become worthless; no one does good, not even one. Their throat is an open grave; they use their tongues to deceive. The venom of asps is under their lips. Their mouth is full of curses and bitterness. Their feet are swift to shed blood; in their paths are ruin and misery, and the way of peace they have not known. There is no fear of God before their eyes." **Titus 1:15**. To the pure, all things are pure, but to the defiled and unbelieving, nothing is pure; but both their minds and their consciences are defiled.

3. They being the root of all mankind, the guilt of this sin was imputed;[1] and the same death in sin, and corrupted nature, conveyed to all their descendants by ordinary generation.[2]

---

1 **Gen. 1:27-28**. So God created man in his own image, in the image of God he created him; male and female he created them. And God blessed them. And God said to them, "Be fruitful and multiply and fill the earth and subdue it and have dominion over the fish of the sea and over the birds of the heavens and over every living thing that moves on the earth." **Gen. 2:16-17**. And the LORD God commanded the man, saying, "You may surely eat of every tree of the garden, but of the tree of the knowledge of good and evil you shall not eat, for in the day that you eat of it you shall surely die." **Acts 17:26**. And he made from one man every nation of mankind to live on all the face of the earth, having determined allotted periods and the boundaries of their dwelling place. **Rom. 5:12,15-19**. Therefore, just as sin came into the world through one man, and death through sin, and so death spread to all men because all sinned. But the free gift is not like the trespass. For if many died through one man's trespass, much more have the grace of God and the free gift by the grace of that one man Jesus Christ abounded for many. And the free gift is not like the result of that one man's sin. For the judgment following one trespass brought condemnation, but the free gift following many trespasses brought justification. For if, because of one man's trespass, death reigned through that one man, much more will those who receive the abundance of grace and the free gift of righteousness reign in life through the one man Jesus Christ. Therefore, as one trespass led to condemnation for all men, so one act of righteousness leads to justification and life for all men. For as by the one man's disobedience the many were made sinners, so by the one man's obedience the many will be made righteous. **1 Cor. 15:21-22,45,49**. For as by a man came death, by a man has come also the resurrection of the dead. For as in Adam all die, so also in Christ shall all be made alive. Thus it is written, "The first man Adam became a living being"; the last Adam became a life-giving spirit. Just as we have borne the image of the man of dust, we shall also bear the image of the man of heaven.

2 **Gen. 5:3**. When Adam had lived 130 years, he fathered a son in his own likeness, after his image, and named him Seth. **Job 14:4**. Who can bring a clean thing out of an unclean? There is not one. **Job 15:14**. What is man, that he can be pure? Or he who is born of a woman, that he can be righteous? **Ps. 51:5**. Behold, I was brought forth in iniquity, and in sin did my mother conceive me.

4. From this original corruption, whereby we are utterly indisposed, disabled, and opposite to all good,[1] and wholly inclined to all evil,[2] do proceed all actual transgressions.[3]

5. This corruption of nature, during this life, does remain in those who are regenerated;[4] and although it be, through Christ, pardoned, and subdued; yet both it, and all the passions it arouses, are truly sin.[5]

---

1 **Rom. 5:6**. For while we were still weak, at the right time Christ died for the ungodly. **Rom. 7:18**. For I know that nothing good dwells in me, that is, in my flesh. For I have the desire to do what is right, but not the ability to carry it out. **Rom. 8:7**. For the mind that is set on the flesh is hostile to God, for it does not submit to God's law; indeed, it cannot. **Col 1:21**. And you, who once were alienated and hostile in mind, doing evil deeds.

2 **Gen. 6:5**. The LORD saw that the wickedness of man was great in the earth, and that every intention of the thoughts of his heart was only evil continually. **Rom. 3:10-12**. as it is written: "None is righteous, no, not one; no one understands; no one seeks for God. All have turned aside; together they have become worthless; no one does good, not even one."

3 **Mt. 15:19**. For out of the heart come evil thoughts, murder, adultery, sexual immorality, theft, false witness, slander. **Eph. 2:2-3**. in which you once walked, following the course of this world, following the prince of the power of the air, the spirit that is now at work in the sons of disobedience—among whom we all once lived in the passions of our flesh, carrying out the desires of the body and the mind, and were by nature children of wrath, like the rest of mankind. **Jas. 1:14-15**. But each person is tempted when he is lured and enticed by his own desire. Then desire when it has conceived gives birth to sin, and sin when it is fully grown brings forth death.

4 **Prov. 20:9**. Who can say, "I have made my heart pure; I am clean from my sin"? **Eccl. 7:20**. Surely there is not a righteous man on earth who does good and never sins. **Rom. 7:14,17-18,23**. For we know that the law is spiritual, but I am of the flesh, sold under sin. So now it is no longer I who do it, but sin that dwells within me. For I know that nothing good dwells in me, that is, in my flesh. For I have the desire to do what is right, but not the ability to carry it out. but I see in my members another law waging war against the law of my mind and making me captive to the law of sin that dwells in my members. **Jas 3:2**. For we all stumble in many ways. And if anyone does not stumble in what he says, he is a perfect man, able also to bridle his whole body. **1 Jn. 1:8,10**. If we say we have no sin, we deceive ourselves, and the truth is not in us. If we say we have not sinned, we make him a liar, and his word is not in us.

5 **Rom. 7:5-8,25**. For while we were living in the flesh, our sinful passions, aroused by the law, were at work in our members to bear fruit for death. But now we are released from the law, having died to that which held us captive, so that we serve in the new way of the Spirit and not in the old way of the written code. The Law and Sin. What then shall we say? That the law is sin? By no means! Yet if it had not been for the law, I would not have known sin. For I would not have known what it is to covet if the law had not said, "You shall not covet." But sin, seizing an opportunity through the commandment, produced in me all kinds of covetousness. For apart from the law, sin lies dead. Thanks be to God through Jesus Christ our Lord! So then, I myself serve the law of God with my mind, but with my flesh I serve the law of sin. **Gal. 5:17**. For the desires of the flesh are against the Spirit, and the desires of the Spirit are against the flesh, for these are opposed to each other, to keep you from doing the things you want to do.

6. Every sin, both original and actual, being a transgression of the righteous law of God, and contrary to it,[1] does in its own nature bring guilt on the sinner,[2] so that he is bound over to the wrath of God,[3] and curse of the law,[4] and so made subject to death,[5] with all miseries spiritual,[6] temporal,[7] and eternal.[8]

---

1 **1 Jn. 3:4**. Everyone who makes a practice of sinning also practices lawlessness; sin is lawlessness.

2 **Rom. 2:15**. They show that the work of the law is written on their hearts, while their conscience also bears witness, and their conflicting thoughts accuse or even excuse them. **Rom. 3:9,19.** What then? Are we Jews any better off? No, not at all. For we have already charged that all, both Jews and Greeks, are under sin. Now we know that whatever the law says it speaks to those who are under the law, so that every mouth may be stopped, and the whole world may be held accountable to God.

3 **Eph. 2:3**. among whom we all once lived in the passions of our flesh, carrying out the desires of the body and the mind, and were by nature children of wrath, like the rest of mankind.

4 **Gal. 3:10**. For all who rely on works of the law are under a curse; for it is written, "Cursed be everyone who does not abide by all things written in the Book of the Law, and do them."

5 **Rom. 6:23**. For the wages of sin is death, but the free gift of God is eternal life in Christ Jesus our Lord.

6 **Eph. 4:18**. They are darkened in their understanding, alienated from the life of God because of the ignorance that is in them, due to their hardness of heart.

7 **Lam. 3:39**. Why should a living man complain, a man, about the punishment of his sins? **Rom. 8:20**. For the creation was subjected to futility, not willingly, but because of him who subjected it, in hope.

8 **Mt. 26:41**. Watch and pray that you may not enter into temptation. The spirit indeed is willing, but the flesh is weak." **2 Thess. 1:9**. They will suffer the punishment of eternal destruction, away from the presence of the Lord and from the glory of his might.

CHAPTER 7

OF GOD'S COVENANT WITH MAN.

1. The distance between God and the creature is so great, that although reasonable creatures do owe obedience to Him as their Creator, yet they could never have any fruition of Him as their blessedness and reward, except by some voluntary condescension on God's part, which He has been pleased to express by way of covenant.[1]

---

1 **1 Sam. 2:25**. If someone sins against a man, God will mediate for him, but if someone sins against the LORD, who can intercede for him?" But they would not listen to the voice of their father, for it was the will of the LORD to put them to death. **Job 9:32-33**. For he is not a man, as I am, that I might answer him, that we should come to trial together. There is no arbiter between us, who might lay his hand on us both. **Job 22:2-3**. Can a man be profitable to God? Surely he who is wise is profitable to himself. Is it any pleasure to the Almighty if you are in the right, or is it gain to him if you make your ways blameless? **Job 35:7-8**. If you are righteous, what do you give to him? Or what does he receive from your hand? Your wickedness concerns a man like yourself, and your righteousness a son of man. **Ps. 100:2-3**. Serve the LORD with gladness! Come into his presence with singing! Know that the LORD, he is God! It is he who made us, and we are his; we are his people, and the sheep of his pasture. **Ps. 113:5-6**. Who is like the LORD our God, who is seated on high, who looks far down on the heavens and the earth? **Isa. 40:13-17**. Who has measured the Spirit of the LORD, or what man shows him his counsel? Whom did he consult, and who made him understand? Who taught him the path of justice, and taught him knowledge, and showed him the way of understanding? Behold, the nations are like a drop from a bucket, and are accounted as the dust on the scales; behold, he takes up the coastlands like fine dust. Lebanon would not suffice for fuel, nor are its beasts enough for a burnt offering. All the nations are as nothing before him, they are accounted by him as less than nothing and emptiness. **Lk. 17:10**. So you also, when you have done all that you were commanded, say, "We are unworthy servants; we have only done what was our duty." **Acts 17:24-25**. The God who made the world and everything in it, being Lord of heaven and earth, does not live in temples made by man, nor is he served by human hands, as though he needed anything, since he himself gives to all mankind life and breath and everything.

2. The first covenant made with man was a covenant of works,[1] in which life was promised to Adam; and in him to his descendants,[2] on condition of perfect and personal obedience.[3]

3. Man, by his fall, having made himself incapable of life by that covenant, the Lord was pleased to make a second,[4] commonly called the covenant of grace; in which He freely offers to sinners life and salvation by Jesus Christ; requiring of them faith in Him, that they may

---

1 **Gal. 3:12.** But the law is not of faith, rather "The one who does them shall live by them."

2 **Rom. 5:12-20.** Therefore, just as sin came into the world through one man, and death through sin, and so death spread to all men because all sinned—for sin indeed was in the world before the law was given, but sin is not counted where there is no law. Yet death reigned from Adam to Moses, even over those whose sinning was not like the transgression of Adam, who was a type of the one who was to come. But the free gift is not like the trespass. For if many died through one man's trespass, much more have the grace of God and the free gift by the grace of that one man Jesus Christ abounded for many. And the free gift is not like the result of that one man's sin. For the judgment following one trespass brought condemnation, but the free gift following many trespasses brought justification. For if, because of one man's trespass, death reigned through that one man, much more will those who receive the abundance of grace and the free gift of righteousness reign in life through the one man Jesus Christ. Therefore, as one trespass led to condemnation for all men, so one act of righteousness leads to justification and life for all men. For as by the one man's disobedience the many were made sinners, so by the one man's obedience the many will be made righteous. Now the law came in to increase the trespass, but where sin increased, grace abounded all the more. **Rom. 10:5.** For Moses writes about the righteousness that is based on the law, that the person who does the commandments shall live by them.

3 **Gen. 2:17.** "but of the tree of the knowledge of good and evil you shall not eat, for in the day that you eat of it you shall surely die." **Gal. 3:10.** For all who rely on works of the law are under a curse; for it is written, "Cursed be everyone who does not abide by all things written in the Book of the Law, and do them."

4 **Gen. 3:15.** I will put enmity between you and the woman, and between your offspring and her offspring; he shall bruise your head, and you shall bruise his heel. **Isa. 42:6.** I am the LORD; I have called you in righteousness; I will take you by the hand and keep you; I will give you as a covenant for the people, a light for the nations, **Rom. 3:20-21.** For by works of the law no human being will be justified in his sight, since through the law comes knowledge of sin. But now the righteousness of God has been manifested apart from the law, although the Law and the Prophets bear witness to it. **Rom. 8:3.** For God has done what the law, weakened by the flesh, could not do. By sending his own Son in the likeness of sinful flesh and for sin, he condemned sin in the flesh. **Gal. 3:21.** Is the law then contrary to the promises of God? Certainly not! For if a law had been given that could give life, then righteousness would indeed be by the law.

be saved,[1] and promising to give to all those who are ordained to eternal life His Holy Spirit, to make them willing, and able to believe.[2]

4. This covenant of grace is frequently set forth in Scripture by the name of a will, in reference to the death of Jesus Christ, and to the everlasting inheritance, with all things belonging to it, bequeathed in it.[3]

5. This covenant was differently administered in the time of the law, and in the time of the Gospel:[4] under the law it was administered by promises, prophecies, sacrifices, circumcision, the paschal lamb, and other types and ordinances delivered to the people of the Jews,

---

1 **Mk. 16:15-16.** And he said to them, "Go into all the world and proclaim the gospel to the whole creation. Whoever believes and is baptized will be saved, but whoever does not believe will be condemned." **Jn. 3:16.** For God so loved the world, that he gave his only Son, that whoever believes in him should not perish but have eternal life. **Rom. 10:6-9.** But the righteousness based on faith says, "Do not say in your heart, 'Who will ascend into heaven?'" (that is, to bring Christ down) or "'Who will descend into the abyss?'" (that is, to bring Christ up from the dead). But what does it say? "The word is near you, in your mouth and in your heart" (that is, the word of faith that we proclaim); because, if you confess with your mouth that Jesus is Lord and believe in your heart that God raised him from the dead, you will be saved. **Gal. 3.** All of Gal. 3.

2 **Ezek. 36:26-27.** And I will give you a new heart, and a new spirit I will put within you. And I will remove the heart of stone from your flesh and give you a heart of flesh. And I will put my Spirit within you, and cause you to walk in my statutes and be careful to obey my rules. **Jn. 6:44-45.** No one can come to me unless the Father who sent me draws him. And I will raise him up on the last day. It is written in the Prophets, 'And they will all be taught by God.' Everyone who has heard and learned from the Father comes to me.

3 **Lk. 22:20.** And likewise the cup after they had eaten, saying, "This cup that is poured out for you is the new covenant in my blood." **Heb. 7:22.** This makes Jesus the guarantor of a better covenant. **Heb. 9:15-17.** Therefore he is the mediator of a new covenant, so that those who are called may receive the promised eternal inheritance, since a death has occurred that redeems them from the transgressions committed under the first covenant. For where a will is involved, the death of the one who made it must be established. For a will takes effect only at death, since it is not in force as long as the one who made it is alive. **1 Cor. 11:25.** In the same way also he took the cup, after supper, saying, "This cup is the new covenant in my blood. Do this, as often as you drink it, in remembrance of me."

4 **2 Cor. 3:6-9.** who has made us competent to be ministers of a new covenant, not of the letter but of the Spirit. For the letter kills, but the Spirit gives life. Now if the ministry of death, carved in letters on stone, came with such glory that the Israelites could not gaze at Moses' face because of its glory, which was being brought to an end, will not the ministry of the Spirit have even more glory? For if there was glory in the ministry of condemnation, the ministry of righteousness must far exceed it in glory.

all pointing to the Christ to come;[1] which were, for that time, sufficient and effectual, through the operation of the Spirit, to instruct and build up the elect in faith in the promised Messiah,[2] by whom they had full remission of sins, and eternal salvation; and is called the Old Testament.[3]

6. Under the Gospel, when Christ, the man,[4] was exhibited, the ordinances in which this covenant is dispensed are the preaching of the

---

1 **Rom. 4:11**. He received the sign of circumcision as a seal of the righteousness that he had by faith while he was still uncircumcised. The purpose was to make him the father of all who believe without being circumcised, so that righteousness would be counted to them as well. **1 Cor. 5:7**. Cleanse out the old leaven that you may be a new lump, as you really are unleavened. For Christ, our Passover lamb, has been sacrificed. **Col. 2:11-12**. In him also you were circumcised with a circumcision made without hands, by putting off the body of the flesh, by the circumcision of Christ, having been buried with him in baptism, in which you were also raised with him through faith in the powerful working of God, who raised him from the dead. **Heb. 8-10**. All of Heb. 8-10.

2 **Jn. 8:56**. Your father Abraham rejoiced that he would see my day. He saw it and was glad. **1 Cor. 10:1-4**. For I want you to know, brothers, that our fathers were all under the cloud, and all passed through the sea, and all were baptized into Moses in the cloud and in the sea, and all ate the same spiritual food, and all drank the same spiritual drink. For they drank from the spiritual Rock that followed them, and the Rock was Christ. **Heb. 11:13**. These all died in faith, not having received the things promised, but having seen them and greeted them from afar, and having acknowledged that they were strangers and exiles on the earth.

3 **Gal. 3:7-9, 14**. Know then that it is those of faith who are the sons of Abraham. And the Scripture, foreseeing that God would justify the Gentiles by faith, preached the gospel beforehand to Abraham, saying, "In you shall all the nations be blessed." So then, those who are of faith are blessed along with Abraham, the man of faith... so that in Christ Jesus the blessing of Abraham might come to the Gentiles, so that we might receive the promised Spirit through faith.

4 **Col. 2:17**. These are a shadow of the things to come, but the substance belongs to Christ.

Word, and the administration of the sacraments of baptism and the Lord's Supper:[1] which, though fewer in number, and administered with more simplicity, and less outward glory, yet, in them, it is held forth in more fullness, evidence, and spiritual efficacy,[2] to all peoples,

---

1 **Mt. 28:19-20**. Go therefore and make disciples of all nations, baptizing them in the name of the Father and of the Son and of the Holy Spirit, teaching them to observe all that I have commanded you. And behold, I am with you always, to the end of the age." **1 Cor. 11:23-25**. For I received from the Lord what I also delivered to you, that the Lord Jesus on the night when he was betrayed took bread, and when he had given thanks, he broke it, and said, "This is my body which is for you. Do this in remembrance of me." In the same way also he took the cup, after supper, saying, "This cup is the new covenant in my blood. Do this, as often as you drink it, in remembrance of me."

2 **Jer. 31:33-34**. But this is the covenant that I will make with the house of Israel after those days, declares the LORD: I will put my law within them, and I will write it on their hearts. And I will be their God, and they shall be my people. And no longer shall each one teach his neighbor and each his brother, saying, 'Know the LORD,' for they shall all know me, from the least of them to the greatest, declares the LORD. For I will forgive their iniquity, and I will remember their sin no more." **Heb. 12:22-27**. But you have come to Mount Zion and to the city of the living God, the heavenly Jerusalem, and to innumerable angels in festal gathering, and to the assembly of the firstborn who are enrolled in heaven, and to God, the judge of all, and to the spirits of the righteous made perfect, and to Jesus, the mediator of a new covenant, and to the sprinkled blood that speaks a better word than the blood of Abel. See that you do not refuse him who is speaking. For if they did not escape when they refused him who warned them on earth, much less will we escape if we reject him who warns from heaven. At that time his voice shook the earth, but now he has promised, "Yet once more I will shake not only the earth but also the heavens." This phrase, "Yet once more," indicates the removal of things that are shaken—that is, things that have been made—in order that the things that cannot be shaken may remain.

both Jews and Gentiles;[1] and is called the New Testament.[2] There are not therefore two covenants of grace, differing in substance, but one and the same, under various dispensations.[3]

1 **Mt. 28:19**. Go therefore and make disciples of all nations, baptizing them in the name of the Father and of the Son and of the Holy Spirit. **Eph. 2:15-19**. by abolishing the law of commandments expressed in ordinances, that he might create in himself one new man in place of the two, so making peace, and might reconcile us both to God in one body through the cross, thereby killing the hostility. And he came and preached peace to you who were far off and peace to those who were near. For through him we both have access in one Spirit to the Father. So then you are no longer strangers and aliens, but you are fellow citizens with the saints and members of the household of God.

2 **Lk. 22:20**. And likewise the cup after they had eaten, saying, "This cup that is poured out for you is the new covenant in my blood."

3 **Ps. 32:1**. Blessed is the one whose transgression is forgiven, whose sin is covered. **Acts 15:11**. But we believe that we will be saved through the grace of the Lord Jesus, just as they will. **Rom. 3:21-23,30**. But now the righteousness of God has been manifested apart from the law, although the Law and the Prophets bear witness to it—the righteousness of God through faith in Jesus Christ for all who believe. For there is no distinction: for all have sinned and fall short of the glory of God.... since God is one—who will justify the circumcised by faith and the uncircumcised through faith. **Rom. 4:3-6**. For what does the Scripture say? "Abraham believed God, and it was counted to him as righteousness." Now to the one who works, his wages are not counted as a gift but as his due. And to the one who does not work but believes in him who justifies the ungodly, his faith is counted as righteousness, just as David also speaks of the blessing of the one to whom God counts righteousness apart from works. **Rom. 3:16-17**. in their paths are ruin and misery, and the way of peace they have not known." **Rom. 3:23-24**. for all have sinned and fall short of the glory of God, and are justified by his grace as a gift, through the redemption that is in Christ Jesus. **Gal. 3:14**. so that in Christ Jesus the blessing of Abraham might come to the Gentiles, so that we might receive the promised Spirit through faith. **Heb. 13:8**. Jesus Christ is the same yesterday and today and forever.

CHAPTER 8

OF CHRIST THE MEDIATOR.

1. It pleased God, in His eternal purpose, to choose and ordain the Lord Jesus, His only begotten Son, to be the Mediator between God and man;[1] the Prophet,[2] Priest,[3] and King;[4] the Head and Savior of His Church;[5] the Heir of all things;[6] and Judge of the world:[7] to whom

---

1 **Isa. 42:1**. Behold my servant, whom I uphold, my chosen, in whom my soul delights; I have put my Spirit upon him; he will bring forth justice to the nations. **Jn. 3:16**. For God so loved the world, that he gave his only Son, that whoever believes in him should not perish but have eternal life. **1 Tim. 2:5**. For there is one God, and there is one mediator between God and men, the man Christ Jesus. **1 Pet. 1:19-20**. But [you were redeemed] with the precious blood of Christ, like that of a lamb without blemish or spot. He was foreknown before the foundation of the world but was made manifest in the last times for the sake of you.

2 **Acts 3:22**. Moses said, The Lord God will raise up for you a prophet like me from your brothers. You shall listen to him in whatever he tells you.

3 **Heb. 5:5-6**. So also Christ did not exalt himself to be made a high priest, but was appointed by him who said to him, "You are my Son, today I have begotten you"; as he says also in another place, "You are a priest forever, after the order of Melchizedek."

4 **Ps. 2:6**. "As for me, I have set my King on Zion, my holy hill." **Lk. 1:33**. And he will reign over the house of Jacob forever, and of his kingdom there will be no end.

5 **Eph. 5:23**. For the husband is the head of the wife even as Christ is the head of the church, his body, and is himself its Savior.

6 **Heb. 1:2**. But in these last days he has spoken to us by his Son, whom he appointed the heir of all things, through whom also he created the world.

7 **Acts 17:31**. ...because he has fixed a day on which he will judge the world in righteousness by a man whom he has appointed; and of this he has given assurance to all by raising him from the dead.

He did from all eternity give a people, to be His seed,[1] and to be by Him in time redeemed, called, justified, sanctified, and glorified.[2]

2. The Son of God, the second person in the Trinity, being very and eternal God, of one substance and equal with the Father, did, when the fullness of time had come, take upon Him man's nature,[3] with all the essential properties, and common infirmities of a man, yet without sin;[4] being conceived by the power of the Holy Spirit, in the womb of the virgin Mary, of her substance.[5] So that two whole, perfect, and distinct natures, the Godhead and the manhood, were inseparably joined together in one person, without conversion,

---

1 **Ps. 22:30**. Posterity shall serve him; it shall be told of the Lord to the coming generation; **Isa. 53:10**. Yet it was the will of the LORD to crush him; he has put him to grief; when his soul makes an offering for guilt, he shall see his offspring; he shall prolong his days; the will of the LORD shall prosper in his hand. **Jn. 17:6**. I have manifested your name to the people whom you gave me out of the world. Yours they were, and you gave them to me, and they have kept your word.

2 **Isa. 55:4-5**. Behold, I made him a witness to the peoples, a leader and commander for the peoples. Behold, you shall call a nation that you do not know, and a nation that did not know you shall run to you, because of the LORD your God, and of the Holy One of Israel, for he has glorified you. **1 Cor. 1:30**. And because of him you are in Christ Jesus, who became to us wisdom from God, righteousness and sanctification and redemption. **1 Tim. 2:6**. ...who gave himself as a ransom for all, which is the testimony given at the proper time.

3 **Jn. 1:1,14**. In the beginning was the Word, and the Word was with God, and the Word was God. And the Word became flesh and dwelt among us, and we have seen his glory, glory as of the only Son from the Father, full of grace and truth. **Gal. 4:4**. But when the fullness of time had come, God sent forth his Son, born of woman, born under the law. **Phil. 2:6**. Who, though he was in the form of God, did not count equality with God a thing to be grasped. **1 Jn. 5:20.** And we know that the Son of God has come and has given us understanding, so that we may know him who is true; and we are in him who is true, in his Son Jesus Christ. He is the true God and eternal life.

4 **Heb. 2:14,16-17**. Since therefore the children share in flesh and blood, he himself likewise partook of the same things, that through death he might destroy the one who has the power of death, that is, the devil. For surely it is not angels that he helps, but he helps the offspring of Abraham. Therefore he had to be made like his brothers in every respect, so that he might become a merciful and faithful high priest in the service of God, to make propitiation for the sins of the people. **Heb. 4:15**. For we do not have a high priest who is unable to sympathize with our weaknesses, but one who in every respect has been tempted as we are, yet without sin.

5 **Lk. 1:27,31,35**.... to a virgin betrothed to a man whose name was Joseph, of the house of David. And the virgin's name was Mary. And behold, you will conceive in your womb and bear a son, and you shall call his name Jesus. And the angel answered her, The Holy Spirit will come upon you, and the power of the Most High will overshadow you; therefore the child to be born will be called holy—the Son of God. **Gal. 4:4**. But when the fullness of time had come, God sent forth his Son, born of woman, born under the law,

composition, or confusion.[1] This person is very God, and very man, yet one Christ, the only Mediator between God and man.[2]

3. The Lord Jesus, in His human nature thus united to the divine, was sanctified, and anointed with the Holy Spirit, above measure,[3] having in Him all the treasures of wisdom and knowledge;[4] in whom it pleased the Father that all fullness should dwell;[5] to the end that, being holy, harmless, undefiled, and full of grace and truth,[6] He might be thoroughly equipped to execute the office of a Mediator and Guarantee.[7] This office He took not by Himself, but was called to it by His Father,[8] who put all power and judgment into His hand, and gave Him authority to execute the same.[9]

---

1 **Lk 1:35**. And the angel answered her, The Holy Spirit will come upon you, and the power of the Most High will overshadow you; therefore the child to be born will be called holy—the Son of God. **Col. 2:9**. For in him the whole fullness of deity dwells bodily. **1 Tim. 3:16**. Great indeed, we confess, is the mystery of godliness: He was manifested in the flesh, vindicated by the Spirit, seen by angels, proclaimed among the nations, believed on in the world, taken up in glory. **1 Pet 3:18**. For Christ also suffered once for sins, the righteous for the unrighteous, that he might bring us to God, being put to death in the flesh but made alive in the spirit.

2 **Rom. 1:3-4**.... concerning his Son, who was descended from David according to the flesh and was declared to be the Son of God in power according to the Spirit of holiness by his resurrection from the dead, Jesus Christ our Lord. **1 Tim 2:5**. For there is one God, and there is one mediator between God and men, the man Christ Jesus.

3 **Ps. 45:7**. you have loved righteousness and hated wickedness. Therefore God, your God, has anointed you with the oil of gladness beyond your companions; **Jn. 3:34**. For he whom God has sent utters the words of God, for he gives the Spirit without measure.

4 **Col. 2:3**....in whom are hidden all the treasures of wisdom and knowledge.

5 **Col 1:19**. For in him all the fullness of God was pleased to dwell.

6 **Jn. 1:14**. And the Word became flesh and dwelt among us, and we have seen his glory, glory as of the only Son from the Father, full of grace and truth. **Heb. 7:26**. For it was indeed fitting that we should have such a high priest, holy, innocent, unstained, separated from sinners, and exalted above the heavens.

7 **Heb. 7:22**. This makes Jesus the guarantor of a better covenant. **Heb. 12:24**...and to Jesus, the mediator of a new covenant, and to the sprinkled blood that speaks a better word than the blood of Abel. **Acts 10:38**. ... how God anointed Jesus of Nazareth with the Holy Spirit and with power. He went about doing good and healing all who were oppressed by the devil, for God was with him.

8 **Heb. 5:4-5**. And no one takes this honor for himself, but only when called by God, just as Aaron was. So also Christ did not exalt himself to be made a high priest, but was appointed by him who said to him, "You are my Son, today I have begotten you."

9 **Mt. 28:18**. And Jesus came and said to them, All authority in heaven and on earth has been given to me. **Jn. 5:22,27**. The Father judges no one, but has given all judgment to the Son. And he has given him authority to execute judgment, because he is the Son of Man. **Acts 2:36**. Let all the house of Israel therefore know for certain that God has made him both Lord and Christ, this Jesus whom you crucified.

4. This office the Lord Jesus did most willingly undertake;[1] so that He might discharge His duties, He was made under the law,[2] and did perfectly fulfill it.[3] He endured most grievous torments immediately in His soul,[4] and most painful sufferings in His body;[5] was crucified, and died,[6] was buried, and remained under the power of death, yet saw no decay.[7] On the third day He arose from the dead,[8] with the

---

1 **Ps. 40:7-8**. Then I said, "Behold, I have come; in the scroll of the book it is written of me: I delight to do your will, O my God; your law is within my heart." **Jn. 10:18**. "No one takes it from me, but I lay it down of my own accord. I have authority to lay it down, and I have authority to take it up again. This charge I have received from my Father." **Phil. 2:8**. "No one takes it from me, but I lay it down of my own accord. I have authority to lay it down, and I have authority to take it up again. This charge I have received from my Father." **Heb. 10:5-10**. Consequently, when Christ came into the world, he said, "Sacrifices and offerings you have not desired, but a body have you prepared for me; in burnt offerings and sin offerings you have taken no pleasure. Then I said, 'Behold, I have come to do your will, O God, as it is written of me in the scroll of the book.'" When he said above, "You have neither desired nor taken pleasure in sacrifices and offerings and burnt offerings and sin offerings" (these are offered according to the law), then he added, "Behold, I have come to do your will." He does away with the first in order to establish the second. And by that will we have been sanctified through the offering of the body of Jesus Christ once for all.

2 **Gal. 4:4**. But when the fullness of time had come, God sent forth his Son, born of woman, born under the law.

3 **Mt. 3:15**. But Jesus answered him, "Let it be so now, for thus it is fitting for us to fulfill all righteousness." Then he consented. **Mt. 5:17**. "Do not think that I have come to abolish the Law or the Prophets; I have not come to abolish them but to fulfill them."

4 **Mt. 26:37-38**. And taking with him Peter and the two sons of Zebedee, he began to be sorrowful and troubled. Then he said to them, "My soul is very sorrowful, even to death; remain here, and watch with me." **Mt. 27:46**. And about the ninth hour Jesus cried out with a loud voice, saying, "*Eli, Eli, lema sabachthani*?" that is, "My God, my God, why have you forsaken me?" **Lk. 22:44**. And being in an agony he prayed more earnestly; and his sweat became like great drops of blood falling down to the ground.

5 **Mt. 26:27**. And he took a cup, and when he had given thanks he gave it to them, saying, "Drink of it, all of you."

6 **Phil. 2:8**. And being found in human form, he humbled himself by becoming obedient to the point of death, even death on a cross.

7 **Acts 2:23-24,27**...this Jesus, delivered up according to the definite plan and foreknowledge of God, you crucified and killed by the hands of lawless men. God raised him up, loosing the pangs of death, because it was not possible for him to be held by it. For you will not abandon my soul to Hades, or let your Holy One see corruption... **Acts 13:37**. but he whom God raised up did not see corruption. **Rom. 6:9**. We know that Christ, being raised from the dead, will never die again; death no longer has dominion over him.

8 **1 Cor. 15:3-5**. For I delivered to you as of first importance what I also received: that Christ died for our sins in accordance with the Scriptures, that he was buried, that he was raised on the third day in accordance with the Scriptures, 5and that he appeared to Cephas, then to the twelve.

same body in which He suffered,[1] with which also He ascended into heaven, and there sits at the right hand of His Father,[2] making intercession,[3] and shall return, to judge men and angels, at the end of the world.[4]

5. The Lord Jesus, by His perfect obedience and sacrifice of Himself, which He through the eternal Spirit once offered up to God, has fully satisfied the justice of His Father;[5] and purchased not only

---

1 **Jn. 20:25,27**. So the other disciples told him, "We have seen the Lord." But he said to them, "Unless I see in his hands the mark of the nails, and place my finger into the mark of the nails, and place my hand into his side, I will never believe." Then he said to Thomas, "Put your finger here, and see my hands; and put out your hand, and place it in my side. Do not disbelieve, but believe."

2 **Mk. 16:19**. So then the Lord Jesus, after he had spoken to them, was taken up into heaven and sat down at the right hand of God.

3 **Rom. 8:34**. Who is to condemn? Christ Jesus is the one who died—more than that, who was raised—who is at the right hand of God, who indeed is interceding for us. **Heb. 7:25**. Consequently, he is able to save to the uttermost those who draw near to God through him, since he always lives to make intercession for them. **Heb. 9:24**. For Christ has entered, not into holy places made with hands, which are copies of the true things, but into heaven itself, now to appear in the presence of God on our behalf.

4 **Mt. 13:40-42**. Just as the weeds are gathered and burned with fire, so will it be at the close of the age. The Son of Man will send his angels, and they will gather out of his kingdom all causes of sin and all law-breakers, and throw them into the fiery furnace. In that place there will be weeping and gnashing of teeth. **Acts 1:11**. ...and said, "Men of Galilee, why do you stand looking into heaven? This Jesus, who was taken up from you into heaven, will come in the same way as you saw him go into heaven." **Acts 10:42**. And he commanded us to preach to the people and to testify that he is the one appointed by God to be judge of the living and the dead. **Rom. 14:9-10**. For to this end Christ died and lived again, that he might be Lord both of the dead and of the living. Why do you pass judgment on your brother? Or you, why do you despise your brother? For we will all stand before the judgment seat of God. **2 Pet. 2:4**. For if God did not spare angels when they sinned, but cast them into hell and committed them to chains of gloomy darkness to be kept until the judgment. **Jude 6**. And the angels who did not stay within their own position of authority, but left their proper dwelling, he has kept in eternal chains under gloomy darkness until the judgment of the great day.

5 **Rom. 3:25-26**. whom God put forward as a propitiation by his blood, to be received by faith. This was to show God's righteousness, because in his divine forbearance he had passed over former sins. It was to show his righteousness at the present time, so that he might be just and the justifier of the one who has faith in Jesus. **Rom. 5:19**. For as by the one man's disobedience the many were made sinners, so by the one man's obedience the many will be made righteous. **Eph. 5:2**. And walk in love, as Christ loved us and gave himself up for us, a fragrant offering and sacrifice to God. **Heb. 9:14,16**. how much more will the blood of Christ, who through the eternal Spirit offered himself without blemish to God, purify our conscience from dead works to serve the living God. For where a will is involved, the death of the one who made it must be established. **Heb. 10:14**. For by a single offering he has perfected for all time those who are being sanctified.

reconciliation, but an everlasting inheritance in the kingdom of heaven, for all those whom the Father has given to Him.[1]

6. Although the work of redemption was not actually done by Christ till after His incarnation, yet the virtue, efficacy, and benefits of it were communicated to the elect, in all ages successively from the beginning of the world, in and by those promises, types, and sacrifices, through which He was revealed and shown to be the seed of the woman that should crush the serpent's head, and the Lamb slain from the beginning of the world; being yesterday and today the same, and forever.[2]

7. Christ, in the work of mediation, acts according to both natures, by each nature doing that which is proper to itself;[3] yet, by reason of

---

1 **Dan. 9:24,26**. "Seventy weeks are decreed about your people and your holy city, to finish the transgression, to put an end to sin, and to atone for iniquity, to bring in everlasting righteousness, to seal both vision and prophet, and to anoint a most holy place." And after the sixty-two weeks, an anointed one shall be cut off and shall have nothing. And the people of the prince who is to come shall destroy the city and the sanctuary. Its end shall come with a flood, and to the end there shall be war. Desolations are decreed. **Jn. 17:2**. ... since you have given him authority over all flesh, to give eternal life to all whom you have given him. **Eph.1:11,14**. In him we have obtained an inheritance, having been predestined according to the purpose of him who works all things according to the counsel of his will ...who is the guarantee of our inheritance until we acquire possession of it, to the praise of his glory. **Col. 1:19-20**. For in him all the fullness of God was pleased to dwell, and through him to reconcile to himself all things, whether on earth or in heaven, making peace by the blood of his cross. **Heb. 9:12,15**.... he entered once for all into the holy places, not by means of the blood of goats and calves but by means of his own blood, thus securing an eternal redemption. Therefore he is the mediator of a new covenant, so that those who are called may receive the promised eternal inheritance, since a death has occurred that redeems them from the transgressions committed under the first covenant.

2 **Gen. 3:15**."I will put enmity between you and the woman, and between your offspring and her offspring; he shall bruise your head, and you shall bruise his heel." **Gal. 4:4-5**. But when the fullness of time had come, God sent forth his Son, born of woman, born under the law, to redeem those who were under the law, so that we might receive adoption as sons. **Heb. 13:8**. Jesus Christ is the same yesterday and today and forever. **Rev. 13:8**.... and all who dwell on earth will worship it, everyone whose name has not been written before the foundation of the world in the book of life of the Lamb who was slain.

3 **Heb. 9:14**.... how much more will the blood of Christ, who through the eternal Spirit offered himself without blemish to God, purify our conscience from dead works to serve the living God. **1 Pet. 3:18**. For Christ also suffered once for sins, the righteous for the unrighteous, that he might bring us to God, being put to death in the flesh but made alive in the spirit.

the unity of the person, that which is proper to one nature is sometimes in Scripture attributed to the person denominated by the other nature.[1]

8. To all those for whom Christ has purchased redemption, He does certainly and effectually apply and communicate the same;[2] making intercession for them,[3] and revealing to them, in and by the Word, the mysteries of salvation;[4] effectually persuading them by His Spirit to believe and obey, and governing their hearts by His Word and

---

1 **Acts 20:28**. Pay careful attention to yourselves and to all the flock, in which the Holy Spirit has made you overseers, to care for the church of God, which he obtained with his own blood. **Jn. 3:13**. No one has ascended into heaven except he who descended from heaven, the Son of Man. **1 Jn. 3:16**. By this we know love, that he laid down his life for us, and we ought to lay down our lives for the brothers.

2 **Jn. 6:37,39**. All that the Father gives me will come to me, and whoever comes to me I will never cast out. And this is the will of him who sent me, that I should lose nothing of all that he has given me, but raise it up on the last day. **Jn. 10:15-16**. just as the Father knows me and I know the Father; and I lay down my life for the sheep. And I have other sheep that are not of this fold. I must bring them also, and they will listen to my voice. So there will be one flock, one shepherd.

3 **Rom. 8:34**. Who is to condemn? Christ Jesus is the one who died—more than that, who was raised—who is at the right hand of God, who indeed is interceding for us. **1 Jn. 2:1-2**. My little children, I am writing these things to you so that you may not sin. But if anyone does sin, we have an advocate with the Father, Jesus Christ the righteous. He is the propitiation for our sins, and not for ours only but also for the sins of the whole world.

4 **Jn. 15:13,15**. Greater love has no one than this, that someone lay down his life for his friends. No longer do I call you servants, for the servant does not know what his master is doing; but I have called you friends, for all that I have heard from my Father I have made known to you. **Jn. 17:6**. "I have manifested your name to the people whom you gave me out of the world. Yours they were, and you gave them to me, and they have kept your word." **Eph. 1:7-10**. In him we have redemption through his blood, the forgiveness of our trespasses, according to the riches of his grace, which he lavished upon us, in all wisdom and insight making known to us the mystery of his will, according to his purpose, which he set forth in Christ as a plan for the fullness of time, to unite all things in him, things in heaven and things on earth.

Spirit;[1] overcoming all their enemies by His almighty power and wisdom, in such manner and ways as are most in agreement with His wonderful and unsearchable ordering of affairs.[2]

1 **Jn. 14:16**. And I will ask the Father, and he will give you another Helper, to be with you forever. **Jn. 17:17**. Sanctify them in the truth; your word is truth. **Rom. 8:9,14**. You, however, are not in the flesh but in the Spirit, if in fact the Spirit of God dwells in you. Anyone who does not have the Spirit of Christ does not belong to him. For all who are led by the Spirit of God are sons of God. **Rom. 15:18-19**. For I will not venture to speak of anything except what Christ has accomplished through me to bring the Gentiles to obedience—by word and deed, by the power of signs and wonders, by the power of the Spirit of God—so that from Jerusalem and all the way around to Illyricum I have fulfilled the ministry of the gospel of Christ;

2 **Ps. 110:1**. The LORD says to my Lord: "Sit at my right hand, until I make your enemies your footstool." **Mal. 4:2-3**. But for you who fear my name, the sun of righteousness shall rise with healing in its wings. You shall go out leaping like calves from the stall. And you shall tread down the wicked, for they will be ashes under the soles of your feet, on the day when I act, says the LORD of hosts. **1 Cor. 15:25-26**. For he must reign until he has put all his enemies under his feet. The last enemy to be destroyed is death. **Col. 2:15**. He disarmed the rulers and authorities and put them to open shame, by triumphing over them in him.

CHAPTER 9

OF FREE WILL.

1. God has endowed the will of man with that natural liberty, that it is neither forced, nor, by any absolute necessity of nature, determined to good, or evil.[1]

2. Man, in his state of innocence, had freedom and power to will and to do that which was good and well pleasing to God;[2] but yet, alternatively, so that he might fall from it.[3]

3. Man, by his fall into a state of sin, has wholly lost all ability of will to any spiritual good accompanying salvation:[4] so as, a natural man,

---

1 **Deut. 30:19**. I call heaven and earth to witness against you today, that I have set before you life and death, blessing and curse. Therefore choose life, that you and your offspring may live. **Mt. 17:12**. But I tell you that Elijah has already come, and they did not recognize him, but did to him whatever they pleased. So also the Son of Man will certainly suffer at their hands." **Jas. 1:14**. But each person is tempted when he is lured and enticed by his own desire.

2 **Gen. 1:26**. Then God said, "Let us make man in our image, after our likeness. And let them have dominion over the fish of the sea and over the birds of the heavens and over the livestock and over all the earth and over every creeping thing that creeps on the earth." **Eccl. 7:29**. See, this alone I found, that God made man upright, but they have sought out many schemes.

3 **Gen. 2:16-17**. And the LORD God commanded the man, saying, "You may surely eat of every tree of the garden, but of the tree of the knowledge of good and evil you shall not eat, for in the day that you eat of it you shall surely die." **Gen. 3:6**. So when the woman saw that the tree was good for food, and that it was a delight to the eyes, and that the tree was to be desired to make one wise, she took of its fruit and ate, and she also gave some to her husband who was with her, and he ate.

4 **Jn. 15:5**. I am the vine; you are the branches. Whoever abides in me and I in him, he it is that bears much fruit, for apart from me you can do nothing. **Rom. 5:6**. For while we were still weak, at the right time Christ died for the ungodly. **Rom. 8:7**. For the mind that is set on the flesh is hostile to God, for it does not submit to God's law; indeed, it cannot.

being altogether averse from that good,[1] and dead in sin,[2] is not able, by his own strength, to convert himself, or to prepare himself for salvation.[3]

4. When God converts a sinner, and brings him into the state of grace, He frees him from his natural bondage under sin;[4] and, by His grace alone, enables him freely to will and to do that which is spiritually

---

1 **Rom. 3:10,12**. None is righteous, no, not one. All have turned aside; together they have become worthless; no one does good, not even one.

2 **Eph. 2:1,5**. And you were dead in the trespasses and sins.... even when we were dead in our trespasses, made us alive together with Christ—by grace you have been saved. **Col. 2:13**. And you, who were dead in your trespasses and the uncircumcision of your flesh, God made alive together with him, having forgiven us all our trespasses.

3 **Jn. 6:44,65**. No one can come to me unless the Father who sent me draws him. And I will raise him up on the last day. And he said, "This is why I told you that no one can come to me unless it is granted him by the Father." **1 Cor. 2:14**. The natural person does not accept the things of the Spirit of God, for they are folly to him, and he is not able to understand them because they are spiritually discerned. **Eph. 2:2-5**.... in which you once walked, following the course of this world, following the prince of the power of the air, the spirit that is now at work in the sons of disobedience—among whom we all once lived in the passions of our flesh, carrying out the desires of the body and the mind, and were by nature children of wrath, like the rest of mankind. But God, being rich in mercy, because of the great love with which he loved us, even when we were dead in our trespasses, made us alive together with Christ—by grace you have been saved. **Titus 3:3-5**. For we ourselves were once foolish, disobedient, led astray, slaves to various passions and pleasures, passing our days in malice and envy, hated by others and hating one another. But when the goodness and loving kindness of God our Savior appeared, he saved us, not because of works done by us in righteousness, but according to his own mercy, by the washing of regeneration and renewal of the Holy Spirit.

4 **Jn. 8:34,36**. Jesus answered them, "Truly, truly, I say to you, everyone who commits sin is a slave to sin." So if the Son sets you free, you will be free indeed. **Col. 1:13**. He has delivered us from the domain of darkness and transferred us to the kingdom of his beloved Son.

good;[1] yet so, because of his remaining corruption, he does not perfectly, nor only, will that which is good, but does also will that which is evil.[2]

5. The will of man is made perfectly and unchangeably free to do good alone in the state of glory only.[3]

---

1 **Rom. 6:18,22**.... and, having been set free from sin, have become slaves of righteousness. But now that you have been set free from sin and have become slaves of God, the fruit you get leads to sanctification and its end, eternal life. **Phil. 2:13**. For it is God who works in you, both to will and to work for his good pleasure.

2 **Rom. 7:15,18-19,21,23**. For I do not understand my own actions. For I do not do what I want, but I do the very thing I hate. For I know that nothing good dwells in me, that is, in my flesh. For I have the desire to do what is right, but not the ability to carry it out. For I do not do the good I want, but the evil I do not want is what I keep on doing. So I find it to be a law that when I want to do right, evil lies close at hand.... but I see in my members another law waging war against the law of my mind and making me captive to the law of sin that dwells in my members. **Gal. 5:17**. For the desires of the flesh are against the Spirit, and the desires of the Spirit are against the flesh, for these are opposed to each other, to keep you from doing the things you want to do.

3 **Eph. 4:13**.... until we all attain to the unity of the faith and of the knowledge of the Son of God, to mature manhood, to the measure of the stature of the fullness of Christ. **Heb. 12:23**.... and to the assembly of the firstborn who are enrolled in heaven, and to God, the judge of all, and to the spirits of the righteous made perfect. **1 Jn. 3:2**. Beloved, we are God's children now, and what we will be has not yet appeared; but we know that when he appears we shall be like him, because we shall see him as he is. **Jude 24**. Now to him who is able to keep you from stumbling and to present you blameless before the presence of his glory with great joy.

CHAPTER 10

OF EFFECTUAL CALLING.

1. All those whom God has predestined for life, and those only, He is pleased, in His appointed and accepted time, effectually to call,[1] by His Word and Spirit,[2] out of that state of sin and death, in which they are by nature, to grace and salvation, by Jesus Christ;[3] enlightening their minds spiritually and salvifically to understand the things of God,[4] taking away their hearts of stone, and giving them

---

1 **Rom. 8:30**. And those whom he predestined he also called, and those whom he called he also justified, and those whom he justified he also glorified. **Rom. 11:7**. What then? Israel failed to obtain what it was seeking. The elect obtained it, but the rest were hardened. **Eph.1:10-11**.... as a plan for the fullness of time, to unite all things in him, things in heaven and things on earth. In him we have obtained an inheritance, having been predestined according to the purpose of him who works all things according to the counsel of his will.

2 **2 Cor. 3:3,6**. And you show that you are a letter from Christ delivered by us, written not with ink but with the Spirit of the living God, not on tablets of stone but on tablets of human hearts....who has made us competent to be ministers of a new covenant, not of the letter but of the Spirit. For the letter kills, but the Spirit gives life.
2 Thess. 2:13-14. But we ought always to give thanks to God for you, brothers beloved by the Lord, because God chose you as the firstfruits to be saved, through sanctification by the Spirit and belief in the truth. To this he called you through our gospel, so that you may obtain the glory of our Lord Jesus Christ.

3 **Rom. 8:2**. For the law of the Spirit of life has set you free in Christ Jesus from the law of sin and death. **Eph. 2:1-5**. And you were dead in the trespasses and sins in which you once walked, following the course of this world, following the prince of the power of the air, the spirit that is now at work in the sons of disobedience—among whom we all once lived in the passions of our flesh, carrying out the desires of the body and the mind, and were by nature children of wrath, like the rest of mankind. But God, being rich in mercy, because of the great love with which he loved us, even when we were dead in our trespasses, made us alive together with Christ—by grace you have been saved. **2 Tim. 1:9-10**.... who saved us and called us to a holy calling, not because of our works but because of his own purpose and grace, which he gave us in Christ Jesus before the ages began, and which now has been manifested through the appearing of our Savior Christ Jesus, who abolished death and brought life and immortality to light through the gospel,

4 **Acts 26:18**.... to open their eyes, so that they may turn from darkness to light and from the power of Satan to God, that they may receive forgiveness of sins and a place among those who are sanctified by faith in me.' **1 Cor. 2:10,12**.... these things God has revealed to us through the Spirit. For the Spirit searches everything, even the depths of God.

hearts of flesh;[1] renewing their wills, and, by His almighty power, determining them to that which is good,[2] and effectually drawing them to Jesus Christ:[3] yet so, as they come most freely, being made willing by His grace.[4]

2. This effectual call is of God's free and special grace alone, not from anything at all foreseen in man,[5] who is altogether powerless in this, until, being quickened and renewed by the Holy Spirit,[6] he is

---

1 **Ezek. 36:26**. And I will give you a new heart, and a new spirit I will put within you. And I will remove the heart of stone from your flesh and give you a heart of flesh.

2 **Deut. 30:6**. And the LORD your God will circumcise your heart and the heart of your offspring, so that you will love the LORD your God with all your heart and with all your soul, that you may live. **Ezek.11:19**. And I will give them one heart, and a new spirit I will put within them. I will remove the heart of stone from their flesh and give them a heart of flesh. **Ezek. 36:27**. And I will put my Spirit within you, and cause you to walk in my statutes and be careful to obey my rules. **Phil. 2:13**.... for it is God who works in you, both to will and to work for his good pleasure.

3 **Jn. 6:44-45**. No one can come to me unless the Father who sent me draws him. And I will raise him up on the last day. It is written in the Prophets, 'And they will all be taught by God.' Everyone who has heard and learned from the Father comes to me. **Eph.1:19**.... and what is the immeasurable greatness of his power toward us who believe, according to the working of his great might

4 **Ps. 110:3**. Your people will offer themselves freely on the day of your power, in holy garments; from the womb of the morning, the dew of your youth will be yours. **John 6:37**. All that the Father gives me will come to me, and whoever comes to me I will never cast out. **Rom. 6:16-18**. Do you not know that if you present yourselves to anyone as obedient slaves, you are slaves of the one whom you obey, either of sin, which leads to death, or of obedience, which leads to righteousness? But thanks be to God, that you who were once slaves of sin have become obedient from the heart to the standard of teaching to which you were committed, and, having been set free from sin, have become slaves of righteousness.

5 **Rom. 9:11**.... though they were not yet born and had done nothing either good or bad—in order that God's purpose of election might continue, not because of works but because of him who calls. **Eph. 2:4-5**. But God, being rich in mercy, because of the great love with which he loved us, even when we were dead in our trespasses, made us alive together with Christ—by grace you have been saved. **Eph. 2:8-9**. For by grace you have been saved through faith. And this is not your own doing; it is the gift of God, not a result of works, so that no one may boast. **2 Timothy 1:9**.... who saved us and called us to a holy calling, not because of our works but because of his own purpose and grace, which he gave us in Christ Jesus before the ages began. **Titus 3:4-5**. But when the goodness and loving kindness of God our Savior appeared, he saved us, not because of works done by us in righteousness, but according to his own mercy, by the washing of regeneration and renewal of the Holy Spirit.

6 **Rom. 8:7**. For the mind that is set on the flesh is hostile to God, for it does not submit to God's law; indeed, it cannot. **1 Cor. 2:14**. The natural person does not accept the things of the Spirit of God, for they are folly to him, and he is not able to understand them because they are spiritually discerned. **Eph. 2:5**.... even when we were dead in our trespasses, made us alive together with Christ—by grace you have been saved.

thereby enabled to answer this call, and to embrace the grace offered and conveyed in it.[1]

3. Elect infants, dying in infancy, are regenerated, and saved by Christ, through the Spirit,[2] who works when, and where, and how He pleases:[3] so also are all other elect persons who are incapable of being outwardly called by the ministry of the Word.[4]

4. Others, not elected, although they may be called by the ministry of the Word,[5] and may have some common operations of the Spirit,[6] yet they never truly come to Christ, and therefore cannot be saved:[7]

---

1 **Jn. 5:25**. "Truly, truly, I say to you, an hour is coming, and is now here, when the dead will hear the voice of the Son of God, and those who hear will live. **Jn. 6:37**. All that the Father gives me will come to me, and whoever comes to me I will never cast out. **Ezek. 36:27**. And I will put my Spirit within you, and cause you to walk in my statutes and be careful to obey my rules.

2 **Lk. 18:15-16**. Now they were bringing even infants to him that he might touch them. And when the disciples saw it, they rebuked them. But Jesus called them to him, saying, "Let the children come to me, and do not hinder them, for to such belongs the kingdom of God." **Jn. 3:3,5**. Jesus answered him, "Truly, truly, I say to you, unless one is born again he cannot see the kingdom of God."... Jesus answered, "Truly, truly, I say to you, unless one is born of water and the Spirit, he cannot enter the kingdom of God." **Acts 2:38-39**. And Peter said to them, "Repent and be baptized every one of you in the name of Jesus Christ for the forgiveness of your sins, and you will receive the gift of the Holy Spirit. For the promise is for you and for your children and for all who are far off, everyone whom the Lord our God calls to himself." **Rom. 8:9**. You, however, are not in the flesh but in the Spirit, if in fact the Spirit of God dwells in you. Anyone who does not have the Spirit of Christ does not belong to him. **1 Jn. 5:12**. Whoever has the Son has life; whoever does not have the Son of God does not have life.

3 **Jn. 3:8**. The wind blows where it wishes, and you hear its sound, but you do not know where it comes from or where it goes. So it is with everyone who is born of the Spirit.

4 **Acts 4:12**. And there is salvation in no one else, for there is no other name under heaven given among men by which we must be saved. **1 Jn. 5:12**. Whoever has the Son has life; whoever does not have the Son of God does not have life.

5 **Mt. 22:14**. For many are called, but few are chosen.

6 **Mt. 7:22**. On that day many will say to me, 'Lord, Lord, did we not prophesy in your name, and cast out demons in your name, and do many mighty works in your name?' **Mt. 13:20-21**. As for what was sown on rocky ground, this is the one who hears the word and immediately receives it with joy, yet he has no root in himself, but endures for a while, and when tribulation or persecution arises on account of the word, immediately he falls away. **Heb. 6:4-5**. For it is impossible, in the case of those who have once been enlightened, who have tasted the heavenly gift, and have shared in the Holy Spirit, and have tasted the goodness of the word of God and the powers of the age to come.

7 **Jn. 6:64-66**. But there are some of you who do not believe. (For Jesus knew from the beginning who those were who did not believe, and who it was who would betray him.) And he said, "This is why I told you that no one can come to me unless it is granted him by the Father." After this many of his disciples turned back and no longer walked with him. **Jn. 8:24**. I told you that you would die in your sins, for unless you believe that I am he you will die in your sins.

much less can men, not professing the Christian religion, be saved in any other way whatsoever, be they ever so diligent to frame their lives according to the light of nature, and the laws of that religion they do profess.[1] And to assert and maintain that they may, is very pernicious, and to be detested.[2]

---

1 **Jn. 4:22.** You worship what you do not know; we worship what we know, for salvation is from the Jews. **Jn. 14:6.** Jesus said to him, "I am the way, and the truth, and the life. No one comes to the Father except through me." **Jn. 17:3.** And this is eternal life, that they know you the only true God, and Jesus Christ whom you have sent. **Acts 4:12.** And there is salvation in no one else, for there is no other name under heaven given among men by which we must be saved. **Eph. 2:12.** remember that you were at that time separated from Christ, alienated from the commonwealth of Israel and strangers to the covenants of promise, having no hope and without God in the world.

2 **1 Cor. 16:22.** If anyone has no love for the Lord, let him be accursed. Our Lord, come! **Gal. 1:6-8.** I am astonished that you are so quickly deserting him who called you in the grace of Christ and are turning to a different gospel—not that there is another one, but there are some who trouble you and want to distort the gospel of Christ. But even if we or an angel from heaven should preach to you a gospel contrary to the one we preached to you, let him be accursed. **2 Jn. 9-11.** Everyone who goes on ahead and does not abide in the teaching of Christ, does not have God. Whoever abides in the teaching has both the Father and the Son. If anyone comes to you and does not bring this teaching, do not receive him into your house or give him any greeting, for whoever greets him takes part in his wicked works.

CHAPTER 11

OF JUSTIFICATION.

1. Those whom God effectually calls, He also freely justifies:[1] not by infusing righteousness in them, but by pardoning their sins, and by accounting and accepting their persons as righteous; not for anything done in them, or done by them, but for Christ's sake alone; nor by imputing faith itself, the act of believing, or any other evangelical obedience to them, as their righteousness; but by imputing the obedience and satisfaction of Christ to them,[2] they receiving and

---

1 **Rom. 3:24.** and are justified by his grace as a gift, through the redemption that is in Christ Jesus, **Rom. 8:30.** And those he predestined, he also called; those he called, he also justified; those he justified, he also glorified.

2 **Jer. 23:6.** In his days Judah will be saved and Israel will live in safety. This is the name by which he will be called: The LORD Our Righteous Savior. **Rom. 3:22, 24-25, 27-28.** the righteousness of God through faith in Jesus Christ for all who believe. For there is no distinction... and are justified by his grace as a gift, through the redemption that is in Christ Jesus, whom God put forward as a propitiation by his blood, to be received by faith. This was to show God's righteousness, because in his divine forbearance he had passed over former sins...Then what becomes of our boasting? It is excluded. By what kind of law? By a law of works? No, but by the law of faith. For we hold that one is justified by faith apart from works of the law. **Rom. 4:5-8.** And to the one who does not work but believes in him who justifies the ungodly, his faith is counted as righteousness, just as David also speaks of the blessing of the one to whom God counts righteousness apart from works: "Blessed are those whose lawless deeds are forgiven, and whose sins are covered; blessed is the man against whom the Lord will not count his sin." **Rom. 5:17-19.** For if, because of one man's trespass, death reigned through that one man, much more will those who receive the abundance of grace and the free gift of righteousness reign in life through the one man Jesus Christ. Therefore, as one trespass led to condemnation for all men, so one act of righteousness leads to justification and life for all men. For as by the one man's disobedience the many were made sinners, so by the one man's obedience the many will be made righteous. **1 Cor. 1:30-31.** And because of him you are in Christ Jesus, who became to us wisdom from God, righteousness and sanctification and redemption, so that, as it is written, "Let the one who boasts, boast in the Lord." **2 Cor. 5:19,21.** that is, in Christ God was reconciling the world to himself, not counting their trespasses against them, and entrusting to us the message of reconciliation. ...For our sake he made him to be sin who knew no sin, so that in him we might become the righteousness of God. **Eph. 1:7.** In him we have redemption through his blood, the forgiveness of our trespasses, according to the riches of his grace. **Titus 3:5,7.** he saved us, not because of works done by us in righteousness, but according to his own mercy, by the washing of regeneration and renewal of the Holy Spirit,... so that being justified by his grace we might become heirs according to the hope of eternal life.

resting on Him and His righteousness by faith; which faith they have not of themselves, it is the gift of God.[1]

2. Faith, thus receiving and resting on Christ and His righteousness, is the only instrument of justification:[2] yet in the person justified it is not alone, but is ever accompanied with all other saving graces, and is no dead faith, but works by love.[3]

3. Christ, by His obedience and death, did fully discharge the debt of all those who are thus justified, and did make a proper, real, and full

---

1 **Acts 10:43.** To him all the prophets bear witness that everyone who believes in him receives forgiveness of sins through his name. **Acts 13:38-39.** Let it be known to you therefore, brothers, that through this man forgiveness of sins is proclaimed to you, and by him everyone who believes is freed from everything from which you could not be freed by the law of Moses. **Gal. 2:16.** Yet we know that a person is not justified by works of the law but through faith in Jesus Christ, so we also have believed in Christ Jesus, in order to be justified by faith in Christ and not by works of the law, because by works of the law no one will be justified. **Eph. 2:7-8.** so that in the coming ages he might show the immeasurable riches of his grace in kindness toward us in Christ Jesus. For by grace you have been saved through faith. And this is not your own doing; it is the gift of God. **Phil. 3:9.** and be found in him, not having a righteousness of my own that comes from the law, but that which comes through faith in Christ, the righteousness from God that depends on faith—

2 **Jn. 1:12.** But to all who did receive him, who believed in his name, he gave the right to become children of God, **Rom. 3:28.** For we hold that one is justified by faith apart from works of the law. **Rom. 5:1.** Therefore, since we have been justified by faith, we have peace with God through our Lord Jesus Christ.

3 **Gal. 5:6.** For in Christ Jesus neither circumcision nor uncircumcision counts for anything, but only faith working through love. **James 2:17, 22,26.** So also faith by itself, if it does not have works, is dead....You see that faith was active along with his works, and faith was completed by his works.... For as the body apart from the spirit is dead, so also faith apart from works is dead

satisfaction to His Father's justice in their behalf.[1] Yet, in as much as He was given by the Father for them;[2] and His obedience and satisfaction accepted in their stead;[3] and both, freely, not for anything in them; their justification is only of free grace;[4] that both the exact justice, and rich grace of God might be glorified in the justification of sinners.[5]

---

1 **Isa. 53:4-6, 10-12**. Surely he has borne our griefs and carried our sorrows; yet we esteemed him stricken, smitten by God, and afflicted. But he was wounded for our transgressions; he was crushed for our iniquities; upon him was the chastisement that brought us peace, and with his stripes we are healed. All we like sheep have gone astray; we have turned—every one—to his own way; and the LORD has laid on him the iniquity of us all....Yet it was the will of the LORD to crush him; he has put him to grief; when his soul makes an offering for guilt, he shall see his offspring; he shall prolong his days; the will of the LORD shall prosper in his hand. Out of the anguish of his soul he shall see and be satisfied; by his knowledge shall the righteous one, my servant, make many to be accounted righteous, and he shall bear their iniquities. Therefore I will divide him a portion with the many, and he shall divide the spoil with the strong, because he poured out his soul to death and was numbered with the transgressors; yet he bore the sin of many, and makes intercession for the transgressors. **Dan. 9:24,26**. Seventy weeks are decreed about your people and your holy city, to finish the transgression, to put an end to sin, and to atone for iniquity, to bring in everlasting righteousness, to seal both vision and prophet, and to anoint a most holy place.... And after the sixty-two weeks, an anointed one shall be cut off and shall have nothing. And the people of the prince who is to come shall destroy the city and the sanctuary. Its end shall come with a flood, and to the end there shall be war. Desolations are decreed. **Rom. 5:8-10,19**. but God shows his love for us in that while we were still sinners, Christ died for us. Since, therefore, we have now been justified by his blood, much more shall we be saved by him from the wrath of God. For if while we were enemies we were reconciled to God by the death of his Son, much more, now that we are reconciled, shall we be saved by his life.... For as by the one man's disobedience the many were made sinners, so by the one man's obedience the many will be made righteous. **1 Tim. 2:5-6**. For there is one God, and there is one mediator between God and men, the man Christ Jesus, who gave himself as a ransom for all, which is the testimony given at the proper time. **Heb. 10:10,14**. And by that will we have been sanctified through the offering of the body of Jesus Christ once for all.... For by a single offering he has perfected for all time those who are being sanctified.

2 **Rom. 8:32**. He who did not spare his own Son but gave him up for us all, how will he not also with him graciously give us all things?

3 **Mt. 3:17**. and behold, a voice from heaven said, "This is my beloved Son, with whom I am well pleased." **Eph. 5:2**. And walk in love, as Christ loved us and gave himself up for us, a fragrant offering and sacrifice to God.

4 **Rom. 3:24**. and are justified by his grace as a gift, through the redemption that is in Christ Jesus, **Eph. 1:7**. In him we have redemption through his blood, the forgiveness of our trespasses, according to the riches of his grace.

5 **Rom. 3:26**. It was to show his righteousness at the present time, so that he might be just and the justifier of the one who has faith in Jesus. **Eph. 2:7**. so that in the coming ages he might show the immeasurable riches of his grace in kindness toward us in Christ Jesus.

4. God did, from all eternity, decree to justify all the elect,[1] and Christ did, in the fullness of time, die for their sins, and rise for their justification:[2]
nevertheless, they are not justified, until the Holy Spirit does, in due time, actually apply Christ to them.[3]

5. God does continue to forgive the sins of those who are justified;[4] and, although they can never fall from the state of justification,[5] yet they may, by their sins, fall under God's fatherly displeasure, and

---

1 **Rom. 8:30**. And those whom he predestined he also called, and those whom he called he also justified, and those whom he justified he also glorified. **Gal. 3:8**. And the Scripture, foreseeing that God would justify the Gentiles by faith, preached the gospel beforehand to Abraham, saying, "In you shall all the nations be blessed." **1 Peter 1:2, 19-20**. according to the foreknowledge of God the Father, in the sanctification of the Spirit, for obedience to Jesus Christ and for sprinkling with his blood. May grace and peace be multiplied to you....but with the precious blood of Christ, like that of a lamb without blemish or spot. He was foreknown before the foundation of the world but was made manifest in the last times for the sake of you.

2 **Rom. 4:25**. who was delivered up for our trespasses and raised for our justification. **Gal. 4:4**. But when the fullness of time had come, God sent forth his Son, born of woman, born under the law. **1 Tim. 2:6**. who gave himself as a ransom for all, which is the testimony given at the proper time.

3 **Gal. 2:16**. yet we know that a person is not justified by works of the law but through faith in Jesus Christ, so we also have believed in Christ Jesus, in order to be justified by faith in Christ and not by works of the law, because by works of the law no one will be justified. **Col. 1:21-22**. And you, who once were alienated and hostile in mind, doing evil deeds, he has now reconciled in his body of flesh by his death, in order to present you holy and blameless and above reproach before him. **Titus 3:3-7**. For we ourselves were once foolish, disobedient, led astray, slaves to various passions and pleasures, passing our days in malice and envy, hated by others and hating one another. But when the goodness and loving kindness of God our Savior appeared, he saved us, not because of works done by us in righteousness, but according to his own mercy, by the washing of regeneration and renewal of the Holy Spirit, whom he poured out on us richly through Jesus Christ our Savior, so that being justified by his grace we might become heirs according to the hope of eternal life.

4 **Mt. 6:12**. and forgive us our debts, as we also have forgiven our debtors. **1 Jn. 1:7, 9**. But if we walk in the light, as he is in the light, we have fellowship with one another, and the blood of Jesus his Son cleanses us from all sin....If we confess our sins, he is faithful and just to forgive us our sins and to cleanse us from all unrighteousness. **1 Jn. 2:1-2.** My little children, I am writing these things to you so that you may not sin. But if anyone does sin, we have an advocate with the Father, Jesus Christ the righteous. He is the propitiation for our sins, and not for ours only but also for the sins of the whole world.

5 **Lk. 22:32.** but I have prayed for you that your faith may not fail. And when you have turned again, strengthen your brothers. **Jn. 10:28**. I give them eternal life, and they will never perish, and no one will snatch them out of my hand. **Heb. 10:14**. For by a single offering he has perfected for all time those who are being sanctified.

not have the light of His approval restored to them, until they humble themselves, confess their sins, beg pardon, and renew their faith and repentance.[1]

6. The justification of believers under the Old Testament was, in all these respects, one and the same with the justification of believers under the New Testament.[2]

1 **Ps. 32:5**. I acknowledged my sin to you, and I did not cover my iniquity; said, "I will confess my transgressions to the LORD," and you forgave the iniquity of my sin. **Ps. 51:7-12**. Purge me with hyssop, and I shall be clean; wash me, and I shall be whiter than snow. Let me hear joy and gladness; let the bones that you have broken rejoice. Hide your face from my sins, and blot out all my iniquities. Create in me a clean heart, O God, and renew a right spirit within me. Cast me not away from your presence, and take not your Holy Spirit from me. Restore to me the joy of your salvation, and uphold me with a willing spirit. **Ps. 89:31-33**. if they violate my statutes and do not keep my commandments, then I will punish their transgression with the rod and their iniquity with stripes, but I will not remove from him my steadfast love or be false to my faithfulness. **Mt. 26:75**. And Peter remembered the saying of Jesus, "Before the rooster crows, you will deny me three times." And he went out and wept bitterly. **Lk. 1:20**. And behold, you will be silent and unable to speak until the day that these things take place, because you did not believe my words, which will be fulfilled in their time." **1 Cor. 11:30,32**. That is why many of you are weak and ill, and some have died....But when we are judged by the Lord, we are disciplined so that we may not be condemned along with the world.

2 **Rom. 4:22-24**. That is why his faith was "counted to him as righteousness." But the words "it was counted to him" were not written for his sake alone, but for ours also. It will be counted to us who believe in him who raised from the dead Jesus our Lord. **Gal. 3:9, 13-14**. So then, those who are of faith are blessed along with Abraham, the man of faith.... Christ redeemed us from the curse of the law by becoming a curse for us—for it is written, "Cursed is everyone who is hanged on a tree"—so that in Christ Jesus the blessing of Abraham might come to the Gentiles, so that we might receive the promised Spirit through faith. **Heb. 13:8**. Jesus Christ is the same yesterday and today and forever.

CHAPTER 12

OF ADOPTION.

1. All those who are justified, God permitted, in and for His only Son Jesus Christ, to make partakers of the grace of adoption,[1] by which they are taken into the number and enjoy the liberties and privileges of the children of God,[2] have His name put on them,[3] receive the spirit of adoption,[4] have access to the throne of grace with boldness,[5]

---

1 **Gal. 4:4-5**. But when the fullness of time had come, God sent forth his Son, born of woman, born under the law, to redeem those who were under the law, so that we might receive adoption as sons. **Eph. 1:5**. he predestined us for adoption as sons through Jesus Christ, according to the purpose of his will.

2 **Jn. 1:12**. But to all who did receive him, who believed in his name, he gave the right to become children of God, **Rom. 8:17**. and if children, then heirs—heirs of God and fellow heirs with Christ, provided we suffer with him in order that we may also be glorified with him.

3 **Jer. 14:9**. Why should you be like a man confused, like a mighty warrior who cannot save? Yet you, O LORD, are in the midst of us, and we are called by your name; do not leave us. **Rev. 3:12**. The one who conquers, I will make him a pillar in the temple of my God. Never shall he go out of it, and I will write on him the name of my God, and the name of the city of my God, the new Jerusalem, which comes down from my God out of heaven, and my own new name.

4 **Rom. 8:15**. For you did not receive the spirit of slavery to fall back into fear, but you have received the Spirit of adoption as sons, by whom we cry, "Abba! Father!"

5 **Rom. 5:2**. Through him we have also obtained access by faith into this grace in which we stand, and we rejoice in hope of the glory of God. **Eph. 3:12**. in whom we have boldness and access with confidence through our faith in him.

are enabled to cry, Abba, Father,[1] are pitied,[2] protected,[3] provided for,[4] and chastened by Him as by a Father:[5] yet never cast off,[6] but sealed to the day of redemption;[7] and inherit the promises,[8] as heirs of everlasting salvation.[9]

---

1 **Gal. 4:6**. And because you are sons, God has sent the Spirit of his Son into our hearts, crying, "Abba! Father!"
2 **Ps. 103:13**. As a father shows compassion to his children, so the LORD shows compassion to those who fear him.
3 **Prov. 14:26**. In the fear of the LORD one has strong confidence, and his children will have a refuge.
4 **Mt. 6:30,32**. But if God so clothes the grass of the field, which today is alive and tomorrow is thrown into the oven, will he not much more clothe you, O you of little faith?... For the Gentiles seek after all these things, and your heavenly Father knows that you need them all. **1 Pet. 5:7**. casting all your anxieties on him, because he cares for you.
5 **Heb. 12:6**. For the Lord disciplines the one he loves, and chastises every son whom he receives.
6 **Lam. 3:31**. For the Lord will not cast off forever.
7 **Eph. 4:30**. And do not grieve the Holy Spirit of God, by whom you were sealed for the day of redemption.
8 **Heb. 6:12**. so that you may not be sluggish, but imitators of those who through faith and patience inherit the promises.
9 **Heb. 1:14**. Are they not all ministering spirits sent out to serve for the sake of those who are to inherit salvation? **1 Pet. 1:3-4**. Blessed be the God and Father of our Lord Jesus Christ! According to his great mercy, he has caused us to be born again to a living hope through the resurrection of Jesus Christ from the dead, to an inheritance that is imperishable, undefiled, and unfading, kept in heaven for you.

CHAPTER 13

OF SANCTIFICATION.

1. They who are once effectually called, and regenerated, having a new heart, and a new spirit created in them, are further sanctified, really and personally, through the virtue of Christ's death and resurrection,[1] by His Word and Spirit dwelling in them;[2] the dominion of the whole body of sin is destroyed,[3] and the several lusts of it are more and more weakened and destroyed;[4] and they more and

---

1 **Acts 20:32**. And now I commend you to God and to the word of his grace, which is able to build you up and to give you the inheritance among all those who are sanctified. **Rom. 6:5-6**. For if we have been united with him in a death like his, we shall certainly be united with him in a resurrection like his. We know that our old self was crucified with him in order that the body of sin might be brought to nothing, so that we would no longer be enslaved to sin. **1 Cor. 6:11**. And such were some of you. But you were washed, you were sanctified, you were justified in the name of the Lord Jesus Christ and by the Spirit of our God. **Phil. 3:10** ... that I may know him and the power of his resurrection, and may share his sufferings, becoming like him in his death.

2 **Jn. 17:17**. Sanctify them in the truth; your word is truth. **Eph. 5:26** ... that he might sanctify her, having cleansed her by the washing of water with the word. **Thess. 2:13**. But we ought always to give thanks to God for you, brothers beloved by the Lord, because God chose you as the firstfruits to be saved, through sanctification by the Spirit and belief in the truth.

3 **Rom. 6:6, 14**. We know that our old self was crucified with him in order that the body of sin might be brought to nothing, so that we would no longer be enslaved to sin. ... For sin will have no dominion over you, since you are not under the law but under grace.

4 **Rom. 8:13**. For if you live according to the flesh you will die, but if by the Spirit you put to death the deeds of the body, you will live. **Gal. 5:24**. And those who belong to Christ Jesus have crucified the flesh with its passions and desires.

more made alive and strengthened in all saving graces,[1] to the practice of true holiness, without which no man shall see the Lord.[2]

2. This sanctification is throughout, in the whole man;[3] yet imperfect in this life, there remaining some remnants of corruption in every part;[4] from which arises a continual and irreconcilable war, the flesh lusting against the Spirit, and the Spirit against the flesh.[5]

3. In which war, although the remaining corruption, for a time, may much prevail;[6] yet, through the continual supply of strength from

---

1 **Eph. 3:16-19**. ... that according to the riches of his glory he may grant you to be strengthened with power through his Spirit in your inner being, so that Christ may dwell in your hearts through faith—that you, being rooted and grounded in love, may have strength to comprehend with all the saints what is the breadth and length and height and depth, and to know the love of Christ that surpasses knowledge, that you may be filled with all the fullness of God. **Col. 1:11**. May you be strengthened with all power, according to his glorious might, for all endurance and patience with joy.

2 **2 Cor. 7:1**. Since we have these promises, beloved, let us cleanse ourselves from every defilement of body and spirit, bringing holiness to completion in the fear of God. **Heb. 12:14**. Strive for peace with everyone, and for the holiness without which no one will see the Lord.

3 **1 Thess. 5:23**. Now may the God of peace himself sanctify you completely, and may your whole spirit and soul and body be kept blameless at the coming of our Lord Jesus Christ.

4 **Rom. 7:18, 23**. For I know that nothing good dwells in me, that is, in my flesh. For I have the desire to do what is right, but not the ability to carry it out. ...but I see in my members another law waging war against the law of my mind and making me captive to the law of sin that dwells in my members. **Phil. 3:12**. Not that I have already obtained this or am already perfect, but I press on to make it my own, because Christ Jesus has made me his own. **1 Jn. 1:10**. If we say we have not sinned, we make him a liar, and his word is not in us.

5 **Gal. 5:17**. For the desires of the flesh are against the Spirit, and the desires of the Spirit are against the flesh, for these are opposed to each other, to keep you from doing the things you want to do. **1 Pet. 2:11**. Beloved, I urge you as sojourners and exiles to abstain from the passions of the flesh, which wage war against your soul.

6 **Rom. 7:23**. ...but I see in my members another law waging war against the law of my mind and making me captive to the law of sin that dwells in my members.

the sanctifying Spirit of Christ, the regenerate part does overcome;[1] and so, the saints grow in grace,[2] perfecting holiness in the fear of God.[3]

---

1 **Rom. 6:14**. For sin will have no dominion over you, since you are not under law but under grace. **Eph. 4:15-16**. Rather, speaking the truth in love, we are to grow up in every way into him who is the head, into Christ, from whom the whole body, joined and held together by every joint with which it is equipped, when each part is working properly, makes the body grow so that it builds itself up in love. **1 Jn. 5:4**. For everyone who has been born of God overcomes the world. And this is the victory that has overcome the world—our faith.

2 **2 Cor. 3:18**. And we all, with unveiled face, beholding the glory of the Lord, are being transformed into the same image from one degree of glory to another. For this comes from the Lord who is the Spirit. **2 Pet. 3:18**. But grow in the grace and knowledge of our Lord and Savior Jesus Christ. To him be glory both now and forever! Amen.

3 **2 Cor. 7:1**. Since we have these promises, beloved, let us cleanse ourselves from every defilement of body and spirit, bringing holiness to completion in the fear of God.

CHAPTER 14

OF SAVING FAITH.

1. The grace of faith, whereby the elect are enabled to believe to the saving of their souls,[1] is the work of the Spirit of Christ in their hearts,[2] and is ordinarily accomplished by the ministry of the Word,[3] by which also, and by the administration of the sacraments, and prayer, it is increased and strengthened.[4]

---

1 **Heb. 10:39**. But we are not of those who shrink back and are destroyed, but of those who have faith and preserve their souls.

2 **2 Cor. 4:13**. Since we have the same spirit of faith according to what has been written, "I believed, and so I spoke," we also believe, and so we also speak. **Eph. 1:17-19**. that the God of our Lord Jesus Christ, the Father of glory, may give you a spirit of wisdom and of revelation in the knowledge of him, having the eyes of your hearts enlightened, that you may know what is the hope to which he has called you, what are the riches of his glorious inheritance in the saints, and what is the immeasurable greatness of his power toward us who believe, according to the working of his great might. **Eph. 2:8**. For by grace you have been saved through faith. And this is not your own doing; it is the gift of God.

3 **Rom. 10:14,17**. How then will they call on him in whom they have not believed? And how are they to believe in him of whom they have never heard? And how are they to hear without someone preaching? So faith comes from hearing, and hearing through the word of Christ.

4 **Lk 17:5**. The apostles said to the Lord, "Increase our faith!" **Acts 20:32**. And now I commend you to God and to the word of his grace, which is able to build you up and to give you the inheritance among all those who are sanctified. **Rom. 1:16-17**. For I am not ashamed of the gospel, for it is the power of God for salvation to everyone who believes, to the Jew first and also to the Greek. For in it the righteousness of God is revealed from faith for faith, as it is written, "The righteous shall live by faith." **Rom 4:11**. He received the sign of circumcision as a seal of the righteousness that he had by faith while he was still uncircumcised. The purpose was to make him the father of all who believe without being circumcised, so that righteousness would be counted to them as well. **1 Pet. 2:2.** Like newborn infants, long for the pure spiritual milk, that by it you may grow up into salvation

2. By this faith, a Christian believes to be true whatever is revealed in the Word, for the authority of God Himself speaking in it;[1] and acts differently on that which each particular passage of it contains; yielding obedience to the commands,[2] trembling at the warnings,[3] and embracing the promises of God for this life, and that which is to come.[4] But the principal acts of saving faith are accepting, receiving, and resting on Christ alone for justification, sanctification, and eternal life, by virtue of the covenant of grace.[5]

---

1 **Jn 4:42**. They said to the woman, "It is no longer because of what you said that we believe, for we have heard for ourselves, and we know that this is indeed the Savior of the world." **Acts 24:14**. But this I confess to you, that according to the Way, which they call a sect, I worship the God of our fathers, believing everything laid down by the Law and written in the Prophets. **1 Thess. 2:13.** And we also thank God constantly for this, that when you received the word of God, which you heard from us, you accepted it not as the word of men but as what it really is, the word of God, which is at work in you believers. **1 Jn. 5:10.** Whoever believes in the Son of God has the testimony in himself. Whoever does not believe God has made him a liar, because he has not believed in the testimony that God has borne concerning his Son.

2 **Rom. 16:26**. but has now been disclosed and through the prophetic writings has been made known to all nations, according to the command of the eternal God, to bring about the obedience of faith.

3 **Isa. 66:2.** All these things my hand has made, and so all these things came to be, declares the LORD. But this is the one to whom I will look: he who is humble and contrite in spirit and trembles at my word.

4 **1 Tim. 4:8**. for while bodily training is of some value, godliness is of value in every way, as it holds promise for the present life and also for the life to come. **Heb 11:13**. These all died in faith, not having received the things promised, but having seen them and greeted them from afar, and having acknowledged that they were strangers and exiles on the earth.

5 **Jn. 1:12.** But to all who did receive him, who believed in his name, he gave the right to become children of God. **Acts 15:11**. But we believe that we will be saved through the grace of the Lord Jesus, just as they will." **Acts 16:31**. And they said, "Believe in the Lord Jesus, and you will be saved, you and your household." **Gal 2:20**. I have been crucified with Christ. It is no longer I who live, but Christ who lives in me. And the life I now live in the flesh I live by faith in the Son of God, who loved me and gave himself for me.

3. This faith is different in degrees, weak or strong;[1] may be often and many ways assailed, and weakened, but gets the victory:[2] growing up in many to the attainment of a full assurance, through Christ,[3] who is both the author and finisher of our faith.[4]

---

1 **Mt. 6:30**. But if God so clothes the grass of the field, which today is alive and tomorrow is thrown into the oven, will he not much more clothe you, O you of little faith? **Mt. 8:10**. When Jesus heard this, he marveled and said to those who followed him, "Truly, I tell you, with no one in Israel have I found such faith. **Rom. 4:19-20**. He did not weaken in faith when he considered his own body, which was as good as dead (since he was about a hundred years old), or when he considered the barrenness of Sarah's womb. No distrust made him waver concerning the promise of God, but he grew strong in his faith as he gave glory to God. **Heb. 5:13-14**. for everyone who lives on milk is unskilled in the word of righteousness, since he is a child. But solid food is for the mature, for those who have their powers of discernment trained by constant practice to distinguish good from evil.

2 **Lk. 22:31-32**. "Simon, Simon, behold, Satan demanded to have you, that he might sift you like wheat, but I have prayed for you that your faith may not fail. And when you have turned again, strengthen your brothers." **Eph. 6:16**. In all circumstances take up the shield of faith, with which you can extinguish all the flaming darts of the evil one. **1 Jn. 5:4-5**. For everyone who has been born of God overcomes the world. And this is the victory that has overcome the world—our faith. Who is it that overcomes the world except the one who believes that Jesus is the Son of God?

3 **Heb. 6:11-12**. And we desire each one of you to show the same earnestness to have the full assurance of hope until the end, so that you may not be sluggish, but imitators of those who through faith and patience inherit the promises. **Heb. 10:22**. let us draw near with a true heart in full assurance of faith, with our hearts sprinkled clean from an evil conscience and our bodies washed with pure water.

4 **Heb. 12:2**. ...looking to Jesus, the founder and perfecter of our faith, who for the joy that was set before him endured the cross, despising the shame, and is seated at the right hand of the throne of God.

CHAPTER 15

OF REPENTANCE TO LIFE.

1. Repentance to life is an evangelical grace,[1] the doctrine of which is to be preached by every minister of the Gospel, as well as the doctrine of faith in Christ.[2]

2. By it, a sinner, because of the sight and sense not only of the danger, but also of the filthiness and odiousness of his sins, as contrary to the holy nature, and righteous law of God; and upon the understanding of His mercy in Christ to such as are penitent, so grieves for, and

1 **Zech. 12:10**. And I will pour out on the house of David and the inhabitants of Jerusalem a spirit of grace and pleas for mercy, so that, when they look on me, on him whom they have pierced, they shall mourn for him, as one mourns for an only child, and weep bitterly over him, as one weeps over a firstborn. **Acts 11:18**. When they heard these things they fell silent. And they glorified God, saying, "Then to the Gentiles also God has granted repentance that leads to life."

2 **Mk. 1:15**. and saying, "The time is fulfilled, and the kingdom of God is at hand; repent and believe in the gospel." **Lk. 24:47**. and that repentance and forgiveness of sins should be proclaimed in his name to all nations, beginning from Jerusalem. **Acts 20:21**. testifying both to Jews and to Greeks of repentance toward God and of faith in our Lord Jesus Christ.

hates his sins, as to turn from them all to God,[1] intending and endeavoring to walk with Him in all the ways of His commandments.[2]

3. Although repentance is not to be rested in, as any satisfaction for sin, or any cause of the pardon for it,[3] which is the act of God's free

---

1 **Ps. 51:4**. Against you, you only, have I sinned and done what is evil in your sight, so that you may be justified in your words and blameless in your judgment. **Ps. 119:128**. Therefore I consider all your precepts to be right; I hate every false way. **Isa. 30:22**. Then you will defile your carved idols overlaid with silver and your gold-plated metal images. You will scatter them as unclean things. You will say to them, "Be gone!" **Jer. 31:18-19**. I have heard Ephraim grieving, 'You have disciplined me, and I was disciplined, like an untrained calf; bring me back that I may be restored, for you are the LORD my God. For after I had turned away, I relented, and after I was instructed, I struck my thigh; I was ashamed, and I was confounded, because I bore the disgrace of my youth.' **Ezek. 18:30-31**. Therefore I will judge you, O house of Israel, every one according to his ways, declares the Lord GOD. Repent and turn from all your transgressions, lest iniquity be your ruin. Cast away from you all the transgressions that you have committed, and make yourselves a new heart and a new spirit! Why will you die, O house of Israel? **Ezek. 36:31**. Then you will remember your evil ways, and your deeds that were not good, and you will loathe yourselves for your iniquities and your abominations. **Joel 2:12-13**. "Yet even now," declares the LORD, "return to me with all your heart, with fasting, with weeping, and with mourning; and rend your hearts and not your garments." Return to the LORD your God, for he is gracious and merciful, slow to anger, and abounding in steadfast love; and he relents over disaster. **Am. 5:15**. Hate evil, and love good, and establish justice in the gate; it may be that the LORD, the God of hosts, will be gracious to the remnant of Joseph. **2 Cor. 7:11**. For see what earnestness this godly grief has produced in you, but also what eagerness to clear yourselves, what indignation, what fear, what longing, what zeal, what punishment! At every point you have proved yourselves innocent in the matter.

2 **2 Kings 23:25**. Before him there was no king like him, who turned to the LORD with all his heart and with all his soul and with all his might, according to all the Law of Moses, nor did any like him arise after him. **Ps. 119:6, 59, 106**. Then I shall not be put to shame, having my eyes fixed on all your commandments... When I think on my ways, I turn my feet to your testimonies... I have sworn an oath and confirmed it, to keep your righteous rules. **Lk. 1:6.** And they were both righteous before God, walking blamelessly in all the commandments and statutes of the Lord.

3 **Ezek. 16:61-63**. Then you will remember your ways and be ashamed when you take your sisters, both your elder and your younger, and I give them to you as daughters, but not on account of the covenant with you. I will establish my covenant with you, and you shall know that I am the LORD, that you may remember and be confounded, and never open your mouth again because of your shame, when I atone for you for all that you have done, declares the Lord GOD. **Ezek. 36:31-32**. Then you will remember your evil ways, and your deeds that were not good, and you will loathe yourselves for your iniquities and your abominations. It is not for your sake that I will act, declares the Lord GOD; let that be known to you. Be ashamed and confounded for your ways, O house of Israel.

grace in Christ;[1] yet it is of such necessity to all sinners, that none may expect pardon without it.[2]

4. As there is no sin so small, but it deserves damnation;[3] so there is no sin so great, that it can bring damnation on those who truly repent.[4] ALL SIN IS MORTAL BUT IT IS NOT FATAL

5. Men ought not to be content with a general repentance, but it is every man's duty to endeavor to repent of his individual sins, individually.[5]

---

1 **Hos. 14:2, 4**. Take with you words and return to the LORD; say to him, "Take away all iniquity; accept what is good, and we will pay with bulls the vows of our lips"... I will heal their apostasy; I will love them freely, for my anger has turned from them. **Rom. 3:24**. and are justified by his grace as a gift, through the redemption that is in Christ Jesus. **Eph. 1:7**. In him we have redemption through his blood, the forgiveness of our trespasses, according to the riches of his grace.

2 **Lk. 13:3, 5**. No, I tell you; but unless you repent, you will all likewise perish. **Acts 17:30-31**. The times of ignorance God overlooked, but now he commands all people everywhere to repent, because he has fixed a day on which he will judge the world in righteousness by a man whom he has appointed; and of this he has given assurance to all by raising him from the dead.

3 **Mt. 12:36**. I tell you, on the day of judgment people will give account for every careless word they speak. **Rom. 5:12**. Therefore, just as sin came into the world through one man, and death through sin, and so death spread to all men because all sinned. **Rom. 6:23**. For the wages of sin is death, but the free gift of God is eternal life in Christ Jesus our Lord.

4 **Isa. 1:16, 18**. Wash yourselves; make yourselves clean; remove the evil of your deeds from before my eyes; cease to do evil... "Come now, let us reason together," says the LORD: "though your sins are like scarlet, they shall be as white as snow; though they are red like crimson, they shall become like wool." **Isa. 55:7**. Let the wicked forsake his way, and the unrighteous man his thoughts; let him return to the LORD, that he may have compassion on him, and to our God, for he will abundantly pardon. **Rom. 8:1**. There is therefore now no condemnation for those who are in Christ Jesus.

5 **Ps. 19:13**. Keep back your servant also from presumptuous sins; let them not have dominion over me! Then I shall be blameless, and innocent of great transgression. **Lk. 19:8**. And Zacchaeus stood and said to the Lord, "Behold, Lord, the half of my goods I give to the poor. And if I have defrauded anyone of anything, I restore it fourfold." **1 Tim. 1:13,15**. though formerly I was a blasphemer, persecutor, and insolent opponent. But I received mercy because I had acted ignorantly in unbelief...The saying is trustworthy and deserving of full acceptance, that Christ Jesus came into the world to save sinners, of whom I am the foremost.

6. As every man is bound to make private confession of his sins to God, praying for the pardon of them;[1] upon which, and the forsaking of them, he shall find mercy;[2] so, he who brings scandal on his brother, or the Church of Christ, ought to be willing, by a private or public confession, and sorrow for his sin, to declare his repentance to those who are offended,[3] who are then to be reconciled to him, and in love to receive him.[4]

---

1 **Ps. 32:5-6**. I acknowledged my sin to you, and I did not cover my iniquity; I said, "I will confess my transgressions to the LORD," and you forgave the iniquity of my sin. Therefore let everyone who is godly offer prayer to you at a time when you may be found; surely in the rush of great waters, they shall not reach him. **Ps. 51:4-5, 7, 9, 14.** Against you, you only, have I sinned and done what is evil in your sight, so that you may be justified in your words and blameless in your judgment. Behold, I was brought forth in iniquity, and in sin did my mother conceive me... Purge me with hyssop, and I shall be clean; wash me, and I shall be whiter than snow... Hide your face from my sins, and blot out all my iniquities... Deliver me from bloodguiltiness, O God, O God of my salvation, and my tongue will sing aloud of your righteousness.

2 **Prov. 28:13**. Whoever conceals his transgressions will not prosper, but he who confesses and forsakes them will obtain mercy. **1 Jn. 1:9**. If we confess our sins, he is faithful and just to forgive us our sins and to cleanse us from all unrighteousness.

3 **Josh. 7:19**. Then Joshua said to Achan, "My son, give glory to the LORD God of Israel and give praise to him. And tell me now what you have done; do not hide it from me." **Ps. 51**. All of Psalm 51. **Lk. 17:3-4**. Pay attention to yourselves! If your brother sins, rebuke him, and if he repents, forgive him, and if he sins against you seven times in the day, and turns to you seven times, saying, 'I repent,' you must forgive him." **Jas. 5:16**. Therefore, confess your sins to one another and pray for one another, that you may be healed. The prayer of a righteous person has great power as it is working.

4 **2 Cor. 2:8**. So I beg you to reaffirm your love for him.

CHAPTER 16

OF GOOD WORKS.

1. Good works are only such as God has commanded in His holy Word,[1] and not such as, without the warrant of Scripture, are devised by men, out of blind zeal, or on any pretense of good intention.[2]
2. These good works, done in obedience to God's commandments, are the fruits and evidences of a true and living faith:[3] and by them

---

1 **Mic. 6:8**. He has told you, O man, what is good; and what does the LORD require of you but to do justice, and to love kindness, and to walk humbly with your God? **Rom. 12:2**. Do not be conformed to this world, but be transformed by the renewal of your mind, that by testing you may discern what is the will of God, what is good and acceptable and perfect. **Heb. 13:21**. ... equip you with everything good that you may do his will, working in us that which is pleasing in his sight, through Jesus Christ, to whom be glory forever and ever. Amen.

2 **1 Sam. 15:21-23**. But the people took of the spoil, sheep and oxen, the best of the things devoted to destruction, to sacrifice to the LORD your God in Gilgal." And Samuel said, "Has the LORD as great delight in burnt offerings and sacrifices, as in obeying the voice of the LORD? Behold, to obey is better than sacrifice, and to listen than the fat of rams. For rebellion is as the sin of divination, and presumption is as iniquity and idolatry. Because you have rejected the word of the LORD, he has also rejected you from being king." **Isa. 29:13**. And the Lord said: "Because this people draw near with their mouth and honor me with their lips, while their hearts are far from me, and their fear of me is a commandment taught by men." **Mt. 15:9**. ...in vain do they worship me, teaching as doctrines the commandments of men. **Jn. 16:2**. They will put you out of the synagogues. Indeed, the hour is coming when whoever kills you will think he is offering service to God. **Rom. 10:2**. For I bear them witness that they have a zeal for God, but not according to knowledge. **1 Pet. 1:18**. ...knowing that you were ransomed from the futile ways inherited from your forefathers, not with perishable things such as silver or gold.

3 **Jas. 2:18, 22**. But someone will say, "You have faith and I have works." Show me your faith apart from your works, and I will show you my faith by my works. ... You see that faith was active along with his works, and faith was completed by his works.

believers show their thankfulness,[1] strengthen their assurance,[2] teach their brothers,[3] give credibility to their profession of the Gospel,[4] stop the criticism from the adversaries,[5] and glorify God,[6] whose workmanship they are, created in Christ Jesus for such purpose,[7] that, having their fruit of holiness, they may have the end, eternal life.[8]

---

1 **Ps. 116:12-13**. What shall I render to the LORD for all his benefits to me? I will lift up the cup of salvation and call on the name of the LORD. **1 Pet. 2:9**. But you are a chosen race, a royal priesthood, a holy nation, a people for his own possession, that you may proclaim the excellencies of him who called you out of darkness into his marvelous light.

2 **2 Pet. 1:5-10**. For this very reason, make every effort to supplement your faith with virtue, and virtue with knowledge, and knowledge with self-control, and self-control with steadfastness, and steadfastness with godliness, and godliness with brotherly affection, and brotherly affection with love. For if these qualities are yours and are increasing, they keep you from being ineffective or unfruitful in the knowledge of our Lord Jesus Christ. For whoever lacks these qualities is so nearsighted that he is blind, having forgotten that he was cleansed from his former sins. Therefore, brothers, be all the more diligent to make your calling and election sure, for if you practice these qualities you will never fall. **1 Jn. 2:3, 5**. And by this we know that we have come to know him, if we keep his commandments. ...but whoever keeps his word, in him truly the love of God is perfected. By this we may know that we are in him.

3 **Mt. 5:16**. In the same way, let your light shine before others, so that they may see your good works and give glory to your Father who is in heaven. **2 Cor. 9:2**. ...for I know your readiness, of which I boast about you to the people of Macedonia, saying that Achaia has been ready since last year. And your zeal has stirred up most of them.

4 **1 Tim. 6:1**. Let all who are under a yoke as slaves regard their own masters as worthy of all honor, so that the name of God and the teaching may not be reviled. **Titus 2:5, 9-12**. ...to be self-controlled, pure, working at home, kind, and submissive to their own husbands, that the word of God may not be reviled. ... Slaves are to be submissive to their own masters in everything; they are to be well-pleasing, not argumentative, not pilfering, but showing all good faith, so that in everything they may adorn the doctrine of God our Savior. For the grace of God has appeared, bringing salvation for all people, training us to renounce ungodliness and worldly passions, and to live self-controlled, upright, and godly lives in the present age.

5 **1 Pet. 2:15**. For this is the will of God, that by doing good you should put to silence the ignorance of foolish people.

6 **Jn. 15:8**. By this my Father is glorified, that you bear much fruit and so prove to be my disciples. **Phil. 1:11**. ...filled with the fruit of righteousness that comes through Jesus Christ, to the glory and praise of God. **1 Pet. 2:12**. Keep your conduct among the Gentiles honorable, so that when they speak against you as evildoers, they may see your good deeds and glorify God on the day of visitation.

7 **Eph. 2:10**. For we are his workmanship, created in Christ Jesus for good works, which God prepared beforehand, that we should walk in them.

8 **Rom. 6:22**. But now that you have been set free from sin and have become slaves of God, the fruit you get leads to sanctification and its end, eternal life.

3. Their ability to do good works is not at all of themselves, but wholly from the Spirit of Christ.[1] And that they may be enabled to do so, besides the graces they have already received, there is required an actual influence of the same Holy Spirit to work in them to will, and to do, of His good pleasure:[2] yet they are not in this to grow negligent, as if they were not bound to perform any duty unless on a special motion of the Spirit; but they ought to be diligent in stirring up the grace of God that is in them.[3]

4. They who, in their obedience, attain to the greatest height that is possible in this life, are so far from being able to do more than God

---

1 **Ezek. 36:26-27**. And I will give you a new heart, and a new spirit I will put within you. And I will remove the heart of stone from your flesh and give you a heart of flesh. And I will put my Spirit within you, and cause you to walk in my statutes and be careful to obey my rules. **Jn. 15:4-6**. Abide in me, and I in you. As the branch cannot bear fruit by itself, unless it abides in the vine, neither can you, unless you abide in me. I am the vine; you are the branches. Whoever abides in me and I in him, he it is that bears much fruit, for apart from me you can do nothing. If anyone does not abide in me he is thrown away like a branch and withers; and the branches are gathered, thrown into the fire, and burned.

2 **2 Cor. 3:5**. Not that we are sufficient in ourselves to claim anything as coming from us, but our sufficiency is from God. **Phil. 2:13**. ...for it is God who works in you, both to will and to work for his good pleasure. **Phil. 4:13**. I can do all things through him who strengthens me.

3 **Isa. 64:7**. There is no one who calls upon your name, who rouses himself to take hold of you; for you have hidden your face from us, and have made us melt in the hand of our iniquities. **Acts 26:6-7**. And now I stand here on trial because of my hope in the promise made by God to our fathers, to which our twelve tribes hope to attain, as they earnestly worship night and day. And for this hope I am accused by Jews, O king! **Phil. 2:12**. Therefore, my beloved, as you have always obeyed, so now, not only as in my presence but much more in my absence, work out your own salvation with fear and trembling. **2 Tim. 1:6**. For this reason I remind you to fan into flame the gift of God, which is in you through the laying on of my hands. **Heb. 6:11-12**. And we desire each one of you to show the same earnestness to have the full assurance of hope until the end, so that you may not be sluggish, but imitators of those who through faith and patience inherit the promises. **2 Pet. 1:3, 5, 10-11**. His divine power has granted to us all things that pertain to life and godliness, through the knowledge of him who called us to his own glory and excellence ... For this very reason, make every effort to supplement your faith with virtue, and virtue with knowledge ... Therefore, brothers, be all the more diligent to make your calling and election sure, for if you practice these qualities you will never fall. For in this way there will be richly provided for you an entrance into the eternal kingdom of our Lord and Savior Jesus Christ. **Jude 20-21**. But you, beloved, building yourselves up in your most holy faith and praying in the Holy Spirit, keep yourselves in the love of God, waiting for the mercy of our Lord Jesus Christ that leads to eternal life.

requires, that they fall short of much which in duty they are bound to do.[1]

5. We cannot by our best works merit pardon of sin, or eternal life in the presence of God, by reason of the great separation that is between them and the glory to come; and the infinite distance that is between us and God, whom, by our works, we can neither profit, nor satisfy for the debt of our former sins,[2] but when we have done all we can, we have done but our duty, and are unworthy servants:[3] and because, as they are good, they proceed from His Spirit;[4] and as they are done by us, they are defiled, and mixed with so much

---

1 **Neh. 13:22**. Then I commanded the Levites that they should purify themselves and come and guard the gates, to keep the Sabbath day holy. Remember this also in my favor, O my God, and spare me according to the greatness of your steadfast love. **Job 9:2-3**. "Truly I know that it is so: But how can a man be in the right before God? If one wished to contend with him, one could not answer him once in a thousand times." **Lk. 17:10**. So you also, when you have done all that you were commanded, say, 'We are unworthy servants; we have only done what was our duty.' **Gal. 5:17**. For the desires of the flesh are against the Spirit, and the desires of the Spirit are against the flesh, for these are opposed to each other, to keep you from doing the things you want to do.

2 **Job 22:2-3**. "Can a man be profitable to God? Surely he who is wise is profitable to himself. Is it any pleasure to the Almighty if you are in the right, or is it gain to him if you make your ways blameless?" **Job 35:7-8**. If you are righteous, what do you give to him? Or what does he receive from your hand? Your wickedness concerns a man like yourself, and your righteousness a son of man. **Ps. 16:2**. I say to the LORD, "You are my Lord; I have no good apart from you." **Rom. 3:20**. For by works of the law no human being will be justified in his sight, since through the law comes knowledge of sin. **Rom. 4:2, 4, 6**. For if Abraham was justified by works, he has something to boast about, but not before God. ... Now to the one who works, his wages are not counted as a gift but as his due. ... just as David also speaks of the blessing of the one to whom God counts righteousness apart from works. **Rom. 8:18**. For I consider that the sufferings of this present time are not worth comparing with the glory that is to be revealed to us. **Eph. 2:8-9**. For by grace you have been saved through faith. And this is not your own doing; it is the gift of God, not a result of works, so that no one may boast. **Titus 3:5-7**. ...he saved us, not because of works done by us in righteousness, but according to his own mercy, by the washing of regeneration and renewal of the Holy Spirit, whom he poured out on us richly through Jesus Christ our Savior, so that being justified by his grace we might become heirs according to the hope of eternal life.

3 **Lk. 17:10.** So you also, when you have done all that you were commanded, say, 'We are unworthy servants; we have only done what was our duty.'

4 **Gal. 5:22-23**. But the fruit of the Spirit is love, joy, peace, patience, kindness, goodness, faithfulness, gentleness, self-control; against such things there is no law.

weakness and imperfection, that they cannot endure the severity of God's judgment.[1]

6. Notwithstanding, the persons of believers being accepted through Christ, their good works also are accepted in Him;[2] not as though they were in this life wholly undeserving of blame and punishment in God's sight;[3] but that He, looking on them in His Son, is pleased to accept and reward that which is sincere, although accompanied with many weaknesses and imperfections.[4]

7. Works done by unregenerate men, although at the center of them they may be things which God commands; and of good use both to

---

1 **Ps. 130:3**. If you, O LORD, should mark iniquities, O Lord, who could stand? **Ps. 143:2**. Enter not into judgment with your servant, for no one living is righteous before you. **Isa. 64:6**. We have all become like one who is unclean, and all our righteous deeds are like a polluted garment. We all fade like a leaf, and our iniquities, like the wind, take us away. **Rom. 7:15, 18**. For I do not understand my own actions. For I do not do what I want, but I do the very thing I hate. ... For I know that nothing good dwells in me, that is, in my flesh. For I have the desire to do what is right, but not the ability to carry it out. **Gal. 5:17**. For the desires of the flesh are against the Spirit, and the desires of the Spirit are against the flesh, for these are opposed to each other, to keep you from doing the things you want to do.

2 **Gen. 4:4**. ...and Abel also brought of the firstborn of his flock and of their fat portions. And the LORD had regard for Abel and his offering. **Ex. 28:38**. It shall be on Aaron's forehead, and Aaron shall bear any guilt from the holy things that the people of Israel consecrate as their holy gifts. It shall regularly be on his forehead, that they may be accepted before the LORD. **Eph. 1:6**. ...to the praise of his glorious grace, with which he has blessed us in the Beloved. **Heb. 11:4**. By faith Abel offered to God a more acceptable sacrifice than Cain, through which he was commended as righteous, God commending him by accepting his gifts. And through his faith, though he died, he still speaks. **1 Pet. 2:5**. ...you yourselves like living stones are being built up as a spiritual house, to be a holy priesthood, to offer spiritual sacrifices acceptable to God through Jesus Christ.

3 **Job 9:20**. Though I am in the right, my own mouth would condemn me; though I am blameless, he would prove me perverse. **Ps. 143:2**. Enter not into judgment with your servant, for no one living is righteous before you.

4 **Mt. 25:21, 23**. His master said to him, 'Well done, good and faithful servant. You have been faithful over a little; I will set you over much. Enter into the joy of your master.'... His master said to him, 'Well done, good and faithful servant. You have been faithful over a little; I will set you over much. Enter into the joy of your master.' **Heb. 6:10**. For God is not unjust so as to overlook your work and the love that you have shown for his name in serving the saints, as you still do. **Heb. 13:20-21**. Now may the God of peace who brought again from the dead our Lord Jesus, the great shepherd of the sheep, by the blood of the eternal covenant, equip you with everything good that you may do his will, working in us that which is pleasing in his sight, through Jesus Christ, to whom be glory forever and ever. Amen. **2 Cor. 8:12**. For if the readiness is there, it is acceptable according to what a person has, not according to what he does not have.

themselves and others:[1] yet, because they proceed not from a heart purified by faith;[2] nor are done in a right manner, according to the Word;[3] nor to a right end, the glory of God,[4] they are therefore sinful, and cannot please God, or make a man fit to receive grace from

1 **1 Kings. 21:27, 29**. And when Ahab heard those words, he tore his clothes and put sackcloth on his flesh and fasted and lay in sackcloth and went about dejectedly. ... "Have you seen how Ahab has humbled himself before me? Because he has humbled himself before me, I will not bring the disaster in his days; but in his son's days I will bring the disaster upon his house." **2 Kings. 10:30-31**. And the LORD said to Jehu, "Because you have done well in carrying out what is right in my eyes, and have done to the house of Ahab according to all that was in my heart, your sons of the fourth generation shall sit on the throne of Israel." But Jehu was not careful to walk in the law of the LORD, the God of Israel, with all his heart. He did not turn from the sins of Jeroboam, which he made Israel to sin. **Phil. 1:15-16, 18**. Some indeed preach Christ from envy and rivalry, but others from good will. The latter do it out of love, knowing that I am put here for the defense of the gospel. ... What then? Only that in every way, whether in pretense or in truth, Christ is proclaimed, and in that I rejoice.

2 **Gen. 4:5**. ...but for Cain and his offering he had no regard. So Cain was very angry, and his face fell. **Heb. 11:4, 6.** By faith Abel offered to God a more acceptable sacrifice than Cain, through which he was commended as righteous, God commending him by accepting his gifts. And through his faith, though he died, he still speaks. ... And without faith it is impossible to please him, for whoever would draw near to God must believe that he exists and that he rewards those who seek him.

3 **Isa. 1:12**. "When you come to appear before me, who has required of you this trampling of my courts?" **1 Cor. 13:3**. If I give away all I have, and if I deliver up my body to be burned, but have not love, I gain nothing.

4 **Mt. 6:2, 5, 16.** "Thus, when you give to the needy, sound no trumpet before you, as the hypocrites do in the synagogues and in the streets, that they may be praised by others. Truly, I say to you, they have received their reward." ... "And when you pray, you must not be like the hypocrites. For they love to stand and pray in the synagogues and at the street corners, that they may be seen by others. Truly, I say to you, they have received their reward." ... "And when you fast, do not look gloomy like the hypocrites, for they disfigure their faces that their fasting may be seen by others. Truly, I say to you, they have received their reward."

God:[1] and yet, their neglect of them is more sinful and displeasing to God.[2]

1 **Hos. 1:4**. And the LORD said to him, "Call his name Jezreel, for in just a little while I will punish the house of Jehu for the blood of Jezreel, and I will put an end to the kingdom of the house of Israel." **Amos 5:21-22**. "I hate, I despise your feasts, and I take no delight in your solemn assemblies. Even though you offer me your burnt offerings and grain offerings, I will not accept them; and the peace offerings of your fattened animals, I will not look upon them." **Hag. 2:14**. Then Haggai answered and said, "So is it with this people, and with this nation before me, declares the LORD, and so with every work of their hands. And what they offer there is unclean." **Rom. 9:16**. So then it depends not on human will or exertion, but on God, who has mercy. **Titus 1:15**.To the pure, all things are pure, but to the defiled and unbelieving, nothing is pure; but both their minds and their consciences are defiled. **Titus 3:5**. ...he saved us, not because of works done by us in righteousness, but according to his own mercy, by the washing of regeneration and renewal of the Holy Spirit.

2 **Job 21:14-15**. They say to God, 'Depart from us! We do not desire the knowledge of your ways. What is the Almighty, that we should serve him? And what profit do we get if we pray to him?' **Ps. 14:4**. Have they no knowledge, all the evildoers who eat up my people as they eat bread and do not call upon the LORD? **Ps. 36:3**. The words of his mouth are trouble and deceit; he has ceased to act wisely and do good. **Mt. 23:23**. "Woe to you, scribes and Pharisees, hypocrites! For you tithe mint and dill and cumin, and have neglected the weightier matters of the law: justice and mercy and faithfulness. These you ought to have done, without neglecting the others." **Mt. 25: 41-43, 45**. "Then he will say to those on his left, 'Depart from me, you cursed, into the eternal fire prepared for the devil and his angels. For I was hungry and you gave me no food, I was thirsty and you gave me no drink, I was a stranger and you did not welcome me, naked and you did not clothe me, sick and in prison and you did not visit me.' ... Then he will answer them, saying, 'Truly, I say to you, as you did not do it to one of the least of these, you did not do it to me.'

CHAPTER 17

OF THE PERSEVERANCE OF THE SAINTS.

1. They, whom God has accepted in His Beloved, effectually called, and sanctified by His Spirit, can neither totally nor finally fall away from the state of grace, but shall certainly persevere in grace to the end, and be eternally saved.[1]
2. This perseverance of the saints depends not on their own free will, but on the unchangeableness of the decree of election, flowing from the free and unchangeable love of God the Father;[2] upon the efficacy

1 **Phil. 1:6**. And I am sure of this, that he who began a good work in you will bring it to completion at the day of Jesus Christ. **1 Pet. 1:5,9**. who by God's power are being guarded through faith for a salvation ready to be revealed in the last time... obtaining the outcome of your faith, the salvation of your souls. **2 Pet. 1:10**. Therefore, brothers, be all the more diligent to make your calling and election sure, for if you practice these qualities you will never fall. **1 Jn. 3:9**. No one born of God makes a practice of sinning, for God's seed abides in him, and he cannot keep on sinning because he has been born of God.

2 **Jer. 31:3**. the LORD appeared to him from far away. I have loved you with an everlasting love; therefore I have continued my faithfulness to you. **2 Tim. 2:18-19**. who have swerved from the truth, saying that the resurrection has already happened. They are upsetting the faith of some. But God's firm foundation stands, bearing this seal: "The Lord knows those who are his," and, "Let everyone who names the name of the Lord depart from iniquity."

of the merit and intercession of Jesus Christ,[1] the remaining of the Spirit, and of the seed of God within them,[2] and the nature of the covenant of grace:[3] from all of which arise also the certainty and infallibility of it.[4]

---

1 **Lk. 22:32**. but I have prayed for you that your faith may not fail. And when you have turned again, strengthen your brothers. **Jn. 17:11, 24**. And I am no longer in the world, but they are in the world, and I am coming to you. Holy Father, keep them in your name, which you have given me, that they may be one, even as we are one... Father, I desire that they also, whom you have given me, may be with me where I am, to see my glory that you have given me because you loved me before the foundation of the world. **Rom. 8:33-39**. Who shall bring any charge against God's elect? It is God who justifies. Who is to condemn? Christ Jesus is the one who died—more than that, who was raised—who is at the right hand of God, who indeed is interceding for us. Who shall separate us from the love of Christ? Shall tribulation, or distress, or persecution, or famine, or nakedness, or danger, or sword? As it is written, "For your sake we are being killed all the day long; we are regarded as sheep to be slaughtered." No, in all these things we are more than conquerors through him who loved us. For I am sure that neither death nor life, nor angels nor rulers, nor things present nor things to come, nor powers, nor height nor depth, nor anything else in all creation, will be able to separate us from the love of God in Christ Jesus our Lord. **Heb. 7:25**. Consequently, he is able to save to the uttermost those who draw near to God through him, since he always lives to make intercession for them. **Heb. 9:12-15**. He entered once for all into the holy places, not by means of the blood of goats and calves but by means of his own blood, thus securing an eternal redemption. For if the blood of goats and bulls, and the sprinkling of defiled persons with the ashes of a heifer, sanctify for the purification of the flesh, how much more will the blood of Christ, who through the eternal Spirit offered himself without blemish to God, purify our conscience from dead works to serve the living God. Therefore he is the mediator of a new covenant, so that those who are called may receive the promised eternal inheritance, since a death has occurred that redeems them from the transgressions committed under the first covenant. **Heb. 10:10, 14**. And by that will we have been sanctified through the offering of the body of Jesus Christ once for all... For by a single offering he has perfected for all time those who are being sanctified. **Heb. 13:20-21**. Now may the God of peace who brought again from the dead our Lord Jesus, the great shepherd of the sheep, by the blood of the eternal covenant, equip you with everything good that you may do his will, working in us that which is pleasing in his sight, through Jesus Christ, to whom be glory forever and ever. Amen.

2 **Jn. 14:16-17**. And I will ask the Father, and he will give you another Helper, to be with you forever, even the Spirit of truth, whom the world cannot receive, because it neither sees him nor knows him. You know him, for he dwells with you and will be in you. **1 Jn. 2:27**. But the anointing that you received from him abides in you, and you have no need that anyone should teach you. But as his anointing teaches you about everything, and is true, and is no lie—just as it has taught you, abide in him. **1 Jn. 3:9**. No one born of God makes a practice of sinning, for God's seed abides in him, and he cannot keep on sinning because he has been born of God.

3 **Jer. 32:40**. I will make with them an everlasting covenant, that I will not turn away from doing good to them. And I will put the fear of me in their hearts, that they may not turn from me.

4 **Jn. 10:28**. I give them eternal life, and they will never perish, and no one will snatch them out of my hand. **2 Thess. 3:3**. But the Lord is faithful. He will establish you and guard you against the evil one. **1 Jn. 2:19**. They went out from us, but they were not of us; for if they had been of us, they would have continued with us. But they went out, that it might become plain that they all are not of us.

3. Nevertheless, they may, through the temptations of Satan and of the world, the prevalence of corruption remaining in them, and the neglect of the means of their preservation, fall into grievous sins;[1] and, for a time, continue in them:[2] whereby they incur God's displeasure,[3] and grieve His Holy Spirit,[4] come to be deprived of some measure of their graces and comforts,[5] have their hearts hardened,[6] and their consciences wounded;[7] hurt and scandalize others,[8] and bring temporal judgments on themselves.[9]

---

1 **Mt. 26:70, 72, 74**. But he denied it before them all, saying, "I do not know what you mean." ... And again he denied it with an oath: "I do not know the man."... Then he began to invoke a curse on himself and to swear, "I do not know the man." And immediately the rooster crowed.

2 **Ps. 51**. All of Psalm 51.

3 **2 Sam. 11:27**. And when the mourning was over, David sent and brought her to his house, and she became his wife and bore him a son. But the thing that David had done displeased the LORD. **Isa. 64:5, 7, 9**. You meet him who joyfully works righteousness, those who remember you in your ways. Behold, you were angry, and we sinned; in our sins we have been a long time, and shall we be saved?... There is no one who calls upon your name, who rouses himself to take hold of you; for you have hidden your face from us, and have made us melt in the hand of our iniquities... Be not so terribly angry, O LORD, and remember not iniquity forever. Behold, please look, we are all your people.

4 **Eph. 4:30**. And do not grieve the Holy Spirit of God, by whom you were sealed for the day of redemption.

5 **Ps. 51:8, 10, 12**. Let me hear joy and gladness; let the bones that you have broken rejoice... Create in me a clean heart, O God, and renew a right spirit within me... Restore to me the joy of your salvation, and uphold me with a willing spirit.
Song 5:2-4, 6. I slept, but my heart was awake. A sound! My beloved is knocking. "Open to me, my sister, my love, my dove, my perfect one, for my head is wet with dew, my locks with the drops of the night." I had put off my garment; how could I put it on? I had bathed my feet; how could I soil them? My beloved put his hand to the latch, and my heart was thrilled within me... I opened to my beloved, but my beloved had turned and gone. My soul failed me when he spoke. I sought him, but found him not; I called him, but he gave no answer. **Rev 2:4**. But I have this against you, that you have abandoned the love you had at first.

6 **Isa. 63:17**. O LORD, why do you make us wander from your ways and harden our heart, so that we fear you not? Return for the sake of your servants, the tribes of your heritage. **Mk. 6:52**. for they did not understand about the loaves, but their hearts were hardened. **Mk. 16:14**. Afterward he appeared to the eleven themselves as they were reclining at table, and he rebuked them for their unbelief and hardness of heart, because they had not believed those who saw him after he had risen.

7 **Ps. 32:3-4**. For when I kept silent, my bones wasted away through my groaning all day long. 4For day and night your hand was heavy upon me; my strength was dried up as by the heat of summer. **Ps. 51:8**. Let me hear joy and gladness; let the bones that you have broken rejoice.

8 **2 Sam. 12:14**. Nevertheless, because by this deed you have utterly scorned the LORD, the child who is born to you shall die.

9 **Ps. 89:31-32**. If they violate my statutes and do not keep my commandments, then I will punish their transgression with the rod and their iniquity with stripes.
1 Cor. 11:32. But when we are judged by the Lord, we are disciplined so that we may not be condemned along with the world.

CHAPTER 18

OF ASSURANCE OF GRACE AND SALVATION.

1. Although hypocrites and other unregenerate men may vainly deceive themselves with false hopes and worldly presumptions of being in the favor of God, and estate of salvation[1] (the hope of which shall perish):[2] yet such as truly believe in the Lord Jesus, and love Him in sincerity, endeavoring to walk in all good conscience before Him, may, in this life, be certainly assured that they are in the state of grace,[3] and may rejoice in the hope of the glory of God, which hope shall never make them ashamed.[4]
2. This certainty is not merely conjecture and probable conclusion grounded on a fallible hope;[5] but an infallible assurance of faith

---

1 **Deut. 29:19**.... one who, when he hears the words of this sworn covenant, blesses himself in his heart, saying, 'I shall be safe, though I walk in the stubbornness of my heart.' This will lead to the sweeping away of moist and dry alike. **Job 8:13-14**. Such are the paths of all who forget God; the hope of the godless shall perish. His confidence is severed, and his trust is a spider's web. **Mic. 3:11**. Its heads give judgment for a bribe; its priests teach for a price; its prophets practice divination for money; yet they lean on the LORD and say, "Is not the LORD in the midst of us? No disaster shall come upon us." **Jn. 8:41**. You are doing the works your father did." They said to him, "We were not born of sexual immorality. We have one Father—even God."

2 **Mt. 7:22-23**. On that day many will say to me, 'Lord, Lord, did we not prophesy in your name, and cast out demons in your name, and do many mighty works in your name?' And then will I declare to them, 'I never knew you; depart from me, you workers of lawlessness.'

3 **1 Jn. 2:3**. And by this we know that we have come to know him, if we keep his commandments. **1 Jn. 3:14,18-19, 21, 24**. We know that we have passed out of death into life, because we love the brothers. Whoever does not love abides in death. Little children, let us not love in word or talk but in deed and in truth. By this we shall know that we are of the truth and reassure our heart before him. Beloved, if our heart does not condemn us, we have confidence before God. Whoever keeps his commandments abides in God, and God in him. And by this we know that he abides in us, by the Spirit whom he has given us. **1 Jn. 5:13**. I write these things to you who believe in the name of the Son of God that you may know that you have eternal life.

4 **Rom. 5:2,5**. Through him we have also obtained access by faith into this grace in which we stand, and we rejoice in hope of the glory of God.

5 **Heb. 6:11,19**. And we desire each one of you to show the same earnestness to have the full assurance of hope until the end. We have this as a sure and steadfast anchor of the soul, a hope that enters into the inner place behind the curtain.

founded on the divine truth of the promises of salvation,[1] the inward evidence of those graces on which these promises are made,[2] the testimony of the Spirit of adoption witnessing with our spirits that we are the children of God,[3] which Spirit is the deposit on our inheritance, by which we are sealed to the day of redemption.[4]

---

1 **HEB. 6:17-18.** So when God desired to show more convincingly to the heirs of the promise the unchangeable character of his purpose, he guaranteed it with an oath, so that by two unchangeable things, in which it is impossible for God to lie, we who have fled for refuge might have strong encouragement to hold fast to the hope set before us.

2 **2 COR. 2:12.** When I came to Troas to preach the gospel of Christ, even though a door was opened for me in the Lord. **2 PET. 1:4-5,10-11**.... by which he has granted to us his precious and very great promises, so that through them you may become partakers of the divine nature, having escaped from the corruption that is in the world because of sinful desire. For this very reason, make every effort to supplement your faith with virtue, and virtue with knowledge. Therefore, brothers, be all the more diligent to make your calling and election sure, for if you practice these qualities you will never fall. For in this way there will be richly provided for you an entrance into the eternal kingdom of our Lord and Savior Jesus Christ. **1 JN. 2:3.** And by this we know that we have come to know him, if we keep his commandments. **1 JN. 3:14.** We know that we have passed out of death into life, because we love the brothers. Whoever does not love abides in death.

3 **ROM. 8:15-16.** For you did not receive the spirit of slavery to fall back into fear, but you have received the Spirit of adoption as sons, by whom we cry, "Abba! Father!" The Spirit himself bears witness with our spirit that we are children of God.

4 **2 COR. 1:21-22.** And it is God who establishes us with you in Christ, and has anointed us, and who has also put his seal on us and given us his Spirit in our hearts as a guarantee. **EPH. 1:13-14.** In him you also, when you heard the word of truth, the gospel of your salvation, and believed in him, were sealed with the promised Holy Spirit, who is the guarantee of our inheritance until we acquire possession of it, to the praise of his glory. **EPH. 4:30.** And do not grieve the Holy Spirit of God, by whom you were sealed for the day of redemption.

3. This infallible assurance does not so belong to the essence of faith, but that a true believer may wait long, and conflict with many difficulties, before he have it:[1] yet, being enabled by the Spirit to know the things that are freely given him of God, he may, without extraordinary revelation in the right use of ordinary means, attain to it.[2] And therefore it is the duty of everyone to give all diligence to make his calling and election sure,[3] that thereby his heart may be enlarged in peace and joy in the Holy Spirit, in love and thankfulness to God, and in strength and cheerfulness in the duties of

---

1 **Ps. 77:1-12.** I cry aloud to God, aloud to God, and he will hear me. In the day of my trouble I seek the Lord; in the night my hand is stretched out without wearying; my soul refuses to be comforted. When I remember God, I moan; when I meditate, my spirit faints. You hold my eyelids open; I am so troubled that I cannot speak. I consider the days of old, the years long ago. I said, "Let me remember my song in the night; let me meditate in my heart." Then my spirit made a diligent search: "Will the Lord spurn forever, and never again be favorable? Has his steadfast love forever ceased? Are his promises at an end for all time? Has God forgotten to be gracious? Has he in anger shut up his compassion?" Then I said, "I will appeal to this, to the years of the right hand of the Most High." I will remember the deeds of the LORD; yes, I will remember your wonders of old. I will ponder all your work, and meditate on your mighty deeds. **Ps. 88.** All of Psalm 88. **Isa. 50:10.** Who among you fears the LORD and obeys the voice of his servant? Let him who walks in darkness and has no light trust in the name of the LORD and rely on his God. **Mk. 9:24.** Immediately the father of the child cried out and said, "I believe; help my unbelief!" **1 Jn. 5:13.** I write these things to you who believe in the name of the Son of God that you may know that you have eternal life.

2 **1 Cor. 2:12.** Now we have received not the spirit of the world, but the Spirit who is from God, that we might understand the things freely given us by God. **Eph. 3:17.**... so that Christ may dwell in your hearts through faith—that you, being rooted and grounded in love ...**Heb. 6:11-12.** And we desire each one of you to show the same earnestness to have the full assurance of hope until the end, so that you may not be sluggish, but imitators of those who through faith and patience inherit the promises. **1 Jn. 4:13.** By this we know that we abide in him and he in us, because he has given us of his Spirit.

3 **2 Pet. 1:10.** Therefore, brothers, be all the more diligent to make your calling and election sure, for if you practice these qualities you will never fall.

obedience,[1] the proper fruits of this assurance; so far is it from inclining men to indifference.[2]

4. True believers may have the assurance of their salvation shaken in many ways, diminished, and interrupted; as, by negligence in preserving of it, by falling into some special sin that wounds the conscience and grieves the Spirit; by some sudden or vehement

---

1 **Ps. 4:6-7**. There are many who say, "Who will show us some good? Lift up the light of your face upon us, O LORD!" You have put more joy in my heart than they have when their grain and wine abound. **Ps. 119:32**. I will run in the way of your commandments when you enlarge my heart! **Rom. 5:1-2,5**. Therefore, since we have been justified by faith, we have peace with God through our Lord Jesus Christ. Through him we have also obtained access by faith into this grace in which we stand, and we rejoice in hope of the glory of God.... and hope does not put us to shame, because God's love has been poured into our hearts through the Holy Spirit who has been given to us. **Rom. 14:17**. For the kingdom of God is not a matter of eating and drinking but of righteousness and peace and joy in the Holy Spirit. **Rom. 15:13**. May the God of hope fill you with all joy and peace in believing, so that by the power of the Holy Spirit you may abound in hope. **Eph. 1:3-4**. Blessed be the God and Father of our Lord Jesus Christ, who has blessed us in Christ with every spiritual blessing in the heavenly places, even as he chose us in him before the foundation of the world, that we should be holy and blameless before him.

2 **Ps. 130:4**. But with you there is forgiveness, that you may be feared. **Rom. 6:1-2**. What shall we say then? Are we to continue in sin that grace may abound? By no means! How can we who died to sin still live in it? **Rom. 8:1,12**. There is therefore now no condemnation for those who are in Christ Jesus. So then, brothers, we are debtors, not to the flesh, to live according to the flesh. **2 Cor. 7:1**. Since we have these promises, beloved, let us cleanse ourselves from every defilement of body and spirit, bringing holiness to completion in the fear of God. **Titus 2:11-12,14**. For the grace of God has appeared, bringing salvation for all people, training us to renounce ungodliness and worldly passions, and to live self-controlled, upright, and godly lives in the present age ...who gave himself for us to redeem us from all lawlessness and to purify for himself a people for his own possession who are zealous for good works. **1 Jn. 1:6-7.** If we say we have fellowship with him while we walk in darkness, we lie and do not practice the truth. But if we walk in the light, as he is in the light, we have fellowship with one another, and the blood of Jesus his Son cleanses us from all sin. **1 Jn. 2:1-2**. My little children, I am writing these things to you so that you may not sin. But if anyone does sin, we have an advocate with the Father, Jesus Christ the righteous. He is the propitiation for our sins, and not for ours only but also for the sins of the whole world. **1 Jn. 3:2-3**. Beloved, we are God's children now, and what we will be has not yet appeared; but we know that when he appears we shall be like him, because we shall see him as he is. And everyone who thus hopes in him purifies himself as he is pure.

temptation, by God's withdrawing the light of His approval, and permitting even those who fear Him to walk in darkness and to have no light:[1] yet are they never utterly destitute of that seed of God, and life of faith, that love of Christ and the brothers, that sincerity of heart, and conscience of duty, out of which, by the operation of the Spirit, this assurance may, in due time, be revived;[2] and

---

1 **Ps. 31:22.** I had said in my alarm, "I am cut off from your sight." But you heard the voice of my pleas for mercy when I cried to you for help. **Ps. 51:8,12,14**. Let me hear joy and gladness; let the bones that you have broken rejoice. Restore to me the joy of your salvation, and uphold me with a willing spirit. **Ps. 77:1-10**. I cry aloud to God, aloud to God, and he will hear me. In the day of my trouble I seek the Lord; in the night my hand is stretched out without wearying; my soul refuses to be comforted. When I remember God, I moan; when I meditate, my spirit faints. You hold my eyelids open; I am so troubled that I cannot speak. I consider the days of old, the years long ago. I said, "Let me remember my song in the night; let me meditate in my heart." Then my spirit made a diligent search: "Will the Lord spurn forever, and never again be favorable? Has his steadfast love forever ceased? Are his promises at an end for all time? Has God forgotten to be gracious? Has he in anger shut up his compassion?" Then I said, "I will appeal to this, to the years of the right hand of the Most High." **Ps. 88**. All of Psalm 88. **Isa. 50:10**. Who among you fears the LORD and obeys the voice of his servant? Let him who walks in darkness and has no light trust in the name of the LORD and rely on his God. **Mt. 26:69-72**. Now Peter was sitting outside in the courtyard. And a servant girl came up to him and said, "You also were with Jesus the Galilean." But he denied it before them all, saying, "I do not know what you mean." And when he went out to the entrance, another servant girl saw him, and she said to the bystanders, "This man was with Jesus of Nazareth." And again he denied it with an oath: "I do not know the man." **Eph. 4:30-31**. And do not grieve the Holy Spirit of God, by whom you were sealed for the day of redemption. Let all bitterness and wrath and anger and clamor and slander be put away from you, along with all malice.

2 **Job 13:14**. Why should I take my flesh in my teeth and put my life in my hand? **Ps. 51:8,12**. Let me hear joy and gladness; let the bones that you have broken rejoice. Restore to me the joy of your salvation, and uphold me with a willing spirit. **Ps. 73:15**. If I had said, "I will speak thus," I would have betrayed the generation of your children. **Isa. 50:10.** Who among you fears the LORD and obeys the voice of his servant? Let him who walks in darkness and has no light trust in the name of the LORD and rely on his God. **Lk. 22:32**.... but I have prayed for you that your faith may not fail. And when you have turned again, strengthen your brothers." **1 Jn. 3:9.** No one born of God makes a practice of sinning, for God's seed abides in him, and he cannot keep on sinning because he has been born of God.

be that which, in the meantime, they are supported from utter despair.[1]

1 **Ps. 22:1**. My God, my God, why have you forsaken me? Why are you so far from saving me, from the words of my groaning? All of **Ps. 88**. **Isa. 54:7-10**. For a brief moment I deserted you, but with great compassion I will gather you. In overflowing anger for a moment I hid my face from you, but with everlasting love I will have compassion on you," says the LORD, your Redeemer. "This is like the days of Noah to me: as I swore that the waters of Noah should no more go over the earth, so I have sworn that I will not be angry with you, and will not rebuke you. For the mountains may depart and the hills be removed, but my steadfast love shall not depart from you, and my covenant of peace shall not be removed," says the LORD, who has compassion on you. **Jer. 32:40**. I will make with them an everlasting covenant, that I will not turn away from doing good to them. And I will put the fear of me in their hearts, that they may not turn from me. **Mic. 7:7-9**. But as for me, I will look to the LORD; I will wait for the God of my salvation; my God will hear me. Rejoice not over me, O my enemy; when I fall, I shall rise; when I sit in darkness, the LORD will be a light to me. I will bear the indignation of the LORD because I have sinned against him, until he pleads my cause and executes judgment for me. He will bring me out to the light; I shall look upon his vindication.

CHAPTER 19

OF THE LAW OF GOD.

1. God gave to Adam a law, as a covenant of works, by which He bound him and all his posterity, to personal, entire, exact, and perpetual obedience, promised life upon the fulfilling, and threatened death upon the breach of it, and provided him with power and ability to keep it.[1]

2. This law, after his fall, continued to be a perfect rule of righteousness; and, as such, was delivered by God on Mount Sinai, in ten

1 **Gen. 1:26-27**. Then God said, "Let us make man in our image, after our likeness. And let them have dominion over the fish of the sea and over the birds of the heavens and over the livestock and over all the earth and over every creeping thing that creeps on the earth." So God created man in his own image, in the image of God he created him; male and female he created them. **Gen. 2:17**. ...but of the tree of the knowledge of good and evil you shall not eat, for in the day that you eat of it you shall surely die. **Job 28:28**. And he said to man, 'Behold, the fear of the Lord, that is wisdom, and to turn away from evil is understanding.' **Eccl. 7:29**. See, this alone I found, that God made man upright, but they have sought out many schemes. **Rom. 2:14-15**. For when Gentiles, who do not have the law, by nature do what the law requires, they are a law to themselves, even though they do not have the law. They show that the work of the law is written on their hearts, while their conscience also bears witness, and their conflicting thoughts accuse or even excuse them. **Rom. 5:12, 19**. Therefore, just as sin came into the world through one man, and death through sin, and so death spread to all men because all sinned... For as by the one man's disobedience the many were made sinners, so by the one man's obedience the many will be made righteous. **Rom. 10:5**. For Moses writes about the righteousness that is based on the law, that the person who does the commandments shall live by them. **Gal. 3:10, 12**. For all who rely on works of the law are under a curse; for it is written, "Cursed be everyone who does not abide by all things written in the Book of the Law, and do them." ... But the law is not of faith, rather "The one who does them shall live by them."

commandments, and written in two tables:[1] the first four commandments containing our duty toward God; and the other six, our duty toward man.[2]

3. Besides this law, commonly called moral, God was pleased to give to the people of Israel, as a church not yet mature, ceremonial laws, containing several typical ordinances, partly of worship, prefiguring Christ, His graces, actions, sufferings, and benefits;[3] and partly,

1 **Ex. 34:1**. The LORD said to Moses, "Cut for yourself two tablets of stone like the first, and I will write on the tablets the words that were on the first tablets, which you broke." **Deut. 5:32**. You shall be careful therefore to do as the LORD your God has commanded you. You shall not turn aside to the right hand or to the left. **Deut. 10:4**. And he wrote on the tablets, in the same writing as before, the Ten Commandments that the LORD had spoken to you on the mountain out of the midst of the fire on the day of the assembly. And the LORD gave them to me. **Rom. 13:8-9**. Owe no one anything, except to love each other, for the one who loves another has fulfilled the law. For the commandments, "You shall not commit adultery, You shall not murder, You shall not steal, You shall not covet," and any other commandment, are summed up in this word: "You shall love your neighbor as yourself." **Jas. 1:25**. But the one who looks into the perfect law, the law of liberty, and perseveres, being no hearer who forgets but a doer who acts, he will be blessed in his doing. **Jas. 2:8, 10-12**. If you really fulfill the royal law according to the Scripture, "You shall love your neighbor as yourself," you are doing well. ... For whoever keeps the whole law but fails in one point has become accountable for all of it. For he who said, "Do not commit adultery," also said, "Do not murder." If you do not commit adultery but do murder, you have become a transgressor of the law. So speak and so act as those who are to be judged under the law of liberty.

2 **Mt. 22:37-40**. And he said to him, "You shall love the Lord your God with all your heart and with all your soul and with all your mind. This is the great and first commandment. And a second is like it: You shall love your neighbor as yourself. On these two commandments depend all the Law and the Prophets."

3 **Gal. 4:1-3**. I mean that the heir, as long as he is a child, is no different from a slave, though he is the owner of everything, but he is under guardians and managers until the date set by his father. In the same way we also, when we were children, were enslaved to the elementary principles of the world. **Col. 2:17**. These are a shadow of the things to come, but the substance belongs to Christ. **Heb. 9. Heb. 10:1**. For since the law has but a shadow of the good things to come instead of the true form of these realities, it can never, by the same sacrifices that are continually offered every year, make perfect those who draw near.

holding forth various instructions of moral duties.[1] All of these ceremonial laws are now abrogated, under the New Testament.[2]

4. To them also, as a nation, He gave many judicial laws, which expired together with the state of that people; not obliging any other now, further than the general equity of them may require.[3]

5. The moral law does forever bind all, justified persons as well as others, to the obedience of it;[4] and that, not only in regard to the

---

1 **1 Cor. 5:7**. Cleanse out the old leaven that you may be a new lump, as you really are unleavened. For Christ, our Passover lamb, has been sacrificed. **2 Cor. 6:17**. Therefore go out from their midst, and be separate from them, says the Lord, and touch no unclean thing; then I will welcome you. **Jude 23**. ...save others by snatching them out of the fire; to others show mercy with fear, hating even the garment stained by the flesh.

2 **Dan. 9:27**. "And he shall make a strong covenant with many for one week, and for half of the week he shall put an end to sacrifice and offering. And on the wing of abominations shall come one who makes desolate, until the decreed end is poured out on the desolator." **Eph. 2:15-16**. ...by abolishing the law of commandments expressed in ordinances, that he might create in himself one new man in place of the two, so making peace, and might reconcile us both to God in one body through the cross, thereby killing the hostility. **Col. 2:14, 16-17**. ...by canceling the record of debt that stood against us with its legal demands. This he set aside, nailing it to the cross. ... Therefore let no one pass judgment on you in questions of food and drink, or with regard to a festival or a new moon or a Sabbath. These are a shadow of the things to come, but the substance belongs to Christ.

3 **Gen. 49:10**. The scepter shall not depart from Judah, nor the ruler's staff from between his feet, until tribute comes to him; and to him shall be the obedience of the peoples. **Ex. 21. Ex. 22:1-29. Mt. 5:17, 38-39**. "Do not think that I have come to abolish the Law or the Prophets; I have not come to abolish them but to fulfill them." "You have heard that it was said, 'An eye for an eye and a tooth for a tooth.' But I say to you, Do not resist the one who is evil. But if anyone slaps you on the right cheek, turn to him the other also." **1 Cor. 9:8-10**. Do I say these things on human authority? Does not the Law say the same? For it is written in the Law of Moses, "You shall not muzzle an ox when it treads out the grain." Is it for oxen that God is concerned? Does he not speak entirely for our sake? It was written for our sake, because the plowman should plow in hope and the thresher thresh in hope of sharing in the crop. **1 Pet. 2:13-14**. Be subject for the Lord's sake to every human institution, whether it be to the emperor as supreme, or to governors as sent by him to punish those who do evil and to praise those who do good.

4 **Rom. 13:8-9**. Owe no one anything, except to love each other, for the one who loves another has fulfilled the law. For the commandments, "You shall not commit adultery, You shall not murder, You shall not steal, You shall not covet," and any other commandment, are summed up in this word: "You shall love your neighbor as yourself." **Eph. 6:2**. "Honor your father and mother" (this is the first commandment with a promise). **1 Jn. 2:3-4, 7-8**. And by this we know that we have come to know him, if we keep his commandments. Whoever says "I know him" but does not keep his commandments is a liar, and the truth is not in him ... Beloved, I am writing you no new commandment, but an old commandment that you had from the beginning. The old commandment is the word that you have heard. At the same time, it is a new commandment that I am writing to you, which is true in him and in you, because the darkness is passing away and the true light is already shining.

matter contained in it, but also in respect of the authority of God the Creator, who gave it.[1] Neither does Christ, in the Gospel, any way dissolve, but much strengthen this obligation.[2]

6. Although true believers are not under the law, as a covenant of works, to be justified, or condemned by it;[3] yet is it of great use to them, as well as to others; in that, as a rule of life informing them of the will of God, and their duty, it directs and binds them to walk accordingly;[4] discovering also the sinful pollutions of their nature,

---

1 **Jas. 2:10-11.** For whoever keeps the whole law but fails in one point has become accountable for all of it. For he who said, "Do not commit adultery," also said, "Do not murder." If you do not commit adultery but do murder, you have become a transgressor of the law.

2 **Mt. 5:17-19.** "Do not think that I have come to abolish the Law or the Prophets; I have not come to abolish them but to fulfill them. For truly, I say to you, until heaven and earth pass away, not an iota, not a dot, will pass from the Law until all is accomplished. Therefore whoever relaxes one of the least of these commandments and teaches others to do the same will be called least in the kingdom of heaven, but whoever does them and teaches them will be called great in the kingdom of heaven." **Rom. 3:31.** Do we then overthrow the law by this faith? By no means! On the contrary, we uphold the law. **Jas. 2:8.** If you really fulfill the royal law according to the Scripture, "You shall love your neighbor as yourself," you are doing well.

3 **Acts 13:39.** ...and by him everyone who believes is freed from everything from which you could not be freed by the law of Moses. **Rom. 6:14.** For sin will have no dominion over you, since you are not under law but under grace. **Rom. 8:1.** There is therefore now no condemnation for those who are in Christ Jesus. **Gal. 2:16.** ...yet we know that a person is not justified by works of the law but through faith in Jesus Christ, so we also have believed in Christ Jesus, in order to be justified by faith in Christ and not by works of the law, because by works of the law no one will be justified. **Gal. 3:13.** Christ redeemed us from the curse of the law by becoming a curse for us—for it is written, "Cursed is everyone who is hanged on a tree." **Gal. 4:4-5.** But when the fullness of time had come, God sent forth his Son, born of woman, born under the law, to redeem those who were under the law, so that we might receive adoption as sons.

4 **Ps. 119:4-6.** You have commanded your precepts to be kept diligently. Oh that my ways may be steadfast in keeping your statutes! Then I shall not be put to shame, having my eyes fixed on all your commandments. **Rom. 7:12, 22, 25.** So the law is holy, and the commandment is holy and righteous and good. ... For I delight in the law of God, in my inner being... Thanks be to God through Jesus Christ our Lord! So then, I myself serve the law of God with my mind, but with my flesh I serve the law of sin. **1 Cor. 7:19.** For neither circumcision counts for anything nor uncircumcision, but keeping the commandments of God. **Gal. 5:14, 16, 18-23.** For the whole law is fulfilled in one word: "You shall love your neighbor as yourself." ... But I say, walk by the Spirit, and you will not gratify the desires of the flesh. ... But if you are led by the Spirit, you are not under the law. Now the works of the flesh are evident: sexual immorality, impurity, sensuality, idolatry, sorcery, enmity, strife, jealousy, fits of anger, rivalries, dissensions, divisions, envy, drunkenness, orgies, and things like these. I warn you, as I warned you before, that those who do such things will not inherit the kingdom of God. But the fruit of the Spirit is love, joy, peace, patience, kindness, goodness, faithfulness, gentleness, self-control; against such things there is no law.

hearts, and lives;[1] so as, examining themselves thereby, they may come to further conviction of, humiliation for, and hatred against sin,[2] together with a clearer sight of the need they have of Christ, and the perfection of His obedience.[3] It is likewise of use to the regenerate, to restrain their corruptions, in that it forbids sin:[4] and the warnings of it serve to show what even their sins deserve; and what afflictions, in this life, they may expect for them, although freed from the curse threatened in the law.[5] The promises of it, in like manner, show them God's approval of obedience, and what

---

1 **Rom. 3:20**. For by works of the law no human being will be justified in his sight, since through the law comes knowledge of sin. **Rom. 7:7**. What then shall we say? That the law is sin? By no means! Yet if it had not been for the law, I would not have known sin. For I would not have known what it is to covet if the law had not said, "You shall not covet."

2 **Rom. 7:9, 14, 24**. I was once alive apart from the law, but when the commandment came, sin came alive and I died. ... For we know that the law is spiritual, but I am of the flesh, sold under sin. ... Wretched man that I am! Who will deliver me from this body of death? **Jas. 1:23-25**. For if anyone is a hearer of the word and not a doer, he is like a man who looks intently at his natural face in a mirror. For he looks at himself and goes away and at once forgets what he was like. But the one who looks into the perfect law, the law of liberty, and perseveres, being no hearer who forgets but a doer who acts, he will be blessed in his doing.

3 **Rom. 7:24**. Wretched man that I am! Who will deliver me from this body of death? **Rom. 8:3-4**. For God has done what the law, weakened by the flesh, could not do. By sending his own Son in the likeness of sinful flesh and for sin, he condemned sin in the flesh, in order that the righteous requirement of the law might be fulfilled in us, who walk not according to the flesh but according to the Spirit. **Gal. 3:24**. So then, the law was our guardian until Christ came, in order that we might be justified by faith.

4 **Ps. 119:101, 104, 128**. I hold back my feet from every evil way, in order to keep your word. ... Through your precepts I get understanding; therefore I hate every false way. ... Therefore I consider all your precepts to be right; I hate every false way. **Jas. 2:11**. For he who said, "Do not commit adultery," also said, "Do not murder." If you do not commit adultery but do murder, you have become a transgressor of the law.

5 **Ezra 9:13-14**. And after all that has come upon us for our evil deeds and for our great guilt, seeing that you, our God, have punished us less than our iniquities deserved and have given us such a remnant as this, shall we break your commandments again and intermarry with the peoples who practice these abominations? Would you not be angry with us until you consumed us, so that there should be no remnant, nor any to escape?

blessings they may expect for the performance of it:[1] although not as due to them by the law as a covenant of works.[2] So as, a man's doing good, and refraining from evil, because the law encourages to

CALVIN CALLED THE LAW THE WHIP THAT DRIVES US TO CHRIST — FORUS TO PURSUE OUR SALVATION / SANCTIFICATION FOR OUR ENABLEMENT.

LAW OF GOD SERVES AS A RESTRAINT MAKES LIFE MORE FULL + POSSIBLE RESTRAINING WHAT OUR FLESH WOULD WANT TO DO. IT IS FOR OUR BENEFIT THAT MIGHT – IF IT WASN'T THERE – WOULD LEAD TO SELF DESTRUCTION.

---

1 **Lev. 26:1-14**. "You shall not make idols for yourselves or erect an image or pillar, and you shall not set up a figured stone in your land to bow down to it, for I am the LORD your God. You shall keep my Sabbaths and reverence my sanctuary: I am the LORD. "If you walk in my statutes and observe my commandments and do them, then I will give you your rains in their season, and the land shall yield its increase, and the trees of the field shall yield their fruit. Your threshing shall last to the time of the grape harvest, and the grape harvest shall last to the time for sowing. And you shall eat your bread to the full and dwell in your land securely. I will give peace in the land, and you shall lie down, and none shall make you afraid. And I will remove harmful beasts from the land, and the sword shall not go through your land. You shall chase your enemies, and they shall fall before you by the sword. Five of you shall chase a hundred, and a hundred of you shall chase ten thousand, and your enemies shall fall before you by the sword. I will turn to you and make you fruitful and multiply you and will confirm my covenant with you. You shall eat old store long kept, and you shall clear out the old to make way for the new. I will make my dwelling among you, and my soul shall not abhor you. And I will walk among you and will be your God, and you shall be my people. I am the LORD your God, who brought you out of the land of Egypt, that you should not be their slaves. And I have broken the bars of your yoke and made you walk erect. "But if you will not listen to me and will not do all these commandments." **Ps. 19:11**. Moreover, by them is your servant warned; in keeping them there is great reward. **Ps. 37:11.** But the meek shall inherit the land and delight themselves in abundant peace. **Mt. 5:5**. "Blessed are the meek, for they shall inherit the earth." **2 Cor. 6:16**. What agreement has the temple of God with idols? For we are the temple of the living God; as God said, "I will make my dwelling among them and walk among them, and I will be their God, and they shall be my people." **Eph. 6:2-3**. "Honor your father and mother" (this is the first commandment with a promise), "that it may go well with you and that you may live long in the land."

2 **Lk. 17:10**. So you also, when you have done all that you were commanded, say, 'We are unworthy servants; we have only done what was our duty.' **Gal. 2:16**. ...yet we know that a person is not justified by works of the law but through faith in Jesus Christ, so we also have believed in Christ Jesus, in order to be justified by faith in Christ and not by works of the law, because by works of the law no one will be justified.

the one, and deters from the other, is no evidence of his being under the law; and not under grace.[1]

7. Neither are these uses of the law contrary to the grace of the Gospel, but do sweetly comply with it;[2] the Spirit of Christ subduing and enabling the will of man to do that freely, and cheerfully, which the will of God, revealed in the law, requires to be done.[3]

---

1 **Ps. 34:12-16**. What man is there who desires life and loves many days, that he may see good? Keep your tongue from evil and your lips from speaking deceit. Turn away from evil and do good; seek peace and pursue it. The eyes of the LORD are toward the righteous and his ears toward their cry. The face of the LORD is against those who do evil, to cut off the memory of them from the earth. **Rom. 6:12, 14**. Let not sin therefore reign in your mortal body, to make you obey its passions. ... For sin will have no dominion over you, since you are not under law but under grace. **Heb. 12:28-29**. Therefore let us be grateful for receiving a kingdom that cannot be shaken, and thus let us offer to God acceptable worship, with reverence and awe, for our God is all consuming fire. **1 Pet. 3:8-12**. Finally, all of you, have unity of mind, sympathy, brotherly love, a tender heart, and a humble mind. Do not repay evil for evil or reviling for reviling, but on the contrary, bless, for to this you were called, that you may obtain a blessing. For "Whoever desires to love life and see good days, let him keep his tongue from evil and his lips from speaking deceit; let him turn away from evil and do good; let him seek peace and pursue it. For the eyes of the Lord are on the righteous, and his ears are open to their prayer. But the face of the Lord is against those who do evil."

2 **Gal. 3:21**. Is the law then contrary to the promises of God? Certainly not! For if a law had been given that could give life, then righteousness would indeed be by the law.

3 **Jer. 31:33**. But this is the covenant that I will make with the house of Israel after those days, declares the LORD: I will put my law within them, and I will write it on their hearts. And I will be their God, and they shall be my people. **Ezek. 36:27**. And I will put my Spirit within you, and cause you to walk in my statutes and be careful to obey my rules. **Heb. 8:10**. For this is the covenant that I will make with the house of Israel after those days, declares the Lord: I will put my laws into their minds, and write them on their hearts, and I will be their God, and they shall be my people.

CHAP 20 — CHRISTIAN LIBERTY

EXPANDING ON CHAP 19 — USE OF THE LAW — NOW 3RD USE OF LAW IS AS A GUIDE — SO THAT LIFE WILL GO WELL WITH US. UNPACKS THIS FOR HOW THEN DO WE LIVE UNDER THE GOOD LAW UNDER THE LIBERTY OF THE LAW

PARAGRAPH 1 IS A GOOD ONE TO BE READ OVER + OVER TO REMIND US WHAT WE HAVE BEEN FREED FROM!

BOTH POSITIVE + NEGATIVE. AND NT BELIEVERS — FREED FROM CEREMONIAL LAW — ACCESS TO GOD'S THRONE — GIFT OF THE HOLY SPIRIT!

CHAPTER 20

OF CHRISTIAN LIBERTY, AND LIBERTY OF CONSCIENCE.

1. The liberty that Christ has purchased for believers under the Gospel consists in their freedom from the guilt of sin, the condemning wrath of God, the curse of the moral law;[1] and, in their being delivered from this present evil world, bondage to Satan, and dominion of sin;[2] from the evil of afflictions, the sting of death, the victory of the grave, and everlasting damnation;[3] as also, in their free access to God,[4] and their yielding obedience to Him, not out of slavish fear,

NEGATIVE

POSITIVES

---

1 **Gal. 3:13**. Christ redeemed us from the curse of the law by becoming a curse for us—for it is written, "Cursed is everyone who is hanged on a tree." **1 Thess. 1:10**. ...and to wait for his Son from heaven, whom he raised from the dead, Jesus who delivers us from the wrath to come. **Titus 2:14**. who gave himself for us to redeem us from all lawlessness and to purify for himself a people for his own possession who are zealous for good works.

2 **Acts 26:18**. to open their eyes, so that they may turn from darkness to light and from the power of Satan to God, that they may receive forgiveness of sins and a place among those who are sanctified by faith in me.' **Rom. 6:14**. For sin will have no dominion over you, since you are not under law but under grace. **Gal 1:4**. who gave himself for our sins to deliver us from the present evil age, according to the will of our God and Father. **Col. 1:13**. He has delivered us from the domain of darkness and transferred us to the kingdom of his beloved Son,

3 **Ps. 119:7**. It is good for me that I was afflicted, that I might learn your statutes. **Rom 8:1**. There is therefore now no condemnation for those who are in Christ Jesus. **Rom 8:28** And we know that for those who love God all things work together for good, for those who are called according to his purpose. **1 Cor. 15:54-57**. When the perishable puts on the imperishable, and the mortal puts on immortality, then shall come to pass the saying that is written: "Death is swallowed up in victory." "O death, where is your victory? O death, where is your sting?" The sting of death is sin, and the power of sin is the law. But thanks be to God, who gives us the victory through our Lord Jesus Christ.

4 **Rom. 5:1-2**. Therefore, since we have been justified by faith, we have peace with God through our Lord Jesus Christ. Through him we have also obtained access by faith into this grace in which we stand, and we rejoice in hope of the glory of God.

but a child-like love and willing mind.[1] All these were common also to believers under the law.[2] But, under the New Testament, the liberty of Christians is further enlarged, in their freedom from the yoke of the ceremonial law, to which the Jewish church was subjected;[3] and in greater boldness of access to the throne of grace,[4] and in fuller communications of the free Spirit of God, than believers under the law did ordinarily have.[5]

---

1 **Rom. 8:14-15**. For all who are led by the Spirit of God are sons of God. For you did not receive the spirit of slavery to fall back into fear, but you have received the Spirit of adoption as sons, by whom we cry, "Abba! Father!" **1 Jn. 4:18**. There is no fear in love, but perfect love casts out fear. For fear has to do with punishment, and whoever fears has not been perfected in love.

2 **1 Cor. 5:7**. Cleanse out the old leaven that you may be a new lump, as you really are unleavened. For Christ, our Passover lamb, has been sacrificed. **Gal. 3:9, 11, 14**. So then, those who are of faith are blessed along with Abraham, the man of faith; Now it is evident that no one is justified before God by the law, for "The righteous shall live by faith." so that in Christ Jesus the blessing of Abraham might come to the Gentiles, so that we might receive the promised Spirit through faith.

3 **Acts 15:10-11**. Now, therefore, why are you putting God to the test by placing a yoke on the neck of the disciples that neither our fathers nor we have been able to bear? But we believe that we will be saved through the grace of the Lord Jesus, just as they will." **Gal. 4:1-3, 6-7**. I mean that the heir, as long as he is a child, is no different from a slave, though he is the owner of everything, but he is under guardians and managers until the date set by his father. In the same way we also, when we were children, were enslaved to the elementary principles of the world; And because you are sons, God has sent the Spirit of his Son into our hearts, crying, "Abba! Father!" So you are no longer a slave, but a son, and if a son, then an heir through God. **Gal. 5:1**. For freedom Christ has set us free; stand firm therefore, and do not submit again to a yoke of slavery.

4 **Heb. 4:14, 16**. Since then we have a great high priest who has passed through the heavens, Jesus, the Son of God, let us hold fast our confession; Let us then with confidence draw near to the throne of grace, that we may receive mercy and find grace to help in time of need. **Heb. 10:19-22**. Therefore, brothers, since we have confidence to enter the holy places by the blood of Jesus, by the new and living way that he opened for us through the curtain, that is, through his flesh, and since we have a great priest over the house of God, let us draw near with a true heart in full assurance of faith, with our hearts sprinkled clean from an evil conscience and our bodies washed with pure water.

5 **Jn. 7:38-39**. Whoever believes in me, as the Scripture has said, 'Out of his heart will flow rivers of living water.'" Now this he said about the Spirit, whom those who believed in him were to receive, for as yet the Spirit had not been given, because Jesus was not yet glorified. **2 Cor. 3:13, 17-18**. ...not like Moses, who would put a veil over his face so that the Israelites might not gaze at the outcome of what was being brought to an end; Now the Lord is the Spirit, and where the Spirit of the Lord is, there is freedom. And we all, with unveiled face, beholding the glory of the Lord, are being transformed into the same image from one degree of glory to another. For this comes from the Lord who is the Spirit.

2. God alone is Lord of the conscience,[1] and has left it free from the doctrines and commandments of men, which are, in anything, contrary to His Word; or besides it, if matters of faith, or worship.[2] So that, to believe such doctrines, or to obey such commands, out of conscience, is to betray true liberty of conscience:[3] and the requiring of an implicit faith, and an absolute and blind obedience, is to destroy liberty of conscience, and reason also.[4]

---

1 **Rom 14:4**. Who are you to pass judgment on the servant of another? It is before his own master that he stands or falls. And he will be upheld, for the Lord is able to make him stand. **Jas. 4:12**. There is only one lawgiver and judge, he who is able to save and to destroy. But who are you to judge your neighbor?

2 **Mt. 15:9**. In vain do they worship me, teaching as doctrines the commandments of men. **Mt. 23:8-10.** But you are not to be called rabbi, for you have one teacher, and you are all brothers. And call no man your father on earth, for you have one Father, who is in heaven. Neither be called instructors, for you have one instructor, the Christ. **Acts 4:19**. But Peter and John answered them, "Whether it is right in the sight of God to listen to you rather than to God, you must judge. **Acts 5:29**. But Peter and the apostles answered, "We must obey God rather than men. **1 Cor. 7:23**. You were bought with a price; do not become slaves of men. **2 Cor. 1:24**. Not that we lord it over your faith, but we work with you for your joy, for you stand firm in your faith.

3 **Gal. 1:10**. For am I now seeking the approval of man, or of God? Or am I trying to please man? If I were still trying to please man, I would not be a servant of Christ. **Gal. 2:4-5**. Yet because of false brothers secretly brought in—who slipped in to spy out our freedom that we have in Christ Jesus, so that they might bring us into slavery—to them we did not yield in submission even for a moment, so that the Ruth of the gospel might be preserved for you. **Gal. 5:1**. For freedom Christ has set us free; stand firm therefore, and do not submit again to a yoke of slavery. **Col. 2:20, 22-23**. If with Christ you died to the elemental spirits of the world, why, as if you were still alive in the world, do you submit to regulations; (referring to things that all perish as they are used)—according to human precepts and teachings? These have indeed an appearance of wisdom in promoting self-made religion and asceticism and severity to the body, but they are of no value in stopping the indulgence of the flesh.

4 **Isa. 8:20**. To the teaching and to the testimony! If they will not speak according to this word, it is because they have no dawn. **Jer. 8:9**. The wise men shall be put to shame; they shall be dismayed and taken; behold, they have rejected the word of the LORD, so what wisdom is in them? **Hos. 5:11**. Ephraim is oppressed, crushed in judgment, because he was determined to go after filth. **Jn. 4:22**. You worship what you do not know; we worship what we know, for salvation is from the Jews. **Acts 17:11**. Now these Jews were more noble than those in Thessalonica; they received the word with all eagerness, examining the Scriptures daily to see if these things were so. **Rom. 10:17**. So faith comes from hearing, and hearing through the word of Christ. **Rom. 14:23**. But whoever has doubts is condemned if he eats, because the eating is not from faith. For whatever does not proceed from faith is sin. **Rev. 13:12, 16-17**. It exercises all the authority of the first beast in its presence, and makes the earth and its inhabitants worship the first beast, whose mortal wound was healed; Also it causes all, both small and great, both rich and poor, both free and slave, to be marked on the right hand or the forehead, so that no one can buy or sell unless he has the mark, that is, the name of the beast or the number of its name.

3. They who, upon pretense of Christian liberty, do practice any sin, or cherish any lust, do thereby destroy the end of Christian liberty, which is, that being delivered out of the hands of our enemies, we might serve the Lord without fear, in holiness and righteousness before Him, all the days of our lives.[1]

4. And because the powers which God has ordained, and the liberty that Christ has purchased, are not intended by God to destroy, but mutually to uphold and preserve one another, they who, upon pretense of Christian liberty, shall oppose any lawful power, or the lawful exercise of it, whether it be civil or ecclesiastical, resist the ordinance of God.[2]And, for their publishing of such opinions, or maintaining of such practices, as are contrary to the light of nature,

1 **Lk. 1:74-75**. that we, being delivered from the hand of our enemies, might serve him without fear, in holiness and righteousness before him all our days. **Jn. 8:34**. Jesus answered them, "Truly, truly, I say to you, everyone who commits sin is a slave to sin. **Gal. 5:13**. For you were called to freedom, brothers. Only do not use your freedom as an opportunity for the flesh, but through love serve one another. **1 Pet. 2:16.** Live as people who are free, not using your freedom as a cover-up for evil, but living as servants of God. **2 Pet. 2:19**. They promise them freedom, but they themselves are slaves of corruption. For whatever overcomes a person, to that he is enslaved.

2 **Mt. 12:25**. Knowing their thoughts, he said to them, "Every kingdom divided against itself is laid waste, and no city or house divided against itself will stand. **Rom. 13:1-8**. Let every person be subject to the governing authorities. For there is no authority except from God, and those that exist have been instituted by God. Therefore whoever resists the authorities resists what God has appointed, and those who resist will incur judgment. For rulers are not a terror to good conduct, but to bad. Would you have no fear of the one who is in authority? Then do what is good, and you will receive his approval, for he is God's servant for your good. But if you do wrong, be afraid, for he does not bear the sword in vain. For he is the servant of God, an avenger who carries out God's wrath on the wrongdoer. Therefore one must be in subjection, not only to avoid God's wrath but also for the sake of conscience. For because of this you also pay taxes, for the authorities are ministers of God, attending to this very thing. Pay to all what is owed to them: taxes to whom taxes are owed, revenue to whom revenue is owed, respect to whom respect is owed, honor to whom honor is owed. Owe no one anything, except to love each other, for the one who loves another has fulfilled the law. **Heb. 13:17**. Obey your leaders and submit to them, for they are keeping watch over your souls, as those who will have to give an account. Let them do this with joy and not with groaning, for that would be of no advantage to you. **1 Pet. 2:13-14, 16**. Be subject for the Lord's sake to every human institution, whether it be to the emperor as supreme, or to governors as sent by him to punish those who do evil and to praise those who do good; Live as people who are free, not using your freedom as a cover-up for evil, but living as servants of God.

or to the known principles of Christianity (whether concerning faith, worship, or conversation), or to the power of godliness; or, such erroneous opinions or practices, as either in their own nature, or in the manner of publishing or maintaining them, are destructive to the external peace and order which Christ has established in the Church, they may lawfully be called to account.[1]

---

1 **Mt. 18:15-17.** "If your brother sins against you, go and tell him his fault, between you and him alone. If he listens to you, you have gained your brother. But if he does not listen, take one or two others along with you, that every charge may be established by the evidence of two or three witnesses. If he refuses to listen to them, tell it to the church. And if he refuses to listen even to the church, let him be to you as a Gentile and a tax collector. **Rom. 1:32.** Though they know God's decree that those who practice such things deserve to die, they not only do them but give approval to those who practice them. **1 Cor. 5:1,5,11,13.** It is actually reported that there is sexual immorality among you, and of a kind that is not tolerated even among pagans, for a man has his father's wife; you are to deliver this man to Satan for the destruction of the flesh, so that his spirit may be saved in the day of the Lord; But now I am writing to you not to associate with anyone who bears the name of brother if he is guilty of sexual immorality or greed, or is an idolater, reviler, drunkard, or swindler—not even to eat with such a one; God judges those outside. "Purge the evil person from among you." **2 Thess. 3:14.** If anyone does not obey what we say in this letter, take note of that person, and have nothing to do with him, that he may be ashamed. **1 Tim. 1:19-20.** holding faith and a good conscience. By rejecting this, some have made shipwreck of their faith, among whom are Hymenaeus and Alexander, whom I have handed over to Satan that they may learn not to blaspheme. **1 Tim. 6:3-5.** If anyone teaches a different doctrine and does not agree with the sound words of our Lord Jesus Christ and the teaching that accords with godliness, he is puffed up with conceit and understands nothing. He has an unhealthy craving for controversy and for quarrels about words, which produce envy, dissension, slander, evil suspicions, and constant friction among people who are depraved in mind and deprived of the truth, imagining that godliness is a means of gain. **Titus 1:10-11,13.** For there are many who are insubordinate, empty talkers and deceivers, especially those of the circumcision party. They must be silenced, since they are upsetting whole families by teaching for shameful gain what they ought not to teach; This testimony is true. Therefore rebuke them sharply, that they may be sound in the faith. **Titus 3:10.** As for a person who stirs up division, after warning him once and then twice, have nothing more to do with him. **Rev. 2:2, 14-15, 20.** "'I know your works, your toil and your patient endurance, and how you cannot bear with those who are evil, but have tested those who call themselves apostles and are not, and found them to be false; But I have a few things against you: you have some there who hold the teaching of Balaam, who taught Balak to put a stumbling block before the sons of Israel, so that they might eat food sacrificed to idols and practice sexual immorality. So also you have some who hold the teaching of the Nicolaitans; But I have this against you, that you tolerate that woman Jezebel, who calls herself a prophetess and is teaching and seducing my servants to practice sexual immorality and to eat food sacrificed to idols. **Rev. 3:9.** Behold, I will make those of the synagogue of Satan who say that they are Jews and are not, but lie—behold, I will make them come and bow down before your feet and they will learn that I have loved you.

CHAP 27 WORSHIP/SABBATH
PAR. 1
FOUNDATION OF WORSHIP IS THE GOODNESS OF GOD
WE WORSHIP HIM - BECAUSE HE IS GOOD
PSALMIST SAYS - IT'S BECAUSE YOU FORGIVE SINS - YOU ARE FEARED - PSALM 130:4+5. WORSHIP CANNOT BE SLAVISH OR SERVILE OR IT WOULD NOT BE ENTERED INTO WITHOUT A LARGER UNDERSTANDING OF GODS GOODNESS, SOVEREIGN, CARING FOR HIS LOVED ONES. ALSO THIS PARAGRAPH TEACHES HE ONLY SHOULD BE WORSHIPPED AS HE DESIGN/ IN SCRIPTURE → NOT ACCORDING TO MAN'S IMAGINATION + DEVICES.

PAR 2 TRINITY, ROME
ONLY GOD GET'S WORSHIP - NOT MARY, NOT ANGELS SAINTS OR CREATURES

PAR 3. ARE ABOUT PRAYER - IN WORSHIP - THANKSGIVING TO GOD - IN THE SONS NAME - WITH AID OF THE SPIRIT IN A PARTICULAR "POSTURE" UNDERSTANDING, REVERENCE, HUMILITY, PASSION, FAITH LOVE, PERSEVERANCE + IN A KNOWN TONGUE. (ROME/LATIN)

PAR 4
PRAY ACCORDING TO HIS "LAWFUL" WILL + FOR THOSE NOW LIVING + TO COME. NOT FOR THE DEAD.
NOR THOSE THAT HAVE SINNED THE SIN THAT LEADS TO DEATH. WHAT DOES THAT MEAN? GRIEVE THE HS + REJECT THE WORK OF CHRIST. MATT 24:13 - DO NOT ENDURE TO THE END... LIGONIER - ~~[illegible]~~ BE PRAY FOR ONE ANOTHER - BUT DO NOT BE CONCERNED TO PRAY FOR THOSE WHO COMMIT THE SIN LEADING TO DEATH
- BLASPHEMY OF THE HOLY SPIRIT MARK 3:28-30
? - PERSISTANT REFUSAL TO HEAR THE GOSPEL?
APOSTASY FOR THOSE WHO HAVE KNOWLEDGE OF THE TRUTH. 1 JOHN 5:18 - BELIEVERS WILL NOT PERSIST IN UNREPENTANT SIN THAT LEADS TO A FINAL HEART HARDENING - APPLICATION - PRAY FOR ONE ANOTHER + DO NOT BE HASTY TO ASSUME WE KNOW THEIR END

CHAPTER 21

OF RELIGIOUS WORSHIP, AND THE SABBATH DAY.

1. The light of nature shows that there is a God, who has lordship and sovereignty over all, is good, and does good to all, and is therefore to be feared, loved, praised, called upon, trusted in, and served, with all the heart, and with all the soul, and with all the might.[1] But the acceptable way of worshipping the true God is instituted by Him, and so limited by His own revealed will, that He may not be worshipped according to the imaginations and devices of men, or the

---

1 **Josh. 24:14**. Now therefore fear the LORD and serve him in sincerity and in faithfulness. Put away the gods that your fathers served beyond the River and in Egypt, and serve the LORD. **Ps. 18:3.** I call upon the LORD, who is worthy to be praised, and I am saved from my enemies. **Ps. 31:23**. Love the LORD, all you his saints! The LORD preserves the faithful but abundantly repays the one who acts in pride. **Ps. 62:8**. Trust in him at all times, O people; pour out your heart before him; God is a refuge for us. **Ps. 119:68**. You are good and do good; teach me your statutes. **Jer. 10:7**. Who would not fear you, O King of the nations? For this is your due; for among all the wise ones of the nations and in all their kingdoms there is none like you. **Mk. 12:33**. And to love him with all the heart and with all the understanding and with all the strength, and to love one's neighbor as oneself, is much more than all whole burnt offerings and sacrifices. **Acts 17:24**. The God who made the world and everything in it, being Lord of heaven and earth, does not live in temples made by man. **Rom. 1:20**. For his invisible attributes, namely, his eternal power and divine nature, have been clearly perceived, ever since the creation of the world, in the things that have been made. So they are without excuse. **Rom. 10:12**. For there is no distinction between Jew and Greek; for the same Lord is Lord of all, bestowing his riches on all who call on him.

suggestions of Satan, under any visible representation, or any other way not prescribed in the Holy Scripture.[1]

2. Religious worship is to be given to God, the Father, Son, and Holy Spirit; and to Him alone;[2] not to angels, saints, or any other creature:[3] and, since the fall, not without a Mediator; nor in the mediation of any other but of Christ alone.[4]

---

1 **Ex. 20:4-6.** You shall not make for yourself a carved image, or any likeness of anything that is in heaven above, or that is in the earth beneath, or that is in the water under the earth. You shall not bow down to them or serve them, for I the LORD your God am a jealous God, visiting the iniquity of the fathers on the children to the third and the fourth generation of those who hate me, but showing steadfast love to thousands of those who love me and keep my commandments. **Deut. 12:32.** Everything that I command you, you shall be careful to do. You shall not add to it or take from it. **Deut. 4:15-20.** Therefore watch yourselves very carefully. Since you saw no form on the day that the LORD spoke to you at Horeb out of the midst of the fire, beware lest you act corruptly by making a carved image for yourselves, in the form of any figure, the likeness of male or female, the likeness of any animal that is on the earth, the likeness of any winged bird that flies in the air, the likeness of anything that creeps on the ground, the likeness of any fish that is in the water under the earth. And beware lest you raise your eyes to heaven, and when you see the sun and the moon and the stars, all the host of heaven, you be drawn away and bow down to them and serve them, things that the LORD your God has allotted to all the peoples under the whole heaven. But the LORD has taken you and brought you out of the iron furnace, out of Egypt, to be a people of his own inheritance, as you are this day. **Mt. 4:9-10.** And he said to him, "All these I will give you, if you will fall down and worship me." Then Jesus said to him, "Be gone, Satan! For it is written, "You shall worship the Lord your God and him only shall you serve." **Mt. 15:9.** in vain do they worship me, teaching as doctrines the commandments of men. **Acts 17:25.** nor is he served by human hands, as though he needed anything, since he himself gives to all mankind life and breath and everything. **Col. 2:23.** These have indeed an appearance of wisdom in promoting self-made religion and asceticism and severity to the body, but they are of no value in stopping the indulgence of the flesh.

2 **Mt. 4:10.** Then Jesus said to him, "Be gone, Satan! For it is written, "You shall worship the Lord your God and him only shall you serve." **Jn. 5:23.** that all may honor the Son, just as they honor the Father. Whoever does not honor the Son does not honor the Father who sent him. **2 Cor. 13:14.** The grace of the Lord Jesus Christ and the love of God and the fellowship of the Holy Spirit be with you all.

3 **Rom. 1:25.** because they exchanged the truth about God for a lie and worshiped and served the creature rather than the Creator, who is blessed forever! Amen. **Col. 2:18.** Let no one disqualify you, insisting on asceticism and worship of angels, going on in detail about visions, puffed up without reason by his sensuous mind, **Rev. 19:10.** Then I fell down at his feet to worship him, but he said to me, "You must not do that! I am a fellow servant with you and your brothers who hold to the testimony of Jesus. Worship God." For the testimony of Jesus is the spirit of prophecy.

4 **Jn. 14:6.** Jesus said to him, "I am the way, and the truth, and the life. No one comes to the Father except through me. **Eph. 2:18.** For through him we both have access in one Spirit to the Father. **Col. 3:17.** And whatever you do, in word or deed, do everything in the name of the Lord Jesus, giving thanks to God the Father through him. **1 Tim. 2:5.** For there is one God, and there is one mediator between God and men, the man Christ Jesus,

3. Prayer, with thanksgiving, being one special part of religious worship,[1] is by God required of all men:[2] and, that it may be accepted, it is to be made in the name of the Son,[3] by the help of His Spirit,[4] according to His will,[5] with understanding, reverence, humility, passion, faith, love, and perseverance;[6] and, if vocal, in a known tongue.[7]

---

1 **Phil. 4:6**. do not be anxious about anything, but in everything by prayer and supplication with thanksgiving let your requests be made known to God.

2 **Ps. 65:2**. O you who hear prayer, to you shall all flesh come.

3 **Jn. 14:13-14**. Whatever you ask in my name, this I will do, that the Father may be glorified in the Son. If you ask me anything in my name, I will do it. **1 Pet. 2:5**. you yourselves like living stones are being built up as a spiritual house, to be a holy priesthood, to offer spiritual sacrifices acceptable to God through Jesus Christ.

4 **Rom. 8:26**. Likewise the Spirit helps us in our weakness. For we do not know what to pray for as we ought, but the Spirit himself intercedes for us with groanings too deep for words.

5 **1 Jn. 5:14**. And this is the confidence that we have toward him, that if we ask anything according to his will he hears us.

6 **Gen.18:27**. Abraham answered and said, "Behold, I have undertaken to speak to the Lord, I who am but dust and ashes. **Ps. 47:7**. For God is the King of all the earth; sing praises with a psalm! **Eccl. 5:1-2**. Guard your steps when you go to the house of God. To draw near to listen is better than to offer the sacrifice of fools, for they do not know that they are doing evil. Be not rash with your mouth, nor let your heart be hasty to utter a word before God, for God is in heaven and you are on earth. Therefore let your words be few. **Mt. 6:12,14-15**. and forgive us our debts, as we also have forgiven our debtors .... For if you forgive others their trespasses, your heavenly Father will also forgive you, but if you do not forgive others their trespasses, neither will your Father forgive your trespasses. **Mk. 11:24**. Therefore I tell you, whatever you ask in prayer, believe that you have received it, and it will be yours. **Eph. 6:18**. praying at all times in the Spirit, with all prayer and supplication. To that end keep alert with all perseverance, making supplication for all the saints, **Col. 4:2**. Continue steadfastly in prayer, being watchful in it with thanksgiving. **Heb. 12:28**. Therefore let us be grateful for receiving a kingdom that cannot be shaken, and thus let us offer to God acceptable worship, with reverence and awe. **Jas. 1:6-7**. But let him ask in faith, with no doubting, for the one who doubts is like a wave of the sea that is driven and tossed by the wind. For that person must not suppose that he will receive anything from the Lord. **Jas. 5:16**. Therefore, confess your sins to one another and pray for one another, that you may be healed. The prayer of a righteous person has great power as it is working.

7 **1 Cor. 14:14**. For if I pray in a tongue, my spirit prays but my mind is unfruitful.

4. Prayer is to be made for things lawful;[1] and for all sorts of men living, or who shall live hereafter:[2] but not for the dead,[3] nor for those of whom it may be known that they have sinned the sin that leads to death.[4]

5. The reading of the Scriptures with godly fear,[5] the sound preaching[6] and conscientious hearing of the Word, in obedience to God, with understanding, faith and reverence,[7] singing of psalms with

---

1 **1 Jn. 5:14**. And this is the confidence that we have toward him, that if we ask anything according to his will he hears us.

2 **Ruth 4:12**. and may your house be like the house of Perez, whom Tamar bore to Judah, because of the offspring that the LORD will give you by this young woman. **2 Sam. 7:29**. Now therefore may it please you to bless the house of your servant, so that it may continue forever before you. For you, O Lord GOD, have spoken, and with your blessing shall the house of your servant be blessed forever. **Jn. 17:20**. I do not ask for these only, but also for those who will believe in me through their word. **1 Tim. 2:1-2**. First of all, then, I urge that supplications, prayers, intercessions, and thanksgivings be made for all people, for kings and all who are in high positions, that we may lead a peaceful and quiet life, godly and dignified in every way.

3 **2 Sam. 12:21-23**. Then his servants said to him, "What is this thing that you have done? You fasted and wept for the child while he was alive; but when the child died, you arose and ate food." He said, "While the child was still alive, I fasted and wept, for I said, 'Who knows whether the LORD will be gracious to me, that the child may live?' But now he is dead. Why should I fast? Can I bring him back again? I shall go to him, but he will not return to me." **Lk. 16:25-26**. But Abraham said, 'Child, remember that you in your lifetime received your good things, and Lazarus in like manner bad things; but now he is comforted here, and you are in anguish. And besides all this, between us and you a great chasm has been fixed, in order that those who would pass from here to you may not be able, and none may cross from there to us.' **Rev. 14:13**. And I heard a voice from heaven saying, "Write this: Blessed are the dead who die in the Lord from now on." "Blessed indeed," says the Spirit, "that they may rest from their labors, for their deeds follow them!"

4 **1 Jn. 5:16**. If anyone sees his brother committing a sin not leading to death, he shall ask, and God will give him life—to those who commit sins that do not lead to death. There is sin that leads to death; I do not say that one should pray for that.

5 **Acts 15:21**. For from ancient generations Moses has had in every city those who proclaim him, for he is read every Sabbath in the synagogues. **Rev. 1:3**. Blessed is the one who reads aloud the words of this prophecy, and blessed are those who hear, and who keep what is written in it, for the time is near.

6 **2 Tim. 4:2**. preach the word; be ready in season and out of season; reprove, rebuke, and exhort, with complete patience and teaching.

7 **Isa. 66:2**. All these things my hand has made, and so all these things came to be, declares the LORD. But this is the one to whom I will look: he who is humble and contrite in spirit and trembles at my word. **Mt. 13:19**. When anyone hears the word of the kingdom and does not understand it, the evil one comes and snatches away what has been sown in his heart. This is what was sown along the path. **Acts 10:33**. So I sent for you at once, and you have been kind enough to come. Now therefore we are all here in the presence of God to hear all that you have been commanded by the Lord. **Heb. 4:2**. For good news came to us just as to them, but the message they heard did not benefit them, because they were not united by faith with those who listened. **Jas. 1:22**. But be doers of the word, and not hearers only, deceiving yourselves.

grace in the heart;[1] as also, the due administration and worthy receiving of the sacraments instituted by Christ, are all parts of the ordinary religious worship of God:[2] besides religious oaths,[3] vows,[4] solemn fasting,[5] and thanksgiving on special occasions,[6] which are, in their various times and seasons, to be used in a holy and religious manner.[7]

---

1 **Eph. 5:13,19**. But when anything is exposed by the light, it becomes visible.... addressing one another in psalms and hymns and spiritual songs, singing and making melody to the Lord with your heart. **Col. 3:16**. Let the word of Christ dwell in you richly, teaching and admonishing one another in all wisdom, singing psalms and hymns and spiritual songs, with thankfulness in your hearts to God. **Jas. 5:13**. Is anyone among you suffering? Let him pray. Is anyone cheerful? Let him sing praise.

2 **Mt. 28:19**. Go therefore and make disciples of all nations, baptizing them in the name of the Father and of the Son and of the Holy Spirit. **Acts 2:42**. And they devoted themselves to the apostles' teaching and the fellowship, to the breaking of bread and the prayers. **1 Cor. 11:23-29**. For I received from the Lord what I also delivered to you, that the Lord Jesus on the night when he was betrayed took bread, and when he had given thanks, he broke it, and said, "This is my body which is for you. Do this in remembrance of me." In the same way also he took the cup, after supper, saying, "This cup is the new covenant in my blood. Do this, as often as you drink it, in remembrance of me." For as often as you eat this bread and drink the cup, you proclaim the Lord's death until he comes. Whoever, therefore, eats the bread or drinks the cup of the Lord in an unworthy manner will be guilty concerning the body and blood of the Lord. Let a person examine himself, then, and so eat of the bread and drink of the cup. For anyone who eats and drinks without discerning the body eats and drinks judgment on himself.

3 **Deut. 6:13**. It is the LORD your God you shall fear. Him you shall serve and by his name you shall swear. **Neh. 10:29**. join with their brothers, their nobles, and enter into a curse and an oath to walk in God's Law that was given by Moses the servant of God, and to observe and do all the commandments of the LORD our Lord and his rules and his statutes.

4 **Eccl. 5:4-5**. When you vow a vow to God, do not delay paying it, for he has no pleasure in fools. Pay what you vow. It is better that you should not vow than that you should vow and not pay. **Isa. 19:21**. And the LORD will make himself known to the Egyptians, and the Egyptians will know the LORD in that day and worship with sacrifice and offering, and they will make vows to the LORD and perform them.

5 **Esth. 4:16**. "Go, gather all the Jews to be found in Susa, and hold a fast on my behalf, and do not eat or drink for three days, night or day. I and my young women will also fast as you do. Then I will go to the king, though it is against the law, and if I perish, I perish." **Joel 2:12**. "Yet even now," declares the LORD, "return to me with all your heart, with fasting, with weeping, and with mourning." **Mt. 9:15**. And Jesus said to them, "Can the wedding guests mourn as long as the bridegroom is with them? The days will come when the bridegroom is taken away from them, and then they will fast." **1 Cor. 7:5**. Do not deprive one another, except perhaps by agreement for a limited time, that you may devote yourselves to prayer; but then come together again, so that Satan may not tempt you because of your lack of self-control.

6 **Esth. 9:22**. as the days on which the Jews got relief from their enemies, and as the month that had been turned for them from sorrow into gladness and from mourning into a holiday; that they should make them days of feasting and gladness, days for sending gifts of food to one another and gifts to the poor. **Ps. 107**. All of Ps. 107.

7 **Heb. 12:28**. Therefore let us be grateful for receiving a kingdom that cannot be shaken, and thus let us offer to God acceptable worship, with reverence and awe.

6. Neither prayer, nor any other part of religious worship, is now, under the Gospel, either tied to, or made more acceptable by any place in which it is performed, or toward which it is directed:[1] but God is to be worshipped everywhere,[2] in spirit and truth;[3] as, in private families[4] daily,[5] and in secret, each one by himself;[6] so, more

(6) WORSHIP NOT JUST IN RELIGIOUS SERVICE BUT EVERYWHERE — IN SECRET + AS A FAMILY + IN PUBLIC ASSEMBLIES

(7) + (8) NATURE OF SABBATH DAY, OUR HEARTS KEEP IT HOLY — PREPARE + REST SO WORSHIP ON SABBATH — PERFORM ACTS OF MERCY DUTIES OF NECESSITY + MERCY RECREATIONS — WHAT SAY YOU?

---

1 **Jn. 4:21**. Jesus said to her, "Woman, believe me, the hour is coming when neither on this mountain nor in Jerusalem will you worship the Father."

2 **Mal. 1:11**. For from the rising of the sun to its setting my name will be great among the nations, and in every place incense will be offered to my name, and a pure offering. For my name will be great among the nations, says the LORD of hosts. **1 Tim. 2:8**. I desire then that in every place the men should pray, lifting holy hands without anger or quarreling.

3 **Jn. 4:23-24.** But the hour is coming, and is now here, when the true worshipers will worship the Father in spirit and truth, for the Father is seeking such people to worship him. God is spirit, and those who worship him must worship in spirit and truth.

4 **Deut. 6:6-7**. And these words that I command you today shall be on your heart. You shall teach them diligently to your children, and shall talk of them when you sit in your house, and when you walk by the way, and when you lie down, and when you rise. **2 Sam. 6:18,20**. And when David had finished offering the burnt offerings and the peace offerings, he blessed the people in the name of the LORD of hosts. ...And David returned to bless his household. But Michal the daughter of Saul came out to meet David and said, "How the king of Israel honored himself today, uncovering himself today before the eyes of his servants' female servants, as one of the vulgar fellows shamelessly uncovers himself!" **Job 1:5**. And when the days of the feast had run their course, Job would send and consecrate them, and he would rise early in the morning and offer burnt offerings according to the number of them all. For Job said, "It may be that my children have sinned, and cursed God in their hearts." Thus Job did continually. **Jer. 10:25**. Pour out your wrath on the nations that know you not, and on the peoples that call not on your name, for they have devoured Jacob; they have devoured him and consumed him, and have laid waste his habitation. **Acts 10:2**. a devout man who feared God with all his household, gave alms generously to the people, and prayed continually to God. **1 Pet. 3:7**. Likewise, husbands, live with your wives in an understanding way, showing honor to the woman as the weaker vessel, since they are heirs with you of the grace of life, so that your prayers may not be hindered.

5 **Mt. 6:11**. Give us this day our daily bread.

6 **Mt. 6:6**. But when you pray, go into your room and shut the door and pray to your Father who is in secret. And your Father who sees in secret will reward you. **Eph. 6:18.** praying at all times in the Spirit, with all prayer and supplication. To that end keep alert with all perseverance, making supplication for all the saints.

solemnly in the public assemblies, which are not carelessly or willfully to be neglected, or forsaken, when God, by His Word or providence, so calls.[1]

7. As it is the law of nature, that, in general, a due proportion of time be set apart for the worship of God; so, in His Word, by a positive, moral, and perpetual commandment binding all men in all ages, He has particularly appointed one day in seven, for a Sabbath, to be kept holy to him:[2] which, from the beginning of the world to the resurrection of Christ, was the last day of the week; and, from the resurrection of Christ, was changed into the first day of the week,[3]

---

1 **Pr. 1:20-21,24.** Wisdom cries aloud in the street, in the markets she raises her voice; at the head of the noisy streets she cries out; at the entrance of the city gates she speaks. **Pr. 8:34.** Blessed is the one who listens to me, watching daily at my gates, waiting beside my doors. **Isa. 56:6-7.** "And the foreigners who join themselves to the LORD, to minister to him, to love the name of the LORD, and to be his servants, everyone who keeps the Sabbath and does not profane it, and holds fast my covenant—these I will bring to my holy mountain, and make them joyful in my house of prayer; their burnt offerings and their sacrifices will be accepted on my altar; for my house shall be called a house of prayer for all peoples." **Lk. 4:16.** And he came to Nazareth, where he had been brought up. And as was his custom, he went to the synagogue on the Sabbath day, and he stood up to read. **Acts 2:42.** And they devoted themselves to the apostles' teaching and the fellowship, to the breaking of bread and the prayers. **Acts 13:42.** As they went out, the people begged that these things might be told them the next Sabbath. **Heb. 10:25.** not neglecting to meet together, as is the habit of some, but encouraging one another, and all the more as you see the Day drawing near.

2 **Ex. 20:8-11.** Remember the Sabbath day, to keep it holy. Six days you shall labor, and do all your work, but the seventh day is a Sabbath to the LORD your God. On it you shall not do any work, you, or your son, or your daughter, your male servant, or your female servant, or your livestock, or the sojourner who is within your gates. For in six days the LORD made heaven and earth, the sea, and all that is in them, and rested on the seventh day. Therefore the LORD blessed the Sabbath day and made it holy. **Isa. 56:2,4,6-7.** Blessed is the man who does this, and the son of man who holds it fast, who keeps the Sabbath, not profaning it, and keeps his hand from doing any evil For thus says the LORD: "To the eunuchs who keep my Sabbaths, who choose the things that please me and hold fast my covenant, ...And the foreigners who join themselves to the LORD, to minister to him, to love the name of the LORD, and to be his servants, everyone who keeps the Sabbath and does not profane it, and holds fast my covenant—these I will bring to my holy mountain, and make them joyful in my house of prayer; their burnt offerings and their sacrifices will be accepted on my altar; for my house shall be called a house of prayer for all peoples."

3 **Gen. 2:2-3.** And on the seventh day God finished his work that he had done, and he rested on the seventh day from all his work that he had done. So God blessed the seventh day and made it holy, because on it God rested from all his work that he had done in creation. **Acts 20:7.** On the first day of the week, when we were gathered together to break bread, Paul talked with them, intending to depart on the next day, and he prolonged his speech until midnight. **1 Cor. 16:1.** Now concerning the collection for the saints: as I directed the churches of Galatia, so you also are to do.

which, in Scripture, is called the Lord's Day,[1] and is to be continued to the end of the world, as the Christian Sabbath.[2]

8. This Sabbath is then kept holy to the Lord, when men, after a due preparing of their hearts, and ordering of their common affairs beforehand, do not only observe a holy rest all the day from their own works, words, and thoughts about their worldly employments

1 **Rev. 1:10.** I was in the Spirit on the Lord's day, and I heard behind me a loud voice like a trumpet.

2 **Ex. 20:8,10.** Remember the Sabbath day, to keep it holy... but the seventh day is a Sabbath to the LORD your God. On it you shall not do any work, you, or your son, or your daughter, your male servant, or your female servant, or your livestock, or the sojourner who is within your gates. **Mt. 5:17-18.** Do not think that I have come to abolish the Law or the Prophets; I have not come to abolish them but to fulfill them. For truly, I say to you, until heaven and earth pass away, not an iota, not a dot, will pass from the Law until all is accomplished.

and recreations,[1] but also are taken up, the whole time, in the public

1 **Ex. 16:23-26,20-30.** he said to them, "This is what the LORD has commanded: 'Tomorrow is a day of solemn rest, a holy Sabbath to the LORD; bake what you will bake and boil what you will boil, and all that is left over lay aside to be kept till the morning.'" So they laid it aside till the morning, as Moses commanded them, and it did not stink, and there were no worms in it. Moses said, "Eat it today, for today is a Sabbath to the LORD; today you will not find it in the field. Six days you shall gather it, but on the seventh day, which is a Sabbath, there will be none." ... But they did not listen to Moses. Some left part of it till the morning, and it bred worms and stank. And Moses was angry with them. Morning by morning they gathered it, each as much as he could eat; but when the sun grew hot, it melted. On the sixth day they gathered twice as much bread, two omers each. And when all the leaders of the congregation came and told Moses, he said to them, "This is what the LORD has commanded: 'Tomorrow is a day of solemn rest, a holy Sabbath to the LORD; bake what you will bake and boil what you will boil, and all that is left over lay aside to be kept till the morning.'" So they laid it aside till the morning, as Moses commanded them, and it did not stink, and there were no worms in it. Moses said, "Eat it today, for today is a Sabbath to the LORD; today you will not find it in the field. Six days you shall gather it, but on the seventh day, which is a Sabbath, there will be none." On the seventh day some of the people went out to gather, but they found none. And the LORD said to Moses, "How long will you refuse to keep my commandments and my laws? See! The LORD has given you the Sabbath; therefore on the sixth day he gives you bread for two days. Remain each of you in his place; let no one go out of his place on the seventh day." So the people rested on the seventh day. **Ex. 20:8.** Remember the Sabbath day, to keep it holy. **Ex. 31:15-17.** Six days shall work be done, but the seventh day is a Sabbath of solemn rest, holy to the LORD. Whoever does any work on the Sabbath day shall be put to death. Therefore the people of Israel shall keep the Sabbath, observing the Sabbath throughout their generations, as a covenant forever. It is a sign forever between me and the people of Israel that in six days the LORD made heaven and earth, and on the seventh day he rested and was refreshed. **Neh. 13:15-22.** In those days I saw in Judah people treading winepresses on the Sabbath, and bringing in heaps of grain and loading them on donkeys, and also wine, grapes, figs, and all kinds of loads, which they brought into Jerusalem on the Sabbath day. And I warned them on the day when they sold food. Tyrians also, who lived in the city, brought in fish and all kinds of goods and sold them on the Sabbath to the people of Judah, in Jerusalem itself! Then I confronted the nobles of Judah and said to them, "What is this evil thing that you are doing, profaning the Sabbath day? Did not your fathers act in this way, and did not our God bring all this disaster on us and on this city? Now you are bringing more wrath on Israel by profaning the Sabbath." As soon as it began to grow dark at the gates of Jerusalem before the Sabbath, I commanded that the doors should be shut and gave orders that they should not be opened until after the Sabbath. And I stationed some of my servants at the gates, that no load might be brought in on the Sabbath day. Then the merchants and sellers of all kinds of wares lodged outside Jerusalem once or twice. But I warned them and said to them, "Why do you lodge outside the wall? If you do so again, I will lay hands on you." From that time on they did not come on the Sabbath. Then I commanded the Levites that they should purify themselves and come and guard the gates, to keep the Sabbath day holy. Remember this also in my favor, O my God, and spare me according to the greatness of your steadfast love. **Isa. 58:13.** If you turn back your foot from the Sabbath, from doing your pleasure on my holy day, and call the Sabbath a delight and the holy day of the LORD honorable; if you honor it, not going your own ways, or seeking your own pleasure, or talking idly;

and private exercises of His worship, and in the duties of necessity and mercy.[1]

---

1 **Isa. 58:13**. If you turn back your foot from the Sabbath, from doing your pleasure on my holy day, and call the Sabbath a delight and the holy day of the LORD honorable; if you honor it, not going your own ways, or seeking your own pleasure, or talking idly; **Mt. 12:1-13**. At that time Jesus went through the grainfields on the Sabbath. His disciples were hungry, and they began to pluck heads of grain and to eat. But when the Pharisees saw it, they said to him, "Look, your disciples are doing what is not lawful to do on the Sabbath." He said to them, "Have you not read what David did when he was hungry, and those who were with him: how he entered the house of God and ate the bread of the Presence, which it was not lawful for him to eat nor for those who were with him, but only for the priests? Or have you not read in the Law how on the Sabbath the priests in the temple profane the Sabbath and are guiltless? I tell you, something greater than the temple is here. And if you had known what this means, 'I desire mercy, and not sacrifice,' you would not have condemned the guiltless. For the Son of Man is lord of the Sabbath." He went on from there and entered their synagogue. And a man was there with a withered hand. And they asked him, "Is it lawful to heal on the Sabbath?"—so that they might accuse him. He said to them, "Which one of you who has a sheep, if it falls into a pit on the Sabbath, will not take hold of it and lift it out? Of how much more value is a man than a sheep! So it is lawful to do good on the Sabbath." Then he said to the man, "Stretch out your hand." And the man stretched it out, and it was restored, healthy like the other.

CHAPTER 22

OF LAWFUL OATHS AND VOWS.

1. A lawful oath is part of religious worship,[1] in which, on an appropriate occasion, the person swearing solemnly calls God to witness what he asserts, or promises, and to judge him according to the truth or falsehood of what he swears.[2]

2. The name of God only is that by which men ought to swear, and it is to be used with all holy fear and reverence.[3] Therefore, to swear vainly, or rashly, by that glorious and dreadful Name; or, to swear at all by any other thing, is sinful, and to be abhorred.[4] Yet, as in matters of weight and moment, an oath is warranted by the Word of God, under the New Testament as well as under the old;[5] so a

---

1 **Deut. 10:20**. You shall fear the LORD your God. You shall serve him and hold fast to him, and by his name you shall swear.

2 **Ex. 20:7**. "You shall not take the name of the LORD your God in vain, for the LORD will not hold him guiltless who takes his name in vain. Lev. 19:12. You shall not swear by my name falsely, and so profane the name of your God: I am the LORD. **2 Cor. 1:23**. But I call God to witness against me—it was to spare you that I refrained from coming again to Corinth. **2 Chr. 6:22-23**. "If a man sins against his neighbor and is made to take an oath and comes and swears his oath before your altar in this house, then hear from heaven and act and judge your servants, repaying the guilty by bringing his conduct on his own head, and vindicating the righteous by rewarding him according to his righteousness.

3 **Deu.t 6:13**. It is the LORD your God you shall fear. Him you shall serve and by his name you shall swear.

4 **Ex. 20:7**. "You shall not take the name of the LORD your God in vain, for the LORD will not hold him guiltless who takes his name in vain. **Jer. 5:7**. "How can I pardon you? Your children have forsaken me and have sworn by those who are no gods. When I fed them to the full, they committed adultery and trooped to the houses of whores. **Mt. 5:34, 37**. But I say to you, Do not take an oath at all, either by heaven, for it is the throne of God; Let what you say be simply 'Yes' or 'No'; anything more than this comes from evil. **Jas. 5:12**. But above all, my brothers, do not swear, either by heaven or by earth or by any other oath, but let your "yes" be yes and your "no" be no, so that you may not fall under condemnation.

5 **Isa. 65:16**. So that he who blesses himself in the land shall bless himself by the God of truth, and he who takes an oath in the land shall swear by the God of truth; because the former troubles are forgotten and are hidden from my eyes. **2 Cor. 1:23**. But I call God to witness against me—it was to spare you that I refrained from coming again to Corinth. **Heb. 6:16.** For people swear by something greater than themselves, and in all their disputes an oath is final for confirmation.

lawful oath, being imposed by lawful authority, in such matters, ought to be taken.[1]

3. Whoever takes an oath ought to consider the weightiness of so solemn an act, and in it to declare nothing but what he is fully convinced is the truth:[2] neither may any man bind himself by oath to anything but what is good and just, and what he believes to be so, and what he is able and resolved to perform.[3,4]

4. An oath is to be taken in the plain and common sense of the words, without equivocation, or mental reservation.[5] It cannot oblige to sin; but in anything not sinful, being taken, it binds to performance,

---

1 **1 Kings 8:31.** "If a man sins against his neighbor and is made to take an oath and comes and swears his oath before your altar in this house. **Ezra 10:5.** Then Ezra arose and made the leading priests and Levites and all Israel take oath that they would do as had been said. So they took the oath. **Neh. 13:25.** And I confronted them and cursed them and beat some of them and pulled out their hair. And I made them take oath in the name of God, saying, "You shall not give your daughters to their sons, or take their daughters for your sons or for yourselves.

2 **Ex. 20:7.** "You shall not take the name of the LORD your God in vain, for the LORD will not hold him guiltless who takes his name in vain. **Jer. 4:2.** and if you swear, 'As the LORD lives,' in truth, in justice, and in righteousness, then nations shall bless themselves in him, and in him shall they glory."

3 **Gen. 24:2-3,5-6,8-9.** And Abraham said to his servant, the oldest of his household, who had charge of all that he had, "Put your hand under my thigh, that I may make you swear by the LORD, the God of heaven and God of the earth, that you will not take a wife for my son from the daughters of the Canaanites, among whom I dwell; The servant said to him, "Perhaps the woman may not be willing to follow me to this land. Must I then take your son back to the land from which you came?" Abraham said to him, "See to it that you do not take my son back there; But if the woman is not willing to follow you, then you will be free from this oath of mine; only you must not take my son back there." So the servant put his hand under the thigh of Abraham his master and swore to him concerning this matter.

4 Intentionally omitted

5 **Ps. 24:4.** He who has clean hands and a pure heart, who does not lift up his soul to what is false and does not swear deceitfully. **Jer. 4:2.** and if you swear, 'As the LORD lives,' in truth, in justice, and in righteousness, then nations shall bless themselves in him, and in him shall they glory."

even though it may hurt the one making the oath.[1] Nor is it to be violated, although made to heretics, or unbelievers.[2]

5. A vow is like a promissory oath, and ought to be made with similar religious care, and to be performed with the same faithfulness.[3]

---

1 **1 Sam. 25:22,32-34**. God do so to the enemies of David and more also, if by morning I leave so much as one male of all who belong to him." And David said to Abigail, "Blessed be the LORD, the God of Israel, who sent you this day to meet me! Blessed be your discretion, and blessed be you, who have kept me this day from bloodguilt and from avenging myself with my own hand! For as surely as the LORD, the God of Israel, lives, who has restrained me from hurting you, unless you had hurried and come to meet me, truly by morning there had not been left to Nabal so much as one male." **Ps. 15:4**. in whose eyes a vile person is despised, but who honors those who fear the LORD; who swears to his own hurt and does not change;

2 **Josh 9:18-19**. But the people of Israel did not attack them, because the leaders of the congregation had sworn to them by the LORD, the God of Israel. Then all the congregation murmured against the leaders. But all the leaders said to all the congregation, "We have sworn to them by the LORD, the God of Israel, and now we may not touch them. **2 Sam. 21:1**. Now there was a famine in the days of David for three years, year after year. And David sought the face of the LORD. And the LORD said, "There is bloodguilt on Saul and on his house, because he put the Gibeonites to death." **Ezek. 17:16, 18-19**. "As I live, declares the Lord GOD, surely in the place where the king dwells who made him king, whose oath he despised, and whose covenant with him he broke, in Babylon he shall die; He despised the oath in breaking the covenant, and behold, he gave his hand and did all these things; he shall not escape. Therefore thus says the Lord GOD: As I live, surely it is my oath that he despised, and my covenant that he broke. I will return it upon his head.

3 **Ps. 61:8**. So will I ever sing praises to your name, as I perform my vows day after day. **Ps. 66:13-14**. I will come into your house with burnt offerings; I will perform my vows to you, that which my lips uttered and my mouth promised when I was in trouble. **Ecc. 5:4-6**. When you vow a vow to God, do not delay paying it, for he has no pleasure in fools. Pay what you vow. It is better that you should not vow than that you should vow and not pay. Let not your mouth lead you into sin, and do not say before the messenger that it was a mistake. Why should God be angry at your voice and destroy the work of your hands? **Isa. 19:21**. And the LORD will make himself known to the Egyptians, and the Egyptians will know the LORD in that day and worship with sacrifice and offering, and they will make vows to the LORD and perform them.

6. It is not to be made to any creature, but to God alone:[1] and, that it may be accepted, it is to be made voluntarily, out of faith, and conscience of duty, in way of thankfulness for mercy received, or for the obtaining of what we want, whereby we more strictly bind ourselves to necessary duties: or, to other things, so far and so long as they may aptly contribute to the intended result.[2]

7. No man may vow to do anything forbidden in the Word of God, or what would hinder any duty commanded in it, or which is not in his own power, and for the performance of which he has no promise of

---

1 **Ps. 76:11.** Make your vows to the LORD your God and perform them; let all around him bring gifts to him who is to be feared. **Jer. 44:25-26.** Thus says the LORD of hosts, the God of Israel: You and your wives have declared with your mouths, and have fulfilled it with your hands, saying, 'We will surely perform our vows that we have made, to make offerings to the queen of heaven and to pour out drink offerings to her.' Then confirm your vows and perform your vows! Therefore hear the word of the LORD, all you of Judah who dwell in the land of Egypt: Behold, I have sworn by my great name, says the LORD, that my name shall no more be invoked by the mouth of any man of Judah in all the land of Egypt, saying, 'As the Lord GOD lives

2 **Gen. 28:20-22.** Then Jacob made a vow, saying, "If God will be with me and will keep me in this way that I go, and will give me bread to eat and clothing to wear, so that I come again to my father's house in peace, then the LORD shall be my God, and this stone, which I have set up for a pillar, shall be God's house. And of all that you give me I will give a full tenth to you." **Deut. 23:21-23.** "If you make a vow to the LORD your God, you shall not delay fulfilling it, for the LORD your God will surely require it of you, and you will be guilty of sin. But if you refrain from vowing, you will not be guilty of sin. You shall be careful to do what has passed your lips, for you have voluntarily vowed to the LORD your God what you have promised with your mouth. **1 Sam.1:11.** And she vowed a vow and said, "O LORD of hosts, if you will indeed look on the affliction of your servant and remember me and not forget your servant, but will give to your servant a son, then I will give him to the LORD all the days of his life, and no razor shall touch his head." **Ps. 50:14.** Offer to God a sacrifice of thanksgiving, and perform your vows to the Most High. Ps. **66:13-14.** I will come into your house with burnt offerings; I will perform my vows to you, that which my lips uttered and my mouth promised when I was in trouble. **Ps. 132:2-5.** how he swore to the LORD and vowed to the Mighty One of Jacob,"I will not enter my house or get into my bed,I will not give sleep to my eyes or slumber to my eyelids until I find a place for the LORD, a dwelling place for the Mighty One of Jacob."

ability from God.[1] In which respects, Roman Catholic monastical vows of perpetual single life, professed poverty, and regular obedience, are so far from being degrees of higher perfection, that they are superstitious and sinful snares, in which no Christian may entangle himself.[2]

---

1. **Num. 30:5,8,12-13**. But if her father opposes her on the day that he hears of it, no vow of hers, no pledge by which she has bound herself shall stand. And the LORD will forgive her, because her father opposed her; But if, on the day that her husband comes to hear of it, he opposes her, then he makes void her vow that was on her, and the thoughtless utterance of her lips by which she bound herself. And the LORD will forgive her; But if her husband makes them null and void on the day that he hears them, then whatever proceeds out of her lips concerning her vows or concerning her pledge of herself shall not stand. Her husband has made them void, and the LORD will forgive her. Any vow and any binding oath to afflict herself, her husband may establish, or her husband may make void. **Mk. 6:26**. And the king was exceedingly sorry, but because of his oaths and his guests he did not want to break his word to her. **Acts 23:12,14**. When it was day, the Jews made a plot and bound themselves by an oath neither to eat nor drink till they had killed Paul; They went to the chief priests and elders and said, "We have strictly bound ourselves by an oath to taste no food till we have killed Paul.

2 **Mt. 19:11-12**. But he said to them, "Not everyone can receive this saying, but only those to whom it is given. For there are eunuchs who have been so from birth, and there are eunuchs who have been made eunuchs by men, and there are eunuchs who have made themselves eunuchs for the sake of the kingdom of heaven. Let the one who is able to receive this receive it." **1 Cor. 7:2,9**. But because of the temptation to sexual immorality, each man should have his own wife and each woman her own husband; But if they cannot exercise self-control, they should marry. For it is better to marry than to burn with passion. **1 Cor 7:23.** You were bought with a price; do not become slaves of men. **Eph. 4:28**. Let the thief no longer steal, but rather let him labor, doing honest work with his own hands, so that he may have something to share with anyone in need. **1 Pet. 4:2.** so as to live for the rest of the time in the flesh no longer for human passions but for the will of God.

CHAPTER 23

OF THE CIVIL MAGISTRATE.

1. God, the supreme Lord and King of all the world, has ordained civil magistrates to be under Him, over the people, for His own glory, and the public good: and, to this end, has armed them with the power of the sword, for the defense and encouragement of those who are good, and for the punishment of evildoers.[1]
2. It is lawful for Christians to accept and execute the office of a magistrate, when so called:[2] in the managing of it, as they ought especially to maintain piety, justice, and peace, according to the wholesome laws of each commonwealth;[3] so, for that end, they may lawfully,

---

1 **Rom. 13:1-4.** Let every person be subject to the governing authorities. For there is no authority except from God, and those that exist have been instituted by God. Therefore whoever resists the authorities resists what God has appointed, and those who resist will incur judgment. For rulers are not a terror to good conduct, but to bad. Would you have no fear of the one who is in authority? Then do what is good, and you will receive his approval, for he is God's servant for your good. But if you do wrong, be afraid, for he does not bear the sword in vain. For he is the servant of God, an avenger who carries out God's wrath on the wrongdoer. **1 Pet. 2:13-14.** Be subject for the Lord's sake to every human institution, whether it be to the emperor as supreme, or to governors as sent by him to punish those who do evil and to praise those who do good.

2 **Prov. 8:15-16.** By me kings reign, and rulers decree what is just; by me princes rule, and nobles, all who govern justly. **Rom. 13:1-2, 4.** Let every person be subject to the governing authorities. For there is no authority except from God, and those that exist have been instituted by God. Therefore whoever resists the authorities resists what God has appointed, and those who resist will incur judgment. ...for he is God's servant for your good. But if you do wrong, be afraid, for he does not bear the sword in vain. For he is the servant of God, an avenger who carries out God's wrath on the wrongdoer.

3 **2 Sam. 23:3.** The God of Israel has spoken; the Rock of Israel has said to me: When one rules justly over men, ruling in the fear of God. **Ps. 2:10-12.** Now therefore, O kings, be wise; be warned, O rulers of the earth. Serve the LORD with fear, and rejoice with trembling. Kiss the Son, lest he be angry, and you perish in the way, for his wrath is quickly kindled. Blessed are all who take refuge in him. **Ps. 82:3-4.** "Give justice to the weak and the fatherless; maintain the right of the afflicted and the destitute. Rescue the weak and the needy; deliver them from the hand of the wicked." **1 Tim. 2:2.** ... for kings and all who are in high positions, that we may lead a peaceful and quiet life, godly and dignified in every way. **1 Pet. 2:13.** Be subject for the Lord's sake to every human institution, whether it be to the emperor as supreme.

now under the New Testament, wage war, upon just and necessary occasion.[1]

3. Civil magistrates may not assume to themselves the administration of the Word and sacraments;[2] or the power of the keys of the kingdom of heaven;[3] or, in the least, interfere in the matters of faith.[4] Yet, as nursing fathers, it is the duty of civil magistrates to protect the Church of our common Lord, without giving the preference to any denomination of Christians above the rest, in such a manner that all ecclesiastical persons whatever shall enjoy the full, free, and

---

1 **Mt. 8:9-10**. For I too am a man under authority, with soldiers under me. And I say to one, 'Go,' and he goes, and to another, 'Come,' and he comes, and to my servant, 'Do this,' and he does it." When Jesus heard this, he marveled and said to those who followed him, "Truly, I tell you, with no one in Israel have I found such faith." **Lk. 3:14**. Soldiers also asked him, "And we, what shall we do?" And he said to them, "Do not extort money from anyone by threats or by false accusation, and be content with your wages." **Acts 10:1-2**. At Caesarea there was a man named Cornelius, a centurion of what was known as the Italian Cohort, a devout man who feared God with all his household, gave alms generously to the people, and prayed continually to God. **Rom. 13:4**. ...for he is God's servant for your good. But if you do wrong, be afraid, for he does not bear the sword in vain. For he is the servant of God, an avenger who carries out God's wrath on the wrongdoer. **Rev. 17:14, 16**. "They will make war on the Lamb, and the Lamb will conquer them, for he is Lord of lords and King of kings, and those with him are called and chosen and faithful." ... And the ten horns that you saw, they and the beast will hate the prostitute. They will make her desolate and naked, and devour her flesh and burn her up with fire.

2 **2 Chron. 26:18**. ...and they withstood King Uzziah and said to him, "It is not for you, Uzziah, to burn incense to the LORD, but for the priests, the sons of Aaron, who are consecrated to burn incense. Go out of the sanctuary, for you have done wrong, and it will bring you no honor from the LORD God."

3 **Mt. 16:19**. "I will give you the keys of the kingdom of heaven, and whatever you bind on earth shall be bound in heaven, and whatever you loose on earth shall be loosed in heaven." **Mt. 18:17**. If he refuses to listen to them, tell it to the church. And if he refuses to listen even to the church, let him be to you as a Gentile and a tax collector. **Rom. 10:15**. And how are they to preach unless they are sent? As it is written, "How beautiful are the feet of those who preach the good news!" **1 Cor. 4:1-2**. This is how one should regard us, as servants of Christ and stewards of the mysteries of God. Moreover, it is required of stewards that they be found trustworthy. **1 Cor. 12:28-29**. And God has appointed in the church first apostles, second prophets, third teachers, then miracles, then gifts of healing, helping, administrating, and various kinds of tongues. Are all apostles? Are all prophets? Are all teachers? Do all work miracles? **Eph. 4:11-12**. And he gave the apostles, the prophets, the evangelists, the shepherds and teachers, to equip the saints for the work of ministry, for building up the body of Christ. **Heb. 5:4**. And no one takes this honor for himself, but only when called by God, just as Aaron was.

4 **Jn. 18:36**. Jesus answered, "My kingdom is not of this world. If my kingdom were of this world, my servants would have been fighting, that I might not be delivered over to the Jews. But my kingdom is not from the world." **Acts 5:29**. But Peter and the apostles answered, "We must obey God rather than men." **Eph. 4:11-12**. And he gave the apostles, the prophets, the evangelists, the shepherds and teachers, to equip the saints for the work of ministry, for building up the body of Christ.

unquestioned liberty of discharging every part of their sacred functions, without violence or danger.[1] And, as Jesus Christ has appointed a regular government and discipline in His Church, no law of any commonwealth should interfere with, let, or hinder, the due exercise thereof, among the voluntary members of any denomination of Christians, according to their own profession and belief.[2] It is the duty of civil magistrates to protect the person and good name of all their people, in such an effectual manner that no person be permitted, either upon pretense of religion or of infidelity, to offer any indignity, violence, abuse, or injury to any other person whatsoever: and to take order, that all religious and ecclesiastical assemblies be held without molestation or disturbance.[3]

4. It is the duty of people to pray for magistrates,[4] to honor their persons,[5] to pay them tribute or other dues,[6] to obey their lawful commands, and to be subject to their authority, for conscience's

---

1 **Isa. 49:23**. "Kings shall be your foster fathers, and their queens your nursing mothers. With their faces to the ground they shall bow down to you, and lick the dust of your feet. Then you will know that I am the LORD; those who wait for me shall not be put to shame." **Rom. 13:1-6**. Let every person be subject to the governing authorities. For there is no authority except from God, and those that exist have been instituted by God. Therefore whoever resists the authorities resists what God has appointed, and those who resist will incur judgment. For rulers are not a terror to good conduct, but to bad. Would you have no fear of the one who is in authority? Then do what is good, and you will receive his approval, for he is God's servant for your good. But if you do wrong, be afraid, for he does not bear the sword in vain. For he is the servant of God, an avenger who carries out God's wrath on the wrongdoer. Therefore one must be in subjection, not only to avoid God's wrath but also for the sake of conscience. For because of this you also pay taxes, for the authorities are ministers of God, attending to this very thing.

2 **Ps. 105:15**. ...saying, "Touch not my anointed ones, do my prophets no harm!" **Acts 18:14-15**. But when Paul was about to open his mouth, Gallio said to the Jews, "If it were a matter of wrongdoing or vicious crime, O Jews, I would have reason to accept your complaint. But since it is a matter of questions about words and names and your own law, see to it yourselves. I refuse to be a judge of these things."

3 **Rom. 13:4**. ...for he is God's servant for your good. But if you do wrong, be afraid, for he does not bear the sword in vain. For he is the servant of God, an avenger who carries out God's wrath on the wrongdoer. **1 Tim. 2:2**. ...for kings and all who are in high positions, that we may lead a peaceful and quiet life, godly and dignified in every way.

4 **1 Tim. 2:1-2**. First of all, then, I urge that supplications, prayers, intercessions, and thanksgivings be made for all people, for kings and all who are in high positions, that we may lead a peaceful and quiet life, godly and dignified in every way.

5 **1 Pet.2:17**. Honor everyone. Love the brotherhood. Fear God. Honor the emperor.

6 **Rom. 13:6-7**. For because of this you also pay taxes, for the authorities are ministers of God, attending to this very thing. Pay to all what is owed to them: taxes to whom taxes are owed, revenue to whom revenue is owed, respect to whom respect is owed, honor to whom honor is owed.

sake.[1] Infidelity, or difference in religion, does not make void the magistrates' just and legal authority, nor free the people from their due obedience to them:[2] from which ecclesiastical persons are not exempted,[3] much less has the pope any power and jurisdiction over them in their dominions, or over any of their people; and, least of all, to deprive them of their dominions, or lives, if he shall judge them to be heretics, or upon any other pretense whatever.[4]

---

1 **Rom. 13:5**. Therefore one must be in subjection, not only to avoid God's wrath but also for the sake of conscience. **Titus 3:1**. Remind them to be submissive to rulers and authorities, to be obedient, to be ready for every good work.

2 **1 Pet. 2:13-14, 16**. Be subject for the Lord's sake to every human institution, whether it be to the emperor as supreme, or to governors as sent by him to punish those who do evil and to praise those who do good. ... Live as people who are free, not using your freedom as a cover-up for evil, but living as servants of God.

3 **1 Kings 2:35**. The king put Benaiah the son of Jehoiada over the army in place of Joab, and the king put Zadok the priest in the place of Abiathar. **Acts 25:9-11**. But Festus, wishing to do the Jews a favor, said to Paul, "Do you wish to go up to Jerusalem and there be tried on these charges before me?" But Paul said, "I am standing before Caesar's tribunal, where I ought to be tried. To the Jews I have done no wrong, as you yourself know very well. If then I am a wrongdoer and have committed anything for which I deserve to die, I do not seek to escape death. But if there is nothing to their charges against me, no one can give me up to them. I appeal to Caesar." **Rom. 13:1**. Let every person be subject to the governing authorities. For there is no authority except from God, and those that exist have been instituted by God. **2 Pet. 2:1, 10-11**. But false prophets also arose among the people, just as there will be false teachers among you, who will secretly bring in destructive heresies, even denying the Master who bought them, bringing upon themselves swift destruction. ... Bold and willful, they do not tremble as they blaspheme the glorious ones, whereas angels, though greater in might and power, do not pronounce a blasphemous judgment against them before the Lord. **Jude 8-11**. Yet in like manner these people also, relying on their dreams, defile the flesh, reject authority, and blaspheme the glorious ones. But when the archangel Michael, contending with the devil, was disputing about the body of Moses, he did not presume to pronounce a blasphemous judgment, but said, "The Lord rebuke you." But these people blaspheme all that they do not understand, and they are destroyed by all that they, like unreasoning animals, understand instinctively. Woe to them! For they walked in the way of Cain and abandoned themselves for the sake of gain to Balaam's error and perished in Korah's rebellion.

4 **2 Thess. 2:4**. ...who opposes and exalts himself against every so-called god or object of worship, so that he takes his seat in the temple of God, proclaiming himself to be God. **Rev. 13:15-17**. And it was allowed to give breath to the image of the beast, so that the image of the beast might even speak and might cause those who would not worship the image of the beast to be slain. Also it causes all, both small and great, both rich and poor, both free and slave, to be marked on the right hand or the forehead, so that no one can buy or sell unless he has the mark, that is, the name of the beast or the number of its name.

CHAPTER 24

OF MARRIAGE AND DIVORCE.

1. Marriage is to be between one man and one woman: neither is it lawful for any man to have more than one wife, nor for any woman to have more than one husband, at the same time.[1]
2. Marriage was ordained for the mutual help of husband and wife,[2] for the increase of mankind with legitimate descendants, and of the Church with a holy seed;[3] and for preventing of uncleanness.[4]
3. It is lawful for all sorts of people to marry, who are able with judgment to give their consent.[5] Yet it is the duty of Christians to marry only in the Lord.[6] And therefore such as profess the true reformed

---

1 **Gen. 2:24**. Therefore a man shall leave his father and his mother and hold fast to his wife, and they shall become one flesh. **Prov. 2:17**. who forsakes the companion of her youth and forgets the covenant of her God; **Mt. 19:5-6**. and said, 'Therefore a man shall leave his father and his mother and hold fast to his wife, and the two shall become one flesh'? So they are no longer two but one flesh. What therefore God has joined together, let not man separate."

2 **Gen. 2:18**. Then the LORD God said, "It is not good that the man should be alone; I will make him a helper fit for him."

3 **Mal. 2:15**. Did he not make them one, with a portion of the Spirit in their union? And what was the one God seeking? Godly offspring. So guard yourselves in your spirit, and let none of you be faithless to the wife of your youth.

4 **1 Cor. 7:2,9**. But because of the temptation to sexual immorality, each man should have his own wife and each woman her own husband; But if they cannot exercise self-control, they should marry. For it is better to marry than to burn with passion.

5 **1 Cor. 7:36-38**. If anyone thinks that he is not behaving properly toward his betrothed, if his passions are strong, and it has to be, let him do as he wishes: let them marry—it is no sin. But whoever is firmly established in his heart, being under no necessity but having his desire under control, and has determined this in his heart, to keep her as his betrothed, he will do well. So then he who marries his betrothed does well, and he who refrains from marriage will do even better. **1 Tim. 4:3**. who forbid marriage and require abstinence from foods that God created to be received with thanksgiving by those who believe and know the truth. **Heb. 13:4**. Let marriage be held in honor among all, and let the marriage bed be undefiled, for God will judge the sexually immoral and adulterous.

6 **1 Cor. 7:39**. A wife is bound to her husband as long as he lives. But if her husband dies, she is free to be married to whom she wishes, only in the Lord.

religion should not marry with infidels, papists, or other idolaters: neither should such as are godly be unequally yoked, by marrying with such as are notoriously wicked in their lives, or maintain damnable heresies.[1]

---

1 **Gen. 34:14**. They said to them, "We cannot do this thing, to give our sister to one who is uncircumcised, for that would be a disgrace to us. **Ex. 34:16**. and you take of their daughters for your sons, and their daughters whore after their gods and make your sons whore after their gods. **Deut. 7:3-4**. You shall not intermarry with them, giving your daughters to their sons or taking their daughters for your sons, for they would turn away your sons from following me, to serve other gods. Then the anger of the LORD would be kindled against you, and he would destroy you quickly. **1 Kings 11:4.** For when Solomon was old his wives turned away his heart after other gods, and his heart was not wholly true to the LORD his God, as was the heart of David his father. **Neh. 13:25-27**. And I confronted them and cursed them and beat some of them and pulled out their hair. And I made them take oath in the name of God, saying, "You shall not give your daughters to their sons, or take their daughters for your sons or for yourselves. Did not Solomon king of Israel sin on account of such women? Among the many nations there was no king like him, and he was beloved by his God, and God made him king over all Israel. Nevertheless, foreign women made even him to sin. Shall we then listen to you and do all this great evil and act treacherously against our God by marrying foreign women?" **Mal. 2:11-12**. Judah has been faithless, and abomination has been committed in Israel and in Jerusalem. For Judah has profaned the sanctuary of the LORD, which he loves, and has married the daughter of a foreign god. May the LORD cut off from the tents of Jacob any descendant of the man who does this, who brings an offering to the LORD of hosts! **2 Cor. 6:14**. Do not be unequally yoked with unbelievers. For what partnership has righteousness with lawlessness? Or what fellowship has light with darkness?

4. Marriage ought not to be within the degrees of blood relationship or family closeness forbidden by the Word.[1] Nor can such incestuous marriage ever be made by any law of man or consent of parties, so as those persons may live together as man and wife.[2]

5. Adultery or fornication committed after entering into a contract, being detected before marriage, give just occasion to the innocent

---

1 **Lev. 18: 6-17, 24-30.** "None of you shall approach any one of his close relatives to uncover nakedness. I am the LORD. You shall not uncover the nakedness of your father, which is the nakedness of your mother; she is your mother, you shall not uncover her nakedness. You shall not uncover the nakedness of your father's wife; it is your father's nakedness. You shall not uncover the nakedness of your sister, your father's daughter or your mother's daughter, whether brought up in the family or in another home. You shall not uncover the nakedness of your son's daughter or of your daughter's daughter, for their nakedness is your own nakedness. You shall not uncover the nakedness of your father's wife's daughter, brought up in your father's family, since she is your sister. You shall not uncover the nakedness of your father's sister; she is your father's relative. You shall not uncover the nakedness of your mother's sister, for she is your mother's relative. You shall not uncover the nakedness of your father's brother, that is, you shall not approach his wife; she is your aunt. You shall not uncover the nakedness of your daughter-in-law; she is your son's wife, you shall not uncover her nakedness. You shall not uncover the nakedness of your brother's wife; it is your brother's nakedness. You shall not uncover the nakedness of a woman and of her daughter, and you shall not take her son's daughter or her daughter's daughter to uncover her nakedness; they are relatives; it is depravity; "Do not make yourselves unclean by any of these things, for by all these the nations I am driving out before you have become unclean, and the land became unclean, so that I punished its iniquity, and the land vomited out its inhabitants. But you shall keep my statutes and my rules and do none of these abominations, either the native or the stranger who sojourns among you (for the people of the land, who were before you, did all of these abominations, so that the land became unclean), lest the land vomit you out when you make it unclean, as it vomited out the nation that was before you. For everyone who does any of these abominations, the persons who do them shall be cut off from among their people. So keep my charge never to practice any of these abominable customs that were practiced before you, and never to make yourselves unclean by them: I am the LORD your God." **Amos 2:7.** those who trample the head of the poor into the dust of the earth and turn aside the way of the afflicted; a man and his father go in to the same girl, so that my holy name is profaned; **1 Cor 5:1.** It is actually reported that there is sexual immorality among you, and of a kind that is not tolerated even among pagans, for a man has his father's wife.

2 **Lev. 18:24-28.** "Do not make yourselves unclean by any of these things, for by all these the nations I am driving out before you have become unclean, and the land became unclean, so that I punished its iniquity, and the land vomited out its inhabitants. But you shall keep my statutes and my rules and do none of these abominations, either the native or the stranger who sojourns among you (for the people of the land, who were before you, did all of these abominations, so that the land became unclean), lest the land vomit you out when you make it unclean, as it vomited out the nation that was before you. **Mk. 6:18.** For John had been saying to Herod, "It is not lawful for you to have your brother's wife."

party to dissolve that contract.[1] In the case of adultery after marriage, it is lawful for the innocent party to sue out a divorce,[2] and, after the divorce, to marry another, as if the offending party were dead.[3]

6. Although the corruption of man be such that he is apt to study arguments unduly to separate those whom God has joined together in marriage: yet, nothing but adultery, or such willful desertion as can no way be remedied by the Church, or civil magistrate, is sufficient cause for dissolving the bond of marriage:[4] in this, a public and orderly course of proceeding is to be observed; and the persons concerned in it not left to their own wills and discretion in their own case.[5]

---

1 **Mt. 1:18-20**. Now the birth of Jesus Christ took place in this way. When his mother Mary had been betrothed to Joseph, before they came together she was found to be with child from the Holy Spirit. And her husband Joseph, being a just man and unwilling to put her to shame, resolved to divorce her quietly. But as he considered these things, behold, an angel of the Lord appeared to him in a dream, saying, "Joseph, son of David, do not fear to take Mary as your wife, for that which is conceived in her is from the Holy Spirit."

2 **Mt. 5:31-32**. "It was also said, 'Whoever divorces his wife, let him give her a certificate of divorce.' But I say to you that everyone who divorces his wife, except on the ground of sexual immorality, makes her commit adultery, and whoever marries a divorced woman commits adultery.

3 **Mt. 19:9**. And I say to you: whoever divorces his wife, except for sexual immorality, and marries another, commits adultery." **Rom. 7:2-3**. For a married woman is bound by law to her husband while he lives, but if her husband dies she is released from the law of marriage. Accordingly, she will be called an adulteress if she lives with another man while her husband is alive. But if her husband dies, she is free from that law, and if she marries another man she is not an adulteress.

4 **Mt. 19:8-9**. He said to them, "Because of your hardness of heart Moses allowed you to divorce your wives, but from the beginning it was not so. And I say to you: whoever divorces his wife, except for sexual immorality, and marries another, commits adultery." **Mt. 19:6**. So they are no longer two but one flesh. What therefore God has joined together, let not man separate." **1 Cor. 7:15**. But if the unbelieving partner separates, let it be so. In such cases the brother or sister is not enslaved. God has called you to peace.

5 **Deut. 24:1-4**. "When a man takes a wife and marries her, if then she finds no favor in his eyes because he has found some indecency in her, and he writes her a certificate of divorce and puts it in her hand and sends her out of his house, and she departs out of his house, and if she goes and becomes another man's wife, and the latter man hates her and writes her a certificate of divorce and puts it in her hand and sends her out of his house, or if the latter man dies, who took her to be his wife, then her former husband, who sent her away, may not take her again to be his wife, after she has been defiled, for that is an abomination before the LORD. And you shall not bring sin upon the land that the LORD your God is giving you for an inheritance.

CHAPTER 25

OF THE CHURCH.

1. The catholic or universal Church, which is invisible, consists of the whole number of the elect, who have been, are, or shall be gathered into one, under Christ its Head; and is the spouse, the body, the fullness of Him who fills everything in every way.[1]
2. The visible Church, which is also catholic or universal under the Gospel (not confined to one nation, as before under the law), consists of all those throughout the world who profess the true

---

1 **Eph. 1:10, 22-23.** ...as a plan for the fullness of time, to unite all things in him, things in heaven and things on earth. ... And he put all things under his feet and gave him as head over all things to the church, which is his body, the fullness of him who fills all in all. **Eph. 5:23, 27, 32.** For the husband is the head of the wife even as Christ is the head of the church, his body, and is himself its Savior. ...so that he might present the church to himself in splendor, without spot or wrinkle or any such thing, that she might be holy and without blemish. ... This mystery is profound, and I am saying that it refers to Christ and the church. **Col. 1:18.** And he is the head of the body, the church. He is the beginning, the firstborn from the dead, that in everything he might be preeminent.

religion;[1] and of their children:[2] and is the kingdom of the Lord Jesus Christ,[3] the house and family of God,[4] out of which there is no ordinary possibility of salvation.[5]

3. To this catholic visible Church, Christ has given the ministry, Scriptures, and means of grace of God, for the gathering and maturing of the saints, in this life, to the end of the world: and does, by His own

1 **Ps. 2:8.** Ask of me, and I will make the nations your heritage, and the ends of the earth your possession. **Rom. 15:9-12.** ...and in order that the Gentiles might glorify God for his mercy. As it is written, "Therefore I will praise you among the Gentiles, and sing to your name." And again it is said, "Rejoice, O Gentiles, with his people." And again, "Praise the Lord, all you Gentiles, and let all the peoples extol him." And again Isaiah says, "The root of Jesse will come, even he who arises to rule the Gentiles; in him will the Gentiles hope." **1 Cor. 1:2.** To the church of God that is in Corinth, to those sanctified in Christ Jesus, called to be saints together with all those who in every place call upon the name of our Lord Jesus Christ, both their Lord and ours. **1 Cor. 12:12-13.** For just as the body is one and has many members, and all the members of the body, though many, are one body, so it is with Christ. For in one Spirit we were all baptized into one body—Jews or Greeks, slaves or free—and all were made to drink of one Spirit. **Rev. 7:9.** After this I looked, and behold, a great multitude that no one could number, from every nation, from all tribes and peoples and languages, standing before the throne and before the Lamb, clothed in white robes, with palm branches in their hands.

2 **Gen. 3:15.** "I will put enmity between you and the woman, and between your offspring and her offspring; he shall bruise your head, and you shall bruise his heel." **Gen. 17:7.** And I will establish my covenant between me and you and your offspring after you throughout their generations for an everlasting covenant, to be God to you and to your offspring after you. **Ezek. 16:20-21.** And you took your sons and your daughters, whom you had borne to me, and these you sacrificed to them to be devoured. Were your whorings so small a matter that you slaughtered my children and delivered them up as an offering by fire to them? **Acts 2:39.** "For the promise is for you and for your children and for all who are far off, everyone whom the Lord our God calls to himself." **Rom. 11:16.** If the dough offered as firstfruits is holy, so is the whole lump, and if the root is holy, so are the branches. **1 Cor. 7:14.** For the unbelieving husband is made holy because of his wife, and the unbelieving wife is made holy because of her husband. Otherwise your children would be unclean, but as it is, they are holy.

3 **Isa. 9:7.** Of the increase of his government and of peace there will be no end, on the throne of David and over his kingdom, to establish it and to uphold it with justice and with righteousness from this time forth and forevermore. The zeal of the LORD of hosts will do this. **Mt. 13:47.** "Again, the kingdom of heaven is like a net that was thrown into the sea and gathered fish of every kind."

4 **Eph. 2:19.** So then you are no longer strangers and aliens, but you are fellow citizens with the saints and members of the household of God. **Eph. 3:15.** ...from whom every family in heaven and on earth is named.

5 **Acts 2:47.** ...praising God and having favor with all the people. And the Lord added to their number day by day those who were being saved.

presence and Spirit, according to His promise, make them effectual to the saints.[1]

4. This catholic Church has been sometimes more, sometimes less visible.[2] And particular Churches, which are members of it, are more or less pure, to the extent the doctrine of the Gospel is taught and embraced, means of grace administered, and public worship performed more or less purely in them.[3]

---

1 **Isa 59:12.** For our transgressions are multiplied before you, and our sins testify against us; for our transgressions are with us, and we know our iniquities. **Mt. 28:19-20.** "Go therefore and make disciples of all nations, baptizing them in the name of the Father and of the Son and of the Holy Spirit, teaching them to observe all that I have commanded you. And behold, I am with you always, to the end of the age." **1 Cor. 12:28.** And God has appointed in the church first apostles, second prophets, third teachers, then miracles, then gifts of healing, helping, administrating, and various kinds of tongues. **Eph. 4:11-13.** And he gave the apostles, the prophets, the evangelists, the shepherds and teachers, to equip the saints for the work of ministry, for building up the body of Christ, until we all attain to the unity of the faith and of the knowledge of the Son of God, to mature manhood, to the measure of the stature of the fullness of Christ.

2 **Rom. 11:3-4.** "Lord, they have killed your prophets, they have demolished your altars, and I alone am left, and they seek my life." But what is God's reply to him? "I have kept for myself seven thousand men who have not bowed the knee to Baal." **Rev. 12:6, 14.** ...and the woman fled into the wilderness, where she has a place prepared by God, in which she is to be nourished for 1,260 days. ... But the woman was given the two wings of the great eagle so that she might fly from the serpent into the wilderness, to the place where she is to be nourished for a time, and times, and half a time.

3 **1 Cor. 5:6-7.** Your boasting is not good. Do you not know that a little leaven leavens the whole lump? Cleanse out the old leaven that you may be a new lump, as you really are unleavened. For Christ, our Passover lamb, has been sacrificed. **Rev. 2, 3.** All of Revelation 2 and 3.

5. The purest Churches under heaven are subject both to mixture and error;[1] and some have so degenerated as not to be Churches of Christ, but synagogues of Satan.[2] Nevertheless, there shall be always a Church on earth to worship God according to His will.[3]

---

1 **Mt. 13:24-30, 47.** He put another parable before them, saying, "The kingdom of heaven may be compared to a man who sowed good seed in his field, but while his men were sleeping, his enemy came and sowed weeds among the wheat and went away. So when the plants came up and bore grain, then the weeds appeared also. And the servants of the master of the house came and said to him, 'Master, did you not sow good seed in your field? How then does it have weeds?' He said to them, 'An enemy has done this.' So the servants said to him, 'Then do you want us to go and gather them?' But he said, 'No, lest in gathering the weeds you root up the wheat along with them. Let both grow together until the harvest, and at harvest time I will tell the reapers, Gather the weeds first and bind them in bundles to be burned, but gather the wheat into my barn.'" ... "Again, the kingdom of heaven is like a net that was thrown into the sea and gathered fish of every kind." **1 Cor. 13:12.** For now we see in a mirror dimly, but then face to face. Now I know in part; then I shall know fully, even as I have been fully known. **Rev. 2, 3.** All of Rev. 2 and 3.

2 **Rom. 11:18-22.** ...do not be arrogant toward the branches. If you are, remember it is not you who support the root, but the root that supports you. Then you will say, "Branches were broken off so that I might be grafted in." That is true. They were broken off because of their unbelief, but you stand fast through faith. So do not become proud, but fear. For if God did not spare the natural branches, neither will he spare you. Note then the kindness and the severity of God: severity toward those who have fallen, but God's kindness to you, provided you continue in his kindness. Otherwise you too will be cut off. **Rev. 18:2.** And he called out with a mighty voice, "Fallen, fallen is Babylon the great! She has become a dwelling place for demons, a haunt for every unclean spirit, a haunt for every unclean bird, a haunt for every unclean and detestable beast."

3 **Ps. 72:17.** May his name endure forever, his fame continue as long as the sun! May people be blessed in him, all nations call him blessed! **Ps. 102:28.** The children of your servants shall dwell secure; their offspring shall be established before you. **Mt. 16:18.** And I tell you, you are Peter, and on this rock I will build my church, and the gates of hell shall not prevail against it. **Mt. 28:19-20.** "Go therefore and make disciples of all nations, baptizing them in the name of the Father and of the Son and of the Holy Spirit, teaching them to observe all that I have commanded you. And behold, I am with you always, to the end of the age."

6. There is no other head of the Church but the Lord Jesus Christ.[1] Nor can the pope of Rome, in any sense, be head of it.[2]

1 **Eph. 1:22.** And he put all things under his feet and gave him as head over all things to the church. **Col. 1:18**. And he is the head of the body, the church. He is the beginning, the firstborn from the dead, that in everything he might be preeminent.

2 **Mt. 23:8-10**. But you are not to be called rabbi, for you have one teacher, and you are all brothers. And call no man your father on earth, for you have one Father, who is in heaven. Neither be called instructors, for you have one instructor, the Christ. **2 Thess. 2:3-4, 8-9**. Let no one deceive you in any way. For that day will not come, unless the rebellion comes first, and the man of lawlessness is revealed, the son of destruction, who opposes and exalts himself against every so-called god or object of worship, so that he takes his seat in the temple of God, proclaiming himself to be God. ... And then the lawless one will be revealed, whom the Lord Jesus will kill with the breath of his mouth and bring to nothing by the appearance of his coming. The coming of the lawless one is by the activity of Satan with all power and false signs and wonders. **Rev. 13:6**. It opened its mouth to utter blasphemies against God, blaspheming his name and his dwelling, that is, those who dwell in heaven.

CHAPTER 26

OF THE COMMUNION OF SAINTS.

1. All saints, who are united to Jesus Christ their Head, by His Spirit, and by faith, have fellowship with Him in His grace, sufferings, death, resurrection, and glory:[1] and, being united to one another in love, they have communion in each other's gifts and graces,[2] and are obliged to the performance of such duties, public and private, as

---

1 **JN. 1:16**. And from his fullness we have all received, grace upon grace. **ROM. 6:5-6**. For if we have been united with him in a death like his, we shall certainly be united with him in a resurrection like his. We know that our old self was crucified with him in order that the body of sin might be brought to nothing, so that we would no longer be enslaved to sin. **EPH. 2:5-6.** even when we were dead in our trespasses, made us alive together with Christ—by grace you have been saved—and raised us up with him and seated us with him in the heavenly places in Christ Jesus, **EPH. 3:16-18**. that according to the riches of his glory he may grant you to be strengthened with power through his Spirit in your inner being, so that Christ may dwell in your hearts through faith—that you, being rooted and grounded in love, may have strength to comprehend with all the saints what is the breadth and length and height and depth, **PHIL. 3:10**. that I may know him and the power of his resurrection, and may share his sufferings, becoming like him in his death, ... **2 TIM. 2:12**. if we endure, we will also reign with him; if we deny him, he also will deny us; **1 JN. 1:3**. that which we have seen and heard we proclaim also to you, so that you too may have fellowship with us; and indeed our fellowship is with the Father and with his Son Jesus Christ.

2 **1 COR. 3:21-23**. So let no one boast in men. For all things are yours, whether Paul or Apollos or Cephas or the world or life or death or the present or the future—all are yours, and you are Christ's, and Christ is God's. **EPH. 4:15-16**. Rather, speaking the truth in love, we are to grow up in every way into him who is the head, into Christ, from whom the whole body, joined and held together by every joint with which it is equipped, when each part is working properly, makes the body grow so that it builds itself up in love. **COL. 2:19**. and not holding fast to the Head, from whom the whole body, nourished and knit together through its joints and ligaments, grows with a growth that is from God.

do contribute to their mutual good, both in the inward and outward man.[1]

2. Those who profess to be saints are bound to maintain a holy fellowship and communion in the worship of God, and in performing such other spiritual services as tend toward their mutual edification;[2] as also in relieving each other in outward things, according to their various abilities and needs. This communion, as God offers opportunity, is to be extended to all those who, in every place, call on the name of the Lord Jesus.[3]

---

1 **Rom. 1:11-12,14**. For I long to see you, that I may impart to you some spiritual gift to strengthen you—that is, that we may be mutually encouraged by each other's faith, both yours and mine.... I am under obligation both to Greeks and to barbarians, both to the wise and to the foolish. **Gal. 6:10**. So then, as we have opportunity, let us do good to everyone, and especially to those who are of the household of faith. **1 Thess. 5:11,14**. Therefore encourage one another and build one another up, just as you are doing....And we urge you, brothers, admonish the idle, encourage the fainthearted, help the weak, be patient with them all. **1 Jn. 3:16-18**. By this we know love, that he laid down his life for us, and we ought to lay down our lives for the brothers. But if anyone has the world's goods and sees his brother in need, yet closes his heart against him, how does God's love abide in him? Little children, let us not love in word or talk but in deed and in truth.

2 **Isa. 2:3**. and many peoples shall come, and say: "Come, let us go up to the mountain of the LORD, to the house of the God of Jacob, that he may teach us his ways and that we may walk in his paths." For out of Zion shall go the law, and the word of the LORD from Jerusalem. **Acts. 2:42, 46.** And they devoted themselves to the apostles' teaching and the fellowship, to the breaking of bread and the prayers.... And day by day, attending the temple together and breaking bread in their homes, they received their food with glad and generous hearts, ... **1 Cor. 11:20**. When you come together, it is not the Lord's supper that you eat. **Heb. 10:24-25**. And let us consider how to stir up one another to love and good works, not neglecting to meet together, as is the habit of some, but encouraging one another, and all the more as you see the Day drawing near.

3 **Acts 2:44-45.** And all who believed were together and had all things in common. And they were selling their possessions and belongings and distributing the proceeds to all, as any had need. **Acts 11:29-30**. So the disciples determined, everyone according to his ability, to send relief to the brothers living in Judea. And they did so, sending it to the elders by the hand of Barnabas and Saul. **2 Cor. 8,9**. All of 2 Cor. 8 and 9. **1 Jn. 3:17**. But if anyone has the world's goods and sees his brother in need, yet closes his heart against him, how does God's love abide in him?

3. This communion that the saints have with Christ, does not make them in any way partakers of the substance of His Godhead; or to be equal with Christ in any respect: to affirm either of these is irreverent and blasphemous.[1] Nor does their communion with each another, as saints, take away, or infringe on the title or ownership that each man has in his goods and possessions.[2]

---

1 **Ps. 45:7.** you have loved righteousness and hated wickedness. Therefore God, your God, has anointed you with the oil of gladness beyond your companions; **Isa. 42:8.** I am the LORD; that is my name; my glory I give to no other, nor my praise to carved idols. **1 Cor. 8:6.** yet for us there is one God, the Father, from whom are all things and for whom we exist, and one Lord, Jesus Christ, through whom are all things and through whom we exist. **Col. 1:18-19.** And he is the head of the body, the church. He is the beginning, the firstborn from the dead, that in everything he might be preeminent. For in him all the fullness of God was pleased to dwell, **1 Tim. 6:15-16.** which he will display at the proper time—he who is the blessed and only Sovereign, the King of kings and Lord of lords, who alone has immortality, who dwells in unapproachable light, whom no one has ever seen or can see. To him be honor and eternal dominion. Amen. **Heb. 1:6-9.** And again, when he brings the firstborn into the world, he says, "Let all God's angels worship him." Of the angels he says, "He makes his angels winds, and his ministers a flame of fire." But of the Son he says, "Your throne, O God, is forever and ever, the scepter of uprightness is the scepter of your kingdom. You have loved righteousness and hated wickedness; therefore God, your God, has anointed you with the oil of gladness beyond your companions."

2 **Ex. 20:15.** You shall not steal. **Acts 5:4.** While it remained unsold, did it not remain your own? And after it was sold, was it not at your disposal? Why is it that you have contrived this deed in your heart? You have not lied to men but to God. **Eph. 4:28.** Let the thief no longer steal, but rather let him labor, doing honest work with his own hands, so that he may have something to share with anyone in need.

CHAPTER 27

OF THE SACRAMENTS.

1. Sacraments are holy signs and seals of the covenant of grace,[1] directly instituted by God,[2] to represent Christ and His benefits; and to confirm our interest in Him:[3] as also, to put a visible difference between those who belong to the Church and the rest of the world;[4]

---

1 **Gen. 17:7,10.** And I will establish my covenant between me and you and your offspring after you throughout their generations for an everlasting covenant, to be God to you and to your offspring after you; This is my covenant, which you shall keep, between me and you and your offspring after you: Every male among you shall be circumcised. **Rom. 4:11.** He received the sign of circumcision as a seal of the righteousness that he had by faith while he was still uncircumcised. The purpose was to make him the father of all who believe without being circumcised, so that righteousness would be counted to them as well,

2 **Mt. 28:19.** Go therefore and make disciples of all nations, baptizing them in the name of the Father and of the Son and of the Holy Spirit, **1 Cor. 11:23.** For I received from the Lord what I also delivered to you, that the Lord Jesus on the night when he was betrayed took bread,

3 **1 Cor. 10:16.** The cup of blessing that we bless, is it not a participation in the blood of Christ? The bread that we break, is it not a participation in the body of Christ? **1 Cor. 11:25-26.** In the same way also he took the cup, after supper, saying, "This cup is the new covenant in my blood. Do this, as often as you drink it, in remembrance of me." For as often as you eat this bread and drink the cup, you proclaim the Lord's death until he comes. **Gal. 3:17, 27.** This is what I mean: the law, which came 430 years afterward, does not annul a covenant previously ratified by God, so as to make the promise void; For as many of you as were baptized into Christ have put on Christ.

4 **Gen. 34:14.** They said to them, "We cannot do this thing, to give our sister to one who is uncircumcised, for that would be a disgrace to us. **Ex. 12:48.** If a stranger shall sojourn with you and would keep the Passover to the LORD, let all his males be circumcised. Then he may come near and keep it; he shall be as a native of the land. But no uncircumcised person shall eat of it. **Rom. 15:8.** For I tell you that Christ became a servant to the circumcised to show God's truthfulness, in order to confirm the promises given to the patriarchs,

and solemnly to engage them to the service of God in Christ, according to His Word.[1]

2. There is, in every sacrament, a spiritual relationship, or sacramental union, between the sign and the thing signified: so that the names and effects of the one are attributed to the other.[2]

3. The grace that is exhibited in or by the sacraments rightly used, is not conferred by any power in them; neither does the efficacy of a sacrament depend on the piety or intention of him who administers it:[3] but on the work of the Spirit,[4] and the words of institution, which contain, together with a precept authorizing their use, a promise of benefit to those eligible to receive them.[5]

---

1 **Rom. 6:3-4**. Do you not know that all of us who have been baptized into Christ Jesus were baptized into his death? We were buried therefore with him by baptism into death, in order that, just as Christ was raised from the dead by the glory of the Father, we too might walk in newness of life. **1 Cor. 10:16,21**. The cup of blessing that we bless, is it not a participation in the blood of Christ? The bread that we break, is it not a participation in the body of Christ? You cannot drink the cup of the Lord and the cup of demons. You cannot partake of the table of the Lord and the table of demons.

2 **Gen. 17:10**. This is my covenant, which you shall keep, between me and you and your offspring after you: Every male among you shall be circumcised. **Mt. 26:27-28**. And he took a cup, and when he had given thanks he gave it to them, saying, "Drink of it, all of you, for this is my blood of the covenant, which is poured out for many for the forgiveness of sins. **Titus 3:5**. he saved us, not because of works done by us in righteousness, but according to his own mercy, by the washing of regeneration and renewal of the Holy Spiritv

3 **Rom. 2:28-29**. For no one is a Jew who is merely one outwardly, nor is circumcision outward and physical. But a Jew is one inwardly, and circumcision is a matter of the heart, by the Spirit, not by the letter. His praise is not from man but from God. **1 Pet. 3:21**. Baptism, which corresponds to this, now saves you, not as a removal of dirt from the body but as an appeal to God for a good conscience, through the resurrection of Jesus Christ,

4 **Mt. 3:11**. "I baptize you with water for repentance, but he who is coming after me is mightier than I, whose sandals I am not worthy to carry. He will baptize you with the Holy Spirit and fire. **1 Cor. 12:13**. For in one Spirit we were all baptized into one body—Jews or Greeks, slaves or free—and all were made to drink of one Spirit.

5 **Mt. 26:27-28**. And he took a cup, and when he had given thanks he gave it to them, saying, "Drink of it, all of you, for this is my blood of the covenant, which is poured out for many for the forgiveness of sins. **Mt. 28:19-20**. Go therefore and make disciples of all nations, baptizing them in the name of the Father and of the Son and of the Holy Spirit, teaching them to observe all that I have commanded you. And behold, I am with you always, to the end of the age."

4. There are only two sacraments established by Christ our Lord in the Gospel; that is to say, Baptism, and the Lord's Supper: neither of which may be dispensed by any, but by a minister of the Word lawfully ordained.[1]

5. The sacraments of the Old Testament in regard to the spiritual things thereby signified and exhibited, were, for substance, the same as those of the New.[2]

---

1 **Mt. 28:19**. Go therefore and make disciples of all nations, baptizing them in the name of the Father and of the Son and of the Holy Spirit, **1 Cor. 4:1**. This is how one should regard us, as servants of Christ and stewards of the mysteries of God. **1 Cor. 11:20,23**. When you come together, it is not the Lord's supper that you eat; For I received from the Lord what I also delivered to you, that the Lord Jesus on the night when he was betrayed took bread. **Heb. 5:4**. And no one takes this honor for himself, but only when called by God, just as Aaron was.

2 **1 Cor. 10:1-4**. For I want you to know, brothers, that our fathers were all under the cloud, and all passed through the sea, and all were baptized into Moses in the cloud and in the sea, and all ate the same spiritual food, and all drank the same spiritual drink. For they drank from the spiritual Rock that followed them, and the Rock was Christ.

CHAPTER 28

OF BAPTISM.

1. Baptism is a sacrament of the New Testament, established by Jesus Christ,[1] not only for the solemn admission of the party baptized into the visible Church;[2] but also to be for him a sign and seal of the covenant of grace,[3] of his grafting into Christ,[4] of regeneration,[5] of remission of sins,[6] and of his surrender to God, through Jesus Christ, to walk in newness of life.[7] This sacrament is, by Christ's own appointment, to be continued in His Church until the end of the world.[8]
2. The outward element to be used in this sacrament is water, with which the party is to be baptized, in the name of the Father, and of

---

1 **Mt. 28:19**. Go therefore and make disciples of all nations, baptizing them in the name of the Father and of the Son and of the Holy Spirit.

2 **1 Cor. 12:13**. For in one Spirit we were all baptized into one body—Jews or Greeks, slaves or free—and all were made to drink of one Spirit.

3 **Rom. 4:11**. He received the sign of circumcision as a seal of the righteousness that he had by faith while he was still uncircumcised. The purpose was to make him the father of all who believe without being circumcised, so that righteousness would be counted to them as well. **Col. 2:11-12**. In him also you were circumcised with a circumcision made without hands, by putting off the body of the flesh, by the circumcision of Christ, having been buried with him in baptism, in which you were also raised with him through faith in the powerful working of God, who raised him from the dead.

4 **Rom. 6:5**. For if we have been united with him in a death like his, we shall certainly be united with him in a resurrection like his. **Gal. 3:27**. For as many of you as were baptized into Christ have put on Christ.

5 **Titus 3:5**. ...he saved us, not because of works done by us in righteousness, but according to his own mercy, by the washing of regeneration and renewal of the Holy Spirit.

6 **Mk. 1:4**. John appeared, baptizing in the wilderness and proclaiming a baptism of repentance for the forgiveness of sins.

7 **Rom. 6:3-4**. Do you not know that all of us who have been baptized into Christ Jesus were baptized into his death? We were buried therefore with him by baptism into death, in order that, just as Christ was raised from the dead by the glory of the Father, we too might walk in newness of life.

8 **Mt. 28:19-20**. "Go therefore and make disciples of all nations, baptizing them in the name of the Father and of the Son and of the Holy Spirit, teaching them to observe all that I have commanded you. And behold, I am with you always, to the end of the age."

the Son, and of the Holy Spirit, by a minister of the Gospel, lawfully called to that office.[1]

3. Immersion of the person in the water is not necessary; but Baptism is rightly administered by pouring, or sprinkling water on the person.[2]

---

1 **Mt. 3:11.** "I baptize you with water for repentance, but he who is coming after me is mightier than I, whose sandals I am not worthy to carry. He will baptize you with the Holy Spirit and fire." **Mt. 28:19-20.** "Go therefore and make disciples of all nations, baptizing them in the name of the Father and of the Son and of the Holy Spirit, teaching them to observe all that I have commanded you. And behold, I am with you always, to the end of the age." **Jn. 1:33.** I myself did not know him, but he who sent me to baptize with water said to me, 'He on whom you see the Spirit descend and remain, this is he who baptizes with the Holy Spirit.'

2 **Mk. 7:4.** ...and when they come from the marketplace, they do not eat unless they wash. And there are many other traditions that they observe, such as the washing of cups and pots and copper vessels and dining couches. **Acts 2:41.** So those who received his word were baptized, and there were added that day about three thousand souls. **Acts 16:33.** And he took them the same hour of the night and washed their wounds; and he was baptized at once, he and all his family. **Heb. 9:10, 19-22.** ...but deal only with food and drink and various washings, regulations for the body imposed until the time of reformation. ... For when every commandment of the law had been declared by Moses to all the people, he took the blood of calves and goats, with water and scarlet wool and hyssop, and sprinkled both the book itself and all the people, saying, "This is the blood of the covenant that God commanded for you." And in the same way he sprinkled with the blood both the tent and all the vessels used in worship. Indeed, under the law almost everything is purified with blood, and without the shedding of blood there is no forgiveness of sins.

4. Not only those who actually profess faith in and obedience to Christ,[1] but also the infants of one, or both, believing parents, are to be baptized.[2]

5. Although it is a great sin to condemn or neglect this ordinance,[3] yet grace and salvation are not so inseparably attached to it, that no

---

1 **Mk. 16:15-16**. And he said to them, "Go into all the world and proclaim the gospel to the whole creation. Whoever believes and is baptized will be saved, but whoever does not believe will be condemned." **Acts 8:37-38**. And he commanded the chariot to stop, and they both went down into the water, Philip and the eunuch, and he baptized him.

2 **Gen. 17:7-8**. "And I will establish my covenant between me and you and your offspring after you throughout their generations for an everlasting covenant, to be God to you and to your offspring after you. And I will give to you and to your offspring after you the land of your sojournings, all the land of Canaan, for an everlasting possession, and I will be their God." **Mt. 28:19.** Go therefore and make disciples of all nations, baptizing them in the name of the Father and of the Son and of the Holy Spirit. **Mk. 10:13-16**. And they were bringing children to him that he might touch them, and the disciples rebuked them. But when Jesus saw it, he was indignant and said to them, "Let the children come to me; do not hinder them, for to such belongs the kingdom of God. Truly, I say to you, whoever does not receive the kingdom of God like a child shall not enter it." And he took them in his arms and blessed them, laying his hands on them. **Lk. 18:15**. Now they were bringing even infants to him that he might touch them. And when the disciples saw it, they rebuked them. **Acts 2:38-39**. And Peter said to them, "Repent and be baptized every one of you in the name of Jesus Christ for the forgiveness of your sins, and you will receive the gift of the Holy Spirit. For the promise is for you and for your children and for all who are far off, everyone whom the Lord our God calls to himself." **Rom. 4:11-12**. He received the sign of circumcision as a seal of the righteousness that he had by faith while he was still uncircumcised. The purpose was to make him the father of all who believe without being circumcised, so that righteousness would be counted to them as well, and to make him the father of the circumcised who are not merely circumcised but who also walk in the footsteps of the faith that our father Abraham had before he was circumcised. **1 Cor. 7:14.** For the unbelieving husband is made holy because of his wife, and the unbelieving wife is made holy because of her husband. Otherwise your children would be unclean, but as it is, they are holy. **Gal. 3:9, 14**. So then, those who are of faith are blessed along with Abraham, the man of faith. ...so that in Christ Jesus the blessing of Abraham might come to the Gentiles, so that we might receive the promised Spirit through faith. **Col. 2:11-12.** In him also you were circumcised with a circumcision made without hands, by putting off the body of the flesh, by the circumcision of Christ, having been buried with him in baptism, in which you were also raised with him through faith in the powerful working of God, who raised him from the dead.

3 **Ex 4:24-26**. At a lodging place on the way the LORD met him and sought to put him to death. Then Zipporah took a flint and cut off her son's foreskin and touched Moses' feet with it and said, "Surely you are a bridegroom of blood to me!" So he let him alone. It was then that she said, "A bridegroom of blood," because of the circumcision. **Lk 7:30.** ...but the Pharisees and the lawyers rejected the purpose of God for themselves, not having been baptized by him.

person can be regenerated, or saved, without it:[1] or, that all who are baptized are undoubtedly regenerated.[2]

6. The efficacy of Baptism is not tied to that moment of time at which it is administered;[3] yet, notwithstanding, by the right use of this ordinance, the grace promised is not only offered, but really exhibited, and conferred, by the Holy Spirit, to such (whether of age or infants) as that grace belongs to, according to the counsel of God's own will, in His appointed time.[4]
7. The sacrament of Baptism is but once to be administered to any person.[5]

---

1 **Acts 10:2, 4, 22, 31, 45, 47**. ...a devout man who feared God with all his household, gave alms generously to the people, and prayed continually to God. ... And he stared at him in terror and said, "What is it, Lord?" And he said to him, "Your prayers and your alms have ascended as a memorial before God. ... And they said, "Cornelius, a centurion, an upright and God-fearing man, who is well spoken of by the whole Jewish nation, was directed by a holy angel to send for you to come to his house and to hear what you have to say." ...and said, 'Cornelius, your prayer has been heard and your alms have been remembered before God. ... And the believers from among the circumcised who had come with Peter were amazed, because the gift of the Holy Spirit was poured out even on the Gentiles. ... "Can anyone withhold water for baptizing these people, who have received the Holy Spirit just as we have?" **Rom. 4:11**. He received the sign of circumcision as a seal of the righteousness that he had by faith while he was still uncircumcised. The purpose was to make him the father of all who believe without being circumcised, so that righteousness would be counted to them as well.

2 **Acts 8:13, 23**. Even Simon himself believed, and after being baptized he continued with Philip. And seeing signs and great miracles performed, he was amazed. ... "For I see that you are in the gall of bitterness and in the bond of iniquity."

3 **Jn. 3:5, 8**. Jesus answered, "Truly, truly, I say to you, unless one is born of water and the Spirit, he cannot enter the kingdom of God." ... "The wind blows where it wishes, and you hear its sound, but you do not know where it comes from or where it goes. So it is with everyone who is born of the Spirit."

4 **Acts 2:38, 41**. And Peter said to them, "Repent and be baptized every one of you in the name of Jesus Christ for the forgiveness of your sins, and you will receive the gift of the Holy Spirit." ... So those who received his word were baptized, and there were added that day about three thousand souls. **Gal. 3:27**. For as many of you as were baptized into Christ have put on Christ. **Eph. 5:25-26**. Husbands, love your wives, as Christ loved the church and gave himself up for her, that he might sanctify her, having cleansed her by the washing of water with the word. **Titus 3:5**. ...he saved us, not because of works done by us in righteousness, but according to his own mercy, by the washing of regeneration and renewal of the Holy Spirit.

5 **Titus 3:5**. ...he saved us, not because of works done by us in righteousness, but according to his own mercy, by the washing of regeneration and renewal of the Holy Spirit.

CHAPTER 29

OF THE LORD'S SUPPER.

1. Our Lord Jesus, on the night in which He was betrayed, instituted the sacrament of His body and blood, called the Lord's Supper, to be observed in His Church, to the end of the world, for the perpetual remembrance of the sacrifice of Himself in His death; the sealing of all benefits of it to true believers, their spiritual nourishment and growth in Him, their further engagement in and to all duties that they owe to Him; and, to be a bond and pledge of their communion with Him, and with each other, as members of His mystical body.[1]
2. In this sacrament, Christ is not offered up to His Father; nor any real sacrifice made at all, for remission of sins of the living or dead;[2]

---

1 **1 Cor. 10:16-17, 21**. The cup of blessing that we bless, is it not a participation in the blood of Christ? The bread that we break, is it not a participation in the body of Christ? Because there is one bread, we who are many are one body, for we all partake of the one bread. ... You cannot drink the cup of the Lord and the cup of demons. You cannot partake of the table of the Lord and the table of demons. **1 Cor. 11:23-26**. For I received from the Lord what I also delivered to you, that the Lord Jesus on the night when he was betrayed took bread, and when he had given thanks, he broke it, and said, "This is my body which is for you. Do this in remembrance of me." In the same way also he took the cup, after supper, saying, "This cup is the new covenant in my blood. Do this, as often as you drink it, in remembrance of me." For as often as you eat this bread and drink the cup, you proclaim the Lord's death until he comes. **1 Cor. 12:13**. For in one Spirit we were all baptized into one body—Jews or Greeks, slaves or free—and all were made to drink of one Spirit.

2 **Heb. 9:22, 25-26, 28**. Indeed, under the law almost everything is purified with blood, and without the shedding of blood there is no forgiveness of sins. ... Nor was it to offer himself repeatedly, as the high priest enters the holy places every year with blood not his own, for then he would have had to suffer repeatedly since the foundation of the world. But as it is, he has appeared once for all at the end of the ages to put away sin by the sacrifice of himself. ...so Christ, having been offered once to bear the sins of many, will appear a second time, not to deal with sin but to save those who are eagerly waiting for him.

but only a commemoration of that one offering up of Himself, by Himself, upon the cross, once for all: and a spiritual offering of all possible praise to God, for the same:[1] so that the Roman Catholic sacrifice of the mass (as they call it) is most abominably injurious to Christ's one and only sacrifice, the only propitiation for all the sins of His elect.[2]

3. The Lord Jesus has, in this ordinance, appointed His ministers to declare His words of institution to the people; to pray, and to bless the elements of bread and wine, and thereby to set them apart from a common to a holy use; and to take and break the bread, to take the cup, and (they communicating also themselves) to give both to

---

1 **Mt. 26:26-27**. Now as they were eating, Jesus took bread, and after blessing it broke it and gave it to the disciples, and said, "Take, eat; this is my body." And he took a cup, and when he had given thanks he gave it to them, saying, "Drink of it, all of you." **1 Cor. 11:24-26**. ...and when he had given thanks, he broke it, and said, "This is my body which is for you. Do this in remembrance of me." In the same way also he took the cup, after supper, saying, "This cup is the new covenant in my blood. Do this, as often as you drink it, in remembrance of me." For as often as you eat this bread and drink the cup, you proclaim the Lord's death until he comes.

2 **Heb. 7:23-24, 27**. The former priests were many in number, because they were prevented by death from continuing in office, but he holds his priesthood permanently, because he continues forever. ... He has no need, like those high priests, to offer sacrifices daily, first for his own sins and then for those of the people, since he did this once for all when he offered up himself. **Heb. 10:11-12, 14, 18**. And every priest stands daily at his service, offering repeatedly the same sacrifices, which can never take away sins. But when Christ had offered for all time a single sacrifice for sins, he sat down at the right hand of God... For by a single offering he has perfected for all time those who are being sanctified. ... Where there is forgiveness of these, there is no longer any offering for sin.

the communicants;[1] but to none who are not then present in the congregation.[2]

4. Private masses, or receiving this sacrament by a priest, or any other alone;[3] as likewise, the denial of the cup to the people,[4] worshipping the elements, the lifting them up, or carrying them about, for adoration, and the reserving of them for any pretended religious use; are all contrary to the nature of this sacrament, and to the institution of Christ.[5]

---

1 **Mt. 26:26-28.** Now as they were eating, Jesus took bread, and after blessing it broke it and gave it to the disciples, and said, "Take, eat; this is my body." And he took a cup, and when he had given thanks he gave it to them, saying, "Drink of it, all of you, for this is my blood of the covenant, which is poured out for many for the forgiveness of sins." **Mk. 14:22-24.** And as they were eating, he took bread, and after blessing it broke it and gave it to them, and said, "Take; this is my body." And he took a cup, and when he had given thanks he gave it to them, and they all drank of it. And he said to them, "This is my blood of the covenant, which is poured out for many." **Lk. 22:19-20.** And he took the bread, and when he had given thanks, he broke it and gave it to them, saying, "This is my body, which is given for you. Do this in remembrance of me." And likewise the cup after they had eaten, saying, "This cup that is poured out for you is the new covenant in my blood." **1 Cor. 11:23-26.** For I received from the Lord what I also delivered to you, that the Lord Jesus on the night when he was betrayed took bread, and when he had given thanks, he broke it, and said, "This is my body which is for you. Do this in remembrance of me." In the same way also he took the cup, after supper, saying, "This cup is the new covenant in my blood. Do this, as often as you drink it, in remembrance of me." For as often as you eat this bread and drink the cup, you proclaim the Lord's death until he comes.

2 **Acts 20:7.** On the first day of the week, when we were gathered together to break bread, Paul talked with them, intending to depart on the next day, and he prolonged his speech until midnight. **1 Cor. 11:20.** When you come together, it is not the Lord's supper that you eat.

3 **1 Cor. 10:16.** The cup of blessing that we bless, is it not a participation in the blood of Christ? The bread that we break, is it not a participation in the body of Christ?

4 **Mk. 14:23.** And he took a cup, and when he had given thanks he gave it to them, and they all drank of it. **1 Cor. 11:25-29.** In the same way also he took the cup, after supper, saying, "This cup is the new covenant in my blood. Do this, as often as you drink it, in remembrance of me." For as often as you eat this bread and drink the cup, you proclaim the Lord's death until he comes. Whoever, therefore, eats the bread or drinks the cup of the Lord in an unworthy manner will be guilty concerning the body and blood of the Lord. Let a person examine himself, then, and so eat of the bread and drink of the cup. For anyone who eats and drinks without discerning the body eats and drinks judgment on himself.

5 **Mt. 15:9.** ..."'in vain do they worship me, teaching as doctrines the commandments of men.'"

5. The outward elements in this sacrament, duly set apart to the uses ordained by Christ, have such relation to Him crucified, as that, truly, yet sacramentally only, they are sometimes called by the names of the things they represent, to wit, the body and blood of Christ;[1] albeit, in substance and nature, they remain truly and only bread and wine, as they were before.[2]

6. That doctrine that maintains a change of the substance of bread and wine, into the substance of Christ's body and blood (commonly called transubstantiation) by consecration of a priest, or by any other way, is repugnant, not to Scripture alone, but even to common sense, and reason; overthrows the nature of the sacrament; and has been, and is, the cause of many superstitions; even of gross idolatries.[3]

7. Eligible receivers, outwardly partaking of the visible elements, in this sacrament,[4] do then also, inwardly by faith, really and indeed, yet not carnally and corporally but spiritually, receive, and feed on, Christ crucified, and all benefits of His death: the body and blood of Christ being then, not corporally or carnally, in, with, or under the

---

1 **Mt. 26:26-28.** Now as they were eating, Jesus took bread, and after blessing it broke it and gave it to the disciples, and said, "Take, eat; this is my body." And he took a cup, and when he had given thanks he gave it to them, saying, "Drink of it, all of you, for this is my blood of the covenant, which is poured out for many for the forgiveness of sins."

2 **Mt. 26:29.** "I tell you I will not drink again of this fruit of the vine until that day when I drink it new with you in my Father's kingdom." **1 Cor. 11:26-28.** For as often as you eat this bread and drink the cup, you proclaim the Lord's death until he comes. Whoever, therefore, eats the bread or drinks the cup of the Lord in an unworthy manner will be guilty concerning the body and blood of the Lord. Let a person examine himself, then, and so eat of the bread and drink of the cup.

3 **Lk. 24:6, 39.** He is not here, but has risen. Remember how he told you, while he was still in Galilee... "See my hands and my feet, that it is I myself. Touch me, and see. For a spirit does not have flesh and bones as you see that I have." **Acts 3:21.** ...whom heaven must receive until the time for restoring all the things about which God spoke by the mouth of his holy prophets long ago. **1 Cor. 11:24-26.** ...and when he had given thanks, he broke it, and said, "This is my body which is for you. Do this in remembrance of me." In the same way also he took the cup, after supper, saying, "This cup is the new covenant in my blood. Do this, as often as you drink it, in remembrance of me." For as often as you eat this bread and drink the cup, you proclaim the Lord's death until he comes.

4 **1 Cor. 11:28.** Let a person examine himself, then, and so eat of the bread and drink of the cup.

bread and wine; yet, as really, but spiritually, present to the faith of believers in that ordinance, as the elements themselves are to their outward senses.[1]

8. Although ignorant and wicked men receive the outward elements in this sacrament; yet, they receive not the thing signified thereby; but, by their ineligible partaking, are guilty of the body of the Lord, to their own damnation. Wherefore, all ignorant and ungodly persons, as they are unfit to enjoy communion with Him, so are they ineligible for the Lord's table; and cannot, without great sin against Christ, while they remain such, partake of these holy mysteries,[2] or be admitted to them.[3]

---

1 **1 Cor. 10:16**. The cup of blessing that we bless, is it not a participation in the blood of Christ? The bread that we break, is it not a participation in the body of Christ?

2 **1 Cor. 11:27-29**. Whoever, therefore, eats the bread or drinks the cup of the Lord in an unworthy manner will be guilty concerning the body and blood of the Lord. Let a person examine himself, then, and so eat of the bread and drink of the cup. For anyone who eats and drinks without discerning the body eats and drinks judgment on himself. **2 Cor. 6:14, 16**. Do not be unequally yoked with unbelievers. For what partnership has righteousness with lawlessness? Or what fellowship has light with darkness? ... What agreement has the temple of God with idols? For we are the temple of the living God; as God said, "I will make my dwelling among them and walk among them, and I will be their God, and they shall be my people."

3 **Mt. 7:6**. "Do not give dogs what is holy, and do not throw your pearls before pigs, lest they trample them underfoot and turn to attack you." **1 Cor. 5:6-7, 13**. Your boasting is not good. Do you not know that a little leaven leavens the whole lump? Cleanse out the old leaven that you may be a new lump, as you really are unleavened. For Christ, our Passover lamb, has been sacrificed. ... God judges those outside. "Purge the evil person from among you." **2 Thess. 3:6, 14-15**. Now we command you, brothers, in the name of our Lord Jesus Christ, that you keep away from any brother who is walking in idleness and not in accord with the tradition that you received from us. ... If anyone does not obey what we say in this letter, take note of that person, and have nothing to do with him, that he may be ashamed. Do not regard him as an enemy, but warn him as a brother.

CHAPTER 30

OF CHURCH CENSURES.

1. The Lord Jesus, as King and Head of His Church, has in it appointed a government, in the hand of Church officers, distinct from the civil magistrate.[1]
2. To these officers the keys of the kingdom of heaven are committed; by virtue of which, they have power, respectively, to retain, and remit sins; to shut that kingdom against the impenitent, both by the Word, and censures; and to open it to penitent sinners, by the ministry of

---

1 **Isa. 9:6-7**. For to us a child is born, to us a son is given; and the government shall be upon his shoulder, and his name shall be called Wonderful Counselor, Mighty God, Everlasting Father, Prince of Peace. Of the increase of his government and of peace there will be no end, on the throne of David and over his kingdom, to establish it and to uphold it with justice and with righteousness from this time forth and forevermore. The zeal of the LORD of hosts will do this. **Mt. 28:18-20**. And Jesus came and said to them, "All authority in heaven and on earth has been given to me. Go therefore and make disciples of all nations, baptizing them in the name of the Father and of the Son and of the Holy Spirit, teaching them to observe all that I have commanded you. And behold, I am with you always, to the end of the age." **Acts 20:17-18**. Now from Miletus he sent to Ephesus and called the elders of the church to come to him. And when they came to him, he said to them "You yourselves know how I lived among you the whole time from the first day that I set foot in Asia. **1 Cor. 12:28.** And God has appointed in the church first apostles, second prophets, third teachers, then miracles, then gifts of healing, helping, administrating, and various kinds of tongues. **1 Thess. 5:12**. We ask you, brothers, to respect those who labor among you and are over you in the Lord and admonish you, **1 Tim. 5:17**. Let the elders who rule well be considered worthy of double honor, especially those who labor in preaching and teaching. **Heb. 13:7,17,24**. Remember your leaders, those who spoke to you the word of God. Consider the outcome of their way of life, and imitate their faith; Obey your leaders and submit to them, for they are keeping watch over your souls, as those who will have to give an account. Let them do this with joy and not with groaning, for that would be of no advantage to you; Greet all your leaders and all the saints. Those who come from Italy send you greetings.

the Gospel; and by absolution from censures, as occasion shall require.[1]

3. Church censures are necessary, for the reclaiming and gaining of offending brothers, for deterring of others from similar offenses, for purging out of that leaven which might infect the whole lump, for vindicating the honor of Christ, and the holy profession of the Gospel, and for preventing the wrath of God, which might justly fall on the Church, if they should suffer His covenant, and the seals thereof, to be profaned by notorious and obstinate offenders.[2]

---

1 **Mt. 16:19**. I will give you the keys of the kingdom of heaven, and whatever you bind on earth shall be bound in heaven, and whatever you loose on earth shall be loosed in heaven." **Mt. 18:17-18**. If he refuses to listen to them, tell it to the church. And if he refuses to listen even to the church, let him be to you as a Gentile and a tax collector. Truly, I say to you, whatever you bind on earth shall be bound in heaven, and whatever you loose on earth shall be loosed in heaven. **Jn. 20:21-23**. Jesus said to them again, "Peace be with you. As the Father has sent me, even so I am sending you." And when he had said this, he breathed on them and said to them, "Receive the Holy Spirit. If you forgive the sins of any, they are forgiven them; if you withhold forgiveness from any, it is withheld." **2 Cor. 2:6-8.** For such a one, this punishment by the majority is enough, so you should rather turn to forgive and comfort him, or he may be overwhelmed by excessive sorrow. So I beg you to reaffirm your love for him.

2 **Mt. 7:6**. "Do not give dogs what is holy, and do not throw your pearls before pigs, lest they trample them underfoot and turn to attack you. **1 Cor. 5:1-13**. It is actually reported that there is sexual immorality among you, and of a kind that is not tolerated even among pagans, for a man has his father's wife. And you are arrogant! Ought you not rather to mourn? Let him who has done this be removed from among you. For though absent in body, I am present in spirit; and as if present, I have already pronounced judgment on the one who did such a thing. When you are assembled in the name of the Lord Jesus and my spirit is present, with the power of our Lord Jesus, you are to deliver this man to Satan for the destruction of the flesh, so that his spirit may be saved in the day of the Lord. Your boasting is not good. Do you not know that a little leaven leavens the whole lump? Cleanse out the old leaven that you may be a new lump, as you really are unleavened. For Christ, our Passover lamb, has been sacrificed. Let us therefore celebrate the festival, not with the old leaven, the leaven of malice and evil, but with the unleavened bread of sincerity and truth. I wrote to you in my letter not to associate with sexually immoral people—not at all meaning the sexually immoral of this world, or the greedy and swindlers, or idolaters, since then you would need to go out of the world. But now I am writing to you not to associate with anyone who bears the name of brother if he is guilty of sexual immorality or greed, or is an idolater, reviler, drunkard, or swindler—not even to eat with such a one. For what have I to do with judging outsiders? Is it not those inside the church whom you are to judge? God judge those outside. "Purge the evil person from among you." **1 Cor. 11:27**. Whoever, therefore, eats the bread or drinks the cup of the Lord in an unworthy manner will be guilty concerning the body and blood of the Lord. **1 Tim. 1:20**. among whom are Hymenaeus and Alexander, whom I have handed over to Satan that they may learn not to blaspheme. **1 Tim. 5:20**. As for those who persist in sin, rebuke them in the presence of all, so that the rest may stand in fear. **Jude 23**. save others by snatching them out of the fire; to others show mercy with fear, hating even the garment stained by the flesh.

4. For the better attaining of these ends, the officers of the Church are to proceed by admonition, by suspension from the sacrament of the Lord's Supper for a season; and by excommunication from the Church, according to the nature of the crime, and demerit of the person.[1]

1 **Mt. 18:17**. If he refuses to listen to them, tell it to the church. And if he refuses to listen even to the church, let him be to you as a Gentile and a tax collector. **1 Cor. 5:4-5, 13**. When you are assembled in the name of the Lord Jesus and my spirit is present, with the power of our Lord Jesus, you are to deliver this man to Satan for the destruction of the flesh, so that his spirit may be saved in the day of the Lord; God Judge those outside. "Purge the evil person from among you." **1 Thess. 5:12**. We ask you, brothers, to respect those who labor among you and are over you in the Lord and admonish you, **2 Thess. 3:6, 14-15**. Now we command you, brothers, in the name of our Lord Jesus Christ, that you keep away from any brother who is walking in idleness and not in accord with the tradition that you received from us; If anyone does not obey what we say in this letter, take note of that person, and have nothing to do with him, that he may be ashamed. Do not regard him as an enemy, but warn him as a brother. **Titus 3:10**. As for a person who stirs up division, after warning him once and then twice, have nothing more to do with him,

CHAPTER 31

OF SYNODS AND COUNCILS.

1. For the better government, and further edification of the Church, there ought to be such assemblies as are commonly called synods or councils;[1] and it belongs to the overseers and other rulers of the particular churches, by virtue of their office, and the power that Christ has given them for edification and not for destruction, to appoint such assemblies;[2] and to convene together in them, as often as they shall judge it expedient for the good of the Church.[3]
2. It belongs to synods and councils, to determine ministerially controversies of faith, and cases of conscience; to set down rules and directions for the better ordering of the public worship of God, and government of His Church; to receive complaints in cases of improper administration, and to determine authoritatively the same: which decrees and determinations, if consistent with the Word of God, are to be received with reverence and submission; not only for their agreement with the Word, but also for the power by

---

1 **Acts 15:2,4,6.** And after Paul and Barnabas had no small dissension and debate with them, Paul and Barnabas and some of the others were appointed to go up to Jerusalem to the apostles and the elders about this question; When they came to Jerusalem, they were welcomed by the church and the apostles and the elders, and they declared all that God had done with them; The apostles and the elders were gathered together to consider this matter.

2 **Acts 15.** All of Acts 15.

3 **Acts 15:22-23,25.** Then it seemed good to the apostles and the elders, with the whole church, to choose men from among them and send them to Antioch with Paul and Barnabas. They sent Judas called Barsabbas, and Silas, leading men among the brothers, with the following letter: "The brothers, both the apostles and the elders, to the brothers who are of the Gentiles in Antioch and Syria and Cilicia, greetings; it has seemed good to us, having come to one accord, to choose men and send them to you with our beloved Barnabas and Paul,

which they are made, as being an ordinance of God appointed in His Word.[1]

3. All synods or councils, since the apostles' times, whether general or particular, may err; and many have erred. Therefore they are not to be made the rule of faith, or practice; but to be used as a help in both.[2]

4. Synods and councils are to handle, or conclude nothing, but that which is ecclesiastical: and are not to meddle in civil affairs that concern the commonwealth, unless by way of humble petition in extraordinary cases; or, by way of advice, for satisfaction of conscience, if they be required to do so by the civil magistrate.[3]

---

1 **Mt. 18:17-20**. If he refuses to listen to them, tell it to the church. And if he refuses to listen even to the church, let him be to you as a Gentile and a tax collector. Truly, I say to you, whatever you bind on earth shall be bound in heaven, and whatever you loose on earth shall be loosed in heaven. Again I say to you, if two of you agree on earth about anything they ask, it will be done for them by my Father in heaven. For where two or three are gathered in my name, there am I among them." **Acts 15:15,19,24,27-31**. And with this the words of the prophets agree, just as it is written; Therefore my judgment is that we should not trouble those of the Gentiles who turn to God; Since we have heard that some persons have gone out from us and troubled you with words, unsettling your minds, although we gave them no instructions; We have therefore sent Judas and Silas, who themselves will tell you the same things by word of mouth. For it has seemed good to the Holy Spirit and to us to lay on you no greater burden than these requirements: that you abstain from what has been sacrificed to idols, and from blood, and from what has been strangled, and from sexual immorality. If you keep yourselves from these, you will do well. Farewell. "So when they were sent off, they went down to Antioch, and having gathered the congregation together, they delivered the letter. And when they had read it, they rejoiced because of its encouragement. **Acts 16:4**. As they went on their way through the cities, they delivered to them for observance the decisions that had been reached by the apostles and elders who were in Jerusalem.

2 **Acts 17:11**. Now these Jews were more noble than those in Thessalonica; they received the word with all eagerness, examining the Scriptures daily to see if these things were so. **2 Cor. 1:24**. Not that we lord it over your faith, but we work with you for your joy, for you stand firm in your faith. **1 Cor. 2:5**. that your faith might not rest in the wisdom of men but in the power of God. **Eph. 2:20**. built on the foundation of the apostles and prophets, Christ Jesus himself being the cornerstone,

3 **Lk. 12:13-14**. Someone in the crowd said to him, "Teacher, tell my brother to divide the inheritance with me." But he said to him, "Man, who made me a judge or arbitrator over you?" **Jn. 18:36**. Jesus answered, "My kingdom is not of this world. If my kingdom were of this world, my servants would have been fighting, that I might not be delivered over to the Jews. But my kingdom is not from the world."

CHAPTER 32

OF THE STATE OF MEN AFTER DEATH, AND OF THE RESURRECTION OF THE DEAD.

1. The bodies of men, after death, return to dust, and see decay:[1] but their souls, which neither die nor sleep, having an immortal existence, immediately return to God who gave them:[2] the souls of the righteous, being then made perfect in holiness, are received into the highest heavens, where they behold the face of God, in light and glory, waiting for the full redemption of their bodies.[3] And the souls of the wicked are cast into hell, where they remain in torments and

---

1 **Gen. 3:19**. "By the sweat of your face you shall eat bread, till you return to the ground, for out of it you were taken; for you are dust, and to dust you shall return." **Acts 13:36**. For David, after he had served the purpose of God in his own generation, fell asleep and was laid with his fathers and saw corruption.

2 **Eccl. 12:7**. ...and the dust returns to the earth as it was, and the spirit returns to God who gave it. **Lk. 23:43**. And he said to him, "Truly, I say to you, today you will be with me in Paradise."

3 **Acts 3:21**. ...whom heaven must receive until the time for restoring all the things about which God spoke by the mouth of his holy prophets long ago. **2 Cor. 5:1, 6, 8**. For we know that if the tent that is our earthly home is destroyed, we have a building from God, a house not made with hands, eternal in the heavens. ... So we are always of good courage. We know that while we are at home in the body we are away from the Lord. ... Yes, we are of good courage, and we would rather be away from the body and at home with the Lord. **Eph. 4:10**. He who descended is the one who also ascended far above all the heavens, that he might fill all things. **Phil. 1:23**. I am hard pressed between the two. My desire is to depart and be with Christ, for that is far better. **Heb. 12:23**. ...and to the assembly of the firstborn who are enrolled in heaven, and to God, the judge of all, and to the spirits of the righteous made perfect.

utter darkness, reserved to the judgment of the great day.[1] Besides these two places, for souls separated from their bodies, the Scripture acknowledges none.

2. At the last day, such as are found alive shall not die, but be changed:[2] and all the dead shall be raised up, with their own bodies, and none other (although with different qualities), which shall be united again to their souls forever.[3]

3. The bodies of the unjust shall, by the power of Christ, be raised to dishonor: the bodies of the just, by His Spirit, to honor; and be made to conform with His own glorious body.[4]

---

1 **Lk. 16:23-24**. ...and in Hades, being in torment, he lifted up his eyes and saw Abraham far off and Lazarus at his side. And he called out, 'Father Abraham, have mercy on me, and send Lazarus to dip the end of his finger in water and cool my tongue, for I am in anguish in this flame.' **Acts 1:25.** "...to take the place in this ministry and apostleship from which Judas turned aside to go to his own place." **1 Pet. 3:19**. ...in which he went and proclaimed to the spirits in prison. **Jude 6-7**. And the angels who did not stay within their own position of authority, but left their proper dwelling, he has kept in eternal chains under gloomy darkness until the judgment of the great day—just as Sodom and Gomorrah and the surrounding cities, which likewise indulged in sexual immorality and pursued unnatural desire, serve as an example by undergoing a punishment of eternal fire.

2 **1 Cor. 15:51-52**. Listen, I tell you a mystery: We will not all sleep, but we will all be changed—in a flash, in the twinkling of an eye, at the last trumpet. For the trumpet will sound, the dead will be raised imperishable, and we will be changed. **1 Thess. 4:17**. After that, we who are still alive and are left will be caught up together with them in the clouds to meet the Lord in the air. And so we will be with the Lord forever.

3 **Job 19:26-27**. And after my skin has been thus destroyed, yet in my flesh I shall see God, whom I shall see for myself, and my eyes shall behold, and not another. My heart faints within me! **1 Cor. 15:42-44**. So is it with the resurrection of the dead. What is sown is perishable; what is raised is imperishable. It is sown in dishonor; it is raised in glory. It is sown in weakness; it is raised in power. It is sown a natural body; it is raised a spiritual body. If there is a natural body, there is also a spiritual body.

4 **Jn. 5:28-29**. Do not marvel at this, for an hour is coming when all who are in the tombs will hear his voice and come out, those who have done good to the resurrection of life, and those who have done evil to the resurrection of judgment. **Acts 24:15**. ...having a hope in God, which these men themselves accept, that there will be a resurrection of both the just and the unjust. **1 Cor. 15:43**. It is sown in dishonor; it is raised in glory. It is sown in weakness; it is raised in power. **Phil. 3:21**. ...who will transform our lowly body to be like his glorious body, by the power that enables him even to subject all things to himself.

CHAPTER 33

OF THE LAST JUDGMENT.

1. God has appointed a day, on which He will judge the world, in righteousness, by Jesus Christ,[1] to whom all power and judgment are given of the Father.[2] In which day, not only the apostate angels shall be judged,[3] but likewise all persons who have lived on earth shall appear before the tribunal of Christ, to give an account of their thoughts, words, and deeds; and to receive according to what they have done in the body, whether good or evil.[4]
2. The purpose of God's appointing this day is to make known the glory of His mercy, in the eternal salvation of the elect; and of His justice, in the damnation of the reprobate, who are wicked and disobedient. For then shall the righteous go to everlasting life, and

---

1 **Acts 17:31**. "...because he has fixed a day on which he will judge the world in righteousness by a man whom he has appointed; and of this he has given assurance to all by raising him from the dead."

2 **Jn. 5:22, 27**. The Father judges no one, but has given all judgment to the Son... And he has given him authority to execute judgment, because he is the Son of Man.

3 **1 Cor. 6:3**. Do you not know that we are to judge angels? How much more, then, matters pertaining to this life! **2 Pet. 2:4**. For if God did not spare angels when they sinned, but cast them into hell and committed them to chains of gloomy darkness to be kept until the judgment. **Jude 6**. And the angels who did not stay within their own position of authority, but left their proper dwelling, he has kept in eternal chains under gloomy darkness until the judgment of the great day.

4 **Eccl. 12:14**. For God will bring every deed into judgment, with every secret thing, whether good or evil. **Mt. 12:36-37**. "I tell you, on the day of judgment people will give account for every careless word they speak, for by your words you will be justified, and by your words you will be condemned." **Rom. 2:16**. ...on that day when, according to my gospel, God judges the secrets of men by Christ Jesus. **Rom. 14:10, 12**. Why do you pass judgment on your brother? Or you, why do you despise your brother? For we will all stand before the judgment seat of God... So then each of us will give an account of himself to God. **2 Cor. 5:10**. For we must all appear before the judgment seat of Christ, so that each one may receive what is due for what he has done in the body, whether good or evil.

receive that fullness of joy and refreshing, which shall come from the presence of the Lord: but the wicked, who know not God, and obey not the Gospel of Jesus Christ, shall be cast into eternal torments, and be punished with everlasting destruction from the presence of the Lord, and from the glory of His power.[1]

3. As Christ would have us to be certainly convinced that there shall be a day of judgment, both to deter all men from sin; and for the

1 **Mt. 25:21**. His master said to him, 'Well done, good and faithful servant. You have been faithful over a little; I will set you over much. Enter into the joy of your master.' **Mt. 25:31-46**. "When the Son of Man comes in his glory, and all the angels with him, then he will sit on his glorious throne. Before him will be gathered all the nations, and he will separate people one from another as a shepherd separates the sheep from the goats. And he will place the sheep on his right, but the goats on the left. Then the King will say to those on his right, 'Come, you who are blessed by my Father, inherit the kingdom prepared for you from the foundation of the world. For I was hungry and you gave me food, I was thirsty and you gave me drink, I was a stranger and you welcomed me, I was naked and you clothed me, I was sick and you visited me, I was in prison and you came to me.' Then the righteous will answer him, saying, 'Lord, when did we see you hungry and feed you, or thirsty and give you drink? And when did we see you a stranger and welcome you, or naked and clothe you? And when did we see you sick or in prison and visit you?' And the King will answer them, 'Truly, I say to you, as you did it to one of the least of these my brothers, you did it to me.' "Then he will say to those on his left, 'Depart from me, you cursed, into the eternal fire prepared for the devil and his angels. For I was hungry and you gave me no food, I was thirsty and you gave me no drink, I was a stranger and you did not welcome me, naked and you did not clothe me, sick and in prison and you did not visit me.' Then they also will answer, saying, 'Lord, when did we see you hungry or thirsty or a stranger or naked or sick or in prison, and did not minister to you?' Then he will answer them, saying, 'Truly, I say to you, as you did not do it to one of the least of these, you did not do it to me.' And these will go away into eternal punishment, but the righteous into eternal life." **Acts 3:19**. Repent therefore, and turn again, that your sins may be blotted out. **Rom. 2:5-6**. But because of your hard and impenitent heart you are storing up wrath for yourself on the day of wrath when God's righteous judgment will be revealed. He will render to each one according to his works. **Rom. 9:22-23**. What if God, desiring to show his wrath and to make known his power, has endured with much patience vessels of wrath prepared for destruction, in order to make known the riches of his glory for vessels of mercy, which he has prepared beforehand for glory. **2 Thess. 1:7-10**. ...and to grant relief to you who are afflicted as well as to us, when the Lord Jesus is revealed from heaven with his mighty angels in flaming fire, inflicting vengeance on those who do not know God and on those who do not obey the gospel of our Lord Jesus. They will suffer the punishment of eternal destruction, away from the presence of the Lord and from the glory of his might, when he comes on that day to be glorified in his saints, and to be marveled at among all who have believed, because our testimony to you was believed.

greater consolation of the godly in their adversity:[1] so will He have that day unknown to men, that they may shake off all worldly security, and be always watchful, because they know not at what hour the Lord will come; and may be ever prepared to say, Come Lord Jesus, come quickly. Amen.[2]

---

1 **Lk. 21:27-28. Rom. 8:23-25.** And not only the creation, but we ourselves, who have the firstfruits of the Spirit, groan inwardly as we wait eagerly for adoption as sons, the redemption of our bodies. For in this hope we were saved. Now hope that is seen is not hope. For who hopes for what he sees? But if we hope for what we do not see, we wait for it with patience. **2 Cor. 5:10-11.** For we must all appear before the judgment seat of Christ, so that each one may receive what is due for what he has done in the body, whether good or evil. Therefore, knowing the fear of the Lord, we persuade others. But what we are is known to God, and I hope it is known also to your conscience. **2 Thess. 1:5-7.** This is evidence of the righteous judgment of God, that you may be considered worthy of the kingdom of God, for which you are also suffering—since indeed God considers it just to repay with affliction those who afflict you, and to grant relief to you who are afflicted as well as to us, when the Lord Jesus is revealed from heaven with his mighty angels. **2 Pet. 3:11, 14.** Since all these things are thus to be dissolved, what sort of people ought you to be in lives of holiness and godliness... Therefore, beloved, since you are waiting for these, be diligent to be found by him without spot or blemish, and at peace.

2 **Mt. 24:36, 42-44.** "But concerning that day and hour no one knows, not even the angels of heaven, nor the Son, but the Father only. ... Therefore, stay awake, for you do not know on what day your Lord is coming. But know this, that if the master of the house had known in what part of the night the thief was coming, he would have stayed awake and would not have let his house be broken into. Therefore you also must be ready, for the Son of Man is coming at an hour you do not expect." **Mk. 13:35-37.** "Therefore stay awake—for you do not know when the master of the house will come, in the evening, or at midnight, or when the rooster crows, or in the morning—lest he come suddenly and find you asleep. And what I say to you I say to all: Stay awake." **Lk. 12:35-36.** "Stay dressed for action and keep your lamps burning, and be like men who are waiting for their master to come home from the wedding feast, so that they may open the door to him at once when he comes and knocks." **Rev. 22:20.** He who testifies to these things says, "Surely I am coming soon." Amen. Come, Lord Jesus!

The Westminster Larger Catechism

The view of the West Front of Westminster Abbey is one of the best known in the world. The gothic lower part was completed in the fifteenth century; the towers, designed by Nicholas Hawksmoor in a more classical stye, were added at the beginning of the eighteenth century.

Q. 1. What is the chief and highest end of man?

A. Man's chief and highest end is to glorify God,[1] and fully to enjoy Him forever.[2]

1 **Rom. 11.36.** For from him and through him and to him are all things. To him be glory forever. Amen. **1 Cor. 10:31.** So, whether you eat or drink, or whatever you do, do all to the glory of God.

2 **Ps. 73: 24-28.** You guide me with your counsel, and afterward you will receive me to glory. Whom have I in heaven but you? And there is nothing on earth that I desire besides you. My flesh and my heart may fail, but God is the strength of my heart and my portion forever. For behold, those who are far from you shall perish; you put an end to everyone who is unfaithful to you. But for me it is good to be near God; I have made the Lord GOD my refuge, that I may tell of all your works. **Jn. 17:21-23.** ...that they may all be one, just as you, Father, are in me, and I in you, that they also may be in us, so that the world may believe that you have sent me. The glory that you have given me I have given to them, that they may be one even as we are one, I in them and you in me, that they may become perfectly one, so that the world may know that you sent me and loved them even as you loved me.

Q. 2. How does it appear that there is a God?

A. The very light of nature in man, and the works of God, declare plainly that there is a God;[1] but his Word and Spirit only, do sufficiently and effectually reveal Him to men for their salvation.[2]

1 **Ps. 19:1-3.** The heavens declare the glory of God, and the sky above proclaims his handiwork. Day to day pours out speech, and night to night reveals knowledge. There is no speech, nor are there words, whose voice is not heard. **Acts 17:28.** ... for "'In him we live and move and have our being'; as even some of your own poets have said, 'For we are indeed his offspring.'" **Rom. 1:19-20.** For what can be known about God is plain to them, because God has shown it to them. For his invisible attributes, namely, his eternal power and divine nature, have been clearly perceived, ever since the creation of the world, in the things that have been made. So they are without excuse.

2 **Isa. 59:21.** "And as for me, this is my covenant with them," says the LORD: "My Spirit that is upon you, and my words that I have put in your mouth, shall not depart out of your mouth, or out of the mouth of your offspring, or out of the mouth of your children's offspring," says the LORD, "from this time forth and forevermore." **1 Cor. 2:9-10.** But, as it is written, "What no eye has seen, nor ear heard, nor the heart of man imagined, what God has prepared for those who love him"— these things God has revealed to us through the Spirit. For the Spirit searches everything, even the depths of God. **2 Tim. 3:15-17.** ...and how from childhood you have been acquainted with the sacred writings, which are able to make you wise for salvation through faith in Christ Jesus. All Scripture is breathed out by God and profitable for teaching, for reproof, for correction, and for training in righteousness, that the man of God may be complete, equipped for every good work.

Q. 3. What is the Word of God?

A. The holy Scriptures of the Old and New Testaments are the Word of God,[1] the only rule of faith and obedience.[2]

1 **2 Tim. 3:16.** All Scripture is breathed out by God and profitable for teaching, for reproof, for correction, and for training in righteousness. **2 Pet. 1:19-21.** And we have the prophetic word more fully confirmed, to which you will do well to pay attention as to a lamp shining in a dark place, until the day dawns and the morning star rises in your hearts, knowing this first of all, that no prophecy of Scripture comes from someone's own interpretation. For no prophecy was ever produced by the will of man, but men spoke from God as they were carried along by the Holy Spirit.

2 **Isa. 8:20.** To the teaching and to the testimony! If they will not speak according to this word, it is because they have no dawn. But Abraham said, 'They have Moses and the Prophets; let them hear them.' ... He said to him, 'If they do not hear Moses and the Prophets, neither will they be convinced if someone should rise from the dead.' **Gal. 1:8-9.** But even if we or an angel from heaven should preach to you a gospel contrary to the one we preached to you, let him be accursed. As we have said before, so now I say again: If anyone is preaching to you a gospel contrary to the one you received, let him be accursed. **Eph. 2:20.** ...built on the foundation of the apostles and prophets, Christ Jesus himself being the cornerstone. **2 Tim. 3:15-16.** ...and how from childhood you have been acquainted with the sacred writings, which are able to make you wise for salvation through faith in Christ Jesus. All Scripture is breathed out by God and profitable for teaching, for reproof, for correction, and for training in righteousness. **Rev. 22:18-19.** I warn everyone who hears the words of the prophecy of this book: if anyone adds to them, God will add to him the plagues described in this book, and if anyone takes away from the words of the book of this prophecy, God will take away his share in the tree of life and in the holy city, which are described in this book.

Q. 4. How does it appear that the Scriptures are the Word of God?

A. The Scriptures show themselves to be the Word of God, by their majesty[1] and purity;[2] by the unity of all the parts,[3] and the scope of the whole, which is to give all glory to God;[4] by their light and power to convince and convert sinners, to comfort and build up believers toward salvation.[5] But the Spirit of God, bearing witness by and with the Scriptures in the heart of man, is alone able to convince it fully that they are the very Word of God.[6]

1 **Ps. 119:18, 129.** Open my eyes, that I may behold wondrous things out of your law. ... Your testimonies are wonderful; therefore my soul keeps them. **Hos. 8:12.** Were I to write for him my laws by the ten thousands, they would be regarded as a strange thing. **1 Cor. 2:6-7, 13.** Yet among the mature we do impart wisdom, although it is not a wisdom of this age or of the rulers of this age, who are doomed to pass away. But we impart a secret and hidden wisdom of God, which God decreed before the ages for our glory. ... And we impart this in words not taught by human wisdom but taught by the Spirit, interpreting spiritual truths to those who are spiritual.

2 **Ps. 12:6.** The words of the LORD are pure words, like silver refined in a furnace on the ground, purified seven times. **Ps. 119:140.** Your promise is well tried, and your servant loves it.

3 **Acts 10:43.** To him all the prophets bear witness that everyone who believes in him receives forgiveness of sins through his name. **Acts 26:22.** To this day I have had the help that comes from God, and so I stand here testifying both to small and great, saying nothing but what the prophets and Moses said would come to pass.

4 **Rom. 3:19, 27.** Now we know that whatever the law says it speaks to those who are under the law, so that every mouth may be stopped, and the whole world may be held accountable to God. ... Then what becomes of our boasting? It is excluded. By what kind of law? By a law of works? No, but by the law of faith.

5 **Ps. 19:7-9.** The law of the LORD is perfect, reviving the soul; the testimony of the LORD is sure, making wise the simple; the precepts of the LORD are right, rejoicing the heart; the commandment of the LORD is pure, enlightening the eyes; the fear of the LORD is clean, enduring forever; the rules of the LORD are true, and righteous altogether. **Acts 18:28.** ...for he powerfully refuted the Jews in public, showing by the Scriptures that the Christ was Jesus. **Acts 20:32.** And now I commend you to God and to the word of his grace, which is able to build you up and to give you the inheritance among all those who are sanctified. **Rom. 15:4.** For whatever was written in former days was written for our instruction, that through endurance and through the encouragement of the Scriptures we might have hope. **Jas. 1:18.** Of his own will he brought us forth by the word of truth, that we should be a kind of firstfruits of his creatures.

6 **Jn. 16:13-14.** When the Spirit of truth comes, he will guide you into all the truth, for he will not speak on his own authority, but whatever he hears he will speak, and he will declare to you the things that are to come. He will glorify me, for he will take what is mine and declare it to you. **Jn. 20:31.** ...but these are written so that you may believe that Jesus is the Christ, the Son of God, and that by believing you may have life in his name. **1 Jn. 2:20, 27.** But you have been anointed by the Holy One, and you all have knowledge. ... But the anointing that you received from him abides in you, and you have no need that anyone should teach you. But as his anointing teaches you about everything, and is true, and is no lie—just as it has taught you, abide in him.

Q. 5. What do the Scriptures principally teach?

A. The Scriptures principally teach, what man is to believe concerning God, and what duty God requires of man.[1]

1 **2 Tim. 1:13.** Follow the pattern of the sound words that you have heard from me, in the faith and love that are in Christ Jesus.

WHAT MAN OUGHT TO BELIEVE CONCERNING GOD

Q. 6. What do the Scriptures make known of God?

A. The Scriptures make known what God is,[1] the persons in the Godhead,[2] his decrees,[3] and the execution of his decrees.[4]

1 **Heb. 11:6.** And without faith it is impossible to please him, for whoever would draw near to God must believe that he exists and that he rewards those who seek him.

2 **Mt. 28:19-20.** "Go therefore and make disciples of all nations, baptizing them in the name of the Father and of the Son and of the Holy Spirit, teaching them to observe all that I have commanded you. And behold, I am with you always, to the end of the age." **Mt. 3:16-17.** And when Jesus was baptized, immediately he went up from the water, and behold, the heavens were opened to him, and he saw the Spirit of God descending like a dove and coming to rest on him; and behold, a voice from heaven said, "This is my beloved Son, with whom I am well pleased."

3 **Acts 15:14-15, 18.** Simeon has related how God first visited the Gentiles, to take from them a people for his name. And with this the words of the prophets agree, just as it is written. ...known from of old.

4 **Acts 4:27-28.** ...for truly in this city there were gathered together against your holy servant Jesus, whom you anointed, both Herod and Pontius Pilate, along with the Gentiles and the peoples of Israel, to do whatever your hand and your plan had predestined to take place.

Q. 7. What is God?

A. God is a Spirit,[1] in and of Himself infinite in being,[2] glory,[3] blessedness,[4] and perfection;[5] all-sufficient,[6] eternal,[7] unchangeable,[8] incomprehensible,[9] everywhere present,[10] almighty;[11] knowing all things,[12] most wise,[13] most holy,[14] most just,[15] most merciful and gracious, long-suffering, and abundant in goodness and truth.[16]

1 **Jn. 4:24.** "God is spirit, and those who worship him must worship in spirit and truth."

2 **Ex. 3:14.** God said to Moses, "I AM WHO I AM." And he said, "Say this to the people of Israel, 'I AM has sent me to you.'" **Job 11:7-9.** "Can you find out the deep things of God? Can you find out the limit of the Almighty? It is higher than heaven—what can you do? Deeper than Sheol—what can you know? Its measure is longer than the earth and broader than the sea."

3 **Acts 7:2.** "Brothers and fathers, hear me. The God of glory appeared to our father Abraham when he was in Mesopotamia, before he lived in Haran."

4 **1 Tim. 6:15.** ...which he will display at the proper time—he who is the blessed and only Sovereign, the King of kings and Lord of lords."

5 **Mt. 5:48.** You therefore must be perfect, as your heavenly Father is perfect.

6 **Gen. 17:1.** When Abram was ninety-nine years old the LORD appeared to Abram and said to him, "I am God Almighty; walk before me, and be blameless."

7 **Ps. 90:2.** Before the mountains were brought forth, or ever you had formed the earth and the world, from everlasting to everlasting you are God.

8 **Mal. 3:6.** "For I the LORD do not change; therefore you, O children of Jacob, are not consumed.

9 **1 Kings 8:27.** "But will God indeed dwell on the earth? Behold, heaven and the highest heaven cannot contain you; how much less this house that I have built!"

10 **Ps. 139:1-13.** O LORD, you have searched me and known me! You know when I sit down and when I rise up; you discern my thoughts from afar. You search out my path and my lying down and are acquainted with all my ways. Even before a word is on my tongue, behold, O LORD, you know it altogether. You hem me in, behind and before, and lay your hand upon me. Such knowledge is too wonderful for me; it is high; I cannot attain it. Where shall I go from your Spirit? Or where shall I flee from your presence? If I ascend to heaven, you are there! If I make my bed in Sheol, you are there! If I take the wings of the morning and dwell in the uttermost parts of the sea, even there your hand shall lead me, and your right hand shall hold me. If I say, "Surely the darkness shall cover me, and the light about me be night," even the darkness is not dark to you; the night is bright as the day, for darkness is as light with you. For you formed my inward parts; you knitted me together in my mother's womb.

11 **Rev. 4:8.** And the four living creatures, each of them with six wings, are full of eyes all around and within, and day and night they never cease to say, "Holy, holy, holy, is the Lord God Almighty, who was and is and is to come!"

12 **Ps. 147:5.** Great is our Lord, and abundant in power; his understanding is beyond measure. **Heb. 4:13.** And no creature is hidden from his sight, but all are naked and exposed to the eyes of him to whom we must give account.

13 **Rom. 16:27.** ...to the only wise God be glory forevermore through Jesus Christ! Amen.

14 **Isa. 6:3.** And one called to another and said: "Holy, holy, holy is the LORD of hosts; the whole earth is full of his glory!"

15 **Deut. 32:4.** "The Rock, his work is perfect, for all his ways are justice. A God of faithfulness and without iniquity, just and upright is he."

16 **Ex. 34:6.** The LORD passed before him and proclaimed, "The LORD, the LORD, a God merciful and gracious, slow to anger, and abounding in steadfast love and faithfulness."

Q. 8. Are there more Gods than one?

A. There is but one only, the living and true God.[1]

1 **Deut. 6:4.** "Hear, O Israel: The LORD our God, the LORD is one." **Jer. 10:10.** But the LORD is the true God; he is the living God and the everlasting King. At his wrath the earth quakes, and the nations cannot endure his indignation.
1 Cor. 8:4, 6 Therefore, as to the eating of food offered to idols, we know that "an idol has no real existence," and that "there is no God but one." ...yet for us there is one God, the Father, from whom are all things and for whom we exist, and one Lord, Jesus Christ, through whom are all things and through whom we exist.

Q. 9. How many persons are there in the Godhead?

A. There are three persons in the Godhead: the Father, the Son, and the Holy Spirit; and these three are one true, eternal God, the same in substance, equal in power and glory; although distinguished by their personal properties.[1]

1 **Mt. 3:16-17**. And when Jesus was baptized, immediately he went up from the water, and behold, the heavens were opened to him, and he saw the Spirit of God descending like a dove and coming to rest on him; and behold, a voice from heaven said, "This is my beloved Son, with whom I am well pleased." **Mt. 28:19.** Go therefore and make disciples of all nations, baptizing them in the name of the Father and of the Son and of the Holy Spirit. **Jn. 10:30**. "I and the Father are one." **2 Cor. 13:14**. The grace of the Lord Jesus Christ and the love of God and the fellowship of the Holy Spirit be with you all. **1 Jn. 5:7.** For there are three that testify.

Q. 10. What are the personal properties of the three persons in the Godhead?

A. It is the property of the Father to beget His Son,[1] and of the Son to be begotten of the Father,[2] and of the Holy Spirit to proceed from the Father and the Son, from all eternity.[3]

1 **Heb. 1:5-6, 8**. For to which of the angels did God ever say, "You are my Son, today I have begotten you"? Or again, "I will be to him a father, and he shall be to me a son"? And again, when he brings the firstborn into the world, he says, "Let all God's angels worship him." ... But of the Son he says, "Your throne, O God, is forever and ever, the scepter of uprightness is the scepter of your kingdom.

2 **Jn. 1:14, 18**. And the Word became flesh and dwelt among us, and we have seen his glory, glory as of the only Son from the Father, full of grace and truth. ... No one has ever seen God; the only God, who is at the Father's side, he has made him known.

3 **Jn. 15:26**. "But when the Helper comes, whom I will send to you from the Father, the Spirit of truth, who proceeds from the Father, he will bear witness about me." **Gal. 4:6**. And because you are sons, God has sent the Spirit of his Son into our hearts, crying, "Abba! Father!"

Q. 11. How does it appear that the Son and the Holy Spirit are equal with the Father?

A. The Scriptures show that the Son and the Holy Spirit are God equal with the Father, ascribing to them such names,[1] attributes,[2] works,[3] and worship,[4] as are proper to God only.

1 **Isa. 6:3, 5, 8**. And one called to another and said: "Holy, holy, holy is the LORD of hosts; the whole earth is full of his glory!" ... And I said: "Woe is me! For I am

lost; for I am a man of unclean lips, and I dwell in the midst of a people of unclean lips; for my eyes have seen the King, the LORD of hosts!" ... And I heard the voice of the Lord saying, "Whom shall I send, and who will go for us?" Then I said, "Here I am! Send me." **JN. 12:41**. Isaiah said these things because he saw his glory and spoke of him. **ACTS 5:3-4**. But Peter said, "Ananias, why has Satan filled your heart to lie to the Holy Spirit and to keep back for yourself part of the proceeds of the land? While it remained unsold, did it not remain your own? And after it was sold, was it not at your disposal? Why is it that you have contrived this deed in your heart? You have not lied to man but to God." **ACTS 28:25**. And disagreeing among themselves, they departed after Paul had made one statement: "The Holy Spirit was right in saying to your fathers through Isaiah the prophet." **1 JN. 5:20**. And we know that the Son of God has come and has given us understanding, so that we may know him who is true; and we are in him who is true, in his Son Jesus Christ. He is the true God and eternal life.

2 **ISA. 9:6**. For to us a child is born, to us a son is given; and the government shall be upon his shoulder, and his name shall be called Wonderful Counselor, Mighty God, Everlasting Father, Prince of Peace. **JN. 1:1.** In the beginning was the Word, and the Word was with God, and the Word was God. **JN. 2:24-25**. But Jesus on his part did not entrust himself to them, because he knew all people and needed no one to bear witness about man, for he himself knew what was in man. **1 COR. 2:10-11**. ...these things God has revealed to us through the Spirit. For the Spirit searches everything, even the depths of God. For who knows a person's thoughts except the spirit of that person, which is in him? So also no one comprehends the thoughts of God except the Spirit of God.

3 **GEN. 1:2**. The earth was without form and void, and darkness was over the face of the deep. And the Spirit of God was hovering over the face of the waters. **COL. 1:16**. For by him all things were created, in heaven and on earth, visible and invisible, whether thrones or dominions or rulers or authorities—all things were created through him and for him.

4 **MATT. 28:19**. Go therefore and make disciples of all nations, baptizing them in the name of the Father and of the Son and of the Holy Spirit. **2 COR. 13:14.** The grace of the Lord Jesus Christ and the love of God and the fellowship of the Holy Spirit be with you all.

Q. 12. What are the decrees of God?

A. God's decrees are the wise, free, and holy acts of the counsel of His will,[1] whereby, from all eternity, He has, for his own glory, unchangeably foreordained whatever comes to pass in time,[2] especially concerning angels and men.

1 **ROM. 9:14-15, 18**. What shall we say then? Is there injustice on God's part? By no means! For he says to Moses, "I will have mercy on whom I have mercy, and I will have compassion on whom I have compassion."... So then he has mercy on whomever he wills, and he hardens whomever he wills. **ROM. 11:33**. Oh, the depth of the riches and wisdom and knowledge of God! How unsearchable are his judgments and how inscrutable his ways! **EPH. 1:11**. In him we have obtained an inheritance, having been predestined according to the purpose of him who works all things according to the counsel of his will.

2 **Ps. 33:11**. The counsel of the LORD stands forever, the plans of his heart to all generations. **Rom. 9:22-23**. What if God, desiring to show his wrath and to make known his power, has endured with much patience vessels of wrath prepared for destruction, in order to make known the riches of his glory for vessels of mercy, which he has prepared beforehand for glory. **Eph. 1:4, 11**. ...even as he chose us in him before the foundation of the world, that we should be holy and blameless before him. In love... In him we have obtained an inheritance, having been predestined according to the purpose of him who works all things according to the counsel of his will.

Q. 13. What has God especially decreed concerning angels and men?

A. God, by an eternal and unchangeable decree, out of His mere love, for the praise of His glorious grace, to be made known at the appropriate time, has elected some angels to glory;[1] and, in Christ, has chosen some men to eternal life, and the means for this;[2] and also, according to His sovereign power, and the unsearchable counsel of His own will (with which he extends or withholds favor as he pleases), has passed by, and foreordained the rest to dishonor and wrath, to be inflicted because of their sin, to the praise of the glory of His justice.[3]

1 **1 Tim. 5:21**. In the presence of God and of Christ Jesus and of the elect angels I charge you to keep these rules without prejudging, doing nothing from partiality.

2 **Eph. 1:4-6**. ...even as he chose us in him before the foundation of the world, that we should be holy and blameless before him. In love he predestined us for adoption as sons through Jesus Christ, according to the purpose of his will, to the praise of his glorious grace, with which he has blessed us in the Beloved. **2 Thess. 2:13-14**. But we ought always to give thanks to God for you, brothers beloved by the Lord, because God chose you as the firstfruits to be saved, through sanctification by the Spirit and belief in the truth. To this he called you through our gospel, so that you may obtain the glory of our Lord Jesus Christ.

3 **Mt. 11:25-26.** At that time Jesus declared, "I thank you, Father, Lord of heaven and earth, that you have hidden these things from the wise and understanding and revealed them to little children; yes, Father, for such was your gracious will. **Rom. 9:17-18, 21-22**. For the Scripture says to Pharaoh, "For this very purpose I have raised you up, that I might show my power in you, and that my name might be proclaimed in all the earth." So then he has mercy on whomever he wills, and he hardens whomever he wills. ... Has the potter no right over the clay, to make out of the same lump one vessel for honorable use and another for dishonorable use? What if God, desiring to show his wrath and to make known his power, has endured with much patience vessels of wrath prepared for destruction. **2 Tim. 2:20**. Now in a great house there are not only vessels of gold and silver but also of wood and clay, some for honorable use, some for dishonorable. **1 Pet. 2:8**. ...and "A stone of stumbling, and a rock of offense." They stumble because they disobey the word, as they were destined to do. **Jude 4**. For certain people have crept in unnoticed who long ago were designated for this condemnation, ungodly people, who pervert the grace of our God into sensuality and deny our only Master and Lord, Jesus Christ.

Q. 14. How does God execute his decrees?

A. God executes His decrees in the works of creation and providence, according to His infallible foreknowledge, and the free and unchangeable counsel of His own will.[1]

1 **Eph. 1:11.** In him we have obtained an inheritance, having been predestined according to the purpose of him who works all things according to the counsel of his will.

Q. 15. What is the work of creation?

A. The work of creation is that in which God did in the beginning, by the word of his power, make of nothing, the world and all things therein, for Himself, within the space of six days, and all very good.[1]

1 See **Gen. 1. Prov. 16:4**. The LORD has made everything for its purpose, even the wicked for the day of trouble. **Heb. 11:3**. By faith we understand that the universe was created by the word of God, so that what is seen was not made out of things that are visible.

Q. 16. How did God create angels?

A. God created all the angels[1] as spirits,[2] immortal,[3] holy, excelling in knowledge,[4] mighty in power;[5] to execute His commandments, and to praise His name,[6] yet subject to change.[7]

1 **Col. 1:16.** For by him all things were created, in heaven and on earth, visible and invisible, whether thrones or dominions or rulers or authorities—all things were created through him and for him.

2 **Ps. 104:4**. ...he makes his messengers winds, his ministers a flaming fire.

3 **Mt. 22:30**. For in the resurrection they neither marry nor are given in marriage, but are like angels in heaven.

4 **2 Sam. 14:17.** And your servant thought, 'The word of my lord the king will set me at rest,' for my lord the king is like the angel of God to discern good and evil. The LORD your God be with you!" **Mt. 24:36**. "But concerning that day and hour no one knows, not even the angels of heaven, nor the Son, but the Father only.

5 **2 Thess. 1:7**. ...and to grant relief to you who are afflicted as well as to us, when the Lord Jesus is revealed from heaven with his mighty angels.

6 **Ps. 103:20-21**. Bless the LORD, O you his angels, you mighty ones who do his word, obeying the voice of his word! Bless the LORD, all his hosts, his ministers, who do his will!

7 **2 Pet. 2:4**. For if God did not spare angels when they sinned, but cast them into hell and committed them to chains of gloomy darkness to be kept until the judgment.

Q. 17. How did God create man?

A. After God had made all other creatures, He created man, male and female;[1] formed the body of the man of the dust of the ground,[2] and the woman of the rib of man,[3] endued them with living, reasonable, and immortal souls;[4] made them after His own image,[5] in knowledge,[6] righteousness, and holiness,[7] having the law of God written in their hearts,[8] and power to fulfill it,[9] with dominion over the creatures;[10] yet subject to fall.[11]

1 **Gen. 1:27**. So God created man in his own image, in the image of God he created him; male and female he created them.

2 **Gen. 2:7**. ...then the LORD God formed the man of dust from the ground and breathed into his nostrils the breath of life, and the man became a living creature.

3 **Gen 2:22**. And the rib that the LORD God had taken from the man he made into a woman and brought her to the man.

4 **Gen 2:7**. ...then the LORD God formed the man of dust from the ground and breathed into his nostrils the breath of life, and the man became a living creature. **Job 35:11**. '...who teaches us more than the beasts of the earth and makes us wiser than the birds of the heavens?' **Eccl. 12:7**. ...and the dust returns to the earth as it was, and the spirit returns to God who gave it. **Mt. 10:28**. And do not fear those who kill the body but cannot kill the soul. Rather fear him who can destroy both soul and body in hell. **Lk 23:43**. And he said to him, "Truly, I say to you, today you will be with me in Paradise."

5 **Gen. 1:27**. So God created man in his own image, in the image of God he created him; male and female he created them.

6 **Col. 3:10**. ...and have put on the new self, which is being renewed in knowledge after the image of its creator.

7 **Eph. 4:24**. ...and to put on the new self, created after the likeness of God in true righteousness and holiness.

8 **Rom. 2:14-15**. For when Gentiles, who do not have the law, by nature do what the law requires, they are a law to themselves, even though they do not have the law. They show that the work of the law is written on their hearts, while their conscience also bears witness, and their conflicting thoughts accuse or even excuse them.

9 **Eccl. 7:29**. See, this alone I found, that God made man upright, but they have sought out many schemes.

10 **Gen. 1:28**. And God blessed them. And God said to them, "Be fruitful and multiply and fill the earth and subdue it, and have dominion over the fish of the sea and over the birds of the heavens and over every living thing that moves on the earth."

11 **Gen. 3:6**. So when the woman saw that the tree was good for food, and that it was a delight to the eyes, and that the tree was to be desired to make one wise, she took of its fruit and ate, and she also gave some to her husband who was with her, and he ate. **Eccl. 7:29**. See, this alone I found, that God made man upright, but they have sought out many schemes.

Q. 18. What are God's works of providence?

A. God's works of providence are His most holy,[1] wise,[2] and powerful preserving[3] and governing[4] all his creatures; using them, and all their actions,[5] to His own glory.[6]

1 **Ps. 145:17**. The LORD is righteous in all his ways and kind in all his works.

2 **Ps. 104:24**. O LORD, how manifold are your works! In wisdom have you made them all; the earth is full of your creatures.

3 **Heb. 1:3**. He is the radiance of the glory of God and the exact imprint of his nature, and he upholds the universe by the word of his power. After making purification for sins, he sat down at the right hand of the Majesty on high.

4 **Ps. 103:19**. The LORD has established his throne in the heavens, and his kingdom rules over all.

5 **Gen. 45:7**. And God sent me before you to preserve for you a remnant on earth, and to keep alive for you many survivors. **Mt. 10:29-31**. Are not two sparrows sold for a penny? And not one of them will fall to the ground apart from your Father. But even the hairs of your head are all numbered. Fear not, therefore; you are of more value than many sparrows.

6 **Isa. 63:14**. Like livestock that go down into the valley, the Spirit of the LORD gave them rest. So you led your people, to make for yourself a glorious name. **Rom. 11:36**. For from him and through him and to him are all things. To him be glory forever. Amen.

Q. 19. What is God's providence toward the angels?

A. God by his providence permitted some of the angels, willfully and irreversibly, to fall into sin and damnation,[1] limiting and using that, and all their sins, to His own glory;[2] and established the rest in holiness and happiness;[3] employing them all,[4] at His pleasure, in the administration of His power, mercy, and justice.[5]

1 **Jn. 8:44**. You are of your father the devil, and your will is to do your father's desires. He was a murderer from the beginning, and does not stand in the truth, because there is no truth in him. When he lies, he speaks out of his own character, for he is a liar and the father of lies. **Heb. 2:16**. For surely it is not angels that he helps, but he helps the offspring of Abraham. **2 Pet. 2:4**. For if God did not spare angels when they sinned, but cast them into hell and committed them to chains of gloomy darkness to be kept until the judgment. **Jude 6**. And the angels who did not stay within their own position of authority, but left their proper dwelling, he has kept in eternal chains under gloomy darkness until the judgment of the great day.

2 **Job 1:12**. And the LORD said to Satan, "Behold, all that he has is in your hand. Only against him do not stretch out your hand." So Satan went out from the presence of the LORD. **Mt. 8:31**. And the demons begged him, saying, "If you cast us out, send us away into the herd of pigs."

3 **Mk 8:38**. "For whoever is ashamed of me and of my words in this adulterous and sinful generation, of him will the Son of Man also be ashamed when he comes in

the glory of his Father with the holy angels." **1 Tim. 5:21**. In the presence of God and of Christ Jesus and of the elect angels I charge you to keep these rules without prejudging, doing nothing from partiality. **Heb. 12:22**. But you have come to Mount Zion and to the city of the living God, the heavenly Jerusalem, and to innumerable angels in festal gathering.

4 **Ps. 104:4**. ...he makes his messengers winds, his ministers a flaming fire.

5 **2 Kings 19:35**. And that night the angel of the LORD went out and struck down 185,000 in the camp of the Assyrians. And when people arose early in the morning, behold, these were all dead bodies. **Heb. 1:14**. Are they not all ministering spirits sent out to serve for the sake of those who are to inherit salvation?

Q. 20. What was the providence of God toward man in the estate in which he was created?

A. The providence of God toward man in the estate in which he was created was, the placing of him in paradise, appointing him to take care of it, giving him liberty to eat of the fruit of the earth,[1] putting the creatures under his dominion,[2] ordaining marriage for his help,[3] affording him communion with Himself,[4] and instituting the Sabbath;[5] entering into a covenant of life with him, upon condition of personal, perfect, and perpetual obedience,[6] of which the Tree of Life was a pledge;[7] and forbidding him to eat of the Tree of the Knowledge of Good and Evil, on pain of death.[8]

1 **Gen. 2:8, 15-16**. And the LORD God planted a garden in Eden, in the east, and there he put the man whom he had formed. ... The LORD God took the man and put him in the garden of Eden to work it and keep it. And the LORD God commanded the man, saying, "You may surely eat of every tree of the garden."

2 **Gen. 1:28**. And God blessed them. And God said to them, "Be fruitful and multiply and fill the earth and subdue it, and have dominion over the fish of the sea and over the birds of the heavens and over every living thing that moves on the earth."

3 **Gen. 2:18**. Then the LORD God said, "It is not good that the man should be alone; I will make him a helper fit for him."

4 **Gen. 1:26-29**. Then God said, "Let us make man in our image, after our likeness. And let them have dominion over the fish of the sea and over the birds of the heavens and over the livestock and over all the earth and over every creeping thing that creeps on the earth." So God created man in his own image, in the image of God he created him; male and female he created them. And God blessed them. And God said to them, "Be fruitful and multiply and fill the earth and subdue it, and have dominion over the fish of the sea and over the birds of the heavens and over every living thing that moves on the earth." And God said, "Behold, I have given you every plant yielding seed that is on the face of all the earth, and every tree with seed in its fruit. You shall have them for food." **Gen. 3:8**. And they heard the sound of the LORD God walking in the garden in the cool of the day, and the man and his wife hid themselves from the presence of the LORD God among the trees of the garden.

5 **Gen. 2:3**. So God blessed the seventh day and made it holy, because on it God rested from all his work that he had done in creation.

6 **Rom. 10:5.** For Moses writes about the righteousness that is based on the law, that the person who does the commandments shall live by them. **Gal. 3:12.** But the law is not of faith, rather "The one who does them shall live by them."

7 **Gen. 2:9.** And out of the ground the LORD God made to spring up every tree that is pleasant to the sight and good for food. The tree of life was in the midst of the garden, and the tree of the knowledge of good and evil.

8 **Gen. 2:17.** "...but of the tree of the knowledge of good and evil you shall not eat, for in the day that you eat of it you shall surely die."

Q. 21. Did man continue in that estate in which God created him?

A. Our first parents, being left to the freedom of their own will, through the temptation of Satan, transgressed the commandment of God, in eating the forbidden fruit, and thereby fell from the estate of innocence in which they were created.[1]

1 **Gen. 3:6-8, 13.** So when the woman saw that the tree was good for food, and that it was a delight to the eyes, and that the tree was to be desired to make one wise, she took of its fruit and ate, and she also gave some to her husband who was with her, and he ate. Then the eyes of both were opened, and they knew that they were naked. And they sewed fig leaves together and made themselves loincloths. And they heard the sound of the LORD God walking in the garden in the cool of the day, and the man and his wife hid themselves from the presence of the LORD God among the trees of the garden. ... Then the LORD God said to the woman, "What is this that you have done?" The woman said, "The serpent deceived me, and I ate." **Eccl. 7:29.** See, this alone I found, that God made man upright, but they have sought out many schemes. **2 Cor. 11:3.** But I am afraid that as the serpent deceived Eve by his cunning, your thoughts will be led astray from a sincere and pure devotion to Christ.

Q. 22. Did all mankind fall in that first transgression?

A. The covenant being made with Adam as a representative person, not for himself only, but for his descendants, all mankind, descending from him by ordinary generation,[1] sinned in him, and fell with him in that first transgression.[2]

1 **Acts 17:26.** And he made from one man every nation of mankind to live on all the face of the earth, having determined allotted periods and the boundaries of their dwelling place.

2 **Gen. 2:16-17.** And the LORD God commanded the man, saying, "You may surely eat of every tree of the garden, but of the tree of the knowledge of good and evil you shall not eat, for in the day that you eat of it you shall surely die."
Rom. 5:12-20. Therefore, just as sin came into the world through one man, and death through sin, and so death spread to all men because all sinned — for sin indeed was in the world before the law was given, but sin is not counted where there is no law. Yet death reigned from Adam to Moses, even over those whose sinning was not like the transgression of Adam, who was a type of the one who was to come. But the free gift is not like the trespass. For if many died through one man's trespass, much more have the grace of God and the free gift by the grace of that

one man Jesus Christ abounded for many. And the free gift is not like the result of that one man's sin. For the judgment following one trespass brought condemnation, but the free gift following many trespasses brought justification. For if, because of one man's trespass, death reigned through that one man, much more will those who receive the abundance of grace and the free gift of righteousness reign in life through the one man Jesus Christ. Therefore, as one trespass led to condemnation for all men, so one act of righteousness leads to justification and life for all men. For as by the one man's disobedience the many were made sinners, so by the one man's obedience the many will be made righteous. Now the law came in to increase the trespass, but where sin increased, grace abounded all the more. **1 Cor. 15:21-22**. For as by a man came death, by a man has come also the resurrection of the dead. For as in Adam all die, so also in Christ shall all be made alive.

Q. 23. Into what estate did the Fall bring mankind?

A. The Fall brought mankind into an estate of sin and misery.[1]

1 **Rom. 3:23**. ...for all have sinned and fall short of the glory of God. **Rom. 5:12**. Therefore, just as sin came into the world through one man, and death through sin, and so death spread to all men because all sinned.

Q. 24. What is sin?

A. Sin is any lack of conformity to, or transgression of, any law of God, given as a rule to the reasonable creature.[1]

1 **Gal. 3:10, 12.** For all who rely on works of the law are under a curse; for it is written, "Cursed be everyone who does not abide by all things written in the Book of the Law, and do them." ... But the law is not of faith, rather "The one who does them shall live by them." **1 Jn. 3:4**. Everyone who makes a practice of sinning also practices lawlessness; sin is lawlessness.

Q. 25. What is the sinfulness of that estate into which man fell?

A. The sinfulness of that estate into which man fell, consists of the guilt of Adam's first sin,[1] the lack of that righteousness in which he was created, and the corruption of his nature, through which he is made utterly unwilling, unable, and opposite to all that is spiritually good, and wholly inclined to all evil, and that continually;[2] which is commonly called original sin, and from which do proceed all actual transgressions.[3]

1 **Rom. 5:12, 19**. Therefore, just as sin came into the world through one man, and death through sin, and so death spread to all men because all sinned. ... For as by the one man's disobedience the many were made sinners, so by the one man's obedience the many will be made righteous.

2 **Gen. 6:5**. The LORD saw that the wickedness of man was great in the earth, and that every intention of the thoughts of his heart was only evil continually.

Rom. 3:10-19. ...as it is written: "None is righteous, no, not one; no one understands; no one seeks for God. All have turned aside; together they have become worthless; no one does good, not even one. Their throat is an open grave; they use their tongues to deceive. The venom of asps is under their lips. Their mouth is full of curses and bitterness. Their feet are swift to shed blood; in their paths are ruin and misery, and the way of peace they have not known. There is no fear of God before their eyes." Now we know that whatever the law says it speaks to those who are under the law, so that every mouth may be stopped, and the whole world may be held accountable to God. **Rom. 5:6.** For while we were still weak, at the right time Christ died for the ungodly. **Rom. 8:7-8.** For the mind that is set on the flesh is hostile to God, for it does not submit to God's law; indeed, it cannot. Those who are in the flesh cannot please God. **Eph. 2:1-3.** And you were dead in the trespasses and sins in which you once walked, following the course of this world, following the prince of the power of the air, the spirit that is now at work in the sons of disobedience—among whom we all once lived in the passions of our flesh, carrying out the desires of the body and the mind, and were by nature children of wrath, like the rest of mankind.

3 **Mt. 15:19.** For out of the heart come evil thoughts, murder, adultery, sexual immorality, theft, false witness, slander. **Jas. 1:14-15.** But each person is tempted when he is lured and enticed by his own desire. Then desire when it has conceived gives birth to sin, and sin when it is fully grown brings forth death.

Q. 26. How is original sin conveyed from our first parents to their descendants?

A. Original sin is conveyed from our first parents to their descendants by natural generation, so as all that proceed from them in that way, are conceived and born in sin.[1]

1 **Job 14:4.** Who can bring a clean thing out of an unclean? There is not one. **Job 15:14.** What is man, that he can be pure? Or he who is born of a woman, that he can be righteous? **Ps. 51:5.** Behold, I was brought forth in iniquity, and in sin did my mother conceive me. **Jn. 3:6.** That which is born of the flesh is flesh, and that which is born of the Spirit is spirit.

Q. 27. What misery did the Fall bring on mankind?

A. The Fall brought on mankind the loss of communion with God,[1] His displeasure and curse; so as we are by nature children of wrath,[2] bond slaves to Satan,[3] and justly liable to all punishments in this world and that which is to come.[4]

1 **Gen. 3:8, 10, 24.** And they heard the sound of the LORD God walking in the garden in the cool of the day, and the man and his wife hid themselves from the presence of the LORD God among the trees of the garden. ... And he said, "I heard the sound of you in the garden, and I was afraid, because I was naked, and I hid myself." ... He drove out the man, and at the east of the garden of Eden he placed the cherubim and a flaming sword that turned every way to guard the way to the tree of life.

2 **Eph. 2:2-3.** ...in which you once walked, following the course of this world, following the prince of the power of the air, the spirit that is now at work in the sons

of disobedience— among whom we all once lived in the passions of our flesh, carrying out the desires of the body and the mind, and were by nature children of wrath, like the rest of mankind.

3 **2 Tim. 2:26.** ...and they may come to their senses and escape from the snare of the devil, after being captured by him to do his will.

4 **Gen. 2:17.** "...but of the tree of the knowledge of good and evil you shall not eat, for in the day that you eat of it you shall surely die." **Lam. 3:39.** Why should a living man complain, a man, about the punishment of his sins? **Mt. 25:41, 46.** "Then he will say to those on his left, 'Depart from me, you cursed, into the eternal fire prepared for the devil and his angels'. ... And these will go away into eternal punishment, but the righteous into eternal life." **Rom. 6:23.** For the wages of sin is death, but the free gift of God is eternal life in Christ Jesus our Lord. **Jude 7.** ... just as Sodom and Gomorrah and the surrounding cities, which likewise indulged in sexual immorality and pursued unnatural desire, serve as an example by undergoing a punishment of eternal fire.

Q. 28. What are the punishments of sin in this world?

A. The punishments of sin in this world, are either inward, as blindness of mind,[1] a reprobate sense,[2] strong delusions,[3] hardness of heart,[4] horror of conscience,[5] and vile affections;[6] or outward, as the curse of God on the creatures for our sake,[7] and all other evils that befall us in our bodies, names, estates, relations, and employments;[8] together with death itself.[9]

1 **Eph. 4:18.** They are darkened in their understanding, alienated from the life of God because of the ignorance that is in them, due to their hardness of heart.

2 **Rom. 1:28.** And since they did not see fit to acknowledge God, God gave them up to a debased mind to do what ought not to be done.

3 **2 Thess. 2:11.** Therefore God sends them a strong delusion, so that they may believe what is false.

4 **Rom. 2:5.** But because of your hard and impenitent heart you are storing up wrath for yourself on the day of wrath when God's righteous judgment will be revealed.

5 **Gen. 4:13.** Cain said to the LORD, "My punishment is greater than I can bear. **Isa. 33:14.** The sinners in Zion are afraid; trembling has seized the godless: "Who among us can dwell with the consuming fire? Who among us can dwell with everlasting burnings?" **Mt. 27:4.** ...saying, "I have sinned by betraying innocent blood." They said, "What is that to us? See to it yourself."

6 **Rom. 1:26.** For this reason God gave them up to dishonorable passions. For their women exchanged natural relations for those that are contrary to nature.

7 **Gen. 3:17.** And to Adam he said, "Because you have listened to the voice of your wife and have eaten of the tree of which I commanded you, 'You shall not eat of it,' cursed is the ground because of you; in pain you shall eat of it all the days of your life.

8 **Deut. 28:15-18.** "But if you will not obey the voice of the LORD your God or be careful to do all his commandments and his statutes that I command you today, then all these curses shall come upon you and overtake you. Cursed shall you be in the city, and cursed shall you be in the field. Cursed shall be your basket and your kneading bowl. Cursed shall be the fruit of your womb and the fruit of your ground, the increase of your herds and the young of your flock."

9 **Rom. 6:21, 23.** But what fruit were you getting at that time from the things of which you are now ashamed? For the end of those things is death. ... For the wages of sin is death, but the free gift of God is eternal life in Christ Jesus our Lord.

Q. 29. What are the punishments of sin in the world to come?

A. The punishments of sin in the world to come are everlasting separation from the comforting presence of God, and most grievous torments in soul and body, without relief, in hellfire forever.[1]

1 **Mk. 9:43-44, 46, 48.** And if your hand causes you to sin, cut it off. It is better for you to enter life crippled than with two hands to go to hell, to the unquenchable fire. '...where their worm does not die and the fire is not quenched.' **Lk. 16:24.** And he called out, 'Father Abraham, have mercy on me, and send Lazarus to dip the end of his finger in water and cool my tongue, for I am in anguish in this flame.' **2 Thess. 1:9.** They will suffer the punishment of eternal destruction, away from the presence of the Lord and from the glory of his might.

Q. 30. Does God leave all mankind to perish in the estate of sin and misery?

A. God does not leave all men to perish in the estate of sin and misery,[1] into which they fell by the breach of the first covenant, commonly called the Covenant of Works;[2] but of his mere love and mercy delivers His elect out of it, and brings them into an estate of salvation by the second covenant, commonly called the Covenant of Grace.[3]

1 **1 Thess. 5:9.** For God has not destined us for wrath, but to obtain salvation through our Lord Jesus Christ.

2 **Gal. 3:10, 12.** For all who rely on works of the law are under a curse; for it is written, "Cursed be everyone who does not abide by all things written in the Book of the Law, and do them."... But the law is not of faith, rather "The one who does them shall live by them."

3 **Rom. 3:20.** For by works of the law no human being will be justified in his sight, since through the law comes knowledge of sin. **2 Cor. 3:7-9.** Now if the ministry of death, carved in letters on stone, came with such glory that the Israelites could not gaze at Moses' face because of its glory, which was being brought to an end, will not the ministry of the Spirit have even more glory? For if there was glory in the ministry of condemnation, the ministry of righteousness must far exceed it in glory. **Gal. 3:21.** Is the law then contrary to the promises of God? Certainly not! For if a law had been given that could give life, then righteousness would indeed be by the law. **Titus 3:4-7.** But when the goodness and loving kindness of God our Savior appeared, he saved us, not because of works done by us in righteousness, but according to his own mercy, by the washing of regeneration and renewal of the Holy Spirit, whom he poured out on us richly through Jesus Christ our Savior, so that being justified by his grace we might become heirs according to the hope of eternal life.

Q. 31. With whom was the Covenant of Grace made?

A. The Covenant of Grace was made with Christ as the second Adam, and in Him with all the elect as His seed.[1]

1 **Isa. 53:10-11**. Yet it was the will of the LORD to crush him; he has put him to grief; when his soul makes an offering for guilt, he shall see his offspring; he shall prolong his days; the will of the LORD shall prosper in his hand. Out of the anguish of his soul he shall see and be satisfied; by his knowledge shall the righteous one, my servant, make many to be accounted righteous, and he shall bear their iniquities. **Rom. 5:15-21**. But the free gift is not like the trespass. For if many died through one man's trespass, much more have the grace of God and the free gift by the grace of that one man Jesus Christ abounded for many. And the free gift is not like the result of that one man's sin. For the judgment following one trespass brought condemnation, but the free gift following many trespasses brought justification. For if, because of one man's trespass, death reigned through that one man, much more will those who receive the abundance of grace and the free gift of righteousness reign in life through the one man Jesus Christ. Therefore, as one trespass led to condemnation for all men, so one act of righteousness leads to justification and life for all men. For as by the one man's disobedience the many were made sinners, so by the one man's obedience the many will be made righteous. Now the law came in to increase the trespass, but where sin increased, grace abounded all the more, so that, as sin reigned in death, grace also might reign through righteousness leading to eternal life through Jesus Christ our Lord. **Gal. 3:16**. Now the promises were made to Abraham and to his offspring. It does not say, "And to offsprings," referring to many, but referring to one, "And to your offspring," who is Christ.

Q. 32. How is the grace of God shown in the second covenant?

A. The grace of God is shown in the second covenant, in that He freely provides and offers to sinners a Mediator,[1] and life and salvation by Him;[2] and requiring faith as the condition to interest them in Him,[3] promises and gives His Holy Spirit[4] to all His elect, to work in them that faith,[5] with all other saving graces;[6] and to enable them to do all holy obedience,[7] as the evidence of the truth of their faith[8] and of their thankfulness to God,[9] and as the way which he has appointed them to salvation.[10]

1 **Gen. 3:15**. "I will put enmity between you and the woman, and between your offspring and her offspring; he shall bruise your head, and you shall bruise his heel." **Isa. 42:6**. "I am the LORD; I have called you in righteousness; I will take you by the hand and keep you; I will give you as a covenant for the people, a light for the nations." **Jn. 6:27**. "Do not work for the food that perishes, but for the food that endures to eternal life, which the Son of Man will give to you. For on him God the Father has set his seal."

2 4 **Jn. 14:16-17**. And I will ask the Father, and he will give you another Helper, to be with you forever, even the Spirit of truth, whom the world cannot receive,

because it neither sees him nor knows him. You know him, for he dwells with you and will be in you.

3 **Jn. 1:12**. But to all who did receive him, who believed in his name, he gave the right to become children of God. **Jn. 3:16**. "For God so loved the world, that he gave his only Son, that whoever believes in him should not perish but have eternal life."

4 **Prov. 1:23**. If you turn at my reproof, behold, I will pour out my spirit to you; I will make my words known to you.

5 **2 Cor. 4:13.** Since we have the same spirit of faith according to what has been written, "I believed, and so I spoke," we also believe, and so we also speak.

6 **Gal. 5:22-23.** But the fruit of the Spirit is love, joy, peace, patience, kindness, goodness, faithfulness, gentleness, self-control; against such things there is no law.

7 **Ezek. 36:27.** And I will put my Spirit within you, and cause you to walk in my statutes and be careful to obey my rules.

8 **Jas. 2:18, 22.** But someone will say, "You have faith and I have works." Show me your faith apart from your works, and I will show you my faith by my works. ... You see that faith was active along with his works, and faith was completed by his works.

9 **2 Cor. 5:14-15.** For the love of Christ controls us, because we have concluded this: that one has died for all, therefore all have died; and he died for all, that those who live might no longer live for themselves but for him who for their sake died and was raised.

10 **Eph. 2:18.** For through him we both have access in one Spirit to the Father.

Q. 33. Was the Covenant of Grace always administered in one and the same manner?

A. The Covenant of Grace was not always administered in the same manner, but the administrations of it under the Old Testament were different from those under the New.[1]

1 **2 Cor. 3:6-9.** who has made us sufficient to be ministers of a new covenant, not of the letter but of the Spirit. For the letter kills, but the Spirit gives life. Now if the ministry of death, carved in letters on stone, came with such glory that the Israelites could not gaze at Moses' face because of its glory, which was being brought to an end, will not the ministry of the Spirit have even more glory? For if there was glory in the ministry of condemnation, the ministry of righteousness must far exceed it in glory.

Q. 34. How was the Covenant of Grace administered under the Old Testament?

A. The Covenant of Grace was administered under the Old Testament, by promises,[1] prophecies,[2] sacrifices,[3] circumcision,[4] the Passover,[5] and other types and ordinances; which did all signify Christ then to come, and were for that time sufficient to build up the elect in faith in the promised Messiah,[6] by whom they then had full remission of sin and eternal salvation.[7]

1 **ROM. 15:8.** For I tell you that Christ became a servant to the circumcised to show God's truthfulness, in order to confirm the promises given to the patriarchs.

2 **ACTS 3:20, 24.** that times of refreshing may come from the presence of the Lord, and that he may send the Christ appointed for you, Jesus. And all the prophets who have spoken, from Samuel and those who came after him, also proclaimed these days.

3 **HEB. 10:1.** For since the law has but a shadow of the good things to come instead of the true form of these realities, it can never, by the same sacrifices that are continually offered every year, make perfect those who draw near.

4 **ROM. 4:11.** He received the sign of circumcision as a seal of the righteousness that he had by faith while he was still uncircumcised. The purpose was to make him the father of all who believe without being circumcised, so that righteousness would be counted to them as well.

5 **1 COR. 5:7.** Cleanse out the old leaven that you may be a new lump, as you really are unleavened. For Christ, our Passover lamb, has been sacrificed.

6 **HEB. 8-11; 13.** All of Hebrews 8-11; 13.

7 **GAL. 3:7-9, 14.** Know then that it is those of faith who are the sons of Abraham. And the Scripture, foreseeing that God would justify the Gentiles by faith, preached the gospel beforehand to Abraham, saying, "In you shall all the nations be blessed." So then, those who are of faith are blessed along with Abraham, the man of faith.... so that in Christ Jesus the blessing of Abraham might come to the Gentiles, so that we might receive the promised Spirit through faith.

Q. 35. How is the Covenant of Grace administered under the New Testament?

A. Under the New Testament, when Christ appeared in the flesh, the same Covenant of Grace was, and still is to be, administered in the preaching of the Word,[1] and the administration of the sacraments of Baptism,[2] and the Lord's Supper;[3] in which grace and salvation are shown in more fullness, evidence, and efficacy to all nations.[4]

1 **MK. 16:15.** And he said to them, "Go into all the world and proclaim the gospel to the whole creation.

2 **MT. 28:19-20.** "Go therefore and make disciples of all nations, baptizing them in the name of the Father and of the Son and of the Holy Spirit, teaching them to observe all that I have commanded you. And behold, I am with you always, to the end of the age."

3 **1 COR. 11:23-25.** For I received from the Lord what I also delivered to you, that the Lord Jesus on the night when he was betrayed took bread, and when he had given thanks, he broke it, and said, "This is my body which is for you. Do this in remembrance of me." In the same way also he took the cup, after supper, saying, "This cup is the new covenant in my blood. Do this, as often as you drink it, in remembrance of me."

4 **2 COR. 3:6-9.** who has made us sufficient to be ministers of a new covenant, not of the letter but of the Spirit. For the letter kills, but the Spirit gives life. Now if the ministry of death, carved in letters on stone, came with such glory that the Israelites could not gaze at Moses' face because of its glory, which was being brought to an end, will not the ministry of the Spirit have even more glory? For if there was glory in the ministry of condemnation, the ministry of righteousness must far exceed it in glory. **HEB. 8:6, 10-11.** But as it is, Christ has obtained a ministry that

is as much more excellent than the old as the covenant he mediates is better, since it is enacted on better promises.... For this is the covenant that I will make with the house of Israel after those days, declares the Lord: I will put my laws into their minds, and write them on their hearts, and I will be their God, and they shall be my people. And they shall not teach, each one his neighbor and each one his brother, saying, 'Know the Lord,' for they shall all know me, from the least of them to the greatest. **Mt. 28:19.** Go therefore and make disciples of all nations, baptizing them in the name of the Father and of the Son and of the Holy Spirit.

Q. 36. Who is the Mediator of the Covenant of Grace?

A. The only Mediator of the Covenant of Grace is the Lord Jesus Christ,[1] who being the eternal Son of God, of one substance and equal with the Father,[2] in the fullness of time became man,[3] and so was, and continues to be, God and man, in two entire distinct natures, and one person, forever.[4]

1 **1 Tim. 2:5.** For there is one God, and there is one mediator between God and men, the man Christ Jesus.

2 **Jn. 1:1, 14.** In the beginning was the Word, and the Word was with God, and the Word was God.... And the Word became flesh and dwelt among us, and we have seen his glory, glory as of the only Son from the Father, full of grace and truth. **Jn. 10:30.** "I and the Father are one." **Phil. 2:6.** who, though he was in the form of God, did not count equality with God a thing to be grasped.

3 **Gal. 4:4.** But when the fullness of time had come, God sent forth his Son, born of woman, born under the law.

4 **Lk. 1:35.** And the angel answered her, "The Holy Spirit will come upon you, and the power of the Most High will overshadow you; therefore the child to be born will be called holy—the Son of God. **Rom. 9:5.** To them belong the patriarchs, and from their race, according to the flesh, is the Christ, who is God over all, blessed forever. Amen. **Col. 2:9.** For in him the whole fullness of deity dwells bodily. **Heb. 7:24-25.** but he holds his priesthood permanently, because he continues forever. Consequently, he is able to save to the uttermost those who draw near to God through him, since he always lives to make intercession for them.

Q. 37. How did Christ, being the Son of God, become man?

A. Christ, the Son of God, became man by taking to Himself a true body, and a reasonable soul,[1] being conceived by the power of the Holy Spirit, in the womb of the Virgin Mary, of her substance, and born of her,[2] yet without sin.[3]

1 **Jn. 1:14.** And the Word became flesh and dwelt among us, and we have seen his glory, glory as of the only Son from the Father, full of grace and truth. **Mt. 26:38.** Then he said to them, "My soul is very sorrowful, even to death; remain here, and watch with me."

2 **Lk. 1:27, 31, 35, 42.** to a virgin betrothed to a man whose name was Joseph, of the house of David. And the virgin's name was Mary.... And behold, you will conceive in your womb and bear a son, and you shall call his name Jesus.... And the

angel answered her, "The Holy Spirit will come upon you, and the power of the Most High will overshadow you; therefore the child to be born will be called holy—the Son of God".... and she exclaimed with a loud cry, "Blessed are you among women, and blessed is the fruit of your womb!" **GAL. 4:4.** But when the fullness of time had come, God sent forth his Son, born of woman, born under the law.

3 **HEB. 4:15.** For we do not have a high priest who is unable to sympathize with our weaknesses, but one who in every respect has been tempted as we are, yet without sin. **HEB. 7:26.** For it was indeed fitting that we should have such a high priest, holy, innocent, unstained, separated from sinners, and exalted above the heavens.

Q. 38. Why was it necessary that the Mediator should be God?

A. It was necessary that the Mediator should be God; that he might sustain and keep the human nature from sinking under the infinite wrath of God, and the power of death;[1] give worth and efficacy to His sufferings, obedience, and intercession;[2] and to satisfy God's justice,[3] procure His favor,[4] purchase a unique people,[5] give His Spirit to them,[6] conquer all their enemies,[7] and bring them to everlasting salvation.[8]

1 **ACTS 2:24-25.** God raised him up, loosing the pangs of death, because it was not possible for him to be held by it. For David says concerning him, "I saw the Lord always before me, for he is at my right hand that I may not be shaken." **ROM. 1:4.** and was declared to be the Son of God in power according to the Spirit of holiness by his resurrection from the dead, Jesus Christ our Lord. **ROM. 4:25.** who was delivered up for our trespasses and raised for our justification. **HEB. 9:14.** how much more will the blood of Christ, who through the eternal Spirit offered himself without blemish to God, purify our conscience from dead works to serve the living God.

2 **ACTS 20:28.** Pay careful attention to yourselves and to all the flock, in which the Holy Spirit has made you overseers, to care for the church of God, which he obtained with his own blood. **HEB. 7:25-28.** Consequently, he is able to save to the uttermost those who draw near to God through him, since he always lives to make intercession for them. For it was indeed fitting that we should have such a high priest, holy, innocent, unstained, separated from sinners, and exalted above the heavens. He has no need, like those high priests, to offer sacrifices daily, first for his own sins and then for those of the people, since he did this once for all when he offered up himself. For the law appoints men in their weakness as high priests, but the word of the oath, which came later than the law, appoints a Son who has been made perfect forever. **HEB. 9:14.** how much more will the blood of Christ, who through the eternal Spirit offered himself without blemish to God, purify our conscience from dead works to serve the living God.

3 **ROM. 3:24-26.** and are justified by his grace as a gift, through the redemption that is in Christ Jesus, whom God put forward as a propitiation by his blood, to be received by faith. This was to show God's righteousness, because in his divine forbearance he had passed over former sins. It was to show his righteousness at the present time, so that he might be just and the justifier of the one who has faith in Jesus.

4 **EPH. 1:6.** to the praise of his glorious grace, with which he has blessed us in the Beloved. **MT. 3:17.** and behold, a voice from heaven said, "This is my beloved Son, with whom I am well pleased."

5 **Tit. 2:13-14.** waiting for our blessed hope, the appearing of the glory of our great God and Savior Jesus Christ, who gave himself for us to redeem us from all lawlessness and to purify for himself a people for his own possession who are zealous for good works.

6 **Gal. 4:6.** And because you are sons, God has sent the Spirit of his Son into our hearts, crying, "Abba! Father!"

7 **Lk. 1:68-69, 71, 74.** "Blessed be the Lord God of Israel, for he has visited and redeemed his people and has raised up a horn of salvation for us in the house of his servant David...that we should be saved from our enemies and from the hand of all who hate us;...that we, being delivered from the hand of our enemies, might serve him without fear.

8 **Heb. 5:8-9.** Although he was a son, he learned obedience through what he suffered. And being made perfect, he became the source of eternal salvation to all who obey him. **Heb. 9:11-15.** But when Christ appeared as a high priest of the good things that have come, then through the greater and more perfect tent (not made with hands, that is, not of this creation) he entered once for all into the holy places, not by means of the blood of goats and calves but by means of his own blood, thus securing an eternal redemption. For if the blood of goats and bulls, and the sprinkling of defiled persons with the ashes of a heifer, sanctify for the purification of the flesh, how much more will the blood of Christ, who through the eternal Spirit offered himself without blemish to God, purify our conscience from dead works to serve the living God. Therefore he is the mediator of a new covenant, so that those who are called may receive the promised eternal inheritance, since a death has occurred that redeems them from the transgressions committed under the first covenant.

Q. 39. Why was it necessary that the Mediator should be man?

A. It was necessary that the Mediator should be man; that he might advance our nature,[1] perform obedience to the law,[2] suffer and make intercession for us in our nature,[3] have a fellow feeling of our infirmities;[4] that we might receive the adoption of sons,[5] and have comfort and access with boldness to the Throne of Grace.[6]

1 **Heb. 2:16.** For surely it is not angels that he helps, but he helps the offspring of Abraham.

2 **Gal. 4:4.** But when the fullness of time had come, God sent forth his Son, born of woman, born under the law.

3 **Heb. 2:14.** Since therefore the children share in flesh and blood, he himself likewise partook of the same things, that through death he might destroy the one who has the power of death, that is, the devil. **Heb. 7:24-25.** but he holds his priesthood permanently, because he continues forever. Consequently, he is able to save to the uttermost those who draw near to God through him, since he always lives to make intercession for them.

4 **Heb. 4:15.** For we do not have a high priest who is unable to sympathize with our weaknesses, but one who in every respect has been tempted as we are, yet without sin.

5 **Gal. 4:5.** to redeem those who were under the law, so that we might receive adoption as sons.

6 **Heb. 4:16.** Let us then with confidence draw near to the throne of grace, that we may receive mercy and find grace to help in time of need.

Q. 40. Why was it necessary that the Mediator should be God and man in one person?

A. It was necessary that the Mediator, who was to reconcile God and man, should Himself be both God and man, and this in one person; that the proper works of each nature might be accepted of God for us,[1] and relied on by us, as the works of the whole person.[2]

1 **Mt. 1:21, 23.** She will bear a son, and you shall call his name Jesus, for he will save his people from their sins. **Mt. 3:17.** and behold, a voice from heaven said, "This is my beloved Son, with whom I am well pleased." **Heb. 9:14.** how much more will the blood of Christ, who through the eternal Spirit offered himself without blemish to God, purify our conscience from dead works to serve the living God.

2 **1 Pet. 2:6.** For it stands in Scripture: "Behold, I am laying in Zion a stone, a cornerstone chosen and precious, and whoever believes in him will not be put to shame."

Q. 41. Why was our Mediator called Jesus?

A. Our Mediator was called Jesus, because he saves His people from their sins.[1]

1 **Mt. 1:21**. "She will bear a son, and you shall call his name Jesus, for he will save his people from their sins."

Q. 42. Why was our Mediator called Christ?

A. Our Mediator was called Christ, because he was anointed with the Holy Spirit above measure;[1] and so set apart, and fully furnished with all authority and ability,[2] to execute the office of prophet,[3] priest,[4] and king of His church,[5] in the estate both of His humiliation and exaltation.

1 **Ps. 45:7**. ...you have loved righteousness and hated wickedness. Therefore God, your God, has anointed you with the oil of gladness beyond your companions. **Jn. 3:34**. For he whom God has sent utters the words of God, for he gives the Spirit without measure.

2 **Mt. 28:18-20**. And Jesus came and said to them, "All authority in heaven and on earth has been given to me. Go therefore and make disciples of all nations, baptizing them in the name of the Father and of the Son and of the Holy Spirit, teaching them to observe all that I have commanded you. And behold, I am with you always, to the end of the age." **Jn. 6:27.** Do not work for the food that perishes, but for the food that endures to eternal life, which the Son of Man will give to you. For on him God the Father has set his seal.

3 **Lk. 4:18, 21.** "The Spirit of the Lord is upon me, because he has anointed me to proclaim good news to the poor. He has sent me to proclaim liberty to the captives and recovering of sight to the blind, to set at liberty those who are oppressed..." And he began to say to them, "Today this Scripture has been fulfilled in your hearing." **Acts 3:21-22.** ...whom heaven must receive until the time for restoring all the things about which God spoke by the mouth of his holy prophets long ago. Moses said, 'The Lord God will raise up for you a prophet like me from your brothers. You shall listen to him in whatever he tells you.'

4 **Heb. 4:14-15.** Since then we have a great high priest who has passed through the heavens, Jesus, the Son of God, let us hold fast our confession. For we do not have a high priest who is unable to sympathize with our weaknesses, but one who in every respect has been tempted as we are, yet without sin. **Heb. 5:5-7.** So also Christ did not exalt himself to be made a high priest, but was appointed by him who said to him.

5 **Ps. 2:6.** "As for me, I have set my King on Zion, my holy hill." **Isa. 9:6-7.** For to us a child is born, to us a son is given; and the government shall be upon his shoulder, and his name shall be called Wonderful Counselor, Mighty God, Everlasting Father, Prince of Peace. Of the increase of his government and of peace there will be no end, on the throne of David and over his kingdom, to establish it and to uphold it with justice and with righteousness from this time forth and forevermore. The zeal of the LORD of hosts will do this. **Matt. 21:5.** "Say to the daughter of Zion, Behold, your king is coming to you, humble, and mounted on a donkey, on a colt, the foal of a beast of burden.'" **Phil. 2:8-11.** And being found in human form, he humbled himself by becoming obedient to the point of death, even death on a cross. Therefore God has highly exalted him and bestowed on him the name that is above every name, so that at the name of Jesus every knee should bow, in heaven and on earth and under the earth, and every tongue confess that Jesus Christ is Lord, to the glory of God the Father.

Q. 43. How does Christ execute the office of a prophet?

A. Christ executes the office of a prophet, in his revealing to the church[1] in all ages, by his Spirit and Word,[2] in various ways of administration,[3] the whole will of God,[4] in all things concerning their edification and salvation.[5]

1 **Jn. 1:18.** No one has ever seen God; the only God, who is at the Father's side, he has made him known.

2 **1 Pet. 1:10-12.** Concerning this salvation, the prophets who prophesied about the grace that was to be yours searched and inquired carefully, inquiring what person or time the Spirit of Christ in them was indicating when he predicted the sufferings of Christ and the subsequent glories. It was revealed to them that they were serving not themselves but you, in the things that have now been announced to you through those who preached the good news to you by the Holy Spirit sent from heaven, things into which angels long to look.

3 **Heb. 1:1-2.** Long ago, at many times and in many ways, God spoke to our fathers by the prophets, but in these last days he has spoken to us by his Son, whom he appointed the heir of all things, through whom also he created the world.

4 **Jn. 15:15.** No longer do I call you servants, for the servant does not know what his master is doing; but I have called you friends, for all that I have heard from my Father I have made known to you.

5 **Jn. 20:31.** ...but these are written so that you may believe that Jesus is the Christ, the Son of God, and that by believing you may have life in his name. **Acts 20:32.** And now I commend you to God and to the word of his grace, which is able to build you up and to give you the inheritance among all those who are sanctified. **Eph. 4:11-13.** And he gave the apostles, the prophets, the evangelists, the shepherds and teachers, to equip the saints for the work of ministry, for building up the body of Christ, until we all attain to the unity of the faith and of the knowledge of the Son of God, to mature manhood, to the measure of the stature of the fullness of Christ.

Q. 44. How does Christ execute the office of a priest?

A. Christ executes the office of a priest, in His once offering Himself as a sacrifice without imperfection to God,[1] to be a reconciliation for the sins of His people;[2] and in making continual intercession for them.[3]

1 **Heb. 9:14, 28.** ...how much more will the blood of Christ, who through the eternal Spirit offered himself without blemish to God, purify our conscience from dead works to serve the living God. ...so Christ, having been offered once to bear the sins of many, will appear a second time, not to deal with sin but to save those who are eagerly waiting for him.

2 **Heb. 2:17.** Therefore he had to be made like his brothers in every respect, so that he might become a merciful and faithful high priest in the service of God, to make propitiation for the sins of the people.

3 **Heb. 7:25.** Consequently, he is able to save to the uttermost those who draw near to God through him, since he always lives to make intercession for them.

Q. 45. How does Christ execute the office of a king?

A. Christ executes the office of a king, in calling out of the world a people to Himself;[1] and giving them officers,[2] laws,[3] and censures, by which he visibly governs them;[4] in bestowing saving grace on His elect,[5] rewarding their obedience,[6] and correcting them for their sins,[7] preserving and supporting them under all their temptations and sufferings;[8] restraining and overcoming all their enemies,[9] and powerfully ordering all things for His own glory,[10] and their good;[11] and also in taking vengeance on the rest, who know not God, and obey not the Gospel.[12]

1 **Gen. 49:10.** The scepter shall not depart from Judah, nor the ruler's staff from between his feet, until tribute comes to him; and to him shall be the obedience of the peoples. **Ps. 110:3.** Your people will offer themselves freely on the day of your power, in holy garments; from the womb of the morning, the dew of your youth will be yours. **Isa. 55:4-5.** Behold, I made him a witness to the peoples, a leader and commander for the peoples. Behold, you shall call a nation that you do not know, and a nation that did not know you shall run to you, because of the LORD your God, and of the Holy One of Israel, for he has glorified you. **Acts 15:14-16.**

Simeon has related how God first visited the Gentiles, to take from them a people for his name. And with this the words of the prophets agree, just as it is written, "'After this I will return, and I will rebuild the tent of David that has fallen; I will rebuild its ruins, and I will restore it.'"

2 **1 Cor. 12:28**. And God has appointed in the church first apostles, second prophets, third teachers, then miracles, then gifts of healing, helping, administrating, and various kinds of tongues. **Eph. 4:11-12**. And he gave the apostles, the prophets, the evangelists, the shepherds and teachers, to equip the saints for the work of ministry, for building up the body of Christ.

3 **Isa. 33:22**. For the LORD is our judge; the LORD is our lawgiver; the LORD is our king; he will save us.

4 **Mt. 18:17-18**. If he refuses to listen to them, tell it to the church. And if he refuses to listen even to the church, let him be to you as a Gentile and a tax collector. Truly, I say to you, whatever you bind on earth shall be bound in heaven, and whatever you loose on earth shall be loosed in heaven. **1 Cor. 5:4-5**. When you are assembled in the name of the Lord Jesus and my spirit is present, with the power of our Lord Jesus, you are to deliver this man to Satan for the destruction of the flesh, so that his spirit may be saved in the day of the Lord.

5 **Acts 5:31**. God exalted him at his right hand as Leader and Savior, to give repentance to Israel and forgiveness of sins.

6 **Rev. 2:10**. Do not fear what you are about to suffer. Behold, the devil is about to throw some of you into prison, that you may be tested, and for ten days you will have tribulation. Be faithful unto death, and I will give you the crown of life. **Rev. 22:12**. "Behold, I am coming soon, bringing my recompense with me, to repay each one for what he has done."

7 **Rev. 3:19**. Those whom I love, I reprove and discipline, so be zealous and repent.

8 **Isa. 63:9**. In all their affliction he was afflicted, and the angel of his presence saved them; in his love and in his pity he redeemed them; he lifted them up and carried them all the days of old.

9 **Ps. 110:1-2**. The LORD says to my Lord: "Sit at my right hand, until I make your enemies your footstool." The LORD sends forth from Zion your mighty scepter. Rule in the midst of your enemies! **1 Cor. 15:25**. For he must reign until he has put all his enemies under his feet.

10 **Rom. 14:10-11**. Why do you pass judgment on your brother? Or you, why do you despise your brother? For we will all stand before the judgment seat of God; for it is written, "As I live, says the Lord, every knee shall bow to me, and every tongue shall confess to God."

11 **Rom. 8:28**. And we know that for those who love God all things work together for good, for those who are called according to his purpose.

12 **Ps. 2:8-9**. "Ask of me, and I will make the nations your heritage, and the ends of the earth your possession. You shall break them with a rod of iron and dash them in pieces like a potter's vessel." **Thess. 1:8-9**. ...in flaming fire, inflicting vengeance on those who do not know God and on those who do not obey the gospel of our Lord Jesus. They will suffer the punishment of eternal destruction, away from the presence of the Lord and from the glory of his might.

Q. 46. What was the estate of Christ's humiliation?

A. The estate of Christ's humiliation was that low condition, wherein He, for our sakes, emptying himself of His glory, took upon Himself the form of a servant, in His conception and birth, life, death, and after His death until His resurrection.[1]

1 **Lk. 1:31**. And behold, you will conceive in your womb and bear a son, and you shall call his name Jesus. **Acts. 2:24**. God raised him up, loosing the pangs of death, because it was not possible for him to be held by it. **2 Cor. 8:9**. For you know the grace of our Lord Jesus Christ, that though he was rich, yet for your sake he became poor, so that you by his poverty might become rich. **Phil. 2:6-8**. ... who, though he was in the form of God, did not count equality with God a thing to be grasped, but emptied himself, by taking the form of a servant, being born in the likeness of men. And being found in human form, he humbled himself by becoming obedient to the point of death, even death on a cross.

Q. 47. How did Christ humble Himself in his conception and birth?

A. Christ humbled Himself in His conception and birth, in that, being from all eternity the Son of God in the bosom of the Father, he was pleased in the fullness of time to become the Son of Man, made of a woman of low estate, and to be born to her, with various circumstances of more than ordinary deprivation.[1]

1 **Lk. 2:7**. And she gave birth to her firstborn son and wrapped him in swaddling cloths and laid him in a manger, because there was no place for them in the inn. **Jn. 1:14, 18**. And the Word became flesh and dwelt among us, and we have seen his glory, glory as of the only Son from the Father, full of grace and truth. ... No one has ever seen God; the only God, who is at the Father's side, he has made him known. **Gal. 4:4**. But when the fullness of time had come, God sent forth his Son, born of woman, born under the law.

Q. 48. How did Christ humble Himself in His life?

A. Christ humbled Himself in His life, by subjecting Himself to the law,[1] which He perfectly fulfilled,[2] and by enduring the indignities of the world,[3] temptations of Satan,[4] and infirmities in His flesh; whether common to the nature of man, or particularly accompanying His low condition.[5]

1 **Gal. 4:4**. But when the fullness of time had come, God sent forth his Son, born of woman, born under the law.

2 **Mt. 5:17**. "Do not think that I have come to abolish the Law or the Prophets; I have not come to abolish them but to fulfill them." **Rom. 5:19**. For as by the one man's disobedience the many were made sinners, so by the one man's obedience the many will be made righteous.

3 **Ps. 22:6**. But I am a worm and not a man, scorned by mankind and despised by the people. **Heb. 12:2-3**. ...looking to Jesus, the founder and perfecter of our faith, who for the joy that was set before him endured the cross, despising the shame, and is seated at the right hand of the throne of God. Consider him who endured

from sinners such hostility against himself, so that you may not grow weary or fainthearted.

4 **Mt. 4:1-12**. Then Jesus was led up by the Spirit into the wilderness to be tempted by the devil. And after fasting forty days and forty nights, he was hungry. And the tempter came and said to him, "If you are the Son of God, command these stones to become loaves of bread." But he answered, "It is written, "'Man shall not live by bread alone, but by every word that comes from the mouth of God.'" Then the devil took him to the holy city and set him on the pinnacle of the temple and said to him, "If you are the Son of God, throw yourself down, for it is written, "'He will command his angels concerning you,' and "'On their hands they will bear you up, lest you strike your foot against a stone.'" Jesus said to him, "Again it is written, 'You shall not put the Lord your God to the test.'" Again, the devil took him to a very high mountain and showed him all the kingdoms of the world and their glory. And he said to him, "All these I will give you, if you will fall down and worship me." Then Jesus said to him, "Be gone, Satan! For it is written, "'You shall worship the Lord your God and him only shall you serve.'" Then the devil left him, and behold, angels came and were ministering to him. Now when he heard that John had been arrested, he withdrew into Galilee. **Lk. 4:13**. And when the devil had ended every temptation, he departed from him until an opportune time.

5 **Isa. 52:13-14**. Behold, my servant shall act wisely; he shall be high and lifted up, and shall be exalted. As many were astonished at you— his appearance was so marred, beyond human semblance, and his form beyond that of the children of mankind. **Heb. 2:17-18**. Therefore he had to be made like his brothers in every respect, so that he might become a merciful and faithful high priest in the service of God, to make propitiation for the sins of the people. For because he himself has suffered when tempted, he is able to help those who are being tempted. **Heb. 4:15**. For we do not have a high priest who is unable to sympathize with our weaknesses, but one who in every respect has been tempted as we are, yet without sin.

Q. 49. How did Christ humble Himself in His death?

A. Christ humbled Himself in His death in that, having been betrayed by Judas,[1] forsaken by His disciples,[2] scorned and rejected by the world,[3] condemned by Pilate, and tormented by His persecutors;[4] having also conflicted with the terrors of death and the powers of darkness, having felt and borne the weight of God's wrath,[5] He laid down his life an offering for sin,[6] enduring the painful, shameful, and cursed death of the cross.[7]

1 **Mt. 27:4**. ...saying, "I have sinned by betraying innocent blood." They said, "What is that to us? See to it yourself."

2 **Mt. 26:56**. But all this has taken place that the Scriptures of the prophets might be fulfilled." Then all the disciples left him and fled.

3 **Isa. 53:2-3**. For he grew up before him like a young plant, and like a root out of dry ground; he had no form or majesty that we should look at him, and no beauty that we should desire him. He was despised and rejected by men; a man of sorrows, and acquainted with grief; and as one from whom men hide their faces he was despised, and we esteemed him not.

4 **Mt. 27:26-50**. Then he released for them Barabbas, and having scourged Jesus, delivered him to be crucified. Then the soldiers of the governor took Jesus into the governor's headquarters, and they gathered the whole battalion before him. And they stripped him and put a scarlet robe on him, and twisting together a crown of thorns, they put it on his head and put a reed in his right hand. And kneeling before him, they mocked him, saying, "Hail, King of the Jews!" And they spit on him and took the reed and struck him on the head. And when they had mocked him, they stripped him of the robe and put his own clothes on him and led him away to crucify him. As they went out, they found a man of Cyrene, Simon by name. They compelled this man to carry his cross. And when they came to a place called Golgotha (which means Place of a Skull), they offered him wine to drink, mixed with gall, but when he tasted it, he would not drink it. And when they had crucified him, they divided his garments among them by casting lots. Then they sat down and kept watch over him there. And over his head they put the charge against him, which read, "This is Jesus, the King of the Jews." Then two robbers were crucified with him, one on the right and one on the left. And those who passed by derided him, wagging their heads and saying, "You who would destroy the temple and rebuild it in three days, save yourself! If you are the Son of God, come down from the cross." So also the chief priests, with the scribes and elders, mocked him, saying, "He saved others; he cannot save himself. He is the King of Israel; let him come down now from the cross, and we will believe in him. He trusts in God; let God deliver him now, if he desires him. For he said, 'I am the Son of God.'" And the robbers who were crucified with him also reviled him in the same way. Now from the sixth hour there was darkness over all the land until the ninth hour. And about the ninth hour Jesus cried out with a loud voice, saying, "Eli, Eli, lema sabachthani?" that is, "My God, my God, why have you forsaken me?" And some of the bystanders, hearing it, said, "This man is calling Elijah." And one of them at once ran and took a sponge, filled it with sour wine, and put it on a reed and gave it to him to drink. But the others said, "Wait, let us see whether Elijah will come to save him." And Jesus cried out again with a loud voice and yielded up his spirit. **Jn. 19:34**. But one of the soldiers pierced his side with a spear, and at once there came out blood and water.

5 **Mt. 27:46**. And about the ninth hour Jesus cried out with a loud voice, saying, "Eli, Eli, lema sabachthani?" that is, "My God, my God, why have you forsaken me?" **Lk. 22:44**. And being in an agony he prayed more earnestly; and his sweat became like great drops of blood falling down to the ground.

6 **Isa. 53:10**. Yet it was the will of the LORD to crush him; he has put him to grief; when his soul makes an offering for guilt, he shall see his offspring; he shall prolong his days; the will of the LORD shall prosper in his hand.

7 **Gal. 3:13**. Christ redeemed us from the curse of the law by becoming a curse for us—for it is written, "Cursed is everyone who is hanged on a tree." **Phil. 2:8**. And being found in human form, he humbled himself by becoming obedient to the point of death, even death on a cross. **Heb. 12:2**. ...looking to Jesus, the founder and perfecter of our faith, who for the joy that was set before him endured the cross, despising the shame, and is seated at the right hand of the throne of God.

Q. 50. In what did Christ's humiliation consist after His death?

A. Christ's humiliation after His death consisted in His being buried,[1] and continuing in the state of the dead, and under the power of death till the third day,[2] which has been otherwise expressed in these words: "He descended into hell."

1 **1 Cor. 15:3-4**. For I delivered to you as of first importance what I also received: that Christ died for our sins in accordance with the Scriptures, that he was buried, that he was raised on the third day in accordance with the Scriptures.

2 **Ps. 16:10**. For you will not abandon my soul to Sheol, or let your holy one see corruption. **Mt. 12:40**. For just as Jonah was three days and three nights in the belly of the great fish, so will the Son of Man be three days and three nights in the heart of the earth. **Acts 2:24-27, 31**. God raised him up, loosing the pangs of death, because it was not possible for him to be held by it. For David says concerning him, "'I saw the Lord always before me, for he is at my right hand that I may not be shaken; therefore my heart was glad, and my tongue rejoiced; my flesh also will dwell in hope. For you will not abandon my soul to Hades, or let your Holy One see corruption. ...he foresaw and spoke about the resurrection of the Christ, that he was not abandoned to Hades, nor did his flesh see corruption. **Rom. 6:9.** We know that Christ, being raised from the dead, will never die again; death no longer has dominion over him.

Q. 51. What was the estate of Christ's exaltation?

A. The estate of Christ's exaltation is made up of His resurrection,[1] ascension,[2] sitting at the right hand of the Father,[3] and His coming again to judge the world.[4]

1 **1 Cor. 15:4**. ...that he was buried, that he was raised on the third day in accordance with the Scripture.

2 **Mk. 16:19**. So then the Lord Jesus, after he had spoken to them, was taken up into heaven and sat down at the right hand of God.

3 **Eph. 1:20**. ...that he worked in Christ when he raised him from the dead and seated him at his right hand in the heavenly places.

4 **Acts 1:11**. ...and said, "Men of Galilee, why do you stand looking into heaven? This Jesus, who was taken up from you into heaven, will come in the same way as you saw him go into heaven." **Acts 17:31**. "...because he has fixed a day on which he will judge the world in righteousness by a man whom he has appointed; and of this he has given assurance to all by raising him from the dead."

Q. 52. How was Christ exalted in His resurrection?

A. Christ was exalted in His resurrection, in that, not having seen decay in death (in which it was not possible for Him to be held),[1] and having the very same body in which he suffered, with its essential properties[2] (but without mortality and other common infirmities belonging to this life), really united to His soul,[3] He rose again from the dead the third day by His own power;[4] whereby He declared Himself to be the Son of God,[5] to have satisfied divine justice,[6] to have vanquished death and him who had the power of it,[7] and to be Lord of the living and the dead.[8] All this He did as a representative person,[9] the head of His church,[10] for their justification,[11] making them alive in grace,[12] supporting them against enemies,[13] and assuring them of their resurrection from the dead at the last day.[14]

1 **Acts 2:24, 27**. God raised him up, loosing the pangs of death, because it was not possible for him to be held by it. ... For you will not abandon my soul to Hades, or let your Holy One see corruption.

2 **Lk. 24:39**. "See my hands and my feet, that it is I myself. Touch me, and see. For a spirit does not have flesh and bones as you see that I have."

3 **Rom. 6:9**. We know that Christ, being raised from the dead, will never die again; death no longer has dominion over him. **Rev. 1:18**. ...and the living one. I died, and behold I am alive forevermore, and I have the keys of Death and Hades.

4 **Jn. 10:17-18**. "For this reason the Father loves me, because I lay down my life that I may take it up again. No one takes it from me, but I lay it down of my own accord. I have authority to lay it down, and I have authority to take it up again. This charge I have received from my Father."

5 **Rom. 1:4**. ...and was declared to be the Son of God in power according to the Spirit of holiness by his resurrection from the dead, Jesus Christ our Lord.

6 **Rom. 8:34**. Who is to condemn? Christ Jesus is the one who died—more than that, who was raised—who is at the right hand of God, who indeed is interceding for us.

7 **Heb. 2:14**. Since therefore the children share in flesh and blood, he himself likewise partook of the same things, that through death he might destroy the one who has the power of death, that is, the devil.

8 **Rom. 14:9**. For to this end Christ died and lived again, that he might be Lord both of the dead and of the living.

9 **1 Cor. 15:21-22**. For as by a man came death, by a man has come also the resurrection of the dead. For as in Adam all die, so also in Christ shall all be made alive.

10 **Eph. 1:20-23**. ...that he worked in Christ when he raised him from the dead and seated him at his right hand in the heavenly places, far above all rule and authority and power and dominion, and above every name that is named, not only in this age but also in the one to come. And he put all things under his feet and gave him as head over all things to the church, which is his body, the fullness of him who fills all in all. **Col. 1:18**. And he is the head of the body, the church. He is the beginning, the firstborn from the dead, that in everything he might be preeminent.

11 **Rom. 4:25**. ...who was delivered up for our trespasses and raised for our justification.

12 **Eph. 2:1, 5-6**. And you were dead in the trespasses and sins. ...even when we were dead in our trespasses, made us alive together with Christ—by grace you have been saved— and raised us up with him and seated us with him in the heavenly places in Christ Jesus. **Col. 2:12**. ...having been buried with him in baptism, in which you were also raised with him through faith in the powerful working of God, who raised him from the dead.

13 **1 Cor. 15:25-27**. For he must reign until he has put all his enemies under his feet. The last enemy to be destroyed is death. For "God has put all things in subjection under his feet." But when it says, "all things are put in subjection," it is plain that he is excepted who put all things in subjection under him.

14 **1 Cor. 15:20**. But in fact Christ has been raised from the dead, the firstfruits of those who have fallen asleep.

Q. 53. How was Christ exalted in his ascension?

A. Christ was exalted in His ascension, in that having, after His resurrection, often appeared to and conversed with His apostles, speaking to them of the things pertaining to the Kingdom of God,[1] and giving them commission to preach the gospel to all nations;[2] forty days after His resurrection, He, in our nature, and as our Head,[3] triumphing over enemies,[4] visibly went up into the highest heavens, there to receive gifts for men,[5] to raise up our affections in that way,[6] and to prepare a place for us,[7] where He is, and shall continue till His second coming at the end of the world.[8]

1 **Acts 1:2-3**. ...until the day when he was taken up, after he had given commands through the Holy Spirit to the apostles whom he had chosen. He presented himself alive to them after his suffering by many proofs, appearing to them during forty days and speaking about the kingdom of God.

2 **Mt. 28:19-20**. "Go therefore and make disciples of all nations, baptizing them in the name of the Father and of the Son and of the Holy Spirit, teaching them to observe all that I have commanded you. And behold, I am with you always, to the end of the age."

3 **Heb. 6:20**. ...where Jesus has gone as a forerunner on our behalf, having become a high priest forever after the order of Melchizedek.

4 **Eph. 4:8**. Therefore it says, "When he ascended on high he led a host of captives, and he gave gifts to men."

5 **Ps. 66:18**. If I had cherished iniquity in my heart, the Lord would not have listened. **Acts 1:9-11**. And when he had said these things, as they were looking on, he was lifted up, and a cloud took him out of their sight. And while they were gazing into heaven as he went, behold, two men stood by them in white robes, and said, "Men of Galilee, why do you stand looking into heaven? This Jesus, who was taken up from you into heaven, will come in the same way as you saw him go into heaven." **Eph. 4:10**. He who descended is the one who also ascended far above all the heavens, that he might fill all things.

6 **Col. 3:1-2**. If then you have been raised with Christ, seek the things that are above, where Christ is, seated at the right hand of God. Set your minds on things that are above, not on things that are on earth.

7 **Jn. 14:3**. And if I go and prepare a place for you, I will come again and will take you to myself, that where I am you may be also.

8 **Acts 3:21**. ...whom heaven must receive until the time for restoring all the things about which God spoke by the mouth of his holy prophets long ago.

Q. 54. How is Christ exalted in His sitting at the right hand of God?

A. Christ is exalted in His sitting at the right hand of God, in that as God-man He is advanced to the highest favor with God the Father,[1] with all fullness of joy,[2] glory,[3] and power over all things in heaven and earth;[4] and does gather and defend His church, and subdue their enemies; furnishes His ministers and people with gifts and graces,[5] and makes intercession for them.[6]

1 **PHIL. 2:9.** Therefore God has highly exalted him and bestowed on him the name that is above every name.

2 **PS. 16:11.** You make known to me the path of life; in your presence there is fullness of joy; at your right hand are pleasures forevermore. **ACTS 2:28.** 'You have made known to me the paths of life; you will make me full of gladness with your presence.'

3 **JN. 17:5.** And now, Father, glorify me in your own presence with the glory that I had with you before the world existed.

4 **EPH. 1:22.** And he put all things under his feet and gave him as head over all things to the church. **1 PET. 3:22.** ...who has gone into heaven and is at the right hand of God, with angels, authorities, and powers having been subjected to him.

5 **PS. 110:1.** The LORD says to my Lord: "Sit at my right hand, until I make your enemies your footstool." **EPH. 4:10-12.** (He who descended is the one who also ascended far above all the heavens, that he might fill all things.) And he gave the apostles, the prophets, the evangelists, the shepherds and teachers, to equip the saints for the work of ministry, for building up the body of Christ.

6 **ROM. 8:34.** Who is to condemn? Christ Jesus is the one who died—more than that, who was raised—who is at the right hand of God, who indeed is interceding for us.

Q. 55. How does Christ make intercession?

A. Christ makes intercession, by His appearing in our nature continually before the Father in heaven,[1] in the merit of His obedience and sacrifice on earth;[2] declaring His will to have it applied to all believers;[3] answering all accusations against them;[4] and obtaining for them peace of conscience, notwithstanding daily failings,[5] access with boldness to the Throne of Grace,[6] and acceptance of them[7] and their services.[8]

1 **HEB. 9:12, 24.** ...he entered once for all into the holy places, not by means of the blood of goats and calves but by means of his own blood, thus securing an eternal redemption. ... For Christ has entered, not into holy places made with hands, which are copies of the true things, but into heaven itself, now to appear in the presence of God on our behalf.

2 **HEB. 1:3.** He is the radiance of the glory of God and the exact imprint of his nature, and he upholds the universe by the word of his power. After making purification for sins, he sat down at the right hand of the Majesty on high.

3 **JN. 3:16.** "For God so loved the world, that he gave his only Son, that whoever believes in him should not perish but have eternal life." **JN. 17:9, 20, 24.** I am praying for them. I am not praying for the world but for those whom you have given me, for they are yours. ... "I do not ask for these only, but also for those who will believe in me through their word."... Father, I desire that they also, whom you have given me, may be with me where I am, to see my glory that you have given me because you loved me before the foundation of the world.

4 **Rom. 8:33-34**. Who shall bring any charge against God's elect? It is God who justifies. Who is to condemn? Christ Jesus is the one who died—more than that, who was raised—who is at the right hand of God, who indeed is interceding for us.

5 **Rom. 5:1-2**. Therefore, since we have been justified by faith, we have peace with God through our Lord Jesus Christ. Through him we have also obtained access by faith into this grace in which we stand, and we rejoice in hope of the glory of God. **1 Jn. 2:1-2**. My little children, I am writing these things to you so that you may not sin. But if anyone does sin, we have an advocate with the Father, Jesus Christ the righteous. He is the propitiation for our sins, and not for ours only but also for the sins of the whole world.

6 **Heb. 4:16**. Let us then with confidence draw near to the throne of grace, that we may receive mercy and find grace to help in time of need.

7 **Eph. 1:6**. ...to the praise of his glorious grace, with which he has blessed us in the Beloved.

8 **1 Pet. 2:5**. ...you yourselves like living stones are being built up as a spiritual house, to be a holy priesthood, to offer spiritual sacrifices acceptable to God through Jesus Christ.

Q. 56. How is Christ to be exalted in His coming again to judge the world?

A. Christ is to be exalted in his coming again to judge the world, in that He, who was unjustly judged and condemned by wicked men,[1] shall come again at the last day in great power,[2] and in the full display of His own glory, and of His Father's, with all his holy angels,[3] with a shout, with the voice of the archangel, and with the trumpet of God,[4] to judge the world in righteousness.[5]

1 **Acts 3:14-15**. But you denied the Holy and Righteous One, and asked for a murderer to be granted to you, and you killed the Author of life, whom God raised from the dead. To this we are witnesses.

2 **Mt. 24:30**. Then will appear in heaven the sign of the Son of Man, and then all the tribes of the earth will mourn, and they will see the Son of Man coming on the clouds of heaven with power and great glory.

3 **Mt. 25:31**. "When the Son of Man comes in his glory, and all the angels with him, then he will sit on his glorious throne." **Lk. 9:26**. For whoever is ashamed of me and of my words, of him will the Son of Man be ashamed when he comes in his glory and the glory of the Father and of the holy angels.

4 **1 Thess. 4:16**. For the Lord himself will descend from heaven with a cry of command, with the voice of an archangel, and with the sound of the trumpet of God. And the dead in Christ will rise first.

5 **Acts 17:31**. "...because he has fixed a day on which he will judge the world in righteousness by a man whom he has appointed; and of this he has given assurance to all by raising him from the dead."

Q. 57. What benefits has Christ obtained by his mediation?

A. Christ by His mediation has obtained redemption,[1] with all other benefits of the Covenant of Grace.[2]

1 **Heb. 9:12.** ...he entered once for all into the holy places, not by means of the blood of goats and calves but by means of his own blood, thus securing an eternal redemption.

2 **2 Cor. 1:20.** For all the promises of God find their Yes in him. That is why it is through him that we utter our Amen to God for his glory.

Q. 58. How do we come to be made recipients of the benefits that Christ has obtained?

A. We are made recipients of the benefits that Christ has obtained, by the application of them to us,[1] which is the work especially of God the Holy Spirit.[2]

1 **Jn. 1:11-12.** He came to his own, and his own people did not receive him. But to all who did receive him, who believed in his name, he gave the right to become children of God.

2 **Titus 3:5-6.** He saved us, not because of works done by us in righteousness, but according to his own mercy, by the washing of regeneration and renewal of the Holy Spirit, whom he poured out on us richly through Jesus Christ our Savior.

Q. 59. Who are made recipients of redemption through Christ?

A. Redemption is certainly applied, and effectually communicated, to all those for whom Christ has purchased it;[1] who are at the appropriate time enabled by the Holy Spirit to believe in Christ, according to the Gospel.[2]

1 **Jn. 6:37, 39.** All that the Father gives me will come to me, and whoever comes to me I will never cast out. ... And this is the will of him who sent me, that I should lose nothing of all that he has given me, but raise it up on the last day. **Jn. 10:15-16.** ...just as the Father knows me and I know the Father; and I lay down my life for the sheep. And I have other sheep that are not of this fold. I must bring them also, and they will listen to my voice. So there will be one flock, one shepherd. **Eph. 1:13-14.** In him you also, when you heard the word of truth, the gospel of your salvation, and believed in him, were sealed with the promised Holy Spirit, who is the guarantee of our inheritance until we acquire possession of it, to the praise of his glory.

2 **2 Cor. 4:13.** Since we have the same spirit of faith according to what has been written, "I believed, and so I spoke," we also believe, and so we also speak. **Eph. 2:8.** For by grace you have been saved through faith. And this is not your own doing; it is the gift of God.

Q. 60. Can they who have never heard the Gospel, and thus do not know Jesus Christ or believe in Him, be saved by their living according to the light of nature?

A. They who, having never heard the Gospel,[1] do not know Jesus Christ[2] and do not believe in Him, cannot be saved,[3] though they be diligent to frame their lives according to the light of nature,[4] or the laws of that religion which they profess;[5] neither is there salvation in any other, but in Christ alone,[6] who is the Savior only of His body the church.[7]

1 **Rom. 10:14**. How then will they call on him in whom they have not believed? And how are they to believe in him of whom they have never heard? And how are they to hear without someone preaching?

2 **Jn. 1:10-12**. He was in the world, and the world was made through him, yet the world did not know him. He came to his own, and his own people did not receive him. But to all who did receive him, who believed in his name, he gave the right to become children of God. **Eph. 2:12**. ...remember that you were at that time separated from Christ, alienated from the commonwealth of Israel and strangers to the covenants of promise, having no hope and without God in the world. **2 Thess. 1:8-9**. ...in flaming fire, inflicting vengeance on those who do not know God and on those who do not obey the gospel of our Lord Jesus. They will suffer the punishment of eternal destruction, away from the presence of the Lord and from the glory of his might.

3 **Mk. 16:16.** Whoever believes and is baptized will be saved, but whoever does not believe will be condemned. **Jn. 8:24**. "I told you that you would die in your sins, for unless you believe that I am he you will die in your sins."

4 **1 Cor. 1:20-24**. Where is the one who is wise? Where is the scribe? Where is the debater of this age? Has not God made foolish the wisdom of the world? For since, in the wisdom of God, the world did not know God through wisdom, it pleased God through the folly of what we preach to save those who believe. For Jews demand signs and Greeks seek wisdom, but we preach Christ crucified, a stumbling block to Jews and folly to Gentiles, but to those who are called, both Jews and Greeks, Christ the power of God and the wisdom of God.

5 **Jn. 4:22**. You worship what you do not know; we worship what we know, for salvation is from the Jews. **Rom. 9:31-32**. ...but that Israel who pursued a law that would lead to righteousness did not succeed in reaching that law. Why? Because they did not pursue it by faith, but as if it were based on works. They have stumbled over the stumbling stone. **Phil. 3:4-9**. ...though I myself have reason for confidence in the flesh also. If anyone else thinks he has reason for confidence in the flesh, I have more: circumcised on the eighth day, of the people of Israel, of the tribe of Benjamin, a Hebrew of Hebrews; as to the law, a Pharisee; as to zeal, a persecutor of the church; as to righteousness under the law, blameless. But whatever gain I had, I counted as loss for the sake of Christ. Indeed, I count everything as loss because of the surpassing worth of knowing Christ Jesus my Lord. For his sake I have suffered the loss of all things and count them as rubbish, in order that I may gain Christ and be found in him, not having a righteousness of my own that comes from the law, but that which comes through faith in Christ, the righteousness from God that depends on faith.

6 **Acts 4:12**. "And there is salvation in no one else, for there is no other name under heaven given among men by which we must be saved."

7 **Eph. 5:23**. For the husband is the head of the wife even as Christ is the head of the church, his body, and is himself its Savior.

Q. 61. Are all saved who hear the Gospel, and live in the church?

A. All who hear the Gospel, and live in the visible church, are not saved; but only they who are true members of the church invisible.[1]

1 **Mt. 7:21**. "Not everyone who says to me, 'Lord, Lord,' will enter the kingdom of heaven, but the one who does the will of my Father who is in heaven." **Mt. 22:14**. "For many are called, but few are chosen." **Jn. 12:38-40**. ...so that the word spoken by the prophet Isaiah might be fulfilled: "Lord, who has believed what he heard from us, and to whom has the arm of the Lord been revealed?" Therefore they could not believe. For again Isaiah said, "He has blinded their eyes and hardened their heart, lest they see with their eyes, and understand with their heart, and turn, and I would heal them." **Rom. 9:6.** But it is not as though the word of God has failed. For not all who are descended from Israel belong to Israel. **Rom. 11:7**. What then? Israel failed to obtain what it was seeking. The elect obtained it, but the rest were hardened.

Q. 62. What is the visible church?

A. The visible church is a society made up of all persons who in all ages and places of the world do profess the true religion,[1] and of their children.[2]

1 **Ps. 2:8**. Ask of me, and I will make the nations your heritage, and the ends of the earth your possession. **Ps. 22:27-31**. All the ends of the earth shall remember and turn to the LORD, and all the families of the nations shall worship before you. For kingship belongs to the LORD, and he rules over the nations. All the prosperous of the earth eat and worship; before him shall bow all who go down to the dust, even the one who could not keep himself alive. Posterity shall serve him; it shall be told of the Lord to the coming generation; they shall come and proclaim his righteousness to a people yet unborn, that he has done it. **Ps. 45:17**. I will cause your name to be remembered in all generations; therefore nations will praise you forever and ever. **Isa. 59:21**. "And as for me, this is my covenant with them," says the LORD: "My Spirit that is upon you, and my words that I have put in your mouth, shall not depart out of your mouth, or out of the mouth of your offspring, or out of the mouth of your children's offspring," says the LORD, "from this time forth and forevermore." **Mt. 28:19-20**. "Go therefore and make disciples of all nations, baptizing them in the name of the Father and of the Son and of the Holy Spirit, teaching them to observe all that I have commanded you. And behold, I am with you always, to the end of the age." **Rom. 15:9-12**. ...and in order that the Gentiles might glorify God for his mercy. As it is written, "Therefore I will praise you among the Gentiles, and sing to your name." And again it is said, "Rejoice, O Gentiles, with his people." And again, "Praise the Lord, all you Gentiles, and let all the peoples extol him." And again Isaiah says, "The root of Jesse will come, even he who arises to rule the Gentiles; in him will the Gentiles hope." **1 Cor. 1:2**. To the church of God that is in Corinth, to those sanctified in Christ Jesus, called to be saints

together with all those who in every place call upon the name of our Lord Jesus Christ, both their Lord and ours. See **1 Cor. 12**. See **1 Cor. 13. Rev. 7:9**. After this I looked, and behold, a great multitude that no one could number, from every nation, from all tribes and peoples and languages, standing before the throne and before the Lamb, clothed in white robes, with palm branches in their hands.

2 **Gen. 17:7.** And I will establish my covenant between me and you and your offspring after you throughout their generations for an everlasting covenant, to be God to you and to your offspring after you. **Acts 2:39.** "For the promise is for you and for your children and for all who are far off, everyone whom the Lord our God calls to himself." **Rom. 11:16**. If the dough offered as firstfruits is holy, so is the whole lump, and if the root is holy, so are the branches. **1 Cor. 7:14**. For the unbelieving husband is made holy because of his wife, and the unbelieving wife is made holy because of her husband. Otherwise your children would be unclean, but as it is, they are holy.

Q. 63. What are the special privileges of the visible church?

A. The visible church has the privilege of being under God's special care and government;[1] of being protected and preserved in all ages, notwithstanding the opposition of all enemies;[2] and of enjoying the communion of saints, the ordinary means of salvation,[3] and offers of grace by Christ, to all members of it, in the ministry of the Gospel, testifying that whoever believes in Him shall be saved,[4] and excluding none who will come to Him.[5]

1 **Isa. 9:5-6**. For every boot of the tramping warrior in battle tumult and every garment rolled in blood will be burned as fuel for the fire. For to us a child is born, to us a son is given; and the government shall be upon his shoulder, and his name shall be called Wonderful Counselor, Mighty God, Everlasting Father, Prince of Peace. **1 Tim. 4:10**. For to this end we toil and strive, because we have our hope set on the living God, who is the Savior of all people, especially of those who believe.

2 **Ps. 115:1-2, 9**. Not to us, O LORD, not to us, but to your name give glory, for the sake of your steadfast love and your faithfulness! Why should the nations say, "Where is their God?" ... O Israel, trust in the LORD! He is their help and their shield. **Isa. 31:4-5**. For thus the LORD said to me, "As a lion or a young lion growls over his prey, and when a band of shepherds is called out against him he is not terrified by their shouting or daunted at their noise, so the LORD of hosts will come down to fight on Mount Zion and on its hill. Like birds hovering, so the LORD of hosts will protect Jerusalem; he will protect and deliver it; he will spare and rescue it." **Zech. 12:2-4, 8, 9**. "Behold, I am about to make Jerusalem a cup of staggering to all the surrounding peoples. The siege of Jerusalem will also be against Judah. On that day I will make Jerusalem a heavy stone for all the peoples. All who lift it will surely hurt themselves. And all the nations of the earth will gather against it. On that day, declares the LORD, I will strike every horse with panic, and its rider with madness. But for the sake of the house of Judah I will keep my eyes open, when I strike every horse of the peoples with blindness. ... On that day the LORD will protect the inhabitants of Jerusalem, so that the feeblest among

them on that day shall be like David, and the house of David shall be like God, like the angel of the LORD, going before them. ... And on that day I will seek to destroy all the nations that come against Jerusalem.

3 **Acts 2:39, 42.** "For the promise is for you and for your children and for all who are far off, everyone whom the Lord our God calls to himself."... And they devoted themselves to the apostles' teaching and the fellowship, to the breaking of bread and the prayers.

4 **Ps. 147:19-20.** He declares his word to Jacob, his statutes and rules to Israel. He has not dealt thus with any other nation; they do not know his rules. Praise the LORD! **Mk. 16:15-16.** And he said to them, "Go into all the world and proclaim the gospel to the whole creation. Whoever believes and is baptized will be saved, but whoever does not believe will be condemned. **Rom. 9:4.** They are Israelites, and to them belong the adoption, the glory, the covenants, the giving of the law, the worship, and the promises. **Eph. 4:11-12.** And he gave the apostles, the prophets, the evangelists, the shepherds and teachers, to equip the saints for the work of ministry, for building up the body of Christ.

5 **Jn. 6:37.** All that the Father gives me will come to me, and whoever comes to me I will never cast out.

Q. 64. What is the invisible church?

A. The invisible church is the whole number of the elect, who have been, are, or shall be gathered into one under Christ the head.[1]

1 **Jn. 10:16.** And I have other sheep that are not of this fold. I must bring them also, and they will listen to my voice. So there will be one flock, one shepherd. **Jn. 11:52.** ...and not for the nation only, but also to gather into one the children of God who are scattered abroad. **Eph. 1:10, 22-23.** ...as a plan for the fullness of time, to unite all things in him, things in heaven and things on earth. ... And he put all things under his feet and gave him as head over all things to the church, which is his body, the fullness of him who fills all in all.

Q. 65. What special benefits do the members of the invisible church enjoy by Christ?

A. The members of the invisible church, by Christ, enjoy union and communion with Him in grace and glory.[1]

1 **Jn. 17:21, 24.** ...that they may all be one, just as you, Father, are in me, and I in you, that they also may be in us, so that the world may believe that you have sent me. ... Father, I desire that they also, whom you have given me, may be with me where I am, to see my glory that you have given me because you loved me before the foundation of the world. **Eph. 2:5-6.** ...even when we were dead in our trespasses, made us alive together with Christ—by grace you have been saved—and raised us up with him and seated us with him in the heavenly places in Christ Jesus.

Q. 66. What is that union that the elect have with Christ?

A. The union that the elect have with Christ is the work of God's grace,[21] by which they are spiritually and mystically, yet really and inseparably, joined to Christ as their head and husband;[2] which is done in their effectual calling.[3]

1 **Eph. 1:22.** And he put all things under his feet and gave him as head over all things to the church. **Eph. 2:6-7.** ...and raised us up with him and seated us with him in the heavenly places in Christ Jesus, so that in the coming ages he might show the immeasurable riches of his grace in kindness toward us in Christ Jesus.

2 **Jn. 10:28.** I give them eternal life, and they will never perish, and no one will snatch them out of my hand. **1 Cor. 6:17.** But he who is joined to the Lord becomes one spirit with him. **Eph. 5:23, 30.** For the husband is the head of the wife even as Christ is the head of the church, his body, and is himself its Savior. ...because we are members of his body.

3 **1 Cor. 1:9.** God is faithful, by whom you were called into the fellowship of his Son, Jesus Christ our Lord. **1 Pet. 5:10.** And after you have suffered a little while, the God of all grace, who has called you to his eternal glory in Christ, will himself restore, confirm, strengthen, and establish you.

Q. 67. What is effectual calling?

A. Effectual calling is the work of God's almighty power and grace,[1] by which (out of his free and special love to his elect, and from nothing in them moving him to do so)[2] He does in his accepted time invite and draw them to Jesus Christ, by His Word and Spirit;[3] savingly enlightening their minds,[4] renewing and powerfully determining their wills,[5] so as they (although in themselves dead in sin) are hereby made willing and able, freely to answer His call, and to accept and embrace the grace offered and conveyed in it.[6]

1 **Jn. 5:25.** "Truly, truly, I say to you, an hour is coming, and is now here, when the dead will hear the voice of the Son of God, and those who hear will live." **Eph. 1:18-20.** ...having the eyes of your hearts enlightened, that you may know what is the hope to which he has called you, what are the riches of his glorious inheritance in the saints, and what is the immeasurable greatness of his power toward us who believe, according to the working of his great might that he worked in Christ when he raised him from the dead and seated him at his right hand in the heavenly places. **2 Tim. 1:8-9.** Therefore do not be ashamed of the testimony about our Lord, nor of me his prisoner, but share in suffering for the gospel by the power of God, who saved us and called us to a holy calling, not because of our works but because of his own purpose and grace, which he gave us in Christ Jesus before the ages began.

2 **Rom. 9:11.** ... though they were not yet born and had done nothing either good or bad—in order that God's purpose of election might continue, not because of works but because of him who calls. **Eph. 2:4-5, 7-9.** But God, being rich in mercy, because of the great love with which he loved us, even when we were dead in our trespasses, made us alive together with Christ—by grace you have been saved. ...so

that in the coming ages he might show the immeasurable riches of his grace in kindness toward us in Christ Jesus. For by grace you have been saved through faith. And this is not your own doing; it is the gift of God, not a result of works, so that no one may boast. **Titus 3:4-5**. But when the goodness and loving kindness of God our Savior appeared, he saved us, not because of works done by us in righteousness, but according to his own mercy, by the washing of regeneration and renewal of the Holy Spirit.

3 **Jn. 6:44**. No one can come to me unless the Father who sent me draws him. And I will raise him up on the last day. **2 Cor. 5:20**. Therefore, we are ambassadors for Christ, God making his appeal through us. We implore you on behalf of Christ, be reconciled to God. **2 Cor. 6:1-2**. Working together with him, then, we appeal to you not to receive the grace of God in vain. For he says, "In a favorable time I listened to you, and in a day of salvation I have helped you." Behold, now is the favorable time; behold, now is the day of salvation. **2 Thess. 2:13-14.** But we ought always to give thanks to God for you, brothers beloved by the Lord, because God chose you as the firstfruits to be saved, through sanctification by the Spirit and belief in the truth. To this he called you through our gospel, so that you may obtain the glory of our Lord Jesus Christ.

4 **Acts 26:18.** 'to open their eyes, so that they may turn from darkness to light and from the power of Satan to God, that they may receive forgiveness of sins and a place among those who are sanctified by faith in me.' **1 Cor. 2:10, 12**. ...these things God has revealed to us through the Spirit. For the Spirit searches everything, even the depths of God. ... Now we have received not the spirit of the world, but the Spirit who is from God, that we might understand the things freely given us by God.

5 **Ezek. 11:19**. And I will give them one heart, and a new spirit I will put within them. I will remove the heart of stone from their flesh and give them a heart of flesh. **Ezek. 36:26-27**. And I will give you a new heart, and a new spirit I will put within you. And I will remove the heart of stone from your flesh and give you a heart of flesh. And I will put my Spirit within you, and cause you to walk in my statutes and be careful to obey my rules. **Jn. 6:45**. It is written in the Prophets, 'And they will all be taught by God.' Everyone who has heard and learned from the Father comes to me.

6 **Deut. 30:6**. And the LORD your God will circumcise your heart and the heart of your offspring, so that you will love the LORD your God with all your heart and with all your soul, that you may live. **Eph. 2:5**. ...even when we were dead in our trespasses, made us alive together with Christ—by grace you have been saved. **Phil. 2:13**. ...for it is God who works in you, both to will and to work for his good pleasure.

Q. 68. Are the elect only effectually called?

A. All the elect, and they only, are effectually called;[1] although others may be, and often are, outwardly called by the ministry of the Word,[2] and have some common operations of the Spirit,[3] who, for their willful neglect and contempt of the grace offered to them, being justly left in their unbelief, do never truly come to Jesus Christ.[4]

1 **Acts 13:48**. And when the Gentiles heard this, they began rejoicing and glorifying the word of the Lord, and as many as were appointed to eternal life believed.

2 **Mt. 22:14**. "For many are called, but few are chosen."

3 **Mt. 7:22**. On that day many will say to me, 'Lord, Lord, did we not prophesy in your name, and cast out demons in your name, and do many mighty works in your name?' **Mt. 13:20-21**. As for what was sown on rocky ground, this is the one who hears the word and immediately receives it with joy, yet he has no root in himself, but endures for a while, and when tribulation or persecution arises on account of the word, immediately he falls away. **Heb. 6:4-6**. For it is impossible, in the case of those who have once been enlightened, who have tasted the heavenly gift, and have shared in the Holy Spirit, and have tasted the goodness of the word of God and the powers of the age to come, and then have fallen away, to restore them again to repentance, since they are crucifying once again the Son of God to their own harm and holding him up to contempt.

4 **Ps. 81:11-12**. "But my people did not listen to my voice; Israel would not submit to me. So I gave them over to their stubborn hearts, to follow their own counsels." **Jn. 6:64-65**. "But there are some of you who do not believe." (For Jesus knew from the beginning who those were who did not believe, and who it was who would betray him.) And he said, "This is why I told you that no one can come to me unless it is granted him by the Father." **Jn. 12:38-40**. ...so that the word spoken by the prophet Isaiah might be fulfilled: "Lord, who has believed what he heard from us, and to whom has the arm of the Lord been revealed?" Therefore they could not believe. For again Isaiah said, "He has blinded their eyes and hardened their heart, lest they see with their eyes, and understand with their heart, and turn, and I would heal them." **Acts 28:25-27**. And disagreeing among themselves, they departed after Paul had made one statement: "The Holy Spirit was right in saying to your fathers through Isaiah the prophet: "'Go to this people, and say, "You will indeed hear but never understand, and you will indeed see but never perceive." For this people's heart has grown dull, and with their ears they can barely hear, and their eyes they have closed; lest they should see with their eyes and hear with their ears and understand with their heart and turn, and I would heal them.'

Q. 69. What is the communion in grace, which the members of the invisible church have with Christ?

A. The communion in grace, which the members of the invisible church have with Christ, is their partaking of the virtue of His mediation, in their justification,[1] adoption,[2] sanctification, and whatever else in this life demonstrates their union with Him.[3]

1 **Rom. 8:30**. And those whom he predestined he also called, and those whom he called he also justified, and those whom he justified he also glorified.

2 **Eph. 1:5**. ...he predestined us for adoption as sons through Jesus Christ, according to the purpose of his will.

3 **1 Cor. 1:30**. And because of him you are in Christ Jesus, who became to us wisdom from God, righteousness and sanctification and redemption.

Q. 70. What is justification?

A. Justification is an act of God's free grace to sinners,[1] in which He pardons all their sin, accepts and accounts them righteous in His sight;[2] not for anything done in them, or done by them,[3] but only for the perfect obedience and full satisfaction of Christ, imputed to them by God[4] and received by faith alone.[5]

1 **ROM. 3:22, 24-25.** ...the righteousness of God through faith in Jesus Christ for all who believe. For there is no distinction. ...and are justified by his grace as a gift, through the redemption that is in Christ Jesus, whom God put forward as a propitiation by his blood, to be received by faith. This was to show God's righteousness, because in his divine forbearance he had passed over former sins. **ROM. 4:5.** And to the one who does not work but believes in him who justifies the ungodly, his faith is counted as righteousness.

2 **ROM. 3:22, 24-25, 27-28.** ...the righteousness of God through faith in Jesus Christ for all who believe. For there is no distinction. ...and are justified by his grace as a gift, through the redemption that is in Christ Jesus, whom God put forward as a propitiation by his blood, to be received by faith. This was to show God's righteousness, because in his divine forbearance he had passed over former sins. ... Then what becomes of our boasting? It is excluded. By what kind of law? By a law of works? No, but by the law of faith. For we hold that one is justified by faith apart from works of the law. **2 COR. 5:19-21.** ...that is, in Christ God was reconciling the world to himself, not counting their trespasses against them, and entrusting to us the message of reconciliation. Therefore, we are ambassadors for Christ, God making his appeal through us. We implore you on behalf of Christ, be reconciled to God. For our sake he made him to be sin who knew no sin, so that in him we might become the righteousness of God.

3 **EPH. 1:7.** In him we have redemption through his blood, the forgiveness of our trespasses, according to the riches of his grace. **TITUS 3:5, 7.** ...he saved us, not because of works done by us in righteousness, but according to his own mercy, by the washing of regeneration and renewal of the Holy Spirit. ...so that being justified by his grace we might become heirs according to the hope of eternal life.

4 **ROM. 4:6-8.** ...just as David also speaks of the blessing of the one to whom God counts righteousness apart from works: "Blessed are those whose lawless deeds are forgiven, and whose sins are covered; blessed is the man against whom the Lord will not count his sin." **ROM. 5:17-19.** For if, because of one man's trespass, death reigned through that one man, much more will those who receive the abundance of grace and the free gift of righteousness reign in life through the one man Jesus Christ. Therefore, as one trespass led to condemnation for all men, so one act of righteousness leads to justification and life for all men. For as by the one man's disobedience the many were made sinners, so by the one man's obedience the many will be made righteous.

5 **ACTS 10:43.** "To him all the prophets bear witness that everyone who believes in him receives forgiveness of sins through his name." **GAL. 2:16.** ...yet we know that a person is not justified by works of the law but through faith in Jesus Christ, so we also have believed in Christ Jesus, in order to be justified by faith in Christ and not by works of the law, because by works of the law no one will be justified. **PHIL. 3:9.** ...and be found in him, not having a righteousness of my own that comes from the law, but that which comes through faith in Christ, the righteousness from God that depends on faith.

Q. 71. How is justification an act of God's free grace?

A. Although Christ, by his obedience and death, did make a proper, real, and full satisfaction of God's justice on behalf of them who are justified:[1] yet inasmuch as God accepts the satisfaction from a surety, which he might have demanded of them; and did provide this surety, His only Son,[2] imputing his righteousness to them,[3] and requiring nothing of them for their justification, but faith,[4] which also is His gift,[5] their justification is to them of free grace.[6]

1 **Rom. 5:8-10, 19**. ...but God shows his love for us in that while we were still sinners, Christ died for us. Since, therefore, we have now been justified by his blood, much more shall we be saved by him from the wrath of God. For if while we were enemies we were reconciled to God by the death of his Son, much more, now that we are reconciled, shall we be saved by his life. ... For as by the one man's disobedience the many were made sinners, so by the one man's obedience the many will be made righteous.

2 **Isa. 53:4-6, 10-12**. Surely he has borne our griefs and carried our sorrows; yet we esteemed him stricken, smitten by God, and afflicted. But he was pierced for our transgressions; he was crushed for our iniquities; upon him was the chastisement that brought us peace, and with his wounds we are healed. All we like sheep have gone astray; we have turned—every one—to his own way; and the LORD has laid on him the iniquity of us all. ... Yet it was the will of the LORD to crush him; he has put him to grief; when his soul makes an offering for guilt, he shall see his offspring; he shall prolong his days; the will of the LORD shall prosper in his hand. Out of the anguish of his soul he shall see and be satisfied; by his knowledge shall the righteous one, my servant, make many to be accounted righteous, and he shall bear their iniquities. Therefore I will divide him a portion with the many, and he shall divide the spoil with the strong, because he poured out his soul to death and was numbered with the transgressors; yet he bore the sin of many, and makes intercession for the transgressors. **Dan. 9:24, 26**. "Seventy weeks are decreed about your people and your holy city, to finish the transgression, to put an end to sin, and to atone for iniquity, to bring in everlasting righteousness, to seal both vision and prophet, and to anoint a most holy place." ... And after the sixty-two weeks, an anointed one shall be cut off and shall have nothing. And the people of the prince who is to come shall destroy the city and the sanctuary. Its end shall come with a flood, and to the end there shall be war. Desolations are decreed. **Mt. 20:28**. "...even as the Son of Man came not to be served but to serve, and to give his life as a ransom for many." **Rom. 8:32**. He who did not spare his own Son but gave him up for us all, how will he not also with him graciously give us all things? **1 Tim. 2:5-6**. For there is one God, and there is one mediator between God and men, the man Christ Jesus, who gave himself as a ransom for all, which is the testimony given at the proper time. **Heb. 7:22**. This makes Jesus the guarantor of a better covenant. **Heb. 10:10**. And by that will we have been sanctified through the offering of the body of Jesus Christ once for all. **1 Pet. 1:18-19**. ... knowing that you were ransomed from the futile ways inherited from your forefathers, not with perishable things such as silver or gold, but with the precious blood of Christ, like that of a lamb without blemish or spot.

3 **2 Cor. 5:21**. For our sake he made him to be sin who knew no sin, so that in him we might become the righteousness of God.

4 **Rom. 3:24-25.** ...and are justified by his grace as a gift, through the redemption that is in Christ Jesus, whom God put forward as a propitiation by his blood, to be received by faith. This was to show God's righteousness, because in his divine forbearance he had passed over former sins.

5 **Eph. 2:8.** For by grace you have been saved through faith. And this is not your own doing; it is the gift of God.

6 **Eph. 1:17.** ...that the God of our Lord Jesus Christ, the Father of glory, may give you the Spirit of wisdom and of revelation in the knowledge of him.

Q. 72. What is justifying faith?

A. Justifying faith is a saving grace,[1] wrought in the heart of a sinner, by the Spirit[2] and the Word of God;[3] whereby he, being convinced of his sin and misery, and of his own inability and the inability of all other creatures to rescue him from his lost condition,[4] not only assents to the truth of the promise of the Gospel,[5] but receives and rests on Christ and His righteousness held forth in that truth, for pardon of sin,[6] and for the accepting and accounting of him as righteous in the sight of God for salvation.[7]

1 **Heb. 10:39.** But we are not of those who shrink back and are destroyed, but of those who have faith and preserve their souls.

2 **2 Cor. 4:13.** Since we have the same spirit of faith according to what has been written, "I believed, and so I spoke," we also believe, and so we also speak. **Eph. 1:17-19.** ...that the God of our Lord Jesus Christ, the Father of glory, may give you the Spirit of wisdom and of revelation in the knowledge of him, having the eyes of your hearts enlightened, that you may know what is the hope to which he has called you, what are the riches of his glorious inheritance in the saints, and what is the immeasurable greatness of his power toward us who believe, according to the working of his great might.

3 **Rom. 10:14-17.** How then will they call on him in whom they have not believed? And how are they to believe in him of whom they have never heard? And how are they to hear without someone preaching? And how are they to preach unless they are sent? As it is written, "How beautiful are the feet of those who preach the good news!" But they have not all obeyed the gospel. For Isaiah says, "Lord, who has believed what he has heard from us?" So faith comes from hearing, and hearing through the word of Christ.

4 **Jn. 16:8-9.** And when he comes, he will convict the world concerning sin and righteousness and judgment: concerning sin, because they do not believe in me. **Acts 2:37.** Now when they heard this they were cut to the heart, and said to Peter and the rest of the apostles, "Brothers, what shall we do?" **Acts 4:12.** "And there is salvation in no one else, for there is no other name under heaven given among men by which we must be saved." **Acts 16:30.** Then he brought them out and said, "Sirs, what must I do to be saved?" **Rom. 6:8.** Now if we have died with Christ, we believe that we will also live with him. **Eph. 2:1.** And you were dead in the trespasses and sins.

5 **Eph. 1:13.** In him you also, when you heard the word of truth, the gospel of your salvation, and believed in him, were sealed with the promised Holy Spirit.

6 **Jn. 1:12**. But to all who did receive him, who believed in his name, he gave the right to become children of God. **Acts 10:43**. "To him all the prophets bear witness that everyone who believes in him receives forgiveness of sins through his name." **Acts 16:31**. And they said, "Believe in the Lord Jesus, and you will be saved, you and your household."

7 **Acts 15:11**. "But we believe that we will be saved through the grace of the Lord Jesus, just as they will." **Phil. 3:9**. ...and be found in him, not having a righteousness of my own that comes from the law, but that which comes through faith in Christ, the righteousness from God that depends on faith.

Q. 73. How does faith justify a sinner in the sight of God?

A. Faith justifies a sinner in the sight of God, not because of those other graces that always accompany it, or because of good works that are the fruits of it;[1] nor as if the grace of faith, or any act of it, were imputed to him for justification;[2] but only as it is an instrument, by which he receives and applies Christ and His righteousness.[3]

1 **Rom. 3:28**. For we hold that one is justified by faith apart from works of the law. **Gal. 3:11**. Now it is evident that no one is justified before God by the law, for "The righteous shall live by faith."

2 **Rom. 4:5**. And to the one who does not work but believes in him who justifies the ungodly, his faith is counted as righteousness. **Rom. 10:10**. For with the heart one believes and is justified, and with the mouth one confesses and is saved.

3 **Jn. 1:12**. But to all who did receive him, who believed in his name, he gave the right to become children of God. **Gal. 1:16**. ...was pleased to reveal his Son to me, in order that I might preach him among the Gentiles, I did not immediately consult with anyone. **Phil. 3:9**. ...and be found in him, not having a righteousness of my own that comes from the law, but that which comes through faith in Christ, the righteousness from God that depends on faith.

Q. 74. What is adoption?

A. Adoption is an act of the free grace of God,[1] in and for His only Son Jesus Christ,[2] by which all those who are justified are received into the number of His children,[3] have His name put on them,[4] the Spirit of His Son given to them,[5] are under His Fatherly care and dispensations,[6] admitted to all the liberties and privileges of the sons of God, made heirs of all the promises, and fellow heirs with Christ in glory.[7]

1 **1 Jn. 3:1**. See what kind of love the Father has given to us, that we should be called children of God; and so we are. The reason why the world does not know us is that it did not know him.

2 **Gal. 4:4-5**. But when the fullness of time had come, God sent forth his Son, born of woman, born under the law, to redeem those who were under the law, so that we might receive adoption as sons. **Eph. 1:5**. ...he predestined us for adoption as sons through Jesus Christ, according to the purpose of his will.

3 **Jn. 1:12.** But to all who did receive him, who believed in his name, he gave the right to become children of God.

4 **2 Cor. 6:18**. "...and I will be a father to you, and you shall be sons and daughters to me, says the Lord Almighty." **Rev. 3:12.** The one who conquers, I will make him a pillar in the temple of my God. Never shall he go out of it, and I will write on him the name of my God, and the name of the city of my God, the new Jerusalem, which comes down from my God out of heaven, and my own new name.

5 **Gal. 4:6**. And because you are sons, God has sent the Spirit of his Son into our hearts, crying, "Abba! Father!"

6 **Ps. 103:13**. As a father shows compassion to his children, so the LORD shows compassion to those who fear him. **Prov. 14:26**. In the fear of the LORD one has strong confidence, and his children will have a refuge. **Mt. 6:32**. For the Gentiles seek after all these things, and your heavenly Father knows that you need them all.

7 **Heb. 6:12**. ...so that you may not be sluggish, but imitators of those who through faith and patience inherit the promises.

Q. 75. What is sanctification?

A. Sanctification is a work of God's grace, by which they, whom God has, before the foundation of the world, chosen to be holy, are, in time, through the powerful operation of His Spirit,[1] applying the death and resurrection of Christ to them,[2] renewed in their whole man after the image of God;[3] having the seeds of repentance to life, and all other saving graces, put into their hearts,[4] and those graces so stirred up, increased and strengthened,[5] as that they more and more die to sin, and rise to newness of life.[6]

1 **1 Cor. 6:11**. And such were some of you. But you were washed, you were sanctified, you were justified in the name of the Lord Jesus Christ and by the Spirit of our God. **Eph. 1:4**. ...even as he chose us in him before the foundation of the world, that we should be holy and blameless before him. **2 Thess. 2:13.** But we ought always to give thanks to God for you, brothers beloved by the Lord, because God chose you as the firstfruits to be saved, through sanctification by the Spirit and belief in the truth.

2 **Rom. 6:4-6**. We were buried therefore with him by baptism into death, in order that, just as Christ was raised from the dead by the glory of the Father, we too might walk in newness of life. For if we have been united with him in a death like his, we shall certainly be united with him in a resurrection like his. We know that our old self was crucified with him in order that the body of sin might be brought to nothing, so that we would no longer be enslaved to sin.

3 **Eph. 4:23-24**. ...and to be renewed in the spirit of your minds, and to put on the new self, created after the likeness of God in true righteousness and holiness.

4 **Acts 11:18**. When they heard these things they fell silent. And they glorified God, saying, "Then to the Gentiles also God has granted repentance that leads to life."

1 JN. 3:9. No one born of God makes a practice of sinning, for God's seed abides in him, and he cannot keep on sinning because he has been born of God.

5 **EPH. 3:16-19**. ...that according to the riches of his glory he may grant you to be strengthened with power through his Spirit in your inner being, so that Christ may dwell in your hearts through faith—that you, being rooted and grounded in love, may have strength to comprehend with all the saints what is the breadth and length and height and depth, and to know the love of Christ that surpasses knowledge, that you may be filled with all the fullness of God. **COL. 1:10-11**. ...so as to walk in a manner worthy of the Lord, fully pleasing to him, bearing fruit in every good work and increasing in the knowledge of God. May you be strengthened with all power, according to his glorious might, for all endurance and patience with joy. **HEB. 6:11-12**. And we desire each one of you to show the same earnestness to have the full assurance of hope until the end, so that you may not be sluggish, but imitators of those who through faith and patience inherit the promises. **JUDE 20**. But you, beloved, building yourselves up in your most holy faith and praying in the Holy Spirit.

6 **ROM. 6:4, 6, 14**. We were buried therefore with him by baptism into death, in order that, just as Christ was raised from the dead by the glory of the Father, we too might walk in newness of life. ... We know that our old self was crucified with him in order that the body of sin might be brought to nothing, so that we would no longer be enslaved to sin. ... For sin will have no dominion over you, since you are not under law but under grace. **GAL. 5:24**. And those who belong to Christ Jesus have crucified the flesh with its passions and desires.

Q. 76. What is repentance to life?

A. Repentance to life is a saving grace,[1] accomplished in the heart of a sinner by the Spirit[2] and Word of God,[3] by which out of the sight and sense, not only of the danger,[4] but also of the filthiness and odiousness of his sins,[5] and upon the apprehension of God's mercy in Christ to such as are penitent,[6] he so grieves for,[7] and hates his sins,[8] as that he turns from them all to God,[9] desiring and endeavoring constantly to walk with Him in all the ways of new obedience.[10]

1 **2 TIM. 2:25**. ...correcting his opponents with gentleness. God may perhaps grant them repentance leading to a knowledge of the truth.

2 **ZECH. 12:10**. "And I will pour out on the house of David and the inhabitants of Jerusalem a spirit of grace and pleas for mercy, so that, when they look on me, on him whom they have pierced, they shall mourn for him, as one mourns for an only child, and weep bitterly over him, as one weeps over a firstborn."

3 **ACTS 11:18, 20-21**. When they heard these things they fell silent. And they glorified God, saying, "Then to the Gentiles also God has granted repentance that leads to life."... But there were some of them, men of Cyprus and Cyrene, who on coming to Antioch spoke to the Hellenists also, preaching the Lord Jesus. And the hand of the Lord was with them, and a great number who believed turned to the Lord.

4 **EZEK. 18:28, 30, 32**. Because he considered and turned away from all the transgressions that he had committed, he shall surely live; he shall not die. ... "Therefore I will judge you, O house of Israel, every one according to his ways, declares the Lord GOD. Repent and turn from all your transgressions, lest iniquity be your

ruin. ... For I have no pleasure in the death of anyone, declares the Lord GOD; so turn, and live." **Hos. 2:6-7**. Therefore I will hedge up her way with thorns, and I will build a wall against her, so that she cannot find her paths. She shall pursue her lovers but not overtake them, and she shall seek them but shall not find them. Then she shall say, 'I will go and return to my first husband, for it was better for me then than now.' **Lk. 15:17-18**. "But when he came to himself, he said, 'How many of my father's hired servants have more than enough bread, but I perish here with hunger! I will arise and go to my father, and I will say to him, "Father, I have sinned against heaven and before you."

5 **Isa. 30:22**. Then you will defile your carved idols overlaid with silver and your gold-plated metal images. You will scatter them as unclean things. You will say to them, "Be gone!" **Ezek. 36:31**. Then you will remember your evil ways, and your deeds that were not good, and you will loathe yourselves for your iniquities and your abominations.

6 **Joel 2:12-13**. "Yet even now," declares the LORD, "return to me with all your heart, with fasting, with weeping, and with mourning; and rend your hearts and not your garments." Return to the LORD your God, for he is gracious and merciful, slow to anger, and abounding in steadfast love; and he relents over disaster."

7 **Jer. 31:18-19**. I have heard Ephraim grieving, You have disciplined me, and I was disciplined, like an untrained calf; bring me back that I may be restored, for you are the LORD my God. For after I had turned away, I relented, and after I was instructed, I struck my thigh; I was ashamed, and I was confounded, because I bore the disgrace of my youth.'

8 **2 Cor. 7:11**. For see what earnestness this godly grief has produced in you, but also what eagerness to clear yourselves, what indignation, what fear, what longing, what zeal, what punishment! At every point you have proved yourselves innocent in the matter.

9 **1 Kings 8:47-48**. ...yet if they turn their heart in the land to which they have been carried captive, and repent and plead with you in the land of their captors, saying, 'We have sinned and have acted perversely and wickedly,' if they repent with all their mind and with all their heart in the land of their enemies, who carried them captive, and pray to you toward their land, which you gave to their fathers, the city that you have chosen, and the house that I have built for your name. **Ez. 14:6**. "Therefore say to the house of Israel, Thus says the Lord GOD: Repent and turn away from your idols, and turn away your faces from all your abominations." **Acts 26:18**. '...to open their eyes, so that they may turn from darkness to light and from the power of Satan to God, that they may receive forgiveness of sins and a place among those who are sanctified by faith in me.'

10 **2 Kings 23:25**. Before him there was no king like him, who turned to the LORD with all his heart and with all his soul and with all his might, according to all the Law of Moses, nor did any like him arise after him. **Ps. 119:6, 59, 128**. Then I shall not be put to shame, having my eyes fixed on all your commandments. ... When I think on my ways, I turn my feet to your testimonies. ... Therefore I consider all your precepts to be right; I hate every false way. **Lk. 1:6**. And they were both righteous before God, walking blamelessly in all the commandments and statutes of the Lord.

Q. 77. How do justification and sanctification differ?

A. Although sanctification is inseparably joined with justification,[1] they differ in that God, in justification, imputes the righteousness of

Christ;[2] in sanctification, his Spirit infuses grace, and enables the exercise of it;[3] in the former, sin is pardoned;[4] in the other, it is subdued;[5] the one does equally free all believers from the revenging wrath of God, and that is accomplished perfectly in this life, that they never fall into condemnation;[6] the other is neither equal in all,[7] nor in this life perfect in any,[8] but growing up to perfection.[9]

1 **1 Cor. 1:30**. And because of him you are in Christ Jesus, who became to us wisdom from God, righteousness and sanctification and redemption. **1 Cor. 6:11**. And such were some of you. But you were washed, you were sanctified, you were justified in the name of the Lord Jesus Christ and by the Spirit of our God.

2 **Rom. 4:6, 8**. ...just as David also speaks of the blessing of the one to whom God counts righteousness apart from work. ...blessed is the man against whom the Lord will not count his sin.

3 **Ezek. 36:27**. And I will put my Spirit within you, and cause you to walk in my statutes and be careful to obey my rules.

4 **Rom. 3:24-25**. ...and are justified by his grace as a gift, through the redemption that is in Christ Jesus, whom God put forward as a propitiation by his blood, to be received by faith. This was to show God's righteousness, because in his divine forbearance he had passed over former sins.

5 **Rom. 6:6, 14**. We know that our old self was crucified with him in order that the body of sin might be brought to nothing, so that we would no longer be enslaved to sin. ... For sin will have no dominion over you, since you are not under law but under grace.

6 **Rom. 8:33-34**. Who shall bring any charge against God's elect? It is God who justifies. Who is to condemn? Christ Jesus is the one who died—more than that, who was raised—who is at the right hand of God, who indeed is interceding for us.

7 **Heb. 5:12-14**. For though by this time you ought to be teachers, you need someone to teach you again the basic principles of the oracles of God. You need milk, not solid food, for everyone who lives on milk is unskilled in the word of righteousness, since he is a child. But solid food is for the mature, for those who have their powers of discernment trained by constant practice to distinguish good from evil. **1 Jn. 2:12-14**. I am writing to you, little children, because your sins are forgiven for his name's sake. I am writing to you, fathers, because you know him who is from the beginning. I am writing to you, young men, because you have overcome the evil one. I write to you, children, because you know the Father. I write to you, fathers, because you know him who is from the beginning. I write to you, young men, because you are strong, and the word of God abides in you, and you have overcome the evil one.

8 **1 Jn. 1:8, 10**. If we say we have no sin, we deceive ourselves, and the truth is not in us. ... If we say we have not sinned, we make him a liar, and his word is not in us.

9 **2 Cor. 7:1**. Since we have these promises, beloved, let us cleanse ourselves from every defilement of body and spirit, bringing holiness to completion in the fear of God. **Phil. 3:12-14**. Not that I have already obtained this or am already perfect, but I press on to make it my own, because Christ Jesus has made me his own. Brothers, I do not consider that I have made it my own. But one thing I do: forgetting what lies behind and straining forward to what lies ahead, I press on toward the goal for the prize of the upward call of God in Christ Jesus.

Q. 78. From what arises the imperfection of sanctification in believers?

A. The imperfection of sanctification in believers arises from the remnants of sin in every part of them, and the perpetual lusting of the flesh against the Spirit; by which they are often foiled with temptations, and fall into many sins,[1] are hindered in all their spiritual service,[2] and their best works are imperfect and defiled in the sight of God.[3]

1 **Mk. 14:66-72.** And as Peter was below in the courtyard, one of the servant girls of the high priest came, and seeing Peter warming himself, she looked at him and said, "You also were with the Nazarene, Jesus." But he denied it, saying, "I neither know nor understand what you mean." And he went out into the gateway and the rooster crowed. And the servant girl saw him and began again to say to the bystanders, "This man is one of them." But again he denied it. And after a little while the bystanders again said to Peter, "Certainly you are one of them, for you are a Galilean." But he began to invoke a curse on himself and to swear, "I do not know this man of whom you speak." And immediately the rooster crowed a second time. And Peter remembered how Jesus had said to him, "Before the rooster crows twice, you will deny me three times." And he broke down and wept. **Rom. 7:18, 23.** For I know that nothing good dwells in me, that is, in my flesh. For I have the desire to do what is right, but not the ability to carry it out. ...but I see in my members another law waging war against the law of my mind and making me captive to the law of sin that dwells in my members. **Gal. 2:11-12.** But when Cephas came to Antioch, I opposed him to his face, because he stood condemned. For before certain men came from James, he was eating with the Gentiles; but when they came he drew back and separated himself, fearing the circumcision party.

2 **Heb. 12:1.** Therefore, since we are surrounded by so great a cloud of witnesses, let us also lay aside every weight, and sin which clings so closely, and let us run with endurance the race that is set before us.

3 **Ex. 28:38.** It shall be on Aaron's forehead, and Aaron shall bear any guilt from the holy things that the people of Israel consecrate as their holy gifts. It shall regularly be on his forehead, that they may be accepted before the LORD. **Isa. 64:6.** We have all become like one who is unclean, and all our righteous deeds are like a polluted garment. We all fade like a leaf, and our iniquities, like the wind, take us away.

Q. 79. May not true believers, by reason of their imperfections, and the many temptations and sins they are overtaken with, fall away from the state of grace?

A. True believers, by reason of the unchangeable love of God,[1] and His decree and covenant to give them perseverance,[2] their inseparable union with Christ,[3] His continual intercession for them,[4] and the Spirit and seed of God remaining in them,[5] can neither totally nor finally fall away from the state of grace,[6] but are kept by the power of God through faith to salvation.[7]

1 **Jer. 31:3.** ...the LORD appeared to him from far away. I have loved you with an everlasting love; therefore I have continued my faithfulness to you.

2 **2 Sam. 23:5.** "For does not my house stand so with God? For he has made with me an everlasting covenant, ordered in all things and secure. For will he not cause to prosper all my help and my desire?" **2 Tim. 2:19.** But God's firm foundation stands, bearing this seal: "The Lord knows those who are his," and, "Let everyone who names the name of the Lord depart from iniquity." **Heb. 13:20-21.** Now may the God of peace who brought again from the dead our Lord Jesus, the great shepherd of the sheep, by the blood of the eternal covenant, equip you with everything good that you may do his will, working in us that which is pleasing in his sight, through Jesus Christ, to whom be glory forever and ever. Amen.

3 **1 Cor. 1:8-9.** ...who will sustain you to the end, guiltless in the day of our Lord Jesus Christ. God is faithful, by whom you were called into the fellowship of his Son, Jesus Christ our Lord.

4 **Lk. 22:32.** "...but I have prayed for you that your faith may not fail. And when you have turned again, strengthen your brothers." **Heb. 7:25.** Consequently, he is able to save to the uttermost those who draw near to God through him, since he always lives to make intercession for them.

5 **1 Jn. 2:27.** But the anointing that you received from him abides in you, and you have no need that anyone should teach you. But as his anointing teaches you about everything, and is true, and is no lie—just as it has taught you, abide in him. **1 Jn. 3:9.** No one born of God makes a practice of sinning, for God's seed abides in him, and he cannot keep on sinning because he has been born of God.

6 **Jer. 32:40.** I will make with them an everlasting covenant, that I will not turn away from doing good to them. And I will put the fear of me in their hearts, that they may not turn from me. **Jn. 10:28.** I give them eternal life, and they will never perish, and no one will snatch them out of my hand.

7 **1 Pet. 1:5.** ...who by God's power are being guarded through faith for a salvation ready to be revealed in the last time.

Q. 80. Can true believers be infallibly assured that they are in the estate of grace, and that they shall persevere in it to salvation?

A. Such as truly believe in Christ, and endeavor to walk in all good conscience before Him,[1] may, without extraordinary revelation, by faith grounded on the truth of God's promises, and by the Spirit enabling them to discern in themselves those graces to which the promises of life are made,[2] and bearing witness with their spirits that they are the children of God,[3] be infallibly assured that they are in the estate of grace, and shall persevere in it to salvation.[4]

1 **1 Jn. 2:3.** And by this we know that we have come to know him, if we keep his commandments.

2 **1 Cor. 2:12.** Now we have received not the spirit of the world, but the Spirit who is from God, that we might understand the things freely given us by God. **Heb. 6:11-12.** And we desire each one of you to show the same earnestness to have the full assurance of hope until the end, so that you may not be sluggish, but imitators of those who through faith and patience inherit the promises. **1 Jn. 3:14, 18-19, 21, 24.** We know that we have passed out of death into

life, because we love the brothers. Whoever does not love abides in death. ... Little children, let us not love in word or talk but in deed and in truth. By this we shall know that we are of the truth and reassure our heart before him. ...Beloved, if our heart does not condemn us, we have confidence before God. ... Whoever keeps his commandments abides in God, and God in him. And by this we know that he abides in us, by the Spirit whom he has given us. **1 Jn. 4:13, 16**. By this we know that we abide in him and he in us, because he has given us of his Spirit. ... So we have come to know and to believe the love that God has for us. God is love, and whoever abides in love abides in God, and God abides in him.

3 **Rom. 8:16**. The Spirit himself bears witness with our spirit that we are children of God.

4 **1 Jn. 5:13.** I write these things to you who believe in the name of the Son of God that you may know that you have eternal life.

Q. 81. Are all true believers at all times assured of their present being in the estate of grace, and that they shall be saved?

A. Assurance of grace and salvation not being of the essence of faith,[1] true believers may wait long before they obtain it;[2] and, after the enjoyment thereof, may have it weakened and interrupted, through many disturbances, sins, temptations, and desertions;[3] yet are they never left without such a presence and support of the Spirit of God, as keeps them from sinking into utter despair.[4]

1 **Eph. 1:13**. In him you also, when you heard the word of truth, the gospel of your salvation, and believed in him, were sealed with the promised Holy Spirit.

2 **Ps. 88:1-3, 6-7, 9, 10, 13-15**. O LORD, God of my salvation; I cry out day and night before you. Let my prayer come before you; incline your ear to my cry! For my soul is full of troubles, and my life draws near to Sheol. ... You have put me in the depths of the pit, in the regions dark and deep. Your wrath lies heavy upon me, and you overwhelm me with all your waves. ...my eye grows dim through sorrow. Every day I call upon you, O LORD; I spread out my hands to you. ... Do you work wonders for the dead? Do the departed rise up to praise you? ... But I, O LORD, cry to you; in the morning my prayer comes before you. O LORD, why do you cast my soul away? Why do you hide your face from me? Afflicted and close to death from my youth up, I suffer your terrors; I am helpless. **Isa. 50:10**. Who among you fears the LORD and obeys the voice of his servant? Let him who walks in darkness and has no light trust in the name of the LORD and rely on his God.

3 **Ps. 22:1**. My God, my God, why have you forsaken me? Why are you so far from saving me, from the words of my groaning? **Ps. 31:22**. I had said in my alarm, "I am cut off from your sight." But you heard the voice of my pleas for mercy when I cried to you for help. **Ps. 51:8, 12**. Let me hear joy and gladness; let the bones that you have broken rejoice. ... Restore to me the joy of your salvation, and uphold me with a willing spirit. **Ps. 77:1-12**. I cry aloud to God, aloud to God, and he will hear me. In the day of my trouble I seek the Lord; in the night my hand is stretched out without wearying; my soul refuses to be comforted. When I remember God, I moan; when I meditate, my spirit faints. You hold my eyelids open; I am so troubled that I cannot speak. I consider the days of old, the years long ago. I said, "Let me remember my song in the night; let me meditate in my heart." Then my spirit made a diligent search: "Will the Lord spurn forever, and never again be

favorable? Has his steadfast love forever ceased? Are his promises at an end for all time? Has God forgotten to be gracious? Has he in anger shut up his compassion?" Then I said, "I will appeal to this, to the years of the right hand of the Most High." I will remember the deeds of the LORD; yes, I will remember your wonders of old. I will ponder all your work, and meditate on your mighty deeds. **Song 5:2-3, 6.** I slept, but my heart was awake. A sound! My beloved is knocking. "Open to me, my sister, my love, my dove, my perfect one, for my head is wet with dew, my locks with the drops of the night." I had put off my garment; how could I put it on? I had bathed my feet; how could I soil them? ... I opened to my beloved, but my beloved had turned and gone. My soul failed me when he spoke. I sought him, but found him not; I called him, but he gave no answer."

4 **Job 13:15.** Though he slay me, I will hope in him; yet I will argue my ways to his face. **Ps. 73:15, 23.** If I had said, "I will speak thus," I would have betrayed the generation of your children. ... Nevertheless, I am continually with you; you hold my right hand. **Isa. 54:7-10.** For a brief moment I deserted you, but with great compassion I will gather you. In overflowing anger for a moment I hid my face from you, but with everlasting love I will have compassion on you," says the LORD, your Redeemer. "This is like the days of Noah to me: as I swore that the waters of Noah should no more go over the earth, so I have sworn that I will not be angry with you, and will not rebuke you. For the mountains may depart and the hills be removed, but my steadfast love shall not depart from you, and my covenant of peace shall not be removed," says the LORD, who has compassion on you. **1 Jn. 3:9.** No one born of God makes a practice of sinning, for God's seed abides in him, and he cannot keep on sinning because he has been born of God.

Q. 82. What is the communion in glory that the members of the invisible church have with Christ?

A. The communion in glory that the members of the invisible church have with Christ, is in this life,[1] immediately after death,[2] and at last perfected at the resurrection and day of judgment.[3]

1 **2 Cor. 3:18.** And we all, with unveiled face, beholding the glory of the Lord, are being transformed into the same image from one degree of glory to another. For this comes from the Lord who is the Spirit.

2 **Lk. 23:43.** And he said to him, "Truly, I say to you, today you will be with me in Paradise."

3 **1 Thess. 4:17.** Then we who are alive, who are left, will be caught up together with them in the clouds to meet the Lord in the air, and so we will always be with the Lord.

Q. 83. What is the communion in glory with Christ that the members of the invisible church enjoy in this life?

A. The members of the invisible church have communicated to them, in this life, the first fruits of glory with Christ, as they are members of Him their head, and so in Him have a share in the glory that He is fully possessed of;[1] and as a deposit on it, enjoy the sense of God's love,[2] peace of conscience, joy in the Holy Spirit, and hope of glory.[3] As, on the contrary, the sense of God's revenging wrath, horror of conscience, and a fearful expectation of judgment, are to the wicked the beginning of the torment that they shall endure after death.[4]

1 **Eph. 2:5-6.** ...even when we were dead in our trespasses, made us alive together with Christ—by grace you have been saved—and raised us up with him and seated us with him in the heavenly places in Christ Jesus.

2 **Rom. 5:5.** ...and hope does not put us to shame, because God's love has been poured into our hearts through the Holy Spirit who has been given to us. **2 Cor. 1:22.** ...and who has also put his seal on us and given us his Spirit in our hearts as a guarantee.

3 **Rom. 5:1-2.** Therefore, since we have been justified by faith, we have peace with God through our Lord Jesus Christ. Through him we have also obtained access by faith into this grace in which we stand, and we rejoice in hope of the glory of God. **Rom. 14:17.** For the kingdom of God is not a matter of eating and drinking but of righteousness and peace and joy in the Holy Spirit.

4 **Gen. 4:13.** Cain said to the LORD, "My punishment is greater than I can bear." **Mt. 27:4.** ...saying, "I have sinned by betraying innocent blood." They said, "What is that to us? See to it yourself." **Mk. 9:44, 48.** It is better for you to enter life crippled than with two hands to go to hell, to the unquenchable fire. '...where their worm does not die and the fire is not quenched.' **Rom. 2:9.** There will be tribulation and distress for every human being who does evil, the Jew first and also the Greek. **Heb. 10:27.** ...but a fearful expectation of judgment, and a fury of fire that will consume the adversaries.

Q. 84. Shall all men die?

A. Death being threatened as the wages of sin,[1] it is appointed to all men once to die;[2] for that all have sinned.[3]

1 **Rom. 6:23.** For the wages of sin is death, but the free gift of God is eternal life in Christ Jesus our Lord.

2 **Heb. 9:27.** And just as it is appointed for man to die once, and after that comes judgment.

3 **Rom. 5:12.** Therefore, just as sin came into the world through one man, and death through sin, and so death spread to all men because all sinned.

Q. 85. Death being the wages of sin, why are not the righteous delivered from death, seeing all their sins are forgiven in Christ?

A. The righteous shall be delivered from death itself at the last day, and even in death are delivered from the sting and curse of it;[1] so that although they die, yet it is out of God's love,[2] to free them perfectly from sin and misery,[3] and to make them capable of further communion with Christ in glory, which they then enter.[4]

1 **1 Cor. 15:26, 55-57.** The last enemy to be destroyed is death. ..."O death, where is your victory? O death, where is your sting?" The sting of death is sin, and the power of sin is the law. But thanks be to God, who gives us the victory through our Lord Jesus Christ. **Heb. 2:15.** ...and deliver all those who through fear of death were subject to lifelong slavery.

2 **2 Kings 22:20.** "'Therefore, behold, I will gather you to your fathers, and you shall be gathered to your grave in peace, and your eyes shall not see all the disaster that I will bring upon this place.'" And they brought back word to the king. **Isa. 57:1-2.** The righteous man perishes, and no one lays it to heart; devout men are taken away, while no one understands. For the righteous man is taken away from calamity; he enters into peace; they rest in their beds who walk in their uprightness.

3 **Eph. 5:27.** ...so that he might present the church to himself in splendor, without spot or wrinkle or any such thing, that she might be holy and without blemish. **Rev. 14:13.** And I heard a voice from heaven saying, "Write this: Blessed are the dead who die in the Lord from now on." "Blessed indeed," says the Spirit, "that they may rest from their labors, for their deeds follow them!"

4 **Lk. 23:43.** And he said to him, "Truly, I say to you, today you will be with me in Paradise."

Q. 86. What is the communion in glory with Christ that the members of the invisible church enjoy immediately after death?

A. The communion in glory with Christ that the members of the invisible church enjoy immediately after death, is that their souls are then made perfect in holiness,[1] and received into the highest heavens,[2] where they behold the face of God in light and glory;[3] waiting for the full redemption of their bodies,[4] which even in death continue united to Christ,[5] and rest in their graves as in their beds,[6] till at the last day they be again united to their souls.[7] Whereas the souls of the wicked are at their death cast into hell, where they remain in torments and utter darkness; and their bodies kept in their graves, as in their prisons, until the resurrection and judgment of the great day.[8]

1 **Heb. 12:23.** ...and to the assembly of the firstborn who are enrolled in heaven, and to God, the judge of all, and to the spirits of the righteous made perfect.

2 **Acts 3:21.** ...whom heaven must receive until the time for restoring all the things about which God spoke by the mouth of his holy prophets long ago. **2 Cor. 5:1, 6, 8.** For we know that if the tent that is our earthly home is destroyed, we have a building from God, a house not made with hands, eternal in the heavens. ... So we are always of good courage. We know that while we are at home in the body we are away from the Lord. ... Yes, we are of good courage, and we would rather be away from the body and at home with the Lord. **Eph. 4:10.** He who descended is the one who also ascended far above all the heavens, that he might fill all things. **Phil. 1:23.** I am hard pressed between the two. My desire is to depart and be with Christ, for that is far better.

3 **1 Cor. 13:12**. For now we see in a mirror dimly, but then face to face. Now I know in part; then I shall know fully, even as I have been fully known. **1 Jn. 3:2**. Beloved, we are God's children now, and what we will be has not yet appeared; but we know that when he appears we shall be like him, because we shall see him as he is.

4 **Ps. 16:9**. Therefore my heart is glad, and my whole being rejoices; my flesh also dwells secure. **Rom. 8:23**. And not only the creation, but we ourselves, who have the firstfruits of the Spirit, groan inwardly as we wait eagerly for adoption as sons, the redemption of our bodies.

5 **1 Thess. 4:14**. For since we believe that Jesus died and rose again, even so, through Jesus, God will bring with him those who have fallen asleep.

6 **Isa. 57:2**. ...he enters into peace; they rest in their beds who walk in their uprightness.

7 **Job 19:26-27**. And after my skin has been thus destroyed, yet in my flesh I shall see God, whom I shall see for myself, and my eyes shall behold, and not another. My heart faints within me!

8 **Lk. 16:23-24**. ...and in Hades, being in torment, he lifted up his eyes and saw Abraham far off and Lazarus at his side. And he called out, 'Father Abraham, have mercy on me, and send Lazarus to dip the end of his finger in water and cool my tongue, for I am in anguish in this flame.' **Acts 1:25**. "...to take the place in this ministry and apostleship from which Judas turned aside to go to his own place." **Jude 6-7**. And the angels who did not stay within their own position of authority, but left their proper dwelling, he has kept in eternal chains under gloomy darkness until the judgment of the great day—just as Sodom and Gomorrah and the surrounding cities, which likewise indulged in sexual immorality and pursued unnatural desire, serve as an example by undergoing a punishment of eternal fire.

Q. 87. What are we to believe concerning the resurrection?

A. We are to believe that, at the last day, there shall be a general resurrection of the dead, both of the just and unjust;[1] when they that are then found alive shall in a moment be changed; and the actual bodies of the dead that are laid in the grave, being then again united to their souls forever, shall be raised up by the power of Christ.[2] The bodies of the just, by the Spirit of Christ, and by virtue of his resurrection as their Head, shall be raised in power, spiritual, and incorruptible, and made like His glorious body:[3] and the bodies of the wicked shall be raised up in dishonor by Him as an offended judge.[4]

1 **Acts 24:15**. ...having a hope in God, which these men themselves accept, that there will be a resurrection of both the just and the unjust.

2 **Jn. 5:28-29**. Do not marvel at this, for an hour is coming when all who are in the tombs will hear his voice and come out, those who have done good to the resurrection of life, and those who have done evil to the resurrection of judgment. **1 Cor. 15:51-53**. Behold! I tell you a mystery. We shall not all sleep, but we shall all be changed, in a moment, in the twinkling of an eye, at the last trumpet. For the trumpet will sound, and the dead will be raised imperishable, and we shall be changed. For this perishable body must put on the imperishable, and this mortal body must put on immortality. **1 Thess. 4:15-17**. For this we declare to you by a

word from the Lord, that we who are alive, who are left until the coming of the Lord, will not precede those who have fallen asleep. For the Lord himself will descend from heaven with a cry of command, with the voice of an archangel, and with the sound of the trumpet of God. And the dead in Christ will rise first. Then we who are alive, who are left, will be caught up together with them in the clouds to meet the Lord in the air, and so we will always be with the Lord.

3 **1 Cor. 15:21-23, 42-44**. For as by a man came death, by a man has come also the resurrection of the dead. For as in Adam all die, so also in Christ shall all be made alive. But each in his own order: Christ the firstfruits, then at his coming those who belong to Christ. ... So is it with the resurrection of the dead. What is sown is perishable; what is raised is imperishable. It is sown in dishonor; it is raised in glory. It is sown in weakness; it is raised in power. It is sown a natural body; it is raised a spiritual body. If there is a natural body, there is also a spiritual body. **Phil. 3:21**. ...who will transform our lowly body to be like his glorious body, by the power that enables him even to subject all things to himself.

4 **Mt. 25:33**. And he will place the sheep on his right, but the goats on the left. **Jn. 5:27-29**. And he has given him authority to execute judgment, because he is the Son of Man. Do not marvel at this, for an hour is coming when all who are in the tombs will hear his voice and come out, those who have done good to the resurrection of life, and those who have done evil to the resurrection of judgment.

Q. 88. What shall immediately follow after the resurrection?

A. Immediately after the resurrection shall follow the general and final judgment of angels and men,[1] the day and hour of which no man knows, that all may watch and pray, and be ever ready for the coming of the Lord.[2]

1 **Mt. 25:46.** "And these will go away into eternal punishment, but the righteous into eternal life." **2 Pet. 2:4, 6-7, 14-15**. For if God did not spare angels when they sinned, but cast them into hell and committed them to chains of gloomy darkness to be kept until the judgment. ...if by turning the cities of Sodom and Gomorrah to ashes he condemned them to extinction, making them an example of what is going to happen to the ungodly; and if he rescued righteous Lot, greatly distressed by the sensual conduct of the wicked. ... They have eyes full of adultery, insatiable for sin. They entice unsteady souls. They have hearts trained in greed. Accursed children! Forsaking the right way, they have gone astray. They have followed the way of Balaam, the son of Beor, who loved gain from wrongdoing.

2 **Mt. 24:36, 42, 44**. "But concerning that day and hour no one knows, not even the angels of heaven, nor the Son, but the Father only."... Therefore, stay awake, for you do not know on what day your Lord is coming. ... Therefore you also must be ready, for the Son of Man is coming at an hour you do not expect.

Q. 89. What shall be done to the wicked at the day of judgment?

A. At the day of judgment, the wicked shall be set on Christ's left hand,[1] and upon clear evidence, and full conviction of their own consciences,[2] shall have the fearful but just sentence of condemnation pronounced against them;[3] and then shall be cast out from the favorable presence of God, and the glorious fellowship with Christ,

His saints, and all His holy angels, into hell, to be punished with unspeakable torments both of body and soul, with the devil and his angels forever.[4]

1 **Mt. 25:33**. And he will place the sheep on his right, but the goats on the left.

2 **Rom. 2:15-16**. They show that the work of the law is written on their hearts, while their conscience also bears witness, and their conflicting thoughts accuse or even excuse them on that day when, according to my gospel, God judges the secrets of men by Christ Jesus.

3 **Mt. 25:41-43**. "Then he will say to those on his left, 'Depart from me, you cursed, into the eternal fire prepared for the devil and his angels. For I was hungry and you gave me no food, I was thirsty and you gave me no drink, I was a stranger and you did not welcome me, naked and you did not clothe me, sick and in prison and you did not visit me.'"

4 **Lk. 16:26**. 'And besides all this, between us and you a great chasm has been fixed, in order that those who would pass from here to you may not be able, and none may cross from there to us.' **2 Thess. 1:8-9**. ...in flaming fire, inflicting vengeance on those who do not know God and on those who do not obey the gospel of our Lord Jesus. They will suffer the punishment of eternal destruction, away from the presence of the Lord and from the glory of his might.

Q. 90. What shall be done to the righteous at the day of judgment?

A. At the day of judgment, the righteous, being caught up to Christ in the clouds,[1] shall be set on his right hand, and, there openly acknowledged and acquitted,[2] shall join with Him in the judging of wicked angels and men;[3] and shall be received into heaven,[4] where they shall be fully and forever freed from all sin and misery;[5] filled with inconceivable joy;[6] made perfectly holy and happy both in body and soul, in the company of innumerable saints and angels,[17] but especially in the immediate vision and fruition of God the Father, of our Lord Jesus Christ, and of the Holy Spirit, to all eternity.[8] And this is the perfect and full communion that the members of the invisible church shall enjoy with Christ in glory, at the resurrection and day of judgment.

1 **1 Thess. 4:17**. Then we who are alive, who are left, will be caught up together with them in the clouds to meet the Lord in the air, and so we will always be with the Lord.

2 **Mt. 10:32**. So everyone who acknowledges me before men, I also will acknowledge before my Father who is in heaven. **Mt. 25:33**. And he will place the sheep on his right, but the goats on the left.

3 **1 Cor. 6:2-3**. Or do you not know that the saints will judge the world? And if the world is to be judged by you, are you incompetent to try trivial cases? Do you not know that we are to judge angels? How much more, then, matters pertaining to this life!

4 **Mt. 25: 34, 46**. Then the King will say to those on his right, 'Come, you who are blessed by my Father, inherit the kingdom prepared for you from the foundation of the world.' ... "And these will go away into eternal punishment, but the righteous into eternal life."

5 **Eph. 5:27**. ...so that he might present the church to himself in splendor, without spot or wrinkle or any such thing, that she might be holy and without blemish. **Rev. 14:13**. And I heard a voice from heaven saying, "Write this: Blessed are the dead who die in the Lord from now on." "Blessed indeed," says the Spirit, "that they may rest from their labors, for their deeds follow them!"

6 **Ps. 16:11**. You make known to me the path of life; in your presence there is fullness of joy; at your right hand are pleasures forevermore.

7 **Heb. 12:22-23**. But you have come to Mount Zion and to the city of the living God, the heavenly Jerusalem, and to innumerable angels in festal gathering, and to the assembly of the firstborn who are enrolled in heaven, and to God, the judge of all, and to the spirits of the righteous made perfect.

8 **1 Cor. 13:12**. For now we see in a mirror dimly, but then face to face. Now I know in part; then I shall know fully, even as I have been fully known. **1 Thess. 4:17-18**. Then we who are alive, who are left, will be caught up together with them in the clouds to meet the Lord in the air, and so we will always be with the Lord. Therefore encourage one another with these words. **1 Jn. 3:2**. Beloved, we are God's children now, and what we will be has not yet appeared; but we know that when he appears we shall be like him, because we shall see him as he is.

HAVING SEEN WHAT THE SCRIPTURES PRINCIPALLY TEACH US TO BELIEVE CONCERNING GOD, IT FOLLOWS TO CONSIDER WHAT THEY REQUIRE AS THE DUTY OF MAN

Q. 91. What is the duty that God requires of man?

A. The duty that God requires of man is obedience to his revealed will.[1]

1 **1 Sam. 15:22**. And Samuel said, "Has the LORD as great delight in burnt offerings and sacrifices, as in obeying the voice of the LORD? Behold, to obey is better than sacrifice, and to listen than the fat of rams. **Mic. 6:8**. He has told you, O man, what is good; and what does the LORD require of you but to do justice, and to love kindness, and to walk humbly with your God? **Rom. 12:1-2**. I appeal to you therefore, brothers, by the mercies of God, to present your bodies as a living sacrifice, holy and acceptable to God, which is your spiritual worship. Do not be conformed to this world, but be transformed by the renewal of your mind, that by testing you may discern what is the will of God, what is good and acceptable and perfect.

Q. 92. What did God at first reveal to man as the rule of his obedience?

A. The rule of obedience revealed to Adam in the estate of innocence, and to all mankind in him, besides a special command, not to eat of the fruit of the Tree of the Knowledge of Good and Evil, was the moral law.[1]

1 **Gen. 1:26-27.** Then God said, "Let us make man in our image, after our likeness. And let them have dominion over the fish of the sea and over the birds of the heavens and over the livestock and over all the earth and over every creeping thing that creeps on the earth." So God created man in his own image, in the image of God he created him; male and female he created them. **Gen. 2:17.** "...but of the tree of the knowledge of good and evil you shall not eat, for in the day that you eat of it you shall surely die." **Rom. 2:14-15.** For when Gentiles, who do not have the law, by nature do what the law requires, they are a law to themselves, even though they do not have the law. They show that the work of the law is written on their hearts, while their conscience also bears witness, and their conflicting thoughts accuse or even excuse them. **Rom. 10:5.** For Moses writes about the righteousness that is based on the law, that the person who does the commandments shall live by them.

Q. 93. What is the moral law?

A. The moral law is the declaration of the will of God to mankind, directing and binding everyone to personal, perfect, and perpetual conformity and obedience to it, in the frame and disposition of the whole man, soul and body,[1] and in performance of all those duties of holiness and righteousness that he owes to God and man:[2] promising life upon the fulfilling, and threatening death upon the breach of it.[3]

1 **Deut. 5:1-3, 31, 33.** And Moses summoned all Israel and said to them, "Hear, O Israel, the statutes and the rules that I speak in your hearing today, and you shall learn them and be careful to do them. The LORD our God made a covenant with us in Horeb. Not with our fathers did the LORD make this covenant, but with us, who are all of us here alive today. ... 'But you, stand here by me, and I will tell you the whole commandment and the statutes and the rules that you shall teach them, that they may do them in the land that I am giving them to possess.' ... You shall walk in all the way that the LORD your God has commanded you, that you may live, and that it may go well with you, and that you may live long in the land that you shall possess. **Lk. 10:26-27.** He said to him, "What is written in the Law? How do you read it?" And he answered, "You shall love the Lord your God with all your heart and with all your soul and with all your strength and with all your mind, and your neighbor as yourself." **Gal. 3:10.** For all who rely on works of the law are under a curse; for it is written, "Cursed be everyone who does not abide by all things written in the Book of the Law, and do them." **1 Thess. 5:23.** Now may the God of peace himself sanctify you completely, and may your whole spirit and soul and body be kept blameless at the coming of our Lord Jesus Christ.

42 **Lk. 1:75.** ...in holiness and righteousness before him all our days. **Acts 24:16.** So I always take pains to have a clear conscience toward both God and man.

3 **Rom. 10:5**. For Moses writes about the righteousness that is based on the law, that the person who does the commandments shall live by them. **Gal. 3:10, 13**. For all who rely on works of the law are under a curse; for it is written, "Cursed be everyone who does not abide by all things written in the Book of the Law, and do them."

Q. 94. Is there any use of the moral law to man since the Fall?

A. Although no man since the Fall can attain to righteousness and life by the moral law,[1] yet there is great use for it, common to all men, as specific either to the unregenerate, or the regenerate.[2]

1 **Rom. 8:3**. For God has done what the law, weakened by the flesh, could not do. By sending his own Son in the likeness of sinful flesh and for sin, he condemned sin in the flesh. **Gal. 2:16**. ...yet we know that a person is not justified by works of the law but through faith in Jesus Christ, so we also have believed in Christ Jesus, in order to be justified by faith in Christ and not by works of the law, because by works of the law no one will be justified.

2 **1 Tim. 1:8**. Now we know that the law is good, if one uses it lawfully.

Q. 95. Of what use is the moral law to all men?

A. The moral law is of use to all men, to inform them of the holy nature and will of God,[1] and of their duty binding them to walk accordingly;[2] to convince them of their inability to keep it, and of the sinful pollution of their nature, hearts, and lives,[3] to humble them in the sense of their sin and misery,[4] and thereby help them to a clearer sight of the need they have of Christ,[5] and of the perfection of His obedience.[6]

1 **Lev. 11:44-45**. "For I am the LORD your God. Consecrate yourselves therefore, and be holy, for I am holy. You shall not defile yourselves with any swarming thing that crawls on the ground. For I am the LORD who brought you up out of the land of Egypt to be your God. You shall therefore be holy, for I am holy." **Lev. 20:7-8**. Consecrate yourselves, therefore, and be holy, for I am the LORD your God. Keep my statutes and do them; I am the LORD who sanctifies you. **Rom. 8:12**. So then, brothers, we are debtors, not to the flesh, to live according to the flesh.

2 **Mic. 6:8**. He has told you, O man, what is good; and what does the LORD require of you but to do justice, and to love kindness, and to walk humbly with your God? **Jas. 2:10-11**. For whoever keeps the whole law but fails in one point has become accountable for all of it. For he who said, "Do not commit adultery," also said, "Do not murder." If you do not commit adultery but do murder, you have become a transgressor of the law.

3 **Ps. 19:11-12**. Moreover, by them is your servant warned; in keeping them there is great reward. Who can discern his errors? Declare me innocent from hidden faults. **Rom. 3:20**. For by works of the law no human being will be justified in his sight, since through the law comes knowledge of sin. **Rom. 7:7**. What then shall we say? That the law is sin? By no means! Yet if it had not been for the law, I

would not have known sin. For I would not have known what it is to covet if the law had not said, "You shall not covet."

4 **Rom. 3:9, 23**. What then? Are we Jews any better off? No, not at all. For we have already charged that all, both Jews and Greeks, are under sin. ...for all have sinned and fall short of the glory of God.

5 **Gal. 3:21-22**. Is the law then contrary to the promises of God? Certainly not! For if a law had been given that could give life, then righteousness would indeed be by the law. But the Scripture imprisoned everything under sin, so that the promise by faith in Jesus Christ might be given to those who believe.

6 **Rom. 10:4**. For Christ is the end of the law for righteousness to everyone who believes.

Q. 96. What particular use is there of the moral law to unregenerate men?

A. The moral law is of use to unregenerate men, to awaken their consciences to flee from the wrath to come,[1] and to drive them to Christ;[2] or, upon their continuance in the estate and way of sin, to leave them inexcusable,[3] and under the curse of it.[4]

1 **1 Tim. 1:9-10**. ...understanding this, that the law is not laid down for the just but for the lawless and disobedient, for the ungodly and sinners, for the unholy and profane, for those who strike their fathers and mothers, for murderers, the sexually immoral, men who practice homosexuality, enslavers, liars, perjurers, and whatever else is contrary to sound doctrine.

2 **Gal. 3:24**. So then, the law was our guardian until Christ came, in order that we might be justified by faith.

3 **Rom. 1:20**. For his invisible attributes, namely, his eternal power and divine nature, have been clearly perceived, ever since the creation of the world, in the things that have been made. So they are without excuse. **Rom. 2:15**. They show that the work of the law is written on their hearts, while their conscience also bears witness, and their conflicting thoughts accuse or even excuse them.

4 **Gal. 3:10**. For all who rely on works of the law are under a curse; for it is written, "Cursed be everyone who does not abide by all things written in the Book of the Law, and do them."

Q. 97. What special use is there of the moral law to the regenerate?

A. Although they who are regenerate and believe in Christ are delivered from the moral law as a Covenant of Works,[1] so as by it they are neither justified[2] nor condemned:[3] yet, besides the general uses of it common to them with all men, it is of special use to show them how much they are bound to Christ for his fulfilling it, and enduring the curse of it, in their place and for their good;[4] and thereby to provoke them to more thankfulness,[5] and to express the same in their greater care to conform themselves to it as the rule of their obedience.[6]

1 **Rom. 6:14**. For sin will have no dominion over you, since you are not under law but under grace. **Rom. 7:4, 6**. Likewise, my brothers, you also have died to the law through the body of Christ, so that you may belong to another, to him who has been raised from the dead, in order that we may bear fruit for God. ... But now we are released from the law, having died to that which held us captive, so that we serve in the new way of the Spirit and not in the old way of the written code. **Gal. 4:4-5**. But when the fullness of time had come, God sent forth his Son, born of woman, born under the law, to redeem those who were under the law, so that we might receive adoption as sons.

2 **Rom. 3:20**. For by works of the law no human being will be justified in his sight, since through the law comes knowledge of sin.

3 **Rom. 8:1**. There is therefore now no condemnation for those who are in Christ Jesus. **Gal. 5:23**. ...gentleness, self-control; against such things there is no law.

4 **Rom. 7:24-25**. Wretched man that I am! Who will deliver me from this body of death? Thanks be to God through Jesus Christ our Lord! So then, I myself serve the law of God with my mind, but with my flesh I serve the law of sin. **Rom. 8:3-4**. For God has done what the law, weakened by the flesh, could not do. By sending his own Son in the likeness of sinful flesh and for sin, he condemned sin in the flesh, in order that the righteous requirement of the law might be fulfilled in us, who walk not according to the flesh but according to the Spirit. **Gal. 3:13-14**. Christ redeemed us from the curse of the law by becoming a curse for us—for it is written, "Cursed is everyone who is hanged on a tree"— so that in Christ Jesus the blessing of Abraham might come to the Gentiles, so that we might receive the promised Spirit through faith.

5 **Lk. 1:68-69, 74-75**. "Blessed be the Lord God of Israel, for he has visited and redeemed his people and has raised up a horn of salvation for us in the house of his servant David." ...that we, being delivered from the hand of our enemies, might serve him without fear, in holiness and righteousness before him all our days. **Col. 1:12-14**. ...giving thanks to the Father, who has qualified you to share in the inheritance of the saints in light. He has delivered us from the domain of darkness and transferred us to the kingdom of his beloved Son, in whom we have redemption, the forgiveness of sins.

6 **Rom. 7:22**. For I delight in the law of God, in my inner being. **Rom. 12:2**. Do not be conformed to this world, but be transformed by the renewal of your mind, that by testing you may discern what is the will of God, what is good and acceptable and perfect. **Titus 2:11-14**. For the grace of God has appeared, bringing salvation for all people, training us to renounce ungodliness and worldly passions, and to live self-controlled, upright, and godly lives in the present age, waiting for our blessed hope, the appearing of the glory of our great God and Savior Jesus Christ, who gave himself for us to redeem us from all lawlessness and to purify for himself a people for his own possession who are zealous for good works.

Q. 98. Where is the moral law found to be summarized?

A. The moral law is found summarized in the Ten Commandments, which were delivered by the voice of God on Mount Sinai, and written by Him on two tablets of stone;[1] and are recorded in the twentieth chapter of Exodus; the first four commandments containing our duty to God, and the other six our duty to man.[2]

1 **Ex. 34:1-4.** The LORD said to Moses, "Cut for yourself two tablets of stone like the first, and I will write on the tablets the words that were on the first tablets, which you broke. Be ready by the morning, and come up in the morning to Mount Sinai, and present yourself there to me on the top of the mountain. No one shall come up with you, and let no one be seen throughout all the mountain. Let no flocks or herds graze opposite that mountain." So Moses cut two tablets of stone like the first. And he rose early in the morning and went up on Mount Sinai, as the LORD had commanded him, and took in his hand two tablets of stone.
Deut. 10:4. And he wrote on the tablets, in the same writing as before, the Ten Commandments that the LORD had spoken to you on the mountain out of the midst of the fire on the day of the assembly. And the LORD gave them to me.

2 **Mt. 22:37-40.** And he said to him, "You shall love the Lord your God with all your heart and with all your soul and with all your mind. This is the great and first commandment. And a second is like it: You shall love your neighbor as yourself. On these two commandments depend all the Law and the Prophets."

Q. 99. What rules are to be observed for the right understanding of the Ten Commandments?

A. For the right understanding of the Ten Commandments, these rules are to be observed:

1. That the law is perfect, and binds everyone to full conformity in the whole man to the righteousness of it, and to entire obedience forever; so as to require the utmost perfection of every duty, and to forbid the least degree of every sin.[1]
2. That it is spiritual, and so reaches the understanding, will, affections, and all other powers of the soul; as well as words, works, and gestures.[2]
3. That one and the same thing, in various respects, is required or forbidden in several commandments.[3]
4. That as, where a duty is commanded, the contrary sin is forbidden;[4] and where a sin is forbidden, the contrary duty is commanded;[5] so, where a promise is attached, the contrary threatening is included;[6] and where a threatening is attached, the contrary promise is included.[7]
5. That what God forbids, is at no time to be done;[8] what he commands is always our duty;[9] and yet every particular duty is not to be done at all times.[10]
6. That, under one sin or duty, all of the same kind are forbidden or commanded; together with all the causes, means, occasions, and appearances of it, and provocations to it.[11]

7. That what is forbidden or commanded to us, we are bound, according to our situations, to endeavor that it may be avoided or performed by others, according to the duty of their situations.[12]
8. That in what is commanded to others, we are bound, according to our situations and callings, to be helpful to them;[13] and to take heed of participating with others in what is forbidden them.[14]

1 **Ps. 19:7**. The law of the LORD is perfect, reviving the soul; the testimony of the LORD is sure, making wise the simple. **Mt. 5:21-22**. "You have heard that it was said to those of old, 'You shall not murder; and whoever murders will be liable to judgment.' But I say to you that everyone who is angry with his brother will be liable to judgment; whoever insults his brother will be liable to the council; and whoever says, 'You fool!' will be liable to the hell of fire.'" **Jas. 2:10**. For whoever keeps the whole law but fails in one point has become accountable for all of it.

2 **Deut. 6:5**. You shall love the LORD your God with all your heart and with all your soul and with all your might. **Mt. 5:21-22, 27-28, 33-34, 37-39, 43-44**. "You have heard that it was said to those of old, 'You shall not murder; and whoever murders will be liable to judgment.' But I say to you that everyone who is angry with his brother will be liable to judgment; whoever insults his brother will be liable to the council; and whoever says, 'You fool!' will be liable to the hell of fire.'" ... "You have heard that it was said, 'You shall not commit adultery.' But I say to you that everyone who looks at a woman with lustful intent has already committed adultery with her in his heart." ... "Again you have heard that it was said to those of old, 'You shall not swear falsely, but shall perform to the Lord what you have sworn.' But I say to you, Do not take an oath at all, either by heaven, for it is the throne of God." ... Let what you say be simply 'Yes' or 'No'; anything more than this comes from evil. "You have heard that it was said, 'An eye for an eye and a tooth for a tooth.' But I say to you, Do not resist the one who is evil. But if anyone slaps you on the right cheek, turn to him the other also." ... "You have heard that it was said, 'You shall love your neighbor and hate your enemy.' But I say to you, Love your enemies and pray for those who persecute you." **Mt. 22:37-39**. And he said to him, "You shall love the Lord your God with all your heart and with all your soul and with all your mind. This is the great and first commandment. And a second is like it: You shall love your neighbor as yourself. **Rom. 7:14**. For we know that the law is spiritual, but I am of the flesh, sold under sin.

3 **Prov. 1:19**. Such are the ways of everyone who is greedy for unjust gain; it takes away the life of its possessors. **Am. 8:5**. ...saying, "When will the new moon be over, that we may sell grain? And the Sabbath, that we may offer wheat for sale, that we may make the ephah small and the shekel great and deal deceitfully with false balances. **Col. 3:4**. When Christ who is your life appears, then you also will appear with him in glory. **1 Tim. 6:10**. For the love of money is a root of all kinds of evils. It is through this craving that some have wandered away from the faith and pierced themselves with many pangs.

4 **Deut. 6:13**. It is the LORD your God you shall fear. Him you shall serve and by his name you shall swear. **Isa. 58:13**. "If you turn back your foot from the Sabbath, from doing your pleasure on my holy day, and call the Sabbath a delight and the holy day of the LORD honorable; if you honor it, not going your own ways, or seeking your own pleasure, or talking idly. **Mt. 4:9-10**. And he said to him, "All these I will give you, if you will fall down and worship me." Then Jesus said to

him, "Be gone, Satan! For it is written, "'You shall worship the Lord your God and him only shall you serve.'" **Mt. 15:4-6**. For God commanded, 'Honor your father and your mother,' and, 'Whoever reviles father or mother must surely die.' But you say, 'If anyone tells his father or his mother, "What you would have gained from me is given to God," he need not honor his father.' So for the sake of your tradition you have made void the word of God.

5 **Mt. 5:21-25**. "You have heard that it was said to those of old, 'You shall not murder; and whoever murders will be liable to judgment.' But I say to you that everyone who is angry with his brother will be liable to judgment; whoever insults his brother will be liable to the council; and whoever says, 'You fool!' will be liable to the hell of fire. So if you are offering your gift at the altar and there remember that your brother has something against you, leave your gift there before the altar and go. First be reconciled to your brother, and then come and offer your gift. Come to terms quickly with your accuser while you are going with him to court, lest your accuser hand you over to the judge, and the judge to the guard, and you be put in prison." **Eph. 4:28**. Let the thief no longer steal, but rather let him labor, doing honest work with his own hands, so that he may have something to share with anyone in need.

6 **Ex. 20:12**. "Honor your father and your mother, that your days may be long in the land that the LORD your God is giving you." **Prov. 30:17**. The eye that mocks a father and scorns to obey a mother will be picked out by the ravens of the valley and eaten by the vultures.

7 **Ex. 20:7**. "You shall not take the name of the LORD your God in vain, for the LORD will not hold him guiltless who takes his name in vain." **Ps. 15:1, 4-5**. O LORD, who shall sojourn in your tent? Who shall dwell on your holy hill?...in whose eyes a vile person is despised, but who honors those who fear the LORD; who swears to his own hurt and does not change; who does not put out his money at interest and does not take a bribe against the innocent. He who does these things shall never be moved. **Ps. 24:4-5**. He who has clean hands and a pure heart, who does not lift up his soul to what is false and does not swear deceitfully. He will receive blessing from the LORD and righteousness from the God of his salvation. **Jer. 18:7-8**. If at any time I declare concerning a nation or a kingdom, that I will pluck up and break down and destroy it, and if that nation, concerning which I have spoken, turns from its evil, I will relent of the disaster that I intended to do to it.

8 **Job 13:7-8**. Will you speak falsely for God and speak deceitfully for him? Will you show partiality toward him? Will you plead the case for God? **Job 36:21**. Take care; do not turn to iniquity, for this you have chosen rather than affliction. **Rom. 3:8**. And why not do evil that good may come?—as some people slanderously charge us with saying. Their condemnation is just. **Heb. 11:25**. ...choosing rather to be mistreated with the people of God than to enjoy the fleeting pleasures of sin.

9 **Deut. 4:8-9**. And what great nation is there, that has statutes and rules so righteous as all this law that I set before you today? "Only take care, and keep your soul diligently, lest you forget the things that your eyes have seen, and lest they depart from your heart all the days of your life. Make them known to your children and your children's children.

10 **Mt. 12:7**. And if you had known what this means, 'I desire mercy, and not sacrifice,' you would not have condemned the guiltless.

11 **Mt. 5:21-22, 27-28**. "You have heard that it was said to those of old, 'You shall not murder; and whoever murders will be liable to judgment.' But I say to you that everyone who is angry with his brother will be liable to judgment; whoever insults his brother will be liable to the council; and whoever says, 'You fool!' will be liable to the hell of fire." ... "You have heard that it was said, 'You shall not commit adultery.' But I say to you that everyone who looks at a woman with lustful intent has

already committed adultery with her in his heart." **Mt. 15:4-6**. For God commanded, 'Honor your father and your mother,' and, 'Whoever reviles father or mother must surely die.' But you say, 'If anyone tells his father or his mother, "What you would have gained from me is given to God," he need not honor his father.' So for the sake of your tradition you have made void the word of God. **Gal. 5:26**. Let us not become conceited, provoking one another, envying one another. **Col. 3:21**. Fathers, do not provoke your children, lest they become discouraged. **1 Thess. 5:22**. Abstain from every form of evil. **Heb. 10:24-25**. And let us consider how to stir up one another to love and good works, not neglecting to meet together, as is the habit of some, but encouraging one another, and all the more as you see the Day drawing near. **Jude 23**. ...save others by snatching them out of the fire; to others show mercy with fear, hating even the garment stained by the flesh.

12 **Gen. 18:19**. "For I have chosen him, that he may command his children and his household after him to keep the way of the LORD by doing righteousness and justice, so that the LORD may bring to Abraham what he has promised him." **Ex. 20:10**. ...but the seventh day is a Sabbath to the LORD your God. On it you shall not do any work, you, or your son, or your daughter, your male servant, or your female servant, or your livestock, or the sojourner who is within your gates. **Lev. 19:17**. "You shall not hate your brother in your heart, but you shall reason frankly with your neighbor, lest you incur sin because of him." **Deut. 6:6-7**. And these words that I command you today shall be on your heart. You shall teach them diligently to your children, and shall talk of them when you sit in your house, and when you walk by the way, and when you lie down, and when you rise. **Josh. 14:15**. Now the name of Hebron formerly was Kiriath-arba. (Arba was the greatest man among the Anakim.) And the land had rest from war.

13 **2 Cor. 1:24**. Not that we lord it over your faith, but we work with you for your joy, for you stand firm in your faith.

14 **Eph. 5:11**. Take no part in the unfruitful works of darkness, but instead expose them. **1 Tim. 5:22**. Do not be hasty in the laying on of hands, nor take part in the sins of others; keep yourself pure.

Q. 100. What special things are we to consider in the Ten Commandments?

A. We are to consider in the Ten Commandments: the preface, the substances of the commandments themselves, and the several reasons attached to some of them to encourage greater enforcement of them.

Q. 101. What is the preface to the Ten Commandments?

A. The preface to the Ten Commandments is contained in these words: "I am the LORD your God, who brought you out of the land of Egypt, out of the house of slavery."[1] With this God makes known His sovereignty, as being Yahweh, the eternal, unchangeable, and almighty God;[2] having His existence in and of Himself,[3] and giving existence to all His words[4] and works;[5] and that He is a God in covenant, as with Israel of old, so with all His people;[6]

who as He brought them out of their bondage in Egypt, so He delivered us from our spiritual bondage;[7] and that therefore we are bound to take Him for our God alone, and to keep all his commandments.[8]

1 **Ex. 20:2.** "I am the LORD your God, who brought you out of the land of Egypt, out of the house of slavery."

2 **Isa. 44:6.** Thus says the LORD, the King of Israel and his Redeemer, the LORD of hosts: "I am the first and I am the last; besides me there is no god."

3 **Ex. 3:14.** God said to Moses, "I AM WHO I AM." And he said, "Say this to the people of Israel, 'I AM has sent me to you.'"

4 **Ex. 6:3.** I appeared to Abraham, to Isaac, and to Jacob, as God Almighty, but by my name the LORD I did not make myself known to them.

5 **Acts 17:24, 28.** The God who made the world and everything in it, being Lord of heaven and earth, does not live in temples made by man. ... "'In him we live and move and have our being'; as even some of your own poets have said, "'For we are indeed his offspring.'"

6 **Gen. 17:7.** And I will establish my covenant between me and you and your offspring after you throughout their generations for an everlasting covenant, to be God to you and to your offspring after you. **Rom. 3:9.** What then? Are we Jews any better off? No, not at all. For we have already charged that all, both Jews and Greeks, are under sin.

7 **Lk. 1:74-75.** ...that we, being delivered from the hand of our enemies, might serve him without fear, in holiness and righteousness before him all our days.

8 **Lev. 18:30.** "So keep my charge never to practice any of these abominable customs that were practiced before you, and never to make yourselves unclean by them: I am the LORD your God." **Lev. 19:37.** "And you shall observe all my statutes and all my rules, and do them: I am the LORD." **1 Pet. 1:15, 17-18.** ...but as he who called you is holy, you also be holy in all your conduct. ... And if you call on him as Father who judges impartially according to each one's deeds, conduct yourselves with fear throughout the time of your exile, knowing that you were ransomed from the futile ways inherited from your forefathers, not with perishable things such as silver or gold.

Q. 102. What is the sum of the four commandments that contain our duty to God?

A. The sum of the four commandments containing our duty to God is, to love the Lord our God with all our heart, and with all our soul, and with all our strength, and with all our mind.[1]

1 **Lk. 10:27.** And he answered, "You shall love the Lord your God with all your heart and with all your soul and with all your strength and with all your mind, and your neighbor as yourself."

Q. 103. Which is the First Commandment?

A. The First Commandment is, "You shall have no other gods before me."[1]

1 **Ex. 20:3**. "You shall have no other gods before me."

Q. 104. What are the duties required in the First Commandment?

A. The duties required in the First Commandment are: the knowing and acknowledging of God to be the only true God, and our God;[1] and to worship and glorify him accordingly;[2] by thinking,[3] meditating,[4] remembering,[5] highly esteeming,[6] honoring,[7] adoring,[8] choosing,[9] loving,[10] desiring,[11] fearing him;[12] believing Him;[13] trusting,[14] hoping,[15] delighting,[16] rejoicing in Him;[17] being zealous for Him;[18] calling upon Him, giving all praise and thanks,[19] and yielding all obedience and submission to Him with the whole man;[20] being careful in all things to please Him,[21] and sorrowful when in anything He is offended;[22] and walking humbly with Him.[23]

1 **Deut. 26:7**. Then we cried to the LORD, the God of our fathers, and the LORD heard our voice and saw our affliction, our toil, and our oppression. **1 Chron. 28:9**. "And you, Solomon my son, know the God of your father and serve him with a whole heart and with a willing mind, for the LORD searches all hearts and understands every plan and thought. If you seek him, he will be found by you, but if you forsake him, he will cast you off forever." **Isa. 43:10**. "You are my witnesses," declares the LORD, "and my servant whom I have chosen, that you may know and believe me and understand that I am he. Before me no god was formed, nor shall there be any after me. **Jer. 14:22**. Are there any among the false gods of the nations that can bring rain? Or can the heavens give showers? Are you not he, O LORD our God? We set our hope on you, for you do all these things.

2 **Ps. 29:2**. Ascribe to the LORD the glory due his name; worship the LORD in the splendor of holiness. **Ps. 95:6-7**. Oh come, let us worship and bow down; let us kneel before the LORD, our Maker! For he is our God, and we are the people of his pasture, and the sheep of his hand. Today, if you hear his voice. **Mt. 4:10**. "'You shall worship the Lord your God and him only shall you serve.'"

3 **Mal. 3:16**. Then those who feared the LORD spoke with one another. The LORD paid attention and heard them, and a book of remembrance was written before him of those who feared the LORD and esteemed his name.

4 **Ps. 63:6**. ...when I remember you upon my bed, and meditate on you in the watches of the night.

5 **Eccl. 12:1**. Remember also your Creator in the days of your youth, before the evil days come and the years draw near of which you will say, "I have no pleasure in them."

6 **Ps. 71:19**. Your righteousness, O God, reaches the high heavens. You who have done great things, O God, who is like you?

7 **Mal. 1:6**. "A son honors his father, and a servant his master. If then I am a father, where is my honor? And if I am a master, where is my fear? says the LORD of

hosts to you, O priests, who despise my name. But you say, 'How have we despised your name?'"

8 **Isa. 45:23**. By myself I have sworn; from my mouth has gone out in righteousness a word that shall not return: To me every knee shall bow, every tongue shall swear allegiance.'

9 **Josh. 24:15, 22**. "And if it is evil in your eyes to serve the LORD, choose this day whom you will serve, whether the gods your fathers served in the region beyond the River, or the gods of the Amorites in whose land you dwell. But as for me and my house, we will serve the LORD."... Then Joshua said to the people, "You are witnesses against yourselves that you have chosen the LORD, to serve him." And they said, "We are witnesses."

10 **Deut. 6:5**. You shall love the LORD your God with all your heart and with all your soul and with all your might.

11 **Ps. 73:25**. Whom have I in heaven but you? And there is nothing on earth that I desire besides you.

12 **Isa. 8:13**. But the LORD of hosts, him you shall honor as holy. Let him be your fear, and let him be your dread.

13 **Ex. 14:31**. Israel saw the great power that the LORD used against the Egyptians, so the people feared the LORD, and they believed in the LORD and in his servant Moses.

14 **Isa. 26:4**. Trust in the LORD forever, for the LORD GOD is an everlasting rock.

15 **Ps. 130:7**. O Israel, hope in the LORD! For with the LORD there is steadfast love, and with him is plentiful redemption.

16 **Ps. 37:4**. Delight yourself in the LORD, and he will give you the desires of your heart.

17 **Ps. 32:11**. Be glad in the LORD, and rejoice, O righteous, and shout for joy, all you upright in heart!

18 **Num. 25:11**. "Phinehas the son of Eleazar, son of Aaron the priest, has turned back my wrath from the people of Israel, in that he was jealous with my jealousy among them, so that I did not consume the people of Israel in my jealousy." **Rom. 12:11**. Do not be slothful in zeal, be fervent in spirit, serve the Lord.

19 **Phil. 4:6**. ...do not be anxious about anything, but in everything by prayer and supplication with thanksgiving let your requests be made known to God.

20 **Jer. 7:23**. But this command I gave them: 'Obey my voice, and I will be your God, and you shall be my people. And walk in all the way that I command you, that it may be well with you.' **Jas. 4:7**. Submit yourselves therefore to God. Resist the devil, and he will flee from you.

21 **1 Jn. 3:22**. ...and whatever we ask we receive from him, because we keep his commandments and do what pleases him.

22 **Ps. 119:136**. My eyes shed streams of tears, because people do not keep your law. **Jer. 31:18**. I have heard Ephraim grieving, 'You have disciplined me, and I was disciplined, like an untrained calf; bring me back that I may be restored, for you are the LORD my God.'

23 **Mic. 6:8**. He has told you, O man, what is good; and what does the LORD require of you but to do justice, and to love kindness, and to walk humbly with your God?

Q. 105. What are the sins forbidden in the First Commandment?

A. The sins forbidden in the First Commandment are: atheism, in denying or not having a God;[1] idolatry, in having or worshiping more gods than one, or any with, or instead of the true God;[2] the not having and acknowledging Him for God, and our God;[3] the omission or neglect of anything due to him, required in this commandment;[4] ignorance,[5] forgetfulness,[6] misunderstandings,[7] false opinions,[8] unworthy and wicked thoughts of Him;[9] bold and curious searchings into His secrets;[10] all profaneness,[11] hatred of God,[12] self-love,[13] self-seeking,[14] and all other inordinate and immoderate setting of our mind, will, or affections on other things, and taking them off Him in whole or in part;[15] vain gullibility,[16] unbelief,[17] heresy,[18] misbelief,[19] distrust,[20] despair,[21] incorrigibility,[22] and insensibility under judgments,[23] hardness of heart,[24] pride,[25] presumption,[26] carnal security,[27] tempting of God;[28] using unlawful means,[29] and trusting in lawful means;[30] carnal delights and joys,[31] corrupt, blind, and indiscreet zeal;[32] lukewarmness,[33] and deadness in the things of God;[34] estranging ourselves, and apostatizing from God;[35] praying or giving any religious worship to saints, angels, or any other creatures;[36] all compacts and consulting with the devil,[37] and listening to his suggestions;[38] making men the lords of our faith and conscience;[39] slighting and despising God, and His commands;[40] resisting and grieving of His Spirit,[41] discontent and impatience at His dispensations, charging Him foolishly for the evils He inflicts on us;[42] and ascribing the praise of any good that we are, have, or can do, to fortune,[43] idols,[44] ourselves,[45] or any other creature.[46]

1 **Ps. 14:1**. The fool says in his heart, "There is no God." They are corrupt, they do abominable deeds, there is none who does good. **Eph. 2:12**. ...remember that you were at that time separated from Christ, alienated from the commonwealth of Israel and strangers to the covenants of promise, having no hope and without God in the world.

2 **Jer. 2:27-28**. ...who say to a tree, 'You are my father,' and to a stone, 'You gave me birth.' For they have turned their back to me, and not their face. But in the time of their trouble they say, 'Arise and save us!' But where are your gods that you made for yourself? Let them arise, if they can save you, in your time of trouble; for as many as your cities are your gods, O Judah. **1 Thess. 1:9**. For they themselves report concerning us the kind of reception we had among you, and how you turned to God from idols to serve the living and true God.

3 **Ps. 18:11**. He made darkness his covering, his canopy around him, thick clouds dark with water.

4 **Isa. 43:2, 23-24**. When you pass through the waters, I will be with you; and through the rivers, they shall not overwhelm you; when you walk through fire you shall not be burned, and the flame shall not consume you. ... You have not brought me your sheep for burnt offerings, or honored me with your sacrifices. I have not burdened you with offerings, or wearied you with frankincense. You have not bought me sweet cane with money, or satisfied me with the fat of your sacrifices. But you have burdened me with your sins; you have wearied me with your iniquities.

5 **Jer. 4:22**. "For my people are foolish; they know me not; they are stupid children; they have no understanding. They are 'wise'—in doing evil! But how to do good they know not." **Hos. 4:1, 6**. Hear the word of the LORD, O children of Israel, for the LORD has a controversy with the inhabitants of the land. There is no faithfulness or steadfast love, and no knowledge of God in the land. ... My people are destroyed for lack of knowledge; because you have rejected knowledge, I reject you from being a priest to me. And since you have forgotten the law of your God, I also will forget your children.

6 **Jer. 2:32**. Can a virgin forget her ornaments, or a bride her attire? Yet my people have forgotten me days without number.

7 **Acts 17:23, 29**. For as I passed along and observed the objects of your worship, I found also an altar with this inscription, 'To the unknown god.' What therefore you worship as unknown, this I proclaim to you. ... Being then God's offspring, we ought not to think that the divine being is like gold or silver or stone, an image formed by the art and imagination of man.

8 **Isa. 40:18**. To whom then will you liken God, or what likeness compare with him?

9 **Ps. 50:21**. These things you have done, and I have been silent; you thought that I was one like yourself. But now I rebuke you and lay the charge before you.

10 **Deut. 29:29**. "The secret things belong to the LORD our God, but the things that are revealed belong to us and to our children forever, that we may do all the words of this law."

11 **Titus 1:16**. They profess to know God, but they deny him by their works. They are detestable, disobedient, unfit for any good work. **Heb. 12:16**. ...that no one is sexually immoral or unholy like Esau, who sold his birthright for a single meal.

12 **Rom. 1:30**. ...slanderers, haters of God, insolent, haughty, boastful, inventors of evil, disobedient to parents.

13 **2 Tim. 3:2**. For people will be lovers of self, lovers of money, proud, arrogant, abusive, disobedient to their parents, ungrateful, unholy.

14 **Phil. 2:21**. For they all seek their own interests, not those of Jesus Christ.

15 **1 Sam. 2:29**. 'Why then do you scorn my sacrifices and my offerings that I commanded for my dwelling, and honor your sons above me by fattening yourselves on the choicest parts of every offering of my people Israel?' **Col. 2:2, 5**. ...that their hearts may be encouraged, being knit together in love, to reach all the riches of full assurance of understanding and the knowledge of God's mystery, which is Christ. ... For though I am absent in body, yet I am with you in spirit, rejoicing to see your good order and the firmness of your faith in Christ. **1 Jn. 2:15-16**. Do not love the world or the things in the world. If anyone loves the world, the love of the Father is not in him. For all that is in the world—the desires of the flesh and the desires of the eyes and pride of life—is not from the Father but is from the world.

16 **1 Jn. 4:1**. Beloved, do not believe every spirit, but test the spirits to see whether they are from God, for many false prophets have gone out into the world.

17 **Heb. 3:12**. Take care, brothers, lest there be in any of you an evil, unbelieving heart, leading you to fall away from the living God.

18 **Gal. 5:20**. ...idolatry, sorcery, enmity, strife, jealousy, fits of anger, rivalries, dissensions, divisions. **Titus 3:10**. As for a person who stirs up division, after warning him once and then twice, have nothing more to do with him.

19 **Acts 26:9**. "I myself was convinced that I ought to do many things in opposing the name of Jesus of Nazareth."

20 **Ps. 78:22**. ...because they did not believe in God and did not trust his saving power.

21 **Gen. 4:13**. Cain said to the LORD, "My punishment is greater than I can bear."

22 **Jer. 5:3**. O LORD, do not your eyes look for truth? You have struck them down, but they felt no anguish; you have consumed them, but they refused to take correction. They have made their faces harder than rock; they have refused to repent.

23 **Isa. 42:25**. So he poured on him the heat of his anger and the might of battle; it set him on fire all around, but he did not understand; it burned him up, but he did not take it to heart.

24 **Rom. 2:5**. But because of your hard and impenitent heart you are storing up wrath for yourself on the day of wrath when God's righteous judgment will be revealed.

25 **Jer. 13:15**. Hear and give ear; be not proud, for the LORD has spoken.

26 **Ps. 10:13**. Why does the wicked renounce God and say in his heart, "You will not call to account"?

27 **Zeph. 1:12**. At that time I will search Jerusalem with lamps, and I will punish the men who are complacent, those who say in their hearts, 'The LORD will not do good, nor will he do ill.'

28 **Mt. 4:7**. Jesus said to him, "Again it is written, 'You shall not put the Lord your God to the test.'"

29 **Rom. 3:8**. And why not do evil that good may come?—as some people slanderously charge us with saying. Their condemnation is just.

30 **Jer. 17:5**. Thus says the LORD: Cursed is the man who trusts in man and makes flesh his strength, whose heart turns away from the LORD."

31 **2 Tim. 3:4**. ...treacherous, reckless, swollen with conceit, lovers of pleasure rather than lovers of God.

32 **Lk. 9:54-55**. And when his disciples James and John saw it, they said, "Lord, do you want us to tell fire to come down from heaven and consume them?" But he turned and rebuked them." **Jn. 16:2**. They will put you out of the synagogues. Indeed, the hour is coming when whoever kills you will think he is offering service to God. **Rom. 10:2**. For I bear them witness that they have a zeal for God, but not according to knowledge. **Gal. 4:17**. They make much of you, but for no good purpose. They want to shut you out, that you may make much of them.

33 **Rev. 3:16**. So, because you are lukewarm, and neither hot nor cold, I will spit you out of my mouth.

34 **Rev. 2:1**. "To the angel of the church in Ephesus write: 'The words of him who holds the seven stars in his right hand, who walks among the seven golden lampstands.'"

35 **Isa. 1:4-5**. Ah, sinful nation, a people laden with iniquity, offspring of evildoers, children who deal corruptly! They have forsaken the LORD, they have despised the Holy One of Israel, they are utterly estranged. Why will you still be struck down? Why will you continue to rebel? The whole head is sick, and the whole heart faint. **Ezek. 14:5**. ...that I may lay hold of the hearts of the house of Israel, who are all estranged from me through their idols.

36 **Hos. 4:12**. My people inquire of a piece of wood, and their walking staff gives them oracles. For a spirit of whoredom has led them astray, and they have left their God to play the whore. **Mt. 4:10**. "'You shall worship the Lord your God and him only shall you serve.'" **Acts 10:25-26**. When Peter entered, Cornelius met him and fell down at his feet and worshiped him. But Peter lifted him up, saying, "Stand up; I too am a man." **Rom. 1:25**. ...because they exchanged the truth about God for a lie and worshiped and served the creature rather than the Creator, who is blessed forever! Amen. **Rom. 10:13-14**. For "everyone who calls on the name of the Lord will be saved." How then will they call on him in whom they have not believed? And how are they to believe in him of whom they have never heard? And

how are they to hear without someone preaching? **Col. 2:18**. Let no one disqualify you, insisting on asceticism and worship of angels, going on in detail about visions, puffed up without reason by his sensuous mind. **Rev. 19:10**. Then I fell down at his feet to worship him, but he said to me, "You must not do that! I am a fellow servant with you and your brothers who hold to the testimony of Jesus. Worship God." For the testimony of Jesus is the spirit of prophecy.

37 **Lev. 20:6**. "If a person turns to mediums and necromancers, whoring after them, I will set my face against that person and will cut him off from among his people. " **1 Sam. 28:7, 11**. Then Saul said to his servants, "Seek out for me a woman who is a medium, that I may go to her and inquire of her." And his servants said to him, "Behold, there is a medium at En-dor." ... Then the woman said, "Whom shall I bring up for you?" He said, "Bring up Samuel for me." **1 Chron. 10:13-14**. So Saul died for his breach of faith. He broke faith with the LORD in that he did not keep the command of the LORD, and also consulted a medium, seeking guidance. He did not seek guidance from the LORD. Therefore the LORD put him to death and turned the kingdom over to David the son of Jesse.

38 **Acts 5:3**. But Peter said, "Ananias, why has Satan filled your heart to lie to the Holy Spirit and to keep back for yourself part of the proceeds of the land?

39 **Mt. 23:9**. And call no man your father on earth, for you have one Father, who is in heaven. **2 Cor. 1:24**. Not that we lord it over your faith, but we work with you for your joy, for you stand firm in your faith.

40 **Deut. 32:15**. "But Jeshurun grew fat, and kicked; you grew fat, stout, and sleek; then he forsook God who made him and scoffed at the Rock of his salvation. **2 Sam. 12:9**. Why have you despised the word of the LORD, to do what is evil in his sight? You have struck down Uriah the Hittite with the sword and have taken his wife to be your wife and have killed him with the sword of the Ammonites. **Prov. 13:13**. Whoever despises the word brings destruction on himself, but he who reveres the commandment will be rewarded.

41 **Acts 7:51**. "You stiff-necked people, uncircumcised in heart and ears, you always resist the Holy Spirit. As your fathers did, so do you." **Eph. 4:30**. And do not grieve the Holy Spirit of God, by whom you were sealed for the day of redemption.

42 **Job 1:22**. In all this Job did not sin or charge God with wrong. **Ps. 73:2-3, 13-15, 22**. But as for me, my feet had almost stumbled, my steps had nearly slipped. For I was envious of the arrogant when I saw the prosperity of the wicked. ... All in vain have I kept my heart clean and washed my hands in innocence. For all the day long I have been stricken and rebuked every morning. If I had said, "I will speak thus," I would have betrayed the generation of your children. ... I was brutish and ignorant; I was like a beast toward you.

43 **1 Sam. 6:7-9**. "Now then, take and prepare a new cart and two milk cows on which there has never come a yoke, and yoke the cows to the cart, but take their calves home, away from them. And take the ark of the LORD and place it on the cart and put in a box at its side the figures of gold, which you are returning to him as a guilt offering. Then send it off and let it go its way and watch. If it goes up on the way to its own land, to Beth-shemesh, then it is he who has done us this great harm, but if not, then we shall know that it is not his hand that struck us; it happened to us by coincidence."

44 **Dan. 5:23**. ...but you have lifted up yourself against the Lord of heaven. And the vessels of his house have been brought in before you, and you and your lords, your wives, and your concubines have drunk wine from them. And you have praised the gods of silver and gold, of bronze, iron, wood, and stone, which do not see or hear or know, but the God in whose hand is your breath, and whose are all your ways, you have not honored.

45 **Deut. 8:17.** Beware lest you say in your heart, 'My power and the might of my hand have gotten me this wealth.' **Dan. 4:30.** ...and the king answered and said, "Is not this great Babylon, which I have built by my mighty power as a royal residence and for the glory of my majesty?"

46 **Hab. 1:16.** Therefore he sacrifices to his net and makes offerings to his dragnet; for by them he lives in luxury, and his food is rich.

Q. 106. What are we especially taught by the words "before me," in the First Commandment?

A. The words "before me," or "before my face," in the First Commandment, teach us, that God, who sees all things, takes special notice of, and is much displeased with, the sin of having any other God; so that it may be an argument to dissuade us from it, and to emphasize it as a most serious provocation;[1] as also to persuade us to do as in His sight, whatever we do in His service.[2]

1 **Ps. 44:20-21.** If we had forgotten the name of our God or spread out our hands to a foreign god, would not God discover this? For he knows the secrets of the heart. **Ez. 8:5-6.** Then he said to me, "Son of man, lift up your eyes now toward the north." So I lifted up my eyes toward the north, and behold, north of the altar gate, in the entrance, was this image of jealousy. And he said to me, "Son of man, do you see what they are doing, the great abominations that the house of Israel are committing here, to drive me far from my sanctuary? But you will see still greater abominations."

2 **1 Chr. 28:9.** "And you, Solomon my son, know the God of your father and serve him with a whole heart and with a willing mind, for the LORD searches all hearts and understands every plan and thought. If you seek him, he will be found by you, but if you forsake him, he will cast you off forever."

Q. 107. Which is the Second Commandment?

A. The Second Commandment is, "You shall not make for yourself a carved image, or any likeness of anything that is in heaven above, or that is in the earth beneath, or that is in the water under the earth. You shall not bow down to them or serve them, for I the LORD your God am a jealous God, visiting the iniquity of the fathers on the children to the third and the fourth generation of those who hate me, but showing steadfast love to thousands of those who love me and keep my commandments."[1]

1 **Ex. 20:4-6.** "You shall not make for yourself a carved image, or any likeness of anything that is in heaven above, or that is in the earth beneath, or that is in the water under the earth. You shall not bow down to them or serve them, for I the LORD your God am a jealous God, visiting the iniquity of the fathers on the children to the third and the fourth generation of those who hate me, but showing steadfast love to thousands of those who love me and keep my commandments."

Q. 108. What are the duties required in the Second Commandment?

A. The duties required in the Second Commandment are: the receiving, observing, and keeping pure and entire, all such religious worship and ordinances as God has instituted in his Word;[1] particularly prayer and thanksgiving in the name of Christ;[2] the reading, preaching, and hearing of the Word;[3] the administration and receiving of the sacraments;[4] church government and discipline;[5] the ministry and maintenance of them;[6] religious fasting;[7] swearing by the name of God;[8] and vowing to Him:[9] as also the disapproving, detesting, opposing all false worship;[10] and, according to each one's situation and calling, removing it, and all monuments of idolatry.[11]

1 **Deut. 32:46-47**. ...he said to them, "Take to heart all the words by which I am warning you today, that you may command them to your children, that they may be careful to do all the words of this law. For it is no empty word for you, but your very life, and by this word you shall live long in the land that you are going over the Jordan to possess." **Mt. 28:20**. "...teaching them to observe all that I have commanded you. And behold, I am with you always, to the end of the age." **Acts 2:42**. And they devoted themselves to the apostles' teaching and the fellowship, to the breaking of bread and the prayers. **1 Tim. 6:13-14**. I charge you in the presence of God, who gives life to all things, and of Christ Jesus, who in his testimony before Pontius Pilate made the good confession, to keep the commandment unstained and free from reproach until the appearing of our Lord Jesus Christ.

2 **Eph. 5:20**. ...giving thanks always and for everything to God the Father in the name of our Lord Jesus Christ. **Phil. 4:6**. ...do not be anxious about anything, but in everything by prayer and supplication with thanksgiving let your requests be made known to God.

3 **Deut. 17:18-19**. "And when he sits on the throne of his kingdom, he shall write for himself in a book a copy of this law, approved by the Levitical priests. And it shall be with him, and he shall read in it all the days of his life, that he may learn to fear the LORD his God by keeping all the words of this law and these statutes, and doing them." **Acts 10:33**. "So I sent for you at once, and you have been kind enough to come. Now therefore we are all here in the presence of God to hear all that you have been commanded by the Lord." **Acts 15:21**. "For from ancient generations Moses has had in every city those who proclaim him, for he is read every Sabbath in the synagogues." **2 Tim. 4:2**. ...preach the word; be ready in season and out of season; reprove, rebuke, and exhort, with complete patience and teaching. **Jas. 1:21-22**. Therefore put away all filthiness and rampant wickedness and receive with meekness the implanted word, which is able to save your souls. But be doers of the word, and not hearers only, deceiving yourselves.

4 **Mt. 28:19**. Go therefore and make disciples of all nations, baptizing them in the name of the Father and of the Son and of the Holy Spirit. **1 Cor. 11:23-30**. For I received from the Lord what I also delivered to you, that the Lord Jesus on the night when he was betrayed took bread, and when he had given thanks, he broke it, and said, "This is my body which is for you. Do this in remembrance of me." In the same way also he took the cup, after supper, saying, "This cup is the new covenant in my blood. Do this, as often as you drink it, in remembrance of me." For as

often as you eat this bread and drink the cup, you proclaim the Lord's death until he comes. Whoever, therefore, eats the bread or drinks the cup of the Lord in an unworthy manner will be guilty concerning the body and blood of the Lord. Let a person examine himself, then, and so eat of the bread and drink of the cup. For anyone who eats and drinks without discerning the body eats and drinks judgment on himself. That is why many of you are weak and ill, and some have died.

5 **Mt. 16:19**. "I will give you the keys of the kingdom of heaven, and whatever you bind on earth shall be bound in heaven, and whatever you loose on earth shall be loosed in heaven." **Mt. 18:15-17**. "If your brother sins against you, go and tell him his fault, between you and him alone. If he listens to you, you have gained your brother. But if he does not listen, take one or two others along with you, that every charge may be established by the evidence of two or three witnesses. If he refuses to listen to them, tell it to the church. And if he refuses to listen even to the church, let him be to you as a Gentile and a tax collector." See **1 Cor. 5. 1 Cor. 12:28.** And God has appointed in the church first apostles, second prophets, third teachers, then miracles, then gifts of healing, helping, administrating, and various kinds of tongues.

6 **1 Cor. 9:7-15**. Who serves as a soldier at his own expense? Who plants a vineyard without eating any of its fruit? Or who tends a flock without getting some of the milk? Do I say these things on human authority? Does not the Law say the same? For it is written in the Law of Moses, "You shall not muzzle an ox when it treads out the grain." Is it for oxen that God is concerned? Does he not certainly speak for our sake? It was written for our sake, because the plowman should plow in hope and the thresher thresh in hope of sharing in the crop. If we have sown spiritual things among you, is it too much if we reap material things from you? If others share this rightful claim on you, do not we even more? Nevertheless, we have not made use of this right, but we endure anything rather than put an obstacle in the way of the gospel of Christ. Do you not know that those who are employed in the temple service get their food from the temple, and those who serve at the altar share in the sacrificial offerings? In the same way, the Lord commanded that those who proclaim the gospel should get their living by the gospel. But I have made no use of any of these rights, nor am I writing these things to secure any such provision. For I would rather die than have anyone deprive me of my ground for boasting. **Eph. 4:11-12**. And he gave the apostles, the prophets, the evangelists, the shepherds and teachers, to equip the saints for the work of ministry, for building up the body of Christ. **1 Tim. 5:17-18**. Let the elders who rule well be considered worthy of double honor, especially those who labor in preaching and teaching. For the Scripture says, "You shall not muzzle an ox when it treads out the grain," and, "The laborer deserves his wages."

7 **Joel 2:12, 18**. "Yet even now," declares the LORD, "return to me with all your heart, with fasting, with weeping, and with mourning."... Then the LORD became jealous for his land and had pity on his people. **1 Cor. 7:5**. Do not deprive one another, except perhaps by agreement for a limited time, that you may devote yourselves to prayer; but then come together again, so that Satan may not tempt you because of your lack of self-control.

8 **Deut. 6:13**. It is the LORD your God you shall fear. Him you shall serve and by his name you shall swear.

9 **Ps. 76:11**. Make your vows to the LORD your God and perform them; let all around him bring gifts to him who is to be feared. **Isa. 19:21**. And the LORD will make himself known to the Egyptians, and the Egyptians will know the LORD in that day and worship with sacrifice and offering, and they will make vows to the LORD and perform them.

10 **Ps. 16:4**. The sorrows of those who run after another god shall multiply; their drink offerings of blood I will not pour out or take their names on my lips. **Acts 17:16-17**. Now while Paul was waiting for them at Athens, his spirit was provoked within him as he saw that the city was full of idols. So he reasoned in the synagogue with the Jews and the devout persons, and in the marketplace every day with those who happened to be there.

11 **Deut. 7:5**. But thus shall you deal with them: you shall break down their altars and dash in pieces their pillars and chop down their Asherim and burn their carved images with fire. **Isa. 30:22**. Then you will defile your carved idols overlaid with silver and your gold-plated metal images. You will scatter them as unclean things. You will say to them, "Be gone!"

Q. 109. What are the sins forbidden in the Second Commandment?

A. The sins forbidden in the Second Commandment are: all developing,[1] counseling,[12] commanding,[13] using,[4] and in any way approving any religious worship not instituted by God Himself;[5] the making any representation of God, of all, or of any of the three Persons, either inwardly in our mind, or outwardly in any kind of image or likeness of any creature whatsoever;[6] all worshiping of it,[7] or God in it or by it;[8] the making of any representation of false deities,[9] and all worship of them, or service belonging to them;[10] all superstitious devices,[11] corrupting the worship of God,[12] adding to it, or taking from it,[13] whether invented and taken up of ourselves,[14] or received by tradition from others,[15] though under the title of antiquity,[16] custom,[17] devotion,[18] good intent, or any other pretense whatsoever;[19] buying or selling of pardons,[20] sacrilege;[21] all neglect,[22] contempt,[23] hindering,[24] and opposing the worship and ordinances that God has appointed.[25]

1 **Num. 15:39**. And it shall be a tassel for you to look at and remember all the commandments of the LORD, to do them, not to follow after your own heart and your own eyes, which you are inclined to whore after.

2 **Deut. 13:6-8**. "If your brother, the son of your mother, or your son or your daughter or the wife you embrace or your friend who is as your own soul entices you secretly, saying, 'Let us go and serve other gods,' which neither you nor your fathers have known, some of the gods of the peoples who are around you, whether near you or far off from you, from the one end of the earth to the other, you shall not yield to him or listen to him, nor shall your eye pity him, nor shall you spare him, nor shall you conceal him."

3 **Hos. 5:11**. Ephraim is oppressed, crushed in judgment, because he was determined to go after filth. **Mic. 6:16**. "For you have kept the statutes of Omri, and all the works of the house of Ahab; and you have walked in their counsels, that I may make you a desolation, and your inhabitants a hissing; so you shall bear the scorn of my people."

4 **1 Kings 11:33**. ...because they have forsaken me and worshiped Ashtoreth the goddess of the Sidonians, Chemosh the god of Moab, and Milcom the god of the Ammonites, and they have not walked in my ways, doing what is right in my sight

and keeping my statutes and my rules, as David his father did. **1 Kings 12:33**. He went up to the altar that he had made in Bethel on the fifteenth day in the eighth month, in the month that he had devised from his own heart. And he instituted a feast for the people of Israel and went up to the altar to make offerings.

5 **Deut. 12:30-32**. ...take care that you be not ensnared to follow them, after they have been destroyed before you, and that you do not inquire about their gods, saying, 'How did these nations serve their gods?—that I also may do the same.' You shall not worship the LORD your God in that way, for every abominable thing that the LORD hates they have done for their gods, for they even burn their sons and their daughters in the fire to their gods. "Everything that I command you, you shall be careful to do. You shall not add to it or take from it."

6 **Deut. 4:15-19**. "Therefore watch yourselves very carefully. Since you saw no form on the day that the LORD spoke to you at Horeb out of the midst of the fire, beware lest you act corruptly by making a carved image for yourselves, in the form of any figure, the likeness of male or female, the likeness of any animal that is on the earth, the likeness of any winged bird that flies in the air, the likeness of anything that creeps on the ground, the likeness of any fish that is in the water under the earth. And beware lest you raise your eyes to heaven, and when you see the sun and the moon and the stars, all the host of heaven, you be drawn away and bow down to them and serve them, things that the LORD your God has allotted to all the peoples under the whole heaven." **Acts 17:29**. Being then God's offspring, we ought not to think that the divine being is like gold or silver or stone, an image formed by the art and imagination of man. **Rom. 1:21-23, 25**. For although they knew God, they did not honor him as God or give thanks to him, but they became futile in their thinking, and their foolish hearts were darkened. Claiming to be wise, they became fools, and exchanged the glory of the immortal God for images resembling mortal man and birds and animals and creeping things. ...because they exchanged the truth about God for a lie and worshiped and served the creature rather than the Creator, who is blessed forever! Amen.

7 **Dan. 3:18**. "But if not, be it known to you, O king, that we will not serve your gods or worship the golden image that you have set up." **Gal. 4:8**. Formerly, when you did not know God, you were enslaved to those that by nature are not gods.

8 **Ex. 32:5**. When Aaron saw this, he built an altar before it. And Aaron made a proclamation and said, "Tomorrow shall be a feast to the LORD."

9 **Ex. 32:8**. "They have turned aside quickly out of the way that I commanded them. They have made for themselves a golden calf and have worshiped it and sacrificed to it and said, 'These are your gods, O Israel, who brought you up out of the land of Egypt!'"

10 **1 Kings 18:26, 28**. And they took the bull that was given them, and they prepared it and called upon the name of Baal from morning until noon, saying, "O Baal, answer us!" But there was no voice, and no one answered. And they limped around the altar that they had made."... And they cried aloud and cut themselves after their custom with swords and lances, until the blood gushed out upon them. **Isa. 65:11**. But you who forsake the LORD, who forget my holy mountain, who set a table for Fortune and fill cups of mixed wine for Destiny.

11 **Acts 17:22**. So Paul, standing in the midst of the Areopagus, said: "Men of Athens, I perceive that in every way you are very religious." **Col. 2:21-23**. "Do not handle, Do not taste, Do not touch" (referring to things that all perish as they are used)—according to human precepts and teachings? These have indeed an appearance of wisdom in promoting self-made religion and asceticism and severity to the body, but they are of no value in stopping the indulgence of the flesh.

12 **Mal. 1:7-6, 14**. "A son honors his father, and a servant his master. If then I am a father, where is my honor? And if I am a master, where is my fear? says the LORD

of hosts to you, O priests, who despise my name. But you say, 'How have we despised your name?' By offering polluted food upon my altar. But you say, 'How have we polluted you?' By saying that the LORD's table may be despised." ... Cursed be the cheat who has a male in his flock, and vows it, and yet sacrifices to the Lord what is blemished. For I am a great King, says the LORD of hosts, and my name will be feared among the nations.

13 **Deut. 4:2**. You shall not add to the word that I command you, nor take from it, that you may keep the commandments of the LORD your God that I command you.

14 **Ps. 106:39**. Thus they became unclean by their acts, and played the whore in their deeds.

15 **Mt. 15:9**. "'...in vain do they worship me, teaching as doctrines the commandments of men.'"

16 **1 Pet. 1:8**. Though you have not seen him, you love him. Though you do not now see him, you believe in him and rejoice with joy that is inexpressible and filled with glory.

17 **Jer. 44:17**. But we will do everything that we have vowed, make offerings to the queen of heaven and pour out drink offerings to her, as we did, both we and our fathers, our kings and our officials, in the cities of Judah and in the streets of Jerusalem. For then we had plenty of food, and prospered, and saw no disaster.

18 **Isa. 65:3-5**. ...a people who provoke me to my face continually, sacrificing in gardens and making offerings on bricks; who sit in tombs, and spend the night in secret places; who eat pig's flesh, and broth of tainted meat is in their vessels; who say, "Keep to yourself, do not come near me, for I am too holy for you." These are a smoke in my nostrils, a fire that burns all the day. **Gal. 1:13-14**. For you have heard of my former life in Judaism, how I persecuted the church of God violently and tried to destroy it. And I was advancing in Judaism beyond many of my own age among my people, so extremely zealous was I for the traditions of my fathers.

19 **1 Sam. 15:21**. "But the people took of the spoil, sheep and oxen, the best of the things devoted to destruction, to sacrifice to the LORD your God in Gilgal."

20 **Acts 8:18**. Now when Simon saw that the Spirit was given through the laying on of the apostles' hands, he offered them money.

21 **Mal. 3:8**. Will man rob God? Yet you are robbing me. But you say, 'How have we robbed you?' In your tithes and contributions. **Rom. 2:22**. You who say that one must not commit adultery, do you commit adultery? You who abhor idols, do you rob temples?

22 **Ex. 4:24-26**. At a lodging place on the way the LORD met him and sought to put him to death. Then Zipporah took a flint and cut off her son's foreskin and touched Moses' feet with it and said, "Surely you are a bridegroom of blood to me!" So he let him alone. It was then that she said, "A bridegroom of blood," because of the circumcision.

23 **Mal. 1:7, 13**. By offering polluted food upon my altar. But you say, 'How have we polluted you?' By saying that the LORD's table may be despised. ... But you say, 'What a weariness this is,' and you snort at it, says the LORD of hosts. You bring what has been taken by violence or is lame or sick, and this you bring as your offering! Shall I accept that from your hand? says the LORD. **Mt. 22:5**. But they paid no attention and went off, one to his farm, another to his business.

24 **Mt. 23:13**. "But woe to you, scribes and Pharisees, hypocrites! For you shut the kingdom of heaven in people's faces. For you neither enter yourselves nor allow those who would enter to go in."

25 **Acts 13:44-45**. The next Sabbath almost the whole city gathered to hear the word of the Lord. But when the Jews saw the crowds, they were filled with jealousy and

began to contradict what was spoken by Paul, reviling him. **1 Thess. 2:15-16.** ... who killed both the Lord Jesus and the prophets, and drove us out, and displease God and oppose all mankind by hindering us from speaking to the Gentiles that they might be saved—so as always to fill up the measure of their sins. But wrath has come upon them at last!

Q. 110. What are the reasons added to the Second Commandment, the more to enforce it?

A. The reasons added to the Second Commandment, the more to enforce it, contained in these words, "for I the LORD your God am a jealous God, visiting the iniquity of the fathers on the children to the third and the fourth generation of those who hate me, but showing steadfast love to thousands of those who love me and keep my commandments" [1] are, besides God's sovereignty over us, and ownership in us,[2] his fervent zeal for his own worship,[3] his revengeful indignation against all false worship, as being a spiritual prostitution;[4] accounting those who break this commandment such as hate him, and threatening to punish them for several generations,[5] and esteeming those who observe it as those who love him and keep his commandments, and promising mercy to them for many generations.[6]

1 **Ex. 20:5-6.** You shall not bow down to them or serve them, for I the LORD your God am a jealous God, visiting the iniquity of the fathers on the children to the third and the fourth generation of those who hate me, but showing steadfast love to thousands of those who love me and keep my commandments.

2 **Ps. 45:11.** ...and the king will desire your beauty. Since he is your lord, bow to him. **Rev. 15:3-4.** And they sing the song of Moses, the servant of God, and the song of the Lamb, saying, "Great and amazing are your deeds, O Lord God the Almighty! Just and true are your ways, O King of the nations! Who will not fear, O Lord, and glorify your name? For you alone are holy. All nations will come and worship you, for your righteous acts have been revealed."

3 **Ex. 24:13-14.** So Moses rose with his assistant Joshua, and Moses went up into the mountain of God. And he said to the elders, "Wait here for us until we return to you. And behold, Aaron and Hur are with you. Whoever has a dispute, let him go to them."

4 **Deut. 32:16-20.** They stirred him to jealousy with strange gods; with abominations they provoked him to anger. They sacrificed to demons that were no gods, to gods they had never known, to new gods that had come recently, whom your fathers had never dreaded. You were unmindful of the Rock that bore you, and you forgot the God who gave you birth. "The LORD saw it and spurned them, because of the provocation of his sons and his daughters. And he said, 'I will hide my face from them; I will see what their end will be, for they are a perverse generation, children in whom is no faithfulness. **Jer. 7:18-20.** "The children gather wood, the fathers kindle fire, and the women knead dough, to make cakes for the queen of heaven. And they pour out drink offerings to other gods, to provoke me to anger. Is it I whom they provoke? declares the LORD. Is it not themselves, to their own

shame? Therefore thus says the Lord GOD: Behold, my anger and my wrath will be poured out on this place, upon man and beast, upon the trees of the field and the fruit of the ground; it will burn and not be quenched." **Ezek. 16:26-27**. You also played the whore with the Egyptians, your lustful neighbors, multiplying your whoring, to provoke me to anger. Behold, therefore, I stretched out my hand against you and diminished your allotted portion and delivered you to the greed of your enemies, the daughters of the Philistines, who were ashamed of your lewd behavior. **1 Cor. 10:20-22**. No, I imply that what pagans sacrifice they offer to demons and not to God. I do not want you to be participants with demons. You cannot drink the cup of the Lord and the cup of demons. You cannot partake of the table of the Lord and the table of demons. Shall we provoke the Lord to jealousy? Are we stronger than he?

5 **Hos. 2:2-4**. "Plead with your mother, plead— for she is not my wife, and I am not her husband— that she put away her whoring from her face, and her adultery from between her breasts; lest I strip her naked and make her as in the day she was born, and make her like a wilderness, and make her like a parched land, and kill her with thirst. Upon her children also I will have no mercy, because they are children of whoredom."

6 **Deut. 5:29**. Oh that they had such a heart as this always, to fear me and to keep all my commandments, that it might go well with them and with their descendants forever!

Q. 111. Which is the Third Commandment?

A. The Third Commandment is, "You shall not take the name of the LORD your God in vain, for the LORD will not hold him guiltless who takes his name in vain."[1]

1 **Ex. 20:7**. "You shall not take the name of the LORD your God in vain, for the LORD will not hold him guiltless who takes his name in vain."

Q. 112. What is required in the Third Commandment?

A. The Third Commandment requires, that the name of God, His titles, attributes,[1] ordinances,[2] the Word,[3] sacraments,[4] prayer,[5] oaths,[6] vows,[7] casting of lots,[8] His works,[9] and whatever else there is by which he makes Himself known, be used in a holy and reverent manner in thought,[10] meditation,[11] word,[12] and writing;[13] by a holy profession,[14] and answerable conversation[15] to the glory of God,[16] and the good of ourselves[17] and others.[18]

1 **Deut. 28:58**. "If you are not careful to do all the words of this law that are written in this book, that you may fear this glorious and awesome name, the LORD your God." **Ps. 29:2**. Ascribe to the LORD the glory due his name; worship the LORD in the splendor of holiness. **Ps. 68:4**. Sing to God, sing praises to his name; lift up a song to him who rides through the deserts; his name is the LORD; exult before him! **Mt. 11:9**. What then did you go out to see? A prophet? Yes, I tell you, and more than a prophet. **Rev. 15:3-4**. And they sing the song of Moses, the servant of God, and the song of the Lamb, saying, "Great and amazing are your deeds,

O Lord God the Almighty! Just and true are your ways, O King of the nations! Who will not fear, O Lord, and glorify your name? For you alone are holy. All nations will come and worship you, for your righteous acts have been revealed."

2 **Eccl. 5:1**. Guard your steps when you go to the house of God. To draw near to listen is better than to offer the sacrifice of fools, for they do not know that they are doing evil. **Mal. 1:14**. Cursed be the cheat who has a male in his flock, and vows it, and yet sacrifices to the Lord what is blemished. For I am a great King, says the LORD of hosts, and my name will be feared among the nations.

3 **Ps. 138:2**. I bow down toward your holy temple and give thanks to your name for your steadfast love and your faithfulness, for you have exalted above all things your name and your word.

4 **1 Cor. 11:24-25, 28-29**. ...and when he had given thanks, he broke it, and said, "This is my body which is for you. Do this in remembrance of me." In the same way also he took the cup, after supper, saying, "This cup is the new covenant in my blood. Do this, as often as you drink it, in remembrance of me."... Let a person examine himself, then, and so eat of the bread and drink of the cup. For anyone who eats and drinks without discerning the body eats and drinks judgment on himself.

5 **1 Tim. 2:8.** I desire then that in every place the men should pray, lifting holy hands without anger or quarreling.

6 **Jer. 4:2**. ...and if you swear, 'As the LORD lives,' in truth, in justice, and in righteousness, then nations shall bless themselves in him, and in him shall they glory."

7 **Eccl. 5:2-6**. Be not rash with your mouth, nor let your heart be hasty to utter a word before God, for God is in heaven and you are on earth. Therefore let your words be few. For a dream comes with much business, and a fool's voice with many words. When you vow a vow to God, do not delay paying it, for he has no pleasure in fools. Pay what you vow. It is better that you should not vow than that you should vow and not pay. Let not your mouth lead you into sin, and do not say before the messenger that it was a mistake. Why should God be angry at your voice and destroy the work of your hands?

8 **Acts 1:24, 26**. And they prayed and said, "You, Lord, who know the hearts of all, show which one of these two you have chosen." ... And they cast lots for them, and the lot fell on Matthias, and he was numbered with the eleven apostles.

9 **Job 36:24**. "Remember to extol his work, of which men have sung."

10 **Mal. 3:16**. Then those who feared the LORD spoke with one another. The LORD paid attention and heard them, and a book of remembrance was written before him of those who feared the LORD and esteemed his name.

11 Ps. **8:1, 3-4, 9**. O LORD, our Lord, how majestic is your name in all the earth! You have set your glory above the heavens. ... When I look at your heavens, the work of your fingers, the moon and the stars, which you have set in place, what is man that you are mindful of him, and the son of man that you care for him?... O LORD, our Lord, how majestic is your name in all the earth!

12 **Ps. 105:2, 5**. Sing to him, sing praises to him; tell of all his wondrous works! ... Remember the wondrous works that he has done, his miracles, and the judgments he uttered. **Col. 3:17**. And whatever you do, in word or deed, do everything in the name of the Lord Jesus, giving thanks to God the Father through him.

13 **Ps. 102:18**. Let this be recorded for a generation to come, so that a people yet to be created may praise the LORD.

14 **Mic. 4:5.** For all the peoples walk each in the name of its god, but we will walk in the name of the LORD our God forever and ever. **1 Pet. 3:15**. ... but in your hearts honor Christ the Lord as holy, always being prepared to make a defense to anyone who asks you for a reason for the hope that is in you; yet do it with gentleness and respect.

15 **Phil. 1:27.** Only let your manner of life be worthy of the gospel of Christ, so that whether I come and see you or am absent, I may hear of you that you are standing firm in one spirit, with one mind striving side by side for the faith of the gospel.

16 **1 Cor. 10:31.** So, whether you eat or drink, or whatever you do, do all to the glory of God.

17 **Jer. 32:39.** I will give them one heart and one way, that they may fear me forever, for their own good and the good of their children after them.

18 **1 Pet. 2:12.** Keep your conduct among the Gentiles honorable, so that when they speak against you as evildoers, they may see your good deeds and glorify God on the day of visitation.

Q. 113. What are the sins forbidden in the Third Commandment?

A. The sins forbidden in the Third Commandment are: the failure to use God's name as is required;[1] and the abuse of it in an ignorant,[2] vain,[3] irreverent, profane,[4] superstitious,[5] or wicked mentioning or otherwise using the titles, attributes,[6] ordinances,[7] or works;[8] by blasphemy;[9] perjury;[10] all sinful cursing,[11] oaths,[12] vows,[13] and casting of lots;[14] violating our oaths and vows, if lawful;[15] and fulfilling them, if of things unlawful;[16] murmuring and quarreling at,[17] curious prying into,[18] and misapplying of God's decrees[19] and providence;[20] misinterpreting,[21] misapplying,[22] or any way perverting the Word, or any part of it,[23] to profane jokes,[24] curious and unprofitable questions, vain discord, or the maintaining of false doctrines;[25] abusing it, the creatures, or anything contained under the name of God, to charms,[26] or sinful lusts and practices;[27] the maligning,[28] scorning,[29] verbally abusing,[30] or any way opposing of God's truth, grace, and ways;[31] making profession of religion in hypocrisy, or for sinister ends;[32] being ashamed of it,[33] or a shame to it, by uncomfortable,[34] unwise,[35] unfruitful,[36] and offensive departing[37] or backsliding from it.[38]

1 **Mal. 2:2.** If you will not listen, if you will not take it to heart to give honor to my name, says the LORD of hosts, then I will send the curse upon you and I will curse your blessings. Indeed, I have already cursed them, because you do not lay it to heart.

2 **Acts 17:23.** For as I passed along and observed the objects of your worship, I found also an altar with this inscription, 'To the unknown god.' What therefore you worship as unknown, this I proclaim to you.

3 **Prov. 30:9.** ...lest I be full and deny you and say, "Who is the LORD?" or lest I be poor and steal and profane the name of my God.

4 **Mal. 1:6:7, 12.** "A son honors his father, and a servant his master. If then I am a father, where is my honor? And if I am a master, where is my fear? says the LORD of hosts to you, O priests, who despise my name. But you say, 'How have we despised your name?' By offering polluted food upon my altar. But you say, 'How have we polluted you?' By saying that the LORD's table may be despised." ... But

you profane it when you say that the Lord's table is polluted, and its fruit, that is, its food may be despised. **Mal. 3:14**. You have said, 'It is vain to serve God. What is the profit of our keeping his charge or of walking as in mourning before the LORD of hosts?'

5 **1 Sam. 4:3-5**. And when the people came to the camp, the elders of Israel said, "Why has the LORD defeated us today before the Philistines? Let us bring the ark of the covenant of the LORD here from Shiloh, that it may come among us and save us from the power of our enemies." So the people sent to Shiloh and brought from there the ark of the covenant of the LORD of hosts, who is enthroned on the cherubim. And the two sons of Eli, Hophni and Phinehas, were there with the ark of the covenant of God. As soon as the ark of the covenant of the LORD came into the camp, all Israel gave a mighty shout, so that the earth resounded.
Jer. 7:4, 9-10, 14, 31. Do not trust in these deceptive words: 'This is the temple of the LORD, the temple of the LORD, the temple of the LORD.' ... Will you steal, murder, commit adultery, swear falsely, make offerings to Baal, and go after other gods that you have not known, and then come and stand before me in this house, which is called by my name, and say, 'We are delivered!'—only to go on doing all these abominations? ...therefore I will do to the house that is called by my name, and in which you trust, and to the place that I gave to you and to your fathers, as I did to Shiloh. ... And they have built the high places of Topheth, which is in the Valley of the Son of Hinnom, to burn their sons and their daughters in the fire, which I did not command, nor did it come into my mind. **Col. 2:20-22**. If with Christ you died to the elemental spirits of the world, why, as if you were still alive in the world, do you submit to regulations – "Do not handle, Do not taste, Do not touch" (referring to things that all perish as they are used) – according to human precepts and teachings?

6 **Ex. 5:2**. But Pharaoh said, "Who is the LORD, that I should obey his voice and let Israel go? I do not know the LORD, and moreover, I will not let Israel go."
2 Kings 18:30, 35. 'Do not let Hezekiah make you trust in the LORD by saying, The LORD will surely deliver us, and this city will not be given into the hand of the king of Assyria.' ... "'Who among all the gods of the lands have delivered their lands out of my hand, that the LORD should deliver Jerusalem out of my hand?'"
Ps. 139:20. They speak against you with malicious intent; your enemies take your name in vain.

7 **Ps. 50:16-17**. But to the wicked God says: "What right have you to recite my statutes or take my covenant on your lips? For you hate discipline, and you cast my words behind you."

8 **Isa. 5:12**. They have lyre and harp, tambourine and flute and wine at their feasts, but they do not regard the deeds of the LORD, or see the work of his hands.

9 **Lev. 24:11**. ...and the Israelite woman's son blasphemed the Name, and cursed. Then they brought him to Moses. His mother's name was Shelomith, the daughter of Dibri, of the tribe of Dan. **2 Kings 19:22**. "Whom have you mocked and reviled? Against whom have you raised your voice and lifted your eyes to the heights? Against the Holy One of Israel!"

10 **Zech. 5:4**. "I will send it out, declares the LORD of hosts, and it shall enter the house of the thief, and the house of him who swears falsely by my name. And it shall remain in his house and consume it, both timber and stones." **Zech. 8:17**. "...do not devise evil in your hearts against one another, and love no false oath, for all these things I hate, declares the LORD."

11 **1 Sam. 17:43**. And the Philistine said to David, "Am I a dog, that you come to me with sticks?" And the Philistine cursed David by his gods. **2 Sam. 16:5**. When King David came to Bahurim, there came out a man of the family of the house of

Saul, whose name was Shimei, the son of Gera, and as he came he cursed continually.

12 **Jer. 5:7**. "How can I pardon you? Your children have forsaken me and have sworn by those who are no gods. When I fed them to the full, they committed adultery and trooped to the houses of whores." **Jer. 23:10**. For the land is full of adulterers; because of the curse the land mourns, and the pastures of the wilderness are dried up. Their course is evil, and their might is not right.

13 **Deut. 23:18**. You shall not bring the fee of a prostitute or the wages of a dog into the house of the LORD your God in payment for any vow, for both of these are an abomination to the LORD your God. **Acts 23:12, 14**. When it was day, the Jews made a plot and bound themselves by an oath neither to eat nor drink till they had killed Paul. ... They went to the chief priests and elders and said, "We have strictly bound ourselves by an oath to taste no food till we have killed Paul."

14 **Esth. 3:7**. In the first month, which is the month of Nisan, in the twelfth year of King Ahasuerus, they cast Pur (that is, they cast lots) before Haman day after day; and they cast it month after month till the twelfth month, which is the month of Adar. **Esth. 9:24**. For Haman the Agagite, the son of Hammedatha, the enemy of all the Jews, had plotted against the Jews to destroy them, and had cast Pur (that is, cast lots), to crush and to destroy them. **Ps. 22:18**. ...they divide my garments among them, and for my clothing they cast lots.

15 **Ps. 4:4**. Be angry, and do not sin; ponder in your own hearts on your beds, and be silent. **Ezek. 17:16, 18-19**. "As I live, declares the Lord GOD, surely in the place where the king dwells who made him king, whose oath he despised, and whose covenant with him he broke, in Babylon he shall die." ... He despised the oath in breaking the covenant, and behold, he gave his hand and did all these things; he shall not escape. Therefore thus says the Lord GOD: As I live, surely it is my oath that he despised, and my covenant that he broke. I will return it upon his head.

16 **Mk. 6:26**. And the king was exceedingly sorry, but because of his oaths and his guests he did not want to break his word to her. **1 Sam. 25:22, 32-34**. "God do so to the enemies of David and more also, if by morning I leave so much as one male of all who belong to him." ... And David said to Abigail, "Blessed be the LORD, the God of Israel, who sent you this day to meet me! Blessed be your discretion, and blessed be you, who have kept me this day from bloodguilt and from working salvation with my own hand! For as surely as the LORD, the God of Israel, lives, who has restrained me from hurting you, unless you had hurried and come to meet me, truly by morning there had not been left to Nabal so much as one male."

17 **Rom. 9:14, 19-20**. What shall we say then? Is there injustice on God's part? By no means! ... You will say to me then, "Why does he still find fault? For who can resist his will?" But who are you, O man, to answer back to God? Will what is molded say to its molder, "Why have you made me like this?"

18 **Deut. 29:29**. "The secret things belong to the LORD our God, but the things that are revealed belong to us and to our children forever, that we may do all the words of this law."

19 **Rom. 3:5-7**. But if our unrighteousness serves to show the righteousness of God, what shall we say? That God is unrighteous to inflict wrath on us? (I speak in a human way.) By no means! For then how could God judge the world? But if through my lie God's truth abounds to his glory, why am I still being condemned as a sinner? **Rom. 6:1**. What shall we say then? Are we to continue in sin that grace may abound?

20 **Ps. 39**. I said, "I will guard my ways, that I may not sin with my tongue; I will guard my mouth with a muzzle, so long as the wicked are in my presence." I was mute and silent; I held my peace to no avail, and my distress grew worse. My heart

became hot within me. As I mused, the fire burned; then I spoke with my tongue: "O LORD, make me know my end and what is the measure of my days; let me know how fleeting I am! Behold, you have made my days a few handbreadths, and my lifetime is as nothing before you. Surely all mankind stands as a mere breath! Surely a man goes about as a shadow! Surely for nothing they are in turmoil; man heaps up wealth and does not know who will gather! "And now, O Lord, for what do I wait? My hope is in you. Deliver me from all my transgressions. Do not make me the scorn of the fool! I am mute; I do not open my mouth, for it is you who have done it. Remove your stroke from me; I am spent by the hostility of your hand. When you discipline a man with rebukes for sin, you consume like a moth what is dear to him; surely all mankind is a mere breath! "Hear my prayer, O LORD, and give ear to my cry; hold not your peace at my tears! For I am a sojourner with you, a guest, like all my fathers. Look away from me, that I may smile again, before I depart and am no more!" **Eccl. 8:11**. Because the sentence against an evil deed is not executed speedily, the heart of the children of man is fully set to do evil. **Eccl. 9:3**. This is an evil in all that is done under the sun, that the same event happens to all. Also, the hearts of the children of man are full of evil, and madness is in their hearts while they live, and after that they go to the dead.

21 **Mt. 5:21-48**. "You have heard that it was said to those of old, 'You shall not murder; and whoever murders will be liable to judgment.' But I say to you that everyone who is angry with his brother will be liable to judgment; whoever insults his brother will be liable to the council; and whoever says, 'You fool!' will be liable to the hell of fire. So if you are offering your gift at the altar and there remember that your brother has something against you, leave your gift there before the altar and go. First be reconciled to your brother, and then come and offer your gift. Come to terms quickly with your accuser while you are going with him to court, lest your accuser hand you over to the judge, and the judge to the guard, and you be put in prison. Truly, I say to you, you will never get out until you have paid the last penny. "You have heard that it was said, 'You shall not commit adultery.' But I say to you that everyone who looks at a woman with lustful intent has already committed adultery with her in his heart. If your right eye causes you to sin, tear it out and throw it away. For it is better that you lose one of your members than that your whole body be thrown into hell. And if your right hand causes you to sin, cut it off and throw it away. For it is better that you lose one of your members than that your whole body go into hell. "It was also said, 'Whoever divorces his wife, let him give her a certificate of divorce.' But I say to you that everyone who divorces his wife, except on the ground of sexual immorality, makes her commit adultery, and whoever marries a divorced woman commits adultery. "Again you have heard that it was said to those of old, 'You shall not swear falsely, but shall perform to the Lord what you have sworn.' But I say to you, Do not take an oath at all, either by heaven, for it is the throne of God, or by the earth, for it is his footstool, or by Jerusalem, for it is the city of the great King. And do not take an oath by your head, for you cannot make one hair white or black. Let what you say be simply 'Yes' or 'No'; anything more than this comes from evil. "You have heard that it was said, 'An eye for an eye and a tooth for a tooth.' But I say to you, Do not resist the one who is evil. But if anyone slaps you on the right cheek, turn to him the other also. And if anyone would sue you and take your tunic, let him have your cloak as well. And if anyone forces you to go one mile, go with him two miles. Give to the one who begs from you, and do not refuse the one who would borrow from you. "You have heard that it was said, 'You shall love your neighbor and hate your enemy.' But I say to you, Love your enemies and pray for those who persecute you, so that you may be sons of your Father who is in heaven. For he makes his sun rise on the evil and on the good, and sends rain on the just and on the unjust. For if you love those who love you, what reward do you have? Do not even the tax collectors do

the same? And if you greet only your brothers, what more are you doing than others? Do not even the Gentiles do the same? You therefore must be perfect, as your heavenly Father is perfect.

22 **Ezek. 13:22**. Because you have disheartened the righteous falsely, although I have not grieved him, and you have encouraged the wicked, that he should not turn from his evil way to save his life.

23 **Mt. 22:23-32**. The same day Sadducees came to him, who say that there is no resurrection, and they asked him a question, saying, "Teacher, Moses said, 'If a man dies having no children, his brother must marry the widow and raise up offspring for his brother.' Now there were seven brothers among us. The first married and died, and having no offspring left his wife to his brother. So too the second and third, down to the seventh. After them all, the woman died. In the resurrection, therefore, of the seven, whose wife will she be? For they all had her." But Jesus answered them, "You are wrong, because you know neither the Scriptures nor the power of God. For in the resurrection they neither marry nor are given in marriage, but are like angels in heaven. And as for the resurrection of the dead, have you not read what was said to you by God: 'I am the God of Abraham, and the God of Isaac, and the God of Jacob'? He is not God of the dead, but of the living." **2 Pet. 3:16**. ...as he does in all his letters when he speaks in them of these matters. There are some things in them that are hard to understand, which the ignorant and unstable twist to their own destruction, as they do the other Scriptures.

24 **Isa. 22:13**. ...and behold, joy and gladness, killing oxen and slaughtering sheep, eating flesh and drinking wine. "Let us eat and drink, for tomorrow we die."
Jer. 23:34, 36, 38. And as for the prophet, priest, or one of the people who says, 'The burden of the LORD,' I will punish that man and his household. ... But 'the burden of the LORD' you shall mention no more, for the burden is every man's own word, and you pervert the words of the living God, the LORD of hosts, our God. ... But if you say, 'The burden of the LORD,' thus says the LORD, 'Because you have said these words, "The burden of the LORD," when I sent to you, saying, "You shall not say, 'The burden of the LORD,'"

25 **1 Tim. 1:4, 6-7**. ...nor to devote themselves to myths and endless genealogies, which promote speculations rather than the stewardship from God that is by faith. ...Certain persons, by swerving from these, have wandered away into vain discussion, desiring to be teachers of the law, without understanding either what they are saying or the things about which they make confident assertions. **1 Tim. 6:4-5, 20**. ...he is puffed up with conceit and understands nothing. He has an unhealthy craving for controversy and for quarrels about words, which produce envy, dissension, slander, evil suspicions, and constant friction among people who are depraved in mind and deprived of the truth, imagining that godliness is a means of gain. ... O Timothy, guard the deposit entrusted to you. Avoid the irreverent babble and contradictions of what is falsely called "knowledge." **2 Tim. 2:14**. Remind them of these things, and charge them before God not to quarrel about words, which does no good, but only ruins the hearers. **Titus 3:9**. But avoid foolish controversies, genealogies, dissensions, and quarrels about the law, for they are unprofitable and worthless.

26 **Deut. 18:10-13**. There shall not be found among you anyone who burns his son or his daughter as an offering, anyone who practices divination or tells fortunes or interprets omens, or a sorcerer or a charmer or a medium or a necromancer or one who inquires of the dead, for whoever does these things is an abomination to the LORD. And because of these abominations the LORD your God is driving them out before you. You shall be blameless before the LORD your God.
Acts 19:13. Then some of the itinerant Jewish exorcists undertook to invoke the

name of the Lord Jesus over those who had evil spirits, saying, "I adjure you by the Jesus whom Paul proclaims."

27 **1 Kings 21:9-10**. And she wrote in the letters, "Proclaim a fast, and set Naboth at the head of the people. And set two worthless men opposite him, and let them bring a charge against him, saying, 'You have cursed God and the king.' Then take him out and stone him to death." **Rom. 13:13-14**. Let us walk properly as in the daytime, not in orgies and drunkenness, not in sexual immorality and sensuality, not in quarreling and jealousy. But put on the Lord Jesus Christ, and make no provision for the flesh, to gratify its desires. **2 Tim. 4:3-4**. For the time is coming when people will not endure sound teaching, but having itching ears they will accumulate for themselves teachers to suit their own passions, and will turn away from listening to the truth and wander off into myths. **Jude 4**. ...or certain people have crept in unnoticed who long ago were designated for this condemnation, ungodly people, who pervert the grace of our God into sensuality and deny our only Master and Lord, Jesus Christ.

28 **Acts 13:45**. But when the Jews saw the crowds, they were filled with jealousy and began to contradict what was spoken by Paul, reviling him. **1 Jn. 3:12**. We should not be like Cain, who was of the evil one and murdered his brother. And why did he murder him? Because his own deeds were evil and his brother's righteous.

29 **Ps. 1:1**. Blessed is the man who walks not in the counsel of the wicked, nor stands in the way of sinners, nor sits in the seat of scoffers. **2 Pet. 3:3**. ...knowing this first of all, that scoffers will come in the last days with scoffing, following their own sinful desires.

30 **1 Pet. 4:4**. With respect to this they are surprised when you do not join them in the same flood of debauchery, and they malign you.

31 **Acts 4:18**. So they called them and charged them not to speak or teach at all in the name of Jesus. **Acts 13:45-46, 50**. But when the Jews saw the crowds, they were filled with jealousy and began to contradict what was spoken by Paul, reviling him. And Paul and Barnabas spoke out boldly, saying, "It was necessary that the word of God be spoken first to you. Since you thrust it aside and judge yourselves unworthy of eternal life, behold, we are turning to the Gentiles. ... But the Jews incited the devout women of high standing and the leading men of the city, stirred up persecution against Paul and Barnabas, and drove them out of their district. **Acts 19:9**. But when some became stubborn and continued in unbelief, speaking evil of the Way before the congregation, he withdrew from them and took the disciples with him, reasoning daily in the hall of Tyrannus. **1 Thess. 2:16**. ...by hindering us from speaking to the Gentiles that they might be saved—so as always to fill up the measure of their sins. But wrath has come upon them at last! **Heb. 10:29**. How much worse punishment, do you think, will be deserved by the one who has trampled underfoot the Son of God, and has profaned the blood of the covenant by which he was sanctified, and has outraged the Spirit of grace?

32 **Mt. 6:1-2, 5, 16.** "Beware of practicing your righteousness before other people in order to be seen by them, for then you will have no reward from your Father who is in heaven. "Thus, when you give to the needy, sound no trumpet before you, as the hypocrites do in the synagogues and in the streets, that they may be praised by others. Truly, I say to you, they have received their reward." ... "And when you pray, you must not be like the hypocrites. For they love to stand and pray in the synagogues and at the street corners, that they may be seen by others. Truly, I say to you, they have received their reward."... "And when you fast, do not look gloomy like the hypocrites, for they disfigure their faces that their fasting may be seen by others. Truly, I say to you, they have received their reward." **Mt. 23:13-15**. "But woe to you, scribes and Pharisees, hypocrites! For you shut the kingdom of heaven in people's faces. For you neither enter yourselves nor allow those who would

enter to go in. Woe to you, scribes and Pharisees, hypocrites! For you travel across sea and land to make a single proselyte, and when he becomes a proselyte, you make him twice as much a child of hell as yourselves. **2 Tim. 3:5**. ...having the appearance of godliness, but denying its power. Avoid such people.

33 **Mk. 8:38**. "For whoever is ashamed of me and of my words in this adulterous and sinful generation, of him will the Son of Man also be ashamed when he comes in the glory of his Father with the holy angels."

34 **Ps. 73:14-15**. For all the day long I have been stricken and rebuked every morning. If I had said, "I will speak thus," I would have betrayed the generation of your children.

35 **1 Cor. 6:5-6**. I say this to your shame. Can it be that there is no one among you wise enough to settle a dispute between the brothers, but brother goes to law against brother, and that before unbelievers? **Eph. 5:15-17**. Look carefully then how you walk, not as unwise but as wise, making the best use of the time, because the days are evil. Therefore do not be foolish, but understand what the will of the Lord is.

36 **Isa. 5:4**. What more was there to do for my vineyard, that I have not done in it? When I looked for it to yield grapes, why did it yield wild grapes? **2 Pet. 1:8-9**. For if these qualities are yours and are increasing, they keep you from being ineffective or unfruitful in the knowledge of our Lord Jesus Christ. For whoever lacks these qualities is so nearsighted that he is blind, having forgotten that he was cleansed from his former sins.

37 **Rom. 2:23-24**. You who boast in the law dishonor God by breaking the law. For, as it is written, "The name of God is blasphemed among the Gentiles because of you."

38 **Gal. 3:1, 3**. O foolish Galatians! Who has bewitched you? It was before your eyes that Jesus Christ was publicly portrayed as crucified. ... Are you so foolish? Having begun by the Spirit, are you now being perfected by the flesh? **Heb. 6:6**. ...and then have fallen away, to restore them again to repentance, since they are crucifying once again the Son of God to their own harm and holding him up to contempt.

Q. 114. What reasons are attached to the Third Commandment?

A. The reasons attached to the Third Commandment, in the words, "the Lord your God," and, "for the LORD will not hold him guiltless who takes his name in vain,"[1] are because He is the Lord and our God, therefore his name is not to be profaned, or any way abused by us;[2] especially because he will be so far from acquitting and sparing the transgressors of this commandment, as that he will not suffer them to escape his righteous judgment,[3] even though many of them escape the censures and punishments of men.[4]

1 **Ex. 20:7**. "You shall not take the name of the LORD your God in vain, for the LORD will not hold him guiltless who takes his name in vain."

2 **Lev. 19:12**. You shall not swear by my name falsely, and so profane the name of your God: I am the LORD.

3 **Deut. 28:58-59**. "If you are not careful to do all the words of this law that are written in this book, that you may fear this glorious and awesome name, the

LORD your God, then the LORD will bring on you and your offspring extraordinary afflictions, afflictions severe and lasting, and sicknesses grievous and lasting." **EZEK. 36:21-23**. But I had concern for my holy name, which the house of Israel had profaned among the nations to which they came. "Therefore say to the house of Israel, Thus says the Lord GOD: It is not for your sake, O house of Israel, that I am about to act, but for the sake of my holy name, which you have profaned among the nations to which you came. And I will vindicate the holiness of my great name, which has been profaned among the nations, and which you have profaned among them. And the nations will know that I am the LORD, declares the Lord GOD, when through you I vindicate my holiness before their eyes." **ZECH. 5:2-4.** And he said to me, "What do you see?" I answered, "I see a flying scroll. Its length is twenty cubits, and its width ten cubits." Then he said to me, "This is the curse that goes out over the face of the whole land. For everyone who steals shall be cleaned out according to what is on one side, and everyone who swears falsely shall be cleaned out according to what is on the other side. I will send it out, declares the LORD of hosts, and it shall enter the house of the thief, and the house of him who swears falsely by my name. And it shall remain in his house and consume it, both timber and stones."

4 **1 SAM. 2:12, 17, 22, 24**. Now the sons of Eli were worthless men. They did not know the LORD. ...Thus the sin of the young men was very great in the sight of the LORD, for the men treated the offering of the LORD with contempt. ...Now Eli was very old, and he kept hearing all that his sons were doing to all Israel, and how they lay with the women who were serving at the entrance to the tent of meeting. ... No, my sons; it is no good report that I hear the people of the LORD spreading abroad. **1 SAM. 3:13**. And I declare to him that I am about to punish his house forever, for the iniquity that he knew, because his sons were blaspheming God, and he did not restrain them.

Q. 115. Which is the Fourth Commandment?

A. The Fourth Commandment is, "Remember the Sabbath day, to keep it holy. Six days you shall labor, and do all your work, but the seventh day is a Sabbath to the LORD your God. On it you shall not do any work, you, or your son, or your daughter, your male servant, or your female servant, or your livestock, or the sojourner who is within your gates. For in six days the LORD made heaven and earth, the sea, and all that is in them, and rested the seventh day. Therefore the LORD blessed the Sabbath day and made it holy."[1]

1 **EX. 20:8-11**. "Remember the Sabbath day, to keep it holy. Six days you shall labor, and do all your work, but the seventh day is a Sabbath to the LORD your God. On it you shall not do any work, you, or your son, or your daughter, your male servant, or your female servant, or your livestock, or the sojourner who is within your gates. For in six days the LORD made heaven and earth, the sea, and all that is in them, and rested on the seventh day. Therefore the LORD blessed the Sabbath day and made it holy."

Q. 116. What is required in the Fourth Commandment?

A. The Fourth Commandment requires of all men the sanctifying or keeping holy to God such set times as He has appointed in His Word, expressly one whole day in seven; which was the seventh from the beginning of the world to the resurrection of Christ, and the first day of the week ever since, and so to continue to the end of the world; which is the Christian Sabbath,[1] and in the New Testament called "the Lord's Day."[2]

1 **Gen. 2:2-3**. And on the seventh day God finished his work that he had done, and he rested on the seventh day from all his work that he had done. So God blessed the seventh day and made it holy, because on it God rested from all his work that he had done in creation. **Deut. 5:12-14**. "'Observe the Sabbath day, to keep it holy, as the LORD your God commanded you. Six days you shall labor and do all your work, but the seventh day is a Sabbath to the LORD your God. On it you shall not do any work, you or your son or your daughter or your male servant or your female servant, or your ox or your donkey or any of your livestock, or the sojourner who is within your gates, that your male servant and your female servant may rest as well as you.'" **Isa. 56:2, 4, 6-7**. "Blessed is the man who does this, and the son of man who holds it fast, who keeps the Sabbath, not profaning it, and keeps his hand from doing any evil." ... For thus says the LORD: "To the eunuchs who keep my Sabbaths, who choose the things that please me and hold fast my covenant."... "And the foreigners who join themselves to the LORD, to minister to him, to love the name of the LORD, and to be his servants, everyone who keeps the Sabbath and does not profane it, and holds fast my covenant— these I will bring to my holy mountain, and make them joyful in my house of prayer; their burnt offerings and their sacrifices will be accepted on my altar; for my house shall be called a house of prayer for all peoples." **Mt. 5:17-18**. "Do not think that I have come to abolish the Law or the Prophets; I have not come to abolish them but to fulfill them. For truly, I say to you, until heaven and earth pass away, not an iota, not a dot, will pass from the Law until all is accomplished." **1 Cor. 16:1-2**. Now concerning the collection for the saints: as I directed the churches of Galatia, so you also are to do. On the first day of every week, each of you is to put something aside and store it up, as he may prosper, so that there will be no collecting when I come.

2 **Rev. 1:10**. I was in the Spirit on the Lord's day, and I heard behind me a loud voice like a trumpet.

Q. 117. How is the Sabbath or Lord's Day to be sanctified?

A. The Sabbath, or Lord's Day, is to be sanctified by a holy resting all that day,[1] not only from such works as are at all times sinful, but even from such worldly employments and recreations as are on other days lawful;[2] and making it our delight to spend the whole time (except so much of it as is to be taken up in works of necessity and mercy)[3] in the public and private exercise of God's worship.[4] And, to that end, we are to prepare our hearts, and with such foresight, diligence, and moderation, to arrange, and to accomplish ahead of time our worldly business, that we may be the more free and prepared for the duties of the day.[5]

1 **Ex. 20:8, 10**. "Remember the Sabbath day, to keep it holy. ...but the seventh day is a Sabbath to the LORD your God. On it you shall not do any work, you, or your son, or your daughter, your male servant, or your female servant, or your livestock, or the sojourner who is within your gates."

2 **Ex. 16:25-28**. Moses said, "Eat it today, for today is a Sabbath to the LORD; today you will not find it in the field. Six days you shall gather it, but on the seventh day, which is a Sabbath, there will be none." On the seventh day some of the people went out to gather, but they found none. And the LORD said to Moses, "How long will you refuse to keep my commandments and my laws?" **Neh. 13:15-22**. In those days I saw in Judah people treading winepresses on the Sabbath, and bringing in heaps of grain and loading them on donkeys, and also wine, grapes, figs, and all kinds of loads, which they brought into Jerusalem on the Sabbath day. And I warned them on the day when they sold food. Tyrians also, who lived in the city, brought in fish and all kinds of goods and sold them on the Sabbath to the people of Judah, in Jerusalem itself! Then I confronted the nobles of Judah and said to them, "What is this evil thing that you are doing, profaning the Sabbath day? Did not your fathers act in this way, and did not our God bring all this disaster on us and on this city? Now you are bringing more wrath on Israel by profaning the Sabbath." As soon as it began to grow dark at the gates of Jerusalem before the Sabbath, I commanded that the doors should be shut and gave orders that they should not be opened until after the Sabbath. And I stationed some of my servants at the gates, that no load might be brought in on the Sabbath day. Then the merchants and sellers of all kinds of wares lodged outside Jerusalem once or twice. But I warned them and said to them, "Why do you lodge outside the wall? If you do so again, I will lay hands on you." From that time on they did not come on the Sabbath. Then I commanded the Levites that they should purify themselves and come and guard the gates, to keep the Sabbath day holy. Remember this also in my favor, O my God, and spare me according to the greatness of your steadfast love. **Jer. 17:21-22**. Thus says the LORD: Take care for the sake of your lives, and do not bear a burden on the Sabbath day or bring it in by the gates of Jerusalem. And do not carry a burden out of your houses on the Sabbath or do any work, but keep the Sabbath day holy, as I commanded your fathers.

3 **Mt. 11:1-13**. When Jesus had finished instructing his twelve disciples, he went on from there to teach and preach in their cities. Now when John heard in prison about the deeds of the Christ, he sent word by his disciples and said to him, "Are you the one who is to come, or shall we look for another?" And Jesus answered them, "Go and tell John what you hear and see: the blind receive their sight and the lame walk, lepers are cleansed and the deaf hear, and the dead are raised up, and the poor have good news preached to them. And blessed is the one who is not offended by me." As they went away, Jesus began to speak to the crowds concerning John: "What did you go out into the wilderness to see? A reed shaken by the wind? What then did you go out to see? A man dressed in soft clothing? Behold, those who wear soft clothing are in kings' houses. What then did you go out to see? A prophet? Yes, I tell you, and more than a prophet. This is he of whom it is written, "'Behold, I send my messenger before your face, who will prepare your way before you.' Truly, I say to you, among those born of women there has arisen no one greater than John the Baptist. Yet the one who is least in the kingdom of heaven is greater than he. From the days of John the Baptist until now the kingdom of heaven has suffered violence, and the violent take it by force. For all the Prophets and the Law prophesied until John.

4 **Lev. 23:3**. "Six days shall work be done, but on the seventh day is a Sabbath of solemn rest, a holy convocation. You shall do no work. It is a Sabbath to the LORD in all your dwelling places." **Ps. 92** (A song for the Sabbath). **Isa. 58:13-14**. "If you turn back your foot from the Sabbath, from doing your pleasure on my holy day, and call the Sabbath a delight and the holy day of the Lord honorable; if you honor it, not going your own ways, or seeking your own pleasure, or talking idly; then you shall take delight in the Lord, and I will make you ride on the heights of the earth; I will feed you with the heritage of Jacob your father, for the mouth of the Lord has spoken." **Isa. 66:23**. From new moon to new moon, and from Sabbath to Sabbath, all flesh shall come to worship before me, declares the LORD. **Lk. 4:16**. And he came to Nazareth, where he had been brought up. And as was his custom, he went to the synagogue on the Sabbath day, and he stood up to read. **Acts 20:7**. On the first day of the week, when we were gathered together to break bread, Paul talked with them, intending to depart on the next day, and he prolonged his speech until midnight. **1 Cor. 16:1-2**. Now concerning the collection for the saints: as I directed the churches of Galatia, so you also are to do. On the first day of every week, each of you is to put something aside and store it up, as he may prosper, so that there will be no collecting when I come.

5 **Ex. 16:22, 25-26, 29**. On the sixth day they gathered twice as much bread, two omers each. And when all the leaders of the congregation came and told Moses. ... Moses said, "Eat it today, for today is a Sabbath to the LORD; today you will not find it in the field. Six days you shall gather it, but on the seventh day, which is a Sabbath, there will be none." ... "See! The LORD has given you the Sabbath; therefore on the sixth day he gives you bread for two days. Remain each of you in his place; let no one go out of his place on the seventh day." **Ex. 20:8**. "Remember the Sabbath day, to keep it holy." **Lk. 23:56**. Then they returned and prepared spices and ointments. On the Sabbath they rested according to the commandment. **Neh. 13:19-22**. As soon as it began to grow dark at the gates of Jerusalem before the Sabbath, I commanded that the doors should be shut and gave orders that they should not be opened until after the Sabbath. And I stationed some of my servants at the gates, that no load might be brought in on the Sabbath day. Then the merchants and sellers of all kinds of wares lodged outside Jerusalem once or twice. But I warned them and said to them, "Why do you lodge outside the wall? If you do so again, I will lay hands on you." From that time on they did not come on the Sabbath. Then I commanded the Levites that they should purify themselves and come and guard the gates, to keep the Sabbath day holy. Remember this also in my favor, O my God, and spare me according to the greatness of your steadfast love.

Q. 118. Why is the responsibility of keeping the Sabbath more particularly directed to heads of families and other superiors?

A. The responsibility of keeping the Sabbath is more particularly directed to heads of families and other superiors, because they are bound not only to keep it themselves, but to see that it is observed by all those who are under their charge; and because they are prone often to hinder them by employments of their own.[1]

1 **Ex. 20:10**. ...but the seventh day is a Sabbath to the LORD your God. On it you shall not do any work, you, or your son, or your daughter, your male servant, or

your female servant, or your livestock, or the sojourner who is within your gates. **Ex. 23:12**. "Six days you shall do your work, but on the seventh day you shall rest; that your ox and your donkey may have rest, and the son of your servant woman, and the alien, may be refreshed." **Josh. 24:15**. "And if it is evil in your eyes to serve the LORD, choose this day whom you will serve, whether the gods your fathers served in the region beyond the River, or the gods of the Amorites in whose land you dwell. But as for me and my house, we will serve the LORD." **Neh. 13:15, 17**. In those days I saw in Judah people treading winepresses on the Sabbath, and bringing in heaps of grain and loading them on donkeys, and also wine, grapes, figs, and all kinds of loads, which they brought into Jerusalem on the Sabbath day. And I warned them on the day when they sold food. ... Then I confronted the nobles of Judah and said to them, "What is this evil thing that you are doing, profaning the Sabbath day?" **Jer. 17:20-22**. ...and say: 'Hear the word of the LORD, you kings of Judah, and all Judah, and all the inhabitants of Jerusalem, who enter by these gates. Thus says the LORD: Take care for the sake of your lives, and do not bear a burden on the Sabbath day or bring it in by the gates of Jerusalem. And do not carry a burden out of your houses on the Sabbath or do any work, but keep the Sabbath day holy, as I commanded your fathers.'

Q. 119. What are the sins forbidden in the Fourth Commandment?

A. The sins in the Fourth Commandment are: all omissions of the duties required,[1] all careless, negligent, and unprofitable performing of them, and being weary of them;[2] all profaning the day by idleness, and doing that which is in itself sinful;[3] and by all needless works, words, and thoughts about our worldly employments and recreations.[4]

1 **Ezek. 22:26**. Her priests have done violence to my law and have profaned my holy things. They have made no distinction between the holy and the common, neither have they taught the difference between the unclean and the clean, and they have disregarded my Sabbaths, so that I am profaned among them.

2 **Ezek. 33:30-32**. "As for you, son of man, your people who talk together about you by the walls and at the doors of the houses, say to one another, each to his brother, 'Come, and hear what the word is that comes from the LORD.' And they come to you as people come, and they sit before you as my people, and they hear what you say but they will not do it; for with lustful talk in their mouths they act; their heart is set on their gain. And behold, you are to them like one who sings lustful songs with a beautiful voice and plays well on an instrument, for they hear what you say, but they will not do it." **Am. 8:5**. ...saying, "When will the new moon be over, that we may sell grain? And the Sabbath, that we may offer wheat for sale, that we may make the ephah small and the shekel great and deal deceitfully with false balances." **Mal. 1:13**. But you say, 'What a weariness this is,' and you snort at it, says the LORD of hosts. You bring what has been taken by violence or is lame or sick, and this you bring as your offering! Shall I accept that from your hand? says the LORD. **Acts 20:7, 9**. On the first day of the week, when we were gathered together to break bread, Paul talked with them, intending to depart on the next day, and he prolonged his speech until midnight. ... And a young man named Eutychus, sitting at the window, sank into a deep sleep as Paul talked still longer. And being overcome by sleep, he fell down from the third story and was taken up dead.

3 **Ezek. 23:38**. Moreover, this they have done to me: they have defiled my sanctuary on the same day and profaned my Sabbaths.

4 **Isa. 58:13**. "If you turn back your foot from the Sabbath, from doing your pleasure on my holy day, and call the Sabbath a delight and the holy day of the LORD honorable; if you honor it, not going your own ways, or seeking your own pleasure, or talking idly." **Jer. 17:24, 27**. "'But if you listen to me, declares the LORD, and bring in no burden by the gates of this city on the Sabbath day, but keep the Sabbath day holy and do no work on it. ... But if you do not listen to me, to keep the Sabbath day holy, and not to bear a burden and enter by the gates of Jerusalem on the Sabbath day, then I will kindle a fire in its gates, and it shall devour the palaces of Jerusalem and shall not be quenched.'"

Q. 120. What are the reasons attached to the Fourth Commandment, the more to enforce it?

A. The reasons attached to the Fourth Commandment, the more to enforce it, are taken from the principles of it, God allowing us six days of seven for our own affairs, and reserving but one for Himself, in the words, "Six days you shall labor, and do all your work"[1]; from God's establishment of a special ownership in that day with the words, "the seventh day is a Sabbath to the LORD your God"[2] from the example of God who "in six days ... made heaven and earth, the sea, and all that is in them, and rested the seventh day"; and from the blessing that God put on the day, not only in sanctifying it to be a holy day for His service, but in ordaining it to be a means of blessing to us in our sanctifying it, "Therefore the LORD blessed the Sabbath day and made it holy."[3]

1 **Ex. 20:9**. Six days you shall labor, and do all your work.

2 **Ex. 20:10**. ...but the seventh day is a Sabbath to the LORD your God. On it you shall not do any work, you, or your son, or your daughter, your male servant, or your female servant, or your livestock, or the sojourner who is within your gates.

3 **Ex. 20:11**. For in six days the LORD made heaven and earth, the sea, and all that is in them, and rested on the seventh day. Therefore the LORD blessed the Sabbath day and made it holy.

Q. 121. Why is the word "remember" set in the beginning of the Fourth Commandment?

A. The word "remember" is set in the beginning of the Fourth Commandment,[1] partly because of the great benefit of remembering it, we being thereby helped in our preparation to keep it;[2] and, in keeping it, better at keeping the rest of the commandments[3] and to continue a thankful remembrance of the two great benefits of creation and redemption, which contain an abridged picture of religion:[4] and partly because we are ready to forget it,[5] for that there is less light of nature for it, and yet it restrains our natural liberty in things at other times lawful;[6] that it comes but once in seven days, and many worldly businesses come between, and too often take our minds away from thinking of it, either to prepare for it, or to sanctify it;[7] and that Satan with his followers try hard to blot out the glory, and even the memory of it, and to bring in all hostility to religion and lack of respect for it.[8]

1 **Ex. 20:8**. "Remember the Sabbath day, to keep it holy."

2 **Ex. 16:23**. ...he said to them, "This is what the LORD has commanded: 'Tomorrow is a day of solemn rest, a holy Sabbath to the LORD; bake what you will bake and boil what you will boil, and all that is left over lay aside to be kept till the morning.'" **Neh. 13:19**. As soon as it began to grow dark at the gates of Jerusalem before the Sabbath, I commanded that the doors should be shut and gave orders that they should not be opened until after the Sabbath. And I stationed some of my servants at the gates, that no load might be brought in on the Sabbath day. **Mk. 15:42**. And when evening had come, since it was the day of Preparation, that is, the day before the Sabbath. **Lk. 23:54, 56**. It was the day of Preparation, and the Sabbath was beginning. ... Then they returned and prepared spices and ointments. On the Sabbath they rested according to the commandment.

3 **Ps. 92:13-14**. They are planted in the house of the LORD; they flourish in the courts of our God. They still bear fruit in old age; they are ever full of sap and green. **Ezek. 20:12, 19-20**. Moreover, I gave them my Sabbaths, as a sign between me and them, that they might know that I am the LORD who sanctifies them. ... I am the LORD your God; walk in my statutes, and be careful to obey my rules, and keep my Sabbaths holy that they may be a sign between me and you, that you may know that I am the LORD your God.

4 **Gen. 2:2-3**. And on the seventh day God finished his work that he had done, and he rested on the seventh day from all his work that he had done. So God blessed the seventh day and made it holy, because on it God rested from all his work that he had done in creation. **Ps. 118:22, 24**. The stone that the builders rejected has become the cornerstone. ... This is the day that the LORD has made; let us rejoice and be glad in it. **Acts 4:10-11**. ...let it be known to all of you and to all the people of Israel that by the name of Jesus Christ of Nazareth, whom you crucified, whom God raised from the dead—by him this man is standing before you well. This Jesus is the stone that was rejected by you, the builders, which has become the cornerstone. **Rev. 1:10**. I was in the Spirit on the Lord's day, and I heard behind me a loud voice like a trumpet.

5 **Ezek. 22:26**. Her priests have done violence to my law and have profaned my holy things. They have made no distinction between the holy and the common, neither have they taught the difference between the unclean and the clean, and they have disregarded my Sabbaths, so that I am profaned among them.

6 **Neh. 9:14**. ...and you made known to them your holy Sabbath and commanded them commandments and statutes and a law by Moses your servant.

7 **Deut. 5:14-15**. ...but the seventh day is a Sabbath to the LORD your God. On it you shall not do any work, you or your son or your daughter or your male servant or your female servant, or your ox or your donkey or any of your livestock, or the sojourner who is within your gates, that your male servant and your female servant may rest as well as you. You shall remember that you were a slave in the land

of Egypt, and the LORD your God brought you out from there with a mighty hand and an outstretched arm. Therefore the LORD your God commanded you to keep the Sabbath day. **Am. 8:5**. ...saying, "When will the new moon be over, that we may sell grain? And the Sabbath, that we may offer wheat for sale, that we may make the ephah small and the shekel great and deal deceitfully with false balances."

8 **Neh. 13:15-23**. In those days I saw in Judah people treading winepresses on the Sabbath, and bringing in heaps of grain and loading them on donkeys, and also wine, grapes, figs, and all kinds of loads, which they brought into Jerusalem on the Sabbath day. And I warned them on the day when they sold food. Tyrians also, who lived in the city, brought in fish and all kinds of goods and sold them on the Sabbath to the people of Judah, in Jerusalem itself! Then I confronted the nobles of Judah and said to them, "What is this evil thing that you are doing, profaning the Sabbath day? Did not your fathers act in this way, and did not our God bring all this disaster on us and on this city? Now you are bringing more wrath on Israel by profaning the Sabbath." As soon as it began to grow dark at the gates of Jerusalem before the Sabbath, I commanded that the doors should be shut and gave orders that they should not be opened until after the Sabbath. And I stationed some of my servants at the gates, that no load might be brought in on the Sabbath day. Then the merchants and sellers of all kinds of wares lodged outside Jerusalem once or twice. But I warned them and said to them, "Why do you lodge outside the wall? If you do so again, I will lay hands on you." From that time on they did not come on the Sabbath. Then I commanded the Levites that they should purify themselves and come and guard the gates, to keep the Sabbath day holy. Remember this also in my favor, O my God, and spare me according to the greatness of your steadfast love. In those days also I saw the Jews who had married women of Ashdod, Ammon, and Moab. **Jer. 17:21-23**. Thus says the LORD: Take care for the sake of your lives, and do not bear a burden on the Sabbath day or bring it in by the gates of Jerusalem. And do not carry a burden out of your houses on the Sabbath or do any work, but keep the Sabbath day holy, as I commanded your fathers. Yet they did not listen or incline their ear, but stiffened their neck, that they might not hear and receive instruction. **Lam. 1:7**. Jerusalem remembers in the days of her affliction and wandering all the precious things that were hers from days of old. When her people fell into the hand of the foe, and there was none to help her, her foes gloated over her; they mocked at her downfall.

Q. 122. What is the sum of the six commandments that contain our duty to man?

A. The sum of the six commandments that contain our duty to man is, to love our neighbor as ourselves,[1] and to do to others what we would have them to do to us.[2]

1 **Mt. 22:39**. And a second is like it: You shall love your neighbor as yourself.

2 **Mt. 7:12.** "So whatever you wish that others would do to you, do also to them, for this is the Law and the Prophets."

Q. 123. Which is the Fifth Commandment?

A. The Fifth Commandment is, "Honor your father and your mother, that your days may be long in the land that the LORD your God is giving you."[1]

1 **Ex. 20:12.** "Honor your father and your mother, that your days may be long in the land that the LORD your God is giving you."

Q. 124. Who are meant by "father" and "mother," in the Fifth Commandment?

A. By "father" and "mother" in the Fifth Commandment, are meant not only natural parents,[1] but all superiors in age[2] and giftedness;[3] and especially such as by God's ordinance are over us in place of authority, whether in family,[4] church,[5] or government.[6]

1 **Prov. 23:22, 25.** Listen to your father who gave you life, and do not despise your mother when she is old. ... Let your father and mother be glad; let her who bore you rejoice. **Eph. 6:1.** Children, obey your parents in the Lord, for this is right.

2 **1 Tim. 5:1-2.** Do not rebuke an older man but encourage him as you would a father, younger men as brothers, [2] older women as mothers, younger women as sisters, in all purity.

3 **Gen. 4:20-22.** Adah bore Jabal; he was the father of those who dwell in tents and have livestock. His brother's name was Jubal; he was the father of all those who play the lyre and pipe. Zillah also bore Tubal-cain; he was the forger of all instruments of bronze and iron. The sister of Tubal-cain was Naamah. **Gen. 45:8.** So it was not you who sent me here, but God. He has made me a father to Pharaoh, and lord of all his house and ruler over all the land of Egypt.

4 **2 Kings 5:13.** But his servants came near and said to him, "My father, it is a great word the prophet has spoken to you; will you not do it? Has he actually said to you, 'Wash, and be clean'?"

5 **2 Kings 2:12.** And Elisha saw it and he cried, "My father, my father! The chariots of Israel and its horsemen!" And he saw him no more. Then he took hold of his own clothes and tore them in two pieces. **2 Kings 13:14.** Now when Elisha had fallen sick with the illness of which he was to die, Joash king of Israel went down to him and wept before him, crying, "My father, my father! The chariots of Israel and its horsemen!" **Gal. 4:19.** ...my little children, for whom I am again in the anguish of childbirth until Christ is formed in you!

6 **Isa. 49:23.** "Kings shall be your foster fathers, and their queens your nursing mothers. With their faces to the ground they shall bow down to you, and lick the dust of your feet. Then you will know that I am the LORD; those who wait for me shall not be put to shame."

Q. 125. Why are superiors styled "father" and "mother"?

A. Superiors are styled "father" and "mother" both to teach them in all duties toward their inferiors, as with natural parents, to express love and tenderness to them, according to their various relationships,[1] and to work inferiors to a greater willingness and cheerfulness in performing their duties to their superiors, as to their parents.[2]

1 **Num. 11:11-12**. Moses said to the LORD, "Why have you dealt ill with your servant? And why have I not found favor in your sight, that you lay the burden of all this people on me? Did I conceive all this people? Did I give them birth, that you should say to me, 'Carry them in your bosom, as a nurse carries a nursing child,' to the land that you swore to give their fathers? **2 Cor. 12:14**. Here for the third time I am ready to come to you. And I will not be a burden, for I seek not what is yours but you. For children are not obligated to save up for their parents, but parents for their children. **Eph. 6:4**. Fathers, do not provoke your children to anger, but bring them up in the discipline and instruction of the Lord. **1 Thess. 2:7-8, 11**. But we were gentle among you, like a nursing mother taking care of her own children. So, being affectionately desirous of you, we were ready to share with you not only the gospel of God but also our own selves, because you had become very dear to us. ... For you know how, like a father with his children.

2 **2 Kings 5:13**. But his servants came near and said to him, "My father, it is a great word the prophet has spoken to you; will you not do it? Has he actually said to you, 'Wash, and be clean'?" **1 Cor. 4:14-16**. I do not write these things to make you ashamed, but to admonish you as my beloved children. For though you have countless guides in Christ, you do not have many fathers. For I became your father in Christ Jesus through the gospel. I urge you, then, be imitators of me.

Q. 126. What is the general scope of the Fifth Commandment?

A. The general scope of the Fifth Commandment is, the performance of those duties that we mutually owe in our various relationships, as inferiors, superiors, or equals.[1]

1 **Rom. 12:10**. Love one another with brotherly affection. Outdo one another in showing honor. **Eph. 5:21**. ...submitting to one another out of reverence for Christ. **1 Pet. 2:17**. Honor everyone. Love the brotherhood. Fear God. Honor the emperor.

Q. 127. What is the honor that inferiors owe to superiors?

A. The honor that inferiors owe to their superiors is: all due reverence in heart,[1] word,[2] and behavior;[3] prayer and thanksgiving for them;[4] imitation of their virtues and graces;[5] willing obedience to their lawful commands and counsels,[6] due submission to their corrections;[7] fidelity to,[8] defense[9] and maintenance of them and their authority, according to their various ranks, and the nature of their situations;[10] bearing with their infirmities, and covering them in love,[11] so that they may be an honor to them and to their government.[12]

1 **Lev. 19:3**. Every one of you shall revere his mother and his father, and you shall keep my Sabbaths: I am the LORD your God. **Mal. 1:6**. "A son honors his father, and a servant his master. If then I am a father, where is my honor? And if I am a master, where is my fear? says the LORD of hosts to you, O priests, who despise my name. But you say, 'How have we despised your name?'"

2 **Prov. 31:28**. Her children rise up and call her blessed; her husband also, and he praises her. **1 Pet. 3:6**. ...as Sarah obeyed Abraham, calling him lord. And you are her children, if you do good and do not fear anything that is frightening.

3 **Lev. 19:32**. "You shall stand up before the gray head and honor the face of an old man, and you shall fear your God: I am the LORD." **1 Kings 2:19**. So Bathsheba went to King Solomon to speak to him on behalf of Adonijah. And the king rose to meet her and bowed down to her. Then he sat on his throne and had a seat brought for the king's mother, and she sat on his right.

4 **1 Tim. 2:1-2**. First of all, then, I urge that supplications, prayers, intercessions, and thanksgivings be made for all people, for kings and all who are in high positions, that we may lead a peaceful and quiet life, godly and dignified in every way.

5 **Phil. 3:17**. Brothers, join in imitating me, and keep your eyes on those who walk according to the example you have in us. **Heb. 13:7**. Remember your leaders, those who spoke to you the word of God. Consider the outcome of their way of life, and imitate their faith.

6 **Ex. 18:19, 24**. Now obey my voice; I will give you advice, and God be with you! You shall represent the people before God and bring their cases to God. ... So Moses listened to the voice of his father-in-law and did all that he had said. **Prov. 4:3-4**. When I was a son with my father, tender, the only one in the sight of my mother, he taught me and said to me, "Let your heart hold fast my words; keep my commandments, and live." **Prov. 23:22**. Listen to your father who gave you life, and do not despise your mother when she is old. **Rom. 13:1-5**. Let every person be subject to the governing authorities. For there is no authority except from God, and those that exist have been instituted by God. Therefore whoever resists the authorities resists what God has appointed, and those who resist will incur judgment. For rulers are not a terror to good conduct, but to bad. Would you have no fear of the one who is in authority? Then do what is good, and you will receive his approval, for he is God's servant for your good. But if you do wrong, be afraid, for he does not bear the sword in vain. For he is the servant of God, an avenger who carries out God's wrath on the wrongdoer. Therefore one must be in subjection, not only to avoid God's wrath but also for the sake of conscience. **Eph. 6:1-2, 6-7.** Children, obey your parents in the Lord, for this is right. "Honor your father and mother" (this is the first commandment with a promise.) ... not by the way of eye-service, as people-pleasers, but as bondservants of Christ, doing the will of God from the heart, rendering service with a good will as to the Lord and not to man. **Heb. 13:17**. Obey your leaders and submit to them, for they are keeping watch over your souls, as those who will have to give an account. Let them do this with joy and not with groaning, for that would be of no advantage to you. **1 Pet. 2:13-14**. Be subject for the Lord's sake to every human institution, whether it be to the emperor as supreme, or to governors as sent by him to punish those who do evil and to praise those who do good.

7 **Heb. 12:9**. Besides this, we have had earthly fathers who disciplined us and we respected them. Shall we not much more be subject to the Father of spirits and live? **1 Pet. 2:18-20**. Servants, be subject to your masters with all respect, not only to the good and gentle but also to the unjust. For this is a gracious thing, when, mindful of God, one endures sorrows while suffering unjustly. For what credit is it if, when you sin and are beaten for it, you endure? But if when you do good and suffer for it you endure, this is a gracious thing in the sight of God.

8 **Titus 2:9-10**. Bondservants are to be submissive to their own masters in everything; they are to be well-pleasing, not argumentative, not pilfering, but showing all good faith, so that in everything they may adorn the doctrine of God our Savior.

9 **1 Sam. 26:15-16**. And David said to Abner, "Are you not a man? Who is like you in Israel? Why then have you not kept watch over your lord the king? For one of the people came in to destroy the king your lord. This thing that you have done is not good. As the LORD lives, you deserve to die, because you have not kept watch over your lord, the LORD's anointed. And now see where the king's spear is and the jar of water that was at his head." **2 Sam. 18:3**. But the men said, "You shall not go out. For if we flee, they will not care about us. If half of us die, they will not care about us. But you are worth ten thousand of us. Therefore it is better that you send us help from the city." **Esth. 6:2**. And it was found written how Mordecai had told about Bigthana and Teresh, two of the king's eunuchs, who guarded the threshold, and who had sought to lay hands on King Ahasuerus.

10 **Gen. 45:11**. 'There I will provide for you, for there are yet five years of famine to come, so that you and your household, and all that you have, do not come to poverty.' **Gen. 47:12**. And Joseph provided his father, his brothers, and all his father's household with food, according to the number of their dependents.
Mt. 22:21. They said, "Caesar's." Then he said to them, "Therefore render to Caesar the things that are Caesar's, and to God the things that are God's."
Rom. 13:6-7. For because of this you also pay taxes, for the authorities are ministers of God, attending to this very thing. Pay to all what is owed to them: taxes to whom taxes are owed, revenue to whom revenue is owed, respect to whom respect is owed, honor to whom honor is owed. **Gal. 6:6**. Let the one who is taught the word share all good things with the one who teaches. **1 Tim. 5:17-18**. Let the elders who rule well be considered worthy of double honor, especially those who labor in preaching and teaching. For the Scripture says, "You shall not muzzle an ox when it treads out the grain," and, "The laborer deserves his wages."

11 **Gen. 9:23**. Then Shem and Japheth took a garment, laid it on both their shoulders, and walked backward and covered the nakedness of their father. Their faces were turned backward, and they did not see their father's nakedness. **Prov. 23:22**. Listen to your father who gave you life, and do not despise your mother when she is old. **1 Pet. 2:18**. Servants, be subject to your masters with all respect, not only to the good and gentle but also to the unjust.

12 **Prov. 31:23**. Her husband is known in the gates when he sits among the elders of the land. Ps. **127:3-5**. Behold, children are a heritage from the LORD, the fruit of the womb a reward. Like arrows in the hand of a warrior are the children of one's youth. Blessed is the man who fills his quiver with them! He shall not be put to shame when he speaks with his enemies in the gat

---

Q. 128. What are the sins of inferiors against their superiors?

A. The sins of inferiors against their superiors are: all neglect of the duties required toward them;[1] envying at,[2] contempt of,[3] and rebellion[4] against them[5] and their status,[6] in their lawful counsels,[7] commands, and corrections;[8] cursing, mocking,[9] and all such obstinate and scandalous posturing, as proves a shame and dishonor to them and their government.[10]

1 **Mt. 15:4-6**. For God commanded, 'Honor your father and your mother,' and, 'Whoever reviles father or mother must surely die.' But you say, 'If anyone tells his

father or his mother, "What you would have gained from me is given to God," he need not honor his father.' So for the sake of your tradition you have made void the word of God.

2 **Num. 11:28-29**. And Joshua the son of Nun, the assistant of Moses from his youth, said, "My lord Moses, stop them." But Moses said to him, "Are you jealous for my sake? Would that all the LORD's people were prophets, that the LORD would put his Spirit on them!"

3 **1 Sam. 8:7**. And the LORD said to Samuel, "Obey the voice of the people in all that they say to you, for they have not rejected you, but they have rejected me from being king over them."

4 **2 Sam. 15:1-12**. After this Absalom got himself a chariot and horses, and fifty men to run before him. And Absalom used to rise early and stand beside the way of the gate. And when any man had a dispute to come before the king for judgment, Absalom would call to him and say, "From what city are you?" And when he said, "Your servant is of such and such a tribe in Israel," Absalom would say to him, "See, your claims are good and right, but there is no man designated by the king to hear you." Then Absalom would say, "Oh that I were judge in the land! Then every man with a dispute or cause might come to me, and I would give him justice." And whenever a man came near to pay homage to him, he would put out his hand and take hold of him and kiss him. Thus Absalom did to all of Israel who came to the king for judgment. So Absalom stole the hearts of the men of Israel. And at the end of four years Absalom said to the king, "Please let me go and pay my vow, which I have vowed to the LORD, in Hebron. For your servant vowed a vow while I lived at Geshur in Aram, saying, 'If the LORD will indeed bring me back to Jerusalem, then I will offer worship to the LORD.'" The king said to him, "Go in peace." So he arose and went to Hebron. But Absalom sent secret messengers throughout all the tribes of Israel, saying, "As soon as you hear the sound of the trumpet, then say, 'Absalom is king at Hebron!'" With Absalom went two hundred men from Jerusalem who were invited guests, and they went in their innocence and knew nothing. And while Absalom was offering the sacrifices, he sent for Ahithophel the Gilonite, David's counselor, from his city Giloh. And the conspiracy grew strong, and the people with Absalom kept increasing.

5 **Ex. 24:15**. Then Moses went up on the mountain, and the cloud covered the mountain.

6 **1 Sam. 10:27**. But some worthless fellows said, "How can this man save us?" And they despised him and brought him no present. But he held his peace.

7 **1 Sam. 2:25**. If someone sins against a man, God will mediate for him, but if someone sins against the LORD, who can intercede for him?" But they would not listen to the voice of their father, for it was the will of the LORD to put them to death.

8 **Deut. 21:18-21**. "If a man has a stubborn and rebellious son who will not obey the voice of his father or the voice of his mother, and, though they discipline him, will not listen to them, then his father and his mother shall take hold of him and bring him out to the elders of his city at the gate of the place where he lives, and they shall say to the elders of his city, 'This our son is stubborn and rebellious; he will not obey our voice; he is a glutton and a drunkard.' Then all the men of the city shall stone him to death with stones. So you shall purge the evil from your midst, and all Israel shall hear, and fear."

9 **Prov. 30:11, 17**. There are those who curse their fathers and do not bless their mothers. ... The eye that mocks a father and scorns to obey a mother will be picked out by the ravens of the valley and eaten by the vultures.

10 **Prov. 19:26**. He who does violence to his father and chases away his mother is a son who brings shame and reproach.

Q. 129. What is required of superiors toward their inferiors?

A. It is required of superiors, according to that power they receive from God, and that relationship in which they stand, to love,[1] pray for,[2] and bless their inferiors;[3] to instruct,[4] counsel, and admonish them;[5] supporting,[6] commending,[7] and rewarding such as do well;[8] and withholding support,[9] rebuking, and chastising such as do ill;[10] protecting,[11] and providing for them all things necessary for soul[12] and body;[13] and, by grave, wise, holy, and exemplary posture, to obtain glory to God,[14] honor to themselves,[15] and so to preserve the authority that God has put on them.[16]

1 **Col. 3:19**. Husbands, love your wives, and do not be harsh with them. **Titus 2:4**. ...and so train the young women to love their husbands and children.

2 **Job 1:5**. And when the days of the feast had run their course, Job would send and consecrate them, and he would rise early in the morning and offer burnt offerings according to the number of them all. For Job said, "It may be that my children have sinned, and cursed God in their hearts." Thus Job did continually.
1 Sam. 12:23. Moreover, as for me, far be it from me that I should sin against the LORD by ceasing to pray for you, and I will instruct you in the good and the right way.

3 **Gen. 49:28**. All these are the twelve tribes of Israel. This is what their father said to them as he blessed them, blessing each with the blessing suitable to him.
1 Kings 8:55-56. And he stood and blessed all the assembly of Israel with a loud voice, saying, "Blessed be the LORD who has given rest to his people Israel, according to all that he promised. Not one word has failed of all his good promise, which he spoke by Moses his servant. **Heb. 7:7**. It is beyond dispute that the inferior is blessed by the superior.

4 **Deut. 6:6-7**. And these words that I command you today shall be on your heart. You shall teach them diligently to your children, and shall talk of them when you sit in your house, and when you walk by the way, and when you lie down, and when you rise.

5 **Eph. 6:4**. Fathers, do not provoke your children to anger, but bring them up in the discipline and instruction of the Lord.

6 **1 Pet. 3:7**. Likewise, husbands, live with your wives in an understanding way, showing honor to the woman as the weaker vessel, since they are heirs with you of the grace of life, so that your prayers may not be hindered.

7 **Rom. 13:3**. For rulers are not a terror to good conduct, but to bad. Would you have no fear of the one who is in authority? Then do what is good, and you will receive his approval. **1 Pet. 2:14**. ...or to governors as sent by him to punish those who do evil and to praise those who do good.

8 **Esth. 6:3**. And the king said, "What honor or distinction has been bestowed on Mordecai for this?" The king's young men who attended him said, "Nothing has been done for him."

9 **Rom. 13:3-4**. For rulers are not a terror to good conduct, but to bad. Would you have no fear of the one who is in authority? Then do what is good, and you will receive his approval, for he is God's servant for your good. But if you do wrong, be afraid, for he does not bear the sword in vain. For he is the servant of God, an avenger who carries out God's wrath on the wrongdoer.

10 **Prov. 29:15**. The rod and reproof give wisdom, but a child left to himself brings shame to his mother. **1 Pet. 2:14**. ...or to governors as sent by him to punish those who do evil and to praise those who do good.

11 **Job 29:13-16**. The blessing of him who was about to perish came upon me, and I caused the widow's heart to sing for joy. I put on righteousness, and it clothed me; my justice was like a robe and a turban. I was eyes to the blind and feet to the lame. I was a father to the needy, and I searched out the cause of him whom I did not know. **Isa. 1:10, 17**. Hear the word of the LORD, you rulers of Sodom! Give ear to the teaching of our God, you people of Gomorrah! ...learn to do good; seek justice, correct oppression; bring justice to the fatherless, plead the widow's cause.

12 **Eph. 6:4**. Fathers, do not provoke your children to anger, but bring them up in the discipline and instruction of the Lord.

13 **1 Tim. 5:8**. But if anyone does not provide for his relatives, and especially for members of his household, he has denied the faith and is worse than an unbeliever.

14 **1 Tim. 4:12**. Let no one despise you for your youth, but set the believers an example in speech, in conduct, in love, in faith, in purity. **Titus 2:3-5**. Older women likewise are to be reverent in behavior, not slanderers or slaves to much wine. They are to teach what is good, and so train the young women to love their husbands and children, to be self-controlled, pure, working at home, kind, and submissive to their own husbands, that the word of God may not be reviled.

15 **1 Kings 3:28**. And all Israel heard of the judgment that the king had rendered, and they stood in awe of the king, because they perceived that the wisdom of God was in him to do justice.

16 **Titus 2:15**. Declare these things; exhort and rebuke with all authority. Let no one disregard you.

Q. 130. What are the sins of superiors?

A. The sins of superiors are, besides the neglect of the duties required of them,[1] an inordinate seeking of themselves,[2] their own glory,[3] ease, profit, or pleasure;[4] commanding things unlawful,[5] or not in the power of inferiors to perform;[6] counseling,[7] encouraging,[8] or favoring them in that which is evil;[9] dissuading, discouraging, or withholding support for them in that which is good;[10] correcting them unnecessarily;[11] carelessly exposing or leaving them to wrong, temptation, and danger;[12] provoking them to wrath;[13] or any way dishonoring themselves, or lessening their authority, by an unjust, indiscreet, rigorous, or negligent behavior.[14]

1 **Ezek. 34:2-4**. "Son of man, prophesy against the shepherds of Israel; prophesy, and say to them, even to the shepherds, Thus says the Lord GOD: Ah, shepherds of Israel who have been feeding yourselves! Should not shepherds feed the sheep? You eat the fat, you clothe yourselves with the wool, you slaughter the fat ones, but you do not feed the sheep. The weak you have not strengthened, the sick you have

not healed, the injured you have not bound up, the strayed you have not brought back, the lost you have not sought, and with force and harshness you have ruled them."

2 **Phil. 2:21**. For they all seek their own interests, not those of Jesus Christ.

3 **Jn. 5:44**. How can you believe, when you receive glory from one another and do not seek the glory that comes from the only God? **Jn. 7:18**. The one who speaks on his own authority seeks his own glory; but the one who seeks the glory of him who sent him is true, and in him there is no falsehood.

4 **Deut. 17:17**. And he shall not acquire many wives for himself, lest his heart turn away, nor shall he acquire for himself excessive silver and gold. **Isa. 56:10-11**. His watchmen are blind; they are all without knowledge; they are all silent dogs; they cannot bark, dreaming, lying down, loving to slumber. The dogs have a mighty appetite; they never have enough. But they are shepherds who have no understanding; they have all turned to their own way, each to his own gain, one and all.

5 **Dan. 3:4-6**. And the herald proclaimed aloud, "You are commanded, O peoples, nations, and languages, that when you hear the sound of the horn, pipe, lyre, trigon, harp, bagpipe, and every kind of music, you are to fall down and worship the golden image that King Nebuchadnezzar has set up. And whoever does not fall down and worship shall immediately be cast into a burning fiery furnace." **Acts 4:17-18**. But in order that it may spread no further among the people, let us warn them to speak no more to anyone in this name." So they called them and charged them not to speak or teach at all in the name of Jesus.

6 **Ex. 5:10-18**. So the taskmasters and the foremen of the people went out and said to the people, "Thus says Pharaoh, 'I will not give you straw. Go and get your straw yourselves wherever you can find it, but your work will not be reduced in the least.'" So the people were scattered throughout all the land of Egypt to gather stubble for straw. The taskmasters were urgent, saying, "Complete your work, your daily task each day, as when there was straw." And the foremen of the people of Israel, whom Pharaoh's taskmasters had set over them, were beaten and were asked, "Why have you not done all your task of making bricks today and yesterday, as in the past?" Then the foremen of the people of Israel came and cried to Pharaoh, "Why do you treat your servants like this? No straw is given to your servants, yet they say to us, 'Make bricks!' And behold, your servants are beaten; but the fault is in your own people." But he said, "You are idle, you are idle; that is why you say, 'Let us go and sacrifice to the LORD.' Go now and work. No straw will be given you, but you must still deliver the same number of bricks." **Mt. 23:2, 4**. "The scribes and the Pharisees sit on Moses' seat. ... They tie up heavy burdens, hard to bear, and lay them on people's shoulders, but they themselves are not willing to move them with their finger."

7 **Mt. 14:8**. Prompted by her mother, she said, "Give me the head of John the Baptist here on a platter." **Mk. 5:24**. And he went with him. And a great crowd followed him and thronged about him.

8 **2 Sam. 13:28**. Then Absalom commanded his servants, "Mark when Amnon's heart is merry with wine, and when I say to you, 'Strike Amnon,' then kill him. Do not fear; have I not commanded you? Be courageous and be valiant."

9 **1 Sam. 3:13**. And I declare to him that I am about to punish his house forever, for the iniquity that he knew, because his sons were blaspheming God, and he did not restrain them.

10 **Ex. 5:17**. But he said, "You are idle, you are idle; that is why you say, 'Let us go and sacrifice to the LORD.'" **Jn. 7:46-49**. The officers answered, "No one ever spoke like this man!" The Pharisees answered them, "Have you also been deceived? Have any of the authorities or the Pharisees believed in him? But this

crowd that does not know the law is accursed." **Col. 3:21**. Fathers, do not provoke your children, lest they become discouraged.

11 **Deut. 25:3**. Forty stripes may be given him, but not more, lest, if one should go on to beat him with more stripes than these, your brother be degraded in your sight. **Heb. 12:10**. For they disciplined us for a short time as it seemed best to them, but he disciplines us for our good, that we may share his holiness. **1 Pet. 2:18-20**. Servants, be subject to your masters with all respect, not only to the good and gentle but also to the unjust. For this is a gracious thing, when, mindful of God, one endures sorrows while suffering unjustly. For what credit is it if, when you sin and are beaten for it, you endure? But if when you do good and suffer for it you endure, this is a gracious thing in the sight of God.

12 **Gen. 38:11, 26**. Then Judah said to Tamar his daughter-in-law, "Remain a widow in your father's house, till Shelah my son grows up"—for he feared that he would die, like his brothers. So Tamar went and remained in her father's house. ... Then Judah identified them and said, "She is more righteous than I, since I did not give her to my son Shelah." And he did not know her again. **Acts 18:17**. And they all seized Sosthenes, the ruler of the synagogue, and beat him in front of the tribunal. But Gallio paid no attention to any of this.

13 **Eph. 6:4**. Fathers, do not provoke your children to anger, but bring them up in the discipline and instruction of the Lord.

14 **Gen. 9:21**. He drank of the wine and became drunk and lay uncovered in his tent. **1 Sam. 2:29-31**. Why then do you scorn my sacrifices and my offerings that I commanded for my dwelling, and honor your sons above me by fattening yourselves on the choicest parts of every offering of my people Israel?' Therefore the LORD, the God of Israel, declares: 'I promised that your house and the house of your father should go in and out before me forever,' but now the LORD declares: 'Far be it from me, for those who honor me I will honor, and those who despise me shall be lightly esteemed. Behold, the days are coming when I will cut off your strength and the strength of your father's house, so that there will not be an old man in your house.' **1 Kings 1:6**. His father had never at any time displeased him by asking, "Why have you done thus and so?" He was also a very handsome man, and he was born next after Absalom. **1 Kings 12:13-16**. And the king answered the people harshly, and forsaking the counsel that the old men had given him, he spoke to them according to the counsel of the young men, saying, "My father made your yoke heavy, but I will add to your yoke. My father disciplined you with whips, but I will discipline you with scorpions." So the king did not listen to the people, for it was a turn of affairs brought about by the LORD that he might fulfill his word, which the LORD spoke by Ahijah the Shilonite to Jeroboam the son of Nebat. And when all Israel saw that the king did not listen to them, the people answered the king, "What portion do we have in David? We have no inheritance in the son of Jesse. To your tents, O Israel! Look now to your own house, David." So Israel went to their tents.

Q. 131. What are the duties of equals?

A. The duties of equals are: to regard the dignity and worth of each other,[1] in giving honor to go before one another,[2] and to rejoice in each other's giftedness and advancement as their own.[3]

1 **1 Pet. 2:17**. Honor everyone. Love the brotherhood. Fear God. Honor the emperor.

2 **Rom. 12:10**. Love one another with brotherly affection. Outdo one another in showing honor.

3 **Rom. 12:15-16**. Rejoice with those who rejoice, weep with those who weep. Live in harmony with one another. Do not be haughty, but associate with the lowly. Never be wise in your own sight. **Phil. 2:3-4**. Do nothing from selfish ambition or conceit, but in humility count others more significant than yourselves. Let each of you look not only to his own interests, but also to the interests of others.

Q. 132. What are the sins of equals?

A. The sins of equals are, besides the neglect of the duties required,[1] the undervaluing of the worth,[2] envying the giftedness,[3] grieving at the advancement or prosperity of the other,[4] and seizing superiority over the other.[5]

1 **Rom. 13:8**. Owe no one anything, except to love each other, for the one who loves another has fulfilled the law.

2 **2 Tim. 3:3**. ...heartless, unappeasable, slanderous, without self-control, brutal, not loving good.

3 **Acts 7:9**. "And the patriarchs, jealous of Joseph, sold him into Egypt; but God was with him." **Gal. 5:26**. Let us not become conceited, provoking one another, envying one another.

4 **Num. 12:2**. And they said, "Has the LORD indeed spoken only through Moses? Has he not spoken through us also?" And the LORD heard it. **Esth. 6:12-13**. Then Mordecai returned to the king's gate. But Haman hurried to his house, mourning and with his head covered. And Haman told his wife Zeresh and all his friends everything that had happened to him. Then his wise men and his wife Zeresh said to him, "If Mordecai, before whom you have begun to fall, is of the Jewish people, you will not overcome him but will surely fall before him."

5 **Lk. 22:24**. A dispute also arose among them, as to which of them was to be regarded as the greatest. **3 Jn. 9**. I have written something to the church, but Diotrephes, who likes to put himself first, does not acknowledge our authority.

Q. 133. What is the reason attached to the Fifth Commandment, the more to enforce it?

A. The reason attached to the Fifth Commandment in these words, "that your days may be long in the land that the LORD your God is giving you,"[1] is an express promise of long life and prosperity, as far as it shall serve for God's glory and their own good, to all such as keep this commandment.[2]

1 **Ex. 20:12**. "Honor your father and your mother, that your days may be long in the land that the LORD your God is giving you."

2 **Deut. 5:16**. "'Honor your father and your mother, as the LORD your God commanded you, that your days may be long, and that it may go well with you in the land that the LORD your God is giving you.'" **1 Kings 8:25**. Now therefore, O LORD, God of Israel, keep for your servant David my father what you have

promised him, saying, 'You shall not lack a man to sit before me on the throne of Israel, if only your sons pay close attention to their way, to walk before me as you have walked before me.' **Eph. 6:2-3.** "Honor your father and mother" (this is the first commandment with a promise), "that it may go well with you and that you may live long in the land."

Q. 134. Which is the Sixth Commandment?

A. The Sixth Commandment is, "You shall not murder."[1]

1 **Ex. 20:13.** "You shall not murder."

Q. 135. What are the duties required in the Sixth Commandment?

A. The duties required in the Sixth Commandment are: all careful studies and lawful endeavors, to preserve the lives of ourselves[1] and others,[2] by resisting all thoughts and purposes,[3] subduing all passions,[4] and avoiding all occasions,[5] temptations,[6] and practices that tend to the unjust taking away the life of any;[7] by just defense of life against violence;[8] patient bearing of the hand of God,[9] quietness of mind,[10] cheerfulness of spirit;[11] a sober use of meat,[12] drink,[13] medicine,[14] sleep,[15] labor,[16] and recreation;[17] by charitable thoughts,[18] love,[19] compassion,[20] meekness, gentleness, kindness;[21] peaceable,[22] mild, and courteous speech and behavior,[23] restraint, readiness to be reconciled, patient bearing and forgiving of injuries, and repaying good for evil;[24] comforting and relieving the distressed, and protecting and defending the innocent.[25]

1 **Eph. 5:28-29.** In the same way husbands should love their wives as their own bodies. He who loves his wife loves himself. For no one ever hated his own flesh, but nourishes and cherishes it, just as Christ does the church.

2 **1 Kings 18:4.** ...and when Jezebel cut off the prophets of the LORD, Obadiah took a hundred prophets and hid them by fifties in a cave and fed them with bread and water.

3 **Jer. 26:15-16.** "Only know for certain that if you put me to death, you will bring innocent blood upon yourselves and upon this city and its inhabitants, for in truth the LORD sent me to you to speak all these words in your ears." Then the officials and all the people said to the priests and the prophets, "This man does not deserve the sentence of death, for he has spoken to us in the name of the LORD our God." **Acts 23:12, 16-17, 21, 27.** When it was day, the Jews made a plot and bound themselves by an oath neither to eat nor drink till they had killed Paul. ... "Now the son of Paul's sister heard of their ambush, so he went and entered the barracks and told Paul. Paul called one of the centurions and said, "Take this young man to the tribune, for he has something to tell him."... "But do not be persuaded by them, for more than forty of their men are lying in ambush for him, who have bound themselves by an oath neither to eat nor drink till they have killed him. And now they are ready, waiting for your consent." ... This man was seized by the Jews

and was about to be killed by them when I came upon them with the soldiers and rescued him, having learned that he was a Roman citizen.

4 **Eph. 4:26-27**. Be angry and do not sin; do not let the sun go down on your anger, and give no opportunity to the devil.

5 **Deut. 22:8**. "When you build a new house, you shall make a parapet for your roof, that you may not bring the guilt of blood upon your house, if anyone should fall from it. **2 Sam. 2:22**. And Abner said again to Asahel, "Turn aside from following me. Why should I strike you to the ground? How then could I lift up my face to your brother Joab?"

6 **Prov. 1:10, 11, 15-16**. My son, if sinners entice you, do not consent. ... If they say, "Come with us, let us lie in wait for blood; let us ambush the innocent without reason." ...my son, do not walk in the way with them; hold back your foot from their paths, for their feet run to evil, and they make haste to shed blood. **Mt. 4:6-7**. ... and said to him, "If you are the Son of God, throw yourself down, for it is written, "'He will command his angels concerning you,' and "'On their hands they will bear you up, lest you strike your foot against a stone.'" Jesus said to him, "Again it is written, 'You shall not put the Lord your God to the test.'"

7 **Gen. 37:21-22**. But when Reuben heard it, he rescued him out of their hands, saying, "Let us not take his life." And Reuben said to them, "Shed no blood; throw him into this pit here in the wilderness, but do not lay a hand on him"—that he might rescue him out of their hand to restore him to his father. **1 Sam. 24:12**. May the LORD judge between me and you, may the LORD avenge me against you, but my hand shall not be against you. **1 Sam. 26:9-11**. But David said to Abishai, "Do not destroy him, for who can put out his hand against the LORD's anointed and be guiltless?" And David said, "As the LORD lives, the LORD will strike him, or his day will come to die, or he will go down into battle and perish. The LORD forbid that I should put out my hand against the LORD's anointed. But take now the spear that is at his head and the jar of water, and let us go."

8 **1 Sam. 14:45**. Then the people said to Saul, "Shall Jonathan die, who has worked this great salvation in Israel? Far from it! As the LORD lives, there shall not one hair of his head fall to the ground, for he has worked with God this day." So the people ransomed Jonathan, so that he did not die. **Ps. 82:4**. "Rescue the weak and the needy; deliver them from the hand of the wicked." **Prov. 24:11-12**. Rescue those who are being taken away to death; hold back those who are stumbling to the slaughter. If you say, "Behold, we did not know this," does not he who weighs the heart perceive it? Does not he who keeps watch over your soul know it, and will he not repay man according to his work?

9 **Heb. 12:9**. Besides this, we have had earthly fathers who disciplined us and we respected them. Shall we not much more be subject to the Father of spirits and live? **Jas. 5:7-11**. Be patient, therefore, brothers, until the coming of the Lord. See how the farmer waits for the precious fruit of the earth, being patient about it, until it receives the early and the late rains. You also, be patient. Establish your hearts, for the coming of the Lord is at hand. Do not grumble against one another, brothers, so that you may not be judged; behold, the Judge is standing at the door. As an example of suffering and patience, brothers, take the prophets who spoke in the name of the Lord. Behold, we consider those blessed who remained steadfast. You have heard of the steadfastness of Job, and you have seen the purpose of the Lord, how the Lord is compassionate and merciful.

10 **Ps. 37:8-11**. Refrain from anger, and forsake wrath! Fret not yourself; it tends only to evil. For the evildoers shall be cut off, but those who wait for the LORD shall inherit the land. In just a little while, the wicked will be no more; though you look carefully at his place, he will not be there. But the meek shall inherit the land and delight themselves in abundant peace. **1 Thess. 4:11**. ...and to aspire to live

quietly, and to mind your own affairs, and to work with your hands, as we instructed you. **1 Pet. 3:3-4**. Do not let your adorning be external—the braiding of hair and the putting on of gold jewelry, or the clothing you wear—but let your adorning be the hidden person of the heart with the imperishable beauty of a gentle and quiet spirit, which in God's sight is very precious.

11 **Prov. 17:22**. A joyful heart is good medicine, but a crushed spirit dries up the bones.

12 **Prov. 25:16, 27**. If you have found honey, eat only enough for you, lest you have your fill of it and vomit it. ... It is not good to eat much honey, nor is it glorious to seek one's own glory.

13 **1 Tim. 5:23**. No longer drink only water, but use a little wine for the sake of your stomach and your frequent ailments.

14 **Isa. 38:21**. Now Isaiah had said, "Let them take a cake of figs and apply it to the boil, that he may recover."

15 **Ps. 127:2**. It is in vain that you rise up early and go late to rest, eating the bread of anxious toil; for he gives to his beloved sleep.

16 **Prov. 16:20**. Whoever gives thought to the word will discover good, and blessed is he who trusts in the LORD. **Eccl. 5:12**. Sweet is the sleep of a laborer, whether he eats little or much, but the full stomach of the rich will not let him sleep. **2 Thess. 3:10, 12**. For even when we were with you, we would give you this command: If anyone is not willing to work, let him not eat. ... Now such persons we command and encourage in the Lord Jesus Christ to do their work quietly and to earn their own living.

17 **Eccl. 3:4, 11**. ...a time to weep, and a time to laugh; a time to mourn, and a time to dance. ... He has made everything beautiful in its time. Also, he has put eternity into man's heart, yet so that he cannot find out what God has done from the beginning to the end.

18 **1 Sam. 19:4-5**. And Jonathan spoke well of David to Saul his father and said to him, "Let not the king sin against his servant David, because he has not sinned against you, and because his deeds have brought good to you. For he took his life in his hand and he struck down the Philistine, and the LORD worked a great salvation for all Israel. You saw it, and rejoiced. Why then will you sin against innocent blood by killing David without cause?" **1 Sam. 22:13-14**. And Saul said to him, "Why have you conspired against me, you and the son of Jesse, in that you have given him bread and a sword and have inquired of God for him, so that he has risen against me, to lie in wait, as at this day?" Then Ahimelech answered the king, "And who among all your servants is so faithful as David, who is the king's son-in-law, and captain over your bodyguard, and honored in your house?"

19 **Rom. 13:10**. Love does no wrong to a neighbor; therefore love is the fulfilling of the law.

20 **Lk. 10:33-34**. But a Samaritan, as he journeyed, came to where he was, and when he saw him, he had compassion. He went to him and bound up his wounds, pouring on oil and wine. Then he set him on his own animal and brought him to an inn and took care of him.

21 **Col. 3:12-13**. Put on then, as God's chosen ones, holy and beloved, compassionate hearts, kindness, humility, meekness, and patience, bearing with one another and, if one has a complaint against another, forgiving each other; as the Lord has forgiven you, so you also must forgive.

22 **Jas. 3:17**. But the wisdom from above is first pure, then peaceable, gentle, open to reason, full of mercy and good fruits, impartial and sincere.

23 **Judg. 8:1-3**. Then the men of Ephraim said to him, "What is this that you have done to us, not to call us when you went to fight against Midian?" And they

accused him fiercely. And he said to them, "What have I done now in comparison with you? Is not the gleaning of the grapes of Ephraim better than the grape harvest of Abiezer? God has given into your hands the princes of Midian, Oreb and Zeeb. What have I been able to do in comparison with you?" Then their anger against him subsided when he said this. **Prov. 15:1**. A soft answer turns away wrath, but a harsh word stirs up anger. **1 Pet. 3:8-11**. Finally, all of you, have unity of mind, sympathy, brotherly love, a tender heart, and a humble mind. Do not repay evil for evil or reviling for reviling, but on the contrary, bless, for to this you were called, that you may obtain a blessing. For "Whoever desires to love life and see good days, let him keep his tongue from evil and his lips from speaking deceit; let him turn away from evil and do good; let him seek peace and pursue it.

24 **Mt. 5:24**. ...leave your gift there before the altar and go. First be reconciled to your brother, and then come and offer your gift. **Rom. 12:17, 20.** Repay no one evil for evil, but give thought to do what is honorable in the sight of all. ... To the contrary, "if your enemy is hungry, feed him; if he is thirsty, give him something to drink; for by so doing you will heap burning coals on his head." **Eph. 5:2, 32**. And walk in love, as Christ loved us and gave himself up for us, a fragrant offering and sacrifice to God. ... This mystery is profound, and I am saying that it refers to Christ and the church.

25 **Job 31:19-20**. ...if I have seen anyone perish for lack of clothing, or the needy without covering, if his body has not blessed me, and if he was not warmed with the fleece of my sheep. **Prov. 31:8-9**. Open your mouth for the mute, for the rights of all who are destitute. Open your mouth, judge righteously, defend the rights of the poor and needy. **Mt. 25:35-36**. 'For I was hungry and you gave me food, I was thirsty and you gave me drink, I was a stranger and you welcomed me, I was naked and you clothed me, I was sick and you visited me, I was in prison and you came to me.' **1 Thess. 5:14**. And we urge you, brothers, admonish the idle, encourage the fainthearted, help the weak, be patient with them all.

Q. 136. What are the sins forbidden in the Sixth Commandment?

A. The sins forbidden in the Sixth Commandment are: all taking away of the lives of ourselves,[1] or of others,[2] except in case of public justice,[3] lawful war,[4] or necessary defense;[5] the neglecting or withdrawing of the lawful or necessary means of preservation of life;[6] sinful anger,[7] hatred,[8] envy,[9] desire for revenge;[10] all excessive passions;[11] distracting cares;[12] immoderate use of meat, drink,[13] labor,[14] and recreation;[15] provoking words;[16] oppression,[17] quarreling,[18] striking, wounding,[19] and whatever else tends to the destruction of the life of anyone.[20]

1 **Acts 16:28**. But Paul cried with a loud voice, "Do not harm yourself, for we are all here."

2 **Gen. 9:6**. "Whoever sheds the blood of man, by man shall his blood be shed, for God made man in his own image."

3 **Num. 35:31, 33**. Moreover, you shall accept no ransom for the life of a murderer, who is guilty of death, but he shall be put to death. ... You shall not pollute the land in which you live, for blood pollutes the land, and no atonement can be made

for the land for the blood that is shed in it, except by the blood of the one who shed it.

4 **Deut. 20:1**. "When you go out to war against your enemies, and see horses and chariots and an army larger than your own, you shall not be afraid of them, for the LORD your God is with you, who brought you up out of the land of Egypt." **Jer. 48:10**. "Cursed is he who does the work of the LORD with slackness, and cursed is he who keeps back his sword from bloodshed."

5 **Ex. 22:2-3**. If a thief is found breaking in and is struck so that he dies, there shall be no bloodguilt for him, but if the sun has risen on him, there shall be bloodguilt for him. He shall surely pay. If he has nothing, then he shall be sold for his theft.

6 **Eccl. 6:1-2**. There is an evil that I have seen under the sun, and it lies heavy on mankind: a man to whom God gives wealth, possessions, and honor, so that he lacks nothing of all that he desires, yet God does not give him power to enjoy them, but a stranger enjoys them. This is vanity; it is a grievous evil. **Mt. 25:42-43**. 'For I was hungry and you gave me no food, I was thirsty and you gave me no drink, I was a stranger and you did not welcome me, naked and you did not clothe me, sick and in prison and you did not visit me.' **Jas. 2:15-16**. If a brother or sister is poorly clothed and lacking in daily food, and one of you says to them, "Go in peace, be warmed and filled," without giving them the things needed for the body, what good is that?

7 **Mt. 5:22**. But I say to you that everyone who is angry with his brother will be liable to judgment; whoever insults his brother will be liable to the council; and whoever says, 'You fool!' will be liable to the hell of fire.

8 **Lev. 19:17**. "You shall not hate your brother in your heart, but you shall reason frankly with your neighbor, lest you incur sin because of him." **1 Jn. 3:15**. Everyone who hates his brother is a murderer, and you know that no murderer has eternal life abiding in him.

9 **Prov. 14:30**. A tranquil heart gives life to the flesh, but envy makes the bones rot.

10 **Rom. 12:19**. Beloved, never avenge yourselves, but leave it to the wrath of God, for it is written, "Vengeance is mine, I will repay, says the Lord."

11 **Eph. 4:31**. Let all bitterness and wrath and anger and clamor and slander be put away from you, along with all malice.

12 **Mt. 6:31, 34**. Therefore do not be anxious, saying, 'What shall we eat?' or 'What shall we drink?' or 'What shall we wear?' ... "Therefore do not be anxious about tomorrow, for tomorrow will be anxious for itself. Sufficient for the day is its own trouble."

13 **Lk. 21:34**. "But watch yourselves lest your hearts be weighed down with dissipation and drunkenness and cares of this life, and that day come upon you suddenly like a trap." **Rom. 13:13**. Let us walk properly as in the daytime, not in orgies and drunkenness, not in sexual immorality and sensuality, not in quarreling and jealousy.

14 **Eccl. 2:22-23**. What has a man from all the toil and striving of heart with which he toils beneath the sun? For all his days are full of sorrow, and his work is a vexation. Even in the night his heart does not rest. This also is vanity. **Eccl. 12:12**. My son, beware of anything beyond these. Of making many books there is no end, and much study is a weariness of the flesh.

15 **Isa. 5:12**. They have lyre and harp, tambourine and flute and wine at their feasts, but they do not regard the deeds of the LORD, or see the work of his hands.

16 **Prov. 12:18**. There is one whose rash words are like sword thrusts, but the tongue of the wise brings healing. **Prov. 15:1**. A soft answer turns away wrath, but a harsh word stirs up anger.

17 **Ex. 1:14**. ...and made their lives bitter with hard service, in mortar and brick, and in all kinds of work in the field. In all their work they ruthlessly made them work as slaves. **Ezek. 18:18**. As for his father, because he practiced extortion, robbed his brother, and did what is not good among his people, behold, he shall die for his iniquity.

18 **Prov. 23:29**. Who has woe? Who has sorrow? Who has strife? Who has complaining? Who has wounds without cause? Who has redness of eyes? **Gal. 5:15**. But if you bite and devour one another, watch out that you are not consumed by one another.

19 **Num. 35:16-18, 21**. "But if he struck him down with an iron object, so that he died, he is a murderer. The murderer shall be put to death. And if he struck him down with a stone tool that could cause death, and he died, he is a murderer. The murderer shall be put to death. Or if he struck him down with a wooden tool that could cause death, and he died, he is a murderer. The murderer shall be put to death." ...or in enmity struck him down with his hand, so that he died, then he who struck the blow shall be put to death. He is a murderer. The avenger of blood shall put the murderer to death when he meets him.

20 **Ex. 21:18-36**. "When men quarrel and one strikes the other with a stone or with his fist and the man does not die but takes to his bed, then if the man rises again and walks outdoors with his staff, he who struck him shall be clear; only he shall pay for the loss of his time, and shall have him thoroughly healed. "When a man strikes his slave, male or female, with a rod and the slave dies under his hand, he shall be avenged. But if the slave survives a day or two, he is not to be avenged, for the slave is his money. "When men strive together and hit a pregnant woman, so that her children come out, but there is no harm, the one who hit her shall surely be fined, as the woman's husband shall impose on him, and he shall pay as the judges determine. But if there is harm, then you shall pay life for life, eye for eye, tooth for tooth, hand for hand, foot for foot, burn for burn, wound for wound, stripe for stripe. "When a man strikes the eye of his slave, male or female, and destroys it, he shall let the slave go free because of his eye. If he knocks out the tooth of his slave, male or female, he shall let the slave go free because of his tooth. "When an ox gores a man or a woman to death, the ox shall be stoned, and its flesh shall not be eaten, but the owner of the ox shall not be liable. But if the ox has been accustomed to gore in the past, and its owner has been warned but has not kept it in, and it kills a man or a woman, the ox shall be stoned, and its owner also shall be put to death. If a ransom is imposed on him, then he shall give for the redemption of his life whatever is imposed on him. If it gores a man's son or daughter, he shall be dealt with according to this same rule. If the ox gores a slave, male or female, the owner shall give to their master thirty shekels of silver, and the ox shall be stoned. "When a man opens a pit, or when a man digs a pit and does not cover it, and an ox or a donkey falls into it, the owner of the pit shall make restoration. He shall give money to its owner, and the dead beast shall be his. "When one man's ox butts another's, so that it dies, then they shall sell the live ox and share its price, and the dead beast also they shall share. Or if it is known that the ox has been accustomed to gore in the past, and its owner has not kept it in, he shall repay ox for ox, and the dead beast shall be his."

Q. 137. Which is the Seventh Commandment?

A. The Seventh Commandment is, "You shall not commit adultery."[1]

1 **Ex. 20:14**. "You shall not commit adultery."

Q. 138. What are the duties required in the Seventh Commandment?

A. The duties required in the Seventh Commandment are: chastity in body, mind, affections,[1] words,[2] and behavior,[3] and the preservation of it in ourselves and others;[4] watchfulness over the eyes and all the senses;[5] temperance,[6] keeping of chaste company,[7] modesty in apparel,[8] marriage by those who do not have the gift of self-restraint,[9] marital love,[10] and cohabitation;[11] diligent labor in our callings;[12] shunning of all occasions of unchastity, and resisting temptations to it.[13]

1 **Job 31:1**. "I have made a covenant with my eyes; how then could I gaze at a virgin?" **1 Cor. 7:34**. ...and his interests are divided. And the unmarried or betrothed woman is anxious about the things of the Lord, how to be holy in body and spirit. But the married woman is anxious about worldly things, how to please her husband. **1 Thess. 4:4**. ...that each one of you know how to control his own body in holiness and honor.

2 **Col. 4:6**. Let your speech always be gracious, seasoned with salt, so that you may know how you ought to answer each person.

3 **1 Pet. 2:3**. ...if indeed you have tasted that the Lord is good.

4 **1 Cor. 7:2, 35-36**. But because of the temptation to sexual immorality, each man should have his own wife and each woman her own husband. ... I say this for your own benefit, not to lay any restraint upon you, but to promote good order and to secure your undivided devotion to the Lord. If anyone thinks that he is not behaving properly toward his betrothed, if his passions are strong, and it has to be, let him do as he wishes: let them marry—it is no sin.

5 **Job 31:1**. "I have made a covenant with my eyes; how then could I gaze at a virgin?"

6 **Acts 24:24-25**. After some days Felix came with his wife Drusilla, who was Jewish, and he sent for Paul and heard him speak about faith in Christ Jesus. And as he reasoned about righteousness and self-control and the coming judgment, Felix was alarmed and said, "Go away for the present. When I get an opportunity I will summon you."

7 **Prov. 2:16-20**. So you will be delivered from the forbidden woman, from the adulteress with her smooth words, who forsakes the companion of her youth and forgets the covenant of her God; for her house sinks down to death, and her paths to the departed; none who go to her come back, nor do they regain the paths of life. So you will walk in the way of the good and keep to the paths of the righteous.

8 **1 Tim. 2:9**. ...likewise also that women should adorn themselves in respectable apparel, with modesty and self-control, not with braided hair and gold or pearls or costly attire.

9 **1 Cor. 7:2, 9**. But because of the temptation to sexual immorality, each man should have his own wife and each woman her own husband. ... But if they cannot exercise self-control, they should marry. For it is better to marry than to burn with passion.

10 **Prov. 5:19-20**. ...a lovely deer, a graceful doe. Let her breasts fill you at all times with delight; be intoxicated always in her love. Why should you be intoxicated, my son, with a forbidden woman and embrace the bosom of an adulteress?

11 **1 Pet. 3:7**. Likewise, husbands, live with your wives in an understanding way, showing honor to the woman as the weaker vessel, since they are heirs with you of the grace of life, so that your prayers may not be hindered.

12 **Prov. 3:11, 27-28**. My son, do not despise the LORD's discipline or be weary of his reproof. ... Do not withhold good from those to whom it is due, when it is in your power to do it. Do not say to your neighbor, "Go, and come again, tomorrow I will give it"—when you have it with you.

13 **Gen. 39:8-10**. But he refused and said to his master's wife, "Behold, because of me my master has no concern about anything in the house, and he has put everything that he has in my charge. He is not greater in this house than I am, nor has he kept back anything from me except you, because you are his wife. How then can I do this great wickedness and sin against God?" And as she spoke to Joseph day after day, he would not listen to her, to lie beside her or to be with her. **Prov. 5:8**. Keep your way far from her, and do not go near the door of her house

---

Q. 139. What are the sins forbidden in the Seventh Commandment?

A. The sins forbidden in the Seventh Commandment, besides the neglect of the duties required,[1] are: adultery, fornication,[2] rape, incest,[3] sodomy, and all unnatural lusts;[4] all unclean imaginations, thoughts, purposes, and affections;[5] all corrupt or filthy communications, or listening to them;[6] lewd looks,[7] impudent or light behavior, immodest apparel,[8] prohibiting of lawful,[9] and dispensing with unlawful marriages;[10] allowing, tolerating, keeping of houses of prostitution, and patronizing them;[11] entangling vows of single life,[12] undue delay of marriage;[13] having more wives or husbands than one at the same time;[14] unjust divorce[15] or desertion;[16] idleness, gluttony, drunkenness,[17] unchaste company;[18] lascivious songs, books, pictures, dances, theater,[19] and all other provocations to, or acts of, uncleanness either in ourselves or others.[20]

1 **Prov. 5:7**. And now, O sons, listen to me, and do not depart from the words of my mouth.

2 **Gal. 5:19**. Now the works of the flesh are evident: sexual immorality, impurity, sensuality. **Heb. 13:4**. Let marriage be held in honor among all, and let the marriage bed be undefiled, for God will judge the sexually immoral and adulterous.

3 **2 Sam. 13:14**. But he would not listen to her, and being stronger than she, he violated her and lay with her. **1 Cor. 5:1**. It is actually reported that there is sexual immorality among you, and of a kind that is not tolerated even among pagans, for a man has his father's wife.

4 **Lev. 20:15-16**. If a man lies with an animal, he shall surely be put to death, and you shall kill the animal. If a woman approaches any animal and lies with it, you shall kill the woman and the animal; they shall surely be put to death; their blood is upon them. **Rom. 1:24, 26-27**. Therefore God gave them up in the lusts of their hearts to impurity, to the dishonoring of their bodies among themselves. ... For this reason God gave them up to dishonorable passions. For their women exchanged natural relations for those that are contrary to nature; and the men likewise gave up natural relations with women and were consumed with passion for

one another, men committing shameless acts with men and receiving in themselves the due penalty for their error.

5 **Mt. 5:28**. But I say to you that everyone who looks at a woman with lustful intent has already committed adultery with her in his heart. **Mt. 15:19**. For out of the heart come evil thoughts, murder, adultery, sexual immorality, theft, false witness, slander. **Col. 3:5**. Put to death therefore what is earthly in you: sexual immorality, impurity, passion, evil desire, and covetousness, which is idolatry.

6 **Prov. 7:5, 21-22**. ...to keep you from the forbidden woman, from the adulteress with her smooth words. ... With much seductive speech she persuades him; with her smooth talk she compels him. All at once he follows her, as an ox goes to the slaughter, or as a stag is caught fast. **Eph. 5:3-4**. But sexual immorality and all impurity or covetousness must not even be named among you, as is proper among saints. Let there be no filthiness nor foolish talk nor crude joking, which are out of place, but instead let there be thanksgiving.

7 **Isa. 3:16**. The LORD said: Because the daughters of Zion are haughty and walk with outstretched necks, glancing wantonly with their eyes, mincing along as they go, tinkling with their feet. **2 Pet. 2:14**. They have eyes full of adultery, insatiable for sin. They entice unsteady souls. They have hearts trained in greed. Accursed children!

8 **Prov. 7:10, 13**. And behold, the woman meets him, dressed as a prostitute, wily of heart. ... She seizes him and kisses him, and with bold face she says to him.

9 **1 Tim. 4:3**. ...who forbid marriage and require abstinence from foods that God created to be received with thanksgiving by those who believe and know the truth.

10 **Lev. 18:1-21**. And the LORD spoke to Moses, saying, “Speak to the people of Israel and say to them, I am the LORD your God. You shall not do as they do in the land of Egypt, where you lived, and you shall not do as they do in the land of Canaan, to which I am bringing you. You shall not walk in their statutes. You shall follow my rules and keep my statutes and walk in them. I am the LORD your God. You shall therefore keep my statutes and my rules; if a person does them, he shall live by them: I am the LORD. “None of you shall approach any one of his close relatives to uncover nakedness. I am the LORD. You shall not uncover the nakedness of your father, which is the nakedness of your mother; she is your mother, you shall not uncover her nakedness. You shall not uncover the nakedness of your father’s wife; it is your father’s nakedness. You shall not uncover the nakedness of your sister, your father’s daughter or your mother’s daughter, whether brought up in the family or in another home. You shall not uncover the nakedness of your son’s daughter or of your daughter’s daughter, for their nakedness is your own nakedness. You shall not uncover the nakedness of your father’s wife’s daughter, brought up in your father’s family, since she is your sister. You shall not uncover the nakedness of your father’s sister; she is your father’s relative. You shall not uncover the nakedness of your mother’s sister, for she is your mother’s relative. You shall not uncover the nakedness of your father’s brother, that is, you shall not approach his wife; she is your aunt. You shall not uncover the nakedness of your daughter-in-law; she is your son’s wife, you shall not uncover her nakedness. You shall not uncover the nakedness of your brother’s wife; it is your brother’s nakedness. You shall not uncover the nakedness of a woman and of her daughter, and you shall not take her son’s daughter or her daughter’s daughter to uncover her nakedness; they are relatives; it is depravity. And you shall not take a woman as a rival wife to her sister, uncovering her nakedness while her sister is still alive. “You shall not approach a woman to uncover her nakedness while she is in her menstrual uncleanness. And you shall not lie sexually with your neighbor’s wife and so make yourself unclean with her. You shall not give any of your children to offer them to Molech, and so profane the name of your God: I am the LORD.

Mal. 2:11-12. Judah has been faithless, and abomination has been committed in Israel and in Jerusalem. For Judah has profaned the sanctuary of the LORD, which he loves, and has married the daughter of a foreign god. May the LORD cut off from the tents of Jacob any descendant of the man who does this, who brings an offering to the LORD of hosts! **Mk. 6:18.** For John had been saying to Herod, "It is not lawful for you to have your brother's wife."

11 **Lev. 19:29**. "Do not profane your daughter by making her a prostitute, lest the land fall into prostitution and the land become full of depravity." **Deut. 23:17-18**. "None of the daughters of Israel shall be a cult prostitute, and none of the sons of Israel shall be a cult prostitute. You shall not bring the fee of a prostitute or the wages of a dog into the house of the LORD your God in payment for any vow, for both of these are an abomination to the LORD your God." **1 Kings 15:12**. He put away the male cult prostitutes out of the land and removed all the idols that his fathers had made. **2 Kings 23:7**. And he broke down the houses of the male cult prostitutes who were in the house of the LORD, where the women wove hangings for the Asherah. **Prov. 7:24-27**. And now, O sons, listen to me, and be attentive to the words of my mouth. Let not your heart turn aside to her ways; do not stray into her paths, for many a victim has she laid low, and all her slain are a mighty throng. Her house is the way to Sheol, going down to the chambers of death. **Jer. 5:7**. "How can I pardon you? Your children have forsaken me and have sworn by those who are no gods. When I fed them to the full, they committed adultery and trooped to the houses of whores."

12 **Mt. 19:10-11**. The disciples said to him, "If such is the case of a man with his wife, it is better not to marry." But he said to them, "Not everyone can receive this saying, but only those to whom it is given."

13 **Gen. 38:26**. Then Judah identified them and said, "She is more righteous than I, since I did not give her to my son Shelah." And he did not know her again. **1 Cor. 7:7-9**. I wish that all were as I myself am. But each has his own gift from God, one of one kind and one of another. To the unmarried and the widows I say that it is good for them to remain single as I am. But if they cannot exercise self-control, they should marry. For it is better to marry than to burn with passion.

14 **Mal. 2:14-15**. But you say, "Why does he not?" Because the LORD was witness between you and the wife of your youth, to whom you have been faithless, though she is your companion and your wife by covenant. Did he not make them one, with a portion of the Spirit in their union? And what was the one God seeking? Godly offspring. So guard yourselves in your spirit, and let none of you be faithless to the wife of your youth. **Mt. 19:5**. ...and said, 'Therefore a man shall leave his father and his mother and hold fast to his wife, and the two shall become one flesh'?

15 **Mal. 2:16**. "For the man who does not love his wife but divorces her, says the LORD, the God of Israel, covers his garment with violence, says the LORD of hosts. So guard yourselves in your spirit, and do not be faithless." **Mt. 5:32**. But I say to you that everyone who divorces his wife, except on the ground of sexual immorality, makes her commit adultery, and whoever marries a divorced woman commits adultery.

16 **1 Cor. 7:12-13**. To the rest I say (I, not the Lord) that if any brother has a wife who is an unbeliever, and she consents to live with him, he should not divorce her. If any woman has a husband who is an unbeliever, and he consents to live with her, she should not divorce him.

17 **Prov. 23:30-33**. Those who tarry long over wine; those who go to try mixed wine. Do not look at wine when it is red, when it sparkles in the cup and goes down smoothly. In the end it bites like a serpent and stings like an adder. Your eyes will see strange things, and your heart utter perverse things. **Ezek. 16:49**.

Behold, this was the guilt of your sister Sodom: she and her daughters had pride, excess of food, and prosperous ease, but did not aid the poor and needy.

18 **Gen. 39:19**. As soon as his master heard the words that his wife spoke to him, "This is the way your servant treated me," his anger was kindled. **Prov. 5:8**. Keep your way far from her, and do not go near the door of her house.

19 **Isa. 3:16**. The LORD said: Because the daughters of Zion are haughty and walk with outstretched necks, glancing wantonly with their eyes, mincing along as they go, tinkling with their feet. **Isa. 23:15-17**. In that day Tyre will be forgotten for seventy years, like the days of one king. At the end of seventy years, it will happen to Tyre as in the song of the prostitute: "Take a harp; go about the city, O forgotten prostitute! Make sweet melody; sing many songs, that you may be remembered." At the end of seventy years, the LORD will visit Tyre, and she will return to her wages and will prostitute herself with all the kingdoms of the world on the face of the earth. **Ezek. 23:14-16**. But she carried her whoring further. She saw men portrayed on the wall, the images of the Chaldeans portrayed in vermilion, wearing belts on their waists, with flowing turbans on their heads, all of them having the appearance of officers, a likeness of Babylonians whose native land was Chaldea. When she saw them, she lusted after them and sent messengers to them in Chaldea. **Mk. 6:22**. For when Herodias's daughter came in and danced, she pleased Herod and his guests. And the king said to the girl, "Ask me for whatever you wish, and I will give it to you." **Rom. 13:13**. Let every person be subject to the governing authorities. For there is no authority except from God, and those that exist have been instituted by God. **Eph. 5:4**. Let there be no filthiness nor foolish talk nor crude joking, which are out of place, but instead let there be thanksgiving. **1 Pet. 4:3**. For the time that is past suffices for doing what the Gentiles want to do, living in sensuality, passions, drunkenness, orgies, drinking parties, and lawless idolatry.

20 **2 Kings 9:30**. When Jehu came to Jezreel, Jezebel heard of it. And she painted her eyes and adorned her head and looked out of the window. **Jer. 4:30**. And you, O desolate one, what do you mean that you dress in scarlet, that you adorn yourself with ornaments of gold, that you enlarge your eyes with paint? In vain you beautify yourself. Your lovers despise you; they seek your life. **Ezek. 23:40**. They even sent for men to come from afar, to whom a messenger was sent; and behold, they came. For them you bathed yourself, painted your eyes, and adorned yourself with ornaments.

Q. 140. Which is the Eighth Commandment?

A. The Eighth Commandment is, "You shall not steal."[1]

1 **Ex. 20:15**. "You shall not steal."

Q. 141. What are the duties required in the Eighth Commandment?

A. The duties required in the Eighth Commandment are: truth, faithfulness, and justice in contracts and commerce between man and man;[1] restitution of goods unlawfully detained from the right owners of them;[2] giving and lending freely, according to our abilities, and the needs of others;[3] moderation of our judgments, wills, and affections, concerning worldly goods;[4] a provident care and study to get,[5] keep, use, and dispose of those things that are necessary and convenient for the support of our nature, and suitable to our condition;[6] a lawful calling,[7] and a diligence in it;[8] frugality;[9] avoiding unnecessary lawsuits,[10] and pledge of security, or other like engagements;[11] and an endeavor by all just and lawful means to obtain, preserve, and further the wealth and outward estate of others, as well as our own.[12]

1 **Ps. 15:2, 4**. He who walks blamelessly and does what is right and speaks truth in his heart. ...in whose eyes a vile person is despised, but who honors those who fear the LORD; who swears to his own hurt and does not change. **Zech. 7:4, 10**. Then the word of the LORD of hosts came to me. "...do not oppress the widow, the fatherless, the sojourner, or the poor, and let none of you devise evil against another in your heart." **Zech. 8:16-17**. "These are the things that you shall do: Speak the truth to one another; render in your gates judgments that are true and make for peace; do not devise evil in your hearts against one another, and love no false oath, for all these things I hate, declares the LORD."

2 **Lev. 6:2-5**. "If anyone sins and commits a breach of faith against the LORD by deceiving his neighbor in a matter of deposit or security, or through robbery, or if he has oppressed his neighbor or has found something lost and lied about it, swearing falsely—in any of all the things that people do and sin thereby— if he has sinned and has realized his guilt and will restore what he took by robbery or what he got by oppression or the deposit that was committed to him or the lost thing that he found or anything about which he has sworn falsely, he shall restore it in full and shall add a fifth to it, and give it to him to whom it belongs on the day he realizes his guilt." **Lk. 19:8**. And Zacchaeus stood and said to the Lord, "Behold, Lord, the half of my goods I give to the poor. And if I have defrauded anyone of anything, I restore it fourfold."

3 **Lk. 6:30, 38**. Give to everyone who begs from you, and from one who takes away your goods do not demand them back. "...give, and it will be given to you. Good measure, pressed down, shaken together, running over, will be put into your lap. For with the measure you use it will be measured back to you." **Gal. 6:10**. So then, as we have opportunity, let us do good to everyone, and especially to those who are of the household of faith. **Eph. 4:28.** Let the thief no longer steal, but rather let him labor, doing honest work with his own hands, so that he may have something to share with anyone in need. **1 Jn. 3:17.** But if anyone has the world's goods and sees his brother in need, yet closes his heart against him, how does God's love abide in him?

4 **Gal. 6:14**. But far be it from me to boast except in the cross of our Lord Jesus Christ, by which the world has been crucified to me, and I to the world. **1 Tim. 6:6-9**. But godliness with contentment is great gain, for we brought nothing into the world, and we cannot take anything out of the world. But if we have food and clothing, with these we will be content. But those who desire to be rich fall into temptation, into a snare, into many senseless and harmful desires that plunge people into ruin and destruction.

5 **1 Tim. 5:8**. But if anyone does not provide for his relatives, and especially for members of his household, he has denied the faith and is worse than an unbeliever.

6 **Prov. 27:23-27**. Know well the condition of your flocks, and give attention to your herds, for riches do not last forever; and does a crown endure to all generations? When the grass is gone and the new growth appears and the vegetation of the mountains is gathered, the lambs will provide your clothing, and the goats the

price of a field. There will be enough goats' milk for your food, for the food of your household and maintenance for your girls. **Eccl. 2:24**. There is nothing better for a person than that he should eat and drink and find enjoyment in his toil. This also, I saw, is from the hand of God. **Eccl. 3:12-13**. I perceived that there is nothing better for them than to be joyful and to do good as long as they live; also that everyone should eat and drink and take pleasure in all his toil—this is God's gift to man. **Isa. 38:1**. In those days Hezekiah became sick and was at the point of death. And Isaiah the prophet the son of Amoz came to him, and said to him, "Thus says the LORD: Set your house in order, for you shall die, you shall not recover." **Mt. 11:8**. What then did you go out to see? A man dressed in soft clothing? Behold, those who wear soft clothing are in kings' houses. **1 Tim. 6:17-18**. As for the rich in this present age, charge them not to be haughty, nor to set their hopes on the uncertainty of riches, but on God, who richly provides us with everything to enjoy. They are to do good, to be rich in good works, to be generous and ready to share.

7 **Gen. 2:15**. The LORD God took the man and put him in the garden of Eden to work it and keep it. **Gen. 3:19.** "By the sweat of your face you shall eat bread, till you return to the ground, for out of it you were taken; for you are dust, and to dust you shall return." **1 Cor. 7:20**. Each one should remain in the condition in which he was called.

8 **Prov. 10:4**. A slack hand causes poverty, but the hand of the diligent makes rich. **Eph. 4:28**. Let the thief no longer steal, but rather let him labor, doing honest work with his own hands, so that he may have something to share with anyone in need.

9 **Prov. 21:20**. Precious treasure and oil are in a wise man's dwelling, but a foolish man devours it. **Jn. 6:12**. And when they had eaten their fill, he told his disciples, "Gather up the leftover fragments, that nothing may be lost."

10 **1 Cor. 6:1-9**. When one of you has a grievance against another, does he dare go to law before the unrighteous instead of the saints? Or do you not know that the saints will judge the world? And if the world is to be judged by you, are you incompetent to try trivial cases? Do you not know that we are to judge angels? How much more, then, matters pertaining to this life! So if you have such cases, why do you lay them before those who have no standing in the church? I say this to your shame. Can it be that there is no one among you wise enough to settle a dispute between the brothers, but brother goes to law against brother, and that before unbelievers? To have lawsuits at all with one another is already a defeat for you. Why not rather suffer wrong? Why not rather be defrauded? But you yourselves wrong and defraud—even your own brothers! Or do you not know that the unrighteous will not inherit the kingdom of God? Do not be deceived: neither the sexually immoral, nor idolaters, nor adulterers, nor men who practice homosexuality.

11 **Prov. 6:1-6**. My son, if you have put up security for your neighbor, have given your pledge for a stranger, if you are snared in the words of your mouth, caught in the words of your mouth, then do this, my son, and save yourself, for you have come into the hand of your neighbor: go, hasten, and plead urgently with your neighbor. Give your eyes no sleep and your eyelids no slumber; save yourself like a gazelle from the hand of the hunter, like a bird from the hand of the fowler. Go to the ant, O sluggard; consider her ways, and be wise. **Prov. 11:15**. Whoever puts up security for a stranger will surely suffer harm, but he who hates striking hands in pledge is secure.

12 **Gen. 47:14, 20**. And Joseph gathered up all the money that was found in the land of Egypt and in the land of Canaan, in exchange for the grain that they bought. And Joseph brought the money into Pharaoh's house. ... So Joseph bought all the land of Egypt for Pharaoh, for all the Egyptians sold their fields, because the

famine was severe on them. The land became Pharaoh's. **Ex. 23:4-5**. "If you meet your enemy's ox or his donkey going astray, you shall bring it back to him. If you see the donkey of one who hates you lying down under its burden, you shall refrain from leaving him with it; you shall rescue it with him." **Lev. 25:35**. "If your brother becomes poor and cannot maintain himself with you, you shall support him as though he were a stranger and a sojourner, and he shall live with you." **Deut. 22:1-4**. "You shall not see your brother's ox or his sheep going astray and ignore them. You shall take them back to your brother. And if he does not live near you and you do not know who he is, you shall bring it home to your house, and it shall stay with you until your brother seeks it. Then you shall restore it to him. And you shall do the same with his donkey or with his garment, or with any lost thing of your brother's, which he loses and you find; you may not ignore it. You shall not see your brother's donkey or his ox fallen down by the way and ignore them. You shall help him to lift them up again." **Mt: 22:39**. And a second is like it: You shall love your neighbor as yourself. **Phil. 2:4**. Let each of you look not only to his own interests, but also to the interests of others.

Q. 142. What are the sins forbidden in the Eighth Commandment?

A. The sins forbidden in the Eighth Commandment, besides the neglect of duties required,[1] are: theft,[2] robbery,[3] man-stealing,[4] and receiving anything that is stolen;[5] fraudulent dealing,[6] false weights and measures,[7] removing property markers,[8] injustice and unfaithfulness in contracts between man and man,[9] or in matters of trust;[10] oppression,[11] extortion,[12] usury,[13] bribery,[14] frivolous lawsuits,[15] unjust confinement and forced migration or genocide;[16] gaining a monopoly on commodities to enhance the price,[17] unlawful callings,[18] and all other unjust or sinful ways of taking or withholding from our neighbor what belongs to him, or of enriching ourselves;[19] covetousness,[20] inordinate prizing of and affection for worldly goods;[21] distrustful and distracting cares and studies in getting, keeping, and using them;[22] envying of the prosperity of others;[23] as likewise idleness,[24] extravagance, wasteful gaming, and all other ways by which we do unnecessarily risk our own outward estate;[25] and defrauding ourselves of the due use and comfort of the estate that God has given us.[26]

1 **Jas. 2:15-16**. If a brother or sister is poorly clothed and lacking in daily food, and one of you says to them, "Go in peace, be warmed and filled," without giving them the things needed for the body, what good is that? **1 Jn. 3:17**. But if anyone has the world's goods and sees his brother in need, yet closes his heart against him, how does God's love abide in him?

2 **Eph. 4:28**. Let the thief no longer steal, but rather let him labor, doing honest work with his own hands, so that he may have something to share with anyone in need.

3 **Ps. 62:10**. Put no trust in extortion; set no vain hopes on robbery; if riches increase, set not your heart on them.

4 **1 Tim. 1:10**. ...the sexually immoral, men who practice homosexuality, enslavers, liars, perjurers, and whatever else is contrary to sound doctrine.

5 **Ps. 50:18**. If you see a thief, you are pleased with him, and you keep company with adulterers. **Prov. 29:24**. The partner of a thief hates his own life; he hears the curse, but discloses nothing.

6 **1 Thess. 4:6**. ...that no one transgress and wrong his brother in this matter, because the Lord is an avenger in all these things, as we told you beforehand and solemnly warned you.

7 **Prov. 11:1**. A false balance is an abomination to the LORD, but a just weight is his delight. **Prov. 20:10**. Unequal weights and unequal measures are both alike an abomination to the LORD.

8 **Deut. 19:14**. "You shall not move your neighbor's landmark, which the men of old have set, in the inheritance that you will hold in the land that the LORD your God is giving you to possess." **Prov. 23:10**. Do not move an ancient landmark or enter the fields of the fatherless.

9 **Ps. 37:21**. The wicked borrows but does not pay back, but the righteous is generous and gives. **Am. 8:5**. ...saying, "When will the new moon be over, that we may sell grain? And the Sabbath, that we may offer wheat for sale, that we may make the ephah small and the shekel great and deal deceitfully with false balances.

10 **Lk. 16:10-12**. "One who is faithful in a very little is also faithful in much, and one who is dishonest in a very little is also dishonest in much. If then you have not been faithful in the unrighteous wealth, who will entrust to you the true riches? And if you have not been faithful in that which is another's, who will give you that which is your own?"

11 **Lev. 25:17**. You shall not wrong one another, but you shall fear your God, for I am the LORD your God. **Ezek. 22:29**. The people of the land have practiced extortion and committed robbery. They have oppressed the poor and needy, and have extorted from the sojourner without justice.

12 **Ezek. 22:12**. In you they take bribes to shed blood; you take interest and profit and make gain of your neighbors by extortion; but me you have forgotten, declares the Lord GOD. **Mt. 23:25**. "Woe to you, scribes and Pharisees, hypocrites! For you clean the outside of the cup and the plate, but inside they are full of greed and self-indulgence."

13 **Ps. 15:5**. ...who does not put out his money at interest and does not take a bribe against the innocent. He who does these things shall never be moved.

14 **Job 15:34**. For the company of the godless is barren, and fire consumes the tents of bribery.

15 **Prov. 3:29-30**. Do not plan evil against your neighbor, who dwells trustingly beside you. Do not contend with a man for no reason, when he has done you no harm. **1 Cor. 6:6-8**. ...but brother goes to law against brother, and that before unbelievers? To have lawsuits at all with one another is already a defeat for you. Why not rather suffer wrong? Why not rather be defrauded? But you yourselves wrong and defraud—even your own brothers!

16 **Isa. 5:8**. Woe to those who join house to house, who add field to field, until there is no more room, and you are made to dwell alone in the midst of the land. **Mic. 2:2**. They covet fields and seize them, and houses, and take them away; they oppress a man and his house, a man and his inheritance.

17 **Prov. 11:26**. The people curse him who holds back grain, but a blessing is on the head of him who sells it.

18 **Acts 19:19, 24-25**. And a number of those who had practiced magic arts brought their books together and burned them in the sight of all. And they counted the value of them and found it came to fifty thousand pieces of silver. ... For a man named Demetrius, a silversmith, who made silver shrines of Artemis, brought no little business to the craftsmen. These he gathered together, with the workmen in similar trades, and said, "Men, you know that from this business we have our wealth.

19 **Job 20:19**. For he has crushed and abandoned the poor; he has seized a house that he did not build. **Prov. 21:6**. The getting of treasures by a lying tongue is a fleeting vapor and a snare of death. Jas. 5:4. Behold, the wages of the laborers who mowed your fields, which you kept back by fraud, are crying out against you, and the cries of the harvesters have reached the ears of the Lord of hosts.

20 **Lk. 12:15**. And he said to them, "Take care, and be on your guard against all covetousness, for one's life does not consist in the abundance of his possessions."

21 **Ps. 62:10**. Put no trust in extortion; set no vain hopes on robbery; if riches increase, set not your heart on them. **Prov. 23:5**. When your eyes light on it, it is gone, for suddenly it sprouts wings, flying like an eagle toward heaven. **Col. 3:2**. Set your minds on things that are above, not on things that are on earth. **1 Tim. 6:5**. ...and constant friction among people who are depraved in mind and deprived of the truth, imagining that godliness is a means of gain.

22 **Eccl. 5:12**. Sweet is the sleep of a laborer, whether he eats little or much, but the full stomach of the rich will not let him sleep. **Mt. 6:25, 31, 34**. "Therefore I tell you, do not be anxious about your life, what you will eat or what you will drink, nor about your body, what you will put on. Is not life more than food, and the body more than clothing?" ... Therefore do not be anxious, saying, 'What shall we eat?' or 'What shall we drink?' or 'What shall we wear?' ... "Therefore do not be anxious about tomorrow, for tomorrow will be anxious for itself. Sufficient for the day is its own trouble."

23 **Ps. 37:1, 7**. Fret not yourself because of evildoers; be not envious of wrongdoers! ... Be still before the LORD and wait patiently for him; fret not yourself over the one who prospers in his way, over the man who carries out evil devices! **Ps. 73:3**. For I was envious of the arrogant when I saw the prosperity of the wicked.

24 **Prov. 18:9**. Whoever is slack in his work is a brother to him who destroys. **2 Thess. 3:11**. For we hear that some among you walk in idleness, not busy at work, but busybodies.

25 **Prov. 21:7**. The violence of the wicked will sweep them away, because they refuse to do what is just. **Prov. 23:20-21**. Be not among drunkards or among gluttonous eaters of meat, for the drunkard and the glutton will come to poverty, and slumber will clothe them with rags. **Prov. 28:19**. Whoever works his land will have plenty of bread, but he who follows worthless pursuits will have plenty of poverty.

26 **Eccl. 4:8**. ...one person who has no other, either son or brother, yet there is no end to all his toil, and his eyes are never satisfied with riches, so that he never asks, "For whom am I toiling and depriving myself of pleasure?" This also is vanity and an unhappy business. **Eccl. 6:2**. ...a man to whom God gives wealth, possessions, and honor, so that he lacks nothing of all that he desires, yet God does not give him power to enjoy them, but a stranger enjoys them. This is vanity; it is a grievous evil. **1 Tim. 5:8**. But if anyone does not provide for his relatives, and especially for members of his household, he has denied the faith and is worse than an unbeliever.

Q. 143. Which is the Ninth Commandment?

A. The Ninth Commandment is, "You shall not bear false witness against your neighbor."[1]

1 **Ex. 20:16.** "You shall not bear false witness against your neighbor."

Q. 144. What are the duties required in the Ninth Commandment?

A. The duties required in the Ninth Commandment are: the preserving and promoting of truth between man and man,[1] and the good name of our neighbor, as well as our own;[2] appearing and standing for the truth;[3] and from the heart,[4] sincerely,[5] freely,[6] clearly,[7] and fully,[8] speaking the truth, and only the truth, in matters of judgment and justice,[9] and in all other things whatsoever;[10] a charitable esteem of our neighbors, [11] loving, desiring, and rejoicing in their good name;[12] sorrowing for,[13] and covering of their infirmities;[14] freely acknowledging of their gifts and graces,[15] defending their innocence;[16] a ready receiving of good report,[17] and unwillingness to admit of an evil report concerning them;[18] discouraging gossips,[19] flatterers,[20] and slanderers;[21] love and care of our own good name, and defending it when necessary;[22] keeping of lawful promises;[23] studying and practicing of whatever things are true, honest, lovely, and of good report.[24]

1 **Zach. 8:16.** These are the things that you shall do: Speak the truth to one another; render in your gates judgments that are true and make for peace.

2 **3 Jn. 12.** Demetrius has received a good testimony from everyone, and from the truth itself. We also add our testimony, and you know that our testimony is true.

3 **Prov. 31:8-9.** Open your mouth for the mute, for the rights of all who are destitute. Open your mouth, judge righteously, defend the rights of the poor and needy.

4 **Ps. 15:2.** He who walks blamelessly and does what is right and speaks truth in his heart.

5 **2 Chr. 19:9.** And he charged them: "Thus you shall do in the fear of the LORD, in faithfulness, and with your whole heart:

6 **1 Sam. 19:4-5.** And Jonathan spoke well of David to Saul his father and said to him, "Let not the king sin against his servant David, because he has not sinned against you, and because his deeds have brought good to you. For he took his life in his hand and he struck down the Philistine, and the LORD worked a great salvation for all Israel. You saw it, and rejoiced. Why then will you sin against innocent blood by killing David without cause?"

7 **Josh. 7:19.** Then Joshua said to Achan, "My son, give glory to the LORD God of Israel and give praise to him. And tell me now what you have done; do not hide it from me."

8 **2 Sam. 14:18-20.** Then the king answered the woman, "Do not hide from me anything I ask you." And the woman said, "Let my lord the king speak." The king said,

"Is the hand of Joab with you in all this?" The woman answered and said, "As surely as you live, my lord the king, one cannot turn to the right hand or to the left from anything that my lord the king has said. It was your servant Joab who commanded me; it was he who put all these words in the mouth of your servant. In order to change the course of things your servant Joab did this. But my lord has wisdom like the wisdom of the angel of God to know all things that are on the earth."

9 **Lev. 19:15**. "You shall do no injustice in court. You shall not be partial to the poor or defer to the great, but in righteousness shall you judge your neighbor. **Prov. 14:5, 25**. A faithful witness does not lie, but a false witness breathes out lies. ...A truthful witness saves lives, but one who breathes out lies is deceitful.

10 **2 Cor. 1:17-18**. Was I vacillating when I wanted to do this? Do I make my plans according to the flesh, ready to say "Yes, yes" and "No, no" at the same time? As surely as God is faithful, our word to you has not been Yes and No. **Eph. 4:25**. Therefore, having put away falsehood, let each one of you speak the truth with his neighbor, for we are members one of another.

11 **1 Cor. 13:7**. Love bears all things, believes all things, hopes all things, endures all things. **Heb. 6:9**. Though we speak in this way, yet in your case, beloved, we feel sure of better things—things that belong to salvation.

12 **Rom. 1:8**. First, I thank my God through Jesus Christ for all of you, because your faith is proclaimed in all the world. **2 Jn. 4.** I rejoiced greatly to find some of your children walking in the truth, just as we were commanded by the Father. **3 Jn. 3-4**. For I rejoiced greatly when the brothers came and testified to your truth, as indeed you are walking in the truth. I have no greater joy than to hear that my children are walking in the truth.

13 **2 Cor. 2:4**. For I wrote to you out of much affliction and anguish of heart and with many tears, not to cause you pain but to let you know the abundant love that I have for you. **2 Cor. 12:21**. I fear that when I come again my God may humble me before you, and I may have to mourn over many of those who sinned earlier and have not repented of the impurity, sexual immorality, and sensuality that they have practiced.

14 **Prov. 17:9**. Whoever covers an offense seeks love, but he who repeats a matter separates close friends. **1 Pet. 4:8**. Above all, keep loving one another earnestly, since love covers a multitude of sins.

15 **1 Cor. 1:4, 5-7**. I give thanks to my God always for you because of the grace of God that was given you in Christ Jesus. ...that in every way you were enriched in him in all speech and all knowledge— even as the testimony about Christ was confirmed among you— so that you are not lacking in any gift, as you wait for the revealing of our Lord Jesus Christ. **2 Tim. 1:4-5**. As I remember your tears, I long to see you, that I may be filled with joy. I am reminded of your sincere faith, a faith that dwelt first in your grandmother Lois and your mother Eunice and now, I am sure, dwells in you as well.

16 **1 Sam. 22:14**. Then Ahimelech answered the king, "And who among all your servants is so faithful as David, who is the king's son-in-law, and captain over your bodyguard, and honored in your house?"

17 **1 Cor. 13:6-7**. ...it does not rejoice at wrongdoing, but rejoices with the truth. Love bears all things, believes all things, hopes all things, endures all things.

18 **Ps. 15:3**. ...who does not slander with his tongue and does no evil to his neighbor, nor takes up a reproach against his friend;

19 **Prov. 25:23**. The north wind brings forth rain, and a backbiting tongue, angry looks.

20 **Prov. 26:24-25**. Whoever hates disguises himself with his lips and harbors deceit in his heart; when he speaks graciously, believe him not, for there are seven abominations in his heart.

21 **Ps. 101:5**. Whoever slanders his neighbor secretly I will destroy. Whoever has a haughty look and an arrogant heart I will not endure.

22 **Prov. 22:1**. A good name is to be chosen rather than great riches, and favor is better than silver or gold. **Jn. 8:49**. Jesus answered, "I do not have a demon, but I honor my Father, and you dishonor me.

23 **Ps. 15:4**. ...in whose eyes a vile person is despised, but who honors those who fear the LORD; who swears to his own hurt and does not change;

24 **Phil. 4:8**. Finally, brothers, whatever is true, whatever is honorable, whatever is just, whatever is pure, whatever is lovely, whatever is commendable, if there is any excellence, if there is anything worthy of praise, think about these things.

Q. 145. What are the sins forbidden in the Ninth Commandment?

A. The sins forbidden in the Ninth Commandment are: all premature judging of the truth, and the good name of our neighbors as well as our own,[1] especially in public administration of justice;[2] giving false evidence,[3] inducing of false witnesses,[4] wittingly appearing and pleading for an evil cause, defiance of and dominance over the truth;[5] passing unjust sentence,[6] calling evil good, and good evil; rewarding the wicked according to the work of the righteous, and the righteous according to the work of the wicked;[7] forgery,[8] concealing the truth, undue silence in a just cause,[9] and holding our peace when iniquity calls for either a reproof from us,[10] or complaint to others;[11] speaking the truth at a poor time,[12] or maliciously to a wrong end,[13] or perverting it to a wrong meaning,[14] or in doubtful and equivocal expression, to the prejudice of truth or justice;[15] speaking untruth,[16] lying,[17] slandering,[18] backbiting,[19] gossiping,[20] whispering,[21] scoffing,[22] using abusive language;[23] rash,[24] harsh,[25] and partial censuring;[26] misconstruing intentions, words, and actions;[27] flattering,[28] vain boasting,[29] thinking or speaking too highly or too poorly of ourselves or others;[30] denying the gifts and graces of God;[31] aggravating smaller faults;[32] hiding, excusing, or extenuating of sins, when called to a free confession;[33] unnecessary discovering of infirmities;[34] raising false rumors;[35] receiving and approving evil reports,[36] and stopping our ears against just defense;[37] evil suspicion;[38] envying or grieving at the deserved credit of anyone;[39] endeavoring or desiring to impair it,[40] rejoicing in the disgrace and bad reputation of anyone;[41] scornful contempt,[42] fond admiration,[43] breach of lawful promises;[44] neglecting such things as are of good report;[45] and practicing or not avoiding ourselves, or not hindering what we can in others, such things as result in an ill name.[46]

1 **1 Sam. 17:28.** Now Eliab his eldest brother heard when he spoke to the men. And Eliab's anger was kindled against David, and he said, "Why have you come down? And with whom have you left those few sheep in the wilderness? I know your presumption and the evil of your heart, for you have come down to see the battle." **2 Sam. 1:9, 10, 15-16.** And he said to me, 'Stand beside me and kill me, for anguish has seized me, and yet my life still lingers.' ... "So I stood beside him and killed him, because I was sure that he could not live after he had fallen. And I took the crown that was on his head and the armlet that was on his arm, and I have brought them here to my lord." ... Then David called one of the young men and said, "Go, execute him." And he struck him down so that he died. And David said to him, "Your blood be on your head, for your own mouth has testified against you, saying, 'I have killed the LORD's anointed.'" **2 Sam. 16:3.** And the king said, "And where is your master's son?" Ziba said to the king, "Behold, he remains in Jerusalem, for he said, 'Today the house of Israel will give me back the kingdom of my father.'"

2 **Lev. 19:15.** "You shall do no injustice in court. You shall not be partial to the poor or defer to the great, but in righteousness shall you judge your neighbor." **Hab. 1:4.** So the law is paralyzed, and justice never goes forth. For the wicked surround the righteous; so justice goes forth perverted.

3 **Prov. 6:16, 19.** There are six things that the LORD hates, seven that are an abomination to him. ...a false witness who breathes out lies, and one who sows discord among brothers. **Prov. 19:5.** A false witness will not go unpunished, and he who breathes out lies will not escape.

4 **Acts 6:13** ...and they set up false witnesses who said, "This man never ceases to speak words against this holy place and the law.

5 **Ps. 12:3-4.** May the LORD cut off all flattering lips, the tongue that makes great boasts, those who say, "With our tongue we will prevail, our lips are with us; who is master over us?" **Ps. 52:1-4.** Why do you boast of evil, O mighty man? The steadfast love of God endures all the day. Your tongue plots destruction, like a sharp razor, you worker of deceit. You love evil more than good, and lying more than speaking what is right. You love all words that devour, O deceitful tongue. **Jer. 9:3, 5.** They bend their tongue like a bow; falsehood and not truth has grown strong in the land; for they proceed from evil to evil, and they do not know me, declares the LORD. ... Everyone deceives his neighbor, and no one speaks the truth; they have taught their tongue to speak lies; they weary themselves committing iniquity. **Acts 24:2, 5.** ...and when he had been summoned, Tertullus began to accuse him, saying: "Since through you we enjoy much peace, and since by your foresight, most excellent Felix, reforms are being made for this nation." ... For we have found this man a plague, one who stirs up riots among all the Jews throughout the world and is a ringleader of the sect of the Nazarenes.

6 **1 Kings 21:9-14.** And she wrote in the letters, "Proclaim a fast, and set Naboth at the head of the people. And set two worthless men opposite him, and let them bring a charge against him, saying, 'You have cursed God and the king.' Then take him out and stone him to death." And the men of his city, the elders and the leaders who lived in his city, did as Jezebel had sent word to them. As it was written in the letters that she had sent to them, they proclaimed a fast and set Naboth at the head of the people. And the two worthless men came in and sat opposite him. And the worthless men brought a charge against Naboth in the presence of the people, saying, "Naboth cursed God and the king." So they took him outside the city and stoned him to death with stones. Then they sent to Jezebel, saying, "Naboth has

been stoned; he is dead." **PROV. 17:15**. He who justifies the wicked and he who condemns the righteous are both alike an abomination to the LORD.

7 **ISA. 5:23**. ...who acquit the guilty for a bribe, and deprive the innocent of his right!

8 **PS. 119:69**. The insolent smear me with lies, but with my whole heart I keep your precepts. **LK. 16:5-7**. So, summoning his master's debtors one by one, he said to the first, 'How much do you owe my master?' He said, 'A hundred measures of oil.' He said to him, 'Take your bill, and sit down quickly and write fifty.' Then he said to another, 'And how much do you owe?' He said, 'A hundred measures of wheat.' He said to him, 'Take your bill, and write eighty.' **LK. 19:8**. And Zacchaeus stood and said to the Lord, "Behold, Lord, the half of my goods I give to the poor. And if I have defrauded anyone of anything, I restore it fourfold."

9 **LEV. 5:1**. "If anyone sins in that he hears a public adjuration to testify, and though he is a witness, whether he has seen or come to know the matter, yet does not speak, he shall bear his iniquity." **DEUT. 13:8**. ...you shall not yield to him or listen to him, nor shall your eye pity him, nor shall you spare him, nor shall you conceal him. **ACTS 5:3, 8-9**. But Peter said, "Ananias, why has Satan filled your heart to lie to the Holy Spirit and to keep back for yourself part of the proceeds of the land?" ... And Peter said to her, "Tell me whether you sold the land for so much." And she said, "Yes, for so much." But Peter said to her, "How is it that you have agreed together to test the Spirit of the Lord? Behold, the feet of those who have buried your husband are at the door, and they will carry you out." **2 TIM. 4:6**. For I am already being poured out as a drink offering, and the time of my departure has come.

10 **LEV. 19:17**. "You shall not hate your brother in your heart, but you shall reason frankly with your neighbor, lest you incur sin because of him." **1 KINGS 1:6**. His father had never at any time displeased him by asking, "Why have you done thus and so?" He was also a very handsome man, and he was born next after Absalom.

11 **ISA. 59:4**. No one enters suit justly; no one goes to law honestly; they rely on empty pleas, they speak lies, they conceive mischief and give birth to iniquity.

12 **PROV. 29:11**. A fool gives full vent to his spirit, but a wise man quietly holds it back.

13 **1 SAM. 22:9-10**. Then answered Doeg the Edomite, who stood by the servants of Saul, "I saw the son of Jesse coming to Nob, to Ahimelech the son of Ahitub, and he inquired of the LORD for him and gave him provisions and gave him the sword of Goliath the Philistine." **PS. 52:1-5**. Why do you boast of evil, O mighty man? The steadfast love of God endures all the day. Your tongue plots destruction, like a sharp razor, you worker of deceit. You love evil more than good, and lying more than speaking what is right. You love all words that devour, O deceitful tongue. But God will break you down forever; he will snatch and tear you from your tent; he will uproot you from the land of the living.

14 **PS. 56:5**. All day long they injure my cause; all their thoughts are against me for evil. **MT. 26:60-61**. ...but they found none, though many false witnesses came forward. At last two came forward and said, "This man said, 'I am able to destroy the temple of God, and to rebuild it in three days.'" **JN. 2:19**. Jesus answered them, "Destroy this temple, and in three days I will raise it up."

15 **GEN. 3:5**. For God knows that when you eat of it your eyes will be opened, and you will be like God, knowing good and evil." **GEN. 26:7, 9**. When the men of the place asked him about his wife, he said, "She is my sister," for he feared to say, "My wife," thinking, "lest the men of the place should kill me because of Rebekah," because she was attractive in appearance. ... So Abimelech called Isaac and said, "Behold, she is your wife. How then could you say, 'She is my sister'?" Isaac said to him, "Because I thought, 'Lest I die because of her.'"

16 **Isa. 59:13**. ...transgressing, and denying the LORD, and turning back from following our God, speaking oppression and revolt, conceiving and uttering from the heart lying words.

17 **Lev. 19:11**. "You shall not steal; you shall not deal falsely; you shall not lie to one another.

18 **Ps. 50:20**. You sit and speak against your brother; you slander your own mother's son.

19 **Jer. 38:4**. Then the officials said to the king, "Let this man be put to death, for he is weakening the hands of the soldiers who are left in this city, and the hands of all the people, by speaking such words to them. For this man is not seeking the welfare of this people, but their harm." **Jas. 4:11**. Do not speak evil against one another, brothers. The one who speaks against a brother or judges his brother, speaks evil against the law and judges the law. But if you judge the law, you are not a doer of the law but a judge.

20 **Lev. 19:19**. "You shall keep my statutes. You shall not let your cattle breed with a different kind. You shall not sow your field with two kinds of seed, nor shall you wear a garment of cloth made of two kinds of material.

21 **Rom. 1:29-30**. They were filled with all manner of unrighteousness, evil, covetousness, malice. They are full of envy, murder, strife, deceit, maliciousness. They are gossips, slanderers, haters of God, insolent, haughty, boastful, inventors of evil, disobedient to parents.

22 **Gen. 21:9**. But Sarah saw the son of Hagar the Egyptian, whom she had borne to Abraham, laughing. **Gal. 4:29**. But just as at that time he who was born according to the flesh persecuted him who was born according to the Spirit, so also it is now.

23 **1 Cor. 6:10**. ...nor thieves, nor the greedy, nor drunkards, nor revilers, nor swindlers will inherit the kingdom of God.

24 **Mt. 7:1**. "Judge not, that you be not judged."

25 **Acts 28:4**. When the native people saw the creature hanging from his hand, they said to one another, "No doubt this man is a murderer. Though he has escaped from the sea, Justice has not allowed him to live."

26 **Gen. 38:24**. About three months later Judah was told, "Tamar your daughter-in-law has been immoral. Moreover, she is pregnant by immorality." And Judah said, "Bring her out, and let her be burned." Rom. 2:1. Therefore you have no excuse, O man, every one of you who judges. For in passing judgment on another you condemn yourself, because you, the judge, practice the very same things.

27 **1 Sam. 1:13-15**. Hannah was speaking in her heart; only her lips moved, and her voice was not heard. Therefore Eli took her to be a drunken woman. And Eli said to her, "How long will you go on being drunk? Put your wine away from you." But Hannah answered, "No, my lord, I am a woman troubled in spirit. I have drunk neither wine nor strong drink, but I have been pouring out my soul before the LORD. **2 Sam. 10:3**. But the princes of the Ammonites said to Hanun their lord, "Do you think, because David has sent comforters to you, that he is honoring your father? Has not David sent his servants to you to search the city and to spy it out and to overthrow it?" **Neh. 6:6-8**. In it was written, "It is reported among the nations, and Geshem also says it, that you and the Jews intend to rebel; that is why you are building the wall. And according to these reports you wish to become their king. And you have also set up prophets to proclaim concerning you in Jerusalem, 'There is a king in Judah.' And now the king will hear of these reports. So now come and let us take counsel together." Then I sent to him, saying, "No such things as you say have been done, for you are inventing them out of your own mind." **Ps. 69:10**. When I wept and humbled my soul with fasting, it became my

reproach. **Rom. 3:8**. And why not do evil that good may come?—as some people slanderously charge us with saying. Their condemnation is just.

28 **Ps. 12:2-3**. Everyone utters lies to his neighbor; with flattering lips and a double heart they speak. May the LORD cut off all flattering lips, the tongue that makes great boasts.

29 **2 Tim. 3:2**. For people will be lovers of self, lovers of money, proud, arrogant, abusive, disobedient to their parents, ungrateful, unholy.

30 **Ex. 4:10-14**. But Moses said to the LORD, "Oh, my Lord, I am not eloquent, either in the past or since you have spoken to your servant, but I am slow of speech and of tongue." Then the LORD said to him, "Who has made man's mouth? Who makes him mute, or deaf, or seeing, or blind? Is it not I, the LORD? Now therefore go, and I will be with your mouth and teach you what you shall speak." But he said, "Oh, my Lord, please send someone else." Then the anger of the LORD was kindled against Moses and he said, "Is there not Aaron, your brother, the Levite? I know that he can speak well. Behold, he is coming out to meet you, and when he sees you, he will be glad in his heart. **Lk. 18:9, 11**. He also told this parable to some who trusted in themselves that they were righteous, and treated others with contempt. ... The Pharisee, standing by himself, prayed thus: 'God, I thank you that I am not like other men, extortioners, unjust, adulterers, or even like this tax collector.' **Acts 12:22**. And the people were shouting, "The voice of a god, and not of a man!" **Rom. 12:16**. Live in harmony with one another. Do not be haughty, but associate with the lowly. Never be wise in your own sight. **1 Cor. 4:6**. I have applied all these things to myself and Apollos for your benefit, brothers, that you may learn by us not to go beyond what is written, that none of you may be puffed up in favor of one against another.

31 **Job 4:6**. Is not your fear of God your confidence, and the integrity of your ways your hope? **Job 27:5, 6**. Far be it from me to say that you are right; till I die I will not put away my integrity from me. ... I hold fast my righteousness and will not let it go; my heart does not reproach me for any of my days.

32 **Mt. 7:3-5**. Why do you see the speck that is in your brother's eye, but do not notice the log that is in your own eye? Or how can you say to your brother, 'Let me take the speck out of your eye,' when there is the log in your own eye? You hypocrite, first take the log out of your own eye, and then you will see clearly to take the speck out of your brother's eye.

33 **Gen. 3:12-13**. The man said, "The woman whom you gave to be with me, she gave me fruit of the tree, and I ate." Then the LORD God said to the woman, "What is this that you have done?" The woman said, "The serpent deceived me, and I ate." **Gen. 4:9**. Then the LORD said to Cain, "Where is Abel your brother?" He said, "I do not know; am I my brother's keeper?" **2 Kings 5:25**. He went in and stood before his master, and Elisha said to him, "Where have you been, Gehazi?" And he said, "Your servant went nowhere." **Prov. 28:13**. Whoever conceals his transgressions will not prosper, but he who confesses and forsakes them will obtain mercy. **Jer. 2:35**. ...you say, 'I am innocent; surely his anger has turned from me.' Behold, I will bring you to judgment for saying, 'I have not sinned.'

34 **Gen. 9:22**. And Ham, the father of Canaan, saw the nakedness of his father and told his two brothers outside. **Prov. 25:9-10**. Argue your case with your neighbor himself, and do not reveal another's secret, lest he who hears you bring shame upon you, and your ill repute have no end.

35 **Ex. 23:1**. "You shall not spread a false report. You shall not join hands with a wicked man to be a malicious witness."

36 **Prov. 29:12**. If a ruler listens to falsehood, all his officials will be wicked.

37 **Job 31:13-14**. "If I have rejected the cause of my manservant or my maidservant, when they brought a complaint against me, what then shall I do when God rises up? When he makes inquiry, what shall I answer him. **Acts 7:56-57**. And he said, "Behold, I see the heavens opened, and the Son of Man standing at the right hand of God." But they cried out with a loud voice and stopped their ears and rushed together at him.

38 **1 Cor. 13:5**. ...or rude. It does not insist on its own way; it is not irritable or resentful. **1 Tim. 6:4**. ...he is puffed up with conceit and understands nothing. He has an unhealthy craving for controversy and for quarrels about words, which produce envy, dissension, slander, evil suspicions.

39 **Num. 11:29**. But Moses said to him, "Are you jealous for my sake? Would that all the LORD's people were prophets, that the LORD would put his Spirit on them!" **Mt. 21:15**. But when the chief priests and the scribes saw the wonderful things that he did, and the children crying out in the temple, "Hosanna to the Son of David!" they were indignant.

40 **Ezra 4:12-13**. ...be it known to the king that the Jews who came up from you to us have gone to Jerusalem. They are rebuilding that rebellious and wicked city. They are finishing the walls and repairing the foundations. Now be it known to the king that if this city is rebuilt and the walls finished, they will not pay tribute, custom, or toll, and the royal revenue will be impaired.

41 **Jer. 48:27**. Was not Israel a derision to you? Was he found among thieves, that whenever you spoke of him you wagged your head?

42 **Ps. 35:15-16, 21**. But at my stumbling they rejoiced and gathered; they gathered together against me; wretches whom I did not know tore at me without ceasing; like profane mockers at a feast, they gnash at me with their teeth. ... They open wide their mouths against me; they say, "Aha, Aha! Our eyes have seen it!" **Mt. 27:28-29**. And they stripped him and put a scarlet robe on him, and twisting together a crown of thorns, they put it on his head and put a reed in his right hand. And kneeling before him, they mocked him, saying, "Hail, King of the Jews!"

43 **Acts 12:22**. And the people were shouting, "The voice of a god, and not of a man!" **Jude 16**. These are grumblers, malcontents, following their own sinful desires; they are loud-mouthed boasters, showing favoritism to gain advantage.

44 **Rom. 1:31**. ...foolish, faithless, heartless, ruthless. **2 Tim. 3:3**. ...heartless, unappeasable, slanderous, without self-control, brutal, not loving good.

45 **1 Sam. 2:24**. No, my sons; it is no good report that I hear the people of the LORD spreading abroad.

46 **2 Sam. 13:12-13**. She answered him, "No, my brother, do not violate me, for such a thing is not done in Israel; do not do this outrageous thing. As for me, where could I carry my shame? And as for you, you would be as one of the outrageous fools in Israel. Now therefore, please speak to the king, for he will not withhold me from you." **Prov. 5:8-9**. Keep your way far from her, and do not go near the door of her house, lest you give your honor to others and your years to the merciless. **Prov. 6:33**. He will get wounds and dishonor, and his disgrace will not be wiped away.

Q. 146. Which is the Tenth Commandment?

A. The Tenth Commandment is, "You shall not covet your neighbor's house; you shall not covet your neighbor's wife, or his male servant, or his female servant, or his ox, or his donkey, or anything that is your neighbor's."[1]

1 **Ex. 20:17**. "You shall not covet your neighbor's house; you shall not covet your neighbor's wife, or his male servant, or his female servant, or his ox, or his donkey, or anything that is your neighbor's."

Q. 147. What are the duties required in the Tenth Commandment?

A. The duties required in the Tenth Commandment are: such a full contentment with our own condition,[1] and such a charitable frame of the whole soul toward our neighbor, so that all our inward motions and affections touching him, tend toward and further all the good that is his.[2]

1 **1 Tim. 6:6**. But godliness with contentment is great gain. **Heb. 13:5**. Keep your life free from love of money, and be content with what you have, for he has said, "I will never leave you nor forsake you."

2 **Job 31:29**. "If I have rejoiced at the ruin of him who hated me, or exulted when evil overtook him." **Esth. 10:3**. For Mordecai the Jew was second in rank to King Ahasuerus, and he was great among the Jews and popular with the multitude of his brothers, for he sought the welfare of his people and spoke peace to all his people. **Ps. 122:7-9**. Peace be within your walls and security within your towers!" For my brothers and companions' sake I will say, "Peace be within you!" For the sake of the house of the LORD our God, I will seek your good. **Rom. 12:15**. Rejoice with those who rejoice, weep with those who weep. **1 Cor. 13:4-7**. Love is patient and kind; love does not envy or boast; it is not arrogant or rude. It does not insist on its own way; it is not irritable or resentful; it does not rejoice at wrongdoing, but rejoices with the truth. Love bears all things, believes all things, hopes all things, endures all things. **1 Tim. 1:5**. The aim of our charge is love that issues from a pure heart and a good conscience and a sincere faith.

Q. 148. What are the sins forbidden in the Tenth Commandment?

A. The sins forbidden in the Tenth Commandment are: discontent with our own estate;[1] envying,[2] and grieving at the good of our neighbor,[3] together with all inordinate motions and affections toward anything that is his.[4]

1 **1 Kings 21:4**. And Ahab went into his house vexed and sullen because of what Naboth the Jezreelite had said to him, for he had said, "I will not give you the inheritance of my fathers." And he lay down on his bed and turned away his face and would eat no food. **Esth. 5:13**. Yet all this is worth nothing to me, so long as I see Mordecai the Jew sitting at the king's gate." **1 Cor. 10:10**. ...nor grumble, as some of them did and were destroyed by the Destroyer.

2 **Gal. 5:26**. Let us not become conceited, provoking one another, envying one another. **Jas. 3:14, 16**. But if you have bitter jealousy and selfish ambition in your hearts, do not boast and be false to the truth. ... For where jealousy and selfish ambition exist, there will be disorder and every vile practice.

3 **Neh. 2:10**. But when Sanballat the Horonite and Tobiah the Ammonite servant heard this, it displeased them greatly that someone had come to seek the welfare of the people of Israel. **Ps. 112:9-10**. He has distributed freely; he has given to the poor; his righteousness endures forever; his horn is exalted in honor. The wicked man sees it and is angry; he gnashes his teeth and melts away; the desire of the wicked will perish!

4 **Deut. 5:21**. "'And you shall not covet your neighbor's wife. And you shall not desire your neighbor's house, his field, or his male servant, or his female servant, his ox, or his donkey, or anything that is your neighbor's.' **Rom. 7:7-8**. For the commandments, "You shall not commit adultery, You shall not murder, You shall not steal, You shall not covet," and any other commandment, are summed up in this word: "You shall love your neighbor as yourself." **Rom. 13:9**. For the commandments, "You shall not commit adultery, You shall not murder, You shall not steal, You shall not covet," and any other commandment, are summed up in this word: "You shall love your neighbor as yourself." **Col. 3:5**. Put to death therefore what is earthly in you: sexual immorality, impurity, passion, evil desire, and covetousness, which is idolatry.

Q. 149. Is any man able perfectly to keep the commandments of God?

A. No man is able, either of himself,[1] or by any grace received in this life, perfectly to keep the commandments of God;[2] but does daily break them in thought,[3] word, and deed.[4]

1 **Jn. 15:5**. I am the vine; you are the branches. Whoever abides in me and I in him, he it is that bears much fruit, for apart from me you can do nothing. **Rom. 8:3**. For God has done what the law, weakened by the flesh, could not do. By sending his own Son in the likeness of sinful flesh and for sin, he condemned sin in the flesh. **Jas. 3:2**. For we all stumble in many ways. And if anyone does not stumble in what he says, he is a perfect man, able also to bridle his whole body.

2 **Eccl. 7:20**. Surely there is not a righteous man on earth who does good and never sins. **Rom. 7:18-19**. For I know that nothing good dwells in me, that is, in my flesh. For I have the desire to do what is right, but not the ability to carry it out. For I do not do the good I want, but the evil I do not want is what I keep on doing. **Gal. 5:17**. For the desires of the flesh are against the Spirit, and the desires of the Spirit are against the flesh, for these are opposed to each other, to keep you from doing the things you want to do. **1 Jn. 1:8, 10**. If we say we have no sin, we deceive ourselves, and the truth is not in us. ... If we say we have not sinned, we make him a liar, and his word is not in us.

3 **Gen. 6:5**. The LORD saw that the wickedness of man was great in the earth, and that every intention of the thoughts of his heart was only evil continually. **Gen. 8:21**. And when the LORD smelled the pleasing aroma, the LORD said in his heart, "I will never again curse the ground because of man, for the intention of man's heart is evil from his youth. Neither will I ever again strike down every living creature as I have done."

4 **Rom. 3:9-19**. What then? Are we Jews any better off? No, not at all. For we have already charged that all, both Jews and Greeks, are under sin, as it is written: "None is righteous, no, not one; no one understands; no one seeks for God. All have turned aside; together they have become worthless; no one does good, not even one. Their throat is an open grave; they use their tongues to deceive. The venom of asps is under their lips. Their mouth is full of curses and bitterness. Their feet are swift to shed blood; in their paths are ruin and misery, and the way

of peace they have not known. There is no fear of God before their eyes." Now we know that whatever the law says it speaks to those who are under the law, so that every mouth may be stopped, and the whole world may be held accountable to God. **Jas. 3:2-13**. For we all stumble in many ways. And if anyone does not stumble in what he says, he is a perfect man, able also to bridle his whole body. If we put bits into the mouths of horses so that they obey us, we guide their whole bodies as well. Look at the ships also: though they are so large and are driven by strong winds, they are guided by a very small rudder wherever the will of the pilot directs. So also the tongue is a small member, yet it boasts of great things. How great a forest is set ablaze by such a small fire! And the tongue is a fire, a world of unrighteousness. The tongue is set among our members, staining the whole body, setting on fire the entire course of life, and set on fire by hell. For every kind of beast and bird, of reptile and sea creature, can be tamed and has been tamed by mankind, but no human being can tame the tongue. It is a restless evil, full of deadly poison. With it we bless our Lord and Father, and with it we curse people who are made in the likeness of God. From the same mouth come blessing and cursing. My brothers, these things ought not to be so. Does a spring pour forth from the same opening both fresh and salt water? Can a fig tree, my brothers, bear olives, or a grapevine produce figs? Neither can a salt pond yield fresh water. Who is wise and understanding among you? By his good conduct let him show his works in the meekness of wisdom.

Q. 150. Are all transgressions of the law of God equally wicked in themselves, and in the sight of God?

A. All transgressions of the law of God are not equally wicked; but some sins in themselves, and by reason of aggravating circumstances, are more wicked in the sight of God than others.[1]

1 **Ps. 78:17, 32, 56**. Yet they sinned still more against him, rebelling against the Most High in the desert. ... In spite of all this, they still sinned; despite his wonders, they did not believe. ... Yet they tested and rebelled against the Most High God and did not keep his testimonies. **Ezek. 8:6, 13, 15**. And he said to me, "Son of man, do you see what they are doing, the great abominations that the house of Israel are committing here, to drive me far from my sanctuary? But you will see still greater abominations." ... He said also to me, "You will see still greater abominations that they commit." ... Then he said to me, "Have you seen this, O son of man? You will see still greater abominations than these." **Jn. 19:11**. Jesus answered him, "You would have no authority over me at all unless it had been given you from above. Therefore he who delivered me over to you has the greater sin." **1 Jn. 5:16**. If anyone sees his brother committing a sin not leading to death, he shall ask, and God will give him life—to those who commit sins that do not lead to death. There is sin that leads to death; I do not say that one should pray for that.

Q. 151. What are those aggravating circumstances that make some sins more wicked than others?

A. Sins receive their aggravated status,

1. From the persons offending:[1] if they be of more mature age,[2] greater experience of grace,[3] high regard for profession,[4] giftedness,[5] place,[6] office,[7] standing as guides to others,[8] and whose example is likely to be followed by others.[9]
2. From the parties offended:[10] if immediately against God,[11] His attributes,[12] and worship;[13] against Christ, and His grace:[14] the Holy Spirit,[15] His witness,[16] and workings;[17] against superiors, men of high standing,[18] and those to whom we stand especially related and engaged;[19] against any of the saints,[20] particularly weak brothers and sisters,[21] the souls of them or any other;[22] and the common good of all or many.[23]
3. From the nature and seriousness of the offense:[24] if it be against the express letter of the law,[25] break many commandments, contain in it many sins:[26] if not only conceived in the heart, but carried out in words and actions,[27] scandalize others,[28] and permit no compensation:[29] if against means,[30] mercies,[31] judgments,[32] light of nature,[33] conviction of conscience,[34] public or private admonition,[35] censures of the church,[36] civil punishments;[37] and our prayers, purposes, promises,[38] vows,[39] covenants,[40] and engagements to God or men:[41] if done deliberately,[42] willfully,[43] presumptuously,[44] impudently,[45] boastingly,[46] maliciously,[47] frequently,[48] obstinately,[49] with light,[50] repeatedly,[51] or relapsing after repentance.[52]
4. From circumstances of time,[53] and place:[54] if on the Lord's Day,[55] or other times of divine worship;[56] or immediately before,[57] or after these,[58] or other situations that should prevent or remedy such miscarriages;[59] if in public, or in the presence of others, who are thereby likely to be provoked or corrupted.[60]

1 **Jer. 2:8**. The priests did not say, 'Where is the LORD?' Those who handle the law did not know me; the shepherds transgressed against me; the prophets prophesied by Baal and went after things that do not profit.

2 **Job 32:7, 9**. I said, 'Let days speak, and many years teach wisdom.' ... It is not the old who are wise, nor the aged who understand what is right. **Eccl. 4:13**. Better was a poor and wise youth than an old and foolish king who no longer knew how to take advice.

3 **1 Kings 11:4, 9**. For when Solomon was old his wives turned away his heart after other gods, and his heart was not wholly true to the LORD his God, as was the heart of David his father. ... And the LORD was angry with Solomon, because his heart had turned away from the LORD, the God of Israel, who had appeared to him twice.

4 **2 Sam. 12:14**. "Nevertheless, because by this deed you have utterly scorned the LORD, the child who is born to you shall die." **1 Cor. 5:1**. It is actually reported that there is sexual immorality among you, and of a kind that is not tolerated even among pagans, for a man has his father's wife.

5 **Lk. 12:47-48**. And that servant who knew his master's will but did not get ready or act according to his will, will receive a severe beating. But the one who did not know, and did what deserved a beating, will receive a light beating. Everyone to whom much was given, of him much will be required, and from him to whom they entrusted much, they will demand the more.

6 **Jer. 5:4-5**. Then I said, "These are only the poor; they have no sense; for they do not know the way of the LORD, the justice of their God. I will go to the great and will speak to them, for they know the way of the LORD, the justice of their God." But they all alike had broken the yoke; they had burst the bonds.

7 **2 Sam. 12:7-9**. Nathan said to David, "You are the man! Thus says the LORD, the God of Israel, 'I anointed you king over Israel, and I delivered you out of the hand of Saul. And I gave you your master's house and your master's wives into your arms and gave you the house of Israel and of Judah. And if this were too little, I would add to you as much more. Why have you despised the word of the LORD, to do what is evil in his sight? You have struck down Uriah the Hittite with the sword and have taken his wife to be your wife and have killed him with the sword of the Ammonites.'" **Ezek. 8:11-12**. And before them stood seventy men of the elders of the house of Israel, with Jaazaniah the son of Shaphan standing among them. Each had his censer in his hand, and the smoke of the cloud of incense went up. Then he said to me, "Son of man, have you seen what the elders of the house of Israel are doing in the dark, each in his room of pictures? For they say, 'The LORD does not see us, the LORD has forsaken the land.'"

8 **Rom. 2:17-24**. But if you call yourself a Jew and rely on the law and boast in God and know his will and approve what is excellent, because you are instructed from the law; and if you are sure that you yourself are a guide to the blind, a light to those who are in darkness, an instructor of the foolish, a teacher of children, having in the law the embodiment of knowledge and truth— you then who teach others, do you not teach yourself? While you preach against stealing, do you steal? You who say that one must not commit adultery, do you commit adultery? You who abhor idols, do you rob temples? You who boast in the law dishonor God by breaking the law. For, as it is written, "The name of God is blasphemed among the Gentiles because of you."

9 **Gal. 2:11-14**. But when Cephas came to Antioch, I opposed him to his face, because he stood condemned. For before certain men came from James, he was eating with the Gentiles; but when they came he drew back and separated himself, fearing the circumcision party. And the rest of the Jews acted hypocritically along with him, so that even Barnabas was led astray by their hypocrisy. But when I saw that their conduct was not in step with the truth of the gospel, I said to Cephas before them all, "If you, though a Jew, live like a Gentile and not like a Jew, how can you force the Gentiles to live like Jews?"

10 **Mt. 21:38-39**. But when the tenants saw the son, they said to themselves, 'This is the heir. Come, let us kill him and have his inheritance.' And they took him and threw him out of the vineyard and killed him.

11 **1 Sam. 2:25**. If someone sins against a man, God will mediate for him, but if someone sins against the LORD, who can intercede for him?" But they would not listen to the voice of their father, for it was the will of the LORD to put them to death. **Ps. 5:4**. For you are not a God who delights in wickedness; evil may not dwell with you. **Acts 5:4**. "While it remained unsold, did it not remain your own? And after it was sold, was it not at your disposal? Why is it that you have contrived this deed in your heart? You have not lied to man but to God."

12 **Rom. 2:4**. Or do you presume on the riches of his kindness and forbearance and patience, not knowing that God's kindness is meant to lead you to repentance?

13 **Mal. 1:8, 14**. When you offer blind animals in sacrifice, is that not evil? And when you offer those that are lame or sick, is that not evil? Present that to your governor; will he accept you or show you favor? says the LORD of hosts. ... Cursed be the cheat who has a male in his flock, and vows it, and yet sacrifices to the Lord what is blemished. For I am a great King, says the LORD of hosts, and my name will be feared among the nations.

14 **Heb. 2:2-3**. For since the message declared by angels proved to be reliable, and every transgression or disobedience received a just retribution, how shall we escape if we neglect such a great salvation? It was declared at first by the Lord, and it was attested to us by those who heard. **Heb. 7:25**. Consequently, he is able to save to the uttermost those who draw near to God through him, since he always lives to make intercession for them.

15 **Mt. 12:31-32**. Therefore I tell you, every sin and blasphemy will be forgiven people, but the blasphemy against the Spirit will not be forgiven. And whoever speaks a word against the Son of Man will be forgiven, but whoever speaks against the Holy Spirit will not be forgiven, either in this age or in the age to come.
Heb. 10:29. How much worse punishment, do you think, will be deserved by the one who has trampled underfoot the Son of God, and has profaned the blood of the covenant by which he was sanctified, and has outraged the Spirit of grace?

16 **Eph. 4:30**. And do not grieve the Holy Spirit of God, by whom you were sealed for the day of redemption.

17 **Heb. 6:4-6**. For it is impossible, in the case of those who have once been enlightened, who have tasted the heavenly gift, and have shared in the Holy Spirit, and have tasted the goodness of the word of God and the powers of the age to come, and then have fallen away, to restore them again to repentance, since they are crucifying once again the Son of God to their own harm and holding him up to contempt.

18 **Num. 12:8-9**. With him I speak mouth to mouth, clearly, and not in riddles, and he beholds the form of the LORD. Why then were you not afraid to speak against my servant Moses?" And the anger of the LORD was kindled against them, and he departed. **Isa. 3:5**. And the people will oppress one another, every one his fellow and every one his neighbor; the youth will be insolent to the elder, and the despised to the honorable. **Jude 8**. Yet in like manner these people also, relying on their dreams, defile the flesh, reject authority, and blaspheme the glorious ones.

19 **Ps. 55:12-15**. For it is not an enemy who taunts me— then I could bear it; it is not an adversary who deals insolently with me— then I could hide from him. But it is you, a man, my equal, my companion, my familiar friend. We used to take sweet counsel together; within God's house we walked in the throng. Let death steal over them; let them go down to Sheol alive; for evil is in their dwelling place and in their heart. **Prov. 30:17**. The eye that mocks a father and scorns to obey a mother will be picked out by the ravens of the valley and eaten by the vultures.
2 Cor. 12:15. I will most gladly spend and be spent for your souls. If I love you more, am I to be loved less?

20 **Zeph. 2:8, 10-11**. "I have heard the taunts of Moab and the revilings of the Ammonites, how they have taunted my people and made boasts against their territory." ... This shall be their lot in return for their pride, because they taunted and boasted against the people of the LORD of hosts. The LORD will be awesome against them; for he will famish all the gods of the earth, and to him shall bow down, each in its place, all the lands of the nations. **Mt. 18:6**. ...but whoever causes one of these little ones who believe in me to sin, it would be better for him to have a great millstone fastened around his neck and to be drowned in the depth of the sea. **1 Cor. 6:8**. But you yourselves wrong and defraud—even your own

brothers! **Rev. 17:6.** And I saw the woman, drunk with the blood of the saints, the blood of the martyrs of Jesus. When I saw her, I marveled greatly.

21 **Rom. 14:13, 15, 21.** Therefore let us not pass judgment on one another any longer, but rather decide never to put a stumbling block or hindrance in the way of a brother. ... For if your brother is grieved by what you eat, you are no longer walking in love. By what you eat, do not destroy the one for whom Christ died. ... It is good not to eat meat or drink wine or do anything that causes your brother to stumble. **1 Cor. 8:11-12.** And so by your knowledge this weak person is destroyed, the brother for whom Christ died. Thus, sinning against your brothers and wounding their conscience when it is weak, you sin against Christ.

22 **Ezek. 13:19.** You have profaned me among my people for handfuls of barley and for pieces of bread, putting to death souls who should not die and keeping alive souls who should not live, by your lying to my people, who listen to lies. **Mt. 23:15.** Woe to you, scribes and Pharisees, hypocrites! For you travel across sea and land to make a single proselyte, and when he becomes a proselyte, you make him twice as much a child of hell as yourselves. **1 Cor. 8:12.** Thus, sinning against your brothers and wounding their conscience when it is weak, you sin against Christ.

23 **Josh. 22:20.** "'Did not Achan the son of Zerah break faith in the matter of the devoted things, and wrath fell upon all the congregation of Israel? And he did not perish alone for his iniquity.'" **1 Thess. 2:15-16.** ...who killed both the Lord Jesus and the prophets, and drove us out, and displease God and oppose all mankind by hindering us from speaking to the Gentiles that they might be saved—so as always to fill up the measure of their sins. But wrath has come upon them at last!

24 **Prov. 6:30-33.** People do not despise a thief if he steals to satisfy his appetite when he is hungry, but if he is caught, he will pay sevenfold; he will give all the goods of his house. He who commits adultery lacks sense; he who does it destroys himself. He will get wounds and dishonor, and his disgrace will not be wiped away.

25 **1 Kings 11:9-10.** And the LORD was angry with Solomon, because his heart had turned away from the LORD, the God of Israel, who had appeared to him twice and had commanded him concerning this thing, that he should not go after other gods. But he did not keep what the LORD commanded. **Ezek. 9:10-12.** As for me, my eye will not spare, nor will I have pity; I will bring their deeds upon their heads." And behold, the man clothed in linen, with the writing case at his waist, brought back word, saying, "I have done as you commanded me."

26 **Josh. 7:21.** ...when I saw among the spoil a beautiful cloak from Shinar, and 200 shekels of silver, and a bar of gold weighing 50 shekels, then I coveted them and took them. And see, they are hidden in the earth inside my tent, with the silver underneath." **Prov. 5:8-12.** Keep your way far from her, and do not go near the door of her house, lest you give your honor to others and your years to the merciless, lest strangers take their fill of your strength, and your labors go to the house of a foreigner, and at the end of your life you groan, when your flesh and body are consumed, and you say, "How I hated discipline, and my heart despised reproof!" **Prov. 6:32-33.** He who commits adultery lacks sense; he who does it destroys himself. He will get wounds and dishonor, and his disgrace will not be wiped away. **Col. 3:5.** Put to death therefore what is earthly in you: sexual immorality, impurity, passion, evil desire, and covetousness, which is idolatry. **1 Tim. 6:10.** For the love of money is a root of all kinds of evils. It is through this craving that some have wandered away from the faith and pierced themselves with many pangs.

27 **Mic. 2:1.** Woe to those who devise wickedness and work evil on their beds! When the morning dawns, they perform it, because it is in the power of their hand. **Mt. 5:22.** But I say to you that everyone who is angry with his brother will be liable to judgment; whoever insults his brother will be liable to the council; and

whoever says, 'You fool!' will be liable to the hell of fire. **JAS. 1:14-15**. But each person is tempted when he is lured and enticed by his own desire. Then desire when it has conceived gives birth to sin, and sin when it is fully grown brings forth death.

28 **MT. 18:7**. "Woe to the world for temptations to sin! For it is necessary that temptations come, but woe to the one by whom the temptation comes! **ROM. 2:23-24**. You who boast in the law dishonor God by breaking the law. For, as it is written, "The name of God is blasphemed among the Gentiles because of you."

29 **DEUT. 22:22, 28-29**. "If a man is found lying with the wife of another man, both of them shall die, the man who lay with the woman, and the woman. So you shall purge the evil from Israel." ... "If a man meets a virgin who is not betrothed, and seizes her and lies with her, and they are found, then the man who lay with her shall give to the father of the young woman fifty shekels of silver, and she shall be his wife, because he has violated her. He may not divorce her all his days." **PROV. 6:32-35**. He who commits adultery lacks sense; he who does it destroys himself. He will get wounds and dishonor, and his disgrace will not be wiped away. For jealousy makes a man furious, and he will not spare when he takes revenge. He will accept no compensation; he will refuse though you multiply gifts.

30 **MT. 11:21-24**. "Woe to you, Chorazin! Woe to you, Bethsaida! For if the mighty works done in you had been done in Tyre and Sidon, they would have repented long ago in sackcloth and ashes. But I tell you, it will be more bearable on the day of judgment for Tyre and Sidon than for you. And you, Capernaum, will you be exalted to heaven? You will be brought down to Hades. For if the mighty works done in you had been done in Sodom, it would have remained until this day. But I tell you that it will be more tolerable on the day of judgment for the land of Sodom than for you." **JN. 15:22**. If I had not come and spoken to them, they would not have been guilty of sin, but now they have no excuse for their sin.

31 **DEUT. 32:6**. Do you thus repay the LORD, you foolish and senseless people? Is not he your father, who created you, who made you and established you? **ISA. 1:3**. "The ox knows its owner, and the donkey its master's crib, but Israel does not know, my people do not understand."

32 **JER. 5:3**. O LORD, do not your eyes look for truth? You have struck them down, but they felt no anguish; you have consumed them, but they refused to take correction. They have made their faces harder than rock; they have refused to repent. **AM. 4:8-11**. ...so two or three cities would wander to another city to drink water, and would not be satisfied; yet you did not return to me," declares the LORD. "I struck you with blight and mildew; your many gardens and your vineyards, your fig trees and your olive trees the locust devoured; yet you did not return to me," declares the LORD. "I sent among you a pestilence after the manner of Egypt; I killed your young men with the sword, and carried away your horses, and I made the stench of your camp go up into your nostrils; yet you did not return to me," declares the LORD. "I overthrew some of you, as when God overthrew Sodom and Gomorrah, and you were as a brand plucked out of the burning; yet you did not return to me," declares the LORD.

33 **ROM. 1:26-27**. For this reason God gave them up to dishonorable passions. For their women exchanged natural relations for those that are contrary to nature; and the men likewise gave up natural relations with women and were consumed with passion for one another, men committing shameless acts with men and receiving in themselves the due penalty for their error.

34 **DAN. 5:22**. And you his son, Belshazzar, have not humbled your heart, though you knew all this. **ROM. 1:32**. Though they know God's righteous decree that those who practice such things deserve to die, they not only do them but give approval to those who practice them. **TITUS 3:10-11**. As for a person who stirs up

division, after warning him once and then twice, have nothing more to do with him, knowing that such a person is warped and sinful; he is self-condemned.

35 **Prov. 29:1**. He who is often reproved, yet stiffens his neck, will suddenly be broken beyond healing.

36 **Mt. 18:17**. If he refuses to listen to them, tell it to the church. And if he refuses to listen even to the church, let him be to you as a Gentile and a tax collector. **Titus 3:10**. As for a person who stirs up division, after warning him once and then twice, have nothing more to do with him.

37 **Pro. 23:35**. "They struck me," you will say, "but I was not hurt; they beat me, but I did not feel it. When shall I awake? I must have another drink." **Prov. 27:22**. Crush a fool in a mortar with a pestle along with crushed grain, yet his folly will not depart from him.

38 **Ps. 78:34-37**. When he killed them, they sought him; they repented and sought God earnestly. They remembered that God was their rock, the Most High God their redeemer. But they flattered him with their mouths; they lied to him with their tongues. Their heart was not steadfast toward him; they were not faithful to his covenant. **Jer. 2:20**. "For long ago I broke your yoke and burst your bonds; but you said, 'I will not serve.' Yes, on every high hill and under every green tree you bowed down like a whore.'" **Jer. 13:5-6, 20-21**. So I went and hid it by the Euphrates, as the Lord commanded me. And after many days the Lord said to me, "Arise, go to the Euphrates, and take from there the loincloth that I commanded you to hide there." ... "Lift up your eyes and see those who come from the north. Where is the flock that was given you, your beautiful flock? What will you say when they set as head over you those whom you yourself have taught to be friends to you? Will not pangs take hold of you like those of a woman in labor?"

39 **Prov. 20:25**. It is a snare to say rashly, "It is holy," and to reflect only after making vows. **Eccl. 5:4-6**. When you vow a vow to God, do not delay paying it, for he has no pleasure in fools. Pay what you vow. It is better that you should not vow than that you should vow and not pay. Let not your mouth lead you into sin, and do not say before the messenger that it was a mistake. Why should God be angry at your voice and destroy the work of your hands?

40 **Lev. 26:25**. And I will bring a sword upon you, that shall execute vengeance for the covenant. And if you gather within your cities, I will send pestilence among you, and you shall be delivered into the hand of the enemy.

41 **Prov. 2:17**. ...who forsakes the companion of her youth and forgets the covenant of her God. **Ezek. 7:18-19**. They put on sackcloth, and horror covers them. Shame is on all faces, and baldness on all their heads. They cast their silver into the streets, and their gold is like an unclean thing. Their silver and gold are not able to deliver them in the day of the wrath of the LORD. They cannot satisfy their hunger or fill their stomachs with it. For it was the stumbling block of their iniquity.

42 **Ps. 36:4**. He plots trouble while on his bed; he sets himself in a way that is not good; he does not reject evil.

43 **Jer. 6:16**. Thus says the LORD: "Stand by the roads, and look, and ask for the ancient paths, where the good way is; and walk in it, and find rest for your souls. But they said, 'We will not walk in it.'"

44 **Ex. 21:14**. But if a man willfully attacks another to kill him by cunning, you shall take him from my altar, that he may die. **Num. 15:30**. But the person who does anything with a high hand, whether he is native or a sojourner, reviles the LORD, and that person shall be cut off from among his people.

45 **Prov. 7:13**. She seizes him and kisses him, and with bold face she says to him. **Jer. 3:3**. Therefore the showers have been withheld, and the spring rain has not come; yet you have the forehead of a whore; you refuse to be ashamed.

46 **Ps. 52:1**. Why do you boast of evil, O mighty man? The steadfast love of God endures all the day.

47 **3 Jn. 10**. So if I come, I will bring up what he is doing, talking wicked nonsense against us. And not content with that, he refuses to welcome the brothers, and also stops those who want to and puts them out of the church.

48 **Num. 15:22**. "But if you sin unintentionally, and do not observe all these commandments that the LORD has spoken to Moses."

49 **Zech. 7:11-12**. But they refused to pay attention and turned a stubborn shoulder and stopped their ears that they might not hear. They made their hearts diamond-hard lest they should hear the law and the words that the LORD of hosts had sent by his Spirit through the former prophets. Therefore great anger came from the LORD of hosts.

50 **Prov. 2:14**. ...who rejoice in doing evil and delight in the perverseness of evil.

51 **Isa. 57:17**. Because of the iniquity of his unjust gain I was angry, I struck him; I hid my face and was angry, but he went on backsliding in the way of his own heart.

52 **Jer. 34:8-11**. The word that came to Jeremiah from the LORD, after King Zedekiah had made a covenant with all the people in Jerusalem to make a proclamation of liberty to them, that everyone should set free his Hebrew slaves, male and female, so that no one should enslave a Jew, his brother. And they obeyed, all the officials and all the people who had entered into the covenant that everyone would set free his slave, male or female, so that they would not be enslaved again. They obeyed and set them free. But afterward they turned around and took back the male and female slaves they had set free, and brought them into subjection as slaves. **2 Pet. 2:20-22**. For if, after they have escaped the defilements of the world through the knowledge of our Lord and Savior Jesus Christ, they are again entangled in them and overcome, the last state has become worse for them than the first. For it would have been better for them never to have known the way of righteousness than after knowing it to turn back from the holy commandment delivered to them. What the true proverb says has happened to them: "The dog returns to its own vomit, and the sow, after washing herself, returns to wallow in the mire."

53 **2 Kings 5:26**. But he said to him, "Did not my heart go when the man turned from his chariot to meet you? Was it a time to accept money and garments, olive orchards and vineyards, sheep and oxen, male servants and female servants?"

54 **Isa. 26:10**. If favor is shown to the wicked, he does not learn righteousness; in the land of uprightness he deals corruptly and does not see the majesty of the LORD. **Jer. 7:10**. ...and then come and stand before me in this house, which is called by my name, and say, 'We are delivered!'—only to go on doing all these abominations?

55 **Ezek. 23:37-39**. For they have committed adultery, and blood is on their hands. With their idols they have committed adultery, and they have even offered up to them for food the children whom they had borne to me. Moreover, this they have done to me: they have defiled my sanctuary on the same day and profaned my Sabbaths. For when they had slaughtered their children in sacrifice to their idols, on the same day they came into my sanctuary to profane it. And behold, this is what they did in my house.

56 **Num. 25:6-7**. And behold, one of the people of Israel came and brought a Midianite woman to his family, in the sight of Moses and in the sight of the whole congregation of the people of Israel, while they were weeping in the entrance of the tent of meeting. When Phinehas the son of Eleazar, son of Aaron the priest, saw it, he rose and left the congregation and took a spear in his hand. **Isa. 58:3-5**. 'Why have we fasted, and you see it not? Why have we humbled ourselves, and you take no knowledge of it?' Behold, in the day of your fast you seek your own pleasure,

and oppress all your workers. Behold, you fast only to quarrel and to fight and to hit with a wicked fist. Fasting like yours this day will not make your voice to be heard on high. Is such the fast that I choose, a day for a person to humble himself? Is it to bow down his head like a reed, and to spread sackcloth and ashes under him? Will you call this a fast, and a day acceptable to the LORD.

57 **1 Cor. 11:20-21**. When you come together, it is not the Lord's supper that you eat. For in eating, each one goes ahead with his own meal. One goes hungry, another gets drunk.

58 **Prov. 7:14-15**. "I had to offer sacrifices, and today I have paid my vows; so now I have come out to meet you, to seek you eagerly, and I have found you." **Jer. 7:8-10**. "Behold, you trust in deceptive words to no avail. Will you steal, murder, commit adultery, swear falsely, make offerings to Baal, and go after other gods that you have not known, and then come and stand before me in this house, which is called by my name, and say, 'We are delivered!'—only to go on doing all these abominations?" **Jn. 13:27, 30**. Then after he had taken the morsel, Satan entered into him. Jesus said to him, "What you are going to do, do quickly." ... So, after receiving the morsel of bread, he immediately went out. And it was night.

59 **Ezra. 9:13-14**. And after all that has come upon us for our evil deeds and for our great guilt, seeing that you, our God, have punished us less than our iniquities deserved and have given us such a remnant as this, shall we break your commandments again and intermarry with the peoples who practice these abominations? Would you not be angry with us until you consumed us, so that there should be no remnant, nor any to escape?

60 **1 Sam. 2:22-24**. Now Eli was very old, and he kept hearing all that his sons were doing to all Israel, and how they lay with the women who were serving at the entrance to the tent of meeting. And he said to them, "Why do you do such things? For I hear of your evil dealings from all these people. No, my sons; it is no good report that I hear the people of the LORD spreading abroad. **2 Sam. 16:22**. So they pitched a tent for Absalom on the roof. And Absalom went in to his father's concubines in the sight of all Israel.

Q. 152. What does every sin deserve at the hands of God?

A. Every sin, even the least, being against the sovereignty,[1] good ness,[2] and holiness of God,[3] and against His righteous law,[4] deserves His wrath and curse,[5] both in this life,[6] and that which is to come;[7] and cannot be expiated but by the blood of Christ.[8]

1 **Jas. 2:10-11**. For whoever keeps the whole law but fails in one point has become accountable for all of it. For he who said, "Do not commit adultery," also said, "Do not murder." If you do not commit adultery but do murder, you have become a transgressor of the law.

2 **Ex. 20:1-2**. And God spoke all these words, saying, "I am the LORD your God, who brought you out of the land of Egypt, out of the house of slavery.

3 **Lev. 10:3**. Then Moses said to Aaron, "This is what the LORD has said: 'Among those who are near me I will be sanctified, and before all the people I will be glorified.'" And Aaron held his peace. **Lev. 11:44-45**. "For I am the LORD your God. Consecrate yourselves therefore, and be holy, for I am holy. You shall not defile yourselves with any swarming thing that crawls on the ground. For I am the LORD who brought you up out of the land of Egypt to be your God. You shall therefore be holy, for I am holy." **Hab. 1:13**. You who are of purer eyes than to see evil and

cannot look at wrong, why do you idly look at traitors and remain silent when the wicked swallows up the man more righteous than he?

4 **Rom. 7:12**. So the law is holy, and the commandment is holy and righteous and good. **1 Jn. 3:4**. Everyone who makes a practice of sinning also practices lawlessness; sin is lawlessness.

5 **Gal. 3:10**. For all who rely on works of the law are under a curse; for it is written, "Cursed be everyone who does not abide by all things written in the Book of the Law, and do them." **Eph. 5:6**. Let no one deceive you with empty words, for because of these things the wrath of God comes upon the sons of disobedience.

6 **Deut. 20:15-20**. Thus you shall do to all the cities that are very far from you, which are not cities of the nations here. But in the cities of these peoples that the LORD your God is giving you for an inheritance, you shall save alive nothing that breathes, but you shall devote them to complete destruction, the Hittites and the Amorites, the Canaanites and the Perizzites, the Hivites and the Jebusites, as the LORD your God has commanded, that they may not teach you to do according to all their abominable practices that they have done for their gods, and so you sin against the LORD your God. **Lam. 3:39**. Why should a living man complain, a man, about the punishment of his sins?

7 **Mt. 25:41**. "Then he will say to those on his left, 'Depart from me, you cursed, into the eternal fire prepared for the devil and his angels."

8 **Heb. 9:22**. Indeed, under the law almost everything is purified with blood, and without the shedding of blood there is no forgiveness of sins. **1 Pet. 1:18-19**. ... knowing that you were ransomed from the futile ways inherited from your forefathers, not with perishable things such as silver or gold, but with the precious blood of Christ, like that of a lamb without blemish or spot.

Q. 153. What does God require of us, that we may escape His wrath and curse due to us by reason of the transgression of the law?

A. That we may escape the wrath and curse of God due to us by reason of the transgression of the law, He requires of us repentance toward God, and faith toward our Lord Jesus Christ,[1] and the diligent use of the outward means by which Christ communicates to us the benefits of His mediation.[2]

1 **Mt. 3:7-8**. But when he saw many of the Pharisees and Sadducees coming to his baptism, he said to them, "You brood of vipers! Who warned you to flee from the wrath to come? Bear fruit in keeping with repentance." **Lk. 13:3, 5**. No, I tell you; but unless you repent, you will all likewise perish. ... "No, I tell you; but unless you repent, you will all likewise perish." **Jn. 3:16, 18**. "For God so loved the world, that he gave his only Son, that whoever believes in him should not perish but have eternal life." ... Whoever believes in him is not condemned, but whoever does not believe is condemned already, because he has not believed in the name of the only Son of God. **Acts 16:30-31**. Then he brought them out and said, "Sirs, what must I do to be saved?" And they said, "Believe in the Lord Jesus, and you will be saved, you and your household." **Acts 20:21**. ...testifying both to Jews and to Greeks of repentance toward God and of faith in our Lord Jesus Christ.

2 **Prov. 2:1-5**. My son, if you receive my words and treasure up my commandments with you, making your ear attentive to wisdom and inclining your heart to understanding; yes, if you call out for insight and raise your voice for understanding, if

you seek it like silver and search for it as for hidden treasures, then you will understand the fear of the LORD and find the knowledge of God. **Prov. 8:33-36**. "Hear instruction and be wise, and do not neglect it. Blessed is the one who listens to me, watching daily at my gates, waiting beside my doors. For whoever finds me finds life and obtains favor from the LORD, but he who fails to find me injures himself; all who hate me love death."

Q. 154. What are the outward means by which Christ communicates to us the benefits of His mediation?

A. The outward and ordinary means, by which Christ communicates to His church the benefits of His mediation, are all His ordinances, especially the Word, sacraments, and prayer, all of which are made effectual to the elect for their salvation.[1]

1 **Mt. 28:19-20**. "Go therefore and make disciples of all nations, baptizing them in the name of the Father and of the Son and of the Holy Spirit, teaching them to observe all that I have commanded you. And behold, I am with you always, to the end of the age." **Acts 2:42, 46-47**. And they devoted themselves to the apostles' teaching and the fellowship, to the breaking of bread and the prayers. ... And day by day, attending the temple together and breaking bread in their homes, they received their food with glad and generous hearts, praising God and having favor with all the people. And the Lord added to their number day by day those who were being saved.

Q. 155. How is the Word made effectual to salvation?

A. The Spirit of God makes the reading, but especially the preaching of the Word, an effectual means of enlightening,[1] convincing, and humbling sinners,[2] of driving them out of themselves, and drawing them to Christ,[3] of conforming them to His image,[4] and subduing them to His will;[5] of strengthening them against temptations and corruptions;[6] of building them up in grace,[7] and establishing their hearts in holiness and comfort through faith to salvation.[8]

1 **Neh. 8:8**. They read from the book, from the Law of God, clearly, and they gave the sense, so that the people understood the reading. **Ps. 19:8**. ...the precepts of the LORD are right, rejoicing the heart; the commandment of the LORD is pure, enlightening the eyes. **Acts 26:18**. '...to open their eyes, so that they may turn from darkness to light and from the power of Satan to God, that they may receive forgiveness of sins and a place among those who are sanctified by faith in me.'

2 **1 Cor. 14:24-25**. But if all prophesy, and an unbeliever or outsider enters, he is convicted by all, he is called to account by all, the secrets of his heart are disclosed, and so, falling on his face, he will worship God and declare that God is really among you. **2 Chr. 34:18, 19, 26-28**. Then Shaphan the secretary told the king, "Hilkiah the priest has given me a book." And Shaphan read from it before the king. ... And when the king heard the words of the Law, he tore his clothes. ... But

to the king of Judah, who sent you to inquire of the LORD, thus shall you say to him, Thus says the LORD, the God of Israel: Regarding the words that you have heard, because your heart was tender and you humbled yourself before God when you heard his words against this place and its inhabitants, and you have humbled yourself before me and have torn your clothes and wept before me, I also have heard you, declares the LORD. Behold, I will gather you to your fathers, and you shall be gathered to your grave in peace, and your eyes shall not see all the disaster that I will bring upon this place and its inhabitants.'" And they brought back word to the king.

3 **ACTS 2:37, 41**. Now when they heard this they were cut to the heart, and said to Peter and the rest of the apostles, "Brothers, what shall we do?" ... So those who received his word were baptized, and there were added that day about three thousand souls. **ACTS 8:27-30, 35-38**. And he rose and went. And there was an Ethiopian, a eunuch, a court official of Candace, queen of the Ethiopians, who was in charge of all her treasure. He had come to Jerusalem to worship and was returning, seated in his chariot, and he was reading the prophet Isaiah. And the Spirit said to Philip, "Go over and join this chariot." So Philip ran to him and heard him reading Isaiah the prophet and asked, "Do you understand what you are reading?" ... Then Philip opened his mouth, and beginning with this Scripture he told him the good news about Jesus. And as they were going along the road they came to some water, and the eunuch said, "See, here is water! What prevents me from being baptized?" And he commanded the chariot to stop, and they both went down into the water, Philip and the eunuch, and he baptized him.

4 **2 COR. 3:18**. And we all, with unveiled face, beholding the glory of the Lord, are being transformed into the same image from one degree of glory to another. For this comes from the Lord who is the Spirit.

5 **ROM. 6:17**. But thanks be to God, that you who were once slaves of sin have become obedient from the heart to the standard of teaching to which you were committed. **2 COR. 10:4-6**. For the weapons of our warfare are not of the flesh but have divine power to destroy strongholds. We destroy arguments and every lofty opinion raised against the knowledge of God, and take every thought captive to obey Christ, being ready to punish every disobedience, when your obedience is complete.

6 **PS. 19:11**. Moreover, by them is your servant warned; in keeping them there is great reward. **MT. 4:4, 7, 10**. But he answered, "It is written, "'Man shall not live by bread alone, but by every word that comes from the mouth of God.'" ... Jesus said to him, "Again it is written, 'You shall not put the Lord your God to the test.'" ...Then Jesus said to him, "Be gone, Satan! For it is written, "'You shall worship the Lord your God and him only shall you serve.'" **1 COR. 10:11**. Now these things happened to them as an example, but they were written down for our instruction, on whom the end of the ages has come. **EPH. 6:16-17**. In all circumstances take up the shield of faith, with which you can extinguish all the flaming darts of the evil one; and take the helmet of salvation, and the sword of the Spirit, which is the word of God.

7 **ACTS 20:32**. And now I commend you to God and to the word of his grace, which is able to build you up and to give you the inheritance among all those who are sanctified. **2 TIM. 3:15-17**. ...and how from childhood you have been acquainted with the sacred writings, which are able to make you wise for salvation through faith in Christ Jesus. All Scripture is breathed out by God and profitable for teaching, for reproof, for correction, and for training in righteousness, that the man of God may be complete, equipped for every good work.

8 **ROM. 1:16**. For I am not ashamed of the gospel, for it is the power of God for salvation to everyone who believes, to the Jew first and also to the Greek.

Rom. 10:13-17. For "everyone who calls on the name of the Lord will be saved." How then will they call on him in whom they have not believed? And how are they to believe in him of whom they have never heard? And how are they to hear without someone preaching? And how are they to preach unless they are sent? As it is written, "How beautiful are the feet of those who preach the good news!" But they have not all obeyed the gospel. For Isaiah says, "Lord, who has believed what he has heard from us?" So faith comes from hearing, and hearing through the word of Christ." **Rom. 15:4**. For whatever was written in former days was written for our instruction, that through endurance and through the encouragement of the Scriptures we might have hope. **Rom. 16:25**. Now to him who is able to strengthen you according to my gospel and the preaching of Jesus Christ, according to the revelation of the mystery that was kept secret for long ages. **1 Thess. 3:2, 10-11, 13**. ... and we sent Timothy, our brother and God's coworker in the gospel of Christ, to establish and exhort you in your faith. ...as we pray most earnestly night and day that we may see you face to face and supply what is lacking in your faith? Now may our God and Father himself, and our Lord Jesus, direct our way to you. ...so that he may establish your hearts blameless in holiness before our God and Father, at the coming of our Lord Jesus with all his saints.

Q. 156. Is the Word of God to be read by all?

A. Although all are not permitted to read the Word publicly to the congregation,[1] yet all sorts of people are bound to read it apart by themselves,[2] and with their families;[3] to which end, the Holy Scriptures are to be translated out of the original into the language of every people to whom they come.[4]

1 **Deut. 31:9, 11-13.** Then Moses wrote this law and gave it to the priests, the sons of Levi, who carried the ark of the covenant of the LORD, and to all the elders of Israel. "...when all Israel comes to appear before the LORD your God at the place that he will choose, you shall read this law before all Israel in their hearing. Assemble the people, men, women, and little ones, and the sojourner within your towns, that they may hear and learn to fear the LORD your God, and be careful to do all the words of this law, and that their children, who have not known it, may hear and learn to fear the LORD your God, as long as you live in the land that you are going over the Jordan to possess." **Neh. 8:2-3**. So Ezra the priest brought the Law before the assembly, both men and women and all who could understand what they heard, on the first day of the seventh month. And he read from it facing the square before the Water Gate from early morning until midday, in the presence of the men and the women and those who could understand. And the ears of all the people were attentive to the Book of the Law. **Neh. 9:3-5**. And they stood up in their place and read from the Book of the Law of the LORD their God for a quarter of the day; for another quarter of it they made confession and worshiped the LORD their God. On the stairs of the Levites stood Jeshua, Bani, Kadmiel, Shebaniah, Bunni, Sherebiah, Bani, and Chenani; and they cried with a loud voice to the LORD their God. Then the Levites, Jeshua, Kadmiel, Bani, Hashabneiah, Sherebiah, Hodiah, Shebaniah, and Pethahiah, said, "Stand up and bless the LORD your God from everlasting to everlasting. Blessed be your glorious name, which is exalted above all blessing and praise.

2 **Deut. 17:19**. And it shall be with him, and he shall read in it all the days of his life, that he may learn to fear the LORD his God by keeping all the words of this law and these statutes, and doing them. **Isa. 34:16**. Seek and read from the book

of the LORD: Not one of these shall be missing; none shall be without her mate. For the mouth of the LORD has commanded, and his Spirit has gathered them. **JN. 5:39**. You search the Scriptures because you think that in them you have eternal life; and it is they that bear witness about me. **REV. 1:8**. "I am the Alpha and the Omega," says the Lord God, "who is and who was and who is to come, the Almighty."

3 **GEN. 18:17, 19**. The LORD said, "Shall I hide from Abraham what I am about to do. ... For I have chosen him, that he may command his children and his household after him to keep the way of the LORD by doing righteousness and justice, so that the LORD may bring to Abraham what he has promised him." **DEUT. 6:6-9**. And these words that I command you today shall be on your heart. You shall teach them diligently to your children, and shall talk of them when you sit in your house, and when you walk by the way, and when you lie down, and when you rise. You shall bind them as a sign on your hand, and they shall be as frontlets between your eyes. You shall write them on the doorposts of your house and on your gates. **PS. 78:5-7**. He established a testimony in Jacob and appointed a law in Israel, which he commanded our fathers to teach to their children, that the next generation might know them, the children yet unborn, and arise and tell them to their children, so that they should set their hope in God and not forget the works of God, but keep his commandments.

4 **1 COR. 14:6, 9, 11-12, 15-16, 24, 27-28**. Now, brothers, if I come to you speaking in tongues, how will I benefit you unless I bring you some revelation or knowledge or prophecy or teaching? ... So with yourselves, if with your tongue you utter speech that is not intelligible, how will anyone know what is said? For you will be speaking into the air. ...but if I do not know the meaning of the language, I will be a foreigner to the speaker and the speaker a foreigner to me. So with yourselves, since you are eager for manifestations of the Spirit, strive to excel in building up the church. ... What am I to do? I will pray with my spirit, but I will pray with my mind also; I will sing praise with my spirit, but I will sing with my mind also. Otherwise, if you give thanks with your spirit, how can anyone in the position of an outsider say "Amen" to your thanksgiving when he does not know what you are saying? ... But if all prophesy, and an unbeliever or outsider enters, he is convicted by all, he is called to account by all. ... If any speak in a tongue, let there be only two or at most three, and each in turn, and let someone interpret. But if there is no one to interpret, let each of them keep silent in church and speak to himself and to God.

Q. 157. How is the Word of God to be read?

A. The Holy Scriptures are to be read with a high and reverent esteem of them;[1] with a firm conviction that they are the very Word of God,[2] and that only He can enable us to understand them;[3] with desire to know, believe, and obey, the will of God revealed in them;[4] with diligence,[5] and attention to the matter and scope of them;[6] with meditation,[7] application,[8] self-denial,[9] and prayer.[10]

1 **EX. 24:7**. Then he took the Book of the Covenant and read it in the hearing of the people.And they said, "All that the LORD has spoken we will do, and we will be obedient." **CHR. 34:27**. ...because your heart was tender and you humbled yourself before God when you heard his words against this place and its inhabitants, and you have humbled yourself before me and have torn your clothes and wept

before me, I also have heard you, declares the LORD. **Neh. 8:3-6, 10**. And he read from it facing the square before the Water Gate from early morning until midday, in the presence of the men and the women and those who could understand. And the ears of all the people were attentive to the Book of the Law. And Ezra the scribe stood on a wooden platform that they had made for the purpose. And beside him stood Mattithiah, Shema, Anaiah, Uriah, Hilkiah, and Maaseiah on his right hand, and Pedaiah, Mishael, Malchijah, Hashum, Hashbaddanah, Zechariah, and Meshullam on his left hand. And Ezra opened the book in the sight of all the people, for he was above all the people, and as he opened it all the people stood. And Ezra blessed the LORD, the great God, and all the people answered, "Amen, Amen," lifting up their hands. And they bowed their heads and worshiped the LORD with their faces to the ground. ... Then he said to them, "Go your way. Eat the fat and drink sweet wine and send portions to anyone who has nothing ready, for this day is holy to our Lord. And do not be grieved, for the joy of the LORD is your strength." **Ps. 19:10**. More to be desired are they than gold, even much fine gold; sweeter also than honey and drippings of the honeycomb. **Isa. 66:2**. All these things my hand has made, and so all these things came to be, declares the LORD. But this is the one to whom I will look: he who is humble and contrite in spirit and trembles at my word.

2 **2 Pet. 1:19-21**. And we have the prophetic word more fully confirmed, to which you will do well to pay attention as to a lamp shining in a dark place, until the day dawns and the morning star rises in your hearts, knowing this first of all, that no prophecy of Scripture comes from someone's own interpretation. For no prophecy was ever produced by the will of man, but men spoke from God as they were carried along by the Holy Spirit.

3 **Lk. 24:45**. Then he opened their minds to understand the Scriptures. **2 Cor. 3:13-16**. ...not like Moses, who would put a veil over his face so that the Israelites might not gaze at the outcome of what was being brought to an end. But their minds were hardened. For to this day, when they read the old covenant, that same veil remains unlifted, because only through Christ is it taken away. Yes, to this day whenever Moses is read a veil lies over their hearts. But when one turns to the Lord, the veil is removed.

4 **Deut. 17:10, 20.** Then you shall do according to what they declare to you from that place that the LORD will choose. And you shall be careful to do according to all that they direct you. ...that his heart may not be lifted up above his brothers, and that he may not turn aside from the commandment, either to the right hand or to the left, so that he may continue long in his kingdom, he and his children, in Israel.

5 **Acts 17:11**. Now these Jews were more noble than those in Thessalonica; they received the word with all eagerness, examining the Scriptures daily to see if these things were so.

6 **Lk. 10:26-28**. He said to him, "What is written in the Law? How do you read it?" And he answered, "You shall love the Lord your God with all your heart and with all your soul and with all your strength and with all your mind, and your neighbor as yourself." And he said to him, "You have answered correctly; do this, and you will live." **Acts 8:30, 34**. So Philip ran to him and heard him reading Isaiah the prophet and asked, "Do you understand what you are reading?" ... And the eunuch said to Philip, "About whom, I ask you, does the prophet say this, about himself or about someone else?"

7 **Ps. 1:2**. ...but his delight is in the law of the LORD, and on his law he meditates day and night. **Ps. 119:97**. Oh how I love your law! It is my meditation all the day.

8 **2 Chr. 34:21**. "Go, inquire of the LORD for me and for those who are left in Israel and in Judah, concerning the words of the book that has been found. For great is

the wrath of the LORD that is poured out on us, because our fathers have not kept the word of the LORD, to do according to all that is written in this book."

9 **Deut. 33:3**. Yes, he loved his people, all his holy ones were in his hand; so they followed in your steps, receiving direction from you. **Prov. 3:5**. Trust in the LORD with all your heart, and do not lean on your own understanding.

10 **Neh. 8:6, 8.** And Ezra blessed the Lord, the great God, and all the people answered, "Amen, Amen," lifting up their hands. And they bowed their heads and worshiped the Lord with their faces to the ground....They read from the book, from the Law of God, clearly, and they gave the sense, so that the people understood the reading. **Ps. 119:18**. Open my eyes, that I may behold wondrous things out of your law. **Prov. 2:1-6.** My son, if you receive my words and treasure up my commandments with you, making your ear attentive to wisdom and inclining your heart to understanding; yes, if you call out for insight and raise your voice for understanding, if you seek it like silver and search for it as for hidden treasures, then you will understand the fear of the LORD and find the knowledge of God. For the LORD gives wisdom; from his mouth come knowledge and understanding.

Q. 158. By whom is the Word of God to be preached?

A. The Word of God is to be preached only by such as are sufficiently gifted,[1] and also duly approved and called to that office.[2]

1 **Hos. 4:6.** My people are destroyed for lack of knowledge; because you have rejected knowledge, I reject you from being a priest to me. And since you have forgotten the law of your God, I also will forget your children. **Mal. 2:7**. For the lips of a priest should guard knowledge, and people should seek instruction from his mouth, for he is the messenger of the LORD of hosts. **2 Cor. 3:6**. ...who has made us sufficient to be ministers of a new covenant, not of the letter but of the Spirit. For the letter kills, but the Spirit gives life. **Eph. 4:8-11**. Therefore it says, "When he ascended on high he led a host of captives, and he gave gifts to men." (In saying, "He ascended," what does it mean but that he had also descended into the lower regions, the earth? He who descended is the one who also ascended far above all the heavens, that he might fill all things.) And he gave the apostles, the prophets, the evangelists, the shepherds and teachers. **1 Tim. 3:2, 6**. Therefore an overseer must be above reproach, the husband of one wife, sober-minded, self-controlled, respectable, hospitable, able to teach. ... He must not be a recent convert, or he may become puffed up with conceit and fall into the condemnation of the devil.

2 **Jer. 14:15**. Therefore thus says the LORD concerning the prophets who prophesy in my name although I did not send them, and who say, 'Sword and famine shall not come upon this land': By sword and famine those prophets shall be consumed. **Rom. 10:15**. And how are they to preach unless they are sent? As it is written, "How beautiful are the feet of those who preach the good news!" **1 Cor. 12:28-29**. And God has appointed in the church first apostles, second prophets, third teachers, then miracles, then gifts of healing, helping, administrating, and various kinds of tongues. Are all apostles? Are all prophets? Are all teachers? Do all work miracles? **1 Tim. 3:10**. And let them also be tested first; then let them serve as deacons if they prove themselves blameless. **1 Tim. 5:22**. Do not be hasty in the laying on of hands, nor take part in the sins of others; keep yourself pure. **1 Tim. 4:14**. Do not neglect the gift you have, which was given you by prophecy when the council of

elders laid their hands on you. **Heb. 5:4**. And no one takes this honor for himself, but only when called by God, just as Aaron was.

Q. 159. How is the Word of God to be preached by those who are called to do so?

A. They who are called to labor in the ministry of the Word are to preach sound doctrine,[1] diligently,[2] in season, and out of season;[3] plainly,[4] not in the enticing words of man's wisdom, but in demonstration of the Spirit, and of power;[5] faithfully,[6] making known the whole counsel of God;[7] wisely,[8] applying themselves to the needs and abilities of the hearers;[9] zealously,[10] with fervent love to God,[11] and the souls of His people;[12] sincerely,[13] aiming at His glory,[14] and their conversion,[15] edification,[16] and salvation.[17]

1 **Titus 2:1, 8**. But as for you, teach what accords with sound doctrine. ...and sound speech that cannot be condemned, so that an opponent may be put to shame, having nothing evil to say about us.

2 **Acts 18:25**. He had been instructed in the way of the Lord. And being fervent in spirit, he spoke and taught accurately the things concerning Jesus, though he knew only the baptism of John.

3 **2 Tim. 4:2**. ...preach the word; be ready in season and out of season; reprove, rebuke, and exhort, with complete patience and teaching.

4 **1 Cor. 14:19**. Nevertheless, in church I would rather speak five words with my mind in order to instruct others, than ten thousand words in a tongue.

5 **1 Cor. 2:4**. ...and my speech and my message were not in plausible words of wisdom, but in demonstration of the Spirit and of power.

6 **Jer. 23:28**. Let the prophet who has a dream tell the dream, but let him who has my word speak my word faithfully. What has straw in common with wheat? declares the LORD. **1 Cor. 4:1-2**. This is how one should regard us, as servants of Christ and stewards of the mysteries of God. Moreover, it is required of stewards that they be found faithful.

7 **Acts 20:27**. ...for I did not shrink from declaring to you the whole counsel of God.

8 **Col. 1:28**. Him we proclaim, warning everyone and teaching everyone with all wisdom, that we may present everyone mature in Christ. **2 Tim. 2:15**. Do your best to present yourself to God as one approved, a worker who has no need to be ashamed, rightly handling the word of truth.

9 **Lk. 12:42**. And the Lord said, "Who then is the faithful and wise manager, whom his master will set over his household, to give them their portion of food at the proper time." **1 Cor. 3:2**. I fed you with milk, not solid food, for you were not ready for it. And even now you are not yet ready. **Heb. 5:12-14**. For though by this time you ought to be teachers, you need someone to teach you again the basic principles of the oracles of God. You need milk, not solid food, for everyone who lives on milk is unskilled in the word of righteousness, since he is a child. But solid food is for the mature, for those who have their powers of discernment trained by constant practice to distinguish good from evil.

10 **Acts 18:25**. He had been instructed in the way of the Lord. And being fervent in spirit, he spoke and taught accurately the things concerning Jesus, though he knew only the baptism of John.

11 **2 Cor. 5:12-14**. We are not commending ourselves to you again but giving you cause to boast about us, so that you may be able to answer those who boast about outward appearance and not about what is in the heart. For if we are beside ourselves, it is for God; if we are in our right mind, it is for you. For the love of Christ controls us, because we have concluded this: that one has died for all, therefore all have died. **Phil. 1:15-17**. Some indeed preach Christ from envy and rivalry, but others from good will. The latter do it out of love, knowing that I am put here for the defense of the gospel. The former proclaim Christ out of selfish ambition, not sincerely but thinking to afflict me in my imprisonment.

12 **2 Cor. 12:15**. I will most gladly spend and be spent for your souls. If I love you more, am I to be loved less? **Col. 4:12**. Epaphras, who is one of you, a servant of Christ Jesus, greets you, always struggling on your behalf in his prayers, that you may stand mature and fully assured in all the will of God.

13 **2 Cor. 2:17**. For we are not, like so many, peddlers of God's word, but as men of sincerity, as commissioned by God, in the sight of God we speak in Christ. **2 Cor. 4:2**. But we have renounced disgraceful, underhanded ways. We refuse to practice cunning or to tamper with God's word, but by the open statement of the truth we would commend ourselves to everyone's conscience in the sight of God.

14 **Jn. 7:18**. The one who speaks on his own authority seeks his own glory; but the one who seeks the glory of him who sent him is true, and in him there is no falsehood. **1 Thess. 2:4-6**. ...but just as we have been approved by God to be entrusted with the gospel, so we speak, not to please man, but to please God who tests our hearts. For we never came with words of flattery, as you know, nor with a pretext for greed—God is witness. Nor did we seek glory from people, whether from you or from others, though we could have made demands as apostles of Christ.

15 **1 Cor. 9:19-22**. For though I am free from all, I have made myself a servant to all, that I might win more of them. To the Jews I became as a Jew, in order to win Jews. To those under the law I became as one under the law (though not being myself under the law) that I might win those under the law. To those outside the law I became as one outside the law (not being outside the law of God but under the law of Christ) that I might win those outside the law. To the weak I became weak, that I might win the weak. I have become all things to all people, that by all means I might save some.

16 **2 Cor. 12:19**. Have you been thinking all along that we have been defending ourselves to you? It is in the sight of God that we have been speaking in Christ, and all for your upbuilding, beloved. **Eph. 4:12**. ...to equip the saints for the work of ministry, for building up the body of Christ.

17 **Acts 26:16-18**. 'But rise and stand upon your feet, for I have appeared to you for this purpose, to appoint you as a servant and witness to the things in which you have seen me and to those in which I will appear to you, delivering you from your people and from the Gentiles—to whom I am sending you to open their eyes, so that they may turn from darkness to light and from the power of Satan to God, that they may receive forgiveness of sins and a place among those who are sanctified by faith in me.' **1 Tim. 4:16**. Keep a close watch on yourself and on the teaching. Persist in this, for by so doing you will save both yourself and your hearers.

Q. 160. What is required of those who hear the Word preached?

A. It is required of those who hear the Word preached, that they attend to it with diligence,[1] preparation,[2] and prayer;[3] examine what they hear by the Scriptures;[4] receive the truth with faith,[5] love,[6] meekness,[7] and readiness of mind,[8] as the Word of God;[9] meditate,[10] and discuss it;[11] hide it in their hearts,[12] and bring forth the fruit of it in their lives.[13]

1 **Prov. 8:34**. Blessed is the one who listens to me, watching daily at my gates, waiting beside my doors.

2 **Lk. 8:18**. "Take care then how you hear, for to the one who has, more will be given, and from the one who has not, even what he thinks that he has will be taken away." **1 Pet. 2:1-2**. So put away all malice and all deceit and hypocrisy and envy and all slander. Like newborn infants, long for the pure spiritual milk, that by it you may grow up into salvation.

3 **Ps. 119:18**. Open my eyes, that I may behold wondrous things out of your law. **Eph. 6:18-19**. ...praying at all times in the Spirit, with all prayer and supplication. To that end keep alert with all perseverance, making supplication for all the saints, and also for me, that words may be given to me in opening my mouth boldly to proclaim the mystery of the gospel.

4 **Acts 17:11**. Now these Jews were more noble than those in Thessalonica; they received the word with all eagerness, examining the Scriptures daily to see if these things were so.

5 **Heb. 4:2**. For good news came to us just as to them, but the message they heard did not benefit them, because they were not united by faith with those who listened.

6 **2 Thess. 2:10**. ...and with all wicked deception for those who are perishing, because they refused to love the truth and so be saved.

7 **Jas. 1:21**. Therefore put away all filthiness and rampant wickedness and receive with meekness the implanted word, which is able to save your souls.

8 **Acts 17:11**. Now these Jews were more noble than those in Thessalonica; they received the word with all eagerness, examining the Scriptures daily to see if these things were so.

9 **1 Thess. 2:13**. And we also thank God constantly for this, that when you received the word of God, which you heard from us, you accepted it not as the word of men but as what it really is, the word of God, which is at work in you believers.

10 **Lk. 9:44**. "Let these words sink into your ears: The Son of Man is about to be delivered into the hands of men." **Heb. 2:1**. Therefore we must pay much closer attention to what we have heard, lest we drift away from it.

11 **Deut. 6:6-7**. And these words that I command you today shall be on your heart. You shall teach them diligently to your children, and shall talk of them when you sit in your house, and when you walk by the way, and when you lie down, and when you rise. **Lk. 24:14**. ...and they were talking with each other about all these things that had happened.

12 **Ps. 119:11**. I have stored up your word in my heart, that I might not sin against you. **Prov. 2:1**. My son, if you receive my words and treasure up my commandments with you.

13 **Lk. 8:15**. As for that in the good soil, they are those who, hearing the word, hold it fast in an honest and good heart, and bear fruit with patience. **Jas. 1:25**. But the one who looks into the perfect law, the law of liberty, and perseveres, being no hearer who forgets but a doer who acts, he will be blessed in his doing.

Q. 161. How do the sacraments become effectual means of salvation?

A. The sacraments become effectual means of salvation, not by any power in them or any virtue derived from the piety or intention of him by whom they are administered; but only by the working of the Holy Spirit, and the blessing of Christ by whom they are instituted.[1]

1 **ACTS 8:13, 23**. Even Simon himself believed, and after being baptized he continued with Philip. And seeing signs and great miracles performed, he was amazed. ... "For I see that you are in the gall of bitterness and in the bond of iniquity." **1 COR. 3:6-7**. I planted, Apollos watered, but God gave the growth. So neither he who plants nor he who waters is anything, but only God who gives the growth. **1 COR. 12:13**. For in one Spirit we were all baptized into one body—Jews or Greeks, slaves or free—and all were made to drink of one Spirit. **1 PET. 3:21**. Baptism, which corresponds to this, now saves you, not as a removal of dirt from the body but as an appeal to God for a good conscience, through the resurrection of Jesus Christ.

Q. 162. What is a sacrament?

A. A sacrament is a holy ordinance instituted by Christ in His church,[1] to signify, seal and exhibit[2] to those who are within the Covenant of Grace,[3] the benefits of His mediation;[4] to strengthen and increase their faith and all other graces;[5] to oblige them to obedience;[6] to testify and cherish their love and communion with one another,[7] and to distinguish them from those who are outside the Covenant of Grace.[8]

1 **Gen. 17:7, 10.** And I will establish my covenant between me and you and your offspring after you throughout their generations for an everlasting covenant, to be God to you and to your offspring after you. ... This is my covenant, which you shall keep, between me and you and your offspring after you: Every male among you shall be circumcised. See **Ex. 12. Mt. 26:26-28.** Now as they were eating, Jesus took bread, and after blessing it broke it and gave it to the disciples, and said, "Take, eat; this is my body." And he took a cup, and when he had given thanks he gave it to them, saying, "Drink of it, all of you, for this is my blood of the covenant, which is poured out for many for the forgiveness of sins. **Mt. 28:19.** Go therefore and make disciples of all nations, baptizing them in the name of the Father and of the Son and of the Holy Spirit.

2 **Rom. 4:11.** He received the sign of circumcision as a seal of the righteousness that he had by faith while he was still uncircumcised. The purpose was to make him the father of all who believe without being circumcised, so that righteousness would be counted to them as well. **1 Cor. 11:24-25.** ...and when he had given thanks, he broke it, and said, "This is my body which is for you. Do this in remembrance of me." In the same way also he took the cup, after supper, saying, "This cup is the new covenant in my blood. Do this, as often as you drink it, in remembrance of me."

3 **Ex. 12:48.** If a stranger shall sojourn with you and would keep the Passover to the LORD, let all his males be circumcised. Then he may come near and keep it; he shall be as a native of the land. But no uncircumcised person shall eat of it. **Rom. 15:8.** For I tell you that Christ became a servant to the circumcised to show God's truthfulness, in order to confirm the promises given to the patriarchs.

4 **Acts 2:38.** And Peter said to them, "Repent and be baptized every one of you in the name of Jesus Christ for the forgiveness of your sins, and you will receive the gift of the Holy Spirit." **1 Cor. 10:16.** The cup of blessing that we bless, is it not a participation in the blood of Christ? The bread that we break, is it not a participation in the body of Christ?

5 **Rom. 4:11.** He received the sign of circumcision as a seal of the righteousness that he had by faith while he was still uncircumcised. The purpose was to make him the father of all who believe without being circumcised, so that righteousness would be counted to them as well. **Gal. 3:27.** For as many of you as were baptized into Christ have put on Christ.

6 **Rom. 6:3-4.** Do you not know that all of us who have been baptized into Christ Jesus were baptized into his death? We were buried therefore with him by baptism into death, in order that, just as Christ was raised from the dead by the glory of the Father, we too might walk in newness of life." **1 Cor. 10:21.** You cannot drink the cup of the Lord and the cup of demons. You cannot partake of the table of the Lord and the table of demons.

7 **1 Cor. 12:13**. For in one Spirit we were all baptized into one body—Jews or Greeks, slaves or free—and all were made to drink of one Spirit. **Eph. 4:2-5**. ... with all humility and gentleness, with patience, bearing with one another in love, eager to maintain the unity of the Spirit in the bond of peace. There is one body and one Spirit—just as you were called to the one hope that belongs to your call—one Lord, one faith, one baptism.

8 **Gen. 34:14**. They said to them, "We cannot do this thing, to give our sister to one who is uncircumcised, for that would be a disgrace to us. **Eph. 2:11-12.** Therefore remember that at one time you Gentiles in the flesh, called "the uncircumcision" by what is called the circumcision, which is made in the flesh by hands— remember that you were at that time separated from Christ, alienated from the commonwealth of Israel and strangers to the covenants of promise, having no hope and without God in the world.

Q. 163. What are the parts of a sacrament?

A. The parts of a sacrament are two: the one, an outward and perceptible sign used according to Christ's own direction; the other, an inward and spiritual grace signified by it.[1]

1 **Mt. 3:11**. "I baptize you with water for repentance, but he who is coming after me is mightier than I, whose sandals I am not worthy to carry. He will baptize you with the Holy Spirit and fire." **Rom. 2:28-29**. For no one is a Jew who is merely one outwardly, nor is circumcision outward and physical. But a Jew is one inwardly, and circumcision is a matter of the heart, by the Spirit, not by the letter. His praise is not from man but from God. **1 Pet. 3:21**. Baptism, which corresponds to this, now saves you, not as a removal of dirt from the body but as an appeal to God for a good conscience, through the resurrection of Jesus Christ.

Q. 164. How many sacraments has Christ instituted under the New Testament?

A. Under the New Testament, Christ has instituted in His church only two sacraments, Baptism, and the Lord's Supper.[1]

1 See **Mt. 26**. See **Mt. 27**. See **Mt. 28**. **Mt. 28:19.** Go therefore and make disciples of all nations, baptizing them in the name of the Father and of the Son and of the Holy Spirit. **1 Cor. 11:20, 23**. When you come together, it is not the Lord's supper that you eat. ... For I received from the Lord what I also delivered to you, that the Lord Jesus on the night when he was betrayed took bread.

Q. 165. What is Baptism?

A. Baptism is a sacrament of the New Testament, in which Christ has ordained the washing with water in the name of the Father, and of the Son, and of the Holy Spirit,[1] to be a sign and seal of ingrafting to Himself,[2] of remission of sins by His blood,[3] and regeneration by His Spirit;[4] of adoption,[5] and resurrection to everlasting life:[6] and by which the parties baptized are solemnly admitted into the visible church,[7] and enter an open and professed engagement to be wholly and only the Lord's.[8]

1 **Mt. 28:19**. Go therefore and make disciples of all nations, baptizing them in the name of the Father and of the Son and of the Holy Spirit.

2 **Gal. 3:27**. For as many of you as were baptized into Christ have put on Christ.

3 **Mk. 1:4**. John appeared, baptizing in the wilderness and proclaiming a baptism of repentance for the forgiveness of sins. **Rev. 1:5**. ...and from Jesus Christ the faithful witness, the firstborn of the dead, and the ruler of kings on earth. To him who loves us and has freed us from our sins by his blood.

4 **Eph. 5:26**. ...that he might sanctify her, having cleansed her by the washing of water with the word. **Titus 3:5**. ...he saved us, not because of works done by us in righteousness, but according to his own mercy, by the washing of regeneration and renewal of the Holy Spirit.

5 **Gal. 3:26-27**. ...for in Christ Jesus you are all sons of God, through faith. For as many of you as were baptized into Christ have put on Christ.

6 **Rom. 6:5**. For if we have been united with him in a death like his, we shall certainly be united with him in a resurrection like his. **1 Cor. 15:29**. Otherwise, what do people mean by being baptized on behalf of the dead? If the dead are not raised at all, why are people baptized on their behalf?

7 **1 Cor. 12:13**. For in one Spirit we were all baptized into one body—Jews or Greeks, slaves or free—and all were made to drink of one Spirit.

8 **Rom. 6:4**. We were buried therefore with him by baptism into death, in order that, just as Christ was raised from the dead by the glory of the Father, we too might walk in newness of life.

Q. 166. To whom is Baptism to be administered?

A. Baptism is not to be administered to any who are out of the visible church, and so strangers from the Covenant of Promise, till they profess their faith in Christ, and obedience to Him;[1] but infants descending from parents, either both or but one of them, professing faith in Christ, and obedience to Him, are, in that respect, within the covenant, and are to be baptized.[2]

1 **Acts 2:38**. And Peter said to them, "Repent and be baptized every one of you in the name of Jesus Christ for the forgiveness of your sins, and you will receive the gift of the Holy Spirit." **Acts 8:36-37**. And as they were going along the road they came to some water, and the eunuch said, "See, here is water! What prevents me from being baptized?"

2 **Gen. 17:7, 9**. And I will establish my covenant between me and you and your offspring after you throughout their generations for an everlasting covenant, to be God to you and to your offspring after you. ... And God said to Abraham, "As for you, you shall keep my covenant, you and your offspring after you throughout their generations." **Mt. 28:19**. Go therefore and make disciples of all nations, baptizing them in the name of the Father and of the Son and of the Holy Spirit. **Lk. 18:15-16**. Now they were bringing even infants to him that he might touch them. And when the disciples saw it, they rebuked them. But Jesus called them to

him, saying, "Let the children come to me, and do not hinder them, for to such belongs the kingdom of God." **Acts 2:38-39**. And Peter said to them, "Repent and be baptized every one of you in the name of Jesus Christ for the forgiveness of your sins, and you will receive the gift of the Holy Spirit. For the promise is for you and for your children and for all who are far off, everyone whom the Lord our God calls to himself." **Rom. 4:11-12**. He received the sign of circumcision as a seal of the righteousness that he had by faith while he was still uncircumcised. The purpose was to make him the father of all who believe without being circumcised, so that righteousness would be counted to them as well, and to make him the father of the circumcised who are not merely circumcised but who also walk in the footsteps of the faith that our father Abraham had before he was circumcised. **Rom. 11:16**. If the dough offered as firstfruits is holy, so is the whole lump, and if the root is holy, so are the branches. **1 Cor. 7:14**. For the unbelieving husband is made holy because of his wife, and the unbelieving wife is made holy because of her husband. Otherwise your children would be unclean, but as it is, they are holy. **Gal. 3:9**. So then, those who are of faith are blessed along with Abraham, the man of faith. **Col. 2:11-12**. In him also you were circumcised with a circumcision made without hands, by putting off the body of the flesh, by the circumcision of Christ, having been buried with him in baptism, in which you were also raised with him through faith in the powerful working of God, who raised him from the dead.

Q. 167. How is our Baptism to be improved by us?

A. The needful but much neglected duty of improving our Baptism, is to be performed by us all of our lives, especially in the time of temptation, and when we are present at the administration of it to others,[1] by serious and thankful consideration of the nature of it and of the ends for which Christ instituted it, the privileges and benefits conferred and sealed by it, and our solemn vow made in it;[2] by being humbled for our sinful corruption, our falling short of, and walking contrary to, the grace of Baptism and our engagements;[3] by growing up to assurance of pardon of sin, and of all other blessings sealed to us in that sacrament;[4] by drawing strength from the death and resurrection of Christ, into whom we are baptized, for the dying to sin, and being made alive in grace;[5] and by endeavoring to live by faith,[6] to have our conversation in holiness and righteousness,[7] as those who have thus given up their names to Christ,[8] and to walk in brotherly love, as being baptized by the same Spirit into one body.[9]

1 **Rom. 6:4, 6, 11**. We were buried therefore with him by baptism into death, in order that, just as Christ was raised from the dead by the glory of the Father, we too might walk in newness of life. ... We know that our old self was crucified with him in order that the body of sin might be brought to nothing, so that we would no longer be enslaved to sin. ... So you also must consider yourselves dead to sin and alive to God in Christ Jesus. **Col. 2:11-12**. In him also you were circumcised with a circumcision made without hands, by putting off the body of the flesh, by the

circumcision of Christ, having been buried with him in baptism, in which you were also raised with him through faith in the powerful working of God, who raised him from the dead.

2 **Rom. 6:3-5.** Do you not know that all of us who have been baptized into Christ Jesus were baptized into his death? We were buried therefore with him by baptism into death, in order that, just as Christ was raised from the dead by the glory of the Father, we too might walk in newness of life. For if we have been united with him in a death like his, we shall certainly be united with him in a resurrection like his.

3 **Rom. 6:2-3**. By no means! How can we who died to sin still live in it? Do you not know that all of us who have been baptized into Christ Jesus were baptized into his death? **1 Cor. 1:11-13**. For it has been reported to me by Chloe's people that there is quarreling among you, my brothers. What I mean is that each one of you says, "I follow Paul," or "I follow Apollos," or "I follow Cephas," or "I follow Christ." Is Christ divided? Was Paul crucified for you? Or were you baptized in the name of Paul?

4 **Rom. 4:11-12**. He received the sign of circumcision as a seal of the righteousness that he had by faith while he was still uncircumcised. The purpose was to make him the father of all who believe without being circumcised, so that righteousness would be counted to them as well, and to make him the father of the circumcised who are not merely circumcised but who also walk in the footsteps of the faith that our father Abraham had before he was circumcised. **1 Pet. 3:21**. Baptism, which corresponds to this, now saves you, not as a removal of dirt from the body but as an appeal to God for a good conscience, through the resurrection of Jesus Christ.

5 **Rom. 6:3-5**. Do you not know that all of us who have been baptized into Christ Jesus were baptized into his death? We were buried therefore with him by baptism into death, in order that, just as Christ was raised from the dead by the glory of the Father, we too might walk in newness of life. For if we have been united with him in a death like his, we shall certainly be united with him in a resurrection like his.

6 **Gal. 3:26-27**. ...for in Christ Jesus you are all sons of God, through faith. For as many of you as were baptized into Christ have put on Christ.

7 **Rom. 6:22**. But now that you have been set free from sin and have become slaves of God, the fruit you get leads to sanctification and its end, eternal life.

8 **Acts 2:38**. And Peter said to them, "Repent and be baptized every one of you in the name of Jesus Christ for the forgiveness of your sins, and you will receive the gift of the Holy Spirit."

9 **1 Cor. 12:13, 25.** For in one Spirit we were all baptized into one body—Jews or Greeks, slaves or free—and all were made to drink of one Spirit. ...that there may be no division in the body, but that the members may have the same care for one another.

Q. 168. What is the Lord's Supper?

A. The Lord's Supper is a sacrament of the New Testament,[1] in which by giving and receiving bread and wine according to the direction of Jesus Christ, His death is shown forth; and they that worthily communicate, feed upon His body and blood to their spiritual nourishment and growth in grace;[2] have their union and communion with Him confirmed;[3] testify and renew their thankfulness[4] and engagement to God,[5] and their mutual love and fellowship with each other, as members of the same mystical body.[6]

1 **Lk. 22:20**. And likewise the cup after they had eaten, saying, "This cup that is poured out for you is the new covenant in my blood."

2 **Mt. 26:26-28**. Now as they were eating, Jesus took bread, and after blessing it broke it and gave it to the disciples, and said, "Take, eat; this is my body." And he took a cup, and when he had given thanks he gave it to them, saying, "Drink of it, all of you, for this is my blood of the covenant, which is poured out for many for the forgiveness of sins." **1 Cor. 11:23-26**. For I received from the Lord what I also delivered to you, that the Lord Jesus on the night when he was betrayed took bread, and when he had given thanks, he broke it, and said, "This is my body which is for you. Do this in remembrance of me." In the same way also he took the cup, after supper, saying, "This cup is the new covenant in my blood. Do this, as often as you drink it, in remembrance of me." For as often as you eat this bread and drink the cup, you proclaim the Lord's death until he comes.

3 **1 Cor. 10:16**. The cup of blessing that we bless, is it not a participation in the blood of Christ? The bread that we break, is it not a participation in the body of Christ?

4 **1 Cor. 11:24**. ...and when he had given thanks, he broke it, and said, "This is my body which is for you. Do this in remembrance of me."

5 **1 Cor. 10:14-16, 21**. Therefore, my beloved, flee from idolatry. I speak as to sensible people; judge for yourselves what I say. The cup of blessing that we bless, is it not a participation in the blood of Christ? The bread that we break, is it not a participation in the body of Christ? ... You cannot drink the cup of the Lord and the cup of demons. You cannot partake of the table of the Lord and the table of demons.

6 **1 Cor. 10:17**. Because there is one bread, we who are many are one body, for we all partake of the one bread.

Q. 169. How has Christ appointed bread and wine to be given and received in the sacrament of the Lord's Supper?

A. Christ has appointed the ministers of His Word in the administration of this sacrament of the Lord's Supper, to set apart the bread and wine from common use by the words of institution, thanksgiving, and prayer; to take and break the bread, and to give both the bread and the wine to the communicants; who are by the same direction to take and eat the bread, and to drink the wine; in thankful remembrance that the body of Christ was broken and given, and His blood shed for them.[1]

1 **Mt. 26:26-28**. Now as they were eating, Jesus took bread, and after blessing it broke it and gave it to the disciples, and said, "Take, eat; this is my body." And he took a cup, and when he had given thanks he gave it to them, saying, "Drink of it, all of you, for this is my blood of the covenant, which is poured out for many for the forgiveness of sins." **Mk 14:22-24**. And as they were eating, he took bread, and after blessing it broke it and gave it to them, and said, "Take; this is my body." And he took a cup, and when he had given thanks he gave it to them, and they all drank of it. And he said to them, "This is my blood of the covenant, which is

poured out for many." **Lk. 22:19-20**. And he took bread, and when he had given thanks, he broke it and gave it to them, saying, "This is my body, which is given for you. Do this in remembrance of me." And likewise the cup after they had eaten, saying, "This cup that is poured out for you is the new covenant in my blood." **1 Cor. 11:23-24**. For I received from the Lord what I also delivered to you, that the Lord Jesus on the night when he was betrayed took bread, and when he had given thanks, he broke it, and said, "This is my body which is for you. Do this in remembrance of me."

Q. 170. How do they who worthily communicate in the Lord's Supper feed upon the body and blood of Christ in it?

A. As the body and the blood of Christ are not corporally or carnally present in, with, or under the bread and wine in the Lord's Supper;[1] and yet are spiritually present to the faith of the receiver, no less truly and really than the elements themselves are to their outward senses;[2] so they who worthily communicate in the sacrament of the Lord's Supper, do in it feed upon the body and blood of Christ, not after a corporal or carnal, but in a spiritual manner; yet truly and really,[3] while by faith they receive and apply to themselves Christ crucified, and all the benefits of His death.[4]

1 **Acts 3:21**. ...whom heaven must receive until the time for restoring all the things about which God spoke by the mouth of his holy prophets long ago.

2 **Mt. 26:26, 28**. Now as they were eating, Jesus took bread, and after blessing it broke it and gave it to the disciples, and said, "Take, eat; this is my body." ...for this is my blood of the covenant, which is poured out for many for the forgiveness of sins.

3 **1 Cor. 11:24-29**. ...and when he had given thanks, he broke it, and said, "This is my body which is for you. Do this in remembrance of me." In the same way also he took the cup, after supper, saying, "This cup is the new covenant in my blood. Do this, as often as you drink it, in remembrance of me." For as often as you eat this bread and drink the cup, you proclaim the Lord's death until he comes. Whoever, therefore, eats the bread or drinks the cup of the Lord in an unworthy manner will be guilty concerning the body and blood of the Lord. Let a person examine himself, then, and so eat of the bread and drink of the cup. For anyone who eats and drinks without discerning the body eats and drinks judgment on himself.

4 **1 Cor. 10:16**. The cup of blessing that we bless, is it not a participation in the blood of Christ? The bread that we break, is it not a participation in the body of Christ?

Q. 171. How are they who receive the sacrament of the Lord's Supper to prepare themselves before they come to it?

A. They who receive the sacrament of the Lord's Supper are, before they come, to prepare themselves for it; by examining themselves,[1] of their being in Christ,[2] of their sins and wants;[3] of the truth and measure of their knowledge,[4] faith,[5] repentance,[6] love to God and the brothers,[7] charity to all men,[8] forgiving those who have done them wrong;[9] of their desires after Christ,[10] and of their new obedience;[11] and by renewing the exercise of these graces,[12] by serious meditation,[13] and fervent prayer.[14]

1 **1 Cor. 11:28**. Let a person examine himself, then, and so eat of the bread and drink of the cup.

2 **1 Cor. 13:5**. ...or rude. It does not insist on its own way; it is not irritable or resentful.

3 **Ex. 12:15**. Seven days you shall eat unleavened bread. On the first day you shall remove leaven out of your houses, for if anyone eats what is leavened, from the first day until the seventh day, that person shall be cut off from Israel. **1 Cor. 5:7**. Cleanse out the old leaven that you may be a new lump, as you really are unleavened. For Christ, our Passover lamb, has been sacrificed.

4 **1 Cor. 11:29**. For anyone who eats and drinks without discerning the body eats and drinks judgment on himself.

5 **Mt. 26:28**. ...for this is my blood of the covenant, which is poured out for many for the forgiveness of sins. **1 Cor. 13:5**. ...or rude. It does not insist on its own way; it is not irritable or resentful.

6 **Zech. 12:10**. "And I will pour out on the house of David and the inhabitants of Jerusalem a spirit of grace and pleas for mercy, so that, when they look on me, on him whom they have pierced, they shall mourn for him, as one mourns for an only child, and weep bitterly over him, as one weeps over a firstborn." **1 Cor. 11:31**. But if we judged ourselves truly, we would not be judged.

7 **Acts 2:46-47**. And day by day, attending the temple together and breaking bread in their homes, they received their food with glad and generous hearts, praising God and having favor with all the people. And the Lord added to their number day by day those who were being saved. **1 Cor. 11:31**. But if we judged ourselves truly, we would not be judged.

8 **1 Cor. 5:8**. Let us therefore celebrate the festival, not with the old leaven, the leaven of malice and evil, but with the unleavened bread of sincerity and truth. **1 Cor. 11:18, 20**. For, in the first place, when you come together as a church, I hear that there are divisions among you. And I believe it in part. ... When you come together, it is not the Lord's supper that you eat.

9 **Mt. 5:23-24**. So if you are offering your gift at the altar and there remember that your brother has something against you, leave your gift there before the altar and go. First be reconciled to your brother, and then come and offer your gift.

10 **Isa. 55:1**. "Come, everyone who thirsts, come to the waters; and he who has no money, come, buy and eat! Come, buy wine and milk without money and without price. **Jn. 7:37**. On the last day of the feast, the great day, Jesus stood up and cried out, "If anyone thirsts, let him come to me and drink.

11 **1 Cor. 5:7-8**. Cleanse out the old leaven that you may be a new lump, as you really are unleavened. For Christ, our Passover lamb, has been sacrificed. Let us therefore celebrate the festival, not with the old leaven, the leaven of malice and evil, but with the unleavened bread of sincerity and truth.

12 **Ps. 26:6**. I wash my hands in innocence and go around your altar, O LORD, **1 Cor. 11:25-26, 28**. In the same way also he took the cup, after supper, saying, "This cup is the new covenant in my blood. Do this, as often as you drink it, in

remembrance of me." For as often as you eat this bread and drink the cup, you proclaim the Lord's death until he comes. ... Let a person examine himself, then, and so eat of the bread and drink of the cup. **Heb. 10:21-22, 24.** ...and since we have a great priest over the house of God, let us draw near with a true heart in full assurance of faith, with our hearts sprinkled clean from an evil conscience and our bodies washed with pure water. ... And let us consider how to stir up one another to love and good works

13 **1 Cor. 11:24-25.** ...and when he had given thanks, he broke it, and said, "This is my body which is for you. Do this in remembrance of me." In the same way also he took the cup, after supper, saying, "This cup is the new covenant in my blood. Do this, as often as you drink it, in remembrance of me."

14 **2 Chr. 30:18-19.** For a majority of the people, many of them from Ephraim, Manasseh, Issachar, and Zebulun, had not cleansed themselves, yet they ate the Passover otherwise than as prescribed. For Hezekiah had prayed for them, saying, "May the good LORD pardon everyone who sets his heart to seek God, the LORD, the God of his fathers, even though not according to the sanctuary's rules of cleanness." **Mt. 26:26.** Now as they were eating, Jesus took bread, and after blessing it broke it and gave it to the disciples, and said, "Take, eat; this is my body."

Q. 172. May one who doubts of his being in Christ, or of his due preparation, come to the Lord's Supper?

A. One who doubts of his being in Christ, or of his due preparation for the sacrament of the Lord's Supper, may have true interest in Christ, though he is not yet assured of it;[1] and in God's account has it, if he is duly affected with the fear of the want of it,[2] and truly desires to be found in Christ,[3] and to depart from iniquity;[4] in which case (because promises are made, and this sacrament is appointed, for the relief even of weak and doubting Christians)[5] he is to grieve his unbelief,[6] and labor to have his doubts resolved;[7] and so doing, he may and ought to come to the Lord's Supper, that he may be further strengthened.[8]

1 **Ps. 77:1-4, 7-10.** I cry aloud to God, aloud to God, and he will hear me. In the day of my trouble I seek the Lord; in the night my hand is stretched out without wearying; my soul refuses to be comforted. When I remember God, I moan; when I meditate, my spirit faints. You hold my eyelids open; I am so troubled that I cannot speak. ... "Will the Lord spurn forever, and never again be favorable? Has his steadfast love forever ceased? Are his promises at an end for all time? Has God forgotten to be gracious? Has he in anger shut up his compassion?" Then I said, "I will appeal to this, to the years of the right hand of the Most High." **Ps. 88.** O LORD, God of my salvation; I cry out day and night before you. Let my prayer come before you; incline your ear to my cry! For my soul is full of troubles, and my life draws near to Sheol. I am counted among those who go down to the pit; I am a man who has no strength, like one set loose among the dead, like the slain that lie in the grave, like those whom you remember no more, for they are cut off from your hand. You have put me in the depths of the pit, in the regions dark and deep. Your wrath lies heavy upon me, and you overwhelm me with all your waves. You have caused my companions to shun me; you have made me a horror to them. I

am shut in so that I cannot escape; my eye grows dim through sorrow. Every day I call upon you, O LORD; I spread out my hands to you. Do you work wonders for the dead? Do the departed rise up to praise you? Is your steadfast love declared in the grave, or your faithfulness in Abaddon? Are your wonders known in the darkness, or your righteousness in the land of forgetfulness? But I, O LORD, cry to you; in the morning my prayer comes before you. O LORD, why do you cast my soul away? Why do you hide your face from me? Afflicted and close to death from my youth up, I suffer your terrors; I am helpless. Your wrath has swept over me; your dreadful assaults destroy me. They surround me like a flood all day long; they close in on me together. You have caused my beloved and my friend to shun me; my companions have become darkness. **Isa. 50:10**. Who among you fears the LORD and obeys the voice of his servant? Let him who walks in darkness and has no light trust in the name of the LORD and rely on his God. **Jn. 2:4**. And Jesus said to her, "Woman, what does this have to do with me? My hour has not yet come." **1 Jn. 5:13**. I write these things to you who believe in the name of the Son of God that you may know that you have eternal life.

2 **Ps. 31:22**. I had said in my alarm, "I am cut off from your sight." But you heard the voice of my pleas for mercy when I cried to you for help. **Ps. 73:13, 22-23**. All in vain have I kept my heart clean and washed my hands in innocence. ... I was brutish and ignorant; I was like a beast toward you. Nevertheless, I am continually with you; you hold my right hand. **Isa. 54:7-10**. For a brief moment I deserted you, but with great compassion I will gather you. In overflowing anger for a moment I hid my face from you, but with everlasting love I will have compassion on you," says the LORD, your Redeemer. "This is like the days of Noah to me: as I swore that the waters of Noah should no more go over the earth, so I have sworn that I will not be angry with you, and will not rebuke you. For the mountains may depart and the hills be removed, but my steadfast love shall not depart from you, and my covenant of peace shall not be removed," says the LORD, who has compassion on you. **Mt. 5:3-4**. "Blessed are the poor in spirit, for theirs is the kingdom of heaven. Blessed are those who mourn, for they shall be comforted."

3 **Ps. 10:17**. O LORD, you hear the desire of the afflicted; you will strengthen their heart; you will incline your ear. **Ps. 42:1-2, 5**. As a deer pants for flowing streams, so pants my soul for you, O God. My soul thirsts for God, for the living God. When shall I come and appear before God? ... Why are you cast down, O my soul, and why are you in turmoil within me? Hope in God; for I shall again praise him, my salvation. **Phil. 3:8-9**. Indeed, I count everything as loss because of the surpassing worth of knowing Christ Jesus my Lord. For his sake I have suffered the loss of all things and count them as rubbish, in order that I may gain Christ and be found in him, not having a righteousness of my own that comes from the law, but that which comes through faith in Christ, the righteousness from God that depends on faith.

4 **Ps. 66:18-20**. If I had cherished iniquity in my heart, the Lord would not have listened. But truly God has listened; he has attended to the voice of my prayer. Blessed be God, because he has not rejected my prayer or removed his steadfast love from me! **Isa. 50:10**. Who among you fears the LORD and obeys the voice of his servant? Let him who walks in darkness and has no light trust in the name of the LORD and rely on his God. **2 Tim. 2:19**. But God's firm foundation stands, bearing this seal: "The Lord knows those who are his," and, "Let everyone who names the name of the Lord depart from iniquity."

5 **Isa. 40:11, 29, 31**. He will tend his flock like a shepherd; he will gather the lambs in his arms; he will carry them in his bosom, and gently lead those that are with young. ... He gives power to the faint, and to him who has no might he increases strength. ...but they who wait for the LORD shall renew their strength; they shall mount up with wings like eagles; they shall run and not be weary; they shall walk

and not faint. **Mt. 11:28**. Come to me, all who labor and are heavy laden, and I will give you rest. **Mt. 12:20.** ...a bruised reed he will not break, and a smoldering wick he will not quench, until he brings justice to victory. **Mt. 26:28**. ...for this is my blood of the covenant, which is poured out for many for the forgiveness of sins.

6 **Mk. 9:24**. Immediately the father of the child cried out and said, "I believe; help my unbelief!"

7 **Acts 2:37**. Now when they heard this they were cut to the heart, and said to Peter and the rest of the apostles, "Brothers, what shall we do?" **Acts 16:30**. Then he brought them out and said, "Sirs, what must I do to be saved?"

8 **Rom. 4:11**. He received the sign of circumcision as a seal of the righteousness that he had by faith while he was still uncircumcised. The purpose was to make him the father of all who believe without being circumcised, so that righteousness would be counted to them as well. **1 Cor. 11:28**. Let a person examine himself, then, and so eat of the bread and drink of the cup.

Q. 173. May any who profess the faith, and desire to come to the Lord's Supper, be kept from it?

A. Those who are found to be ignorant or scandalous, notwithstanding their profession of the faith, and desire to come to the Lord's Supper, may and ought to be kept from that sacrament by the power that Christ has left in His church,[1] until they receive instruction, and demonstrate their reformation.[2]

1 **Mt. 7:6**. "Do not give dogs what is holy, and do not throw your pearls before pigs, lest they trample them underfoot and turn to attack you." See **1 Cor. 5** to the end. **1 Cor. 11:27-31**. Whoever, therefore, eats the bread or drinks the cup of the Lord in an unworthy manner will be guilty concerning the body and blood of the Lord. Let a person examine himself, then, and so eat of the bread and drink of the cup. For anyone who eats and drinks without discerning the body eats and drinks judgment on himself. That is why many of you are weak and ill, and some have died. But if we judged ourselves truly, we would not be judged. **1 Tim. 5:22**. Do not be hasty in the laying on of hands, nor take part in the sins of others; keep yourself pure.

2 **2 Cor. 2:7**. ...so you should rather turn to forgive and comfort him, or he may be overwhelmed by excessive sorrow.

Q. 174. What is required of those who receive the sacrament of the Lord's Supper in the time of the administration of it?

A. It is required of those who receive the sacrament of the Lord's Supper that, during the time of the administration of it, with all holy reverence and attention, they wait upon God in that ordinance;[1] diligently observe the sacramental elements and actions;[2] heedfully discern the Lord's body,[3] and affectionately meditate on His death and sufferings,[4] and thereby stir up themselves to a vigorous exercise of their graces;[5] in judging themselves,[6] and sorrowing for sin;[7] in earnest hungering and thirsting after Christ,[8] feeding on Him by faith,[9] receiving of His fullness,[10] trusting in His merits,[11] rejoicing in His love,[12] giving thanks for His grace;[13] in renewing of their covenant with God,[14] and love to all the saints.[15]

1 **Lev. 10:3**. Then Moses said to Aaron, "This is what the LORD has said: 'Among those who are near me I will be sanctified, and before all the people I will be glorified.'" And Aaron held his peace. **Ps. 5:7**. But I, through the abundance of your steadfast love, will enter your house. I will bow down toward your holy temple in the fear of you. **1 Cor. 11:17, 26-27**. But in the following instructions I do not commend you, because when you come together it is not for the better but for the worse. ... For as often as you eat this bread and drink the cup, you proclaim the Lord's death until he comes. Whoever, therefore, eats the bread or drinks the cup of the Lord in an unworthy manner will be guilty concerning the body and blood of the Lord. **Heb. 12:28**. Therefore let us be grateful for receiving a kingdom that cannot be shaken, and thus let us offer to God acceptable worship, with reverence and awe.

2 **Ex. 24:8**. And Moses took the blood and threw it on the people and said, "Behold the blood of the covenant that the LORD has made with you in accordance with all these words." **Mt. 26:28**. ...for this is my blood of the covenant, which is poured out for many for the forgiveness of sins.

3 **1 Cor. 11:29**. For anyone who eats and drinks without discerning the body eats and drinks judgment on himself.

4 **Lk. 22:29**. ...and I assign to you, as my Father assigned to me, a kingdom.

5 **1 Cor. 10:3-5, 11, 14**. ...and all ate the same spiritual food, and all drank the same spiritual drink. For they drank from the spiritual Rock that followed them, and the Rock was Christ. Nevertheless, with most of them God was not pleased, for they were overthrown in the wilderness. ... Now these things happened to them as an example, but they were written down for our instruction, on whom the end of the ages has come. ... Therefore, my beloved, flee from idolatry. **1 Cor. 11:26**. For as often as you eat this bread and drink the cup, you proclaim the Lord's death until he comes.

6 **1 Cor. 11:31**. But if we judged ourselves truly, we would not be judged.

7 **Zech. 12:10**. "And I will pour out on the house of David and the inhabitants of Jerusalem a spirit of grace and pleas for mercy, so that, when they look on me, on him whom they have pierced, they shall mourn for him, as one mourns for an only child, and weep bitterly over him, as one weeps over a firstborn.

8 **Rev. 22:17.** The Spirit and the Bride say, "Come." And let the one who hears say, "Come." And let the one who is thirsty come; let the one who desires take the water of life without price.

9 **Jn. 6:35**. Jesus said to them, "I am the bread of life; whoever comes to me shall not hunger, and whoever believes in me shall never thirst."

10 **Jn. 1:16**. For from his fullness we have all received, grace upon grace.

11 **Phil. 1:16**. The latter do it out of love, knowing that I am put here for the defense of the gospel.

12 **2 Chr. 30:21**. And the people of Israel who were present at Jerusalem kept the Feast of Unleavened Bread seven days with great gladness, and the Levites and the priests praised the LORD day by day, singing with all their might to the LORD. **Ps. 63:4-5**. So I will bless you as long as I live; in your name I will lift up my

hands. My soul will be satisfied as with fat and rich food, and my mouth will praise you with joyful lips.

13 **Ps. 22:26.** The afflicted shall eat and be satisfied; those who seek him shall praise the LORD! May your hearts live forever!

14 **Ps. 50:5.** "Gather to me my faithful ones, who made a covenant with me by sacrifice!" **Jer. 50:5.** They shall ask the way to Zion, with faces turned toward it, saying, 'Come, let us join ourselves to the LORD in an everlasting covenant that will never be forgotten.'

15 **Acts 2:42.** And they devoted themselves to the apostles' teaching and the fellowship, to the breaking of bread and the prayers.

Q. 175. What is the duty of Christians after they have received the sacrament of the Lord's Supper?

A. The duty of Christians after they have received the sacrament of the Lord's Supper, is seriously to consider how they have behaved themselves in it, and with what success;[1] if they find quickening and comfort, to bless God for it,[2] beg the continuance of it,[3] watch against relapse,[4] fulfill their vows,[5] and encourage themselves to a frequent attendance on that ordinance:[6] but if they find no present benefit, more exactly to review their preparation for, and posture at, the sacrament;[7] in both which if they can approve themselves to God and their own consciences, they are to wait for the fruit of it in due time;[8] but if they see that they have failed in either, they are to be humbled,[9] and to attend upon it afterward with more care and diligence.[10]

1 **Ps. 28:7.** The LORD is my strength and my shield; in him my heart trusts, and I am helped; my heart exults, and with my song I give thanks to him. Ps. 85:8. Let me hear what God the LORD will speak, for he will speak peace to his people, to his saints; but let them not turn back to folly. **1 Cor. 11:7, 30-31.** For a man ought not to cover his head, since he is the image and glory of God, but woman is the glory of man. ... That is why many of you are weak and ill, and some have died. But if we judged ourselves truly, we would not be judged.

2 **2 Chr. 30:21-23, 25-26.** And the people of Israel who were present at Jerusalem kept the Feast of Unleavened Bread seven days with great gladness, and the Levites and the priests praised the LORD day by day, singing with all their might to the LORD. And Hezekiah spoke encouragingly to all the Levites who showed good skill in the service of the LORD. So they ate the food of the festival for seven days, sacrificing peace offerings and giving thanks to the LORD, the God of their fathers. Then the whole assembly agreed together to keep the feast for another seven days. So they kept it for another seven days with gladness. ... The whole assembly of Judah, and the priests and the Levites, and the whole assembly that came out of Israel, and the sojourners who came out of the land of Israel, and the sojourners who lived in Judah, rejoiced. So there was great joy in Jerusalem, for since the time of Solomon the son of David king of Israel there had been nothing like this in Jerusalem. **Acts 2:42, 46-47.** And they devoted themselves to the apostles' teaching and the fellowship, to the breaking of bread and the prayers. ... And day

by day, attending the temple together and breaking bread in their homes, they received their food with glad and generous hearts, praising God and having favor with all the people. And the Lord added to their number day by day those who were being saved.

3 **1 Chr. 29:18**. O LORD, the God of Abraham, Isaac, and Israel, our fathers, keep forever such purposes and thoughts in the hearts of your people, and direct their hearts toward you. **Ps. 36:10**. Oh, continue your steadfast love to those who know you, and your righteousness to the upright of heart! **Song. 3:4**. Scarcely had I passed them when I found him whom my soul loves. I held him, and would not let him go until I had brought him into my mother's house, and into the chamber of her who conceived me.

4 **1 Cor. 10:3-5, 12**. ...and all ate the same spiritual food, and all drank the same spiritual drink. For they drank from the spiritual Rock that followed them, and the Rock was Christ. Nevertheless, with most of them God was not pleased, for they were overthrown in the wilderness. ...Therefore let anyone who thinks that he stands take heed lest he fall.

5 **Ps. 50:14**. Offer to God a sacrifice of thanksgiving, and perform your vows to the Most High.

6 **Acts 2:42, 46**. And they devoted themselves to the apostles' teaching and the fellowship, to the breaking of bread and the prayers. ... And day by day, attending the temple together and breaking bread in their homes, they received their food with glad and generous hearts. **1 Cor. 11:25-26**. In the same way also he took the cup, after supper, saying, "This cup is the new covenant in my blood. Do this, as often as you drink it, in remembrance of me." For as often as you eat this bread and drink the cup, you proclaim the Lord's death until he comes."

7 **Eccl. 5:1-6**. Guard your steps when you go to the house of God. To draw near to listen is better than to offer the sacrifice of fools, for they do not know that they are doing evil. Be not rash with your mouth, nor let your heart be hasty to utter a word before God, for God is in heaven and you are on earth. Therefore let your words be few. For a dream comes with much business, and a fool's voice with many words. When you vow a vow to God, do not delay paying it, for he has no pleasure in fools. Pay what you vow. It is better that you should not vow than that you should vow and not pay. Let not your mouth lead you into sin, and do not say before the messenger that it was a mistake. Why should God be angry at your voice and destroy the work of your hands? **Song. 5:1-6**. I came to my garden, my sister, my bride, I gathered my myrrh with my spice, I ate my honeycomb with my honey, I drank my wine with my milk. Eat, friends, drink, and be drunk with love! I slept, but my heart was awake. A sound! My beloved is knocking. "Open to me, my sister, my love, my dove, my perfect one, for my head is wet with dew, my locks with the drops of the night." I had put off my garment; how could I put it on? I had bathed my feet; how could I soil them? My beloved put his hand to the latch, and my heart was thrilled within me. I arose to open to my beloved, and my hands dripped with myrrh, my fingers with liquid myrrh, on the handles of the bolt. I opened to my beloved, but my beloved had turned and gone. My soul failed me when he spoke. I sought him, but found him not; I called him, but he gave no answer.

8 **Ps. 42:5, 8**. Why are you cast down, O my soul, and why are you in turmoil within me? Hope in God; for I shall again praise him, my salvation. ... By day the LORD commands his steadfast love, and at night his song is with me, a prayer to the God of my life. **Ps. 43:3-5**. Send out your light and your truth; let them lead me; let them bring me to your holy hill and to your dwelling! Then I will go to the altar of God, to God my exceeding joy, and I will praise you with the lyre, O God, my God. Why are you cast down, O my soul, and why are you in turmoil within me? Hope

in God; for I shall again praise him, my salvation and my God. **Ps. 123:1-2**. To you I lift up my eyes, O you who are enthroned in the heavens! Behold, as the eyes of servants look to the hand of their master, as the eyes of a maidservant to the hand of her mistress, so our eyes look to the LORD our God, till he has mercy upon us.

9 **2 Chr. 30:18-19**. For a majority of the people, many of them from Ephraim, Manasseh, Issachar, and Zebulun, had not cleansed themselves, yet they ate the Passover otherwise than as prescribed. For Hezekiah had prayed for them, saying, "May the good LORD pardon everyone who sets his heart to seek God, the LORD, the God of his fathers, even though not according to the sanctuary's rules of cleanness."

10 **1 Chr. 15:12-14**. ...and said to them, "You are the heads of the fathers' houses of the Levites. Consecrate yourselves, you and your brothers, so that you may bring up the ark of the LORD, the God of Israel, to the place that I have prepared for it. Because you did not carry it the first time, the LORD our God broke out against us, because we did not seek him according to the rule." So the priests and the Levites consecrated themselves to bring up the ark of the LORD, the God of Israel. **2 Cor. 7:11**. For see what earnestness this godly grief has produced in you, but also what eagerness to clear yourselves, what indignation, what fear, what longing, what zeal, what punishment! At every point you have proved yourselves innocent in the matter.

Q. 176. In what do the sacraments of Baptism and the Lord's Supper agree?

A. The sacraments of Baptism and the Lord's Supper agree, in that the Author of both is God;[1] the spiritual part of both is Christ and His benefits;[2] both are seals of the same covenant,[3] are to be dispensed by ministers of the Gospel and by none other,[4] and to be continued in the church of Christ until his second coming.[5]

1 **Mt. 28:19**. Go therefore and make disciples of all nations, baptizing them in the name of the Father and of the Son and of the Holy Spirit. **1 Cor. 11:23**. For I received from the Lord what I also delivered to you, that the Lord Jesus on the night when he was betrayed took bread.

2 **Rom. 6:3-4**. Do you not know that all of us who have been baptized into Christ Jesus were baptized into his death? We were buried therefore with him by baptism into death, in order that, just as Christ was raised from the dead by the glory of the Father, we too might walk in newness of life. **1 Cor. 10:16**. The cup of blessing that we bless, is it not a participation in the blood of Christ? The bread that we break, is it not a participation in the body of Christ?

3 **Mt. 26:27-28**. And he took a cup, and when he had given thanks he gave it to them, saying, "Drink of it, all of you, for this is my blood of the covenant, which is poured out for many for the forgiveness of sins." **Rom. 4:11**. He received the sign of circumcision as a seal of the righteousness that he had by faith while he was still uncircumcised. The purpose was to make him the father of all who believe without being circumcised, so that righteousness would be counted to them as well. **Col. 2:12**. ...having been buried with him in baptism, in which you were also raised with him through faith in the powerful working of God, who raised him from the dead.

4 **Mt. 28:19**. Go therefore and make disciples of all nations, baptizing them in the name of the Father and of the Son and of the Holy Spirit. **Jn. 1:33**. I myself did not know him, but he who sent me to baptize with water said to me, 'He on whom you see the Spirit descend and remain, this is he who baptizes with the Holy Spirit.' **1 Cor. 4:1**. This is how one should regard us, as servants of Christ and stewards of the mysteries of God. **1 Cor. 11:23**. For I received from the Lord what I also delivered to you, that the Lord Jesus on the night when he was betrayed took bread. **Heb. 5:4**. And no one takes this honor for himself, but only when called by God, just as Aaron was.

5 **Mt. 28:19-20**. "Go therefore and make disciples of all nations, baptizing them in the name of the Father and of the Son and of the Holy Spirit, teaching them to observe all that I have commanded you. And behold, I am with you always, to the end of the age." **1 Cor. 11:26**. For as often as you eat this bread and drink the cup, you proclaim the Lord's death until he comes.

Q. 177. In what do the sacraments of Baptism and the Lord's Supper differ?

A. The sacraments of Baptism and the Lord's Supper differ in that Baptism is to be administered but once, with water, to be a sign and seal of our regeneration and ingrafting to Christ,[1] and that even to infants;[2] whereas the Lord's Supper is to be administered often, in the elements of bread and wine, to represent and exhibit Christ as spiritual nourishment to the soul,[3] and to confirm our continuance and growth in Him,[4] and that only to those who are of years and ability to examine themselves.[5]

1 **Mt. 3:11**. "I baptize you with water for repentance, but he who is coming after me is mightier than I, whose sandals I am not worthy to carry. He will baptize you with the Holy Spirit and fire." **Gal. 3:27**. For as many of you as were baptized into Christ have put on Christ. **Titus 3:5**. ...he saved us, not because of works done by us in righteousness, but according to his own mercy, by the washing of regeneration and renewal of the Holy Spirit.

2 **Gen. 17:7, 9**. And I will establish my covenant between me and you and your offspring after you throughout their generations for an everlasting covenant, to be God to you and to your offspring after you. ... And God said to Abraham, "As for you, you shall keep my covenant, you and your offspring after you throughout their generations." **Acts 2:38-39**. And Peter said to them, "Repent and be baptized every one of you in the name of Jesus Christ for the forgiveness of your sins, and you will receive the gift of the Holy Spirit. For the promise is for you and for your children and for all who are far off, everyone whom the Lord our God calls to himself." **1 Cor. 7:14**. For the unbelieving husband is made holy because of his wife, and the unbelieving wife is made holy because of her husband. Otherwise your children would be unclean, but as it is, they are holy.

3 **1 Cor. 11:23-26**. For I received from the Lord what I also delivered to you, that the Lord Jesus on the night when he was betrayed took bread, and when he had given thanks, he broke it, and said, "This is my body which is for you. Do this in remembrance of me." In the same way also he took the cup, after supper, saying, "This cup is the new covenant in my blood. Do this, as often as you drink it, in re-

membrance of me." For as often as you eat this bread and drink the cup, you proclaim the Lord's death until he comes.

4 **1 Cor. 10:16**. The cup of blessing that we bless, is it not a participation in the blood of Christ? The bread that we break, is it not a participation in the body of Christ?

5 **1 Cor. 11:28-29**. Let a person examine himself, then, and so eat of the bread and drink of the cup. For anyone who eats and drinks without discerning the body eats and drinks judgment on himself.

Q. 178. What is prayer?

A. Prayer is an offering up of our desires to God,[1] in the name of Christ,[2] by the help of His Spirit,[3] with confession of our sins,[4] and thankful acknowledgment of his mercies.[5]

1 **Ps. 57:8**. Awake, my glory! Awake, O harp and lyre! I will awake the dawn!

2 **Jn. 16:23**. In that day you will ask nothing of me. Truly, truly, I say to you, whatever you ask of the Father in my name, he will give it to you.

3 **Rom. 8:26**. Likewise the Spirit helps us in our weakness. For we do not know what to pray for as we ought, but the Spirit himself intercedes for us with groanings too deep for words.

4 **Ps. 32:5-6**. I acknowledged my sin to you, and I did not cover my iniquity; I said, "I will confess my transgressions to the LORD," and you forgave the iniquity of my sin. Therefore let everyone who is godly offer prayer to you at a time when you may be found; surely in the rush of great waters, they shall not reach him. **Dan. 9:4**. I prayed to the LORD my God and made confession, saying, "O Lord, the great and awesome God, who keeps covenant and steadfast love with those who love him and keep his commandments."

5 **Phil. 4:6**. ...do not be anxious about anything, but in everything by prayer and supplication with thanksgiving let your requests be made known to God.

Q. 179. Are we to pray to God only?

A. God only being able to search the heart,[1] hear the requests,[2] pardon the sins,[3] and fulfill the desires of all,[4] and only to be believed in,[5] and worshiped with religious worship;[6] prayer, which is a special part of it,[7] is to be made by all to Him alone,[8] and to none other.[9]

1 **1 Kings 8:39**. ...then hear in heaven your dwelling place and forgive and act and render to each whose heart you know, according to all his ways (for you, you only, know the hearts of all the children of mankind). **Acts 1:24**. And they prayed and said, "You, Lord, who know the hearts of all, show which one of these two you have chosen." **Rom. 8:27**. And he who searches hearts knows what is the mind of the Spirit, because the Spirit intercedes for the saints according to the will of God.

2 **Ps. 65:2**. O you who hear prayer, to you shall all flesh come.

3 **Mic. 7:18**. Who is a God like you, pardoning iniquity and passing over transgression for the remnant of his inheritance? He does not retain his anger forever, because he delights in steadfast love.

4 **Ps. 145:18**. The LORD is near to all who call on him, to all who call on him in truth.

5 **Rom. 10:14**. How then will they call on him in whom they have not believed? And how are they to believe in him of whom they have never heard? And how are they to hear without someone preaching?

6 **Mt. 4:10**. Then Jesus said to him, "Be gone, Satan! For it is written, "'You shall worship the Lord your God and him only shall you serve.'"

7 **1 Cor. 1:2**. To the church of God that is in Corinth, to those sanctified in Christ Jesus, called to be saints together with all those who in every place call upon the name of our Lord Jesus Christ, both their Lord and ours.

8 **Ps. 50:15**. "...and call upon me in the day of trouble; I will deliver you, and you shall glorify me."

9 **Rom. 10:14**. How then will they call on him in whom they have not believed? And how are they to believe in him of whom they have never heard? And how are they to hear without someone preaching?

Q. 180. What is it to pray in the name of Christ?

A. To pray in the name of Christ is, in obedience to His command, and with confidence in His promises, to ask mercy for His sake:[1] not by bare mentioning of His name;[2] but by drawing our encouragement to pray, and our boldness, strength, and hope of acceptance in prayer, from Christ and His mediation.[3]

1 **Dan. 9:17**. Now therefore, O our God, listen to the prayer of your servant and to his pleas for mercy, and for your own sake, O Lord, make your face to shine upon your sanctuary, which is desolate. **Jn. 14:13-14**. Whatever you ask in my name, this I will do, that the Father may be glorified in the Son. If you ask me anything in my name, I will do it. **Jn. 16:24**. Until now you have asked nothing in my name. Ask, and you will receive, that your joy may be full.

2 **Mt. 7:21**. "Not everyone who says to me, 'Lord, Lord,' will enter the kingdom of heaven, but the one who does the will of my Father who is in heaven."

3 **Heb. 4:14-16**. Since then we have a great high priest who has passed through the heavens, Jesus, the Son of God, let us hold fast our confession. For we do not have a high priest who is unable to sympathize with our weaknesses, but one who in every respect has been tempted as we are, yet without sin. Let us then with confidence draw near to the throne of grace, that we may receive mercy and find grace to help in time of need. **1 Jn. 5:13-15**. I write these things to you who believe in the name of the Son of God that you may know that you have eternal life. And this is the confidence that we have toward him, that if we ask anything according to his will he hears us. And if we know that he hears us in whatever we ask, we know that we have the requests that we have asked of him.

Q. 181. Why are we to pray in the name of Christ?

A. The sinfulness of man, and his distance from God by reason of it, being so great, as that we can have no access into His presence without a mediator,[1] and there being none in heaven or earth appointed to, or fit for, that glorious work but Christ alone,[2] we are to pray in no other name but His only.[3]

1 **Isa. 59:2.** ...but your iniquities have made a separation between you and your God, and your sins have hidden his face from you so that he does not hear. **Jn. 14:6.** Jesus said to him, "I am the way, and the truth, and the life. No one comes to the Father except through me." **Eph. 3:12.** ...in whom we have boldness and access with confidence through our faith in him.

2 **Jn. 6:27.** "Do not work for the food that perishes, but for the food that endures to eternal life, which the Son of Man will give to you. For on him God the Father has set his seal." **1 Tim. 2:5.** For there is one God, and there is one mediator between God and men, the man Christ Jesus. **Heb. 7:25-27.** Consequently, he is able to save to the uttermost those who draw near to God through him, since he always lives to make intercession for them. For it was indeed fitting that we should have such a high priest, holy, innocent, unstained, separated from sinners, and exalted above the heavens. He has no need, like those high priests, to offer sacrifices daily, first for his own sins and then for those of the people, since he did this once for all when he offered up himself.

3 **Col. 3:17.** And whatever you do, in word or deed, do everything in the name of the Lord Jesus, giving thanks to God the Father through him. **Heb. 13:15.** Through him then let us continually offer up a sacrifice of praise to God, that is, the fruit of lips that acknowledge his name.

Q. 182. How does the Spirit help us to pray?

A. Because we do not know for what to pray as we ought, the Spirit helps our weaknesses, by enabling us to understand both for whom, and what, and how prayer is to be made; and by working and making alive in our hearts (although not in all persons, nor at all times in the same measure) those understandings, affections, and graces that are necessary for the right performance of that duty.[1]

1 **Ps. 10:17.** O LORD, you hear the desire of the afflicted; you will strengthen their heart; you will incline your ear. **Zech. 12:10.** "And I will pour out on the house of David and the inhabitants of Jerusalem a spirit of grace and pleas for mercy, so that, when they look on me, on him whom they have pierced, they shall mourn for him, as one mourns for an only child, and weep bitterly over him, as one weeps over a firstborn." **Rom. 8:26-27.** Likewise the Spirit helps us in our weakness. For we do not know what to pray for as we ought, but the Spirit himself intercedes for us with groanings too deep for words. And he who searches hearts knows what is the mind of the Spirit, because the Spirit intercedes for the saints according to the will of God.

Q. 183. For whom are we to pray?

A. We are to pray for the whole church of Christ on earth,[1] for government officials,[2] and ministers,[3] for ourselves,[4] our brothers and sisters,[5] even our enemies,[6] and for all sorts of men living,[7] or who shall live hereafter;[8] but not for the dead,[9] nor for those that are known to have sinned the sin unto death.[10]

1 **Ps. 28:9**. Oh, save your people and bless your heritage! Be their shepherd and carry them forever. **Eph. 6:18**. ...praying at all times in the Spirit, with all prayer and supplication. To that end keep alert with all perseverance, making supplication for all the saints.

2 **1 Tim. 2:1-2**. First of all, then, I urge that supplications, prayers, intercessions, and thanksgivings be made for all people, for kings and all who are in high positions, that we may lead a peaceful and quiet life, godly and dignified in every way.

3 **Col. 4:3**. At the same time, pray also for us, that God may open to us a door for the word, to declare the mystery of Christ, on account of which I am in prison.

4 **Gen. 32:11**. Please deliver me from the hand of my brother, from the hand of Esau, for I fear him, that he may come and attack me, the mothers with the children.

5 **Jas. 5:16**. Therefore, confess your sins to one another and pray for one another, that you may be healed. The prayer of a righteous person has great power as it is working.

6 **Mt. 5:44**. But I say to you, Love your enemies and pray for those who persecute you.

7 See **1 Tim. 1-2**.

8 **2 Sam. 7:29**. "Now therefore may it please you to bless the house of your servant, so that it may continue forever before you. For you, O Lord GOD, have spoken, and with your blessing shall the house of your servant be blessed forever." **Jn. 17:20**. "I do not ask for these only, but also for those who will believe in me through their word."

9 **2 Sam. 12:21-23**. Then his servants said to him, "What is this thing that you have done? You fasted and wept for the child while he was alive; but when the child died, you arose and ate food." He said, "While the child was still alive, I fasted and wept, for I said, 'Who knows whether the LORD will be gracious to me, that the child may live?' But now he is dead. Why should I fast? Can I bring him back again? I shall go to him, but he will not return to me."

10 **1 Jn 5:16**. If anyone sees his brother committing a sin not leading to death, he shall ask, and God will give him life—to those who commit sins that do not lead to death. There is sin that leads to death; I do not say that one should pray for that.

Q. 184. For what things are we to pray?

A. We are to pray for all things tending to the glory of God,[1] the welfare of the church,[2] our own[3] or others' good;[4] but not for anything that is unlawful.[5]

1 **Mt. 6:9**. Pray then like this: "Our Father in heaven, hallowed be your name."

2 **Ps. 51:18**. Do good to Zion in your good pleasure; build up the walls of Jerusalem. **Ps. 122:6**. Pray for the peace of Jerusalem! "May they be secure who love you!"

3 **Mt. 7:11**. If you then, who are evil, know how to give good gifts to your children, how much more will your Father who is in heaven give good things to those who ask him!

4 **Ps. 125:4**. Do good, O LORD, to those who are good, and to those who are upright in their hearts!

5 **1 Jn. 5:14**. And this is the confidence that we have toward him, that if we ask anything according to his will he hears us.

Q. 185. How are we to pray?

A. We are to pray with an awe-inspiring understanding of the majesty of God,[1] and deep sense of our own unworthiness,[2] needs,[3] and sins;[4] with repentant,[5] thankful,[6] and open hearts;[7] with understanding,[8] faith,[9] sincerity,[10] emotion,[11] love,[12] and perseverance,[13] waiting for Him[14] with humble submission to His will.[15]

1 **Eccl. 5:1**. Guard your steps when you go to the house of God. To draw near to listen is better than to offer the sacrifice of fools, for they do not know that they are doing evil.

2 **Gen. 18:27**. Abraham answered and said, "Behold, I have undertaken to speak to the Lord, I who am but dust and ashes." **Gen. 32:10**. I am not worthy of the least of all the deeds of steadfast love and all the faithfulness that you have shown to your servant, for with only my staff I crossed this Jordan, and now I have become two camps.

3 **Lk. 15:17-19**. "But when he came to himself, he said, 'How many of my father's hired servants have more than enough bread, but I perish here with hunger! I will arise and go to my father, and I will say to him, "Father, I have sinned against heaven and before you. I am no longer worthy to be called your son. Treat me as one of your hired servants."'

4 **Lk. 18:13-14**. "But the tax collector, standing far off, would not even lift up his eyes to heaven, but beat his breast, saying, 'God, be merciful to me, a sinner!' I tell you, this man went down to his house justified, rather than the other. For everyone who exalts himself will be humbled, but the one who humbles himself will be exalted."

5 **Ps. 51:17**. The sacrifices of God are a broken spirit; a broken and contrite heart, O God, you will not despise.

6 **Phil. 4:6**. ...do not be anxious about anything, but in everything by prayer and supplication with thanksgiving let your requests be made known to God.

7 **1 Sam. 1:15**. But Hannah answered, "No, my lord, I am a woman troubled in spirit. I have drunk neither wine nor strong drink, but I have been pouring out my soul before the LORD." **1 Sam. 2:1**. And Hannah prayed and said, "My heart exults in the LORD; my horn is exalted in the LORD. My mouth derides my enemies, because I rejoice in your salvation."

8 **1 Cor. 14:15**. What am I to do? I will pray with my spirit, but I will pray with my mind also; I will sing praise with my spirit, but I will sing with my mind also.

9 **Mk. 11:24**. Therefore I tell you, whatever you ask in prayer, believe that you have received it, and it will be yours. **Jas. 1:6**. But let him ask in faith, with no doubting, for the one who doubts is like a wave of the sea that is driven and tossed by the wind.

10 **Ps. 17:1**. Hear a just cause, O LORD; attend to my cry! Give ear to my prayer from lips free of deceit! **Ps. 145:18**. The LORD is near to all who call on him, to all who call on him in truth.

11 **Jas. 5:16**. Therefore, confess your sins to one another and pray for one another, that you may be healed. The prayer of a righteous person has great power as it is working.

12 **1 Tim. 2:8**. I desire then that in every place the men should pray, lifting holy hands without anger or quarreling.

13 **Eph. 6:18**. ...praying at all times in the Spirit, with all prayer and supplication. To that end keep alert with all perseverance, making supplication for all the saints.

14 **Mic. 7:7**. But as for me, I will look to the LORD; I will wait for the God of my salvation; my God will hear me.

15 **Mt. 26:39**. And going a little farther he fell on his face and prayed, saying, "My Father, if it be possible, let this cup pass from me; nevertheless, not as I will, but as you will."

Q. 186. What rule has God given for our direction in the duty of prayer?

A. The whole Word of God is of use to direct us in the duty of praying;[1] but the special rule of direction is that form of prayer that our Savior Christ taught His disciples, commonly called, "the Lord's Prayer."[2]

1 **1 Jn. 5:14**. And this is the confidence that we have toward him, that if we ask anything according to his will he hears us.

2 **Mt. 6:9-13**. Pray then like this: "Our Father in heaven, hallowed be your name. Your kingdom come, your will be done, on earth as it is in heaven. Give us this day our daily bread, and forgive us our debts, as we also have forgiven our debtors. And lead us not into temptation, but deliver us from evil." **Lk. 11:2-4**. And he said to them, "When you pray, say: "Father, hallowed be your name. Your kingdom come. Give us each day our daily bread, and forgive us our sins, for we ourselves forgive everyone who is indebted to us. And lead us not into temptation."

Q. 187. How is the Lord's Prayer to be used?

A. The Lord's Prayer is not only for direction, as a pattern according to which we are to make other prayers; but may be also used itself as a prayer so that it is done with understanding, faith, reverence, and other graces necessary to the right performance of the duty of prayer.[1]

1 **Mt. 6:9**. Pray then like this: "Our Father in heaven, hallowed be your name." **Lk. 11:2**. And he said to them, "When you pray, say: "Father, hallowed be your name. Your kingdom come."

Q. 188. Of how many parts does the Lord's Prayer consist?

A. The Lord's Prayer consists of three parts: a preface, petitions, and a conclusion.

Q. 189. What does the preface of the Lord's Prayer teach us?

A. The preface of the Lord's Prayer (contained in the words, "Our Father in heaven")[1] teaches us, when we pray, to draw near to God with confidence of His fatherly goodness, and our interest in it;[2] with reverence, and all other childlike attitudes,[3] heavenly affections,[4] and due understanding of His sovereign power, majesty, and gracious condescension:[5] as also to pray with and for others.[6]

1 **Mt. 6:9**. Pray then like this: "Our Father in heaven, hallowed be your name."

2 **Lk. 11:13**. "If you then, who are evil, know how to give good gifts to your children, how much more will the heavenly Father give the Holy Spirit to those who ask him!" **Rom. 8:15**. For you did not receive the spirit of slavery to fall back into fear, but you have received the Spirit of adoption as sons, by whom we cry, "Abba! Father!"

3 **Isa. 64:9**. Be not so terribly angry, O LORD, and remember not iniquity forever. Behold, please look, we are all your people.

4 **Ps. 123:1**. To you I lift up my eyes, O you who are enthroned in the heavens! **Lam. 3:41**. Let us lift up our hearts and hands to God in heaven.

5 **Neh. 1:4-6**. As soon as I heard these words I sat down and wept and mourned for days, and I continued fasting and praying before the God of heaven. And I said, "O LORD God of heaven, the great and awesome God who keeps covenant and steadfast love with those who love him and keep his commandments, let your ear be attentive and your eyes open, to hear the prayer of your servant that I now pray before you day and night for the people of Israel your servants, confessing the sins of the people of Israel, which we have sinned against you. Even I and my father's house have sinned." **Isa. 63:15-16**. Look down from heaven and see, from your holy and beautiful habitation. Where are your zeal and your might? The stirring of your inner parts and your compassion are held back from me. For you are our Father, though Abraham does not know us, and Israel does not acknowledge us; you, O LORD, are our Father, our Redeemer from of old is your name.

6 **Acts 12:5**. So Peter was kept in prison, but earnest prayer for him was made to God by the church.

Q. 190. For what do we pray in the first petition?

A. In the first petition (which is, "Hallowed be your name"[1]), acknowledging the utter inability and unwillingness in ourselves and all men to honor God rightly,[2] we pray: that God would by his grace enable and make us and others willing to know, to acknowledge, and highly esteem Him,[3] His titles,[4] attributes,[5] ordinances, Word,[6] works, and whatever He is pleased to make Himself known by;[7] and to glorify Him in thought, word,[8] and deed;[9] that He would prevent and remove atheism,[10] ignorance,[11] idolatry,[12] profaneness,[13] and whatever is dishonoring to Him;[14] and by His overruling providence, direct and arrange all things to His own glory.[15]

1 **Mt. 6:9**. "Our Father in heaven, hallowed be your name."

2 **Ps. 51:15**. O Lord, open my lips, and my mouth will declare your praise. **2 Cor. 3:5**. Not that we are sufficient in ourselves to claim anything as coming from us, but our sufficiency is from God.

3 **Ps. 67:2-3**. ...that your way may be known on earth, your saving power among all nations. Let the peoples praise you, O God; let all the peoples praise you!

4 **Ps. 83:18**. ...that they may know that you alone, whose name is the LORD, are the Most High over all the earth.

5 **Ps. 86:10-13, 15**. For you are great and do wondrous things; you alone are God. Teach me your way, O LORD, that I may walk in your truth; unite my heart to fear your name. I give thanks to you, O Lord my God, with my whole heart, and I will glorify your name forever. For great is your steadfast love toward me; you have delivered my soul from the depths of Sheol. ... But you, O Lord, are a God merciful and gracious, slow to anger and abounding in steadfast love and faithfulness.

6 **Ps. 138:1-3**. I give you thanks, O LORD, with my whole heart; before the gods I sing your praise; I bow down toward your holy temple and give thanks to your name for your steadfast love and your faithfulness, for you have exalted above all things your name and your word. On the day I called, you answered me; my strength of soul you increased. **Ps. 147:19-20**. He declares his word to Jacob, his statutes and rules to Israel. He has not dealt thus with any other nation; they do not know his rules. Praise the LORD! **2 Cor. 2:14-15**. But thanks be to God, who in Christ always leads us in triumphal procession, and through us spreads the fragrance of the knowledge of him everywhere. For we are the aroma of Christ to God among those who are being saved and among those who are perishing. **2 Thess. 3:1**. Finally, brothers, pray for us, that the word of the Lord may speed ahead and be honored, as happened among you.

7 **Ps. 8**. O LORD, our Lord, how majestic is your name in all the earth! You have set your glory above the heavens. Out of the mouth of babies and infants, you have established strength because of your foes, to still the enemy and the avenger. When I look at your heavens, the work of your fingers, the moon and the stars, which you have set in place, what is man that you are mindful of him, and the son of man that you care for him? Yet you have made him a little lower than the heavenly beings and crowned him with glory and honor. You have given him dominion over the works of your hands; you have put all things under his feet, all sheep and oxen, and also the beasts of the field, the birds of the heavens, and the fish of the sea, whatever passes along the paths of the seas. O LORD, our Lord, how majestic is

your name in all the earth! **Ps. 145**. I will extol you, my God and King, and bless your name forever and ever. Every day I will bless you and praise your name forever and ever. Great is the LORD, and greatly to be praised, and his greatness is unsearchable. One generation shall commend your works to another, and shall declare your mighty acts. On the glorious splendor of your majesty, and on your wondrous works, I will meditate. They shall speak of the might of your awesome deeds, and I will declare your greatness. They shall pour forth the fame of your abundant goodness and shall sing aloud of your righteousness. The LORD is gracious and merciful, slow to anger and abounding in steadfast love. The LORD is good to all, and his mercy is over all that he has made. All your works shall give thanks to you, O LORD, and all your saints shall bless you! They shall speak of the glory of your kingdom and tell of your power, to make known to the children of man your mighty deeds, and the glorious splendor of your kingdom. Your kingdom is an everlasting kingdom, and your dominion endures throughout all generations. [The LORD is faithful in all his words and kind in all his works.] The LORD upholds all who are falling and raises up all who are bowed down. The eyes of all look to you, and you give them their food in due season. You open your hand; you satisfy the desire of every living thing. The LORD is righteous in all his ways and kind in all his works. The LORD is near to all who call on him, to all who call on him in truth. He fulfills the desire of those who fear him; he also hears their cry and saves them. The LORD preserves all who love him, but all the wicked he will destroy. My mouth will speak the praise of the LORD, and let all flesh bless his holy name forever and ever.

8 **Ps. 19:14**. Let the words of my mouth and the meditation of my heart be acceptable in your sight, O LORD, my rock and my redeemer. **Ps. 103:1**. Bless the LORD, O my soul, and all that is within me, bless his holy name!

9 **Phil. 1:9, 11**. And it is my prayer that your love may abound more and more, with knowledge and all discernment. ...filled with the fruit of righteousness that comes through Jesus Christ, to the glory and praise of God.

10 **Ps. 67:1-4**. May God be gracious to us and bless us and make his face to shine upon us, that your way may be known on earth, your saving power among all nations. Let the peoples praise you, O God; let all the peoples praise you! Let the nations be glad and sing for joy, for you judge the peoples with equity and guide the nations upon earth.

11 **Eph. 1:17-18**. ...that the God of our Lord Jesus Christ, the Father of glory, may give you the Spirit of wisdom and of revelation in the knowledge of him, having the eyes of your hearts enlightened, that you may know what is the hope to which he has called you, what are the riches of his glorious inheritance in the saints.

12 **Ps. 97:9**. For you, O LORD, are most high over all the earth; you are exalted far above all gods.

13 **Ps. 74:18, 22-23**. Remember this, O LORD, how the enemy scoffs, and a foolish people reviles your name. ... Arise, O God, defend your cause; remember how the foolish scoff at you all the day! Do not forget the clamor of your foes, the uproar of those who rise against you, which goes up continually!

14 **2 Kings 19:15-16**. And Hezekiah prayed before the LORD and said: "O LORD, the God of Israel, enthroned above the cherubim, you are the God, you alone, of all the kingdoms of the earth; you have made heaven and earth. Incline your ear, O LORD, and hear; open your eyes, O LORD, and see; and hear the words of Sennacherib, which he has sent to mock the living God.

15 **2 Chr. 20:6, 10-12**. ...and said, "O LORD, God of our fathers, are you not God in heaven? You rule over all the kingdoms of the nations. In your hand are power and might, so that none is able to withstand you. ... And now behold, the men of Ammon and Moab and Mount Seir, whom you would not let Israel invade when

they came from the land of Egypt, and whom they avoided and did not destroy—behold, they reward us by coming to drive us out of your possession, which you have given us to inherit. O our God, will you not execute judgment on them? For we are powerless against this great horde that is coming against us. We do not know what to do, but our eyes are on you." **Ps. 83**. O God, do not keep silence; do not hold your peace or be still, O God! For behold, your enemies make an uproar; those who hate you have raised their heads. They lay crafty plans against your people; they consult together against your treasured ones. They say, "Come, let us wipe them out as a nation; let the name of Israel be remembered no more!" For they conspire with one accord; against you they make a covenant – the tents of Edom and the Ishmaelites, Moab and the Hagrites, Gebal and Ammon and Amalek, Philistia with the inhabitants of Tyre; Asshur also has joined them; they are the strong arm of the children of Lot. Do to them as you did to Midian, as to Sisera and Jabin at the river Kishon, who were destroyed at En-dor, who became dung for the ground. Make their nobles like Oreb and Zeeb, all their princes like Zebah and Zalmunna, who said, "Let us take possession for ourselves of the pastures of God." O my God, make them like whirling dust, like chaff before the wind. As fire consumes the forest, as the flame sets the mountains ablaze, so may you pursue them with your tempest and terrify them with your hurricane! Fill their faces with shame, that they may seek your name, O LORD. Let them be put to shame and dismayed forever; let them perish in disgrace, that they may know that you alone, whose name is the LORD, are the Most High over all the earth. **Ps. 140:4, 8**. Guard me, O LORD, from the hands of the wicked; preserve me from violent men, who have planned to trip up my feet. ... Grant not, O LORD, the desires of the wicked; do not further their evil plot, or they will be exalted!

Q. 191. For what do we pray in the second petition?

A. In the second petition (which is, "Your kingdom come"[1]), acknowledging ourselves and all mankind to be by nature under the dominion of sin and Satan,[2] we pray: that the kingdom of sin and Satan may be destroyed,[3] the Gospel spread throughout the world,[4] the Jews called,[5] the fullness of the Gentiles brought in;[6] that the church may be furnished with all Gospel officers and ordinances,[7] purged from corruption,[8] approved and maintained by the civil magistrate;[9] that the ordinances of Christ may be purely dispensed, and made effectual to the converting of those who are yet in their sins, and the confirming, comforting, and building up of those who are already converted;[10] that Christ would rule in our hearts here,[11] and hasten the time of His second coming, and our reigning with Him forever;[12] and that He would be pleased so to exercise the kingdom of His power in all the world, as may best bring about these ends.[13]

1 **Mt. 6:10**. Your kingdom come, your will be done, on earth as it is in heaven.

2 **Eph.2:2-3**. ...in which you once walked, following the course of this world, following the prince of the power of the air, the spirit that is now at work in the sons of disobedience among whom we all once lived in the passions of our flesh, carrying

out the desires of the body and the mind, and were by nature children of wrath, like the rest of mankind.

3 **Ps. 68:1**. God shall arise, his enemies shall be scattered; and those who hate him shall flee before him! **Rev. 12:10-11**. And I heard a loud voice in heaven, saying, "Now the salvation and the power and the kingdom of our God and the authority of his Christ have come, for the accuser of our brothers has been thrown down, who accuses them day and night before our God. And they have conquered him by the blood of the Lamb and by the word of their testimony, for they loved not their lives even unto death.

4 **2 Thess. 3:1**. Finally, brothers, pray for us, that the word of the Lord may speed ahead and be honored, as happened among you.

5 **Rom. 10:1**. Brothers, my heart's desire and prayer to God for them is that they may be saved.

6 **Ps. 67**. May God be gracious to us and bless us and make his face to shine upon us, that your way may be known on earth, your saving power among all nations. Let the peoples praise you, O God; let all the peoples praise you! Let the nations be glad and sing for joy, for you judge the peoples with equity and guide the nations upon earth. Let the peoples praise you, O God; let all the peoples praise you! The earth has yielded its increase; God, our God, shall bless us. God shall bless us; let all the ends of the earth fear him! **Jn. 17:9, 20**. I am praying for them. I am not praying for the world but for those whom you have given me, for they are yours. ... "I do not ask for these only, but also for those who will believe in me through their word." **Rom. 11:25-26**. Lest you be wise in your own sight, I do not want you to be unaware of this mystery, brothers: a partial hardening has come upon Israel, until the fullness of the Gentiles has come in. And in this way all Israel will be saved, as it is written, "The Deliverer will come from Zion, he will banish ungodliness from Jacob."

7 **Mt. 9:38**. "...therefore pray earnestly to the Lord of the harvest to send out laborers into his harvest." **2 Thess. 3:1**. Finally, brothers, pray for us, that the word of the Lord may speed ahead and be honored, as happened among you.

8 **Zeph. 3:9**. "For at that time I will change the speech of the peoples to a pure speech, that all of them may call upon the name of the LORD and serve him with one accord." **Mal. 1:11**. For from the rising of the sun to its setting my name will be great among the nations, and in every place incense will be offered to my name, and a pure offering. For my name will be great among the nations, says the LORD of hosts.

9 **1 Tim. 2:1-2**. First of all, then, I urge that supplications, prayers, intercessions, and thanksgivings be made for all people, for kings and all who are in high positions, that we may lead a peaceful and quiet life, godly and dignified in every way.

10 **Acts 4:29-30**. "And now, Lord, look upon their threats and grant to your servants to continue to speak your word with all boldness, while you stretch out your hand to heal, and signs and wonders are performed through the name of your holy servant Jesus." **Rom. 15:29-30, 32**. I know that when I come to you I will come in the fullness of the blessing of Christ. I appeal to you, brothers, by our Lord Jesus Christ and by the love of the Spirit, to strive together with me in your prayers to God on my behalf. ...so that by God's will I may come to you with joy and be refreshed in your company. **Eph. 6:18-20**. ...praying at all times in the Spirit, with all prayer and supplication. To that end keep alert with all perseverance, making supplication for all the saints, and also for me, that words may be given to me in opening my mouth boldly to proclaim the mystery of the gospel, for which I am an ambassador in chains, that I may declare it boldly, as I ought to speak.
2 Thess. 1:11. To this end we always pray for you, that our God may make you worthy of his calling and may fulfill every resolve for good and every work of faith

by his power. **2 Thess. 2:16-17**. Now may our Lord Jesus Christ himself, and God our Father, who loved us and gave us eternal comfort and good hope through grace, comfort your hearts and establish them in every good work and word.

11 **Eph. 3:14-20**. For this reason I bow my knees before the Father, from whom every family in heaven and on earth is named, that according to the riches of his glory he may grant you to be strengthened with power through his Spirit in your inner being, so that Christ may dwell in your hearts through faith—that you, being rooted and grounded in love, may have strength to comprehend with all the saints what is the breadth and length and height and depth, and to know the love of Christ that surpasses knowledge, that you may be filled with all the fullness of God. Now to him who is able to do far more abundantly than all that we ask or think, according to the power at work within us.

12 **Rev. 22:20**. He who testifies to these things says, "Surely I am coming soon." Amen. Come, Lord Jesus!

13 **Isa. 64:1-2**. Oh that you would rend the heavens and come down, that the mountains might quake at your presence— as when fire kindles brushwood and the fire causes water to boil— to make your name known to your adversaries, and that the nations might tremble at your presence! **Rev. 4:8-11**. And the four living creatures, each of them with six wings, are full of eyes all around and within, and day and night they never cease to say, "Holy, holy, holy, is the Lord God Almighty, who was and is and is to come!" And whenever the living creatures give glory and honor and thanks to him who is seated on the throne, who lives forever and ever, the twenty-four elders fall down before him who is seated on the throne and worship him who lives forever and ever. They cast their crowns before the throne, saying, "Worthy are you, our Lord and God, to receive glory and honor and power, for you created all things, and by your will they existed and were created."

Q. 192. For what do we pray in the third petition?

A. In the third petition (which is, "Your will be done, on earth as it is in heaven"[1]), acknowledging that by nature we and all men are not only utterly unable and unwilling to know and do the will of God,[2] but prone to rebel against His Word,[3] to complain and murmur against his providence,[4] and wholly inclined to do the will of the flesh, and of the devil:[5] we pray that God would by His Spirit take away from us and others all blindness,[6] weakness,[7] unwillingness,[8] and perverseness of heart,[9] and by His grace make us able and willing to know, do, and submit to His will in all things,[10] with the like humility,[11] cheerfulness,[12] faithfulness,[13] diligence,[14] zeal,[15] sincerity,[16] and faithfulness,[17] as the angels do in heaven.[18]

1 **Mt. 6:10**. Your kingdom come, your will be done, on earth as it is in heaven.

2 **Job 21:14**. They say to God, 'Depart from us! We do not desire the knowledge of your ways. **Rom. 7:18**. For I know that nothing good dwells in me, that is, in my flesh. For I have the desire to do what is right, but not the ability to carry it out. **1 Cor. 2:14**. The natural person does not accept the things of the Spirit of God, for they are folly to him, and he is not able to understand them because they are spiritually discerned.

3 **Rom. 8:7**. For the mind that is set on the flesh is hostile to God, for it does not submit to God's law; indeed, it cannot.

4 **Ex. 17:7**. And he called the name of the place Massah and Meribah, because of the quarreling of the people of Israel, and because they tested the LORD by saying, "Is the LORD among us or not?" **Num. 14:2**. And all the people of Israel grumbled against Moses and Aaron. The whole congregation said to them, "Would that we had died in the land of Egypt! Or would that we had died in this wilderness!"

5 **Eph. 2:2**. ...in which you once walked, following the course of this world, following the prince of the power of the air, the spirit that is now at work in the sons of disobedience.

6 **Eph. 1:17-18**. ...that the God of our Lord Jesus Christ, the Father of glory, may give you the Spirit of wisdom and of revelation in the knowledge of him, having the eyes of your hearts enlightened, that you may know what is the hope to which he has called you, what are the riches of his glorious inheritance in the saints

7 **Eph. 3:16**. ...that according to the riches of his glory he may grant you to be strengthened with power through his Spirit in your inner being.

8 **Mt. 26:40-41**. And he came to the disciples and found them sleeping. And he said to Peter, "So, could you not watch with me one hour? Watch and pray that you may not enter into temptation. The spirit indeed is willing, but the flesh is weak."

9 **Jer. 31:18-19**. I have heard Ephraim grieving, 'You have disciplined me, and I was disciplined, like an untrained calf; bring me back that I may be restored, for you are the LORD my God. For after I had turned away, I relented, and after I was instructed, I struck my thigh; I was ashamed, and I was confounded, because I bore the disgrace of my youth.'

10 **Ps. 119:1, 8, 35-36**. Blessed are those whose way is blameless, who walk in the law of the LORD! ... I will keep your statutes; do not utterly forsake me! ... Lead me in the path of your commandments, for I delight in it. Incline my heart to your testimonies, and not to selfish gain! **Acts 21:14**. And since he would not be persuaded, we ceased and said, "Let the will of the Lord be done."

11 **Mic. 6:8.** He has told you, O man, what is good; and what does the LORD require of you but to do justice, and to love kindness, and to walk humbly with your God?

12 **2 Sam. 15:25-26**. Then the king said to Zadok, "Carry the ark of God back into the city. If I find favor in the eyes of the LORD, he will bring me back and let me see both it and his dwelling place. But if he says, 'I have no pleasure in you,' behold, here I am, let him do to me what seems good to him." **Job 1:21**. And he said, "Naked I came from my mother's womb, and naked shall I return. The LORD gave, and the LORD has taken away; blessed be the name of the LORD." **Ps. 100:2**. Serve the LORD with gladness! Come into his presence with singing!

13 **Isa. 38:3**. ...and said, "Please, O LORD, remember how I have walked before you in faithfulness and with a whole heart, and have done what is good in your sight." And Hezekiah wept bitterly."

14 **Ps. 119:4-5**. You have commanded your precepts to be kept diligently. Oh that my ways may be steadfast in keeping your statutes!

15 **Rom. 12:11**. Do not be slothful in zeal, be fervent in spirit, serve the Lord.

16 **Ps. 119:80**. May my heart be blameless in your statutes, that I may not be put to shame!

17 **Ps. 119:112**. I incline my heart to perform your statutes forever, to the end.

18 **Isa. 6:2-3**. Above him stood the seraphim. Each had six wings: with two he covered his face, and with two he covered his feet, and with two he flew. And one called to another and said: "Holy, holy, holy is the LORD of hosts; the whole earth

is full of his glory!" **Mt. 18:10**. "See that you do not despise one of these little ones. For I tell you that in heaven their angels always see the face of my Father who is in heaven."

Q. 193. For what do we pray in the fourth petition?

A. In the fourth petition (which is, "Give us this day our daily bread"[1]), acknowledging that in Adam, and by our own sin, we have forfeited our right to all the outward blessings of this life, and deserve to be wholly deprived of them by God, and to have them cursed to us in the use of them;[2] and that these outward blessings alone are unable to sustain us,[3] nor can we merit them,[4] or by our own work obtain them,[5] but we are prone to desire,[6] get,[7] and use them unlawfully:[8] we pray for ourselves and others, that both they and we, waiting on the providence of God from day to day in the use of lawful means may, of his free gift, and as to his fatherly wisdom shall seem best, enjoy a sufficient portion of them,[9] and have the same continued and blessed to us in our holy and comfortable use of them,[10] and contentment in them;[11] and be kept from all things that are contrary to our material support and comfort.[12]

1 **Mt. 6:11**. Give us this day our daily bread.

2 **Gen. 2:17**. "...but of the tree of the knowledge of good and evil you shall not eat, for in the day that you eat of it you shall surely die." **Gen. 3:17**. And to Adam he said, "Because you have listened to the voice of your wife and have eaten of the tree of which I commanded you, 'You shall not eat of it,' cursed is the ground because of you; in pain you shall eat of it all the days of your life." **Deut. 28:15-17**. "But if you will not obey the voice of the LORD your God or be careful to do all his commandments and his statutes that I command you today, then all these curses shall come upon you and overtake you. Cursed shall you be in the city, and cursed shall you be in the field. Cursed shall be your basket and your kneading bowl." **Jer. 5:25**. Your iniquities have turned these away, and your sins have kept good from you. **Rom. 8:20-22**. For the creation was subjected to futility, not willingly, but because of him who subjected it, in hope that the creation itself will be set free from its bondage to corruption and obtain the freedom of the glory of the children of God. For we know that the whole creation has been groaning together in the pains of childbirth until now.

3 **Deut. 8:3**. And he humbled you and let you hunger and fed you with manna, which you did not know, nor did your fathers know, that he might make you know that man does not live by bread alone, but man lives by every word that comes from the mouth of the LORD.

4 **Gen. 32:10**. I am not worthy of the least of all the deeds of steadfast love and all the faithfulness that you have shown to your servant, for with only my staff I crossed this Jordan, and now I have become two camps.

5 **Deut. 8:17-18**. Beware lest you say in your heart, 'My power and the might of my hand have gotten me this wealth.' You shall remember the LORD your God, for it

is he who gives you power to get wealth, that he may confirm his covenant that he swore to your fathers, as it is this day.

6 **Jer. 6:13**. "For from the least to the greatest of them, everyone is greedy for unjust gain; and from prophet to priest, everyone deals falsely." **Mk. 7:21-22**. For from within, out of the heart of man, come evil thoughts, sexual immorality, theft, murder, adultery, coveting, wickedness, deceit, sensuality, envy, slander, pride, foolishness.

7 **Hos. 12:7**. A merchant, in whose hands are false balances, he loves to oppress.

8 **Jas. 4:3**. You ask and do not receive, because you ask wrongly, to spend it on your passions.

9 **Gen. 28:20**. Then Jacob made a vow, saying, "If God will be with me and will keep me in this way that I go, and will give me bread to eat and clothing to wear." **Gen. 43:12-14**. "Take double the money with you. Carry back with you the money that was returned in the mouth of your sacks. Perhaps it was an oversight. Take also your brother, and arise, go again to the man. May God Almighty grant you mercy before the man, and may he send back your other brother and Benjamin. And as for me, if I am bereaved of my children, I am bereaved." **Eph. 4:8**. Therefore it says, "When he ascended on high he led a host of captives, and he gave gifts to men." **Phil. 4:6**. ...do not be anxious about anything, but in everything by prayer and supplication with thanksgiving let your requests be made known to God. **2 Thess. 3:11-12**. For we hear that some among you walk in idleness, not busy at work, but busybodies. Now such persons we command and encourage in the Lord Jesus Christ to do their work quietly and to earn their own living.

10 **1 Tim. 4:3-5**. ...who forbid marriage and require abstinence from foods that God created to be received with thanksgiving by those who believe and know the truth. For everything created by God is good, and nothing is to be rejected if it is received with thanksgiving, for it is made holy by the word of God and prayer.

11 **1 Tim. 6:6-8**. But godliness with contentment is great gain, for we brought nothing into the world, and we cannot take anything out of the world. But if we have food and clothing, with these we will be content.

12 **Prov. 30:8-9**. Remove far from me falsehood and lying; give me neither poverty nor riches; feed me with the food that is needful for me, lest I be full and deny you and say, "Who is the LORD?" or lest I be poor and steal and profane the name of my God.

Q. 194. For what do we pray for in the fifth petition?

A. In the fifth petition (which is, "Forgive us our debts, as we also have forgiven our debtors"[1]), acknowledging that we and all others are guilty both of original and actual sin, and thereby become debtors to the justice of God, and neither we nor any other creature can make the least satisfaction for that debt:[2] we pray for ourselves and others, that God of his free grace would, through the obedience and satisfaction of Christ understood and applied by faith, acquit us both from the guilt and punishment of sin,[3] accept us in His Beloved,[4] continue His favor and grace to us,[5] pardon our daily failings,[6] and fill us with peace and joy, in giving us daily more and more assurance of forgiveness;[7] which we are more emboldened to ask, and encouraged to expect, when we have this testimony in ourselves, that we from the heart forgive others their offenses.[8]

1 **Mt. 6:12**. ...and forgive us our debts, as we also have forgiven our debtors.

2 **Ps. 130:3-4**. If you, O LORD, should mark iniquities, O Lord, who could stand? But with you there is forgiveness, that you may be feared. **Mt. 18:24-25**. When he began to settle, one was brought to him who owed him ten thousand talents. And since he could not pay, his master ordered him to be sold, with his wife and children and all that he had, and payment to be made. **Rom. 3:9-12, 19**. What then? Are we Jews any better off? No, not at all. For we have already charged that all, both Jews and Greeks, are under sin, as it is written: "None is righteous, no, not one; no one understands; no one seeks for God. All have turned aside; together they have become worthless; no one does good, not even one." ... Now we know that whatever the law says it speaks to those who are under the law, so that every mouth may be stopped, and the whole world may be held accountable to God.

3 **Rom. 3:24-26**. ...and are justified by his grace as a gift, through the redemption that is in Christ Jesus, whom God put forward as a propitiation by his blood, to be received by faith. This was to show God's righteousness, because in his divine forbearance he had passed over former sins. It was to show his righteousness at the present time, so that he might be just and the justifier of the one who has faith in Jesus. **Heb. 9:22**. Indeed, under the law almost everything is purified with blood, and without the shedding of blood there is no forgiveness of sins.

4 **Eph. 1:6-7**. ...to the praise of his glorious grace, with which he has blessed us in the Beloved. In him we have redemption through his blood, the forgiveness of our trespasses, according to the riches of his grace.

5 **2 Pet. 1:2**. May grace and peace be multiplied to you in the knowledge of God and of Jesus our Lord.

6 **Jer. 14:7**. "Though our iniquities testify against us, act, O LORD, for your name's sake; for our backslidings are many; we have sinned against you." **Hos. 14:2**. Take with you words and return to the LORD; say to him, "Take away all iniquity; accept what is good, and we will pay with bulls the vows of our lips.

7 **Ps. 51:7-10, 12**. Purge me with hyssop, and I shall be clean; wash me, and I shall be whiter than snow. Let me hear joy and gladness; let the bones that you have broken rejoice. Hide your face from my sins, and blot out all my iniquities. Create in me a clean heart, O God, and renew a right spirit within me. **Rom. 15:13**. Restore to me the joy of your salvation, and uphold me with a willing spirit.

8 **Mt. 6:14-15**. For if you forgive others their trespasses, your heavenly Father will also forgive you, but if you do not forgive others their trespasses, neither will your Father forgive your trespasses. **Mt. 18:35**. "So also my heavenly Father will do to every one of you, if you do not forgive your brother from your heart." **Lk. 11:4**. "... and forgive us our sins, for we ourselves forgive everyone who is indebted to us. And lead us not into temptation."

Q. 195. For what do we pray in the sixth petition?

A. In the sixth petition (which is, "And lead us not into temptation, but deliver us from evil"[1]), acknowledging that the most wise, righteous, and gracious God, for various holy and just ends, may so order things that we may be assaulted, foiled, and for a time led captive by temptations;[2] that Satan,[3] the world,[4] and the flesh, are ready powerfully to draw us aside and ensnare us;[5] and that we, even after the pardon of our sins, by reason of our corruption,[6] weakness, and lack of watchfulness,[7] are not only subject to be tempted, and quick to expose ourselves to temptations,[8] but also of ourselves unable and unwilling to resist them, to recover from them, and to use them to our benefit;[9] and worthy to be left under the power of them;[10] we pray: that God would so overrule the world and all in it,[11] subdue the flesh,[12] and restrain Satan,[13] order all things,[14] bestow and bless all means of grace,[15] and alert us to watchfulness in the use of them, that we and all His people may by His providence be kept from being tempted to sin;[16] or, if tempted, that by His Spirit we may be powerfully supported and enabled to stand in the hour of temptation;[17] or, when fallen, raised again and recovered from it,[18] and have a sanctified use and benefit from it;[19] that our sanctification and salvation may be perfected,[20] Satan crushed under our feet,[21] and we fully freed from sin, temptation, and all evil forever.[22]

1 **Mt. 6:13**. And lead us not into temptation, but deliver us from evil.

2 **2 Chr. 32:31**. And so in the matter of the envoys of the princes of Babylon, who had been sent to him to inquire about the sign that had been done in the land, God left him to himself, in order to test him and to know all that was in his heart.

3 **1 Chr. 21:1**. Then Satan stood against Israel and incited David to number Israel.

4 **Mk. 4:19**. ...but the cares of the world and the deceitfulness of riches and the desires for other things enter in and choke the word, and it proves unfruitful. **Lk. 21:34**. "But watch yourselves lest your hearts be weighed down with dissipation and drunkenness and cares of this life, and that day come upon you suddenly like a trap."

5 **Jas. 1:14**. But each person is tempted when he is lured and enticed by his own desire.

6 **Gal. 5:17**. For the desires of the flesh are against the Spirit, and the desires of the Spirit are against the flesh, for these are opposed to each other, to keep you from doing the things you want to do.

7 **Mt. 26:41**. "Watch and pray that you may not enter into temptation. The spirit indeed is willing, but the flesh is weak."

8 **2 Chr. 18:3**. Ahab king of Israel said to Jehoshaphat king of Judah, "Will you go with me to Ramoth-gilead?" He answered him, "I am as you are, my people as your people. We will be with you in the war." **2 Chr. 19:2**. But Jehu the son of Hanani the seer went out to meet him and said to King Jehoshaphat, "Should you help the wicked and love those who hate the LORD? Because of this, wrath has gone out against you from the LORD." **Mt. 26:69-72**. Now Peter was sitting outside in the courtyard. And a servant girl came up to him and said, "You also were with Jesus the Galilean." But he denied it before them all, saying, "I do not know what you mean." And when he went out to the entrance, another servant girl saw him, and she said to the bystanders, "This man was with Jesus of Nazareth." And again he denied it with an oath: "I do not know the man." **Gal. 2:11-14**. But when Cephas came to Antioch, I opposed him to his face, because he stood condemned.

For before certain men came from James, he was eating with the Gentiles; but when they came he drew back and separated himself, fearing the circumcision party. And the rest of the Jews acted hypocritically along with him, so that even Barnabas was led astray by their hypocrisy. But when I saw that their conduct was not in step with the truth of the gospel, I said to Cephas before them all, "If you, though a Jew, live like a Gentile and not like a Jew, how can you force the Gentiles to live like Jews?"

9 **1 Chr. 21:1-4**. Then Satan stood against Israel and incited David to number Israel. So David said to Joab and the commanders of the army, "Go, number Israel, from Beersheba to Dan, and bring me a report, that I may know their number." But Joab said, "May the LORD add to his people a hundred times as many as they are! Are they not, my lord the king, all of them my lord's servants? Why then should my lord require this? Why should it be a cause of guilt for Israel?" But the king's word prevailed against Joab. So Joab departed and went throughout all Israel and came back to Jerusalem. **2 Chr. 16:7-10**. At that time Hanani the seer came to Asa king of Judah and said to him, "Because you relied on the king of Syria, and did not rely on the LORD your God, the army of the king of Syria has escaped you. Were not the Ethiopians and the Libyans a huge army with very many chariots and horsemen? Yet because you relied on the LORD, he gave them into your hand. For the eyes of the LORD run to and fro throughout the whole earth, to give strong support to those whose heart is blameless toward him. You have done foolishly in this, for from now on you will have wars." Then Asa was angry with the seer and put him in the stocks in prison, for he was in a rage with him because of this. And Asa inflicted cruelties upon some of the people at the same time. **Rom. 7:23-24**. ...but I see in my members another law waging war against the law of my mind and making me captive to the law of sin that dwells in my members. Wretched man that I am! Who will deliver me from this body of death?

10 **Ps. 81:11-12**. "But my people did not listen to my voice; Israel would not submit to me. So I gave them over to their stubborn hearts, to follow their own counsels."

11 **Jn. 17:15**. I do not ask that you take them out of the world, but that you keep them from the evil one.

12 **Ps. 51:10**. Create in me a clean heart, O God, and renew a right spirit within me. **Ps. 119:133**. Keep steady my steps according to your promise, and let no iniquity get dominion over me.

13 **2 Cor. 12:7-8**. So to keep me from becoming conceited because of the surpassing greatness of the revelations, a thorn was given me in the flesh, a messenger of Satan to harass me, to keep me from becoming conceited. Three times I pleaded with the Lord about this, that it should leave me.

14 **1 Cor. 10:12-13**. Therefore let anyone who thinks that he stands take heed lest he fall. No temptation has overtaken you that is not common to man. God is faithful, and he will not let you be tempted beyond your ability, but with the temptation he will also provide the way of escape, that you may be able to endure it.

15 **Heb. 13:20-21**. Now may the God of peace who brought again from the dead our Lord Jesus, the great shepherd of the sheep, by the blood of the eternal covenant, equip you with everything good that you may do his will, working in us that which is pleasing in his sight, through Jesus Christ, to whom be glory forever and ever. Amen.

16 **Ps. 19:13**. Keep back your servant also from presumptuous sins; let them not have dominion over me! Then I shall be blameless, and innocent of great transgression. **Mt. 26:41**. "Watch and pray that you may not enter into temptation. The spirit indeed is willing, but the flesh is weak."

17 **Eph. 3:14-17**. For this reason I bow my knees before the Father, from whom every family in heaven and on earth is named, that according to the riches of his glory he may grant you to be strengthened with power through his Spirit in your inner being, so that Christ may dwell in your hearts through faith—that you, being rooted and grounded in love. **1 Thess. 3:13**. ...so that he may establish your hearts blameless in holiness before our God and Father, at the coming of our Lord Jesus with all his saints. **Jude 24**. Now to him who is able to keep you from stumbling and to present you blameless before the presence of his glory with great joy.

18 **Ps. 51:12**. Restore to me the joy of your salvation, and uphold me with a willing spirit.

19 **1 Pet. 5:8-10**. Be sober-minded; be watchful. Your adversary the devil prowls around like a roaring lion, seeking someone to devour. Resist him, firm in your faith, knowing that the same kinds of suffering are being experienced by your brotherhood throughout the world. And after you have suffered a little while, the God of all grace, who has called you to his eternal glory in Christ, will himself restore, confirm, strengthen, and establish you.

20 **2 Cor. 13:7, 9**. But we pray to God that you may not do wrong—not that we may appear to have met the test, but that you may do what is right, though we may seem to have failed. ...For we are glad when we are weak and you are strong. Your restoration is what we pray for.

21 **Zech. 3:2**. And the LORD said to Satan, "The LORD rebuke you, O Satan! The LORD who has chosen Jerusalem rebuke you! Is not this a brand plucked from the fire?" **Lk. 22:31-32**. "Simon, Simon, behold, Satan demanded to have you, that he might sift you like wheat, but I have prayed for you that your faith may not fail. And when you have turned again, strengthen your brothers." **Rom. 16:20**. The God of peace will soon crush Satan under your feet. The grace of our Lord Jesus Christ be with you.

22 **Jn. 17:15**. I do not ask that you take them out of the world, but that you keep them from the evil one. **1 Thess. 5:23**. Now may the God of peace himself sanctify you completely, and may your whole spirit and soul and body be kept blameless at the coming of our Lord Jesus Christ.

Q. 196. What does the conclusion of the Lord's Prayer teach us?

A. The conclusion of the Lord's Prayer (which is, "For yours is the kingdom and the power and the glory, forever. Amen."[1]), teaches us to enforce our petitions with arguments[2] that are to be taken, not from any worthiness in ourselves, or in any other creature, but from God,[3] and with our prayers to join praises,[4] ascribing to God alone eternal sovereignty, omnipotence, and glorious excellence;[5] in regard to which, as He is able and willing to help us,[6] so we by faith are emboldened to plead with Him that He would,[7] and to rely quietly on Him that he will, fulfill our requests.[8] And to testify our desires and assurance, we say, "Amen."[9]

1 **Mt. 6:13**. And lead us not into temptation, but deliver us from evil.

2 **Rom. 15:30**. I appeal to you, brothers, by our Lord Jesus Christ and by the love of the Spirit, to strive together with me in your prayers to God on my behalf.

3 **Dan. 9:4, 7-9, 16-19**. I prayed to the LORD my God and made confession, saying, "O Lord, the great and awesome God, who keeps covenant and steadfast love with those who love him and keep his commandments." ... To you, O Lord, belongs righteousness, but to us open shame, as at this day, to the men of Judah, to the inhabitants of Jerusalem, and to all Israel, those who are near and those who are far away, in all the lands to which you have driven them, because of the treachery that they have committed against you. To us, O LORD, belongs open shame, to our kings, to our princes, and to our fathers, because we have sinned against you. To the Lord our God belong mercy and forgiveness, for we have rebelled against him." ... "O Lord, according to all your righteous acts, let your anger and your wrath turn away from your city Jerusalem, your holy hill, because for our sins, and for the iniquities of our fathers, Jerusalem and your people have become a byword among all who are around us. Now therefore, O our God, listen to the prayer of your servant and to his pleas for mercy, and for your own sake, O Lord, make your face to shine upon your sanctuary, which is desolate. O my God, incline your ear and hear. Open your eyes and see our desolations, and the city that is called by your name. For we do not present our pleas before you because of our righteousness, but because of your great mercy. O Lord, hear; O Lord, forgive. O Lord, pay attention and act. Delay not, for your own sake, O my God, because your city and your people are called by your name."

4 **Phil. 4:6**. ...do not be anxious about anything, but in everything by prayer and supplication with thanksgiving let your requests be made known to God.

5 **1 Chr. 29:10-13**. Therefore David blessed the LORD in the presence of all the assembly. And David said: "Blessed are you, O LORD, the God of Israel our father, forever and ever. Yours, O LORD, is the greatness and the power and the glory and the victory and the majesty, for all that is in the heavens and in the earth is yours. Yours is the kingdom, O LORD, and you are exalted as head above all. Both riches and honor come from you, and you rule over all. In your hand are power and might, and in your hand it is to make great and to give strength to all. And now we thank you, our God, and praise your glorious name."

6 **Lk. 11:13**. "If you then, who are evil, know how to give good gifts to your children, how much more will the heavenly Father give the Holy Spirit to those who ask him!" **Eph. 3:20-21**. Now to him who is able to do far more abundantly than all that we ask or think, according to the power at work within us, to him be glory in the church and in Christ Jesus throughout all generations, forever and ever. Amen.

7 **2 Chr. 20:6, 11**. ...and said, "O LORD, God of our fathers, are you not God in heaven? You rule over all the kingdoms of the nations. In your hand are power and might, so that none is able to withstand you." ...behold, they reward us by coming to drive us out of your possession, which you have given us to inherit.

8 **2 Chr. 14:11**. And Asa cried to the LORD his God, "O LORD, there is none like you to help, between the mighty and the weak. Help us, O LORD our God, for we rely on you, and in your name we have come against this multitude. O LORD, you are our God; let not man prevail against you."

9 **1 Cor. 14:16**. Otherwise, if you give thanks with your spirit, how can anyone in the position of an outsider say "Amen" to your thanksgiving when he does not know what you are saying? **Rev. 22:20-21**. He who testifies to these things says, "Surely I am coming soon." Amen. Come, Lord Jesus! The grace of the Lord Jesus be with all. Amen.

The Westminster Shorter Catechism

The Rose Window and the North Transept of Westminster where William Wilberforce is buried next to his friend William Pitt the Younger.

Q. 1. What is the chief end of man?

A. Man's chief end is to glorify God,[1] and to enjoy him forever.[2]

1 **1 Cor. 10:31.** So, whether you eat or drink, or whatever you do, do all to the glory of God.

2 **Ps. 73:25-28.** Whom have I in heaven but you? And there is nothing on earth that I desire besides you. My flesh and my heart may fail, but God is the strength of my heart and my portion forever. For behold, those who are far from you shall perish; you put an end to everyone who is unfaithful to you. But for me it is good to be near God; I have made the Lord GOD my refuge, that I may tell of all your works.

Q. 2. What rule has God given to direct us how we may glorify and enjoy him?

A. The Word of God which is contained in the Scriptures of the Old and New Testaments[1] is the only rule to direct us how we may glorify and enjoy him.[2]

1 **Eph. 2:20.** ...built on the foundation of the apostles and prophets, Christ Jesus himself being the cornerstone. **2 Tim. 3:16.** All Scripture is breathed out by God and profitable for teaching, for reproof, for correction, and for training in righteousness.

2 **1 Jn. 1:3-4.** ...that which we have seen and heard we proclaim also to you, so that you too may have fellowship with us; and indeed our fellowship is with the Father and with his Son Jesus Christ. And we are writing these things so that our joy may be complete.

Q. 3. What do the Scriptures principally teach?

A. The Scriptures principally teach what man is to believe concerning God, and what duty God requires of man.[1]

1 **2 Tim. 1:13.** Follow the pattern of the sound words that you have heard from me, in the faith and love that are in Christ Jesus.

Q. 4. What is God?

A. God is a Spirit,[1] infinite,[2] eternal[3] and unchangeable,[4] in his being,[5] wisdom,[6] power,[7] holiness,[8] justice, goodness, and truth.[9]

1 **Jn. 4:24.** "God is spirit, and those who worship him must worship in spirit and truth."

2 **Job 11:7-9.** "Can you find out the deep things of God? Can you find out the limit of the Almighty? It is higher than heaven—what can you do? Deeper than Sheol —what can you know? Its measure is longer than the earth and broader than the sea."

3 **Ps. 90:2**. Before the mountains were brought forth, or ever you had formed the earth and the world, from everlasting to everlasting you are God.

4 **Jas. 1:17**. Every good gift and every perfect gift is from above, coming down from the Father of lights with whom there is no variation or shadow due to change.

5 **Ex. 3:14**. God said to Moses, "I AM WHO I AM." And he said, "Say this to the people of Israel, 'I AM has sent me to you.'"

6 **Ps. 104:24**. O Lord, how manifold are your works! In wisdom have you made them all; the earth is full of your creatures. **Rom. 11:33-34**. Oh, the depth of the riches and wisdom and knowledge of God! How unsearchable are his judgments and how inscrutable his ways! "For who has known the mind of the Lord, or who has been his counselor?" **Heb. 4:13**. And no creature is hidden from his sight, but all are naked and exposed to the eyes of him to whom we must give account. **1 Jn. 3:20**. ...for whenever our heart condemns us, God is greater than our heart, and he knows everything.

7. **Rev. 1:8.** "I am the Alpha and the Omega," says the Lord God, "who is, and who was, and who is to come, the Almighty."

8 **Rev. 15:4**. "Who will not fear, O Lord, and glorify your name? For you alone are holy. All nations will come and worship you, for your righteous acts have been revealed."

9 **Ex. 34:6-7**. The LORD passed before him and proclaimed, "The LORD, the LORD, a God merciful and gracious, slow to anger, and abounding in steadfast love and faithfulness, keeping steadfast love for thousands, forgiving iniquity and transgression and sin, but who will by no means clear the guilty, visiting the iniquity of the fathers on the children and the children's children, to the third and the fourth generation."

Q. 5. Are there more Gods than one?

A. There is but one only, the living and true God.[1]

1 **Deut. 6:4**. "Hear, O Israel: The LORD our God, the LORD is one."

Q. 6. How many Persons are there in the Godhead?

A. There are three Persons in the Godhead: the Father, the Son, and the Holy Spirit; and these three are one God, the same in substance, equal in power and glory.[1]

1 **Mt. 28:19**. Go therefore and make disciples of all nations, baptizing them in the name of the Father and of the Son and of the Holy Spirit. **1 Jn. 5:7**. For there are three that testify.

Q. 7. What are the decrees of God?

A. The decrees of God are His eternal purpose, according to the counsel of His will, by which, for His own glory, He has foreordained whatever comes to pass.[1]

1 **Rom. 9:22-23**. What if God, desiring to show his wrath and to make known his power, has endured with much patience vessels of wrath prepared for destruction, in order to make known the riches of his glory for vessels of mercy, which he has prepared beforehand for glory. **Eph. 1:4, 11**. ...even as he chose us in him before the foundation of the world, that we should be holy and blameless before him. In love. ... In him we have obtained an inheritance, having been predestined according to the purpose of him who works all things according to the counsel of his will.

Q. 8. How does God execute His decrees?

A. God executes His decrees in the works of creation and providence.

Q. 9. What is the work of creation?

A. The work of creation is God's making all things from nothing, by the word of His power, in the space of six days, and all very good.[1]

1 See **Gen. 1. Heb. 11:3**. By faith we understand that the universe was created by the word of God, so that what is seen was not made out of things that are visible.

Q. 10. How did God create man?

A. God created man male and female, after His own image, in knowledge, righteousness, and holiness, with dominion over the creatures.[1]

1 **Gen. 1:26-28**. Then God said, "Let us make man in our image, after our likeness. And let them have dominion over the fish of the sea and over the birds of the heavens and over the livestock and over all the earth and over every creeping thing that creeps on the earth." So God created man in his own image, in the image of God he created him; male and female he created them. And God blessed them. And God said to them, "Be fruitful and multiply and fill the earth and subdue it, and have dominion over the fish of the sea and over the birds of the heavens and over every living thing that moves on the earth." **Eph. 4:24**. ...and to put on the new self, created after the likeness of God in true righteousness and holiness. **Col. 3:10**. ...and have put on the new self, which is being renewed in knowledge after the image of its creator.

Q. 11. What are God's works of providence?

A. God's works of providence are His most holy,[1] wise,[2] and powerful preserving[3] and governing all His creatures, and all their actions.[4]

1 **Ps. 145:17**. The LORD is righteous in all his ways and kind in all his works.

2 **Ps. 104:24**. O LORD, how manifold are your works! In wisdom have you made them all; the earth is full of your creatures. **Isa. 28:29**. This also comes from the LORD of hosts; he is wonderful in counsel and excellent in wisdom.

3 **Heb. 1:3**. He is the radiance of the glory of God and the exact imprint of his nature, and he upholds the universe by the word of his power. After making purification for sins, he sat down at the right hand of the Majesty on high.

4 **Ps. 103:19**. The LORD has established his throne in the heavens, and his kingdom rules over all. **Mt. 10:29-31**. Are not two sparrows sold for a penny? And not one of them will fall to the ground apart from your Father. But even the hairs of your head are all numbered. Fear not, therefore; you are of more value than many sparrows.

Q. 12. What special act of providence did God exercise toward man, in the estate in which he was created?

A. When God created man, He entered into a covenant of life with him, on condition of perfect obedience; forbidding him to eat of the Tree of the Knowledge of Good and Evil, on the pain of death.[1]

1 **Gen. 2:17**. "...but of the tree of the knowledge of good and evil you shall not eat, for in the day that you eat of it you shall surely die." **Gal. 3:12.** But the law is not of faith, rather "The one who does them shall live by them."

Q. 13. Did our first parents continue in the estate in which they were created?

A. Our first parents, being left to the freedom of their own will, fell from the estate in which they were created, by sinning against God.[1]

1 **Gen. 3:6-8**. So when the woman saw that the tree was good for food, and that it was a delight to the eyes, and that the tree was to be desired to make one wise, she took of its fruit and ate, and she also gave some to her husband who was with her, and he ate. Then the eyes of both were opened, and they knew that they were naked. And they sewed fig leaves together and made themselves loincloths. And they heard the sound of the LORD God walking in the garden in the cool of the day, and the man and his wife hid themselves from the presence of the LORD God among the trees of the garden. **Eccl. 7:29**. See, this alone I found, that God made man upright, but they have sought out many schemes.

Q. 14. What is sin?

A. Sin is any lack of conformity to, or transgression of, the law of God.[1]

1 **1 Jn. 3:4**. Everyone who makes a practice of sinning also practices lawlessness; sin is lawlessness.

Q. 15. What was the sin by which our first parents fell from the estate in which they were created?

A. The sin by which our first parents fell from the estate in which they were created was their eating of the forbidden fruit.[1]

1 **GEN. 3:6**. So when the woman saw that the tree was good for food, and that it was a delight to the eyes, and that the tree was to be desired to make one wise, she took of its fruit and ate, and she also gave some to her husband who was with her, and he ate.

Q. 16. Did all mankind fall in Adam's first transgression?

A. The covenant being made with Adam, not only for himself, but for his descendants, all mankind, descending from him by ordinary generation, sinned in him, and fell with him, in his first transgression.[1]

1 **GEN. 2:16-17**. And the LORD God commanded the man, saying, "You may surely eat of every tree of the garden, but of the tree of the knowledge of good and evil you shall not eat, for in the day that you eat of it you shall surely die." **ROM. 5:12**. Therefore, just as sin came into the world through one man, and death through sin, and so death spread to all men because all sinned. **1 COR. 15:21-22**. For as by a man came death, by a man has come also the resurrection of the dead. For as in Adam all die, so also in Christ shall all be made alive.

Q. 17. Into what estate did the Fall bring mankind?

A. The Fall brought mankind into an estate of sin and misery.[1]

1 **ROM. 5:12**. Therefore, just as sin came into the world through one man, and death through sin, and so death spread to all men because all sinned

---

Q. 18. What is the sinfulness of that estate into which man fell?

A. The sinfulness of that estate into which man fell consists of: the guilt of Adam's first sin, the lack of original righteousness, and the corruption of his whole nature, which is commonly called original sin, together with all actual transgressions that proceed from it.[1]

1 **Mt. 15:19**. For out of the heart come evil thoughts, murder, adultery, sexual immorality, theft, false witness, slander. **Rom. 5:10-20**. For if while we were enemies we were reconciled to God by the death of his Son, much more, now that we are reconciled, shall we be saved by his life. More than that, we also rejoice in God through our Lord Jesus Christ, through whom we have now received reconciliation. Therefore, just as sin came into the world through one man, and death through sin, and so death spread to all men because all sinned— for sin indeed was in the world before the law was given, but sin is not counted where there is no law. Yet death reigned from Adam to Moses, even over those whose sinning was not like the transgression of Adam, who was a type of the one who was to come. But the free gift is not like the trespass. For if many died through one man's trespass, much more have the grace of God and the free gift by the grace of that one man Jesus Christ abounded for many. And the free gift is not like the result of that one man's sin. For the judgment following one trespass brought condemnation, but the free gift following many trespasses brought justification. For if, because of one man's trespass, death reigned through that one man, much more will those who receive the abundance of grace and the free gift of righteousness reign in life through the one man Jesus Christ. Therefore, as one trespass led to condemnation for all men, so one act of righteousness leads to justification and life for all men. For as by the one man's disobedience the many were made sinners, so by the one man's obedience the many will be made righteous. Now the law came in to increase the trespass, but where sin increased, grace abounded all the more. **Rom. 5:12, 19**. Therefore, just as sin came into the world through one man, and death through sin, and so death spread to all men because all sinned. ... For as by the one man's disobedience the many were made sinners, so by the one man's obedience the many will be made righteous. **Eph. 2:1-3**. And you were dead in the trespasses and sins in which you once walked, following the course of this world, following the prince of the power of the air, the spirit that is now at work in the sons of disobedience— among whom we all once lived in the passions of our flesh, carrying out the desires of the body and the mind, and were by nature children of wrath, like the rest of mankind. **Jas. 1:14-15**. But each person is tempted when he is lured and enticed by his own desire. Then desire when it has conceived gives birth to sin, and sin when it is fully grown brings forth death.

Q. 19. What is the misery of that estate into which man fell?

A. All mankind, by their fall, lost communion with God,[1] are under His wrath and curse,[2] and so made liable to all miseries of this life, to death itself, and to the pains of hell forever.[3]

1 **Gen. 3:8, 10, 24**. And they heard the sound of the LORD God walking in the garden in the cool of the day, and the man and his wife hid themselves from the presence of the LORD God among the trees of the garden. ... And he said, "I heard the sound of you in the garden, and I was afraid, because I was naked, and I hid

myself." ... He drove out the man, and at the east of the garden of Eden he placed the cherubim and a flaming sword that turned every way to guard the way to the tree of life.

2 **Gal. 3:10**. For all who rely on works of the law are under a curse; for it is written, "Cursed be everyone who does not abide by all things written in the Book of the Law, and do them." **Eph. 2:2-3**. ...in which you once walked, following the course of this world, following the prince of the power of the air, the spirit that is now at work in the sons of disobedience— among whom we all once lived in the passions of our flesh, carrying out the desires of the body and the mind, and were by nature children of wrath, like the rest of mankind.

3 **Lam. 3:39**. Why should a living man complain, a man, about the punishment of his sins? **Mt. 25:41, 46**. "Then he will say to those on his left, 'Depart from me, you cursed, into the eternal fire prepared for the devil and his angels. ... And these will go away into eternal punishment, but the righteous into eternal life." **Rom. 6:23**. For the wages of sin is death, but the free gift of God is eternal life in Christ Jesus our Lord.

Q. 20. Did God leave all mankind to perish in the estate of sin and misery?

A. God, having out of his mere good pleasure, from all eternity, elected some to everlasting life,[1] did enter into a covenant of grace, to deliver them out of the estate of sin and misery, and to bring them into an estate of salvation by a Redeemer.[2]

1 **Eph. 1:4**. ...even as he chose us in him before the foundation of the world, that we should be holy and blameless before him. In love.

2 **Rom. 3:20-22**. For by works of the law no human being will be justified in his sight, since through the law comes knowledge of sin. But now the righteousness of God has been manifested apart from the law, although the Law and the Prophets bear witness to it— the righteousness of God through faith in Jesus Christ for all who believe. For there is no distinction. **Gal. 3:21-22**. Is the law then contrary to the promises of God? Certainly not! For if a law had been given that could give life, then righteousness would indeed be by the law. But the Scripture imprisoned everything under sin, so that the promise by faith in Jesus Christ might be given to those who believe.

Q. 21. Who is the Redeemer of God's elect?

A. The only Redeemer of God's elect is the Lord Jesus Christ,[1] who, being the eternal Son of God, became man,[2] and so was, and continues to be, God and man, in two distinct natures, and one Person forever.[3]

1 **1 Tim. 2:5-6**. For there is one God, and there is one mediator between God and men, the man Christ Jesus, who gave himself as a ransom for all, which is the testimony given at the proper time.

2 **Jn. 1:14**. And the Word became flesh and dwelt among us, and we have seen his glory, glory as of the only Son from the Father, full of grace and truth. **Gal. 4:4**.

But when the fullness of time had come, God sent forth his Son, born of woman, born under the law.

3 **Lk. 1:35**. And the angel answered her, "The Holy Spirit will come upon you, and the power of the Most High will overshadow you; therefore the child to be born will be called holy—the Son of God." **Rom. 9:5**. To them belong the patriarchs, and from their race, according to the flesh, is the Christ, who is God over all, blessed forever. Amen. **Col. 2:9**. For in him the whole fullness of deity dwells bodily. **Heb. 7:24-25**. ...but he holds his priesthood permanently, because he continues forever. Consequently, he is able to save to the uttermost those who draw near to God through him, since he always lives to make intercession for them.

Q. 22. How did Christ, being the Son of God, become man?

A. Christ, the Son of God, became man, by taking to Himself a true body[1] and a reasonable soul,[2] being conceived by the power of the Holy Spirit, in the womb of the Virgin Mary, and born of her,[3] yet without sin.[4]

1 **Heb. 2:14, 16**. Since therefore the children share in flesh and blood, he himself likewise partook of the same things, that through death he might destroy the one who has the power of death, that is, the devil. ... For surely it is not angels that he helps, but he helps the offspring of Abraham. **Heb. 10:5**. Consequently, when Christ came into the world, he said, "Sacrifices and offerings you have not desired, but a body have you prepared for me."

2 **Mt. 26:38**. Then he said to them, "My soul is very sorrowful, even to death; remain here, and watch with me."

3 **Lk. 1:27, 31, 35, 42**. ...to a virgin betrothed to a man whose name was Joseph, of the house of David. And the virgin's name was Mary. ... And behold, you will conceive in your womb and bear a son, and you shall call his name Jesus. ... And the angel answered her, "The Holy Spirit will come upon you, and the power of the Most High will overshadow you; therefore the child to be born will be called holy—the Son of God. ...and she exclaimed with a loud cry, "Blessed are you among women, and blessed is the fruit of your womb! **Gal. 4:4**. But when the fullness of time had come, God sent forth his Son, born of woman, born under the law.

4 **Heb. 4:15**. For we do not have a high priest who is unable to sympathize with our weaknesses, but one who in every respect has been tempted as we are, yet without sin. **Heb. 7:26**. For it was indeed fitting that we should have such a high priest, holy, innocent, unstained, separated from sinners, and exalted above the heavens.

Q. 23. What offices does Christ execute as our Redeemer?

A. Christ, as our Redeemer, executes the offices of a prophet, of a priest, and of a king, both in His estate of humiliation and exaltation.[1]

1 **Ps. 2:6, 8-11**. "As for me, I have set my King on Zion, my holy hill." ... Ask of me, and I will make the nations your heritage, and the ends of the earth your possession. You shall break them with a rod of iron and dash them in pieces like a potter's vessel." Now therefore, O kings, be wise; be warned, O rulers of the earth. Serve the Lord with fear, and rejoice with trembling. **Isa. 9:6-7**. For to us a child

is born, to us a son is given; and the government shall be upon his shoulder, and his name shall be called Wonderful Counselor, Mighty God, Everlasting Father, Prince of Peace. Of the increase of his government and of peace there will be no end, on the throne of David and over his kingdom, to establish it and to uphold it with justice and with righteousness from this time forth and forevermore. The zeal of the Lord of hosts will do this. **Mt. 21:5**. "Say to the daughter of Zion, 'Behold, your king is coming to you, humble, and mounted on a donkey, on a colt, the foal of a beast of burden.'" **Acts 3:21-22**. ...whom heaven must receive until the time for restoring all the things about which God spoke by the mouth of his holy prophets long ago. Moses said, 'The Lord God will raise up for you a prophet like me from your brothers. You shall listen to him in whatever he tells you. **2 Cor. 13:3**. ...since you seek proof that Christ is speaking in me. He is not weak in dealing with you, but is powerful among you. **Heb. 5:5-7**. So also Christ did not exalt himself to be made a high priest, but was appointed by him who said to him, "You are my Son, today I have begotten you"; as he says also in another place, "You are a priest forever, after the order of Melchizedek." In the days of his flesh, Jesus offered up prayers and supplications, with loud cries and tears, to him who was able to save him from death, and he was heard because of his reverence. **Heb. 7:25**. Consequently, he is able to save to the uttermost those who draw near to God through him, since he always lives to make intercession for them. **Heb. 12:25**. See that you do not refuse him who is speaking. For if they did not escape when they refused him who warned them on earth, much less will we escape if we reject him who warns from heaven.

Q. 24. How does Christ execute the office of a prophet?

A. Christ executes the office of a prophet in revealing to us, by His Word and Spirit, the will of God for our salvation.[1]

1 **Jn. 1:18**. No one has ever seen God; the only God, who is at the Father's side, he has made him known. **Jn. 15:15**. No longer do I call you servants, for the servant does not know what his master is doing; but I have called you friends, for all that I have heard from my Father I have made known to you. **Jn. 20:31**. ...but these are written so that you may believe that Jesus is the Christ, the Son of God, and that by believing you may have life in his name. **1 Pet. 1:10-12**. Concerning this salvation, the prophets who prophesied about the grace that was to be yours searched and inquired carefully, inquiring what person or time the Spirit of Christ in them was indicating when he predicted the sufferings of Christ and the subsequent glories. It was revealed to them that they were serving not themselves but you, in the things that have now been announced to you through those who preached the good news to you by the Holy Spirit sent from heaven, things into which angels long to look.

Q. 25. How does Christ execute the office of a priest?

A. Christ executes the office of a priest in his once offering up of Himself a sacrifice to satisfy divine justice,[1] and reconcile us to God,[2] and in making continual intercession for us.[3]

1 **Heb. 9:14, 28.** ...how much more will the blood of Christ, who through the eternal Spirit offered himself without blemish to God, purify our conscience from dead works to serve the living God. ...so Christ, having been offered once to bear the sins of many, will appear a second time, not to deal with sin but to save those who are eagerly waiting for him.

2 **Heb. 2:17.** Therefore he had to be made like his brothers in every respect, so that he might become a merciful and faithful high priest in the service of God, to make propitiation for the sins of the people.

3 **Heb. 7:24-25.** ...but he holds his priesthood permanently, because he continues forever. Consequently, he is able to save to the uttermost those who draw near to God through him, since he always lives to make intercession for them.

Q. 26. How does Christ execute the office of a king?

A. Christ executes the office of a king in subduing us to Himself, in ruling and defending us,[1] and in restraining and conquering all His and our enemies.[2]

1 **Ps. 110:3.** Your people will offer themselves freely on the day of your power, in holy garments; from the womb of the morning, the dew of your youth will be yours. **Mt. 28:18-20.** And Jesus came and said to them, "All authority in heaven and on earth has been given to me. Go therefore and make disciples of all nations, baptizing them in the name of the Father and of the Son and of the Holy Spirit, teaching them to observe all that I have commanded you. And behold, I am with you always, to the end of the age." **Jn. 17:2.** ...since you have given Him authority over all flesh, to give eternal life to all whom you have given Him. **Col. 1:13.** He has delivered us from the domain of darkness and transferred us to the kingdom of his beloved Son.

2 **Ps. 2:6-9.** "As for me, I have set my King on Zion, my holy hill." I will tell of the decree: The Lord said to me, "You are my Son; today I have begotten you. As of me, and I will make the nations your heritage, and the ends of the earth your possession. You shall break them with a rod of iron and dash them in pieces like a potter's vessel." **Ps. 110:1-2.** The Lord says to my Lord: "Sit at my right hand, until I make your enemies your footstool." The Lord sends forth from Zion your mighty scepter. Rule in the midst of your enemies! **Mt. 12:28.** But if it is by the Spirit of God that I cast out demons, then the kingdom of God has come upon you. **1 Cor. 15:24-26.** Then comes the end, when he delivers the kingdom to God the Father after destroying every rule and every authority and power. For he must reign until he has put all his enemies under his feet. The last enemy to be destroyed is death. **Col. 2:15.** He disarmed the rulers and authorities and put them to open shame, by triumphing over them in him.

Q. 27. What was Christ's humiliation?

A. Christ's humiliation consisted in His being born, and that in a low condition,[1] made under the law,[2] undergoing the miseries of this life,[3] the wrath of God,[4] and the cursed death of the cross;[5] in being buried,[6] and continuing under the power of death for a time.[7]

1 **Lk. 2:7**. And she gave birth to her firstborn son and wrapped him in swaddling cloths and laid him in a manger, because there was no place for them in the inn.

2 **Gal. 4:4**. But when the fullness of time had come, God sent forth his Son, born of woman, born under the law.

3 **Isa. 53:2-3**. For he grew up before him like a young plant, and like a root out of dry ground; he had no form or majesty that we should look at him, and no beauty that we should desire him. He was despised and rejected by men; a man of sorrows, and acquainted with grief;and as one from whom men hide their faces he was despised, and we esteemed him not. **Heb. 12:2-3**. ...looking to Jesus, the founder and perfecter of our faith, who for the joy that was set before him endured the cross, despising the shame, and is seated at the right hand of the throne of God. Consider him who endured from sinners such hostility against himself, so that you may not grow weary or fainthearted.

4 **Mt. 27:46**. And about the ninth hour Jesus cried out with a loud voice, saying, "Eli, Eli, lema sabachthani?" that is, "My God, my God, why have you forsaken me?" **Lk. 22:44**. And being in an agony he prayed more earnestly; and his sweat became like great drops of blood falling down to the ground.

5 **Phil. 2:8**. And being found in human form, he humbled himself by becoming obedient to the point of death, even death on a cross.

6 **1 Cor. 15:3-4**. For I delivered to you as of first importance what I also received: that Christ died for our sins in accordance with the Scriptures, that he was buried, that he was raised on the third day in accordance with the Scriptures.

7 **Acts 2:24-27, 31**. God raised him up, loosing the pangs of death, because it was not possible for him to be held by it. For David says concerning him, "'I saw the Lord always before me, for he is at my right hand that I may not be shaken; therefore my heart was glad, and my tongue rejoiced; my flesh also will dwell in hope. For you will not abandon my soul to Hades, or let your Holy One see corruption. ... he foresaw and spoke about the resurrection of the Christ, that he was not abandoned to Hades, nor did his flesh see corruption.

Q. 28. What is Christ's exaltation?

A. Christ's exaltation consists in His rising again from the dead on the third day,[1] in ascending into heaven,[2] in sitting at the right hand of God the Father,[3] and in coming to judge the world at the last day.[4]

1 **1 Cor. 15:4**. ...that he was buried, that he was raised on the third day in accordance with the Scriptures.

2 **Mk. 16:19**. So then the Lord Jesus, after he had spoken to them, was taken up into heaven and sat down at the right hand of God.

3 **Eph. 1:20**. ...that he worked in Christ when he raised him from the dead and seated him at his right hand in the heavenly places.

4 **Acts 1:11**. ...and said, "Men of Galilee, why do you stand looking into heaven? This Jesus, who was taken up from you into heaven, will come in the same way as you saw him go into heaven." **Acts 17:31**. "...because he has fixed a day on which he will judge the world in righteousness by a man whom he has appointed; and of this he has given assurance to all by raising him from the dead."

Q. 29. How do we take part in the redemption purchased by Christ?

A. We take part in the redemption purchased by Christ by the effectual application of it to us[1] by His Holy Spirit.[2]

1 **Jn. 1:11-12**. He came to his own, and his own people did not receive him. But to all who did receive him, who believed in his name, he gave the right to become children of God.

2 **Titus 3:5-6**. ...he saved us, not because of works done by us in righteousness, but according to his own mercy, by the washing of regeneration and renewal of the Holy Spirit, whom he poured out on us richly through Jesus Christ our Savior.

Q. 30. How does the Spirit apply to us the redemption purchased by Christ?

A. The Spirit applies to us the redemption purchased by Christ by working faith in us,[1] and thereby uniting us to Christ in our effectual calling.[2]

1 **Jn. 6:37-39**. All that the Father gives me will come to me, and whoever comes to me I will never cast out. For I have come down from heaven, not to do my own will but the will of him who sent me. And this is the will of him who sent me, that I should lose nothing of all that he has given me, but raise it up on the last day. **Eph. 1:13-14**. In him you also, when you heard the word of truth, the gospel of your salvation, and believed in him, were sealed with the promised Holy Spirit, who is the guarantee of our inheritance until we acquire possession of it, to the praise of his glory. **Eph. 2:8**. For by grace you have been saved through faith. And this is not your own doing; it is the gift of God.

2 **1 Cor. 1:9**. God is faithful, by whom you were called into the fellowship of his Son, Jesus Christ our Lord. **Eph. 3:17**. ...so that Christ may dwell in your hearts through faith—that you, being rooted and grounded in love.

Q. 31. What is effectual calling?

A. Effectual calling is the work of God's Spirit,[1] by which, convincing us of our sin and misery,[2] enlightening our minds in the knowledge of Christ,[3] and renewing our wills,[4] he persuades and enables us to embrace Jesus Christ, freely offered to us in the Gospel.[5]

1 **2 Thess. 2:13-14**. But we ought always to give thanks to God for you, brothers beloved by the Lord, because God chose you as the firstfruits to be saved, through sanctification by the Spirit and belief in the truth. To this he called you through our gospel, so that you may obtain the glory of our Lord Jesus Christ. **2 Tim. 1:9**.

...who saved us and called us to a holy calling, not because of our works but because of his own purpose and grace, which he gave us in Christ Jesus before the ages began.

2 **Acts 2:37**. Now when they heard this they were cut to the heart, and said to Peter and the rest of the apostles, "Brothers, what shall we do?"

3 **Acts 26:18**. '...to open their eyes, so that they may turn from darkness to light and from the power of Satan to God, that they may receive forgiveness of sins and a place among those who are sanctified by faith in me.'

4 **Ezek. 36:26-27**. And I will give you a new heart, and a new spirit I will put within you. And I will remove the heart of stone from your flesh and give you a heart of flesh. And I will put my Spirit within you, and cause you to walk in my statutes and be careful to obey my rules.

5 **Jn. 6:44-45**. No one can come to me unless the Father who sent me draws him. And I will raise him up on the last day. It is written in the Prophets, 'And they will all be taught by God.' Everyone who has heard and learned from the Father comes to me. **Phil. 2:13**. ...for it is God who works in you, both to will and to work for his good pleasure.

Q. 32. What benefits are there in this life for those who are effectually called?

A. Those who are effectually called partake in justification,[1] adoption,[2] sanctification, and the other benefits that, in this life, do either accompany them or flow from them.[3]

1 **Rom. 8:30**. And those whom he predestined he also called, and those whom he called he also justified, and those whom he justified he also glorified.

2 **Eph. 1:5**. ...he predestined us for adoption as sons through Jesus Christ, according to the purpose of his will.

3 **1 Cor. 1:26, 30**. For consider your calling, brothers: not many of you were wise according to worldly standards, not many were powerful, not many were of noble birth. ...And because of him you are in Christ Jesus, who became to us wisdom from God, righteousness and sanctification and redemption.

Q. 33. What is justification?

A. Justification is an act of God's free grace, in which He pardons all our sins,[1] and accepts us as righteous in His sight,[2] only for the righteousness of Christ imputed to us,[3] and received by faith alone.[4]

1 **Rom. 3:24-25**. ...and are justified by his grace as a gift, through the redemption that is in Christ Jesus, whom God put forward as a propitiation by his blood, to be received by faith. This was to show God's righteousness, because in his divine forbearance he had passed over former sins. **Rom. 4:6-8**. ...just as David also speaks of the blessing of the one to whom God counts righteousness apart from works: "Blessed are those whose lawless deeds are forgiven, and whose sins are covered; blessed is the man against whom the Lord will not count his sin."

2 **2 Cor. 5:19, 21.** ...that is, in Christ God was reconciling the world to himself, not counting their trespasses against them, and entrusting to us the message of reconciliation. ... For our sake he made him to be sin who knew no sin, so that in him we might become the righteousness of God.

3 **Rom. 5:17-19.** For if, because of one man's trespass, death reigned through that one man, much more will those who receive the abundance of grace and the free gift of righteousness reign in life through the one man Jesus Christ. Therefore, as one trespass led to condemnation for all men, so one act of righteousness leads to justification and life for all men. For as by the one man's disobedience the many were made sinners, so by the one man's obedience the many will be made righteous.

4 **Gal. 2:16.** ...yet we know that a person is not justified by works of the law but through faith in Jesus Christ, so we also have believed in Christ Jesus, in order to be justified by faith in Christ and not by works of the law, because by works of the law no one will be justified. **Phil. 3:9.** ...and be found in him, not having a righteousness of my own that comes from the law, but that which comes through faith in Christ, the righteousness from God that depends on faith.

Q. 34. What is adoption?

A. Adoption is an act of God's free grace,[1] by which we are received as sons of God, and have a right to all the privileges of that standing.[2]

1 **1 Jn. 3:1.** See what kind of love the Father has given to us, that we should be called children of God; and so we are. The reason why the world does not know us is that it did not know him.

2 **Jn. 1:12.** But to all who did receive him, who believed in his name, he gave the right to become children of God. **Rom. 8:17.** ...and if children, then heirs—heirs of God and fellow heirs with Christ, provided we suffer with him in order that we may also be glorified with him.

Q. 35. What is sanctification?

A. Sanctification is the work of God's free grace,[1] by which we are renewed in the whole man after the image of God,[2] and are enabled more and more to die to sin and live to righteousness.[3]

1 **2 Thess. 2:13.** But we ought always to give thanks to God for you, brothers beloved by the Lord, because God chose you as the firstfruits to be saved, through sanctification by the Spirit and belief in the truth.

2 **Eph. 4:23-24.** ...and to be renewed in the spirit of your minds, and to put on the new self, created after the likeness of God in true righteousness and holiness.

3 **Rom. 6:4, 6.** We were buried therefore with him by baptism into death, in order that, just as Christ was raised from the dead by the glory of the Father, we too might walk in newness of life. ... We know that our old self was crucified with him in order that the body of sin might be brought to nothing, so that we would no longer be enslaved to sin. **Rom. 8:1.** There is therefore now no condemnation for those who are in Christ Jesus.

Q. 36. What are the benefits that in this life accompany or flow from justification, adoption, and sanctification?

A. The benefits that in this life do accompany or flow from justification, adoption, and sanctification are: assurance of God's love, peace of conscience,[1] joy in the Holy Spirit,[2] increase of grace,[3] and perseverance to the end.[4]

1 **Rom. 5:1-2, 5**. Therefore, since we have been justified by faith, we have peace with God through our Lord Jesus Christ. Through him we have also obtained access by faith into this grace in which we stand, and we rejoice in hope of the glory of God. ...and hope does not put us to shame, because God's love has been poured into our hearts through the Holy Spirit who has been given to us.

2 **Rom. 14:17**. For the kingdom of God is not a matter of eating and drinking but of righteousness and peace and joy in the Holy Spirit.

3 **Prov. 4:18**. But the path of the righteous is like the light of dawn, which shines brighter and brighter until full day.

4 **1 Pet. 1:5**. ...who by God's power are being guarded through faith for a salvation ready to be revealed in the last time. **1 Jn. 5:13**. I write these things to you who believe in the name of the Son of God that you may know that you have eternal life.

Q. 37. What benefits do believers receive from Christ at death?

A. The souls of believers are at their deaths made perfect in holiness,[1] and do immediately pass into glory;[2] and their bodies, being still united to Christ,[3] do rest in their graves[4] till the resurrection.[5]

1 **Heb. 12:23**. ...and to the assembly of the firstborn who are enrolled in heaven, and to God, the judge of all, and to the spirits of the righteous made perfect.

2 **Lk. 23:43**. And he said to him, "Truly, I say to you, today you will be with me in Paradise." **2 Cor. 5:1, 6, 8**. For we know that if the tent that is our earthly home is destroyed, we have a building from God, a house not made with hands, eternal in the heavens. ... So we are always of good courage. We know that while we are at home in the body we are away from the Lord. ... Yes, we are of good courage, and we would rather be away from the body and at home with the Lord. **Phil. 1:23**. I am hard pressed between the two. My desire is to depart and be with Christ, for that is far better.

3 **1 Thess. 4:14**. For since we believe that Jesus died and rose again, even so, through Jesus, God will bring with him those who have fallen asleep.

4 **Isa. 57:2**. ...he enters into peace; they rest in their beds who walk in their uprightness.

5 **Job 19:26-27**. And after my skin has been thus destroyed, yet in my flesh I shall see God, whom I shall see for myself, and my eyes shall behold, and not another. My heart faints within me!

Q. 38. What benefits do believers receive from Christ at the resurrection?

A. At the resurrection, believers, being raised up in glory,[1] shall be openly acknowledged and acquitted in the day of judgment,[2] and made perfectly blessed in the full enjoying of God[3] to all eternity.[4]

1 **1 Cor. 15:43**. It is sown in dishonor; it is raised in glory. It is sown in weakness; it is raised in power.

2 **Mt. 10:32**. So everyone who acknowledges me before men, I also will acknowledge before my Father who is in heaven. **Mt. 25:23**. His master said to him, 'Well done, good and faithful servant. You have been faithful over a little; I will set you over much. Enter into the joy of your master.'

3 **1 Cor. 13:12**. For now we see in a mirror dimly, but then face to face. Now I know in part; then I shall know fully, even as I have been fully known. **1 Jn. 3:2**. Beloved, we are God's children now, and what we will be has not yet appeared; but we know that when he appears we shall be like him, because we shall see him as he is.

4 **1 Thess. 4:17-18**. Then we who are alive, who are left, will be caught up together with them in the clouds to meet the Lord in the air, and so we will always be with the Lord. Therefore encourage one another with these words.

Q. 39. What is the duty that God requires of man?

A. The duty that God requires of man is obedience to His revealed will.[1]

1 **1 Sam. 15:22**. And Samuel said, "Has the Lord as great delight in burnt offerings and sacrifices, as in obeying the voice of the Lord? Behold, to obey is better than sacrifice, and to listen than the fat of rams." **Mic. 6:8**. He has told you, O man, what is good; and what does the Lord require of you but to do justice, and to love kindness, and to walk humbly with your God?

Q. 40. What did God at first reveal to man for the rule of his obedience?

A. The rule that God at first revealed to man for his obedience was the moral law.[1]

1 **Rom. 2:14-15**. For when Gentiles, who do not have the law, by nature do what the law requires, they are a law to themselves, even though they do not have the law. They show that the work of the law is written on their hearts, while their conscience also bears witness, and their conflicting thoughts accuse or even excuse them. **Rom. 10:5**. For Moses writes about the righteousness that is based on the law, that the person who does the commandments shall live by them.

Q. 41. Where is the moral law found to be summarized?

A. The moral law is found summarized in the Ten Commandments.[1]

1 **Deut. 10:4.** And he wrote on the tablets, in the same writing as before, the Ten Commandments that the Lord had spoken to you on the mountain out of the midst of the fire on the day of the assembly. And the Lord gave them to me.
Mt. 19:17. And he said to him, "Why do you ask me about what is good? There is only one who is good. If you would enter life, keep the commandments."

Q. 42. What is the sum of the Ten Commandments?

A. The sum of the Ten Commandments is: to love the Lord our God with all our heart, with all our soul, with all our strength, and with all our mind; and our neighbor as ourselves.[1]

1 **Mt. 22:37-40.** And he said to him, "You shall love the Lord your God with all your heart and with all your soul and with all your mind. This is the great and first commandment. And a second is like it: You shall love your neighbor as yourself. On these two commandments depend all the Law and the Prophets."

Q. 43. What is the preface to the Ten Commandments?

A. The preface to the Ten Commandments is in these words: "I am the LORD your God, who brought you out of the land of Egypt, out of the house of slavery."[1]

1 **Ex. 20:2.** "I am the Lord your God, who brought you out of the land of Egypt, out of the house of slavery."

Q. 44. What does the preface to the Ten Commandments teach us?

A. The preface to the Ten Commandments teaches us that because God is the Lord, and our God and Redeemer, therefore we are bound to keep all His commandments.[1]

1 **Lk. 1:74-75.** ...that we, being delivered from the hand of our enemies, might serve him without fear, in holiness and righteousness before him all our days.
1 Pet. 1:15-18. ...but as he who called you is holy, you also be holy in all your conduct, since it is written, "You shall be holy, for I am holy." And if you call on him as Father who judges impartially according to each one's deeds, conduct yourselves with fear throughout the time of your exile, knowing that you were ransomed from the futile ways inherited from your forefathers, not with perishable things such as silver or gold.

Q. 45. Which is the First Commandment?

A. The First Commandment is, "You shall have no other gods before me."[1]

1 **Ex. 20:3**. "You shall have no other gods before me.

Q. 46. What is required in the First Commandment?

A. The First Commandment requires us to know and acknowledge God to be the only true God, and our God;[1] and to worship and glorify Him accordingly.[2]

1 **Deut. 26:17**. You have declared today that the Lord is your God, and that you will walk in his ways, and keep his statutes and his commandments and his rules, and will obey his voice. **1 Chr. 28:9**. "And you, Solomon my son, know the God of your father and serve him with a whole heart and with a willing mind, for the Lord searches all hearts and understands every plan and thought. If you seek him, he will be found by you, but if you forsake him, he will cast you off forever."

2 **Ps. 29:2**. Ascribe to the Lord the glory due his name; worship the Lord in the splendor of holiness. **Mt. 4:10**. Then Jesus said to him, "Be gone, Satan! For it is written, "'You shall worship the Lord your God and him only shall you serve.'"

Q. 47. What is forbidden in the First Commandment?

A. The First Commandment forbids the denying,[1] or not worshiping and glorifying, the true God as God,[2] and our God;[3] and the giving to any other of that worship and glory due to Him alone.[4]

1 **Ps. 14:1**. The fool says in his heart, "There is no God." They are corrupt, they do abominable deeds, there is none who does good.

2 **Rom. 1:21**. For although they knew God, they did not honor him as God or give thanks to him, but they became futile in their thinking, and their foolish hearts were darkened.

3 **Ps. 81:10-11**. I am the Lord your God, who brought you up out of the land of Egypt. Open your mouth wide, and I will fill it. "But my people did not listen to my voice; Israel would not submit to me."

4 **Rom. 1:25-26**. ...because they exchanged the truth about God for a lie and worshiped and served the creature rather than the Creator, who is blessed forever! Amen. For this reason God gave them up to dishonorable passions. For their women exchanged natural relations for those that are contrary to nature.

Q. 48. What are we especially taught by the words, "before me," in the First Commandment?

A. These words, "before me," in the First Commandment teach us that God, who sees all things, takes notice of, and is much displeased with, the sin of having any other god.[1]

1 **Ps. 44:20-21**. If we had forgotten the name of our God or spread out our hands to a foreign god, would not God discover this? For he knows the secrets of the heart. **Ezek. 8:5-6**. Then he said to me, "Son of man, lift up your eyes now toward the north." So I lifted up my eyes toward the north, and behold, north of the altar gate, in the entrance, was this image of jealousy. And he said to me, "Son of man, do you see what they are doing, the great abominations that the house of Israel are committing here, to drive me far from my sanctuary? But you will see still greater abominations."

Q. 49. Which is the Second Commandment?

A. The Second Commandment is, "You shall not make for yourself a carved image, or any likeness of anything that is in heaven above, or that is in the earth beneath, or that is in the water under the earth. You shall not bow down to them or serve them, for I the LORD your God am a jealous God, visiting the iniquity of the fathers on the children to the third and the fourth generation of those who hate me, but showing steadfast love to thousands of those who love me and keep my commandments."[1]

1 **Ex. 20:4-6**. "You shall not make for yourself a carved image, or any likeness of anything that is in heaven above, or that is in the earth beneath, or that is in the water under the earth. You shall not bow down to them or serve them, for I the Lord your God am a jealous God, visiting the iniquity of the fathers on the children to the third and the fourth generation of those who hate me, but showing steadfast love to thousands of those who love me and keep my commandments."

Q. 50. What is required in the Second Commandment?

A. The Second Commandment requires the receiving, observing, and keeping pure and entire all such religious worship and ordinances as God has appointed in His Word.[1]

1 **Deut. 32:46.** ...he said to them, "Take to heart all the words by which I am warning you today, that you may command them to your children, that they may be careful to do all the words of this law." **Mt. 28:20.** "...teaching them to observe all that I have commanded you. And behold, I am with you always, to the end of the age." **Acts 2:42.** And they devoted themselves to the apostles' teaching and the fellowship, to the breaking of bread and the prayers.

Q. 51. What is forbidden in the Second Commandment?

A. The Second Commandment forbids the worshiping of God by images,[1] or any other way not appointed in His Word.[2]

1 **Ex. 32:5, 8**. When Aaron saw this, he built an altar before it. And Aaron made a proclamation and said, "Tomorrow shall be a feast to the Lord." ... "They have turned aside quickly out of the way that I commanded them. They have made for themselves a golden calf and have worshiped it and sacrificed to it and said, 'These are your gods, O Israel, who brought you up out of the land of Egypt!'" **Deut. 4:15-19**. "Therefore watch yourselves very carefully. Since you saw no form on the day that the Lord spoke to you at Horeb out of the midst of the fire, beware lest you act corruptly by making a carved image for yourselves, in the form of any figure, the likeness of male or female, the likeness of any animal that is on the earth, the likeness of any winged bird that flies in the air, the likeness of anything that creeps on the ground, the likeness of any fish that is in the water under the earth. And beware lest you raise your eyes to heaven, and when you see the sun and the moon and the stars, all the host of heaven, you be drawn away and bow down to them and serve them, things that the Lord your God has allotted to all the peoples under the whole heaven." **Rom. 1:22-23.** Claiming to be wise, they became fools, and exchanged the glory of the immortal God for images resembling mortal man and birds and animals and creeping things.

2 **Deut. 12:31-32.** You shall not worship the Lord your God in that way, for every abominable thing that the Lord hates they have done for their gods, for they even burn their sons and their daughters in the fire to their gods. "Everything that I command you, you shall be careful to do. You shall not add to it or take from it."

Q. 52. What are the reasons attached to the Second Commandment?

A. The reasons attached to the Second Commandment are: God's sovereignty over us,[1] His ownership in us,[2] and the zeal he has for His own worship.[3]

1 **Ps. 95:2-3**. Let us come into his presence with thanksgiving; let us make a joyful noise to him with songs of praise! For the Lord is a great God, and a great King above all gods.

2 **Ps. 45:11**. ...and the king will desire your beauty. Since he is your lord, bow to him.

3 **Ex. 34:13-14**. You shall tear down their altars and break their pillars and cut down their Asherim (for you shall worship no other god, for the Lord, whose name is Jealous, is a jealous God.)

Q. 53. Which is the Third Commandment?

A. The Third Commandment is, "You shall not take the name of the LORD your God in vain, for the LORD will not hold him guiltless who takes his name in vain."[1]

1 **Ex. 20:7.** "You shall not take the name of the Lord your God in vain, for the Lord will not hold him guiltless who takes his name in vain."

Q. 54. What is required in the Third Commandment?

A. The Third Commandment requires the holy and reverent use of God's names,[1] titles,[2] attributes,[3] ordinances,[4] Word,[5] and works.[6]

1 **Deut. 28:58.** "If you are not careful to do all the words of this law that are written in this book, that you may fear this glorious and awesome name, the Lord your God." **Mt. 6:9.** Pray then like this: "Our Father in heaven, hallowed be your name."

2 **Ps. 68:4.** Sing to God, sing praises to his name; lift up a song to him who rides through the deserts; his name is the Lord; exult before him!

3 **Rev. 15:3-4.** And they sing the song of Moses, the servant of God, and the song of the Lamb, saying, "Great and amazing are your deeds, O Lord God the Almighty! Just and true are your ways, O King of the nations! Who will not fear, O Lord, and glorify your name? For you alone are holy. All nations will come and worship you, for your righteous acts have been revealed."

4 **Mal. 1:11, 14.** For from the rising of the sun to its setting my name will be great among the nations, and in every place incense will be offered to my name, and a pure offering. For my name will be great among the nations, says the Lord of hosts. ... Cursed be the cheat who has a male in his flock, and vows it, and yet sacrifices to the Lord what is blemished. For I am a great King, says the Lord of hosts, and my name will be feared among the nations.

5 **Ps. 138:1-2.** I give you thanks, O Lord, with my whole heart; before the gods I sing your praise; I bow down toward your holy temple and give thanks to your name for your steadfast love and your faithfulness, for you have exalted above all things your name and your word.

6 **Rev. 4:11.** "Worthy are you, our Lord and God, to receive glory and honor and power, for you created all things, and by your will they existed and were created." **Ps. 107:21-22.** Let them thank the Lord for his steadfast love, for his wondrous works to the children of man! And let them offer sacrifices of thanksgiving, and tell of his deeds in songs of joy!

Q. 55. What is forbidden in the Third Commandment?

A. The Third Commandment forbids all profaning or abusing of anything by which God makes Himself known.[1]

1 **Mal. 1:6-7, 12.** "A son honors his father, and a servant his master. If then I am a father, where is my honor? And if I am a master, where is my fear? says the Lord of hosts to you, O priests, who despise my name. But you say, 'How have we despised your name?' By offering polluted food upon my altar. But you say, 'How have we polluted you?' By saying that the Lord's table may be despised." ... But you profane it when you say that the Lord's table is polluted, and its fruit, that is, its food may be despised. **Mal. 2:2.** If you will not listen, if you will not take it to heart to give honor to my name, says the Lord of hosts, then I will send the curse upon you and I will curse your blessings. Indeed, I have already cursed them, because you do not lay it to heart. **Mal. 3:14.** You have said, 'It is vain to serve God.

What is the profit of our keeping his charge or of walking as in mourning before the Lord of hosts?'

Q. 56. What is the reason attached to the Third Commandment?

A. The reason attached to the Third Commandment is that, however those who break this commandment may escape punishment from men, yet the Lord our God will not allow them to escape His righteous judgment.[1]

1 **Deut. 28:58-59**. "If you are not careful to do all the words of this law that are written in this book, that you may fear this glorious and awesome name, the Lord your God, then the Lord will bring on you and your offspring extraordinary afflictions, afflictions severe and lasting, and sicknesses grievous and lasting."
1 Sam. 2:12, 17, 22, 29. Now the sons of Eli were worthless men. They did not know the Lord. ... Thus the sin of the young men was very great in the sight of the Lord, for the men treated the offering of the Lord with contempt. ... Now Eli was very old, and he kept hearing all that his sons were doing to all Israel, and how they lay with the women who were serving at the entrance to the tent of meeting. ... 'Why then do you scorn my sacrifices and my offerings that I commanded for my dwelling, and honor your sons above me by fattening yourselves on the choicest parts of every offering of my people Israel?' **1 Sam. 3:13**. And I declare to him that I am about to punish his house forever, for the iniquity that he knew, because his sons were blaspheming God, and he did not restrain them.

Q. 57. Which is the Fourth Commandment?

A. The Fourth Commandment is, "Remember the Sabbath day, to keep it holy. Six days you shall labor, and do all your work, but the seventh day is a Sabbath to the LORD your God. On it you shall not do any work, you, or your son, or your daughter, your male servant, or your female servant, or your livestock, or the sojourner who is within your gates. For in six days the LORD made heaven and earth, the sea, and all that is in them, and rested the seventh day. Therefore the LORD blessed the Sabbath day and made it holy."[1]

1 **Ex. 20:8-11**. "Remember the Sabbath day, to keep it holy. Six days you shall labor, and do all your work, but the seventh day is a Sabbath to the Lord your God. On it you shall not do any work, you, or your son, or your daughter, your male servant, or your female servant, or your livestock, or the sojourner who is within your gates. For in six days the Lord made heaven and earth, the sea, and all that is in them, and rested on the seventh day. Therefore the Lord blessed the Sabbath day and made it holy."

Q. 58. What is required in the Fourth Commandment?

A. The Fourth Commandment requires the keeping holy to God such set times as He has appointed in His Word; expressly one whole day in seven, to be a holy Sabbath to Himself.[1]

1 **Deut. 5:12-14**. "'Observe the Sabbath day, to keep it holy, as the Lord your God commanded you. Six days you shall labor and do all your work, but the seventh day is a Sabbath to the Lord your God. On it you shall not do any work, you or your son or your daughter or your male servant or your female servant, or your ox or your donkey or any of your livestock, or the sojourner who is within your gates, that your male servant and your female servant may rest as well as you.'"

Q. 59. Which day of the seven has God appointed to be the weekly Sabbath?

A. From the beginning of the world to the resurrection of Christ, God appointed the seventh day of the week to be the weekly Sabbath; and the first day of the week ever since, to continue to the end of the world, which is the Christian Sabbath.[1]

1 **Gen. 2:2-3**. And on the seventh day God finished his work that he had done, and he rested on the seventh day from all his work that he had done. So God blessed the seventh day and made it holy, because on it God rested from all his work that he had done in creation. **Acts 20:7**. On the first day of the week, when we were gathered together to break bread, Paul talked with them, intending to depart on the next day, and he prolonged his speech until midnight. **1 Cor. 16:1-2**. Now concerning the collection for the saints: as I directed the churches of Galatia, so you also are to do. On the first day of every week, each of you is to put something aside and store it up, as he may prosper, so that there will be no collecting when I come.

Q. 60. How is the Sabbath to be sanctified?

A. The Sabbath is to be sanctified by a holy resting all that day,[1] even from such worldly employments and recreations as are lawful on other days;[2] and spending the whole time in the public and private exercises of God's worship,[3] except so much as is to be taken up in the works of necessity and mercy.[4]

1 **Ex. 16:25-28**. Moses said, "Eat it today, for today is a Sabbath to the Lord; today you will not find it in the field. Six days you shall gather it, but on the seventh day, which is a Sabbath, there will be none." On the seventh day some of the people went out to gather, but they found none. And the Lord said to Moses, "How long will you refuse to keep my commandments and my laws? **Ex. 20:8, 10**. "Remember the Sabbath day, to keep it holy. ...but the seventh day is a Sabbath to the Lord your God. On it you shall not do any work, you, or your son, or your daughter, your male servant, or your female servant, or your livestock, or the sojourner who is within your gates."

2 **Neh. 13:15-19**. In those days I saw in Judah people treading winepresses on the Sabbath, and bringing in heaps of grain and loading them on donkeys, and also wine, grapes, figs, and all kinds of loads, which they brought into Jerusalem on the Sabbath day. And I warned them on the day when they sold food. Tyrians also, who lived in the city, brought in fish and all kinds of goods and sold them on the Sabbath to the people of Judah, in Jerusalem itself! Then I confronted the nobles of Judah and said to them, "What is this evil thing that you are doing, profaning the Sabbath day? Did not your fathers act in this way, and did not our God bring all this disaster on us and on this city? Now you are bringing more wrath on Israel by profaning the Sabbath." As soon as it began to grow dark at the gates of Jerusalem before the Sabbath, I commanded that the doors should be shut and gave orders that they should not be opened until after the Sabbath. And I stationed some of my servants at the gates, that no load might be brought in on the Sabbath day.

3 **Ps. 92**. It is good to give thanks to the Lord, to sing praises to your name, O Most High; to declare your steadfast love in the morning, and your faithfulness by night, to the music of the lute and the harp, to the melody of the lyre. For you, O Lord, have made me glad by your work; at the works of your hands I sing for joy. How great are your works, O Lord! Your thoughts are very deep! The stupid man cannot know; the fool cannot understand this: that though the wicked sprout like grass and all evildoers flourish, they are doomed to destruction forever; but you, O Lord, are on high forever. For behold, your enemies, O Lord, for behold, your enemies shall perish; all evildoers shall be scattered. But you have exalted my horn like that of the wild ox; you have poured over me fresh oil. My eyes have seen the downfall of my enemies; my ears have heard the doom of my evil assailants. The righteous flourish like the palm tree and grow like a cedar in Lebanon. They are planted in the house of the Lord; they flourish in the courts of our God. They still bear fruit in old age; they are ever full of sap and green, to declare that the Lord is upright; he is my rock, and there is no unrighteousness in him. **Isa. 66:23**. From new moon to new moon, and from Sabbath to Sabbath, all flesh shall come to worship before me, declares the Lord. **Lk. 4:16**. And he came to Nazareth, where he had been brought up. And as was his custom, he went to the synagogue on the Sabbath day, and he stood up to read. **Acts 20:7**. On the first day of the week, when we were gathered together to break bread, Paul talked with them, intending to depart on the next day, and he prolonged his speech until midnight.

4 See **Matt. 12:1-31**

Q. 61. What is forbidden in the Fourth Commandment?

A. The Fourth Commandment forbids the omission, or careless performance, of the duties required,[1] and the profaning the day by idleness,[2] or doing that which is in itself sinful,[3] or by unnecessary thoughts, words, or works, about our worldly employments or recreations.[4]

1 **Ezek. 22:26**. Her priests have done violence to my law and have profaned my holy things. They have made no distinction between the holy and the common, neither have they taught the difference between the unclean and the clean, and they have disregarded my Sabbaths, so that I am profaned among them. Am. 8:5. ...saying, "When will the new moon be over, that we may sell grain? And the Sabbath, that we may offer wheat for sale, that we may make the ephah small and the shekel great and deal deceitfully with false balances." **Mal. 1:13**. But you say,

'What a weariness this is,' and you snort at it, says the Lord of hosts. You bring what has been taken by violence or is lame or sick, and this you bring as your offering! Shall I accept that from your hand? says the Lord.

2 **Acts 20:7, 9**. On the first day of the week, when we were gathered together to break bread, Paul talked with them, intending to depart on the next day, and he prolonged his speech until midnight. ... And a young man named Eutychus, sitting at the window, sank into a deep sleep as Paul talked still longer. And being overcome by sleep, he fell down from the third story and was taken up dead.

3 **Ezek. 23:38**. Moreover, this they have done to me: they have defiled my sanctuary on the same day and profaned my Sabbaths.

4 **Isa. 58:13**. "If you turn back your foot from the Sabbath, from doing your pleasure on my holy day, and call the Sabbath a delight and the holy day of the Lord honorable; if you honor it, not going your own ways, or seeking your own pleasure, or talking idly. **Jer. 17:24-26**. "'But if you listen to me, declares the Lord, and bring in no burden by the gates of this city on the Sabbath day, but keep the Sabbath day holy and do no work on it, then there shall enter by the gates of this city kings and princes who sit on the throne of David, riding in chariots and on horses, they and their officials, the men of Judah and the inhabitants of Jerusalem. And this city shall be inhabited forever. And people shall come from the cities of Judah and the places around Jerusalem, from the land of Benjamin, from the Shephelah, from the hill country, and from the Negeb, bringing burnt offerings and sacrifices, grain offerings and frankincense, and bringing thank offerings to the house of the Lord.

Q. 62. What are the reasons attached to the Fourth Commandment?

A. The reasons attached to the Fourth Commandment are: God's allowing us six days of the week for our own employments,[1] His establishment of a special ownership in the seventh, His own example, and His blessing the Sabbath day.[2]

1 **Ex. 20:9**. Six days you shall labor, and do all your work.

2 **Ex. 20:11**. For in six days the Lord made heaven and earth, the sea, and all that is in them, and rested on the seventh day. Therefore the Lord blessed the Sabbath day and made it holy.

Q. 63. Which is the Fifth Commandment?

A. The Fifth Commandment is, "Honor your father and your mother, that your days may be long in the land that the LORD your God is giving you."[1]

1 **Ex. 20:12**. "Honor your father and your mother, that your days may be long in the land that the Lord your God is giving you."

Q. 64. What is required in the Fifth Commandment?

A. The Fifth Commandment requires the preserving of the honor, and performing the duties, belonging to everyone in their various situations and relationships, as superiors,[1] inferiors,[2] or equals.[3]

1 **Eph. 5:21.** ...submitting to one another out of reverence for Christ.

2 **1 Pet. 2:17.** Honor everyone. Love the brotherhood. Fear God. Honor the emperor.

3 **Rom. 12:10.** Love one another with brotherly affection. Outdo one another in showing honor.

Q. 65. What is forbidden in the Fifth Commandment?

A. The Fifth Commandment forbids the neglecting of, or doing anything against, the honor and duty that belong to everyone in their various situations and relationships.[1]

1 **Ezek. 34:2-4.** "Son of man, prophesy against the shepherds of Israel; prophesy, and say to them, even to the shepherds, Thus says the Lord God: Ah, shepherds of Israel who have been feeding yourselves! Should not shepherds feed the sheep? You eat the fat, you clothe yourselves with the wool, you slaughter the fat ones, but you do not feed the sheep. The weak you have not strengthened, the sick you have not healed, the injured you have not bound up, the strayed you have not brought back, the lost you have not sought, and with force and harshness you have ruled them." **Mt. 15:4-6.** For God commanded, 'Honor your father and your mother,' and, 'Whoever reviles father or mother must surely die.' But you say, 'If anyone tells his father or his mother, "What you would have gained from me is given to God," he need not honor his father.' So for the sake of your tradition you have made void the word of God. **Rom. 13:8.** Owe no one anything, except to love each other, for the one who loves another has fulfilled the law.

Q. 66. What is the reason attached to the Fifth Commandment?

A. The reason attached to the Fifth Commandment is a promise of long life and prosperity (as far as it shall serve for God's glory, and their own good) to all who keep this commandment.[1]

1 **Deut. 5:16.** "'Honor your father and your mother, as the Lord your God commanded you, that your days may be long, and that it may go well with you in the land that the Lord your God is giving you.'" **Eph. 6:2-3.** "Honor your father and mother" (this is the first commandment with a promise),"that it may go well with you and that you may live long in the land."

Q. 67. Which is the Sixth Commandment?

A. The Sixth Commandment is, "You shall not murder."[1]

1 **Ex. 20:13**. "You shall not murder."

Q. 68. What is required in the Sixth Commandment?

A. The Sixth Commandment requires all lawful endeavors to preserve our own lives,[1] and the lives of others.[2]

1 **Eph. 5:28-29**. In the same way husbands should love their wives as their own bodies. He who loves his wife loves himself. For no one ever hated his own flesh, but nourishes and cherishes it, just as Christ does the church.

2 **1 Kings 18:4.** And when Jezebel cut off the prophets of the Lord, Obadiah took a hundred prophets and hid them by fifties in a cave and fed them with bread and water.

Q. 69. What is forbidden in the Sixth Commandment?

A. The Sixth Commandment forbids the taking away of our own lives or the lives of our neighbors unjustly, or whatever tends to do so.[1]

1 **Gen. 9:6**. "Whoever sheds the blood of man, by man shall his blood be shed, for God made man in his own image." **Acts 16:28.** But Paul cried with a loud voice, "Do not harm yourself, for we are all here."

Q. 70. Which is the Seventh Commandment?

A. The Seventh Commandment is, "You shall not commit adultery."[4]

1 **Ex. 20:14**. "You shall not commit adultery."

Q. 71. What is required in the Seventh Commandment?

A. The Seventh Commandment requires the preservation of our own and our neighbor's chastity, in heart, speech, and behavior.[1]

1 **1 Cor. 7:2-3, 5, 34, 36**. But because of the temptation to sexual immorality, each man should have his own wife and each woman her own husband. The husband should give to his wife her conjugal rights, and likewise the wife to her husband. ... Do not deprive one another, except perhaps by agreement for a limited time, that you may devote yourselves to prayer; but then come together again, so that Satan may not tempt you because of your lack of self-control. ...and his interests are divided. And the unmarried or betrothed woman is anxious about the things of the Lord, how to be holy in body and spirit. But the married woman is anxious about worldly things, how to please her husband. ... If anyone thinks that he is not behaving properly toward his betrothed, if his passions are strong, and it has to be,

let him do as he wishes: let them marry—it is no sin. **Col. 4:6**. Let your speech always be gracious, seasoned with salt, so that you may know how you ought to answer each person. **1 Pet. 3:2.** ...when they see your respectful and pure conduct.

Q. 72. What is forbidden in the Seventh Commandment?

A. The Seventh Commandment forbids all unchaste thoughts, words, and actions.[1]

1 **Mt. 5:28**. But I say to you that everyone who looks at a woman with lustful intent has already committed adultery with her in his heart. **Mt. 15:19**. For out of the heart come evil thoughts, murder, adultery, sexual immorality, theft, false witness, slander.

Q. 73. Which is the Eighth Commandment?

A. The Eighth Commandment is, "You shall not steal."[1]

1 **Ex. 20:15**. "You shall not steal."

Q. 74. What is required in the Eighth Commandment?

A. The Eighth Commandment requires that we utilize only lawful means in obtaining and furthering the wealth and outward estate of ourselves and others.[1]

1 **Gen. 30:30**. "For you had little before I came, and it has increased abundantly, and the Lord has blessed you wherever I turned. But now when shall I provide for my own household also?" **Gen. 47:14, 20**. And Joseph gathered up all the money that was found in the land of Egypt and in the land of Canaan, in exchange for the grain that they bought. And Joseph brought the money into Pharaoh's house. ... So Joseph bought all the land of Egypt for Pharaoh, for all the Egyptians sold their fields, because the famine was severe on them. The land became Pharaoh's. **Ex. 23:4-5**. "If you meet your enemy's ox or his donkey going astray, you shall bring it back to him. If you see the donkey of one who hates you lying down under its burden, you shall refrain from leaving him with it; you shall rescue it with him." **Lev. 25:35**. "If your brother becomes poor and cannot maintain himself with you, you shall support him as though he were a stranger and a sojourner, and he shall live with you." **Deut. 22:1-5**. "You shall not see your brother's ox or his sheep going astray and ignore them. You shall take them back to your brother. And if he does not live near you and you do not know who he is, you shall bring it home to your house, and it shall stay with you until your brother seeks it. Then you shall restore it to him. And you shall do the same with his donkey or with his garment, or with any lost thing of your brother's, which he loses and you find; you may not ignore it. You shall not see your brother's donkey or his ox fallen down by the way and ignore them. You shall help him to lift them up again. A woman shall not wear a man's garment, nor shall a man put on a woman's cloak, for whoever does these things is an abomination to the Lord your God." **1 Tim. 5:8**. But if anyone does not provide for his relatives, and especially for members of his household, he has denied the faith and is worse than an unbeliever.

Q. 75. What is forbidden in the Eighth Commandment?

A. The Eighth Commandment forbids whatever does, or may, unjustly hinder our own, or our neighbor's, wealth or outward estate.[1]

1 **Prov. 21:17.** Whoever loves pleasure will be a poor man; he who loves wine and oil will not be rich. **Prov. 23:20-21.** Be not among drunkards or among gluttonous eaters of meat, for the drunkard and the glutton will come to poverty, and slumber will clothe them with rags. **Prov. 28:19.** Whoever works his land will have plenty of bread, but he who follows worthless pursuits will have plenty of poverty. **Eph. 4:28.** Let the thief no longer steal, but rather let him labor, doing honest work with his own hands, so that he may have something to share with anyone in need.

Q. 76. Which is the Ninth Commandment?

A. The Ninth Commandment is, "You shall not bear false witness against your neighbor."[1]

1 **Ex. 20:16.** "You shall not bear false witness against your neighbor."

Q. 77. What is required in the Ninth Commandment?

A. The Ninth Commandment requires the maintaining and promoting of truth between man and man,[1] and of our own and our neighbor's good name,[2] especially in testifying as witnesses.[3]

1 **Zech. 8:16.** These are the things that you shall do: Speak the truth to one another; render in your gates judgments that are true and make for peace.

2 **3 Jn. 12.** Demetrius has received a good testimony from everyone, and from the truth itself. We also add our testimony, and you know that our testimony is true.

3 **Prov. 14:5, 25.** A faithful witness does not lie, but a false witness breathes out lies. A truthful witness saves lives, but one who breathes out lies is deceitful.

Q. 78. What is forbidden in the Ninth Commandment?

A. The Ninth Commandment forbids whatever is prejudicial to truth, or injurious to our own or our neighbor's good name.[1]

1 **Lev. 19:16.** You shall not go around as a slanderer among your people, and you shall not stand up against the life of your neighbor: I am the Lord. **1 Sam. 17:28.** Now Eliab his eldest brother heard when he spoke to the men. And Eliab's anger was kindled against David, and he said, "Why have you come down? And with whom have you left those few sheep in the wilderness? I know your presumption and the evil of your heart, for you have come down to see the battle." **Ps. 15:3.** ... who does not slander with his tongue and does no evil to his neighbor, nor takes up a reproach against his friend.

Q. 79. Which is the Tenth Commandment?

A. The Tenth Commandment is, "You shall not covet your neighbor's house; you shall not covet your neighbor's wife, or his male servant, or his female servant, or his ox, or his donkey, or anything that is your neighbor's."[1]

1 **Ex. 20:17.** "You shall not covet your neighbor's house; you shall not covet your neighbor's wife, or his male servant, or his female servant, or his ox, or his donkey, or anything that is your neighbor's."

Q. 80. What is required in the Tenth Commandment?

A. The Tenth Commandment requires full contentment with our own condition,[1] with a right and charitable frame of spirit toward our neighbor and all that is his.[2]

1 **1 Tim. 6:6.** But godliness with contentment is great gain. **Heb. 13:5.** Keep your life free from love of money, and be content with what you have, for he has said, "I will never leave you nor forsake you."

2 **Rom. 12:15.** Rejoice with those who rejoice, weep with those who weep. **1 Cor. 13:4-7.** Love is patient and kind; love does not envy or boast; it is not arrogant or rude. It does not insist on its own way; it is not irritable or resentful; it does not rejoice at wrongdoing, but rejoices with the truth. Love bears all things, believes all things, hopes all things, endures all things. **Phil. 2:4.** Let each of you look not only to his own interests, but also to the interests of others.

Q. 81. What is forbidden in the Tenth Commandment?

A. The Tenth Commandment forbids all discontentment with our own estate,[1] envying or grieving at the good of our neighbor,[2] and all unreasonable motions and affections toward anything that is his.[3]

1 **1 Kings 21:4.** And Ahab went into his house vexed and sullen because of what Naboth the Jezreelite had said to him, for he had said, "I will not give you the inheritance of my fathers." And he lay down on his bed and turned away his face and would eat no food. **Esth. 5:13.** "Yet all this is worth nothing to me, so long as I see Mordecai the Jew sitting at the king's gate." **1 Cor. 10:10.** ...nor grumble, as some of them did and were destroyed by the Destroyer.

2 **Gal. 5:26.** Let us not become conceited, provoking one another, envying one another. **Jas. 3:14, 16.** But if you have bitter jealousy and selfish ambition in your hearts, do not boast and be false to the truth. ... For where jealousy and selfish ambition exist, there will be disorder and every vile practice.

3 **Deut. 5:21.** "'And you shall not covet your neighbor's wife. And you shall not desire your neighbor's house, his field, or his male servant, or his female servant, his ox, or his donkey, or anything that is your neighbor's.'" **Rom. 7:7-8.** What then shall we say? That the law is sin? By no means! Yet if it had not been for the law, I would not have known sin. For I would not have known what it is to covet if the

law had not said, "You shall not covet."But sin, seizing an opportunity through the commandment, produced in me all kinds of covetousness. For apart from the law, sin lies dead. **Rom. 13:9**. For the commandments, "You shall not commit adultery, You shall not murder, You shall not steal, You shall not covet," and any other commandment, are summed up in this word: "You shall love your neighbor as yourself." **Gal. 5:26.** Let us not become conceited, provoking one another, envying one another. **Col. 3:5**. Put to death therefore what is earthly in you: sexual immorality, impurity, passion, evil desire, and covetousness, which is idolatry.

Q. 82. Is any man able to keep perfectly the commandments of God?

A. No mere man, since the Fall, is able, in this life, to keep perfectly the commandments of God,[1] but does break them daily, in thought, word, and deed.[2]

1 **Eccl. 7:20**. Surely there is not a righteous man on earth who does good and never sins. **Gal. 5:17**. For the desires of the flesh are against the Spirit, and the desires of the Spirit are against the flesh, for these are opposed to each other, to keep you from doing the things you want to do. **1 Jn. 1:8, 10**. If we say we have no sin, we deceive ourselves, and the truth is not in us. ... If we say we have not sinned, we make him a liar, and his word is not in us.

2 **Gen. 6:5**. The Lord saw that the wickedness of man was great in the earth, and that every intention of the thoughts of his heart was only evil continually. **Gen. 8:21**. And when the Lord smelled the pleasing aroma, the Lord said in his heart, "I will never again curse the ground because of man, for the intention of man's heart is evil from his youth. Neither will I ever again strike down every living creature as I have done. **Rom. 3:9-21**. What then? Are we Jews any better off? No, not at all. For we have already charged that all, both Jews and Greeks, are under sin, as it is written: "None is righteous, no, not one; no one understands; no one seeks for God. All have turned aside; together they have become worthless; no one does good, not even one. Their throat is an open grave; they use their tongues to deceive. The venom of asps is under their lips. Their mouth is full of curses and bitterness. Their feet are swift to shed blood; in their paths are ruin and misery, and the way of peace they have not known. There is no fear of God before their eyes." Now we know that whatever the law says it speaks to those who are under the law, so that every mouth may be stopped, and the whole world may be held accountable to God. For by works of the law no human being will be justified in his sight, since through the law comes knowledge of sin. But now the righteousness of God has been manifested apart from the law, although the Law and the Prophets bear witness to it. **Jas. 3:2-13**. For we all stumble in many ways. And if anyone does not stumble in what he says, he is a perfect man, able also to bridle his whole body. If we put bits into the mouths of horses so that they obey us, we guide their whole bodies as well. Look at the ships also: though they are so large and are driven by strong winds, they are guided by a very small rudder wherever the will of the pilot directs. So also the tongue is a small member, yet it boasts of great things. How great a forest is set ablaze by such a small fire! And the tongue is a fire, a world of unrighteousness. The tongue is set among our members, staining the whole body, setting on fire the entire course of life, and set on fire by hell. For every kind of beast and bird, of reptile and sea creature, can be tamed and has been tamed by mankind, but no human being can tame the tongue. It is a restless evil, full of deadly poison. With it we bless our Lord and Father, and with it we curse people who are made in the likeness of God. From the same

mouth come blessing and cursing. My brothers, these things ought not to be so. Does a spring pour forth from the same opening both fresh and salt water? Can a fig tree, my brothers, bear olives, or a grapevine produce figs? Neither can a salt pond yield fresh water. Who is wise and understanding among you? By his good conduct let him show his works in the meekness of wisdom.

Q. 83. Are all transgressions of the law equally wicked?

A. Some sins in themselves, and by reason of aggravating circumstances, are more wicked in the sight of God than others.[1]

1 **Ps. 78:17, 32, 56**. Yet they sinned still more against him, rebelling against the Most High in the desert. ... In spite of all this, they still sinned; despite his wonders, they did not believe. ... Yet they tested and rebelled against the Most High God and did not keep his testimonies. **Ezek. 8:6, 13, 15**. And he said to me, "Son of man, do you see what they are doing, the great abominations that the house of Israel are committing here, to drive me far from my sanctuary? But you will see still greater abominations." ... He said also to me, "You will see still greater abominations that they commit." ... Then he said to me, "Have you seen this, O son of man? You will see still greater abominations than these." **1 Jn. 5:16**. If anyone sees his brother committing a sin not leading to death, he shall ask, and God will give him life—to those who commit sins that do not lead to death. There is sin that leads to death; I do not say that one should pray for that.

Q. 84. What does every sin deserve?

A. Every sin deserves God's wrath and curse, both in this life and that which is to come.[1]

1 **Lam. 3:39**. Why should a living man complain, a man, about the punishment of his sins? **Mt. 25:41**. "Then he will say to those on his left, 'Depart from me, you cursed, into the eternal fire prepared for the devil and his angels.'" **Gal. 3:10**. For all who rely on works of the law are under a curse; for it is written, "Cursed be everyone who does not abide by all things written in the Book of the Law, and do them." **Eph. 5:6**. Let no one deceive you with empty words, for because of these things the wrath of God comes upon the sons of disobedience.

Q. 85. What does God require of us, that we may escape his wrath and curse, due to us for sin?

A. To escape the wrath and curse of God, due to us for sin, God requires of us faith in Jesus Christ, repentance to life,[1] with the diligent use of all the outward means by which Christ communicates to us the benefits of redemption.[2]

1 **Acts 20:21**. ...testifying both to Jews and to Greeks of repentance toward God and of faith in our Lord Jesus Christ.

2 **Prov. 21:1-5**. The king's heart is a stream of water in the hand of the Lord; he turns it wherever he will. Every way of a man is right in his own eyes, but the Lord

weighs the heart. To do righteousness and justice is more acceptable to the Lord than sacrifice. Haughty eyes and a proud heart, the lamp of the wicked, are sin. The plans of the diligent lead surely to abundance, but everyone who is hasty comes only to poverty. **PROV. 8:33-36**. Hear instruction and be wise, and do not neglect it. Blessed is the one who listens to me, watching daily at my gates, waiting beside my doors. For whoever finds me finds life and obtains favor from the Lord, but he who fails to find me injures himself; all who hate me love death." **ISA. 55:3**. Incline your ear, and come to me; hear, that your soul may live; and I will make with you an everlasting covenant, my steadfast, sure love for David.

Q. 86. What is faith in Jesus Christ?

A. Faith in Jesus Christ is a saving grace,[1] by which we receive and rest on Him alone for salvation, as He is offered to us in the Gospel.[2]

1 **EPH. 2:8-9**. For by grace you have been saved through faith. And this is not your own doing; it is the gift of God, not a result of works, so that no one may boast.

2 **JN. 1:12**. But to all who did receive him, who believed in his name, he gave the right to become children of God. **GAL. 2:16**. ...yet we know that a person is not justified by works of the law but through faith in Jesus Christ, so we also have believed in Christ Jesus, in order to be justified by faith in Christ and not by works of the law, because by works of the law no one will be justified. **PHIL. 3:9**. ...and be found in him, not having a righteousness of my own that comes from the law, but that which comes through faith in Christ, the righteousness from God that depends on faith.

Q. 87. What is repentance to life?

A. Repentance to life is a saving grace,[1] by which a sinner, out of a true sense of his sin,[2] and understanding of the mercy of God in Christ,[3] does, with grief and hatred of his sin, turn from it to God,[4] with full intention of, and endeavor after, new obedience.[5]

1 **ACTS 11:18**. When they heard these things they fell silent. And they glorified God, saying, "Then to the Gentiles also God has granted repentance that leads to life."

2 **ACTS 2:37-38**. Now when they heard this they were cut to the heart, and said to Peter and the rest of the apostles, "Brothers, what shall we do?" And Peter said to them, "Repent and be baptized every one of you in the name of Jesus Christ for the forgiveness of your sins, and you will receive the gift of the Holy Spirit.

3 **JER. 3:22**. "Return, O faithless sons; I will heal your faithlessness. Behold, we come to you, for you are the Lord our God." **JOEL 2:12**. "Yet even now," declares the Lord, "return to me with all your heart, with fasting, with weeping, and with mourning.

4 **JER. 31:18-19.** I have heard Ephraim grieving, 'You have disciplined me, and I was disciplined, like an untrained calf; bring me back that I may be restored, for you are the Lord my God. For after I had turned away, I relented, and after I was instructed, I struck my thigh; I was ashamed, and I was confounded, because I bore the disgrace of my youth.' **EZEK. 36:31**. Then you will remember your evil ways, and your deeds that were not good, and you will loathe yourselves for your iniquities and your abominations.

5 **Isa. 1:16-17**. Wash yourselves; make yourselves clean; remove the evil of your deeds from before my eyes; cease to do evil, learn to do good; seek justice, correct oppression; bring justice to the fatherless, plead the widow's cause. **2 Cor. 7:11**. For see what earnestness this godly grief has produced in you, but also what eagerness to clear yourselves, what indignation, what fear, what longing, what zeal, what punishment! At every point you have proved yourselves innocent in the matter.

Q. 88. What are the outward means by which Christ communicates to us the benefits of redemption?

A. The outward and ordinary means by which Christ communicates to us the benefits of redemption are His ordinances, especially the Word, sacraments, and prayer, all of which are made effectual to the elect for salvation.[1]

1 **Mt. 28:19-20**. "Go therefore and make disciples of all nations, baptizing them in the name of the Father and of the Son and of the Holy Spirit, teaching them to observe all that I have commanded you. And behold, I am with you always, to the end of the age." **Acts 2:42, 46-47**. And they devoted themselves to the apostles' teaching and the fellowship, to the breaking of bread and the prayers. ... And day by day, attending the temple together and breaking bread in their homes, they received their food with glad and generous hearts, praising God and having favor with all the people. And the Lord added to their number day by day those who were being saved.

Q. 89. How is the Word made effectual to salvation?

A. The Spirit of God makes the reading, but especially the preaching, of the Word an effectual means of convincing and converting sinners, and of building them up in holiness and comfort, through faith to salvation.[1]

1 **Neh. 8:8**. They read from the book, from the Law of God, clearly, and they gave the sense, so that the people understood the reading. **Ps. 19:8**. ...the precepts of the Lord are right, rejoicing the heart; the commandment of the Lord is pure, enlightening the eyes. **Acts 20:32**. And now I commend you to God and to the word of his grace, which is able to build you up and to give you the inheritance among all those who are sanctified. **Acts 25:18**. When the accusers stood up, they brought no charge in his case of such evils as I supposed. **Rom. 1:16**. For I am not ashamed of the gospel, for it is the power of God for salvation to everyone who believes, to the Jew first and also to the Greek. **Rom. 10:13-17**. For "everyone who calls on the name of the Lord will be saved." How then will they call on him in whom they have not believed? And how are they to believe in him of whom they have never heard? And how are they to hear without someone preaching? And how are they to preach unless they are sent? As it is written, "How beautiful are the feet of those who preach the good news!" But they have not all obeyed the gospel. For Isaiah says, "Lord, who has believed what he has heard from us?" So faith comes from hearing, and hearing through the word of Christ." **Rom. 15:4**. For whatever was written in former days was written for our instruction, that through endurance and through the encouragement of the Scriptures we might have hope.

1 Cor. 14:24-25. But if all prophesy, and an unbeliever or outsider enters, he is convicted by all, he is called to account by all, the secrets of his heart are disclosed, and so, falling on his face, he will worship God and declare that God is really among you. **2 Tim. 3:15-17**. ...and how from childhood you have been acquainted with the sacred writings, which are able to make you wise for salvation through faith in Christ Jesus. All Scripture is breathed out by God and profitable for teaching, for reproof, for correction, and for training in righteousness, that the man of God may be complete, equipped for every good work.

Q. 90. How is the Word to be read and heard, that it may become effectual to salvation?

A. That the Word may become effectual to salvation we must attend to it with diligence,[1] preparation,[2] and prayer;[3] receive it with faith and love;[4] lay it up in our hearts;[5] and practice it in our lives.[6]

1 **Prov. 8:34**. Blessed is the one who listens to me, watching daily at my gates, waiting beside my doors.

2 **1 Pet. 2:1-2**. So put away all malice and all deceit and hypocrisy and envy and all slander. Like newborn infants, long for the pure spiritual milk, that by it you may grow up into salvation.

3 **Ps. 119:18**. Open my eyes, that I may behold wondrous things out of your law.

4 **2 Thess. 2:10**. ...and with all wicked deception for those who are perishing, because they refused to love the truth and so be saved. **Heb. 4:2**. For good news came to us just as to them, but the message they heard did not benefit them, because they were not united by faith with those who listened.

5 **Ps. 119:11**. I have stored up your word in my heart, that I might not sin against you.

6 **Lk. 8:15**. As for that in the good soil, they are those who, hearing the word, hold it fast in an honest and good heart, and bear fruit with patience. **Jas. 1:25**. But the one who looks into the perfect law, the law of liberty, and perseveres, being no hearer who forgets but a doer who acts, he will be blessed in his doing.

Q. 91. How do the sacraments become effectual means of salvation?

A. The sacraments become effectual means of salvation, not from any virtue in them, or in him who administers them, but only by the blessing of Christ,[1] and the working of His Spirit in those who by faith receive them.[2]

1 **Mt. 3:11**. "I baptize you with water for repentance, but he who is coming after me is mightier than I, whose sandals I am not worthy to carry. He will baptize you with the Holy Spirit and fire." **1 Cor. 3:6-7**. I planted, Apollos watered, but God gave the growth. So neither he who plants nor he who waters is anything, but only God who gives the growth. **1 Pet. 3:21**. Baptism, which corresponds to this, now saves you, not as a removal of dirt from the body but as an appeal to God for a good conscience, through the resurrection of Jesus Christ.

2 **1 Cor. 12:13**. For in one Spirit we were all baptized into one body— Jews or Greeks, slaves or free—and all were made to drink of one Spirit.

Q. 92. What is a sacrament?

A. A sacrament is a holy ordinance instituted by Christ, in which, by perceptible signs, Christ and the benefits of the new covenant are represented, sealed, and applied to believers.[1]

1 **Gen. 17:7, 10.** And I will establish my covenant between me and you and your offspring after you throughout their generations for an everlasting covenant, to be God to you and to your offspring after you. ... This is my covenant, which you shall keep, between me and you and your offspring after you: Every male among you shall be circumcised. See **Ex. 12. 1 Cor. 11:23, 26.** For I received from the Lord what I also delivered to you, that the Lord Jesus on the night when he was betrayed took bread. ... For as often as you eat this bread and drink the cup, you proclaim the Lord's death until he comes.

Q. 93. Which are the sacraments of the New Testament?

A. The sacraments of the New Testament are Baptism[1] and the Lord's Supper.[2]

1 **Mt. 28:19.** Go therefore and make disciples of all nations, baptizing them in the name of the Father and of the Son and of the Holy Spirit.

2 **Mt. 26:26-28.** Now as they were eating, Jesus took bread, and after blessing it broke it and gave it to the disciples, and said, "Take, eat; this is my body." And he took a cup, and when he had given thanks he gave it to them, saying, "Drink of it, all of you, for this is my blood of the covenant, which is poured out for many for the forgiveness of sins.

Q. 94. What is Baptism?

A. Baptism is a sacrament, in which the washing with water, in the name of the Father, and of the Son, and of the Holy Spirit,[1] does signify and seal our grafting into Christ, and receiving of the benefits of the Covenant of Grace, and our engagement to be the Lord's.[2]

1 **Mt. 28:19.** Go therefore and make disciples of all nations, baptizing them in the name of the Father and of the Son and of the Holy Spirit.

2 **Rom. 6:4.** We were buried therefore with him by baptism into death, in order that, just as Christ was raised from the dead by the glory of the Father, we too might walk in newness of life. **Gal. 3:27.** For as many of you as were baptized into Christ have put on Christ.

Q. 95. To whom is Baptism to be administered?

A. Baptism is not to be administered to any who are out of the visible church, till they profess their faith in Christ and obedience to him;[1] but the infants of those who are members of the visible Church are to be baptized.[2]

1 **Acts 2:38**. And Peter said to them, "Repent and be baptized every one of you in the name of Jesus Christ for the forgiveness of your sins, and you will receive the gift of the Holy Spirit." **Acts 8:36-38**. And as they were going along the road they came to some water, and the eunuch said, "See, here is water! What prevents me from being baptized?" And he commanded the chariot to stop, and they both went down into the water, Philip and the eunuch, and he baptized him.

2 **Gen. 17:10**. This is my covenant, which you shall keep, between me and you and your offspring after you: Every male among you shall be circumcised. **Acts 2:38-39**. And Peter said to them, "Repent and be baptized every one of you in the name of Jesus Christ for the forgiveness of your sins, and you will receive the gift of the Holy Spirit. For the promise is for you and for your children and for all who are far off, everyone whom the Lord our God calls to himself." **1 Cor. 7:14**. For the unbelieving husband is made holy because of his wife, and the unbelieving wife is made holy because of her husband. Otherwise your children would be unclean, but as it is, they are holy. **Col. 2:11-12**. In him also you were circumcised with a circumcision made without hands, by putting off the body of the flesh, by the circumcision of Christ, having been buried with him in baptism, in which you were also raised with him through faith in the powerful working of God, who raised him from the dead.

Q. 96. What is the Lord's Supper?

A. The Lord's Supper is a sacrament, in which by giving and receiving bread and wine, according to Christ's direction, His death is shown forth; and the worthy receivers are, not after a corporal and carnal manner, but by faith, made partakers of His body and blood, with all His benefits, to their spiritual nourishment and growth in grace.[1]

1 **1 Cor. 11:23-26**. For I received from the Lord what I also delivered to you, that the Lord Jesus on the night when he was betrayed took bread, and when he had given thanks, he broke it, and said, "This is my body which is for you. Do this in remembrance of me." In the same way also he took the cup, after supper, saying, "This cup is the new covenant in my blood. Do this, as often as you drink it, in remembrance of me." For as often as you eat this bread and drink the cup, you proclaim the Lord's death until he comes.

Q. 97. What is required to be worthy of receiving the Lord's Supper?

A. It is required of those who would receive the Lord's Supper worthily that they examine themselves, as to their knowledge to discern the Lord's body,[1] as to their faith to feed on Him,[2] and as to their repentance,[3] love,[4] and new obedience;[5] lest, coming unworthily, they eat and drink judgment on themselves.[6]

1 **1 Cor. 11:28-29.** Let a person examine himself, then, and so eat of the bread and drink of the cup. For anyone who eats and drinks without discerning the body eats and drinks judgment on himself.

2 **1 Cor. 13:5.** ...or rude. It does not insist on its own way; it is not irritable or resentful.

3 **1 Cor. 11:31.** But if we judged ourselves truly, we would not be judged.

4 **1 Cor. 10:16-17.** The cup of blessing that we bless, is it not a participation in the blood of Christ? The bread that we break, is it not a participation in the body of Christ? Because there is one bread, we who are many are one body, for we all partake of the one bread.

5 **1 Cor. 5:7-8.** Cleanse out the old leaven that you may be a new lump, as you really are unleavened. For Christ, our Passover lamb, has been sacrificed. Let us therefore celebrate the festival, not with the old leaven, the leaven of malice and evil, but with the unleavened bread of sincerity and truth.

6 **1 Cor. 11:28-29.** Let a person examine himself, then, and so eat of the bread and drink of the cup. For anyone who eats and drinks without discerning the body eats and drinks judgment on himself.

Q. 98. What is prayer?

A. Prayer is an offering up of our desires to God,[1] for things agreeable to His will,[2] in the name of Christ,[3] with confession of our sins,[4] and thankful acknowledgment of His mercies.[5]

1 **Ps. 62:8.** Trust in him at all times, O people; pour out your heart before him; God is a refuge for us.

2 **1 Jn. 5:14.** And this is the confidence that we have toward him, that if we ask anything according to his will he hears us.

3 **Jn. 16:23.** In that day you will ask nothing of me. Truly, truly, I say to you, whatever you ask of the Father in my name, he will give it to you.

4 **Ps. 32:5-6.** I acknowledged my sin to you, and I did not cover my iniquity; I said, "I will confess my transgressions to the Lord," and you forgave the iniquity of my sin. Therefore let everyone who is godly offer prayer to you at a time when you may be found; surely in the rush of great waters, they shall not reach him.
Dan. 9:4. I prayed to the Lord my God and made confession, saying, "O Lord, the great and awesome God, who keeps covenant and steadfast love with those who love him and keep his commandments."

5 **Phil. 4:6.** ...do not be anxious about anything, but in everything by prayer and supplication with thanksgiving let your requests be made known to God.

Q. 99. What rule has God given for our direction in prayer?

A. The whole Word of God is of use to direct us in prayer;[1] but the special rule of direction is the form of prayer that Christ taught His disciples, commonly called "the Lord's Prayer."[2]

1 **1 Jn. 5:14**. And this is the confidence that we have toward him, that if we ask anything according to his will he hears us.

2 **Mt. 6:9-13**. Pray then like this: "Our Father in heaven, hallowed be your name. Your kingdom come, your will be done, on earth as it is in heaven. Give us this day our daily bread, and forgive us our debts, as we also have forgiven our debtors. And lead us not into temptation, but deliver us from evil." **Lk. 11:2-4**. And he said to them, "When you pray, say: "Father, hallowed be your name. Your kingdom come. Give us each day our daily bread, and forgive us our sins, for we ourselves forgive everyone who is indebted to us. And lead us not into temptation."

Q. 100. What does the preface of the Lord's Prayer teach us?

A. The preface of the Lord's Prayer, which is, "Our Father in heaven,"[1] teaches us to draw near to God with all holy reverence and confidence, as children to a father, able and ready to help us;[2] and that we should pray with and for others.[3]

1 **Mt. 6:9.** Pray then like this: "Our Father in heaven, hallowed be your name."

2 **Lk. 11:13**. "If you then, who are evil, know how to give good gifts to your children, how much more will the heavenly Father give the Holy Spirit to those who ask him!" **Rom. 8:15.** For you did not receive the spirit of slavery to fall back into fear, but you have received the Spirit of adoption as sons, by whom we cry, "Abba! Father!"

3 **Acts 12:5**. So Peter was kept in prison, but earnest prayer for him was made to God by the church. **1 Tim. 2:1-2.** First of all, then, I urge that supplications, prayers, intercessions, and thanksgivings be made for all people, for kings and all who are in high positions, that we may lead a peaceful and quiet life, godly and dignified in every way.

Q. 101. For what do we pray in the first petition?

A. In the first petition, which is, "Hallowed be your name,"[1] we pray that God would enable us, and others, to glorify Him in all the means by which he makes Himself known,[2] and that he would arrange all things to His own glory.[3]

1 **Mt. 6:9.** Pray then like this: "Our Father in heaven, hallowed be your name."

2 **Ps. 67:2-3**. ...that your way may be known on earth, your saving power among all nations. Let the peoples praise you, O God; let all the peoples praise you!

3 **Ps. 83**. O God, do not keep silence; do not hold your peace or be still, O God! For behold, your enemies make an uproar; those who hate you have raised their heads. They lay crafty plans against your people; they consult together against your treasured ones. They say, "Come, let us wipe them out as a nation; let the name of Israel be remembered no more!" For they conspire with one accord; against you they make a covenant— the tents of Edom and the Ishmaelites, Moab and the Hagrites, Gebal and Ammon and Amalek, Philistia with the inhabitants of Tyre; Asshur also has joined them; they are the strong arm of the children of Lot. Do to them as you did to Midian, as to Sisera and Jabin at the river Kishon, who were destroyed at En-dor, who became dung for the ground. Make their nobles like Oreb and Zeeb, all their princes like Zebah and Zalmunna, who said, "Let us take possession for ourselves of the pastures of God." O my God, make them like whirling dust, like chaff before the wind. As fire consumes the forest, as the flame sets the mountains ablaze, so may you pursue them with your tempest and terrify them with your hurricane! Fill their faces with shame, that they may seek your name, O Lord. Let them be put to shame and dismayed forever; let them perish in disgrace, that they may know that you alone, whose name is the Lord, are the Most High over all the earth.

Q. 102. For what do we pray in the second petition?

A. In the second petition, which is, "Your kingdom come,"[1] we pray that Satan's kingdom may be destroyed,[2] and that the kingdom of grace may be advanced,[3] ourselves and others brought into it, and kept in it,[4] and that the kingdom of glory may be hastened.[5]

1 **Mt. 6:10**. Your kingdom come, your will be done, on earth as it is in heaven.

2 **Ps. 68:1, 18**. God shall arise, his enemies shall be scattered; and those who hate him shall flee before him! ... You ascended on high, leading a host of captives in your train and receiving gifts among men, even among the rebellious, that the Lord God may dwell there.

3 **Rev. 12:10-11**. And I heard a loud voice in heaven, saying, "Now the salvation and the power and the kingdom of our God and the authority of his Christ have come, for the accuser of our brothers has been thrown down, who accuses them day and night before our God. And they have conquered him by the blood of the Lamb and by the word of their testimony, for they loved not their lives even unto death.

4 **Jn. 17:9, 20**. I am praying for them. I am not praying for the world but for those whom you have given me, for they are yours. ... "I do not ask for these only, but also for those who will believe in me through their word." **Rom. 10:1**. Brothers, my heart's desire and prayer to God for them is that they may be saved. **2 Thess. 3:1**. Finally, brothers, pray for us, that the word of the Lord may speed ahead and be honored, as happened among you.

5 **Rev. 22:20**. He who testifies to these things says, "Surely I am coming soon." Amen. Come, Lord Jesus!

Q. 103. For what do we pray in the third petition?

A. In the third petition, which is, "Your will be done, on earth as it is in heaven,"[1] we pray that God, by His grace, would make us able and willing to know, obey, and submit to His will in all things,[2] as the angels do in heaven.[3]

1 **Mt. 6:10.** Your kingdom come, your will be done, on earth as it is in heaven.

2 **2 Sam. 15:25.** Then the king said to Zadok, "Carry the ark of God back into the city. If I find favor in the eyes of the Lord, he will bring me back and let me see both it and his dwelling place." **Job 1:21.** And he said, "Naked I came from my mother's womb, and naked shall I return. The Lord gave, and the Lord has taken away; blessed be the name of the Lord." **Ps.67.** May God be gracious to us and bless us and make his face to shine upon us, that your way may be known on earth, your saving power among all nations. Let the peoples praise you, O God; let all the peoples praise you! Let the nations be glad and sing for joy, for you judge the peoples with equity and guide the nations upon earth. Let the peoples praise you, O God; let all the peoples praise you! The earth has yielded its increase; God, our God, shall bless us. God shall bless us; let all the ends of the earth fear him! **Ps. 119:36.** Incline my heart to your testimonies, and not to selfish gain! **Mt. 26:39.** And going a little farther he fell on his face and prayed, saying, "My Father, if it be possible, let this cup pass from me; nevertheless, not as I will, but as you will."

3 **Ps. 103:20-21.** Bless the Lord, O you his angels, you mighty ones who do his word, obeying the voice of his word! Bless the Lord, all his hosts, his ministers, who do his will!

Q. 104. For what do we pray in the fourth petition?

A. In the fourth petition, which is, "Give us this day our daily bread,"[1] we pray that, of God's free gift, we may receive a sufficient portion of the good things of this life, and enjoy His blessing with them.[2]

1 **Mt. 6:11.** Give us this day our daily bread.

2 **Prov. 30:8-9.** Remove far from me falsehood and lying; give me neither poverty nor riches; feed me with the food that is needful for me, lest I be full and deny you and say, "Who is the Lord?" or lest I be poor and steal and profane the name of my God. **1 Tim. 4:4-5.** For everything created by God is good, and nothing is to be rejected if it is received with thanksgiving, for it is made holy by the word of God and prayer.

Q. 105. For what do we pray in the fifth petition?

A. In the fifth petition, which is, "Forgive us our debts, as we also have forgiven our debtors,"[1] we pray that God, for Christ's sake, would freely pardon all our sins;[2] which we are more encouraged to ask because by His grace we are enabled from the heart to forgive others.[3]

1 **Mt. 6:12.** ...and forgive us our debts, as we also have forgiven our debtors.

2 **Ps. 51:1-2, 7, 9.** Have mercy on me, O God, according to your steadfast love; according to your abundant mercy blot out my transgressions. Wash me thoroughly from my iniquity, and cleanse me from my sin! ... Purge me with hyssop, and I shall be clean; wash me, and I shall be whiter than snow. ... Hide your face from my sins, and blot out all my iniquities. **Dan. 9:17-19.** "Now therefore, O our God, listen to the prayer of your servant and to his pleas for mercy, and for your own sake, O Lord, make your face to shine upon your sanctuary, which is desolate. O my God, incline your ear and hear. Open your eyes and see our desolations, and the city that is called by your name. For we do not present our pleas before you because of our righteousness, but because of your great mercy. O Lord, hear; O Lord, forgive. O Lord, pay attention and act. Delay not, for your own sake, O my God, because your city and your people are called by your name."

3 **Mt. 13:35.** This was to fulfill what was spoken by the prophet: "I will open my mouth in parables; I will utter what has been hidden since the foundation of the world." **Lk. 11:4.** "...and forgive us our sins, for we ourselves forgive everyone who is indebted to us. And lead us not into temptation."

Q. 106. For what do we pray in the sixth petition?

A. In the sixth petition, which is, "And lead us not into temptation, but deliver us from evil,"[1] we pray that God would either keep us from being tempted to sin,[2] or support and deliver us when we are tempted.[3]

1 **Mt. 6:13.** And lead us not into temptation, but deliver us from evil.

2 **Mt. 26:41.** "Watch and pray that you may not enter into temptation. The spirit indeed is willing, but the flesh is weak."

3 **2 Cor. 12:7-8.** So to keep me from becoming conceited because of the surpassing greatness of the revelations, a thorn was given me in the flesh, a messenger of Satan to harass me, to keep me from becoming conceited. Three times I pleaded with the Lord about this, that it should leave me.

Q. 107. What does the conclusion of the Lord's Prayer teach us?

A. The conclusion of the Lord's Prayer, which is, "For yours is the kingdom and the power and the glory, forever. Amen,"[1] teaches us to take our encouragement in prayer from God only,[2] and in our prayers to praise Him, ascribing kingdom, power, and glory to Him;[3] and in testimony of our desire and assurance to be heard, we say, "Amen."[4]

1 **MT. 6:13**. And lead us not into temptation, but deliver us from evil.

2 **DAN. 9:4, 7-9, 16-19.** I prayed to the Lord my God and made confession, saying, "O Lord, the great and awesome God, who keeps covenant and steadfast love with those who love him and keep his commandments." ... To you, O Lord, belongs righteousness, but to us open shame, as at this day, to the men of Judah, to the inhabitants of Jerusalem, and to all Israel, those who are near and those who are far away, in all the lands to which you have driven them, because of the treachery that they have committed against you. To us, O Lord, belongs open shame, to our kings, to our princes, and to our fathers, because we have sinned against you. To the Lord our God belong mercy and forgiveness, for we have rebelled against him. ... "O Lord, according to all your righteous acts, let your anger and your wrath turn away from your city Jerusalem, your holy hill, because for our sins, and for the iniquities of our fathers, Jerusalem and your people have become a byword among all who are around us. Now therefore, O our God, listen to the prayer of your servant and to his pleas for mercy, and for your own sake, O Lord, make your face to shine upon your sanctuary, which is desolate. O my God, incline your ear and hear. Open your eyes and see our desolations, and the city that is called by your name. For we do not present our pleas before you because of our righteousness, but because of your great mercy. O Lord, hear; O Lord, forgive. O Lord, pay attention and act. Delay not, for your own sake, O my God, because your city and your people are called by your name."

3 **1 CHR. 29:10-13**. Therefore David blessed the Lord in the presence of all the assembly. And David said: "Blessed are you, O Lord, the God of Israel our father, forever and ever. Yours, O Lord, is the greatness and the power and the glory and the victory and the majesty, for all that is in the heavens and in the earth is yours. Yours is the kingdom, O Lord, and you are exalted as head above all. Both riches and honor come from you, and you rule over all. In your hand are power and might, and in your hand it is to make great and to give strength to all. And now we thank you, our God, and praise your glorious name.

4 **1 COR. 14:16**. Otherwise, if you give thanks with your spirit, how can anyone in the position of an outsider say "Amen" to your thanksgiving when he does not know what you are saying? **REV. 22:20-21**. He who testifies to these things says, "Surely I am coming soon." Amen. Come, Lord Jesus! The grace of the Lord Jesus be with all. Amen.

CPSIA information can be obtained
at www.ICGtesting.com
Printed in the USA
BVHW042348091220
595243BV00001B/82

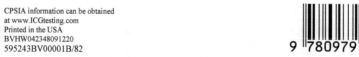

9 780979 371882